Intonation Systems

Andrew Linn

Sheffield 2000

Intonation Systems

A Survey of Twenty Languages

EDITED BY

DANIÉL HIRST

AND

ALBERT DI CRISTO

CNRS Laboratoire Parole et Langage
Institut de Phonétique, Université de Provence

CAMBRIDGE
UNIVERSITY PRESS

PUBLISHED BY THE PRESS SYNDICATE OF THE UNIVERSITY OF CAMBRIDGE

The Pitt Building. Trumpington Street, Cambridge CB2 1RP, United Kingdom

CAMBRIDGE UNIVERSITY PRESS

The Edinburgh Building, Cambridge, CB2 2RU, United Kingdom   http://www.cup.cam.ac.uk

40 West 20th Street, New York, NY 10011–4211, USA   http://www.cup.org

10 Stamford Road, Oakleigh, Melbourne 3166, Australia

First published 1998

Printed in the United Kingdom at the University Press, Cambridge

Typeset in Times [DJH]

A catalogue record for this book is available from the British Library

Library of Congress cataloguing in publication data

Intonation Systems. A Survey of Twenty Languages / edited by Daniel Hirst and Albert Di Cristo.
    p.   cm.
Includes bibliographical references and index.
ISBN 0 521 39513 5 (hardback) ISBN 0 521 39550 X (paperback)
1. Intonation (Phonetics). 2. Grammar, Comparative and general – Phonology. 3. Linguistic typology.
I. Hirst, Daniel 1946– II. Di Cristo, Albert

ISBN 0 521 39513 5 (hardback)
ISBN 0 521 39550 X (paperback)

Contents

Contents

Organisation of the Chapters

In order to facilitate comparisons across languages, almost all the chapters in this volume*, including our introductory chapter (A survey of intonation systems), are organised following the same general outline as follows:

1. Background.

1.1   General prosodic characteristics of the language.

1.2   Theoretical background and approach.

2. Description of intonation patterns.

2.1   Description of a basic non-emphatic pattern.

2.2   Mode and expressivity.

2.3   Focalisation and contextual effects.

2.4   Phrasing and textual organisation.

2.5   Other patterns (e.g. stereotyped or stylised patterns).

3. Comparisons with other intonation systems.

3.1   Comparisons with other dialects.

3.2   Comparisons with other languages.

4. Implications and conclusions.

---

* The chapters which do not follow this outline are Chapter 2 (Intonation in American English by Dwight Bolinger) and Chapter 23 (Intonation in Beijing Chinese by Paul Kratochvil), see notes at the beginning of these chapters.

Contributors

ISAMU ABE *Department of Liberal Arts, Asia University, Tokyo; Language Research Laboratory, Tokyo Institute of Technology*

SANTIAGO ALCOBA *Departamente de Filologia Espanola, Universidad Autónoma de Barcelona*

THAMI BENKIRANE *Department of Linguistics and Phonetics, University of Fez*

†DWIGHT BOLINGER *Department of Linguistics, Harvard University*

ANTONIS BOTINIS *Department of Linguistics, Philosophical Faculty, University of Athens*

GEORGES BOULAKIA *Laboratoire de Phonétique UFRL, Université de Paris VII*

MADALENA CRUZ-FERREIRA *Department of English Language and Literature, National University of Singapore*

LAURENŢIA DASCĂLU-JINGA *Institutul de Cercetari Etnologice şi Dialectologice, Bucharest*

ALBERT DI CRISTO *Institut de Phonétique, Université de Provence, CNRS Laboratoire Parole et Langage*

ĐÕ THẾ DUNG *ILPGA, Université de Paris III; University of Ho Chi Minh-Ville*

IVAN FÓNAGY *Institut d'Etudes Linguistiques et Phonétiques, Paris*

EVA GÅRDING *Department of Linguistics and Phonetics, Lund University*

DAFYDD GIBBON *Fakultät für Linguistik und Literaturwissenschaft, Universität Bielefeld*

Contributors

NINA GRØNNUM *Institute of General and Applied Linguistics, University of Copenhagen*

JOHAN 'T HART *Instituut voor Perceptie Onderzoek, Eindhoven*

DANIEL HIRST *Institut de Phonétique, Université de Provence, CNRS, Laboratoire Parole et Langage*

TRẦN THIEN HUONG *Laboratoire de Phonétique UFRL, Université de Paris VII*

ANTTI IIVONEN *Department of Phonetics, University of Helsinki*

PAUL KRATOCHVIL *Faculty of Oriental Studies, University of Cambridge*

SUDAPORN LUKSANEEYANAWIN *Department of Linguistics, Chulalongkorn University, Bangkok*

†ANASTASIA MISHEVA *Bulgarian Language Institute, Sofia*

JOÃO ANTÔNIO DE MORAES *Department of Linguistics, Universidade Federal do Rio de Janeiro*

JULIO MURILLO *Universidad Autónoma de Barcelona*

MICHEL NIKOV *Department of Romance Studies, University of Sofia*

MARIO ROSSI *Institut de Phonétique, Université de Provence, CNRS Laboratoire Parole et Langage*

NATALIA SVETOZAROVA *Department of Phonetics, University of St. Petersburg*

Preface

Because I had not been called upon to write a preface of this sort before, when asked to do so I did a rapid trawl along my bookshelves looking at prefaces. I found that prefaces to multi-authored works were either written by the editors themselves or were included as tributes in volumes which were in the nature of festschrifts to esteemed scholars. It is a tribute to this book that it falls into neither category but still greatly deserves a preface. The editors present here a unique advance in the study of intonation.

Books which have presented systematic comparisons of many languages or of grammars or of phonologies have been available for at least the last decade. But the enormous problems to be faced in achieving anything comparable for intonation have meant that no-one has dared to take on the task. Indeed the editors probably did not initially realise the enormity of this task and hence how long the gestation period would be (I have myself seen two earlier versions which were considerably different).

What we have now is a volume which enables intonationists and others to compare languages systematically on the variables which are the important ones in intonational comparison, e.g. what is the unmarked contour for simple, declarative sentences and what marks the contours for various types of question and for non-finality? This comparison shows up intonational differences but at the same time also brings out the considerable similarities in intonational form and function across languages.

This highlighting of differences and similarities has been achieved despite the plethora of theoretical approaches which the individual authors have brought to the subject. Moreover the editors also introduce their own theory-neutral transcription system for intonation, which is used by many of the contributors to the volume and hence makes comparison easier. The information contained in the articles has been expertly surveyed by the editors in their Introduction, which itself will become obligatory reading for all those interested in the typological and theoretical study of intonation. This book will be a sourcebook for all cross-linguistic researchers. It represents a landmark in the study of intonation.

ALAN CRUTTENDEN
Manchester

Acknowledgements

This book has been a very long time in the making – it is now over ten years since we first circulated a questionnaire on the intonation of different languages. We should like to take this opportunity of thanking the authors for having agreed to take part in the project in the first place and then for accepting the numerous revisions and changes of plan that we sprang on them. We should particularly like to thank Antonis Botinis, Eva Gårding, Dafydd Gibbon, Hans 't Hart and Nina Grønnum for constructive suggestions and help at various stages in the preparation of the manuscript. Eva Gårding generously remarked: "As it happens, Swedish intonation has not changed so much during the last decade!"

We were extremely sad to learn of the loss of two of our contributors: Dwight Bolinger and Anastasia Misheva. We should like to dedicate this volume to their memory and to that of our teacher and friend Georges Faure who, we know, would have been proud to see this publication by two of his former students.

Over the years the list of people we should like to thank has grown so long that it is impossible for us to name them all here. The editorial staff of Cambridge University Press was remarkably patient, helpful and encouraging. Our thanks first to Penny Carter for her enthusiasm for the project right from the beginning, then to Marion Smith, Catherine Max, Judith Ayling, Joanna West, Lucy Munro, Natalie Davies, Kate Brett, Andrew Winnard, Nicole Webster, Anne Rex and Caroline Murray, to name just those with whom we corresponded. Alan Cruttenden and another anonymous reviewer gave us a lot of very useful advice and comments on earlier versions of the book. We obviously owe a great deal to the support and encouragement of our colleagues from the Institut de Phonétique d'Aix, as well as to all our students with whom we discussed much of the material in the introduction together with our individual chapters and from whom we learned more than they suspect. Special thanks are also due to Christian Cavé for help with proof-reading, to Annie Rival for expert help with typing, and to Marilyn Sahnouni for her invaluable editorial assistance without which this book would have taken even longer to complete. Our final thanks (and apologies) to our families, especially Yvette hirst and Nicole Di Cristo, for their having put up with sharing weekends and holidays with *le bouquin* for so long.

DANIEL HIRST
ALBERT DI CRISTO

1

A survey of intonation systems

DANIEL HIRST and ALBERT DI CRISTO

1. Background

The description of the intonation system of a particular language or dialect is a particularly difficult task since intonation is paradoxically at the same time one of the most universal and one of the most language specific features of human language.

Intonation is universal first of all because every language possesses intonation. Hockett (1963) made this one of his list of ten significant empirical generalisations about languages: generalisations which we should not necessarily want to include in the definition of what constitutes a language but which just happen to be true. Intonation is universal also because many of the linguistic and paralinguistic functions of intonation systems seem to be shared by languages of widely different origins. It has often been noted, for example, that in a vast majority of languages some sort of raised pitch (final or non-final) can be used in contrast with lower pitch to indicate that an utterance is intended as a question rather than as a statement. In this sense the universal status of intonation is rather different from that observed for other phonological systems such as vowels or consonants for example. While it is true that all languages have vowel and consonant systems, and even that similar patterns of vowels and consonants can be found in languages which are only very distantly related, these systems do not convey meanings directly in the way that intonation seems to. There is, for example, no systematic universal meaning which can be ascribed to the difference between front vowels and back vowels or between stops and fricatives.

Despite this universal character, the specific features of a particular speaker's intonation system are also highly dependent on the language, the dialect, and even the style, the mood and the attitude of the speaker. Experimental research has shown (Ohala and Gilbert 1981, Maidment 1983) that speakers are capable of distinguishing languages in which utterances are spoken on the basis of their prosody alone. Recent results obtained using low-pass filtered recordings (Mehler *et al.* 1988) suggest the striking fact that as early as four days after birth infants have already acquired (presumably during the last months of pregnancy) the ability to distinguish the prosody of their native language from that of other languages. The prosodic characteristics of a language are not only probably the first phonetic features acquired by a child (Kaplan 1970, Crystal 1973, Lieberman 1986, Levitt 1993, Konopczynski forthcoming), but also the last to be lost either through aphasia (Caplan 1987) or during the acquisition of another language or dialect (Cruz-Ferreira 1984, Touati 1990).

In recent years there has been an increasing awareness of the importance of intonation not only for phoneticians and linguists, but also for psycholinguists (cf. papers in Cutler and Ladd 1983) and for speech engineers working on technological applications such as automatic speech synthesis and speech recognition by machines (cf. Lea 1980, Holmes 1988, Waibel 1988, Vaissière 1989 and papers in Bailly and Benoît 1992). It has become obvious, for example, that to synthesise a continuous text in such a way that a listener can understand it without making a strenuous effort, needs a fairly sophisticated approach to the intonation of the text. In the same way, the fact that listeners obviously pay a great deal of attention to prosodic cues in the process of perceiving and understanding spoken language (cf. Darwin 1975, Cutler 1984, Bannert 1987, House 1990) seems to imply that automatic speech understanding systems should be drawing more information from prosodic features than is currently the case.

Paradoxically, it is still difficult to find in the literature a succinct and precise statement of the specific characteristics which make one language sound prosodically different from another. This is true not only of the vast majority of the world's languages whose intonation has never been described at all, but even for those languages which have been the object of considerable research.

There are probably a number of reasons which can explain this state of affairs. First of all it often seems to be felt that it is difficult, if not impossible, to describe the intonation of a language without being a native or near-native speaker. A consequence of this is that comparatively few linguists have undertaken comparative studies of intonation systems dealing with more than two languages (although cf. Delattre 1965, Gårding 1981, 1984, 't Hart *et al.* 1990) or typological studies of prosodic systems (but cf. Bolinger 1978b, 1989,

Cruttenden 1981, Fox 1985, Bruce *et al.* 1988, Bertinetto 1989). Linked to this, as both cause and consequence, is the fact that there have been strikingly few attempts to provide a language independent prosodic transcription system comparable to that of the International Phonetic Alphabet for segmental transcription (cf. Bruce 1989). The fact that intonation is not written down means that it is difficult for a non-native speaker to decide if two utterances are tokens of the same intonation pattern or not. A preliminary proposal for an international transcription system for intonation is given below (§1.2) and the system described here has been used by several of the authors in their contributions to this book.

The aim of this volume is to assemble, for the first time, a sample of descriptions of the intonation systems of a number of different languages, written by specialists of intonation, most of whom are also native speakers of the language described and/or working in the country where the language is spoken. We thus hope to have made a first step in the direction of establishing a prosodic typology by bringing together some of the material necessary for describing the variability of intonation systems across languages.

Although we tried to include as wide a sample of languages as possible, we are perfectly conscious that the descriptions presented here are more a reflection of the present state of the art in the field of intonation studies than a statistically significant sample of the variety of intonational forms in human language. A recent evaluation (Ruhlen 1987) estimates that there are about 5000 distinct extant languages in the world which can be grouped into 17 major groupings or phyla. Thirteen of the twenty languages in our sample are from the Indo-European phylum.

We try to emphasise in this survey the ways in which the intonation systems of the different languages described in this volume differ, rather than ways in which they are similar to each other, in the hope that by describing some of the ways in which the individual languages vary we can make some progress towards identifying the different dimensions along which they can be contrasted. At the same time we attempt to provide a thematic guided tour of the material contained in the individual chapters.

Before we look at the different descriptions, a few words concerning terminology may prove useful. We warn the reader, however, that here as in the rest of this chapter, the distinctions we make and the conclusions we draw are in no way intended to imply that all the contributors to this book would agree with us.

The term **intonation** has often been used interchangeably in the literature with that of **prosody**. When a distinction is made between the two words, this is often not explicit. The difference of usage varies considerably from one author to another and can, in our opinion, be traced to a double ambiguity in the use of the term **intonation** itself.

The first ambiguity depends on whether or not intonation is defined in a **broad** sense, that is as including factors such as word-stress, tone and quantity which can be an essential part of the lexical identity of words, or in a **narrow** sense, as excluding such factors. The term *prosody*, like that of *suprasegmentals* can be reserved for the broad sense as opposed to *intonation proper* which is then restricted to what are sometimes called **supralexical**, **postlexical** or simply **non-lexical** characteristics, consisting of such phenomena as the overall form of pitch patterns, declination, boundary phenomena *etc.*, which we describe in more detail in §2 below. This usage can be summarised by the following diagram:

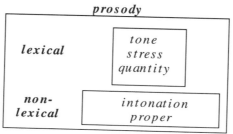

The second ambiguity depends on a distinction between levels of analysis and description. In phonetics, as in all sciences, a distinction may be made between the **physical** level, that of observable and measurable physical parameters, and the **formal** level, which is a rather more abstract level of representation set up as a model in an attempt to describe and explain the observed data. In the case of language, the abstract **linguistic** level attempts to account for a speaker's linguistic **competence**, the implicit knowledge about the language which he is assumed to possess.

On the physical level, intonation is used to refer to variations of one or more acoustic parameters. Of these, fundamental frequency (F_0) is universally acknowledged to be the primary parameter. Many authors, however, have drawn attention to the pluriparametric nature of intonation which besides fundamental frequency involves variations of intensity and segmental duration (Rossi *et al.* 1981, Beckman 1986). Some authors in particular include under the term intonation aspects of temporal organisation or **rhythm** which besides intensity and duration may be reflected in variations of spectral characteristics such as for example distinctions between full and reduced vowels (Crystal 1969).

A distinction between physical and linguistic levels of representation is perhaps more obvious on the level of segmental phonology, corresponding to the distinction between the acoustic data obtained for example from spectrographic analyses (physical) and phonological transcriptions (linguistic). It is worth noting that linguists and phoneticians have always approached segmental phonology by setting up formal linguistic categories (phonemes, distinctive features *etc.*) and then describing the physical characteristics of these categories. Trying to establish the inventory of abstract categories by direct observation of speech signals would amount to assuming that all problems of automatic speech recognition have been solved. Ladd and Cutler (1983) proposed a distinction between what they described as **concrete** and **abstract** approaches to prosody. In our view, for the reasons we have just exposed (although we are aware that this in no way reflects a universal consensus), any attempt to define intonation on a physical basis (Ladd and Cutler's "concrete approach") necessarily implies a formal (abstract) definition, even if this is never made explicit (for an interesting discussion of the abstract nature of intonation cf. Collier 1972).

The two distinctions we made above: **lexical** *vs.* **non-lexical**, and **linguistic** *vs.* **physical** are not in fact entirely independent of each other, since something like the following pattern is commonly assumed:

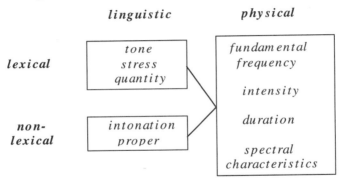

Among non-specialists, a particularly widespread hypothesis concerning intonation was that of a one to one correspondence between formal prosodic characteristics in general and their physical manifestation, corresponding to a physical equivalent of the formal lexical/non-lexical distinction. It was thus often believed that in English, for example, the formal exponents of lexical prosodic characteristics (word stress) and non-lexical prosodic characteristics (intonation) are mapped onto the physical parameters of intensity and fundamental frequency respectively. Something like this is implicit in Trager and Smith's (1951) description of English by means of four stress phonemes and four entirely independent pitch phonemes. This assumption, which could not have been made if English had been a tone language, has been extremely hard-wearing. In recent years, however, it has been demonstrated that the correspondence between abstract prosodic characteristics and acoustic features is far from simple. On the one hand it has been known for a long time that fundamental frequency (F_0) is a far more efficient cue for stress than either duration or intensity alone (Jassem 1952, Bolinger 1958, Fry 1958, Lehiste 1970, Faure *et al.* 1980). On the other hand, many writers have observed that intensity and duration are more systematically correlated with stress in a language such as English than is F_0 (Beckman 1986). A possible explanation for this was proposed by Hirst (1983a) who suggested that there is an asymmetry between production and perception, so that while duration and intensity differences are the most systematic correlates of stress in speech production, the dominant perceptual cue is fundamental frequency. For a slightly different interpretation, however, cf. Botinis (this volume chapter 16).

One other way to attempt to establish a physical definition of intonation has been to maintain that there is a difference of **scale** between **global** prosodic properties of an utterance put down to intonation proper, and **local** properties which are lexically determined, together with a third lower order level of **segmental** or microprosodic properties (Di Cristo and Hirst 1986, Grønnum this volume). It seems clear, however, that a distinction between microprosody, lexical prosody and intonation cannot be maintained on purely physical grounds since it depends on a prior identification of the relevant linguistic constituents: phoneme, morpheme, word, phrase, sentence *etc.* which are clearly of a formal linguistic nature.

The dichotomy between linguistic and physical levels of analysis, like most dichotomies, is not as water-tight as it might look at first sight. Many, if not most, definitions of intonation fall somewhere in between the formal and the physical extremes, and refer to the speaker's or listener's **impression** of physical characteristics. The terms **pitch**, **loudness**, **length** and **timbre** are often used in this sense as auditory correlates of **fundamental frequency**, **intensity**, **duration** and **spectral characteristics** respectively. Such impressions are evidently determined not only by the physical characteristics of the speech signal but also by the speaker's linguistic knowledge and they somehow straddle the boundary between the physical world and a speaker's abstract (cognitive) representation of that world.

This no-man's-land between the formal and the physical has been the object of much discussion in recent years. A number of writers (Fromkin 1975, Keating 1988) have been concerned with exploring the "phonology/phonetics interface". By contrast, Ohala (1990) has recently suggested that "there is no interface between phonology and phonetics" and has rather pleaded for the integration of phonetics and phonology into a single field of research. Our own view is that while Ohala is right in claiming that phonetics and phonology do not constitute autonomous domains, the concept of an interface is a useful metaphor to describe the link between, on the one hand, an abstract, cognitive level of phonological description and, on the other hand, the physical levels of description provided by acoustics and physiology *etc.* It should be clear, however, that in this sense it is the whole field of phonetics which should be seen as constituting this interface between the cognitive and the physical levels as in the following:

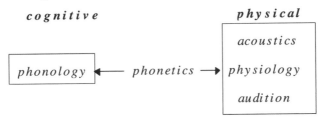

We propose, then, to continue to use the term **prosody** in its most general sense to cover both the abstract cognitive systems and the physical parameters onto which these systems are mapped. On the abstract, phonological level, prosody consists of a number of lexical systems (tone, stress and quantity) and one non-lexical system: **intonation**. We also propose to use the term **intonation** with a second meaning, to refer to a specifically **phonetic** characteristic of utterances, a construction by which the prosodic primitives on the lexical level and the non-lexical level, however we choose to represent these formally, are related to acoustic prosodic parameters. This phonetic interpretation of intonation as the interface between prosodic systems and prosodic parameters is illustrated in the following figure:

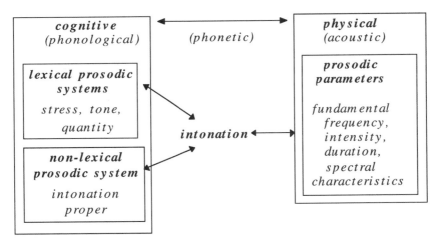

1.1 General prosodic characteristics of the languages

It follows from the definitions given in the preceding section that it is impossible to describe the intonation system of a language without at the same time giving an account of the other relevant prosodic characteristics, since at a physical level, which after all is the only level which is directly observable, the two sets are inextricably mingled.

Classical phonological descriptions provide a typological framework (for a thorough overview cf. Fox 1985) for discussing these lexical properties, depending on whether the language in question makes lexical distinctions based on quantity, stress or tone. In the case of stress, a distinction is often made (Trubetzkoy 1939; Garde 1968) between languages with fixed stress and languages with free stress. It seems probable however that such distinctions can only be made on formal grounds. There is not, in other words, necessarily any *acoustic* cue for the fact that word stress is lexically distinctive in certain languages such as German, Greek, Russian, Spanish, Arabic, Chinese but not in others such as French, Hungarian, and Vietnamese. In the same way there is no logical necessity for there to exist an *acoustic* distinction between tone languages and stress languages. As Wang (1967) remarked:

It is extremely difficult to distinguish utterances in certain types of tone languages (*e.g.* Mandarin) from those in a non-tone language (*e.g.* English) by just examining the pitch measurements of these utterances. (pp. 99–100).

One possibility (developed in Hirst 1987) is that in fact all languages make use of tone and stress (and presumably quantity) at some point in the representation of utterances. Prosodic differences between languages, under this interpretation, would arise from the fact that the different prosodic primitives can be introduced into the phonological representation at different levels. When the prosodic characteristics of a word are not lexically specified, they will need to be introduced by rules which are assumed to convert an underlying representation into a surface representation. It would follow from this that the fact that surface forms are similar in different languages is no guarantee that the lexical representations will be the same. It is not obvious, in other words, that lexical characteristics will translate in any simple one to one fashion into acoustic characteristics, although of course there must be some way in which the language learner makes a choice between different possible underlying lexical representations. It seems more reasonable, however, given the present state of knowledge, to assume that the distinguishing criteria are formal rather than physical ones (cf. discussion by Van der Hulst and Smith 1988).

Most recent work in the framework of non-linear (generative) phonology has assumed that tone is formally represented in the lexicon of a tone language as a sequence of tonal segments (H and L for example), together with language specific rules specifying how the tones are to be associated to the segments or syllables of the word. Word stress, on the other hand, has been represented in a number of different ways: as a distinctive feature of segments (Chomsky and Halle 1968), as an abstract diacritic symbol (*) associated with one syllable of a lexical item (Goldsmith 1976), or, in more recent work, as a **hierarchical prosodic structure** in which a sequence of syllables is grouped into a higher order unit, one syllable of which is specified as the strongest element or **head** of the sequence (cf. work in the framework of **metrical phonology**: Liberman 1975, Selkirk 1981, Giegerich 1985, Nespor and Vogel 1986, Halle and Vergnaud 1987, Goldsmith 1990).

Of the languages described in this book, three are clear-cut cases of tone languages. These are: Vietnamese (Đô, Trân and Boulakia), Thai (Luksaneeyanawin) and Chinese (Kratochvil). Chinese is traditionally described as possessing four lexical tones: High, Rising, Low and Falling, although as Kratochvil demonstrates, an adequate characterisation of tonal phenomena in Chinese needs to account for both pitch and intensity variations. Thai is described as possessing five distinctive tones: High, Mid, Low, Rising and Falling; while (North) Vietnamese has six distinctive tones: Rising, Static and Glottalised with High and Low variants of each category. Besides their tonal characteristics, all three tone languages are described as possessing a distinction between stressed and unstressed syllables which is lexically distinctive in Chinese but not in Vietnamese or Thai.

Two other languages presented in this volume: Japanese (Abe) and Swedish (Gårding) are notorious for the fact that they are often described as being somehow intermediate between stress and tone systems. It has been suggested (cf. McCawley 1978, Van der Hulst and Smith 1988) that the classical typological distinction between **stress** languages and **tone** languages should be extended to a three-way distinction between **stress** languages like English, Dutch, Russian *etc.*, sometimes called "dynamic stress" languages or "stress-accent" languages,[1] **tone** languages (like Chinese, Vietnamese and Thai) and **pitch accent** or **tonal accent** languages (like Japanese and perhaps Swedish). In support of such a distinction, Beckman (1986) has presented experimental evidence that accentual contrasts in Japanese make less use of differences in what she calls "total amplitude" (a function of intensity and duration) than they do in English. It remains, however, to be seen whether comparable experimental data from other languages will provide direct evidence for a binary distinction of this sort, or whether it would be preferable to think of languages as forming a continuous scale defined by the average ratio between the duration of stressed and unstressed syllables in the language. Botinis (this volume) suggests such a scale for Swedish > Danish > Italian > Greek >Spanish.

Abe (this volume), points out that contrary to what is observed in stress systems, where only the **position** of stress is significant, words in Japanese need also to be characterised by a contrast between **presence** and **absence** of stress (his T1 and T2 words). This difference has been accounted for in the literature in a number of different ways. In a phonological analysis of the lexical prosodic systems of various dialects of Japanese, Haraguchi (1977) adopted

Goldsmith's (1976) use of a diacritic symbol (*) to indicate the place of the accent. Other writers, (cf. Pulleyblank 1986), have suggested that rather than use an abstract diacritic symbol, a pitch accent system can be better accounted for by assuming that for some words a single high tone (H) is "pre-linked" to one vowel in the lexical representation. A possible way to account for the distinction between dynamic stress systems and pitch accent systems would be to suppose, as suggested above, that in dynamic stress languages one syllable is lexically marked as the "head" of the word, whereas in pitch accent systems the relevant lexical characteristic is the presence or absence (and if present the position) of a single lexically specified tone. This allows a simple explanation for the fact that in a stress system the maximum number of potential contrasts is equal to the number of syllables (in practice in many stress systems the position of the head is restricted to a smaller number of possible positions). Thus for disyllabic words in a stress language like Greek (Botinis this volume) we find a two-way distinction such as /nómos/ (law) and /nomós/ (county). In a pitch accent system, by contrast, the potential number of contrasts is one more than the number of syllables since it is possible for accentless words to occur. Thus in Japanese, disyllabic words show a potential three-way lexical distinction with examples like *káki* (oyster) *kakí* (fence) and *kaki* (persimmon). In the dialect of Tokyo, described in this book, the distinction between final accent and no accent is only manifested when there is a following syllable such as the subject particle *-ga*.

Japanese thus appears in some sense halfway between a tone language and a stress language or, as Abe puts it, as "a tonal language but not strictly a tone language". Contrasts in Japanese are **syntagmatic** as in a stress language, rather than **paradigmatic** as in tone languages (Garde 1968) but, as in a tone language, the lexical specification directly encodes relative pitch height rather than simply an abstract position. This also accounts for the fact that in a stress language the actual pitch accent associated with accented syllables may vary according to the intonation (see section 2.1 below) whereas in a tonal accent language this does not appear to be the case.

Swedish (Bruce and Gårding 1978, Gårding this volume) possesses two distinct word accents called Accent 1 (acute) and Accent 2 (grave) which can be contrastive except that only Accent 1 can occur on word-final syllables. Gårding discusses several different analyses which have been made of these accents: as an underlying distinction between High and Low, as a sequence High + Low with different association lines linking the tones to the syllables, or as peaks with delayed onset *etc.* The tonal nature of these word accents is apparent from the fact that, just as in a tone language, their overall shape is not modified by the overall intonation pattern. One possibility which is suggested by the present typology is that as in German, Dutch, Danish and English *etc.*, syllables in Swedish can be marked syntagmatically as prosodic heads, but that as in

Japanese, Swedish also allows a paradigmatic contrast between presence and absence of lexically distinctive (High) tone on non-final stressed syllables. For a similar analysis of East Norwegian pitch accents cf. Withgott and Halvorsen (1988).

Swedish and Japanese thus both appear to possess characteristics of both paradigmatic (tonal) and syntagmatic (accentual) prosodic systems. A difference between the two systems seems to be that Japanese is predominantly tonal and only secondarily accentual whereas Swedish is the opposite. The possible patterns for disyllabic words could be summarised as follows for Japanese:

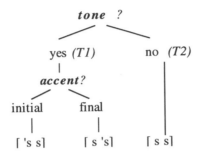

whereas the patterns for Swedish disyllabic words would be:

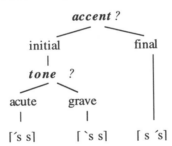

To distinguish the two systems, we could call the prosodic system of Swedish a **tonal accent** system, since the tonal contrast is restricted to a subset of the accentual contrasts, whereas we could describe Japanese as an **accentual tone** system since the accentual contrast is restricted to a subset of the tonal contrasts.

The different types of lexical prosodic systems described above can be summarised as in table 1 below.

It should be noted that it is only the **lexically distinctive** characteristics of a given prosodic system that are recorded in this table so that it is claimed that in a language like Finnish, for example, words have neither lexically distinctive tone, nor lexically distinctive stress, although as suggested above the

Table 1. *A classification of languages on the basis of their lexical prosody.*

type	example	number of lexical tones	lexical stress
fixed stress	*Finnish*	0	no
free stress	*Greek*	0	yes
accentual tone	*Japanese*	1	no
tonal accent	*Swedish*	1	yes
tone	*Thai*	>1	no
tone and stress	*Chinese*	>1	yes

phonological system of Finnish will specify that stress will be assigned to the first syllable of each word and that this stress will be manifested by a particular tonal configuration. Similarly, both Japanese and Swedish are described as possessing a single lexically distinctive tone which is present only on a subset of lexical items (T1 words in Japanese, A2 words in Swedish).

Once again it is assumed that the phonological systems of these languages will determine those accentual and tonal properties of words which are not lexically specified.

A number of linguistic models have been proposed in recent years to account for the way in which phonologically distinctive features such as accent and tone are converted into the relevant acoustic characteristics of an utterance. Ladd (1983a) proposed a distinction between two basic types of intonation models which he called the **Contour Interaction** type and the **Tone Sequence** type. In the Contour Interaction type, the intonation contour is seen as the result of superposing on each other pitch configurations of different sizes. In the Tone Sequence type:

The pitch movements associated with accented syllables are themselves what make up sentence intonation. (p. 40)

Contour Interaction models have their origin in attempts to apply techniques of analysis by synthesis to fundamental frequency curves, factoring out the observed values into two interacting components: word intonation and sentence intonation. Such a model, building on earlier work by Öhman (1967), has been developed in a number of publications by Fujisaki and his colleagues (Fujisaki and Nagashima 1969; Fujisaki, Hirose and Sugito 1979; Fujisaki 1988) who argue in particular that the model adequately reflects the dynamic characteristics of the physiological mechanisms underlying pitch control in speech. The same basic idea, that an intonation contour is the result of the superposition of contours defined on different hierarchical levels, has been applied on a slightly abstract level to the analysis of intonation contours of Swedish and several other languages by Gårding and her colleagues (Gårding *et al.* 1982, Gårding 1983, Gårding this volume) as well as to Danish (Thorsen 1983b, Grønnum [Thorsen] this volume).

Unlike Contour Interaction models (as well as most descriptive accounts of intonation in particular languages), Tone Sequence models have been particularly concerned with integrating the description of intonation into an overall view of phonological representation. This is particularly evident in the version presented by Pierrehumbert (1980) which builds on earlier work by Goldsmith (1974, 1976) and Leben (1976), themselves following in the tradition of Newman (1946) and Trager and Smith (1951). Pierrehumbert's work explores the possibility that the linguistic primitives involved in models of intonation are not formally distinct from those involved in lexical tone systems. In addition to an inventory of tones, restricted for English to H(igh) and L(ow), Pierrehumbert makes use of diacritic symbols, distinguishing for example between "H%" representing a **boundary tone**, "H*" representing the "strong" tone of a pitch accent and "H-" representing a phrase accent. She points out that:

both H* and H% are equally H tones but they differ in how they are associated with the text. (p. 29)

A synthesis of aspects of both Contour Interaction and Tone Sequence models seems the most promising direction for future research. In particular, as we suggested above, rather than make use of ad-hoc diacritic symbols, the representation of hierarchical prosodic structures makes it possible to distinguish the different types of tones directly by associating them with different levels of prosodic structure (Hirst 1983a, 1987, Bruce 1988, Pierrehumbert and Beckman 1988), assuming that the same formal apparatus used to describe lexically distinctive prosodic characteristics (tone, quantity and stress) is available for the phonological representation of utterances in all languages. Just as it is obviously impossible to speak without variations of fundamental frequency, intensity and segmental duration, so it is impossible, following this idea, to speak without tonal segments and hierarchical prosodic structures. Typological distinctions would arise then not from what phonological primitives are used in a representation, but at what level of the representation (lexical or nonlexical) these primitives are introduced.

1.2 Theoretical background

Despite our attempts to facilitate comparisons between the different chapters, and despite the fact that the authors were specifically asked to emphasise description rather than theory, it nonetheless remains inescapable that the description of a language is a complex interaction between the language itself and the linguist who describes the language from the viewpoint of his own theoretical commitments and convictions. A wide variety of different approaches are represented in this volume. We have made no attempt to harmonise the theoretical standpoints of the individual authors, feeling that such an attempt would be premature, given the limited character of our present day knowledge of the nature of intonation in general. To improve the state of this knowledge, considerable research remains to be done into the ways in which intonation systems vary before we may even begin to formulate an overall theory of the different formal parameters involved in prosodic typology.

We mentioned above the quite remarkable absence of any consensus concerning the transcription of intonation. The absence of any other transcription system led us to develop our own system which, following a suggestion by Hans 't Hart, we call: **INTSINT** (an **IN**ternational **T**ranscription **S**ystem for **INT**onation). INTSINT obviously owes a great deal to a number of other transcription systems which have been proposed in the past although most of these have generally been designed for the transcription of a single language. An international transcription system needs to embody a certain number of hypotheses about what possible variations of prosodic features are significant across languages. Since the original development of the INTSINT system a new system called ToBI (for **T**one and **B**reak **I**ndices) has been proposed for transcribing the intonation of American English (Silverman *et al.* 1992) based on research by Pierrehumbert (1980), Pierrehumbert and Beckman (1988) Wightman *et al.* (1991) and others. There has been much interest in the last few years in the possibility of adapting this system to other languages (see Gibbon (this volume) for its application to German), although the authors of ToBI have pointed out on several occasions that they do not believe it can be used directly for describing other languages or dialects, since, like a broad phonemic transcription, it presupposes that the inventory of tonal patterns of the language is already established. By contrast, INTSINT can be considered the equivalent of a narrow phonetic transcription and can consequently be used for gathering data on languages which have not already been described.

One specific original motivation for INTSINT was an attempt to develop a system which could be used for transcribing both English and French. Transcription systems devised for English intonation are not generally suitable for transcribing French intonation, since in French (Di Cristo, this volume) rhythmic groups **culminate** with a prominent syllable rather than beginning with one as in English (Wenk and Wioland 1982), for further discussion see below §2.1). This characteristic of French intonation makes it impossible to use the same symbols to mark the boundaries of the groups, the position of the prominent syllables, and the pitch movement involved, as is the case with many transcription systems devised for English. To avoid this problem, in INTSINT the transcription symbols are written on a separate line below the orthographic or phonetic text so that pitch patterns can be transcribed independently of the division into stress groups.

In contrast with many transcription systems in which pitch **movements** are taken to be the primitive elements, it is assumed in INTSINT that the phonetic representation of an utterance is most adequately defined as a sequence of static points (cf. the "turning points" of Gårding 1977a) each of which is linked to the neighbouring points by an appropriate transition function. We have used a phonetic representation of this type for a number of years now for modelling F_0 curves of utterances in several languages (Hirst 1983a, 1987, 1991, Hirst *et al.* 1993). Recent work has concentrated on developing algorithms for automatic analysis of prosodic features. For an overview and a discussion of the relationship between different levels of representation cf. Hirst *et al.* (in press).

All the pitch symbols in INTSINT are used to define a pitch **point** or **target**, the height of which is determined in one of two ways.

The first possibility is for pitch points to be defined as relatively **higher**, **lower** or the **same** as the immediately preceding pitch point:

(1)

Higher	Lower	Same
↑	↓	→

Two further symbols make it possible to represent a slight **Downstepping** (lowering) or **Upstepping** (raising) of pitch relative to the preceding pitch point:

(2)

Downstep	Upstep
>	<

In most cases, Higher and Lower correspond to peaks and valleys, respectively, whereas Downstep and Upstep correspond to a levelling off in a falling or rising stretch of pitch.[2] The possibility is also, however, left open to make a quantitative distinction, in that Downstep and Upstep are assumed to imply a smaller pitch change than that transcribed as Lower or Higher.

A second possibility is for the symbol to refer more globally to an extreme value with respect to the speaker's range of voice, in which case it may take the value **Top** or **Bottom**:

(3)

Top	Bottom
⇑	⇓

Beyond a certain length, utterances tend to be divided into units which can be, but are not necessarily, separated by pauses. Square brackets are used in INTSINT to mark the **boundaries** of these units which we shall refer to as **intonation units** (for discussion of this and other terminology see below §2.1 and §2.4).

An extreme **initial pitch** in an intonation unit can be marked inside the initial bracket as **Top** or **Bottom**. An unmarked initial bracket is taken as meaning a **Mid** initial pitch.

(4)

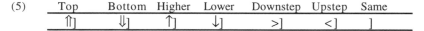

Final pitch in an intonation unit can be marked inside the final boundary as **Top, Bottom, Higher, Lower, Upstep, Downstep**. An unmarked final boundary is interpreted as **Same**.

(5)

Top	Bottom	Higher	Lower	Downstep	Upstep	Same
⇑]	⇓]	↑]	↓]	>]	<]	]

A typical pitch pattern such as that of the Finnish sentence *Laina lainaa Lainalle lainen.* (Laina lends Laina a loan) (Iivonen this volume):

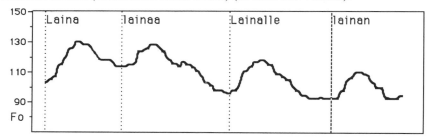

Figure 1. the fundamental frequency curve for a non-emphatic declarative sentence in Finnish (from Iivonen this volume).

can consequently be transcribed simply as:

(6)

LAIna		LAInaa		LAInalle		LAInan	
[⇑	↓	↑	↓	↑	↓	↑	⇓]

The relative scaling of the points within an Intonation Unit need not be specifically marked since it is assumed that the most important factor is the height of each successive point relative to the previous point.

It is probable that no language will need to make use of all of the potential contrasts provided by INTSINT, just as no language uses all the segmental symbols provided by IPA. The description of the intonation system of a given language will consequently need to specify which sequences of symbols constitute well formed intonation patterns in that language and how the symbols relate to the prosodic structure of the utterance.

Note, finally, that the names of the different symbols have been chosen so that the initial letter of the name: **T**op, **B**ottom, **H**igher, **L**ower, **S**ame, **U**pstep,

Downstep can be used for transcription when an appropriate set of graphic symbols is not available.

One voluntary limitation of INTSINT is that it is (at least in its present form) restricted to the transcription of pitch. There is of course no logical reason why it should not be extended to include other prosodic features such as duration and loudness although these can perhaps be more easily integrated into the segmental transcription of an utterance.

In its present form INTSINT provides no way of scaling relative pitch heights **between** Intonation Units although this obviously will be necessary when dealing with the intonation of continuous texts or dialogues. It might however seem reasonable to assume that in the absence of any other specification the **Top** level in successive Intonation Units is gradually lowered. We should then simply require a symbol to indicate resetting: one possibility would be to use double initial brackets ([[ ) to indicate this. In the same way a double final bracket (]]) could be used to indicate prosodic structuring on the paragraph level when this is prosodically signalled *e.g.* by extra-high or extra-low pitch (cf. Hirst this volume). We need, consequently to add the following possibilities:

(7)	Resetting	Extreme Top	Extreme Bottom
	[[	⇑]]	⇓]]

The last of these symbols can also be used in such cases as that described in European Portuguese by Cruz-Ferreira (this volume) for example, where there is a contrast between a low final pitch and an extra-low final pitch, the latter often accompanied by creaky voice.

We mentioned above that INTSINT has been used in ten of the chapters of this book (Hirst, Alcoba and Murillo, Cruz-Ferreira, Moraes, Di Cristo, Dascălu-Jinga, Svetozarova, Misheva and Nikov, Benkirane, Abe). Most of the other chapters use raw or stylised acoustic data for illustration (Gårding, Grønnum, Botinis, Fónagy, Luksaneeyanawin, Đỗ, Trần and Boulakia, Kratochvil). Two other authors, ('t Hart, Iivonen) make use of a simple two-level curve through the text similar to that which had been used by Pike (1945).

(8) a 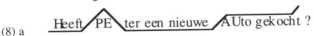 Heeft PEter een nieuwe AUto gekocht ?

This could of course be transcoded directly into INTSINT as follows:

(8) b	Heeft	PEter	een nieuwe	AUto	gekocht?
	[→	⇑	↓ →	↑ →	⇑]]

Note that when pitch is described as remaining static, as in the sequence *-ter een nieuwe* above, we need to specify this explicitly by means of the symbol Same (→) since without this the pitch would be assumed to rise continuously from the low pitch on *-ter* to the high pitch on *AU-*.

Rossi's description of Italian intonation makes use of a rather more abstract system of representation which he has in previous studies applied to the analysis of French intonation. According to this system, an intonation pattern consists of a linear sequence of stress and intonation morphemes functioning at different syntactic levels.

Gibbon's chapter on German, as we mentioned above, uses an adaptation for German of the ToBI system which has recently been proposed as a standard for transcribing the intonation of American English (Silverman *et al.* 1992).

Bolinger, finally, transcribes pitch using the squiggly lines of text which he introduced in Bolinger (1955).[3] This system of representation is in fact very similar to the analogical systems described above and the same remarks apply concerning the fact that behind such a transcription there is an implicit system of discrete contrasts. Notice for example in the following illustration (from Bolinger this volume):

(9)   I've lost ^{more} $\text{pa}_{\text{tients that}}$ ^{way}!

the accented syllable **pa-** is represented with a static pitch slightly lower than the level of the preceding accented syllable *more*, whereas the following unstressed syllable *-tients* is represented as a continuously descending sequence interpolating between *pa-* and *that*.

With INTSINT the sentence could be transcribed:

(10)   I've lost more patients that way!
        [→   ⇑   >   ⇓   ↑]

2. Description of intonation patterns

2.1 Description of a basic non-emphatic pattern

Some authors have cast doubt on the existence of such a thing as a "basic neutral unmarked intonation pattern", cf. in particular Schmerling (1976) and Selkirk (1984). For a critical discussion of Schmerling's arguments see Ladd (1980, pp. 73–76). The concept is, however, one which has proved a useful starting point for much research and probably will continue to do so in the future.

A "simple basic pattern" can be defined in several different ways. It can be identified with the pattern observed on "simple syntactic structures" such as simple sentences, clauses ('t Hart), noun phrases (Di Cristo), or even single words (Luksaneeyanawin). Another approach is to define it as the pattern observed on simple semantic or pragmatic units such as "sense groups", "information units" *etc.* (Luksaneeyanawin). It can be defined finally by phonetic criteria, as a sequence not containing pauses, a "breath group" (Kratochvil) or as a sequence containing only a single major pitch movement or nuclear tone (Cruz-Ferreira). In most cases all these approaches converge on the same **prosodic** unit, variously called by such names as "prosodic phrase", "intonation unit", "tone group" *etc.* In this section we shall be concerned with the way in which the general prosodic characteristics of languages described in §1.1 contribute to the overall intonation pattern of simple declarative non-emphatic utterances constituting a single Intonation Unit. The question of the complex pragmatic, semantic, syntactic and phonological constraints on the constitution of intonation units is beyond the scope of this chapter, but for some discussion see §2.4 below.

To describe the variable intonation patterns observed in the different languages we make a distinction between **global characteristics** – affecting the whole intonation unit, **local characteristics** – affecting a single point in the sequence and **recurrent patterns** which occur several times on a smaller sequence usually containing just one stressed syllable. This classification leads us to examine the way in which various authors have made use of the notion of **rhythmic grouping** and this in turn suggests an interesting typological classification.

Many of the intonation patterns we describe below as typical for a given language are also to be found as stylistic or dialectal variants for other languages. Unless otherwise mentioned, we shall be concerned with the pattern which is described as being stylistically the most neutral for each language.

Practically all the languages in this sample are described as having a globally rising-falling pitch movement in simple unemphatic declarative utterances which form a single intonation unit. This overall pattern generally finishes on an extreme low pitch. In Finnish (Iivonen) this low pitch is often accompanied by aperiodic voicing or "creaky voice". Exceptions to the general rule are mentioned for dialectal variants as in some Midland and Northern dialects of British English as well as in the Extremadura dialect of Spanish and in the Corfu dialect of Greek where declaratives are said to end with a raised final pitch.

Following the British tradition of analysis, we shall refer to the pitch movement associated with the final stressed syllable as the **nuclear** pitch, or **nucleus**. Standard Danish is claimed to be unlike most Germanic languages in that in most dialects (with the exception of that of Bornholm) there is no specific nuclear pitch movement at all. In most theoretical frameworks the nuclear pitch movement is given a special phonological status (referred to as "sentence accent" or "primary stress"). An alternative analysis is to treat the nucleus as the combination of a normal pitch accent and the boundary of an Intonation Unit. Within such a framework Danish would need to be analysed as exceptional in not having any specific pitch manifestation for the end of Intonation Units.

Tone and intonation in tone languages interact to a certain extent so that when rising tones are associated with final falling intonation the result can override the expected tonal configuration as in Chinese (Kratochvil), although without destroying the tonal identity of the morpheme. Abe states that:

Tones by their nature resist being perturbed by intonation.

Similarly, Luksaneeyanawin notes that in Thai:

The **Tune System** of intonation does not contaminate the phonological system of tones in the language. Each phonological tone still keeps its phonetic features distinct from the other phonological tones.

In most languages the falling nucleus is generally prepared by a rising pitch occurring on the first stressed syllable of the unit. Following Crystal (1969) we shall refer to this early rise as the pitch **onset**. One exception to the general tendency for a rising onset is Western Arabic where the pre-nuclear pattern is described as usually more or less flat followed by a nuclear pitch itself consisting of a rising-falling pitch movement. The combination of rising onset and falling nucleus however is an extremely common feature of most other languages in the sample.

When no other pitch movement occurs in the Intonation Unit between the rising onset and the falling nucleus, the resulting pitch pattern corresponds to what has been described for Dutch intonation ('t Hart this volume) as the "hat-pattern":

Besides Dutch, this pattern is described as common in European Portuguese, German, British and American English.

Between the onset and nucleus an overall globally declining pattern seems to be the unmarked case, so that the "hat" is in fact slightly cocked:

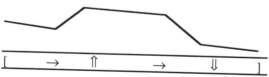

We leave it an open question as to whether the difference between these two patterns should be explicitly marked in the transcription (for example by replacing the symbol Same (→) by the symbol Downstep (>), or whether such general declination should be assumed by default.

In Danish the **degree** of declination is said to vary in function of the modality of the sentence (see §2.2 below), whereas in German it is described as a stylistic variable. Greek is described as having declination only at final junctures but Botinis suggests that the declination observed in many languages is perhaps an artefact of laboratory speech where individual sentences constitute a complete "turn-unit", and that work on spontaneous rather than laboratory speech may find little or no declination at all.

Although there is quite a considerable literature describing F_0 declination in various languages, recent work has shown that the nature and generalisation of the phenomenon are far from uncontroversial. First of all, declination has been interpreted either as an actively controlled process or as a by-product of a peripheral mechanism (see, for a review and discussion: Cohen *et al.* (1982), Gelfer *et al.* (1983), Ladd (1984), Bruce (1984a), 't Hart (1986)). Secondly, while declination has been regularly observed in laboratory speech, its manifestation in other circumstances is less evident. Spontaneous speech samples that typically lack declination have been reported by Lieberman and Tseng (1981) and by Umeda (1982). To what extent declination is situation-dependent remains an open question, as does its relevance for phonological and phonetic descriptions of intonation. It seems probable in fact that the notion of declination covers quite a range of different phenomena which interact at different levels. Ladd (1984) gives a useful discussion of the different theoretical assumptions that this notion has been made to cover. Connell and Ladd (1990) suggest that instead of declination, a more general term "downtrends" should be used to cover a number of phonological and phonetic characteristics including in particular the following:

(i)   **declination**: a strictly phonetic characteristic of utterances consisting of a continuous lowering from the beginning to the end of the intonation unit.

(ii)   **downdrift**: an iterative lowering of successive high pitches within an intonation unit separated by intermediate low points.

(iii)   **downstep:**[4] an iterative lowering of successive high points within an intonation unit without intervening low tones.

(iv)   **final lowering**: a rapid lowering occurring before the final boundary of an intonation unit.

For many of the languages in this volume, besides a globally falling pattern over the Intonation Unit, a series of pitch movements is described, typically associated in some way with the stressed syllables. In the case of tone languages, the form of these pitch movements is determined by the lexically specified tone of each lexical item. For languages with no lexical tone, the same pattern usually re-occurs on each stressed syllable of an Intonation Unit (often with the exception of the final nuclear syllable which may be given special treatment). Many languages have a choice of various recurrent pitch movements for different expressive and stylistic functions but by far the most common pattern described is a rising pitch on each stressed syllable except for the last. A pattern of this type seems to be basic for Dutch, German, French, Italian, Russian, Greek, Brazilian Portuguese, and Finnish.

In some languages, a falling rather than a rising pattern occurs on the stressed syllables. This seems to be the most common pattern in American English, Spanish and Hungarian as well as a fairly common variant for German.

Another common pattern is a step-down in pitch for each stressed syllable between the onset and the nuclear movement. This seems to be the most common pattern in British English and perhaps Romanian. A similar pattern is described for Danish although unlike the basic pattern for British English this downstep to the stressed syllables is followed by a step-up and a falling pattern on any subsequent unstressed syllables.

A distinction between stressed and unstressed syllables does not logically require reference to any higher-level structuring. Stress is, however, often seen as fulfilling some sort of **grouping function** (Bruce 1985) in that each stressed syllable combines in some way with adjacent unstressed syllables to form a "stress-foot" or "stress group". Among the arguments which are presented here in favour of such hierarchical structure are: a more satisfactory account of rhythmic characteristics (Hirst) as well as a simplification of the description of intonation patterns (Grønnum).

If we assume such a hierarchical structure, the recurrent pitch movements can be described as occurring not on the stressed syllable but on a higher-order prosodic unit. In British English and Danish this higher order unit is explicitly defined as consisting of one stressed syllable and any following unstressed syllables.

(11)   (S s s...) (S s s...) (S s s...) ...

where **S** represents a stressed syllable and **s** an unstressed syllable. We shall refer to this using the terminology of metrical phonology (Selkirk 1984, Nespor and Vogel 1986, Halle and Vergnaud 1987) as a **left-headed** stress group. This is the rhythmic unit which Abercrombie (1964) called the **foot**, borrowing the term from traditional poetics, and which he used to describe the rhythm of English verse and speech. Abercrombie specifically claimed that the foot is "independent of word boundaries" (p. 17) so that a sentence like

(12)   We reGREtted his eLECtion.

would be analysed as:

(13)   We re- (GREtted his e-)(LECtion.)

where (...) corresponds to foot boundaries.

A more sophisticated model of prosodic structure in English had been proposed earlier by Jassem (1952) (cf. Hirst this volume) who makes a distinction between rhythmic structure and tonal structure. The **stress group** as described here corresponds more closely to the tonal structure of Jassem's description. A similar distinction is made by Grønnum (this volume) who suggests in fact that the prosodic stress group should be analysed as beginning with the stressed **vowel** rather than with the onset of the stressed **syllable**. This is obviously an area in which much work remains to be done. It remains to be seen, in particular, whether rhythm and melody can be accounted for on a cross-language basis by a single explanatory model of prosodic structure.

In French (Di Cristo) and Italian (Rossi), the stress group is described as consisting of one stressed syllable and any **preceding** unstressed syllables:

(14)   (s s S) (s s S) (s s S) ...

We shall refer to this structure as a **right-headed** stress group. The typological distinction implied here is similar to that proposed by Wenk and Wioland (1982) between "trailer-timed" languages (left-headed) and "leader-timed" languages (right-headed). This distinction is obviously closely linked to that between "syllable-timed" and "stress-timed" languages, a distinction which has been commonly made since Pike (1945) but which has proved surprisingly recalcitrant to objective measurement (for a recent survey cf. Bertinetto 1989).

The case of Portuguese is particularly interesting. Neither Cruz-Ferrreira nor Moraes makes explicit use of the concept of stress group. Something similar is implicit, however, in Cruz-Ferreira's analysis of an intonation pattern into Pre-head, Head and Nuclear tone along the lines of the English school of analysis:

(15)   pre-head   head   nuclear tone
          s s s   S s s S s s   S s s

In particular, it should be noted that her analysis implies that unstressed syllables always belong to the same group as the preceding stressed syllable. Recent experimental work on the temporal organisation of stressed and unstressed syllables in Brazilian Portuguese (Reis 1995) seems to suggest a rhythmic organisation into right-headed stress groups. Whether European Portuguese also uses right-headed stress groups remains an open question: an analysis of the different phonological conditions on Portuguese clitic placement in European and Brazilian Portuguese (de Carvalho 1989) has in fact suggested quite independently that stress groups are left-headed in European Portuguese but right-headed in Brazilian Portuguese.

Several authors either do not mention any tendency to group unstressed syllables at all, or else assume that any such grouping will follow lexical and/or syntactic boundaries (cf. Alcoba and Murillo (this volume) for Spanish). It should, however, be noted that, as we mentioned above, similar proposals have also been made for English so that the analysis of rhythmic patterns by means of a single type of stress group in a given language is never uncontroversial. It would however be an extremely interesting result if it could be shown that left/right-headedness is a language specific typological parameter. If we analyse the prosodic classification of Indo-European languages under this assumption we find a good correspondence with language families, since Germanic languages as a whole seem to make use of left-headed feet whereas Romance languages (except perhaps European Portuguese?) might all use right-headed feet, as in the following, extremely tentative, table:

Table 2. *Typology of non-lexical prosodic systems.*

pitch on stress group	GERMANIC (left-headed)	ROMANCE (right-headed)
Low High [↓ ↑]	Dutch, German, Danish, Swedish	French, Italian, Portuguese (?)
High Low [↑ ↓]	US English	Spanish
Downstepping [>]	GB English	Romanian

Note that the pitch movement described is that which occurs on the stress group as a whole rather than just on the stressed syllable.

The existence of such a language specific characteristic for stress groups seems a promising area for future research into objective criteria for typological prosodic parameters. It remains to be seen in particular whether reliable phonetic correlates of left/right-headedness, such as different durational patterns, can be established on a cross-language basis.

2.2 Mode and expressivity

It has often been assumed, although this assumption has of course been questioned, that one of the most uncontroversial functions of intonation is that of conveying different illocutionary aspects, or **modes.**[5] Thus it is commonly maintained that a distinction between declarative and interrogative modes is one of the most universal characteristics of intonation systems and it is also often claimed that intonation contributes to the expression of other modes such as imperatives, vocatives, hortatives, optatives *etc.*, categories which gradually shade into what some authors see as a distinct category of expressive functions.

Even in the case of interrogative versus declarative, however, the nature of the distinction is far from uncontroversial since a question can be said to differ from a corresponding statement in its syntax, its semantics and its pragmatics, as well as any combination of the three. We shall not be concerned here directly with the different syntactic, semantic and/or pragmatic theories which have been proposed to account for these distinctions. While some authors in this volume claim that there is no specific intonation pattern systematically associated with questions, ('t Hart, Botinis, Iivonen this volume), in a great number of languages, differences in the intonation contours of utterances are said to correspond more regularly to differences in the mode of those utterances, on whatever level this is described. In the following section we briefly compare the various prosodic features which are associated with various modes in the languages described in this volume.

a. Unemphatic yes/no questions
The distinctive properties of intonation patterns associated with non-declarative utterances, in particular with questions, can be classified, like the patterns associated with the corresponding declarative utterances, as **global, local** or **recurrent** characteristics, according to the part of the contour which is affected by these properties.

i. Global characteristics One of the most frequent characteristics described concerning interrogative utterances is a raising of the pitch of all or part of the utterance (US English, Swedish, Brazilian Portuguese, Finnish, Hungarian, Western Arabic, Vietnamese, Thai) whether or not the utterance finishes with a final rise.

In two languages (Danish, Vietnamese), questions are said to contrast with declaratives by an absence of global declination.

ii. Recurrent patterns In French, questions are said to contrast with declaratives through the choice of a different range of recurrent pitch patterns on the stress groups of the unit. The unmarked recurrent pattern is described as rising for declaratives but downstepping for questions, whether or not the question is marked with a final rise.

iii. Local characteristics. By far the most commonly described characteristic of questions is a high final pitch. This corresponds to the intuition that questions have rising intonation whereas declaratives have falling intonation. Bolinger (1978b) reported that about 70% of a sample of nearly 250 languages were said to use a rising terminal to signal questions and that the remaining 30% used a higher over-all pitch for questions than for non-questions.

In this volume a high final pitch for non-emphatic yes/no questions is said to be a common pattern for all the languages except Danish, Finnish, Hungarian, Bulgarian, Russian, Western Arabic and Brazilian Portuguese. In Danish, Finnish and Western Arabic, there is no local pitch characteristic for straightforward yes/no questions, and these are consequently distinguished from statements only by the global characteristics described above. In the case of Brazilian Portuguese, Romanian, Bulgarian, Russian and Hungarian, there is said to be a distinctive pattern on questions which constitutes a final rise only when the last stressed syllable is in sentence final position. Otherwise the pattern consists of a rise on the last stressed syllable followed by a falling pattern on the subsequent unstressed syllables.

For the remaining languages a high final pitch is described as the unmarked pattern for yes/no questions although several authors note, as Bolinger (this volume) puts it:

There are both questions without rises and rises without questions.

When yes/no questions are pronounced without a final rise in these languages they are often said to be perceived as having added connotations.

b. WH-questions

In many languages (English, Spanish, Romanian, Russian, Greek) the intonation of WH-questions is described as being more similar to that of statements than that of yes-no questions. In French, unmarked WH-questions are pronounced with a falling final pitch like statements but the recurrent rising pattern found in statements is frequently replaced by the downstepping pattern observed in yes-no questions. As with imperatives, a rising intonation in these languages can be felt to mark the utterance as "friendly". In Romanian and Greek, however, WH-questions are said to be more like emphatic declaratives and rising intonation is said to be rare. Finally, in British English at least (see §2.4), there seems to be a stronger constraint against breaking up utterances into smaller intonation units in the case of questions than in the case of statements.

c. Repeat questions

One particular type of question seems to be systematically produced with rising intonation in many languages. This is the type that either repeats or calls for a repetition. For example, in:

(16)   – How do you like it?
         – How do I like it?

the repeat question echoes the original question and in:

(17)   – John came last week.
         – When?
         – Last week.

the question calls for a repetition of all or part of what was said. The latter may be compared with:

(18)   – John came last week.
         – When?
         – On Tuesday.

in which the question tends to fall because no repetition is involved. These repeat questions could probably be translated into a number of different languages with the same distinction.

Echo questions are said to be invariably rising in English, Swedish, French, Portuguese, Romanian and Finnish. The rise is said to begin and end higher than in ordinary questions in European Portuguese.

d. Tag questions

An utterance pronounced as a statement can be turned into a question in several languages by adding a question tag (...don't you?) which generally constitutes a separate intonation unit with the normal intonation for a yes-no question. These question tags are described for English, French, Romanian, Portuguese and Western Arabic but are certainly more widespread.

e. Unfinished utterances

Like questions, unfinished utterances or continuatives are commonly pronounced with rising intonation in many languages. In fact a raised final pitch is perhaps even more common for continuatives than for questions: thus both Finnish and Bulgarian are described as using a raised final pitch for continuatives but not for questions. Bolinger takes non-finality to be a universal criterion entailing rising or high pitch on both statements and questions.

In Greek and British English, it is said that the final rise in continuatives can be just as high (in spontaneous dialogue) as in questions. French, European Portuguese, Russian and Romanian are described as using a fuller rise for questions than for continuatives, Thai is said to show a "tense-ending rise" for questions and a "lax-ending rise" for continuatives, while in Japanese a question is said to end with a rise, and a continuative with a level pitch. In Danish unfinished statements are said to exhibit a slightly declining pattern, intermediate between that of statements and that of questions.

f. Other modes and expressivity

A number of other correspondences between intonation and mode or expressivity are described sporadically in various chapters. Thus for example some languages are said to use rising pitch to distinguish requests from commands (although Bolinger suggests that while a command usually goes down a repeated command may rise), others are said to use high pitch to express *surprise*, Vietnamese uses high register to express *obviousness*, Finnish uses a delayed peak to express a *hinting* connotation, Brazilian Portuguese is said to have specific patterns for "commands, requests, suggestions, advice and threats" *etc.* Intonation is not alone in conveying these expressive functions. As both Gårding and Cruz-Ferreira point out, we also need to mention voice quality and other "paralinguistic" features for some distinctions. There are, in fact, few cases where the description of such correspondences seems to reflect any strikingly language specific characteristics. The expressiveness of intonation seems to be the area where universality is at its greatest although of course it is quite possible that this reflects more the state of the art than the state of the world.

2.3 Contextual effects and focalisation

One of the most important functions which has been ascribed to prosody is the part it plays in the way speakers organise and listeners identify information in an utterance. This has given rise to much recent work dealing with the pragmatics of accents, intonation and temporal organisation (cf. for example: Brown and Yule 1983, Eaddy and Cooper 1986, Terken 1985, papers in Johns-Lewis (ed.) 1986, Nooteboom and Kruyt 1987, Pierrehumbert and Hirschberg 1990).

These studies make use of a number of related concepts such as theme/rheme, topic/comment, given/new, presupposition/focus, psychological subject /psychological predicate, background/foreground *etc.* which have been proposed at various times to describe the complex nature of the pragmatic organisation of an utterance and its relation to the discourse context. There is, however, no overall pragmatic framework generally accepted today which is capable of taking into account all the different aspects of this organisation.

Sperber and Wilson, in a recent attempt (1986) to provide such a general pragmatic framework remark that:

there is a huge descriptive literature in this area, but nothing approaching an explanatory theory of the relation between linguistic structure and pragmatic effects. (p. 203)

a. Ground and figure

The basic idea behind all work in this area is that communication takes place against a background of shared knowledge so that the way a listener interprets an utterance will be partly dependent on the (situational) context in which the utterance occurs.

This idea follows a more general principle which had been proposed in the beginning of the century by the Czech psychologist Wertheimer [1886–1943], one of the founders of the Gestalt School of psychology, according to which the perception of a stimulus, particularly in the case of vision, generally consists in attributing a structure in which one part of the stimulus, called the **figure**, seems to stand out against the rest of the stimulus, called the **ground** (cf. Thomson 1968 chapter 13). Under different conditions, the same stimulus can be structured differently into figure and ground, giving rise to a number of familiar optical illusions.

The first person to apply a similar idea to language was another Czech, the linguist Mathesius [1882–1945], founder of the Prague Linguistic Circle, whose theory of **Functional Sentence Perspective** was taken up and developed by other linguists of the Prague School such as Daneš and Firbas. According to this theory, as expounded by Daneš (1967), utterances generally have a bipartite structure consisting of, on the one hand, what the utterance is about: its subject, theme or topic, and, on the other hand, what the utterance says about it. According to Daneš, the original Czech terms **základ** (or **téma**) and **jádro** were first translated by "some Czech scholars" as respectively **theme** and **rheme,** and then later by Y.R. Chao, followed by Hockett (1963) and Daneš himself, as **topic** and **comment**.

The idea that utterances contain a third level of organisation besides syntax and semantics and that one of the main exponents of this organisation is rhythm and intonation (cf. Daneš 1964) was taken up by Halliday in an influential series of publications (1963a,b,c, 1967a,b, 1970) in which he argued, following Mathesius, that besides the thematic structure of an utterance **theme/rheme,** there is a parallel **contextual structure,** according to which information is classified into on the one hand what is **old, already known** or **given** and on the other hand what is **new.**

Halliday also introduced the expression **information focus** (1963b), (although the term "focal accent" had been used by Sharp 1958) to refer to the part of an utterance which is highlighted by pitch prominence. The term focus was taken up later by generative linguists after Chomsky (1970) suggested that the semantic interpretation of an utterance needs to refer to the focus and presupposition, where:

The focus is the phrase containing the intonation center and the presupposition is determined by replacing the focus by a variable. (p. 91)

The link between presupposition/focus, theme/rheme and given/new was made explicit by Jackendoff (1972):

The focus and presupposition designate what information in the sentence is intended to be new and what is intended to be old. (p. 3)

It would obviously take us too far afield to discuss the more recent history of these concepts in any detail but for general discussion from various points of view cf. Firbas 1964, Chafe 1970, 1976, Haviland and Clark 1974, Prince 1981, Reinhart 1981, Culicover and Rochemont 1983. For discussion of their relevance to the study of intonation cf. Ladd 1980, Rossi *et al.* 1981, Brown 1983, Fuchs 1984, Gussenhoven 1984, Schaffer 1984, Selkirk 1984, Rossi 1985, Couper-Kuhlen 1986, Cruttenden 1986, Bolinger 1986b, 1989. There seem to be two basic uses which have been made of these dichotomies and which are reflected in the contributions to this book. The basic distinction is obviously a **cognitive** one. As Chafe puts it:

Given (or old) information is that knowledge which the speaker assumes to be in the consciousness of the addressee at the time of the utterance.

While it seems difficult to dispute the cognitive relevance of such distinctions, opinions differ as to whether it is necessary to set up formal linguistic categories as exponents of them.

Hirst (1989, this volume) following Sperber and Wilson (1986) claims explicitly that these categories are not necessary:

Once we find a way of accounting for these phenomena along the pragmatic lines Sperber and Wilson suggest, we are free to assume that neither focus, nor theme, nor topic have any place in the linguistic description of sentences. (p. 141)

A similar position seems to be implicit in the usage of some authors in this volume (Gibbon, Cruz-Ferreira, Moraes) who make use of the distinction old/new or theme/rheme only in a cognitive sense. In other cases, it is felt necessary to use a different term so that, for example, given/new is used as a cognitive label and theme/rheme as a linguistic category defining a constituent of the utterance (Rossi). For Bolinger "theme/rheme" is defined both cognitively ("what the utterance is about" *vs.* "what is said about the theme") and to refer to constituents of an utterance: "the rheme contains the most important – new, contrastive, interesting – information."

Halliday's original claim was that intonation provides a way of breaking up an utterance into "information units" and that the nucleus (or "tonic" in Halliday's terminology) of each unit marks the end of the new information.

This claim that there is a one-one correspondence between prosody and information has been the subject of much controversy. Thus it has been argued that in sentences like *The TElevision has just exploded*, the nucleus does not necessarily mark the end of new information (Schmerling 1976), that an Intonation Unit can have more than one nucleus (Brown 1983), that given information can be just as accented as new information (Nooteboom and Kruyt 1987) and finally that the distinction between given and new is scalar rather than binary, reflecting different degrees of *givenness* for different items (Terken 1981).

Some authors in this book claim that there is a specific type of accent which acts as a marker of a rhematic element (Gibbon, Alcoba and Murillo, Di Cristo, Svetozarova, Iivonen) or that the distinction corresponds to different levels of accentuation with a higher accent for rheme and a lower one for theme (Bolinger, Iivonen, Nikov and Misheva, Svetozarova). There is, however, fairly general agreement on the fact that the specific pitch patterns of theme and rheme depend on the mode of the utterance (statement or question) as well as, for the theme, on its position in the utterance.

For statements with neutral word order, *i.e.* theme followed by rheme, a continuative pattern for the theme (rising movement or final rise) is described for several different languages (American English, Brazilian Portuguese, French,

Italian, Russian, Bulgarian). In French and Italian, an initial element pronounced as a question is described as constituting an emphatic theme. When the theme follows the rheme, the pitch pattern is variously described as rising or accentless (American English), low falling (Brazilian Portuguese and Bulgarian) or low flat (French and Italian).

The only languages for which the treatment of the theme in questions is discussed are Brazilian Portuguese, Romanian and French. When the theme comes first it has a final fall in Brazilian Portuguese and a globally falling (downstepped) pattern in French. When the theme is postposed it is pronounced with a rise in Brazilian Portuguese and with a high flat pattern or a rise in French.

The rheme is generally said to be characterised by a terminal pitch pattern regardless of its position in the utterance. This pattern is described as falling or rising-falling for statements (French, Italian, Brazilian Portuguese) and rising for questions (French, Brazilian Portuguese, Russian).

b. Focalisation and emphasis
So far we have presented the notion of focus/presupposition as equivalent to that of theme/rheme, given/new or topic/comment. In fact focus is a more general notion than the others which attempts to account by means of a single mechanism both for the given/new aspects of an utterance and at the same time for what has traditionally been treated under a separate heading as **emphasis** or **contrast**. **Contrast** has traditionally been held to be a subset of **emphasis.**

Chafe (1976) remarks that:

Contrastiveness is different from other statuses, and particularly the status of focus of contrast is different from the status of new. There are confusions of contrastiveness with the given-new distinction. There is an unfortunate tendency of both linguists and psychologists to pick foci of contrast as paradigm examples of new information.

Both focalisation and emphasis may be simply defined as the speaker's highlighting of part of an utterance. This is sometimes called **narrow focus** as opposed to **broad focus** in which all the parts of an utterance are given equal prominence (Ladd 1980). A similar distinction is made by Luksaneeyanawin (expressive focus/end focus) and by Nikov and Misheva (emphatic focus/neutral focus). Most contributors to this book, however, use the term **focus** or **focal accent** in its narrow sense.

Some authors prefer the term **emphasis** (Hirst, Dascălu-Jinga, Abe), **pragmatic accent** (Rossi) or **special prominence** (Svetozarova) to that of **focus**. Not much depends on this terminological choice, except for the fact that whereas emphasis is basically a paradigmatic notion, *i.e.* a given item is either emphatic or non-emphatic, focus is basically syntagmatic: focus is on one element of a sequence (more strictly it applies to one node of a tree). This implies that while it is possible to refer to emphatic and non-emphatic versions of an utterance consisting of a single word, (such as *no. vs. NO!*) it is not possible within standard treatments of focus to distinguish broad and narrow focus on a single item (for discussion cf. Hirst this volume).

The traditional distinction between **emphasis for intensity** and **emphasis for contrast,** which Jones (1918) attributes to Coleman (1914), is adopted by a number of authors under various different names including, respectively: **expressive / informative focus** (Gårding): **focus for intensification / focus for contrast** (Di Cristo), **emphasis / contrast** (Dascălu-Jinga, Svetozarova, Nikov and Misheva, Iivonen).

Most languages provide both textual means and prosodic means for emphasising an element of an utterance: very often the textual means is not sufficient by itself. Thus in Western Arabic (Benkirane) an emphasised word is likely to be followed by the morpheme /lli/ and accompanied by an emphatic accent.

It is interesting that emphasis **can** be manifested by intonation alone, without any modification of the syntactic structure. This seems to be the case for all the languages described in this book. It is often claimed that any word of an utterance, including functional words, can receive contrastive emphasis (as for example in French and Chinese).

In European Portuguese (Cruz-Ferreira), a relatively free word order, combined with a principle of **end focus**, has the effect of creating a strong pressure for the word with the highest informational content to be placed at the end of the intonation group, especially in the case of contrast.

(19)   Eu prefiro que ela VENHA   (I prefer her to come).
(20)   Eu prefiro que venha ELA.   (I prefer HER to come).

There are however limits to the freedom of word order and intonational devices take over in cases where grammatical constraints forbid the shifting of a contrasted word to final position. In this case, in Portuguese too, any word within an utterance may be given prominence and take the nucleus.

In the majority of languages described in this volume, focalisation and/or emphasis is said to be manifested by an extra pitch prominence, giving rise to larger F_0 movements often accompanied by extra intensity and duration.

In some languages, it is said that focalisation does not imply the use of a specific pitch pattern. This is the case for Dutch ('t Hart) where focalisation for contrast may be achieved by simply flattening out the surrounding pitch accents. According to 't Hart, contrast is not always deducible from the shape of the pitch contour alone and the interpretation of an accent as contrastive in Dutch needs to refer to the context. Other languages which are described as not having a specific emphatic pitch pattern are Swedish (southern dialects) where the rising-falling pattern of the focused word is similar to that of the sentence accent, and Copenhagen Danish which has no specific emphatic form as opposed to the dialect of Bornholm which uses a rising-falling pattern, similar to a final sentence accent.

When focalisation is accompanied by extra prominence this may be **aligned** with a specific syllable of the focused word: this can be the main stressed syllable as in American English, Romanian, Spanish, Bulgarian *etc.* or an earlier unstressed or secondary stressed syllable as in Brazilian Portuguese, Finnish, French and Chinese. In some cases, (French, Japanese, Chinese) the extra-pitch prominence may spread over the entire word. In a few languages, focalisation is manifested by a rising pitch movement, which may spread over the emphasised word, as in Hungarian and Arabic, or which is more locally defined, as in the dialect of Stockholm (Bruce 1977, quoted by Gårding this volume) where the rise follows the fall of the preceding word accent, with different timing depending on the accent. The last emphatic pitch pattern described by contributors to this volume is a rising-falling one (French, Italian, Russian, and Greek). The timing of the rise and the fall is not specified for Russian, but in Italian and Greek the rise is aligned with the stressed syllable and the fall takes place on the post-nuclear syllable. In French (focalisation for contrast), the rise can take place on any syllable of the focused word, and the last full (stressed) syllable receives a terminal fall, delimiting the focused item as an independent intonation unit. In the case of a focalisation for expressive contrast, both the rise and the fall are compressed onto the final stressed syllable.

The focalisation of part of an utterance leads to modifications of the global pitch pattern which are more or less important depending on the language and/or the dialect. In some languages, focalisation is accompanied by a reduction of surrounding pitch accents both before and after the nucleus. In Danish the flattening of surrounding accents is said to be more important than the upward boosting of the emphasised syllable, while in Dutch, as mentioned above, the surrounding accents may be completely deleted. Western Arabic is said to have no accentual prominence outside the focused word and in Chinese the underlying prominence pattern in the focus domain is occasionally overridden.

After focus, practically all languages in this volume are described as exhibiting an accentless pattern (*i.e.* a low or parenthetic F_0 plateau): French, Italian, Brazilian Portuguese, Danish (non-contrastive focalisation in Copenhagen) and Greek. The only exception described in this collection is Swedish (Southern dialects) where the accented syllables (word accents) often retain their pitch prominence after focus although both phrase and sentence accents are said to be deleted. In general, the pre-focal part does not seem to show such drastic modifications: the prefocal pitch pattern is described as unmodified in Swedish, Italian and Brazilian Portuguese and simply reduced in Danish.

2.4 Phrasing and textual organisation

a. Levels of representation

A very serious problem facing any description of intonation is, as we saw above in section §1.2, that of representation. Specifically we need to decide how we are to represent the fact that the phonetic events that constitute an intonation pattern (however these are themselves represented *i.e.* as tones, turning points, pitch accents *etc.*) seem to have a certain autonomy with respect to the segmental phonematic material, just as in a song the words and the music each have a certain autonomy.

One of the first formal solutions proposed for this problem was to think, as in the representation of a song, in terms of two more or less independent lines where the constituents of intonation were referred to as "prosodemes" (Bloch and Trager 1942), "suprasegmentals" (Hockett 1942), "long components" (Harris 1944) or "prosodies" (Firth 1948). Since the two lines are obviously not entirely independent there must be some way of linking them at various points just as the bar-lines in musical notation provide a point of synchronisation between the text and the music. This was done by postulating a certain number of "secondary phonemes" (Bloomfield 1933) or "juncture phonemes" (Trager and Bloch 1942, Trager and Smith 1951). These junctures were later taken over into the theory of generative phonology (Halle 1959, Chomsky and Halle 1968) and have left their mark on much subsequent work on intonation within a generative framework (Leben 1973, Goldsmith 1976, Pierrehumbert 1980 *etc.*)

Another way of synchronising the segmental and the suprasegmental elements of a representation was to assume that intonation has a hierarchical structure and that it is this structure which is linked to the segmental material. This approach has been characteristic of the British school of analysis[6] from Palmer (1922) to Cruttenden (1986) and Couper-Kuhlen (1986) although the first person to have proposed such an analysis in print seems to have been Klinghardt in his analysis of the intonation of English (Klinghardt and Klemm 1920), where he breaks down a "speech measure" (Sprechtakt) into component parts:

(21) **Auftakt** **Taktkopf** **Neuhebung Tiefton** **Abtakt**
(Pre-measure) (Head) (Re-raising) (Low tone) (Post-measure)

This analysis, with only slight modification, was to become the familiar structure as described (with some slight variation) for example by Palmer (1922), Kingdon (1958), O'Connor and Arnold (1961), Crystal (1969):

(22) **Pre-head** **Head** **Nucleus** **Tail**

A systematically hierarchical analysis of intonation patterns was introduced by Jassem (1952). This model proposed a two-level structure by which a complete utterance can be segmented into a discrete sequence of **tone groups**, each tone group being itself segmented into a discrete sequence of **tonal units**. Jassem's tonal unit is in fact identical to the **stress-foot** introduced later by Abercrombie (1964) and adopted for describing intonation by Halliday (1967a). Abercrombie and Halliday, as we saw earlier, however, adopted the same unit for modelling rhythm and intonation whereas Jassem describes distinct structures: the rhythm unit and the tonal unit.

In this volume, a two-level structure is used by several authors under different names as in table 3. A similar binary hierarchy is implied in the use of major and minor continuatives (Dascălu-Jinga) or intonation morphemes and accent morphemes (Rossi).

It remains an empirical question whether it can be shown that more than two levels are necessary for an adequate theory of intonation. Liberman and Prince (1977) proposed a theory of binary branching phonological structure which contains a potentially infinite number of levels. Martin's (1977, 1981) model of intonation also allows the same sort of infinite recursivity. A more highly articulated model of phonological structure has been proposed by Selkirk (1978) and developed by Nespor and Vogel (1986). According to this model a phonological representation consists of a nested structure of phonological categories ranging from Utterance to Segment, which include Intonation Phrase, Phonological Phrase, Clitic Group, Phonological Word, Foot and Syllable, each category consisting of a discrete sequence of categories of the next lowest level. Other authors have suggested that a more satisfactory approach might be to use a smaller number of constituent types but with a certain degree of recursivity (Hirst 1983b, 1987, Ladd 1986). There is obviously a great deal of work which remains to be done in this area in order to examine how the constituent structures defined by these authors correspond to the generally simpler structures used in describing intonation patterns.

In this volume several authors feel the need for at least one intermediate level between the intonation unit and the stress-foot.

It has sometimes been suggested (e.g. Trim 1959) that there is additional structure **above** the level of the Intonation Unit. Fox (1973) proposed the term "paratone" for a higher order level of this type. Misheva and Nikov refer to "phono-paragraphs". Several authors in this volume (Gibbon, Gårding, Grønnum, Botinis, Iivonen) mention the problem of intonational structuring in continuous discourse and dialogue. Botinis uses the terms "turn-unit" and "sub-turn-unit" for units of dialogue structure.

b. Acoustic marks of intonation boundaries

Most authors assume that the boundary of an Intonation Unit is signalled by a terminal pitch movement (English, German, Dutch, Spanish, Romanian, Italian, Japanese, Finnish, Western Arabic) or by the presence of a final sentence accent or nucleus (Portuguese, Greek, Thai). Other cues which are mentioned are silent or filled pauses (Swedish, European Portuguese, French, Russian,

Table 3. *Three-level hierarchical structures used by authors in this volume.*

Level 1	Level 2	Level 3	authors
prosodic sentence	prosodic phrase	prosodic word	Gårding
			Botinis
prosodic sentence	prosodic phrase	stress group	Grønnum
intonation unit	prosodic word	tonal unit	Di Cristo
phrase	syntagma	phonetic word	Misheva & Nikov
phrase	speech measure	foot	Iivonen

Finnish, Thai), final lengthening (Spanish, French, Italian), rhythmic cohesion (German), change of tempo (European Portuguese) and pitch resetting (Dutch).

c. Syntactic and pragmatic constraints

Since the earliest studies of intonation, there has been a debate over to what extent Intonation Units are syntactically, semantically or pragmatically determined. Extreme positions have been vigorously defended at both ends of the spectrum. A reasonably general consensus (which is however somewhat short of unanimity), seems to have been reached to the conclusion that while pragmatic reasons for dividing an utterance ultimately prevail there are nonetheless a number of syntactic constraints which need to be respected.

The idea that intonation units somehow constitute units of information or sense units is agreed on by most contributors (Bolinger, Hirst, Gårding, Grønnum, Cruz-Ferreira, Moraes, Di Cristo, Rossi, Misheva and Nikov, Svetozarova, Luksaneeyanawin). They also generally agree that while there is no one-one correspondence between syntax and prosody, there is a tendency for intonation units to correspond to clauses (German, Dutch, Portuguese).

It will be clear from the above that there appears to be no evidence that different languages make use of a different number of levels of intonation structure. Nor do the different languages seem to show much difference in the way pragmatic and syntactic constraints determine the division of an utterance into intonation groups: rather the data from each language needs to be weighed in order to establish empirical evidence for an appropriate model for representing intonation which would be valid for the description of the intonation system of all languages.

2.5 Stereotyped patterns

An extremely interesting variety of intonation patterns called "stereotyped patterns", "stylised patterns" or "intonation clichés" have been described for a number of different languages (Pike 1945, Abe 1962, Gibbon 1975, Ladd 1978, Fónagy and Fónagy 1983). These patterns are characterised by the fact that they give the impression of being halfway between speech and song. In this volume, the most frequently cited use of these chants is for calling: a pattern of this type is mentioned for English, German, Dutch, French, Romanian, Japanese and Thai. Another fairly common usage is in jeering chants particularly (but not exclusively) in children's speech (English, German, French). Other uses mentioned include greetings (German), warnings (Thai), enumerations (Spanish, French, German). Stereotyped patterns are certainly more widespread than this but have not yet been studied in several languages. There is some indication of language specific use of these patterns which seem to have wider use in German (Gibbon) and French (Di Cristo) than in English (Bolinger, Hirst) for example.

3. Comparisons with other systems

3.1 Comparisons within languages

Theoretically, there is no reason why differences observed between different languages should not also be observed between dialects of the same language (assuming of course that a distinction between dialects and languages can be founded on linguistic rather than political or sociological criteria). After all, differences between Indo-European languages presumably derive at least in part from differences between earlier dialects of Proto-Indo-European. We can, however, reasonably suppose that, on average, differences between distinct languages will be greater than differences between dialects of the same language, and we should thus expect to find that dialectal variations are statistically more often minor or superficial differences rather than major fundamental ones. In so far as the prosodic characteristics we have described in this chapter are concerned, it seems reasonable to assume that lexical characteristics are more fundamental than non-lexical ones. There does not, however, appear to be any *a priori* reason to classify other prosodic characteristics as fundamental or superficial. The study of dialectal variation could consequently provide a useful tool for this task.

a. Lexical characteristics

Dialectal variations can affect the lexical characteristics of a prosodic system although in this volume there are far fewer cases of this type than those concerning non-lexical characteristics.

In respect of the typology of lexical prosodic systems we proposed above (§1.1, table 3) there is only one case where a dialect would need to be classified under a different category from that of the standard language. In the dialect of Swedish spoken in Finland (Gårding) the distinction between Accent 1 and Accent 2 is neutralised so that this dialect would be classified as a free stress system rather than as a tonal accent system.

In other cases, lexical characteristics vary between dialects but without changing the typological category of the system. The Emilian dialect of Italian (Rossi) is characterised by a tendency for final word stress rather than penultimate stress which is predominant in most other dialects. In Japanese (Abe) the tonal systems are manifested differently in different dialects, the same morpheme being pronounced low-high-high in Tokyo, high-high-high in Kyoto and low-low-high in Kyushu for example. Dialects of South Vietnam differ from those of the North by a neutralisation of one of the tonal contrasts observed in the standard dialect. Dialects of central Vietnam are said to show greater variety than in either the North or the South. In some central dialects a certain degree of neutralisation of tonal contrasts occurs so that speakers from these regions are said to speak "with a level voice".

b. Non-lexical characteristics

These characteristics fall into three main categories: rhythm and temporal organisation, sentence accent and pitch patterns.

i. Rhythm and temporal organisation. We suggested above (§2.1) that there is some evidence that stress groups in European and Brazilian dialects of Portuguese may be organised into left-headed and right-headed structures respectively. If this proves to be the case it would be the only example in this volume of a dialectal variation of this type although this is an area which has yet to be explored for many languages.

European Portuguese is also said to be characterised by a faster speech rate than Brazilian Portuguese (Moraes), an effect which is partly due to the fact that, contrary to Brazilian Portuguese, pre-nuclear central vowels are frequently dropped in European Portuguese.

Dialectal variations of rhythm are briefly mentioned as typical of some dialects of Finnish (Iivonen), Russian (Svetozarova) and French (Di Cristo) where a number of dialects from the North of France are characterised by a strongly marked stress on the initial or final syllable of words, which sounds like an emphatic stress to speakers of General French.

ii. Sentence accent. In Danish (Grønnum), the dialect of Bornholm can be distinguished from Standard (Copenhagen) Danish and other dialects by the fact that it possesses a sentence accent. Furthermore, whereas in Standard Danish, final lengthening is said to be "slight and non compulsory", the dialect of Bornholm exhibits a shortening of final syllables. This means that in Bornholm dialect a final syllable bearing a default or sentence accent is generally shorter than a non-final one, despite large pitch variations.

Final lengthening also has a different effect in two Southern French dialects (Provence and Languedoc), where schwa is maintained in the final syllable of an utterance. Final lengthening affects the last full syllable in Provence but the final unstressed syllable in Languedoc. These differences give the impression that the final contour in statements and yes/no questions is mainly realised on the nuclear syllable in Provence and on the post-nuclear syllable in Languedoc.

In Swedish (Gårding), dialectal variations are characterised by different manifestations of sentence accent: a two-peaked Accent 2 is found in central dialects in which sentence accent and word accent remain distinct, while a single-peaked Accent 2 is observable in Bergstaden and Gotland where sentence accent and word accent coincide.

The form of the focal accent in yes/no questions is different in dialects of Romanian (Dascălu-Jinga), being manifested by a positive pitch-obtrusion in North-Western dialects but with a negative one in Standard Romanian.

iii. Pitch patterns. The choice of a particular type of recurrent pitch pattern (§2.1 table 5) is described as a dialectal variation in English (Hirst), where the unemphatic pre-nuclear pattern is described as a sequence of falling pitch accents in several American and Scottish dialects but as a downstepping sequence in Standard British and as a sequence of rising accents in Welsh English. A similar variability is said to occur in German dialects (Gibbon). In Western Arabic (Benkirane) the pre-nuclear pattern is described as generally flat or rising whereas Syrian and Egyptian varieties of Eastern Arabic are said to show more melodic variation together with a distinct declination effect.

Qualitative pitch differences relative to the distinction between statements and yes/no questions are observed in dialects of Danish, Portuguese, Spanish, Romanian, Greek and Arabic. Sentence mode is said to be signalled globally (by declination slope) in Standard Danish and a number of other dialects, but locally in Bornholm and Sonderberg by a characteristic pitch rise located within the last stress group. In European Portuguese, yes/no questions are usually pronounced with a falling pitch on the nucleus followed by a rise on the final unstressed syllables (Cruz-Ferrreira), while in Brazilian Portuguese, pitch rises on the nucleus and drops on the final unstressed syllables (Moraes). In the Muscel (South Carpatian) dialect of Romanian (Dascălu-Jinga) yes/no questions have a rising terminal contour in all cases, whereas in standard Romanian, the final rise is determined both by the placement of the question focus and by the stress pattern of the final word. Questions in Eastern Arabic dialects are said to be commonly pronounced with a final rise whereas this is described as very uncommon in Western Arabic (Benkirane).

Contours with a final high pitch are found in declarative utterances in a number of Northern dialects of British English (Hirst) as well as in the Extramadura and Tucuman dialects of Spanish (Alcoba and Murillo). A similar observation is made for the Greek dialect of Corfu where statements may sound like questions to speakers of standard Greek (Botinis). Contours of this type are also said to be more frequent in Southern dialects of American English, particularly among younger speakers (Bolinger).

A rising-falling variant of the falling nuclear pitch pattern is described for dialects of three romance languages: Portuguese, Spanish and French. This pattern is frequently used in European Portuguese (Cruz-Ferreira), and is interpreted as attitudinal in Brazilian Portuguese (Moraes). Puerto Rican Spanish also has a pitch pattern of this type in declaratives and questions with interrogative pronouns. In French, a similar pattern is frequently observed in the final contour of Intonation Units in Corsica and Auvergne. A similar dialectal variant is described for German (Gibbon) where the neutral nuclear pitch pattern is described as being typically high with glide to low in the same syllable for Coastal dialects but with a delayed high pitch and slow post-nuclear fall to mid for Rhenish dialects.

In the light of the observations made by the authors of the chapters in this volume, it seems, as might be expected, that lexical prosodic characteristics are those which are the most resistant to dialectal variation, together possibly with the left/right-headed nature of the stress group. Among the parameters which seem more susceptible to dialectal variation are the recurrent pattern typical of unemphatic declaratives, the presence or absence of a final high pitch on yes/no questions as well as the presence or absence of a final high pitch on unemphatic declaratives. This list is of course extremely tentative but may perhaps suggest an extremely interesting direction for future research.

3.2 Comparisons across languages

As we mentioned in the beginning of this survey, (§1.2), the description of an intonation system is the result of a complex interaction between a language and an explicit or implicit theory. This fact is particularly apparent when we attempt to establish comparisons across languages since it is very often difficult to decide whether differences between descriptions are due to different theoretical and/or methodological approaches or whether they are to be put down to genuine differences between the systems constituting language specific prosodic parameters. In this section we briefly list a number of possible candidates for such parameters suggested either by the individual descriptions or by direct comparisons made by the different authors. It will be obvious that in the present state of our knowledge such a list can be neither exhaustive nor well-established: it constitutes rather a number of questions which we feel need to be addressed in future research.

a. Lexical characteristics
These are probably the most heavily theory-dependent of all prosodic characteristics. We suggested (§1.1 table 3) a typology defined by two

independent parameters: accent and tone. It is not at all evident what objective criteria might be used for establishing these parameters since, as we emphasised, the fact that stress or tone is lexically distinctive in a given language does not necessarily imply any easily identifiable acoustic pattern.

b. Non-lexical characteristics

As with dialectal variations, these can be grouped under three headings: rhythm and temporal organisation, sentence accent (and emphasis) and pitch patterns.

i. Rhythm and temporal organisation. There are few direct comparisons between the rhythmic characteristics of different languages but the fact that such characteristics are mentioned as typical of dialectal variations (Portuguese, French, Russian, Finnish) suggests that contrastive studies might well be able to identify systematic cross-language differences in this area. One suggestion (Botinis) is that the average ratio between stressed and unstressed syllables in languages forms a scale along which different languages can be situated.

We proposed a tentative prosodic parameter distinguishing **left-headed** languages, those in which unstressed syllables are grouped with a preceding stressed syllable, and **right-headed** languages where unstressed syllables are grouped with a following stressed syllable. We also suggested that if such structuring is in fact part of the mental representation of speech, we should expect this to give rise to different durational patternings in these languages. It remains, however, to be seen whether all languages can be classified according to this parameter, and whether a simple prosodic structure such as the stress group is sufficient or whether more complex structures need to be posited.

ii. Sentence accent and emphasis. One obvious candidate for a language specific prosodic parameter is the presence or absence of a specific type of pitch pattern for the final stress of unemphatic utterances (Grønnum). As mentioned above, it remains an open question whether the observed differences are best interpreted as different types of prominence or as different ways of signalling prosodic boundaries. Final lengthening also seems to apply differently across languages. Interestingly, Grønnum points out that this phenomenon is not an automatic correlate of a specific nuclear accent. There is also evidence from Grønnum's discussion of Germanic languages that the degree of final lengthening varies from one language to another.   Another possible parameter concerns the existence of a specific emphatic pattern signalled other than simply by the reduction or suppression of pitch accents before and/or after the nucleus.

iii. Pitch patterns. We have distinguished three types of characteristics of pitch patterns which we refer to as **global**, **recurrent** or **local**.

Global characteristics. For these, an obvious question which springs to mind is whether some languages are spoken on a higher overall pitch than others. Such a possibility is not mentioned in any of the chapters of this book but there is, as far as we know, little or no empirical data bearing on this issue. A similar question concerns the range of pitch variations used in different languages. In this respect, 't Hart notes that while two pitch levels were sufficient to model Dutch intonation patterns, three levels were needed to model English patterns adequately. It remains to be seen, however, whether an empirical procedure could be defined which would bring this characteristic to light.

Another global characteristic concerns the presence or absence of declination in an utterance. Botinis notes that little or no declination is to be observed in spontaneous Greek utterances but ascribes this rather to the nature of the speech sample than to a language specific characteristic. It is not known whether the difference of declination depending on sentence mode described for Danish is also observed in any other languages.

Recurrent characteristics. Recurrent pitch patterns coinciding with the stress group can be characterised as typically rising, falling or downstepping. Although this is a strikingly obvious characteristic of intonation patterns, considerable variability is found within individual languages depending on such factors as sentence modality (French), expressivity or dialectal variation (English, German).

Local characteristics. In all standard dialects of the languages described in this book, unemphatic statements are said to finish typically on a low pitch. In a few non-standard dialects (English, Spanish and Greek and no doubt other languages), however, the unmarked pattern appears to be one which finishes on a high pitch.

One of the most obvious local characteristics is the use or not of final high pitch in questions. Final high pitch is said to be a common way of signalling questions in most of the languages described here but is described as uncommon in a number of languages from different phyla (*e.g.* Danish, Finnish and Western Arabic). It is worth noting, however, that some of these languages commonly use final rising pitch for unfinished utterances. In a number of languages, two different types of rises, one for unfinished utterances and another for questions, are described although it is not known how widespread or how systematic such a distinction is.

4. Conclusions

We have emphasised over and over again during this introduction the fact that it is extremely difficult to factor out the language specific prosodic characteristics of a language from the theoretical assumptions and background of the author. In order to establish a typology of prosodic parameters more firmly, it will, in our view, be necessary to undertake systematic co-operative research on an international basis. The most promising direction would perhaps be to attempt to establish a list of objective procedures making as few theoretical assumptions as possible with a view to establishing empirical evidence for the existence of language specific prosodic parameters. It is to be expected that the wider availability of modern technology, including in particular high quality synthesis applied to a large number of languages, will prove an extremely effective tool for this type of research.

One interesting, and to our mind extremely promising, line of research for coming years will be into dialectal variations of intonation systems. It is, after all, arguably easier for one linguist to familiarise himself with three or four dialects of his native language than it is for him to attain an equivalent degree of competence in three or four different languages. As we mentioned above, the variability observed in the intonation systems of different languages is also reflected to a great extent in the variability between dialects of the same language. The study of dialectal variation may provide a valuable source of information as to which parameters of an intonation system are deeply anchored in the system and which are more superficial and hence more susceptible to variation from one dialect to another.

Another aspect which will probably prove important for future research concerns the type of corpus submitted to analysis. The majority of the work reported in this volume is based on the analysis of a form of speech which has come to be known, sometimes rather disparagingly, as "laboratory speech", consisting of isolated sentences pronounced out of context, usually read rather than produced spontaneously (but cf. in particular the chapters by Grønnum, Botinis and Kratochvil). An obvious question which needs to be answered is how far does variability in the situations in which speech is produced influence the results obtained under these conditions? To what degree do generalisations obtained from isolated sentences apply to more spontaneous situations of communication? Do speakers make use of the same prosodic competence in all cases or are completely different processes at work? There is obviously still a great deal of work to be done in this area before we can even begin to answer these questions.

Finally, it is to be hoped that progress will be made in the next decade towards what one of us has referred to elsewhere as a "Third Generation"model of intonation (Hirst 1991), which would go beyond single language descriptions (first generation) and multi-language descriptions (second generation) by defining a number of independent levels of representation determined by more general linguistic principles. Such a model can only come about as the result of a concentration of collaborative work. It is our hope that this volume will be a first step in that direction.

Notes

1   The terms stress and accent are perhaps those where the greatest divergence of usage is to be observed. For some (e.g. Bolinger 1958) the term stress refers to a lexical characteristic whereas accent refers to a physical manifestation. For others, stress refers essentially to loudness and accent to pitch. Yet others (Beckman 1986) use stress for a physical characteristic (intensity and duration) and accent for a syntagmatic manifestation of prominence. In the rest of this chapter we use the two terms practically interchangeably and specify when necessary on what level they are intended to apply.

2   See note 4 below for the distinction between downstep and downdrift.

3   Bolinger quotes a similar typographic representation of an intonation pattern by Mark Twain in chapter 5 of *Tom Sawyer*.

4   This distinction between **downdrift** and **downstep** is fairly standard in the field of lexical tone systems. It has, however, unfortunately become quite common practice in recent work on intonation to use the term **downstep** (instead of **downdrift**) for the lowering of the second of two High tones separated by an intervening Low.

5   This is also sometimes called "modality", "mood", "modus" etc. depending whether emphasis is placed on the syntactic, semantic or pragmatic aspect of the distinctions). We use the term **mode** here as a global cover term for all these distinctions.

6   For a historical account cf Gibbon (1976b) chapter 3 and Cruttenden (1990).

2

Intonation in American English

DWIGHT BOLINGER

[Note: *Dwight Bolinger's global semiotic approach to intonation is rather different to that of most of the other contributions to this volume. For this reason, the chapter on American English does not follow the outline used in the other chapters.* The Editors.]

With minor differences, American English shares a single intonation system with English in general, particularly Southern British. The differences are not in the configurations (presence *versus* absence, or sameness *versus* difference of meaning) but in frequency and pragmatic choice. As with intonation in general, that of American English is highly iconic and must be studied in relation to the entire gestural setting, especially facial expression and expressive body language. A higher pitch is typically associated with higher positions of the eyebrows, shoulders, and often hands and arms, though these movements may be masked or even reversed for complicated effects. For example, a declarative sentence like *You're going, then?* may show its degree of assurance by falling pitch, but still be signalled as a question – as needing confirmation – by raised eyebrows and possibly raised corners of the mouth. Or the opposite can happen – rising pitch calling for the answer (confirmation) and a dour expression pointing to something that is not "upbeat", perhaps unpleasant consequences.

American English has neither word tones nor segmental tones. The connections are affective and sporadic, depending on the speaker's immediate intentions – for example, lowering the pitch in describing something as *big, big*, raising it for *tiny, tiny*, and lengthening the syllable for *long, long (a long,*

long way). These changes are phonesthematic (high pitch generally accompanied by raising and fronting the vowel or even altering it, *tiny* → *teeny*), not intonational in any patterned sense. There are, however, many intonational idioms. Some consist of more or less stereotyped connections between intonation and particular locutions, *e.g.*

(1)   Big
           de al!

(2)   I'll
           show him a thing or two!

for dismissing the importance of something and mildly vengeful threat respectively. Others are tied to some grammatical construction, *e.g.* the casual exclamation using a comparative or superlative such as *I had the strangest experience the other day!* or *I've lost more patients that way!*, using the shape:

(3)   I've lost   more pa
                    tients that way!

which would suggest that the speaker did not take the loss seriously, contrasting with

(4)   I've lost more   pa
                    tients that way!

to explain why a certain medical procedure was not being followed. Yet even here the connection between the intonation and the locutions is loose, the intonation retaining its underlying meaning. In the case of *Big deal!* the configuration is the same as with *Ho, hum!*, suggesting "boredom" – hence "I'm bored with (I don't respect) your idea of the importance of this"; the two can be combined: *Ho, hum!, Big deal!*

At the border between intonation and music there are certain chants whose rhythms are musical rather than intonational, the best known of which are the jeering chant used by children,

(5)   Freddie   a sweet
             has   heart!

and the calling tune, which is more intonational because an impatient caller is apt to vary it in the expected direction, up, if it is necessary to repeat:

(6)   Fe li cia!   cia!
                  Feli

46

As with other intonation systems, fundamental pitch in American English, in its productive (non-stereotyped) aspects, has three main functions in its interaction with linguistic structure: to form accents, closures, and contours.

Accents are abrupt changes in pitch usually combined with increases in length and loudness, imposed, as a rule, on the "stressed" syllable of a word that is to be highlighted. Highlighting may be for the sake of **interest** – the word in question (or a phrase containing it) arouses the speaker, who makes it stand out in pitch, and the hearer interprets that as something focused for "contrast", "importance", "informativeness", *etc.*, whatever excites interest. (Accent alone suffices, though certain grammatical devices serve as backup, *e.g.* "clefting": *It was JOHN who said that* alongside *JOHN said that*.) Or accent may be for impact: the more accents an utterance carries, the more **power** it has, and utterances of any length ordinarily have at least two, an annunciatory one at or near the beginning and a conclusive one at or near the end. The power aspect of accent makes the utterance persuasive: a declarative sentence depends on it for degree of assertiveness, a question for degree of pleading, *etc.* It is possible, for maximum impact, to accent every syllable of an utterance, even to stretch a single syllable and put more than one accent on it, as in a super-emphatic pronunciation of *No—o—o!* And redundant words may be thrown in for the sake of extra accents, as in *I did it with my OWN TWO HANDS*.

The two sides of accent, power and interest, are balanced against each other. As a rule, utterances are adjusted so that accents of interest can also serve as accents of power.

Compare

(7)   I know he went, but I don't know (to) WHERE.

(8)   I know he went, but I don't know where TO.

(9)   * I know he went, but I don't know WHERE to.

(10)   I've got to do it sómewhere, but I don't know WHERE to.

(7) and (8) are satisfactory because they put key directional words (the meaning is directional, and both *where* and *to* are relevant and can be accented for their own sake) in the key power position, as close as possible to the end. (9) is not satisfactory because even though *where* is accented, and that sufficed in (7), the end position is unaccented when it could be accented (directional *to* is just as important as directional *where*) – accent of interest is partially satisfied but accent of power is not. But (10) presents no problem, since the *to* is the *to* of the infinitive and is of little intrinsic interest. (Even there, however, a surge of power could shift the main accent to *to*, giving the interpretation *I don't know where TO do it*.)

Closures in spoken language are crudely represented in writing by punctuation marks: period for fall, question mark for rise, semicolon for shallow fall, comma for slight rise or sustention, parentheses for overall lowering of pitch (an "aside"). Children learn closures in association with pause, which is simply "separation" in speech corresponding to separation of ideas; adults may continue to imagine a pause where the intonation behaves as if the pause were still there. Though essential to the segmentation of speech and to that extent "grammatical", closures are basically metaphorical: a fall is "finality" in any sense (end of a series, end of a main part, "nothing more worth saying" hence positiveness); a rise or high pitch is non-finality in any sense ("not through speaking", "answer my question", "incomplete utterance", "too excited to calm down", "give me feedback"). Each of these pitch movements is graded: a deeper fall makes for greater finality (for example end of a paragraph as against end of a sentence), and a fall that ends on a level non-low tone may resemble a rise as a signal of non-finality. A higher rise makes for higher excitement, a more demanding question, a wider separation, *etc.* Wider separation has grammatical uses to mark the rank of clauses. In both (11) and (12),

(11)   If you see him when you get there, call me.

(12)   If you see him, when you get there call me.

there may be simple rises on *him* and *there*, but the higher rise is at the comma – the "major separation" is marked with the wider excursion of pitch, usually along with pause.

Contours (or intonation groups) are the melodic shapes of utterances, more or less delimited by closures, within which accents are grouped along with unaccented material. A contour is to a profile (shape of an individual accent) approximately what a sentence is to a phrase. There are as many profiles in a contour as there are accents, and a single profile may constitute a contour, as in:

(13)   I ^{tóld} _{you!}

(14)   ^I tóld _{you!}

both answering the question *How was I supposed to know?* There is one accent, on *told*, marked by the wide downward pitch jump after that word. (A less important feature, the pitch of *I*, marks (14) as more "aroused" – possibly the speaker is indignant.)

In place of a fall-from the accent, the one-profile contour here could have a **fall-to** the accent:

(15) ^I tóld y^{ou}!

The accent is "held down" and the effect is one of polite restraint, placation, reassurance, or whatever "holding down" may serve for, metaphorically.

Complex contours incorporate more than one profile:

(16) The ^{rég} ^{Ár} _{ular} _{my}

(17) A ^{régular ár} _{my}

– (16) has two falling profiles and (17) has a high level (or it could be rising) profile plus a falling one. The contrast shows the different functions of the fall and the rise – the fall after *reg-* in (16) suggests "separately important" (the fall metaphorically "cuts off" the preceding element from the following one), whereas the rise in (17) suggests "linked up" with what follows. In (16), *regular* differentiates that army from the irregulars; in (17), *regular* merely intensifies, as in *A regular army of ants crawled over the ground.*

There are practical but no theoretical limits to the number of profiles in a contour. From the standpoint of power the tendency is to have major accents at or near the beginning and the end (this is one of the clues to the completion of a contour) and minor ones, if any, in the middle. And it must be remembered that prominence may be achieved by a downward obtrusion as well as an upward one, *e.g.*

(18) Just dó it the ^{you} bést cáⁿ·

with the triple reassurance of the three down-to accents plus a downward tangent to all three. (The tangent could be up, and then the effect would be somewhat flip.) The opposite effect – strong impact – is achieved with a series of falling profiles but with a **rising** tangent on the accents:

(19) The wá_{lls came} túm_{bling with a} mígh_{ty} ró_{ar!}

Here too the tangent could fall if the speaker is rather "deeply impressed" than "excited" with the event.

In American English, as in English generally, there is no defining relationship between intonation and grammar; intonation conveys affect and attitude. Although a terminal rise is highly frequent in certain kinds of questions – and may in some instances be the hearer's only clue to the fact that the utterance is "a question", *e.g.*

(20)   Your $^{ná\ m\ e}$?

(21)   Your ^{ná} m $_e$.

("What is your name?" and "Tell me your name" respectively) – there are both questions without rises and rises that are not on questions. WH-questions more often than not have a terminal fall-from or a fall-to rather than a rise-to the accent:

(22)   Where's she ^{stáy}i$_{ng?}$

(23)   Where's she stáyi^{ng}?

Even Yes-No questions have been shown to fall about as often as they rise, though a particular sub-variety does almost invariably rise, namely a question that repeats for confirmation something that the other person has just said (an echo question):

(24)   Are you OK? – *Am I OK?* – Yes, that's what I asked. – Yes, I'm fine.

The same is true of a question calling for a repetition (a reclamatory question):

(25)   Are you OK? – *Eh? (What? Am I what?)* – Are you OK? – Oh, sure, fine.

But what we may imagine to be a grammatical dependency in the case of such "repeating" questions is simply a higher degree of tension. Substitute some other attitude for the immediate need-to-know and the shapes change. An indignant reclamatory question, say in response to *Are you a wife-beater?,* might look like:

(26)   Am $_I$ whát!

Though configurations are not definitive, overall **level** tends to be higher for questions – but that is true probably of most languages. The speaker is keyed up, pleading for an answer.

Lack of grammatical dependency does not mean lack of grammatical ties. In particular situations we need intonational differences – for instance, to distinguish between a WH-question that is original and one that is reclamatory.

(27)   John came last week. – *When?* – Last week. (rise, reclamatory)

(28)   John came last week. – *When?* – On Tuesday. (fall, original)

As with questions, so with other grammatical categories – no defining relationship between intonation and commands, statements, or exclamations. But again there are tendencies. Exclamations favour a high level followed by a fall from the accent:

(29)   For   heaven's   sáke!

(30)   Well   I'll be   dámned!

Statements tend to take two forms, depending on whether they introduce something or answer something. In both cases there is usually a terminal fall, but in one the intonation line, particularly the tangent to the accents, has a downward trend, whereas in the other it tends to go up. (31) brings up the subject:

(31)   It's a   béau ti ful   dáy   outside!

but (32) answers *Why do you insist on going outdoors?*

(32)   It's a béau ti ful   dáy   outside!

Since commands usually bring up the subject (or more accurately since the speaker is in control and does not have to "plead" as happens with questions), they too usually go down:

(33)   Hánd me the phóne book will you?

But a repeated command may reverse this:

(34)   Hánd me the phóne book!

(34) also shows what may happen to the unaccented syllables that precede and follow the accented ones. This speaker is irritated to the extent of raising each pitch from *hand* to *phone*. He is in the mood to ask *Are you deaf or something?* *Hand me the* could also be given a downward slant (though still with jump up on *phone*, so that the tangent remains rising), and then a likely interpretation would be "The speaker is really mad and trying to control his feelings".

There are thematic as well as grammatical ties, *i.e.* intonation helps in marking themes (what the utterance is about) and rhemes (what is said about the theme).
A sentence like

(35) Jó^{hn,} ^{sit} dó$_{wn.}$

addresses *John*, the theme, then tells John what to do. The normal order is theme + rheme, each having a major accent (nicely fitting the scheme of power), and with the theme showing its connectedness by its terminal rise. If the two are reversed, the theme can still be shown simply by keeping the same rise, now on the end:

(36) ^{Sit} dó$_{w_{n,}}$ Jó$^{hn.}$

or by giving the theme no accent at all, implying that everyone already knows who or what the utterance is about:

(37) ^{Sit} dó$_{w_{n,}}$ Jóhn.

Relative height of the accents also tells us something about themes *versus* rhemes. In answer to *Does Harrington own the first house on the street?*, which establishes *Harrington* as the theme, either (38) or (39) will do:

(38) Hár$_{rington}$^{,s} is the $\quad$ thírd $\quad$ $_{o}n_{e.}$

(39) The $\quad$ thírd $\quad$ $^{o}n_{e}$ $_{is}$ Hár$_{rington}$$^{,s.}$

The higher accent goes to the rheme, the lower to the theme, regardless of order. (There is more to the story, but no room to expand on it here.) In general the rhematic accent is the stronger, which reflects its privileged status; the rheme contains the most important – new, contrastive, interesting – information, and may occur alone, as in the response to *What are you going to do with this property?*

(40) (What I'm going to do is) $\quad$ séll $\quad$ $_{it.}$

The phonological apparatus by which intonation attaches itself to verbal locutions is heavily dependent on two features of the syllable: (a) whether or not the syllable is stressed within the word (by and large we can say that there is one stress per word), and (b) whether the vowel of the syllable is reduced or full.

(a) A stressed syllable is one that **can** receive an accent. Whether it **will** or not depends on the implementation of power and interest along the contour. An example of pure power, in which only one syllable (*God*) in the entire utterance receives an accent, is:

(41) Gó

       d how I hate this place!

An example of interest is

           yóu   trú

(42) Only   know what you   ly w_{ant}.

where *you* contrasts with *others* and *truly* contrasts with *fictitiously*. (The accents, one toward the beginning and the other toward the end, also nicely serve the power of the utterance as a whole.) In (41) and (42) we notice two different ways in which a fall can be carried out: with *God* it is **within** the syllable; with *you* and *truly* it is **between** one syllable and the next. The first method is more emphatic. The unaccented syllables (all those except *God*, *you* and *tru-*) provide the ground against which the accents stand out as figures.

(b) A reduced vowel defines a reduced syllable, which is regularly unaccented. In the word *séparableness* all syllables but the first are reduced; *sep-* is full, and the dictionary marks it as stressed, so that syllable will take the accent if the word is accented. In the word *reputation* the syllables *-pu-* and *-tion* are reduced, which leaves *re-* and *-ta-* as candidates for accent; the dictionary says that *-ta-* is the stressed syllable, and accordingly *-ta-* will be accented if the speaker chooses to accent that word. But under some circumstances a full syllable that is not the stressed one may receive an additional accent. It is required to be a syllable **preceding** the stressed one. So, in answer to *What suffered most?* we may have either (43) or (44):

(43) His repu ^{ta} t_{io}n.

(44) His ^{re}pu ^{ta} t_{io}n.

In (44) there is an accent on *re-* in addition to the one on *-ta-* (the stressed syllable). What (44) shows is the tendency of short utterances (even when not "complete sentences") to assume the same contour as long ones, with beginning and ending accents, when there is a full syllable in the right place. Nothing can be done to put a second accent on *séparableness*, because only *sep-* is full. Nor can a second accent go on the word *cómradeship*, because *-ship*, though full, is in the wrong position, **after** the stress on *com-*. So in answer to *What do you most desire?* one would have

(45) Your ^{com}$_{rade}$$_{ship.}$

with only *com-* standing out.

A different contour would realise the accents in a different way, *e.g.*

(46) His $_{re}$pu ^{ta} ^{ti}$_{on.}$

(47) His ^{re}pu $_{ta}$ ^{ti}$_{on.}$

(48) His $_{re}$pu $_{ta}$ tion.

with accents protruding down as well as up.

English has a "rhythm rule" that causes a secondary accent sometimes to replace a main one. The word *predetérmined* has full syllables *pre-* and *-ter-*. In the phrase *A predetermined goal*, the most likely contour (say to answer *What does one need to succeed?*) would be:

(49) A ^{pre} determined ^{go}$_{al.}$

with an accent on *pre-* instead of *-ter-*. This is simply another example of the favoured beginning-and-ending accents. For more power, an accent may be put on *-ter-* as well.

The rule against putting an accent on a reduced syllable or on a full one to the right of the stressed syllable is occasionally broken under conditions of extreme power, especially at the end of a contour where the accent tends to shift rightward anyway when the speaker feels an urge to be very emphatic, as in the attested example:

(50) Do it immediateLY!

The ultimate of power is when the speaker accents every syllable:

(51) AB-SO-LUTE-LY!

When a reduced syllable gets such an accent, it is upgraded to full – the schwa [ə] in the second syllable of (51), for example, becomes a full [o].

American English is distinguished from Southern British mainly by a less frequent use of high initial pitches (hence fewer steep falls) and a more frequent use of high final ones especially in yes-no questions. A frequent question pattern in Southern British illustrates both differences:

(52)   Would you ^like some _tea?

or without the final rise:

(53)   Would you ^like some _tea?

American English would be more apt to have

(54)   Would you like some ^tea?

The British intonation strikes the American ear as unduly concerned (the "cordiality" is carried too far); the American English strikes the British ear as too businesslike. But both dialects use both patterns where warranted. The American English speaker will be truly "concerned" with something like (55) and hence use the same pattern as (52),

(55)   Do you ^think I'm to _blame?

and the British speaker would feel that

(56)   Is it going to ^rain?

is suitably businesslike.

As in all other speech communities, American English has its regional differences, but again they have at least some association with affective choice. A noteworthy one is the higher frequency of rising terminals in some varieties of Southern speech, adding suspense, as in (the pitch goes up at the accent mark):

(57)   We played gámes and went for híkes and had the most wónderful tíme!

or asking for feedback (the listener is expected to give some sign of paying attention):

(58)   Our number-one car was broken dówn, and I had to take the number-two, the státion-wagon, to go pick up the pícnic supplies, and...

and this extends to more routine utterances, *e.g.* answering *Where are you from?* with:

(59)   From ^Texas.

This can also be related to a generational difference – younger speakers favour the rises.

3

Intonation in
British English

DANIEL HIRST

1. Background

English is the official language of nearly 50 different countries and is currently spoken as a first language by over 300 million people (Crystal 1988). Among the numerous dialects of English spoken throughout the world, two, usually referred to as (Standard) American English and (Standard) British English, have a rather special status in that they are considered distinct standards for the teaching of English as a foreign language. Both dialects of English are spoken with a number of different accents.

For British English, one particular accent: "Received Pronunciation", or "RP" (for a detailed description see Gimson 1962), traditionally defined as the accent of those educated in public schools, is generally presented as a model for foreign learners as well as a standard for BBC newsreaders. It has been estimated that the proportion of the population of England who actually speak RP is as small as 3% (Hughes and Trudgill 1979). It has been suggested (Brown 1977 p. 12) that RP today should be given a wider interpretation to include all speakers of "educated Southern English". It does seem fairly safe to assume that the intonation system of RP is common to a rather wider section of the native population of (particularly Southern) Britain and it is to this system to which I shall refer below (unless otherwise stated) as "British English Intonation" but considerably more research into the intonation of other accents (see §3.1 below) will obviously be necessary before we shall be in a position to claim, as Palmer (1922) did, that we are describing:

that system of intonation which is used by most of the natives of England. (p. ix)

1.1 General prosodic characteristics

There is a considerable literature on the nature of word stress in English and its relation to the segmental structure of the word (cf. Kingdon 1958a, Chomsky and Halle 1968, Guierre 1979, Hayes 1984, Fudge 1984, Halle and Vergnaud 1986). In particular, in contrast with earlier work which held that the position of word stress is entirely unpredictable, it has been argued in the framework of generative phonology that English word stress can be accounted for by a restricted number of fairly general phonological rules with lexical idiosyncrasies being reduced essentially to marking the final syllables of certain words as either inherently stressed or as **extrametrical** (*i.e.* invisible for the stress rules).

Typologically, English has a hybrid stress-system: on the level of the word, stress rules are in many ways similar to those of Romance languages in that the pattern of stress is basically determined with reference to the right edge of the word (with stress on the penultimate or antepenultimate syllable); Germanic suffixes, however, such as *-ing* and *-ly*, generally do not affect stress, and compound words in English, as in other Germanic languages, are generally stressed on the initial element.

Some authors distinguish more than two degrees of stress/accent. The final or most prominent pitch accent of an intonation unit is often referred to as carrying **primary stress**; a syllable which contains a full rather than a reduced vowel is sometimes said to carry **tertiary stress**. Whether or not an accented syllable is manifested by pitch or solely by duration and/or loudness is sometimes treated as a further degree of accentuation. For this chapter, I assume (following Bolinger 1958) one binary distinction between accented and unaccented syllables on the level of phonetic realisation and another binary distinction between stressed and unstressed syllables on the level of lexical representation.

1.2 Outline of the approach adopted in the chapter

In the following section I shall not present any new data on the intonation of British English but attempt simply to give a brief guide to what seem to me some significant results from the vast and ever-growing literature on the subject. The most exhaustive description of British English intonation is that of Crystal (1969). For discussion of more recent work see Couper-Kuhlen 1986, Cruttenden 1986. In §3.1, I outline some important differences which have been described in the intonation systems of other accents of the British Isles and in §4

I attempt to show how these descriptions can relate to a more general phonological theory of intonation.

2. Description of intonation patterns

2.1 Description of a basic non-emphatic pattern

a. Rhythmic structure
A number of linguists have claimed that intonation patterns are best described by means of a hierarchically organised structure with syllables being grouped into higher order prosodic constituents, each containing one accented syllable. This is often referred to as the **foot**, following Abercrombie (1964), who, in an extremely influential article, borrowed the term from traditional poetics to describe a sequence of syllables containing one stressed syllable followed by any number of unstressed syllables. Abercrombie specifically claimed that the foot is "independent of word boundaries" (p. 17) so that a sentence like

(1) a   They preDICted his eLECtion.

would be analysed as:

(1) b   They pre- | DICted his e- | LECtion. |

where "|" corresponds to foot boundaries.

A more sophisticated model of rhythmic structure had earlier been proposed by Jassem (1952), according to which English speech is organised into two kinds of units: the **Narrow Rhythm Unit**, which like the Abercrombian foot consists of a stressed syllable followed by a sequence of unstressed syllables, and the **Anacrusis** consisting of a sequence of proclitic unstressed syllables. Anacrusis and Narrow Rhythm Unit combine to constitute the **Total Rhythm Unit**. Jassem claimed in particular that the rhythmic organisation of these two types of constituents is completely different: unstressed syllables in the Anacrusis tend to be pronounced "extremely rapidly" whereas the duration of each syllable in a Narrow Rhythm Unit tends to be inversely proportional to the number of syllables in that unit giving rise to the impression of isochrony which has often been attributed to languages like English (Lehiste 1977, Adams 1979). In a statistical analysis of a corpus containing both isolated sentences and a continuous dialogue (Units 30 and 39 of Halliday 1970), Jassem, Hill and Witten (1984) present persuasive evidence that Jassem's model gives a better account of durational patterns of English rhythm than does the Abercrombian model. Jassem's model also appears compatible with data from a recent corpus study based on a twenty-minute continuous recording of a short story read by a professional actor (Campbell 1992 and personal communication). It is not, however, clear whether it is possible to account for both rhythm and melody by a single model of prosodic structure. In particular, it is noteworthy that Jassem

(1952) makes no use of Total Rhythm Units in his description of the melodic patterns of English but instead groups Anacrusis with the preceding Narrow Rhythm Unit (cf. pp. 49–50) to form **Tonal Units** which are said to be the domain of accentual pitch movements. The prosodic structure implied by this model can consequently be summarised as follows:

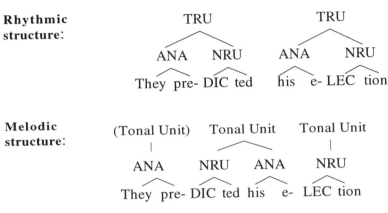

Figure 1. Jassem's model of rhythmic and melodic structure: TRU = Total Rhythm Unit; NRU = Narrow Rhythm Unit; ANA = Anacrusis.

This is obviously a field in which much work still remains to be done, in particular in so far as cross-language studies are concerned. In the rest of this chapter (cf. also Hirst and Di Cristo 1984; Hirst 1987) I shall use Jassem's term **Tonal Unit** to refer to an appropriate constituent for modelling intonation patterns on this level with the proviso that a more complex structure such as that discussed above may eventually prove necessary for a more complete description.

Above the level of the Tonal Unit, a further level of prosodic structure is generally considered necessary, referred to variously as the **Tone Group** (Palmer 1922; Schubiger 1958; Halliday 1967a, 1970; Gussenhoven 1984) the **Tune** (Armstrong and Ward 1926; Schubiger 1935; Jassem 1952; Kingdon 1958) the **Tone Unit** (Crystal 1969; Couper-Kuhlen 1986) or the **Intonation Group** (Cruttenden 1986). In parallel with the term **Tonal Unit** as defined above I shall refer to this higher-level structure here as the **Intonation Unit** (Hirst and Di Cristo 1984; Hirst 1987).

b. Stress and accent

The final accent of an Intonation Unit has often been given special status in descriptions and has been referred to since Palmer (1922) as the **nucleus**. For a historical account of the concept of nucleus in intonation studies see Cruttenden

(1990). The nucleus can occur before the last stressable syllable without in any way implying contrastiveness or emphasis. Thus in a dialogue like:

(2) a   – I've got some nice lamb chops for lunch.

   b   – I'm sorry, I'm afraid I don't eat meat.

there is no contrasting sentence "I (VERB) meat" which (2b) is intended to imply: the final accent falls on *eat* by default, simply because *meat* is de-accented. For discussion of "default accent" cf. Ladd (1980), Fuchs (1984).

Another very interesting case consists of sentences with intransitive verbs which can be pronounced with either a single accent on the subject or with one accent on the subject and another on the verb (cf. Schmerling 1976, Ladd 1980, 1983) Allerton and Cruttenden (1979), Gussenhoven (1984), Faber (1987). All these studies show that accenting and de-accenting imply a complex linguistic process which, despite considerable research, is still not fully understood but which cannot be reduced to a simple question of informativeness or predictability. For a contrary point of view see Bolinger (1989).

c. Tonal structure

One of the simplest accounts of British English intonation was that of Armstrong and Ward (1926) who proposed to analyse the intonation of unemphatic sentences by means of two "tunes". The first of these is said to be used in "ordinary, definite, decided statements (word, phrase or sentence)" (p. 9) while the second is said to be used mainly with questions, requests and incomplete groups (p. 22). Tune 2 will be dealt with in §2.2 below; Tune 1 is described as follows:

The stressed syllables form a descending scale. Within the last stressed syllable, the pitch of the voice falls to a lower level. (p. 4)

Armstrong and Ward illustrate this Tune 1 with examples like the following:

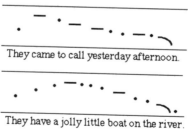

Figure 2. Illustration of the intonation pattern of "Tune 1" from Armstrong and Ward 1922.

In order to transcribe sentences such as these using the INTSINT transcription system (Hirst and Di Cristo this volume) we need to decide whether stressed syllables other than the first and the last in each group carry a pitch accent or not. Armstrong and Ward state that unstressed syllables:

may either descend gradually to the next stress, remain level, be on a slightly higher or a slightly lower level. From our experience we find that it is more usual for the pitch of these unstressed syllables to descend gradually to the next stress. (p. 5)

Palmer (1922) discussing a similar pattern (his "Tone Group 1 with superior head") notes that:

unstressed syllables may tend to remain on the same level as the syllable immediately preceding. (p. 45)

Whether or not the unstressed syllables stay on the same level is obviously important for the transcription. O'Connor and Arnold (1961) make an explicit distinction between stressed and accented syllables:

If a stress occurs in this head without a downward step in pitch, the word concerned is **not** accented. (p. 18)

but this distinction is no longer maintained in the second edition of their book published in 1973.

If there is no intermediate pitch accent we should transcribe the sentences:

(3) a   They CAME to call yesterday afterNOON.
[⇑   >   ⇓]

b   They have a JOlly little boat on the RIver.
[⇑   > ⇓]

If, on the other hand, there is a marked drop in pitch at the beginning of each stressed syllable, these sentences should be transcribed:

(4) a   They CAME to CALL YESterday AFterNOON.
[⇑   >   >   >   >   ⇓]

b   They have a JOlly little BOAT on the RIver
[⇑   >   > ⇓]

It is not always easy to decide from an F_0 curve whether or not a syllable actually carries a pitch accent of this type. In fairly slow deliberate speech, the "downstepping" effect can be quite striking as in the following figure illustrating the F_0 curve for a sequence of syllables *ma 'ma 'ma 'ma 'ma ma* produced imitating the intonation of the sentence *But who stole Jane's bracelet?*:

A pitch curve such as this, re-synthesised on a continuous vowel, is quite sufficient for a listener to identify the number of stresses. In spontaneous speech the actual size of the pitch drop will tend to be more reduced than this and in the extreme case it may become practically imperceptible giving rise to the "hat" or

Figure 3. The F_0 curve for the sequence *ma 'ma 'ma 'ma 'ma ma* imitating the intonation of the sentence *But who stole Jane's bracelet?*

"bridge" type of pattern of sentences (3a) and (3b) that has been described as typical of unemphatic utterances in a number of different languages (see 't Hart this volume and references there).

Whether the downstepped pitch accent is actually suppressed in these cases (as suggested by Knowles 1984 p. 232 and by Hirst 1984 p. 53) or whether the amplitude of the downstep is simply reduced, is, as mentioned above, not always easy to decide from simple observation of F_0 curves. Knowles (1987) makes the same point and claims that:

accent suppression is not all-or-none, it is a process that can apply to a greater or lesser degree. (p. 126)

Reliable empirical criteria will require closer modelling of F_0 curves as well as more work on the psycho-acoustic perceptibility of this type of accent.

Most descriptive studies of English intonation list a variety of different recurrent tonal patterns which can occur in the **head**, *i.e.* the sequence of accents preceding the nucleus. Palmer (1922) lists four varieties of heads: "inferior", "superior" "scandent" (=sequence of rising accents) and "heterogeneous". O'Connor and Arnold (1961) identify "low", "stepping" and "sliding" (=sequence of falling accents) heads although once again this classification is to some extent abandoned in the 1973 revision of their book. The most detailed classification of different patterns was that of Crystal (1969 pp. 225–233) who, on the basis of an extensive corpus study based on a total of about three hours of recording from thirty different speakers, distinguished four categories of globally falling heads, two categories of globally rising heads as well as two mixed categories. The stepping category described above as "neutral non-emphatic" is the most frequent single category of head, occurring in about 30% of Crystal's data. Crystal also notes that whereas "low heads" and "sliding heads" are practically non-existent in his corpus, the two globally rising categories account for another 30% of his data. I shall return to "sliding" heads below (§3.1) in a discussion of intonation patterns of other varieties of English; "scandent" and "globally rising" heads will be discussed under the heading of emphatic variants.

2.2 *Mode and expressivity*

Armstrong and Ward's second basic tune is said to be used in four essential cases:

(a) statements with implications
(b) Yes-No questions
(c) requests
(d) incomplete utterances.

They describe the pitch pattern of Tune 2 as follows:

The outline of the first tune is followed until the last stressed syllable is reached. This is on a low note, and any syllables that follow rise from this point. (p. 20)

To anyone outside the field of intonation studies, the very idea that intonation can contribute to the meaning of an utterance is indissociably linked with the distinction between declarative and interrogative intonation patterns distinguished essentially by a falling as against a rising pitch movement at the end of the utterance. Many linguists however have made use of one single rising pattern to describe both continuative and interrogative patterns. When a distinction is made between low rise and high rise, the low rise is generally held to correspond to a statement which is either unfinished or carries implications of some sort, whereas the high rise is said to correspond to a question. Even when such a distinction is made, however, a number of different positions need to be distinguished.

The strongest claim is that the high rise is exclusively used for questions. This seems to be the position of Kingdon (1958b), since, although he does not say so explicitly, in all his examples the high rise is found only on questions and his low rise never occurs on questions except for sequences of alternative questions where the low rise is marked for every group except the last. A slightly weaker position was held by Palmer (1922) who claimed that the high rise could be used both on questions and statements but that the low rise:

is confined to Statements and Commands, it cannot be used for Questions. (p. 84).

A similar position was taken by Halliday (1967a, 1970):

the difference, though gradual, is best regarded as phonetic overlap (...) the one being merely lower than the other (...) But the meanings are fairly distinct. In most cases the speaker is clearly using one of the other; but sometimes one meets an instance which could be either. (p. 21)

By contrast, O'Connor and Arnold (1961) maintain that a low rise is:

by far the most common way of asking Yes/No questions. It should be regarded as the normal way. (p. 55) but that to turn a statement into a question, a high rise (tone group 8) is needed "as in so many other European languages." (p. 57). Similarly, Jones (1918) describes a potential distinction between *yes* said with a low rise, meaning *Yes, I understand that, please continue* from *yes* said with a high rise, meaning *Is it really so?* (p. 277). In all the examples of transcription which follow, however, all other interrogative forms are marked with a low rise (pp. 282–283).

A fundamental problem underlying these descriptions is the fact that an utterance which is perceived as a question in a given context may no longer be perceived as a question when taken out of this context. This has been demonstrated experimentally for Edinburgh English (Brown, Currie and Kenworthy 1980) and is almost certainly true also for RP, indeed probably for all languages. The effect of this context dependence is that when asked to produce an interrogative pattern out of context, subjects are liable to produce patterns which may be far less common in spontaneous speech.

A rather different explanation for the distinction between high and low rises was proposed by Cruttenden (1970) who suggested that:

The meaning of a rise ending high which is required to turn *you're coming* into a question is probably better described as "surprise". Questions already signalled by the syntax will not usually have high rise but low rise or fall (...). If such questions do have high rise (...) then the element of surprise is added to the question. (p. 188)

It has, in fact, been suggested by several authors (in particular by Bolinger in a number of publications) that it is a mistake to equate the choice of final pitch movement in an utterance with sentence type since, as any study based on utterances produced in spontaneous conditions quickly discovers, it is perfectly possible to find both rising pitch without questions and questions without rising pitch. As Couper-Kuhlen (1986) notes, we need to make a distinction between syntactic sentence type and pragmatic speech act. She goes on to claim that despite the final rise, a sentence such as:

(5)   You've FInished?

is not a syntactic question since "if it were it would have subject-operator inversion." This argument, as it stands, appears somewhat circular – it is not sufficient to simply stipulate that subject-operator inversion is necessary for syntactic questions. There is, however, independent evidence, as I have argued elsewhere (Hirst 1983b) that Couper-Kuhlen is right. It is a well-known fact of English syntax that unlike (6a) a sentence such as (6b) is unacceptable with the indicated stressing:

(6) a   He BOUGHT something

    b   *He BOUGHT anything.

but that in syntactic questions, both *something* and *anything* are acceptable:

(7) a   Did he BUY something?

b   Did he BUY anything?

The crucial fact is that sentence (6b), unlike (6a) is still unacceptable even when it is provided with rising intonation (or, in a written text, with a question mark):

(8) a   He BOUGHT something?

b   *He BOUGHT anything?

This seems to be conclusive evidence that rising intonation is not, contrary to what has often been claimed, a way of turning a statement into a (syntactic) question, but is rather a way of indicating that a syntactic statement is being used pragmatically as a request for information.

In fact, in spontaneous conversation it is quite possible to produce a syntactic statement with falling intonation which is used as a request for information. The following figure shows the F_0 curve of a sentence (from a published collection of recordings: Dickinson and Mackin 1969 p. 78) taken from a recording of a visit to an optician who asks her patient:

(9)   You MAnage in the DIStance alright?

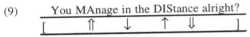

which is quite clearly intended as a question in the context and is interpreted as such by the patient.

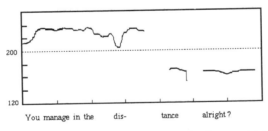

Figure 4. F_0 curve for the "real-life" question *You manage in the distance alright?*

As Lindsey (1985, 1991) points out, questions with declarative form and falling pitch are far more common than is often thought.

We conclude, then, that in English at least, while it is fairly common to use rising intonation for questions, it is by no means compulsory; nor can a rising pattern in itself transform a statement into a syntactic question. We might then ask whether there is some more general pragmatic characteristic which underlies the use of rising pitch both on questions and on statements.

One of the most commonly proposed candidates for such a characteristic has been that of "incompleteness" (cf. Faure 1962 p. 73). Coleman (1914) suggested that Yes/No questions are incomplete alternative questions in which the alternative "or not" has been suppressed and a similar argument has been proposed by a number of linguists although Bolinger (1978a) has convincingly shown that this analysis cannot be correct.

A number of recent proposals, in particular Brazil (1975) and Gussenhoven (1984), have built on an earlier suggestion by Jassem (1952) that:

Falling nuclear tones have proclamatory value. Rising nuclear tones have evocative value. (p. 70)

Under this analysis the basic function of the distinction between falling contours and rising contours is to indicate to the listener how he is intended to process the propositional content of the utterance. A falling contour can be interpreted as an assurance that this propositional content is intended to be added to what **Relevance Theory** (Sperber and Wilson 1986) calls the "mutual cognitive environment" of speaker and listener: the set of facts which at any given moment speaker and listener can share (and can be aware of sharing). This approach seems very promising (see Hirst 1989 for dicussion) but much research remains to be done before the numerous insights which have been proposed can be integrated into a formal theory of the pragmatic interpretation of prosody. For a recent attempt cf. Vandepitte (1989). For a similar approach within a somewhat different framework cf. Pierrehumbert and Hirschberg (1990).

2.3 Focalisation and contextual effects

The term **focus**, more specifically **narrow focus**, has in a number of recent works replaced the more traditional term of **emphasis** to refer to the way in which a speaker gives an optional prosodic highlighting to part of an utterance.

Whether we choose to use the term "focus" or "emphasis" may consequently appear to be a trivial question of vocabulary (or fashion). There does, however, appear to be at least one case where the two notions are not entirely identical. Whereas emphasis is basically a **paradigmatic** notion, in that any given item is either emphatic or non-emphatic, focus is basically **syntagmatic** since it applies to one element of a sequence (more strictly to one node of a tree). This implies that while it is quite possible to refer to emphatic and non-emphatic versions of an utterance consisting of a single word, (such as "NO." *vs.* "NO!"), it is not possible, in standard treatments of focus, to distinguish broad and narrow focus on a single item. The choice between the two notions would then boil down to answering the empirical question: is there a categorical distinction between emphatic and non-emphatic readings of a single word? I assume that such a distinction does exist in British English and shall consequently prefer the concept of emphasis to that of focus.

Classical descriptions of English intonation, since Coleman (1914), refer to two types of emphasis: **contrast emphasis** and **intensity emphasis**. Jones (1918) remarks that:

Contrast emphasis may be applied to almost any word, but intensity emphasis can only be applied to certain words expressing qualities which are measurable. (p. 298)

Intensity emphasis is simpler to define in that it is semantically approximately equivalent to adding an intensifying adverb such as "absolutely". Thus (10a) with intensity emphasis has approximately the same interpretation as (10b):

(10) a   This chocolate is <u>delicious</u>.

     b   This chocolate is absolutely delicious.

When intensity emphasis is applied to the first auxiliary of an utterance the result is the equivalent of an exclamative formed with *How* or *What* so that (11a) is equivalent to (11b):

(11) a   This chocolate <u>is</u> delicious!

     b   How delicious this chocolate is!

The two types of emphasis described above obviously have much in common. In particular, the final (nuclear) pitch accent typically rises to a higher level than that of the preceding syllable, unlike the pattern described in §2.1 for unemphatic utterances. A minimal emphatic reading of (10a) (whether contrastive or intensive) would consequently be:

(12) a   <u>This CHOcolate is deLIcious.</u>
    [⇑   > ↑ ⇓]

Very often, the effect of the high-falling final pitch accent is reinforced by a low-pitched initial accent, itself often preceded by high-pitched unstressed syllables giving a rising head:

(12) b   <u>This CHOcolate is deLIcious.</u>
    [⇑   ⇓   ⇑ ⇓]

The difference between the low initial accent in (12b) and the high initial accent as in (12a) is a qualitative difference, unlike the difference between a high-falling and a low-falling nucleus which is simply a question of degree. It is perhaps for this reason that this is a very common way of signalling emphasis. Interestingly, the same pattern can occur on a single word containing more than one stress as in:

(13)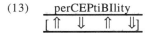

The fact that a single word can be pronounced with a pattern of this type is further evidence that, as mentioned above, it is a paradigmatic opposition which is involved here rather than a syntagmatic contrast.

The pattern consisting of a rising head followed by a high-falling nucleus can be used to express other types of meanings which cannot all be put down to intensive or contrastive emphasis. A similar contour is discussed by Liberman and Sag (1974) and Liberman (1975) for American English with an explicit comparison with British English patterns of the same form. These authors assume that the pattern expresses a global meaning which they call **surprise/redundancy**. In many cases, if not all, the meaning could just as appropriately be labelled **exclamative**, a label which, as we saw above, can also be applied to most of the cases described as "intensity emphasis".

On a longer sentence, any stressed syllables between the initial low accent and the final high-falling accent will be on an intermediate pitch. Just as with the downstepping head described in §2.1, any accented syllables in a rising head of this type are liable to be signalled by a flattening out of the F_0 curve on the accented syllable, and will be consequently transcribed as in (14):

(14)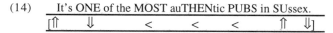

Upstepping accents of this sort have not always been considered genuine pitch accents. Thus Cruttenden (1986) gives an example which he transcribes:

Why did you do that ?

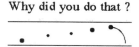

Figure 5. Schematic illustration of a rising head (from Cruttenden 1986).

Cruttenden states that whereas **Why** and **that** carry pitch accents, **do** has only tertiary stress (dependent on length and/or loudness alone) (p. 56). It is of course an empirical question whether in any given utterance an upstepping pitch accent is actually present (once more a subject for further research!) but in the affirmative I should transcribe Cruttenden's example as:

(15) WHY did you DO THAT?
[⇓ < ↑ ⇓]

A further variant of the rising head (O'Connor and Arnold (1969 2nd edition 1973) call this the "climbing head") consists of a recurrent sequence of local rises from each accented syllable giving the following pattern:

(16)   It's ONE of the MOST auTHENtic PUBS in SUssex.

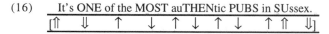

The way in which emphasis interacts with the basic opposition between rising and falling tunes is, once again, a subject of some controversy. Armstrong and Ward (1926) considered that the falling-rising nucleus was the emphatic form of the rising nucleus. This analysis has been implicitly accepted by many authors although others have explicitly rejected it. Halliday (1967a), for example, claimed that there are five basic nuclear tones: falling, high rising, low rising, falling-rising and rising-falling, none of which can be considered modifications of other tones and most of which have secondary variants. Brazil (1975), claimed that it is the fall-rise which is basic and that the simple rising pattern is an emphatic modification of the fall-rise. Gussenhoven (1984) has claimed that there are three primary tones: falling, rising and falling-rising, each of which can exhibit secondary modifications.

It is not at all obvious how one might hope to settle a controversy of this sort other than by appealing to theory-internal criteria. One possible direction is that taken by Lindsay and Ainsworth (1985) who attempt to show that a five-tone analysis makes better predictions than a two-tone analysis concerning discrimination functions derived from listeners' judgements on synthetic stimuli. Another type of experiment was conducted by Gussenhoven (op. cit. chapter 7) who asked listeners to judge the similarity/difference of synthetic stimuli. Gussenhoven interprets his results as evidence against Brazil's analysis. Both of these experiments, however, suffer from weaknesses in the choice of stimuli as well as in their reliance on synthetic speech. Neither can be considered sufficiently convincing to constitute reliable proof of one analysis or the other. Both, however, constitute extremely interesting attempts to provide much needed empirical evidence for phonological analyses.

2.4 Phrasing and textual organisation

Crystal (1969) noted that the average length of Intonation Units in his corpus was of five words and that 80% of the Units were less than eight words long. When utterances are longer than this, they are usually broken up into two or more Intonation Units. WH-questions appear to impose greater restrictions on the possible intonation breaks during the utterance so that a long question will still tend to be produced as a single Intonation Unit even in a sentence containing as many as eight accents:

(17)   WHAT MADE JOHN TELL ANNE NOT to GO HOME?

[⇑   >   >   >   >   >   >   >   ⇓]

Apart from this type of question, it is fairly rare to find utterances in spontaneous speech which contain more than three or four pitch accents in a single Intonation Unit.

There has been considerable disagreement as to what criteria, syntactic, semantic or pragmatic, are relevant for this phrasing. For a summary of arguments for and against syntactic constraints on phrasing cf. Couper-Kuhlen (1986 especially chapter VIII). Many of the arguments which have been presented against such constraints, however, no longer hold if we assume a less trivial correspondence between syntax and phonology than has generally been proposed. Thus it has generally been supposed that a grammatical account of phrasing must show a one-one correspondence between syntactic units and prosodic units. This is obviously not the case in utterances like the following (from Couper-Kuhlen 1986; the symbol / indicates the observed boundaries):

(18)a /They feel like they're a forgotten bit / of a war / that nobody wants to solve /
   b /They'll leave it alone / till it splatters out / to a deadly end/
   c /So here I am / in the middle of the most enormous / movement /
   d /as if the whole world / is hanging waiting on our decision /
   e /which I found one of the most fascinating and most interesting / times of my life/

Couper-Kuhlen consequently draws the conclusion:

it is virtually impossible to predict where boundaries will come. (p. 153)

I have suggested (Hirst 1987, 1993) an alternative explanation for this apparent lack of correspondence between syntactic and phonological constituents. While pragmatic and phonological constraints are obviously the ultimate criteria by which a speaker decides where he **will** place a boundary, syntactic criteria define where these boundaries **may** occur. In all the examples in (18), as well as in others given by the same author, it is striking that each boundary occurs **before** a complete syntactic constituent extending to the end of the sentence. The reason why the correspondence between syntactic and prosodic constituents breaks down is that syntactic constituents may be interrupted by a prosodic boundary at the beginning of an internal syntactic constituent provided that a prosodic boundary is also placed at the end of that constituent. Thus in (18) for example, the syntactic structure relevant to the phrasings noted is:

(19)a [They feel like they're a forgotten bit [of a war [that nobody wants to solve]]]
   b [They'll leave it alone [till it splatters out [to a deadly end]]]
   c [So here I am [in the middle of the most enormous [movement]]]
   d [as if the whole world [is hanging waiting on our decision]]
   e [which I found one of the most fascinating and most interesting [times
     of my life]]

This interpretation thus predicts that while several different phrasings may be theoretically possible, many others will be ruled out; in particular internal boundaries are predicted not to occur before a constituent the end of which is not also marked by a boundary.

While there is, as we saw above, quite a remarkable consensus concerning the existence of prosodic constituents equivalent to what I have called Intonation Units, there is considerably less agreement as to whether larger prosodic units need to be identified.

It has been suggested that Intonation Units are organised into higher-order "paratone-groups" (Fox 1973, 1984) or "major paratones" (Yule 1980), which are signalled essentially by a change of overall width of pitch range or "key" (Brazil 1975, Brown, Currie and Kenworthy 1980).

The beginning of a paratone is said to be usually marked by extra high pitch on the first accent while the end is usually marked with extra-low pitch. When the end of a paratone is marked in this way but not the beginning, the result is what Yule has called a "minor paratone". It seems however equally possible to mark the beginning of a paratone but not the end. This suggests that rather than distinguish major and minor paratones we might make a four-way distinction between Intonation Units which are marked as paratone-initial, paratone-final, or both or neither. Such a distinction could be marked in an INTSINT transcription by simply doubling the initial or final square bracket of an intonation unit so that it would be possible to have a sequence such as:

(20)   [[A] [B] [[C] [D]] [E]]

where A and C are marked as paratone-initial and D and E as paratone-final, even though the sequence as a whole is not properly bracketed and cannot be divided into a sequence of independent paratones.

Another line of research concerns the prosodic structure of conversation and the role of pitch in "turn-taking" (Cutler and Pearson 1986) and "interruption-management" (French and Local 1986). Both of these fields obviously need to be developed (for an overview see Couper-Kuhlen 1986 chapter XI) although on the basis of preliminary results it does not seem very likely that the various strategies described will show many language specific characteristics which need to be accounted for in the phonological description of a given language.

2.5 Stylised patterns

Like many languages, English makes use of a certain number of patterns which strike the listener as being somehow intermediate between speech and song. The common prosodic characteristic of these patterns is that instead of consisting of a continuous sequence of movements from one target-point to the next as in normal speech, the contour is produced as a sequence of static level tones.

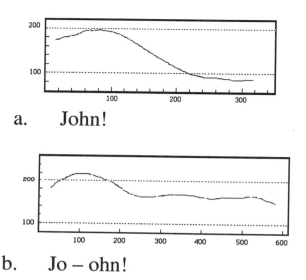

a. John!

b. Jo – ohn!

Figure 6. F_0 curve for the non-stylised contour (a) and the stylised contour (b) used for calling. Horizontal lines correspond to 100 and 200 Hz.

The semantic effect of these contours has been discussed in detail by Ladd (1978) who has aptly called them **stylised** patterns, the common feature being one of stereotyped, conventional almost ritual behaviour. It has often been noted that these patterns are particularly frequent in children's speech, particularly in jeering chants like

(21)   MOlly is a BA- by
        [→ ↓ ↑ > >]

Stylised patterns which are common in adult speech are vocatives ("Jo-ohn!"), and greetings (Good Morning!) particularly in situations such as answering the phone, for example, where the speaker repeats the same message many times throughout the day.

3. Comparisons with other systems

3.1 Comparisons within the same language

British English, as mentioned in §1, is spoken with a number of different accents, some of which exhibit quite strikingly specific intonation variants, concerning both the recurrent patterns found on the head as well as the pattern occurring at the nucleus. Unfortunately, studies of these regional characteristics are few and far between.

a. Recurrent patterns

The downstepping pattern described in §2.1(c) as typical of unemphatic statements is replaced in a number of dialects by a sequence of falling pitch accents (the "sliding head" mentioned above) so that instead of (4a) we find:

(22)   They CAME to CALL YESterday AFterNOON

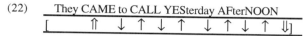

This has been described as typical of Scottish accents, both Western (McClure 1980) and Edinburgh (Brown, Currie and Kenworthy 1980). Neither Palmer (1922) nor O'Connor and Arnold (1961) nor Crystal (1969) describe this as a variant of the unemphatic pattern for Standard British. According to O'Connor and Arnold the sliding head is only found before a falling-rising nucleus. The pattern is probably gaining ground throughout England possibly due to the influence of American speech where the pattern is very common (cf. Pike 1945, Bolinger this volume).

A sequence of rising pitch accents has been described by a number of authors as typical of Welsh accents although I am unaware of any detailed study of the intonation of Welsh English.

b. Nuclear patterns

English accents from Northern Britain, particularly Belfast (Cruttenden and Jarman 1976), Liverpool (Knowles 1974, 1978), Birmingham, Glasgow (Brown, Currie and Kenworthy 1980) and Tyneside (Pellowe and Jones 1978, Local 1986)) are notorious for the fact that, unlike what has been described for most languages, they commonly make use of an intonation pattern with high or rising final pitch in what native speakers perceive as perfectly ordinary statements. For recent discussion cf. Knowles 1984, Cruttenden 1986, Bolinger 1989). Knowles suggested that these rising pitch movements should in fact be interpreted as falls (he calls them "Irish" falls which, perversely, go up) and concludes that the existence of such pitch contours shows up a major weakness in most current systems of analysis which classify patterns according to predetermined phonetic characteristics. An comprehensive account of these rising patterns is to be found in Cruttenden (1994) together with a comparison with superficially similar but functionally different patterns found in an area which Cruttenden refers to as the "pacific rim" (*i.e.* West Coast USA, Australia *etc.*). (see also Bolinger this volume). It has been suggested that the British pattern is of Celtic origin which would explain some of the distribution in the West of the British Isles. This would not however explain why the pattern is far less common in Eire than in Northern Ireland, nor why it is to be found in the Newcastle area. An intriguing possibility would be that this pattern is in fact a trace of the Viking occupation of Britain – similar pattterns have been described for East Norwegian (Fretheim and Nilsen 1989) and West Swedish (Gårding this volume.

4. Theoretical implications and conclusions: the phonology of English intonation

One of the basic aims of phonological theory is to attempt to explain how and why languages differ from one another phonetically, by setting up a limited number of phonological parameters which can combine in various ways to generate the appropriate range of phonetic variability.

This section sketches a theory of phonological representations of intonation which attempts to account for some of these parameters as well as some of the dialectal variations mentioned above.

I assume here, as proposed in the framework of autosegmental phonology (Goldsmith 1976, 1990) that phonological representations in all languages consist of two distinct lines of phonetically interpreted segments: tonal segments (or tones) and phonematic segments (or phones). I also assume, contrary to standard autosegmental theory, but following Hirst 1983a, 1984 (see also Pierrehumbert and Beckman 1988) that these two lines are related to each other **indirectly** via a hierarchical structure containing at least two levels of constituents: Tonal Units and Intonation Units.

Since English is not a tone language, tonal segments are not specified in the lexical entry for each word but are rather added to the phonological representation respecting a phonological template which for English could be of the form:

$$
\begin{array}{ll}
\overset{\text{TU}}{\frown} & \overset{\text{IU}}{\frown} \\
\text{(23)a \quad H \quad L} & \text{b \quad L \ \{L;H\}}
\end{array}
$$

If we assume that the appropriate prosodic structure for a sentence such as:

(24)   It's almost impossible.

is:

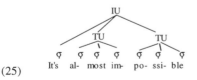

(25)

(where σ represents the syllable constituent) then, in order to respect the tonal templates (23a,b), tonal segments will need to be added. Assuming for example that terminal intonation is chosen, this will give:

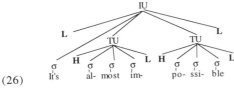

(26)

Such a representation, however, is not pronounceable, since the tonal segments are only partially ordered. Total ordering could be achieved either by reassociating the tones assigned to the Intonation Unit to Tonal Units (as suggested in Hirst 1986) or, perhaps more appropriately, following Pierrehumbert and Beckman (1988) by assuming that tonal segments are all projected onto the same tier but remain linked to different hierarchical constituents.[1] This would result in:

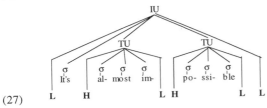

(27)

The advantage of such a representation is that information concerning the hierarchical level of the constituent to which a tonal segment is attached is available to the rules of phonetic interpretation which convert (27) into something like:

(28)   It's ALmost imPOssible.

I shall not go into any more detail here concerning the phonetic rules which are assumed to derive a representation such as (28) from (27). Note simply that two consecutive L tones may be interpreted as a single low phonetic target pitch.

The intonation contour generated in (27) is not that described above as the basic unemphatic pattern for British English, but rather that which is described as basic for American and Scottish dialects (§3.1). In order to derive the British English pattern we need to assume a further parameter converting a sequence of falls into a downstepping pattern. In lexical tone languages, a downstepped tone is standardly analysed (following Clements and Ford 1979) as a high tone preceded by a "floating" low tone – *i.e.* a low tone which is not phonetically realised as a pitch target but which has the effect of lowering the following high tone. This can be achieved very simply by a further rule specific to British English which "delinks" the second of two linked tones in all but the last Tonal Unit:

75

(29)

where **T** is either **H** or **L**

Applied to (27) this will result in:

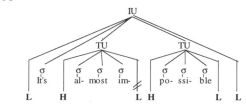

(30)

which is then interpreted as:

(31)   It's ALmost imPOssible.

[⇑   >   ⇓]

The emphatic patterns discussed in (§2.4) could be derived in a number of ways. I have suggested (Hirst 1983b) that these contours contain an emphatic morpheme consisting of a single floating High tone. Another possibility would be to assume that a new prosdic constituent **E** is introduced into the prosodic structure between the Intonation Unit and the Tonal Units and that this constituent is assigned the same tonal segments as the Tonal Unit. This would result, after delinking of the low tone in the first Tonal Unit, in the following structure:

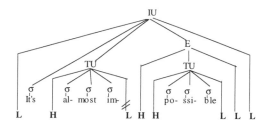

(32)

which can be interpreted as:

(33)   It's ALmost imPOssible

[⇑   > ↑   ⇓]

The emphatic patterns with "rising head" (= sequence of upstepped accents) and "climbing head" (= sequence of rising pitch accents) suggest the possibility that an alternative template for the Tonal Unit is available with the sequence [L H] instead of [H L]. Applied to (25) this would result in:

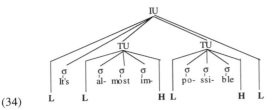

(34)

interpreted as:

(35)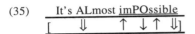

or alternatively, if (29) applied, in:

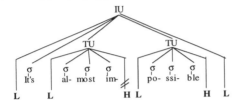

(36)

interpreted as:

(37)   It's ALmost imPOssible
        [⇓   < ↑   ⇓]

A number of questions remain unanswered concerning both the way in which phonological representations of intonation structures are derived and the way in which these representations are interpreted phonetically. The brief outline given in this section, however, does seem to possess at least some of the characteristics of what a phonological theory of intonation might look like, as well as how such a theory might apply to generate the observed variety of patterns in British English.

Note

1   Note that Pierrehumbert and Beckman (1988) assume in addition that tonal segments can be multiply linked to constituents of the hierarchical structure, a suggestion which I do not follow.

4

Intonation in German

DAFYDD GIBBON

1. Background

German is a West Germanic language, closely related to Dutch and English, with about 100 million native speakers in Germany, Austria and the northern parts of Switzerland, as well as small enclaves in Russia and neighbouring countries, in Romania, and in North and South America. Unlike other European standard languages, Standard German is not the language of a specific social stratum in a specific geographical dialect area. Rather, it is perhaps best identified in terms of the pronunciation of the written standard language as codified in the publications of the **Duden** dictionary publishers.

Standard German, **Hochdeutsch** (High German), should not be confused with **Hochdeutsch** as a technical term for the group of Southern German dialects which underwent the High German Consonant Shift in the early Middle Ages. The pronunciation of Standard German is sometimes called **Bühnenaussprache** (stage pronunciation). Standard German is a superstrate which is associated historically with the formal speech of the educated classes in the Lutheran areas of North Germany. However, the distinctive regional pronunciation of speakers in the major German cultural centres is also acceptable in public life.

The main regional standards are associated with Berlin, Hamburg, Hanover, Cologne, Frankfurt, Stuttgart, Munich, Leipzig. Vienna provides the standard for Austrian German and Zurich for Swiss German (see §3.1). A remarkable feature of the German of educated speakers in many parts of Germany is socially triggered dialect switching, between a local dialect, the regional standard, and the standard superstrate. As in other countries, the mass media tend to support spreading of the standard superstrate.

Regional standard accents are characterised both by differences in the vowel and consonant systems, and also by a conspicuous variety of intonation patterns. The prosodic systems of the regional standards do not differ fundamentally from those of the standard superstrate, however. German pronunciation and its relation to other varieties is described by Kohler (1995).

1.1 General prosodic characteristics

The forms and structures of German prosody fall into three main hierarchical domains, the **syllable** and its consonant and vowel constituents, the **foot** and its role in accent and rhythm, and the domain of **phrase** intonation.

a. Syllable structure

In comparison with the other West Germanic languages, German has the most complex syllable structure. There are two main kinds of syllable (Carson-Berndsen 1993), which may be referred to as **major** and **minor** syllables.

Major syllables have the basic pattern, $C_1^3VXC_0^3$ *i.e.* between 1 and 3 consonants, followed by a vowel, a segment X, and between 0 and 3 consonants, where X is a sonorant or a glide or short vowel in a diphthong, or a vowel lengthening. A variant type of major syllable is $C_1^3VC_1^3$, that is, a closed syllable with a short (lax) vowel and at least one obstruent. Syllable-final obstruent clusters are always voiceless (which is not reflected in German spelling), resulting in neutralisation of the voicing contrast in obstruents. German shares this final devoicing with the major Slavic languages; it figures prominently in a "German accent" in other languages. An example[1] is /raʊp ˍ raʊ.bə/ *Raub-Raube* (robbery-robberies). Major syllables may be argued to be **bimoraic**, *i.e.* with two timing elements, essentially V and X. Like English, German has a form of post-vocalic r-vocalisation known as the **a-schwa**: /baːɐ/ *bar* (bar [*e.g.* pub]). There are two main points of interest about the analysis of main syllables. The first concerns whether the initial consonant cluster should be C_1^3 or C_0^3 because vowel-initial major syllables predictably start with a glottal stop: /ʔɪç ʔɛ.sə ʔaɪ.nən ʔap.fəl / *Ich esse einen Apfel* (contrast English /aɪ iːt ən æp.l/ *I eat an apple.*. The second concerns the proliferation of syllable-final voiceless alveolar obstruents and obstruent clusters /t/, /s/ which are either inflectional affixes or historically derived from inflectional affixes; these are generally described as **extrasyllabic**. Major syllables are prosodically rather stable, and tend not to be subject to rhythmic reduction.

Examples of major syllable structures where *C, G, V* are consonant, glide, vowel respectively, are: *CVG* /haɪ/ *Hai* (shark), *CCVV* /ʃneː/ *Schnee* (snow), *CCCVGCCC* /ʃtraɪfst/ *streifst* (you (singular-familiar) touch).

In words of Germanic origin, minor syllables in general contain an optional initial consonant and a weak vowel (the *e-schwa* /ə/, with an optional final consonant, or the *a-schwa* /ɐ/), which realises /r/ in syllable-final position. In combinations of schwa and sonorant /əl, ən, əm/, the schwa elides in fast speech, influencing the rhythmic pattern. A famous example of different fast speech elisions is /çbɪ.mɪm/ in /çbɪ.mɪm faː.raːt.gə.kɔm/ for /ɪç bɪn mɪt deːm faː.raːt gə.kɔ.mən/ *ich bin mit dem Fahrrad gekommen* (I came by bicycle). In non-native words, minor syllables may contain other vowels, as in /teː.o/ *Theo* (Theo [male proper name]).

Fewer than 10^4 syllables are attested in lexical items, out of well over 10^5 theoretically possible syllables based on combinations of onset consonant clusters, syllable nuclei and syllable codas. Syllable nuclei are in general easy to identify but syllable boundary identification is not so easy. The following cases may be distinguished:

1. Lexical roots: in VCV contexts, the syllable boundary precedes the consonant. In VCCV contexts, etc., lack of syllable-final devoicing in the first consonant motivates syllable boundary placement before the consonant, e.g. /vaː.gnɐ/ (Wagner), though the criterion may lead to strange onset clusters, as in /aː.dlɐ/ (eagle).

2. Compound words and derivational prefixes: the syllable boundary coincides with the morphological boundary (see examples in the text).

3. Derivational and inflexional suffixes: the syllable boundary is determined by the Maximal Onset Principle, not the morphological boundary ("re-syllabification", *e.g.* /fɛɐ.bɪnd +. ʊŋ/ → /fɛɐ.bɪn.d+ʊŋ/ *Verbindung* (connection). In C+C contexts, variation may occur, *e.g.* fast speech /vaɪ.b+lɪç/ (female) vs. careful speech /vaɪp +.lɪç/ with syllable-final obstruent devoicing as criterion.

b. Word stress

Word stress, following Bolinger (1958), is the position in a word to which a phonetic accent may be assigned. In German, word stress is assigned on lexical and morphological grounds. In simplex words, stress is closely related to the two main types of syllable: minor syllables are unstressed (and are "hypercorrected" into major syllables if contrasted), and most analysts agree that major syllables may be assigned primary, secondary or no stress. Word stress is initial on native roots, final or penult on non-native roots. On monosyllabic and disyllabic roots, these criteria are indistinguishable, but inflected forms may distinguish the cases by stress-shifting in the more complex form: /dˈɔk.toɐ/ – /dɔk.tˈoː.rən/ *Doktor–Doktoren* (doctor–doctors).

Derivation falls into three main prosodic classes: with stress-shifting, stressed and stress-neutral affixes. The case of stress-shifting and stressed affixes is illustrated by /rɛ.fˈɔɐm - rɛ.fɔɐ.mˈiː.rən - rɛ.fɔ.ma.tsjˈoːn/ *Reform–reformieren–Reformation* (reform–to reform–reformation). Other affixes, mainly of Germanic origin, do not affect stress. Derivational prefixes are unstressed. The stress-shifting and stressed affixes are described at Level I in Lexical Phonology, stress-neutral affixes at Level II (see Wiese 1995).

Stress in nominal and verbal compounds is on the first element, more consistently so than in English: /ʃrˈaɪp.tɪʃ/ *Schreibtisch* (writing desk), /vˈaː.gner.ʃtrˈaː.sə/ *Wagnerstraße* (Wagner Street), /vˈaː.gner.ʔa.lˈeː/ *Wagnerallee* (Wagner avenue).

A systematic taxonomy of German word stress types is given by Bleiching (Bleiching 1992, for simplex words and Bleiching 1994, for compounds and derivations).

c. Phrasal stress and the prosodic hierarchy

The functions of prosody in phrases are characterised by complex interactions between word order and phrase stress (often called **sentence stress**). German is a highly inflecting language, with relatively free word order, and it has been suggested that this has consequences for the use of intonation. Unlike languages such as English, with few inflections and relatively fixed word order, in German word order is a major focalisation device, used for topicalisation and for marking new information in utterances. This means that the **functional load** on prosody in this connection may well be lower than in English (see Schubiger 1958, 1980 and Ehlich 1979).

Furthermore, word order in German, as in Dutch, is predominantly **Subject-Object-Verb**; this SOV order contrasts with the SVO order of English or French, or the VSO order of Welsh. Subordinate clauses are regularly SOV, but main clauses are hybrid: simple verbs or auxiliaries have SVO position and infinitives are in final position, with VOS in polar interrogatives, imperatives and some conditionals. These conditions lead to relatively complicated principles of phrasal stress assignment.

Finally, spoken German has many quasi-parenthetic discourse particles, such as the modal particles like *ja* (yes; as we both well know) *doch* (yes on the contrary; as you well know) *wohl* (presumably) *also* (thus) and focus particles like *sogar, auch* (even), whose functions are to convey kinds of information which may be characteristic of intonation in other languages, such as "obviousness", "imputed shared presupposition", or "contradiction". These devices may be fairly freely combined. An example, compared with the use of intonation in English, is the following:

DEN Apfel hast du doch wohl meiner Tochter gegeben!
the[acc-focus] apple have[present-singular-2nd] you[nominative-singular]
contrary[doch]' obviously [wohl] my-dative-singular daughter given

(You even gave my daughter THAT apple!)

In the unmarked case, phrasal stress is assigned to the final noun, much as in other West Germanic languages (see Ladd 1980), but because of German SOV word order it is not sufficient to specify only "phrase-final lexical word" as it would be for the analogous case in English.

1.2 Outline of the approach adopted in this chapter

The information reviewed in this chapter is keyed more to consensus views than to novel insights. The main assumptions underlying the presentation are, first, that intonation in German is embedded into a prosodic hierarchy, with syllable constituents as the smallest elements and the intonation patterns of dialogue turns as the largest, and second, that the study of intonation should be based on certain specific empirical procedures.

a. The prosodic hierarchy
The idea that intonation in German is hierarchically organised has many sources. It is an old idea, and underlies many traditional and generative descriptions (see Klinghardt and Klemm (1920), von Essen (1956a); Bierwisch (1966) and the overview in Gibbon (1976a)). Intonation units consist of syllables structured into rhythmic sequences with superimposed tonal patterns. Newer developments in theoretical phonology support this idea of a prosodic hierarchy from syllable constituents through the syllable, the metrical foot, to phrase and paragraph (or "paratone") sised discourse units.

More recently, formal hierarchical models of intonation within the framework of automatic speech recognition and synthesis have been proposed (see Grønnum 1992 and Bannert 1983) for German. Feature-based theories also suggest the possibility of hierarchical structure (Gibbon 1995).

However, the hierarchical view has been relativised by the success of models which claim that intonation patterns are linear in the technical sense that they can be modelled by finite state machines ('t Hart and Cohen 1973 for Dutch and Adriaens 1991 for German). Applications of Fujisaki's Japanese model to German (see Möbius 1993) also support this view.

The apparent conflict is discussed by Ladd (1980) and Grønnum (1988). I suggest that the conflict is not an empirical one, but based on different implicit understandings of the concept of hierarchy (which is generally not defined formally in intonation studies). Mathematically, linear patterns are equivalent to exclusively right-branching or exclusively left-branching hierarchies, and other hierarchies with finite depth are also equivalent to linear patterns. But this does

Table 1. *ToBI labels for German.*[2]

Type	ToBI	Interpretation
Pitch	*T+T**	*T* = accented part*
accents	*T*+T*	
	H*	Normal upward pitch peak
	L+H*	Slightly delayed pitch peak
	L*+H	Right-displaced pitch peak
	L*	Downward pitch "valley"
	H+L*	Left-displaced pitch peak
	H+!H*	Left-displaced weak pitch peak
Boundary	*T-T%*	*T- = phrase tone*
tones		*T% = boundary tone*
	L-L%	Terminal fall, "final"
	L-H%	Slight rise in terminal syllable
	H-L%	Mid level, "progredient"
	H-H%	Terminal rise, "interrogative"
Break	B1	Normal word boundary
indices	B2	Fragment, hesitation boundary
	B3	Phrase boundary
	B4	Intonation phrase boundary

not apply to hierarchies with recursive centre-embedding (such as relative clauses in non-final noun phrases, or logical expressions) or with more complex structural dependencies than this. The hierarchies described in the literature belong to the class of structures which are equivalent to linear patterns, but whose topology may also be legitimately be described with the term "hierarchy". For example, the German intonation hierarchy shown in figure 1 is of the finite depth type, and can therefore still be modelled as a linear structure by a finite state machine.

At the lowest levels of the hierarchy, the elementary items are syllables, on the one hand, and elementary prosodic units on the other, which are mapped on to each other by rules of association. The traditional **tonetic** school of intonation description assumes a small inventory of prosodic categories based on pitch contour percepts (types of rise, fall, level tone) from which more complex patterns may be constructed. These accents or tones are symbolised by iconic "tonetic stress marks", such as acute and grave accents for rising and falling tones. Different scholars assume different inventories, from two "level switches" (see Isačenko and Schädlich 1966) through the three standard categories of rise, fall and level (von Essen 1956a) to more elaborate inventories (Pheby 1975). More recently, procedures which decompose the contours into sequences of pitch target levels have been introduced into German intonation research.

b. Corpora and procedures
Prosodic analysis is rarely performed nowadays on a purely auditory basis. A typical procedure for describing the prosody of spoken utterances is to record the utterances on digital tape or directly to a computer storage medium, transcribe them, and then align the transcription symbols with a visual representation of the signal (as an oscillogramme, spectral display, and/or fundamental frequency pattern). The digital technique of prosodic annotation, or prosodic labelling, has been available for about a decade, and has received increasing attention during the past few years because of interest from the area of automatic speech analysis and synthesis.

The symbol inventory which is most commonly used for the prosodic annotation of German is currently an adaptation of the ToBI system (Silverman *et al.* 1992), in which contours are represented as sequences of tone height and boundary marks as shown in table 1 (see also Reyelt *et al.* 1996).

2. Description of intonation patterns
2.1 Description of a basic non-emphatic pattern
There is widespread agreement about basic non-emphatic patterns in formal German speech, and the literature describing these goes back at least to the beginning of the twentieth century. The standard description is by von Essen (1956a). The study of prosody in spontaneous speech in dialogue contexts is, in comparison, still in its infancy.

a. Rhythmic structure
The basic rhythmic skeleton of non-emphatic patterns, typically used in matter-of-fact assertions, and with unmarked SVO and SOV word orders, is similar to that of the other West Germanic languages. The arguments of Jassem (1952) and others about the basic rhythmic structure of English apply, with some modifications, to German. In contemporary analyses, the basic unit is the **foot**, consisting of an accented syllable followed by one or more unaccented syllables, somewhat like (though simpler than) Jassem's **Narrow Rhythm Unit**. In addition to the basic trochaic or dactylic structure of these units, Jassem introduces an additional iambic element, the **Anacrusis**, of unaccented syllables before the accented syllable, creating a **Total Rhythm Unit** (see Jassem and Gibbon 1980). A sequence of feet with a tendency to isochrony, or equal length in time, will be referred to as a **rhythm sequence**, in German

"rhythmischer Körper". It appears that there may also be a higher level of temporal organisation, that is a **paragraph unit**, within which shorter rhythmic sequences are embedded (Gibbon 1981).

The rhythm of German is, like that of English, isochronous only in a weak sense of the term: accented syllables tend to be perceived, like any other kind of audible rhythm, as being evenly spaced in time. Different parts of the overall pattern, especially the unaccented syllables, are not isochronous but may be shortened to support the tendency towards isochrony. It should be added, however, that recent research on details of isochrony in German is lacking. The rhythm sequence provides the fundamental temporal frame within which tonal patterns are associated.

Numerous descriptions of the German rhythm sequences have been based on the von Essen model (1956a), originally designed for teaching formal elocution, in which the constituents of the basic pattern are defined as follows:

1. *Vorlauf (prehead):* a sequence of unstressed syllables.
2. *Rhythmischer Körper (body, rhythm sequence):* a sequence of one or more stressed syllables, the last being the "Schwerpunkt" (nucleus), each optionally followed by a sequence of unstressed syllables,
3. *Schwerpunkt (nucleus):* the last stressed syllable in a rhythmic sequence,
4. *Nachlauf (tail):* an optional sequence of unstressed syllables following the nucleus.

The following examples illustrate the basic von Essen model on two sentences with different rhythmic patterns, *Er kommt mit dem Wagen* (He comes by car), and *Wir wollten doch heute Nachmittag einkaufen gehen* (But we were planning to go shopping this afternoon).

Vorlauf	*Rhythmischer Körper* (*Schwerpunkt* italicised)	*Nachlauf*
er	KOMMT mit dem *WA-*	gen
Wir	WOLLten doch heute NACHmittag *EIN-*	kaufen gehen

An analysis of the rhythm sequence into a foot sequence produces a different grouping. Figure 1 illustrates both the von Essen model and the superimposed foot structure of the Rhythmic Sequence model.[3]

A third, more differentiated model, is that of Jassem. It is not possible on the basis of current evidence to decide which model provides the best description of German rhythm. It seems likely that more than one may be relevant: a rhythm structure for the assignment of accentual patterns, and other global structures for the assignment of melodic patterns.

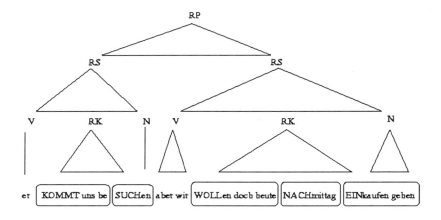

Figure 1. Foot and accent oriented prosodic structures.

b. Stress and accent

Stress is an abstract positional property of linguistic units which denotes the position at which a non-contrastive accent can occur. The stress position is determined by the structure of words and phrases. Pitch accent, on the other hand, is an approximately syllable-sised pitch modulation of the speech signal which lends perceptual prominence. The modulation may be a frequency change away from the basic carrier frequency line and back to it, resulting in the perceptual impression of a pitch peak (a pitch accent); the duration of the relevant syllable may be extended, and the overall energy of the signal may also increase round this syllable. It is generally accepted that pitch and duration changes are more significant than amplitude changes.

In figure 2, an orthographically labelled pitch tracing of a spontaneous utterance in a corpus of scheduling dialogues is reproduced: *ich FINde es zwar AUCH ganz SCHÖN was mir da ge-* (I find it basically quite good what we (did) there). The pitch modulations on *FINde, AUCH* and *SCHÖN* are prominent in the F_0 curve, and correspond to auditory impressions of the rhythmic accent positions. The emphatic focal accent on *AUCH* (also) has the strongest pitch modulation.

c. Tonal structure: statements and questions

In the traditional linguistic and elocutionary literature, statements and questions are associated with falling and rising intonations, respectively, with W-questions (*wer, wie, was, wo, wann,* analogous to English WH-questions with *who, how, what/which, where, when*), associated with falling tones in the unmarked cases. With increasing awareness of the variety of the uses of prosody in different situations, however, these claims are now widely regarded as too simplistic.

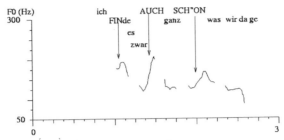

Figure 2. Pitch accent sequence in spontaneous speech.

The first detailed linguistic analysis of sentence mood and intonation in German was Pheby's (1975) study in the framework of systemic linguistics. Pheby distinguishes fifty systems of contrast, some of which are hierarchically related to others, starting with five main sentence classes:

1. statement, answer, question, request, exclamation;
2. familiarity, unfamiliarity;
3. emphatic, unemphatic;
4. contrastive, non-contrastive;
5. expressiveness, unexpressiveness.

In Pheby's analysis, these systems and their subsystems are realised by the tones (simplified characterisations of Pheby's systemic functions are given in parentheses):

1. falling (statements, exclamations);
2. rising (non-final, questions);
3. level (progredience, incompleteness);
4. falling-rising (uncertainty);
5. rising-falling (certainty, obviousness).

An even more detailed analysis, founded in detailed interpretative analyses of an impressively large quantity of spontaneous informal speech and a sophisticated functional account of dialogue processes, with a detailed intonation transcription system, is given by Selting (1991). However, these analyses do not cover the full range of tones which can be observed in colloquial German (cf. §2.4, for example).

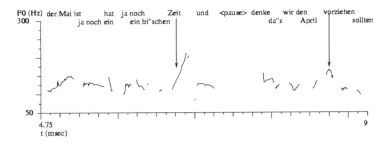

Figure 3. Rising pitch medially, falling terminally in spontaneous speech.

2.2 Mode and expressivity

More attention has been paid in studies of German intonation to the correlation between sentence mood and intonation than to the correlation between intonation and semantic and pragmatic categories such as modality and illocutionary force or speech act type (see Altmann 1988).

a. Sentence type and speech acts

In formal speech, a distinction is, as noted above, generally made between three kinds of terminal or nuclear tone which characterise different speech acts: the falling terminal, typically associated with assertions; the rising terminal, typically associated with yes/no questions; and the mid-level terminal, typically called progredient or *weiterweisend*, *i.e.* continuative. In spontaneous speech the mid-level progredient appears to be rare, except in stylised contexts (see §2.4), and rising nuclei are used for a range of functions, from progredience to questions, but they may also have connotations of deference, politeness, or uncertainty, as shown in figure 3 on the utterance *der Mai ist ja noch ein hat ja noch ein bißchen Zeit und <pause> denke daß wir den April vorziehen sollten* (May is of course still there's still a little time and <pause> [I] think that we should prefer April). A range of interrelations between syntactic mood and speech act type is shown in table 2.

Selting (1995) has demonstrated that in spontaneous German dialogue numerous different question types occur, each of which has a complex relation to intonation and syntax. This means that the traditional categorisation, which applies to less colloquial speech styles such as reading aloud, may not be applicable to everyday speech.

Table 2. *Relations between sentence mood and function.*

Mood	Tone	Function
Declarative	Fall	Assertion
	Rise	Echo question
		Uncertain statement
Imperative	Fall	Command
	Rise	Request, plea
Interrogative	Fall	Peremptory question
(auxiliary	Rise	Neutral question
inversion)		
W-question	Fall	Neutral question
wer, wie, ...	Rise	Interested or echo question

b. Monotony and excitement

The indexical function of pitch height to indicate degree of excitement is widespread, and certainly it occurs in German. However, the range of pitch modulation in German is in general much less than in English and many other languages in otherwise comparable situations, which may lead to misjudgements of intention or attitude. British female voices, in general relatively high-pitched, tend to sound aggressive and over-excited to the German hearer, and, conversely, German males may sound "bored" or "unfriendly" to the British hearer. Misjudgements of this kind indicate elements of cultural convention in an area of intonation which is often taken to be universal.

2.3 Focalisation and contextual effects

German has three main ways of signalling focalisation and related aspects of functional sentence perspective: with **focus particles**, with word order, and with accentuation. The three signalling devices do not have to coincide, and can therefore be assumed to relate to slightly different aspects of focalisation. This will be illustrated with reference to variants of the example given above.

a. Focal accents

In a simpler version of the example already given, *DEN Apfel hast du meiner Tochter gegeben*, accent, word order and focus particle combine to select the definite article *den*. But starting with a basic, unmarked formulation, six types of combination of marked utterance turn out to be possible:

1. *Unmarked word order, normal accent, no focus particle:*
   Du hast meiner Tochter den APFel gegeben.
   you[singular-familiar] have[present-singular-second] my[dative] daughter the[accusative] apple given
   (You have given my daughter the apple.)
2. *Unmarked word order, marked accent, no focus particle:*
   Du hast meiner TOCHter den Apfel gegeben.
3. *Unmarked word order, unmarked accent, focus particle:*
   Du hast sogar meiner Tochter den APFel gegeben.
4. *Marked word order, normal accent, focus particle:*
   Meiner Tochter hast Du sogar den APFel gegeben.
   Den Apfel hast Du sogar meiner TOCHter gegeben.
5. *Marked word order, marked accent, no focus particle:*
   Meiner Tochter hast DU den Apfel gegeben.
   Den Apfel HAST Du meiner Tochter gegeben.
6. *Marked word order, marked accent, focus particle:*
   Meiner Tochter hast DU sogar den Apfel gegeben.
   Den Apfel hast DU sogar meiner Tochter gegeben.

More variations in word order and in the positioning of accent and focus particles are possible for this example sentence than can be illustrated here: effectively, any syllable or combination of syllables can be accented for contrastive or emphatic purposes, any Noun Phrase or Adverbial can be fronted, and a focus particle can occur before or after the focused constituent.

Focalisation is one of the most challenging areas in the study of German intonation, and the largest number of recent studies on German intonation have treated related aspects such as topic and comment, focus and background, given and new information, signalling of the scope of semantic operators; an overview is given by Féry (1993). In German linguistics the field is often referred to as "functional sentence perspective", *funktionale Satzperspektive*, a term introduced in the Prague School of linguistics (see Sgall and Hajičova 1983).

b. Anaphoric, contrastive, and emphatic accent

In broader contexts, most of the marked accent assignments described above have contrastive function. One of the contrastive functions of accent, optionally accompanied by tone group boundary marking such as a pause or a different nuclear tone, is to localise the scope of a semantic operator such as negation, as in English:[4] *Er KAM nicht, weil er viel zu TUN hatte* (He didn't COME, because he had a lot to DO) as opposed to *Er kam nicht, weil er viel zu TUN hatte ...sondern weil er LUST dazu hatte.* (He didn't come because he had a lot to DO...but because he WANTED to). In the first case he came, in the second he did not come.

The standard preference for assigning a nuclear accent to the final noun in a group is overridden by the discourse condition of anaphoric or co-referential nominal groups: *Kennen Sie Herrn Buschkamp? – Ja, ich KENNE Herrn Buschkamp.* (Do you know Mr Buschkamp? – Yes, I KNOW Mr Buschkamp.) The noun Buschkamp is anaphoric; the verb KENNE is neither focused nor contrastively accented; in fact, it is also anaphoric (see Gibbon 1987). There is apparently no striking acoustic difference between this form of accentuation in anaphoric contexts and contrastive accent, though experimental evidence on this is lacking. Accent assignment in these anaphoric contexts is sometimes misleadingly referred to as **de-accenting** and **default accent**, but there is no reason to suppose that in such cases the anaphoric expression is in some sense first accented and then de-accented

Emphatic or emotive accents are not necessarily different in kind from other accents, but basically just have "more of everything". For example they have broader frequency modulation and more extreme syllable lengthening than non-emphatic accents, as in /ʃøːn/ *Schön!* (lovely!), where the *ö* may be extremely long.

2.4 Stylised patterns

The "chanted", flat or stylised pitch contour is used in German to signal the opening, sustaining and closing of a channel of communication (Jakobson's **phatic** function of language). These are the contours which are often called "call contours". In German, they are indeed used specifically in calls, but they have a range of other phatic functions, such as greeting, leave-taking, thanking, and, unlike other languages, in signalling cases of discourse repairs caused by mishearing (see Gibbon 1976a, 1976b, 1984).

1. Call:

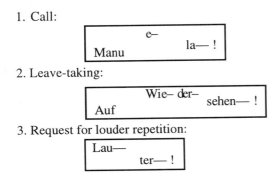

2. Leave-taking:

3. Request for louder repetition:

Dafydd Gibbon

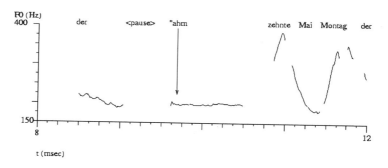

Figure 4. Flat stylised contour on a hesitation particle.

4. Repetition after mishearing:

> Ich habe "Jo— hann" — ge — sagt — !

It has often been pointed out that the pitch drop in this contour may approximate to a musical interval, such as a minor third, though this has not been experimentally established. Unlike English, German does not have a rising stylised contour.

A different form of stylised contour occurs with hesitation particles such as *ehm* or *ähm*, and can also be classified as having a variety of phatic functions. The hesitation contour is flat, and is accompanied by conspicuous lengthening of the associated vowel. Figure 4 illustrates this contour, with the utterance fragment *der <pause> ähm zehnte Mai Montag der* (the <pause> erm tenth of May Monday the), The stylised hesitation vocalisation is followed by a pitch accent on the immediately following lexical selection *zehnte* (tenth) and a rising nucleus on *Mai* (May). It is not known whether the hesitation contour, or indeed the other stylised contours with phatic functions, are universal.

3. Comparisons with other intonation systems

3.1 Comparisons with other dialects

a. Recurrent patterns

It was noted at the outset that the main regional standards are associated with the cities of Berlin, Hamburg, Hanover, Cologne, Frankfurt, Stuttgart, Munich and Leipzig, as well as Vienna for Austrian German, and Zurich for Swiss German, and that fundamentally these varieties share the same prosodic properties. However they have characteristic differences in detail.

92

A characteristic shared by all these German dialects is the regular foot-based rhythm, with syllable reduction on weak syllables. In many dialects, however, the inflectional affixes are much weaker than in the standard language superstrate, or have disappeared. Most inflectional affixes being word-final weak syllables such as /ʾən, əl, əm, əs, ə, ɐ/, this has led to small differences in rhythmic pattern between dialects and the standard language. The reductions are particularly characteristic of Southern varieties, but are also to be found in many other dialects.

Rhythm is based on the regular recurrence of prominent syllables, either with or without enhancement by pitch modulation. Dialects (as well as styles of speaking) vary in the details of this modulation. In general, Southern dialects are associated with a **right-displaced prominence peak**, that is, the syllable perceived as being accented has low pitch, and a pitch rise, often followed by a peak, occurs on one of the following syllables (ToBI $L*+H$, similar to Bolinger's Accent C in English, (Bolinger 1958)). In the standard pronunciation, the peak tends to occur on the accented syllable itself, though in some speech styles, such as telling stories to children, the right-displaced peak rhythm occurs.

The North German coastal dialects in general display features which are quite close to those of dialects of north-eastern England. There have been no comparative studies of the intonation patterns of these areas, however.

b. Nuclear patterns

Conspicuous prosodic differences between German dialects are found in the pitch contours of falling nuclei associated with plain statements. Three main varieties are to be found: fall from the nuclear syllable, a high fall from the nuclear syllable followed by a low rise, and a delayed rise to high following the nuclear syllable, with a fall to mid or low.

The fall from the nuclear syllable is characteristic of Standard Pronunciation in formal situations, and of many dialects. The other two varieties are distinctly regional, however. The high fall from the nuclear syllable followed by a low rise (ToBI $H*+L\ L-H\%$) is characteristic of the intonation of Hamburg and of neighbouring coastal dialects. The delayed rise to high following the nuclear syllable, with fall to mid or low (ToBI $L*+H\ H-H\%$), is common to a chain of dialects along the Rhine valley, from Switzerland ("Schwyzer Dütsch") to Cologne ("Kölsch"). Phonetically, the delayed rise is similar to displaced pitch accents and tones in other languages. Kohler has demonstrated that nuclear accent displacement of this kind is an option associated with different attitudinal meanings in Standard German pronunciation (see Kohler 1995).

3.2 Comparison with other languages

German is a foot-timed language, with a small amount of lexical and morphological stress contrast and no lexical tone or lexical pitch accent. Consequently, German prosody differs greatly both from that of pitch accent languages such as Japanese or Swedish, and that of tone languages such as those of Africa and South East Asia.

Dutch and English are both typologically and historically very close to German, and have fundamentally quite similar prosodic systems. The stress systems of both Dutch and German are less complex than that of English, and have more pronounced tendencies towards initial stress assignment. Sentence stress in both German and Dutch is influenced by the predominant SOV word order, which reduces the tendency to sentence-final stress, in contrast to English. Several factors result in different rhythmic patterns. German is a relatively highly inflecting language, and syllabic inflexional suffixes contribute to a pronounced trochaic rhythm. The distribution and degree of vowel reduction differ in German from those in English; in loan words, vowel quantity and quality tends to be preserved, thus German /fo.n'eː.tɪk/ *Phonetik* (phonetics) as opposed to English /fə.n'ɛ.tɪks/ *phonetics*. The distribution of /ə/ -elision before sonorants (nasals, laterals) in German differs subtly from that in English. There are also differences in the prosodic inventory; English has a rising "call contour", which is absent in German, but the falling German call contour has a broader range of functions than its English counterpart (see Gibbon 1976a, 1976b) Schubiger (1980) claims that in German, modal particles such as *doch*, *wohl*, *ja* play similar roles to certain intonation tunes in English, which does not have such a wide range of particles and particle combinations, while German does not have such a wide range of intonation patterns as English. This claim has a *prima facie* plausibility, but has not been extensively or systematically investigated.

The main central European German-speaking area (Austria, Germany, the Swiss German area) has border contacts with a variety of major languages (Czech, Danish, Dutch, French, Hungarian, Polish, Italian, Slovak and Slovenian), and there are German-speaking minorities in each of these other areas. The Slavic languages Polish, Czech, Slovak and Slovene are also stress timed, and their prosodic systems are similar in many general respects. But the detailed phonetic realisation of prosodic patterns differs markedly, with pronounced differences in rhythm and the bandwidth of pitch modulation.

4. Implications and conclusions

The intonation of German has received considerable attention from linguists and phoneticians, and currently there is an upsurge of interest stemming from speech technology. The goals of providing natural speech synthesis, and, in automatic speech recognition, of disambiguating alternative analyses and of identifying speaker intentions, have received prominence in the context of large research and development projects.

It seems likely that this activity will continue, and be extended to cover increasingly sophisticated problems such as phonostylistic (e.g. fast speech) and dialectal differences, coupled with adaptive techniques for coping with them. A major heuristic contribution of these efforts has been the creation of large speech corpora which have been prosodically analysed, and the development of tractable computer-aided techniques of prosodic corpus analysis (see the overview in Gibbon 1994).

On the side of semantics and pragmatics, and independently of these technological developments, two main centres of linguistic interest can be currently identified: the application of interpretative methods from discourse analysis to the description of intonation, and investigation of the role of focus in formal semantics (see Quasthoff 1994). In these areas, increasingly detailed analyses of the functions of prosody are emerging, which cast doubt on the validity of simple functional labels such as "question intonation", "impatient intonation" and the like in view of insights into the complexity of such notions as "question" and "emotion".

Notes

1 Notation: /./ syllable boundary, /'/ primary stress, /"/ secondary stress (placed before syllable nucleus), /+/ morpheme boundary, /#/ word boundary in compounds; syllable boundaries are placed after morphological boundaries.

2 The symbols in the table have the following meanings: L = low, H = high, ! = downstepped tone (^ is also used for upstepping), - = phrase tone marker, % = boundary tone marker, * = accent position, + = concatenation of tone constituents in a pitch accent.

3 The abbreviations in figure 1 have the following meanings: PU is a Paragraph Unit, RS is a Rhythmic Sequence, V is a *Vorlauf*, RK is a body, *rhythmischer Körper*, N is a tail, *rhythmischer Nachlauf*.

4 Note that comma punctuation in German is determined by grammar, and does not correlate as closely with intonation as in English.

5

Intonation in
Dutch

JOHAN 'T HART

1. Background

1.1 General prosodic characteristics

The intonation system of Dutch can be characterised as a hierarchical system, in which intonation patterns figure at the highest level, and changes of F_0 or pitch movements (rather than levels), at the lowest. It is convenient to consider the clause as the domain of the intonation patterns (but see §2.4), and the syllable as that of the pitch movements. The choice of pattern dictates the nature and order of the pitch movements ('t Hart and Collier 1979), and a grammar specifies their combination possibilities ('t Hart and Collier 1975).

Pitch movements can be divided into abrupt and gradual movements. The latter spread out over several consecutive syllables. Abrupt movements typically have a shorter duration than that of the syllable in which they occur. It appears to be necessary to characterise these movements according to their position in the syllable: early, rather late, very late. Abrupt movements can be divided into those involved in accentuation and those that are not. The accent-lending capacity of pitch movements is related to their position in the syllable; however, the meaning of the individual words is not affected by a difference in pitch movements: Dutch has no tones or tonemes. Since an accent-lending rise must be early in one kind of pattern, but rather late in another, interpretative

96

differences may be experienced between two utterances as a whole with identical segmental content.

See, for instance, figures 1a and 1b. Whereas (a) will be interpreted as a straightforward establishment of a fact, (b) has the implication (for this sentence) that the speaker is anxious that something terrible may have happened to Peter, since usually, he is never late.

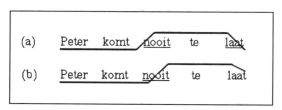

Figure 1. Stylised representation of two different intonation patterns on the same word string (Peter comes never too late), giving rise to a difference in interpretation (see the next).

The relation between pitch accents and lexical stress is simple on the one hand, but complicated on the other. As can already be established auditorily, pitch accents virtually always occur on syllables that bear lexical stress; acoustically, the F_0 changes associated with the pitch accents take place somewhere in those syllables. So far the seemingly simple aspect.

A first complication is that a text-to-speech system should know the lexically stressed syllable of each polysyllabic word (which is not fixed in Dutch, contrary to *e.g.* French, Czech, *etc.*). Attempts to derive lexical stress from segmental content have been rather successful lately (Berendsen, Langeweg and Van Leeuwen 1986; Berendsen and Don 1987), but a situation in which only a limited number of exceptions has to be stored in a memory is still remote. Moreover, the Dutch lexicon contains some minimal pairs distinguished by lexical stress, for instance:

b'eken	= plural of noun *beek* (brook)
bek'en	= confess (imperative)
b'edelen	= to beg, to ask for charity
bed'elen	= to endow, to bestow alms on the poor
v'oorkomen	= to occur, to happen, to appear in court
voork'omen	= to anticipate, to avert, to prevent, to avoid

For a very limited number of words, lexical stress depends on position in the sentence, *e.g. alt'ijd* (always) if it is the last accented word in the clause, but *'altijd* otherwise. The general trend, however, is that lexical stress is independent of higher-order structuring, although occasionally, rhythmical requirements may call for a stress shift, as in:

pass'ief gedr'ag	(passive behaviour), (normal stress), *vs.*
p'assief r'oken	(passive smoking), (shifted stress);
direct'eur Verm'eer	(director Vermeer), *vs.*
d'irecteur J'ansen.	(director Jansen)

A second, more serious complication is that, as in many other Germanic languages, in Dutch not every content word in a sentence receives a pitch accent. For quite a number of cases, rules can be and have been formulated which specify which words in a sentence should be accented, especially on the basis of syntactic considerations. Many other cases still pose problems. Part of these problems are unsolvable, since the intention of the speaker is not always predictable. As a consequence, a text-to-speech system will inevitably make mistakes.

Apart from accentuation, another general characteristic is the possibility to mark syntactic boundaries by means of various different intonational features. These will be dealt with at several instances in §2.

1.2 Outline of the approach

a. Experimental approach
i. Materials. In the study of Dutch intonation, we started with isolated words in citation form, followed by radio interviews, news bulletins and university lectures, and ended up with a corpus of about 1400 utterances in six fragments of theatre plays of about ten minutes each, in which lively conversation was supposed to take place, plus one fragment of ten minutes of spontaneous speech by four, later five different speakers.

In an attempt to examine whether the research methods followed (see next sub-section) would be feasible not only in the analysis of Dutch intonation, but also for other languages, we undertook a comparable approach of British English intonation. In that study, we started with an analysis of examples recorded on the tapes that go with the courses on intonation by Halliday (1970) and by O'Connor and Arnold (1973); later, we analysed interviews as selected by departments of applied linguistics of two Dutch universities; finally, we analysed recordings of spontaneous speech in broadcasts of the British Forces Broadcasting Station in Germany.

ii. Research methods. Basing ourselves on the assumption that only those aspects of the course of F_0 are relevant to the perception of the speech melody that are intended by the speaker, we separate voluntary from involuntary changes of F_0 by applying a stylisation method. This consists of constructing a piecewise linear approximation to the F_0 curve in such a way that the following twofold condition is met: the stylised contour should contain the lowest possible number of straight-line segments and yet be auditorily indistinguishable from the original course of pitch. Contours stylised with the lowest possible number of segments and yet perceptually equal to the originals have been named close-copy stylisations. They contain all and only the perceptually relevant pitch movements.

Subsequently, auditorily comparable pitch movements in close-copy stylisations are given standard specifications as to their slopes, their sizes, and their positions in the syllable. The standard specifications are inspired by averages of the values obtained in close-copy stylisations. The standardised stylisations should sound like successful imitations of the close-copy stylisations (as being perceptually equivalent to them) and in any case, they should sound acceptable as such (in later synthesis-by-rule only the second requirement is relevant). The stylised, artificial contours are made interactively on a computer in which an LPC analysis-resynthesis system is implemented, thus enabling the experimenters to monitor the perceptual effects of their manipulations. The aim of making standard stylisations is to ultimately attain the generalisations that are necessary to disclose the systematic properties in the intonation of the language under investigation. The perceptual equality of close-copy stylisations, and the perceptual equivalence and the acceptability of standardised stylisations, are tested in formal experiments (for British English: De Pijper 1983) with native speakers of the language at issue.

Two (or more) contours that lack mutual perceptual equivalence may nevertheless sound similar in a more abstract way. This has led to a hypothetical categorisation of the melodic possibilities of both Dutch and British English into a number of so-called basic patterns (see §§2.1, 2.5). The validity of these categorisations has been tested in "sorting" and "matching" experiments. With respect to Dutch, some of these have been dealt with in 't Hart and Collier (1975), others in Collier and 't Hart (1972) and in Collier (1975).

b. Summary of main acoustic/phonetic results
The analysis by means of the stylisation method has yielded results that can be divided into the following categories:
- characteristics of movements;
- relation between movements and patterns;
- declination.

i. Acoustic/phonetic characteristics of movements. Dutch standard stylisations can be described by means of ten different perceptually relevant pitch movements, apart from declination. They fall apart according to their direction (rise or fall), slope (abrupt or gradual), and size (full or half), whereas for the full abrupt rises and falls three positions with respect to the syllable are distinguished. A full account is given in Collier (1972) and in 't Hart and Collier (1975). (Comparable data for British English can be found in De Pijper

1983, and Williems, Collier, and 't Hart 1988.) In addition, there is a course of Dutch intonation (Collier and 't Hart 1981), written in Dutch.

ii. Relation between movements and patterns. By our definition of an intonation pattern, a pattern is an abstract category; by virtue of its abstractness, it possesses a fair amount of versatility in its concrete manifestation. One aspect of this versatility can be called **elasticity**: two contours differing in number of syllables between rise and fall are both realisations of the same basic pattern, provided that the types of rise and of fall are the same. The choice of basic pattern thus dictates, in general, the nature and the order of the pitch movements, but not their location in the string of syllables. The timing of pitch movements with respect to the syllables in which they occur has, however, been specified explicitly. See the references mentioned in (i).

The combinatory possibilities and restrictions are mapped out in what has been called a grammar of intonation. This is an algorithm which generates (nearly) all and only those successions of pitch movements that lead to an acceptable intonational result.

iii. Declination. Declination, the gradual tapering off of F_0 throughout an utterance, is observed as a regularly occurring phenomenon. As Maeda (1976) found in his material, we also observed that, at least within one speaker, the utterance-final frequency varies very little. But whereas Maeda found reasons to propose a fixed start frequency as well, we found that longer utterances start higher than shorter utterances (as has also been reported by other authors, *e.g.* Cooper and Sorensen 1981). In Cohen *et al.* (1982), a formula is given which specifies the slope of an uninterrupted lower declination line, or baseline, as a function of utterance duration, and which reflects that property for utterances up to five seconds long. This empirical formula was based on Dutch read-out material, but it gives a nice fit for read-out British English as well, as has been demonstrated by Willems (also cited in Cohen *et al.* 1982). However, his additional observations on spontaneous speech show that, although the slope predicted by the formula is very close to the average of the measured slopes, the individual declination slopes may vary considerably.

We have found no evidence in favour of a dependence of declination slope on sentence category. In an independent study, at our Institute, on dialogues, in which it is easy to check whether an utterance is interpreted by the listener as a statement or a question, it was found that in a limited number of cases utterances lacked apparent declination, but these were evenly distributed over questions and statements (Beun 1988).

iv. Some functional aspects. The main concern of the bottom-up approach in the IPO studies on intonation (first for Dutch, later for British English, still later for

German and Russian) has been and is still to examine what are regularly occurring phenomena in speech pitch, and to try to describe these in terms of discrete events, the pitch movements, and of their combinatory possibilities in configurations and entire contours. Although functional aspects come in the second place in such an approach, the analysis of large amounts of materials confronts the experimenters in a natural way with the conditions in which the various intonational phenomena may occur. And this may inspire them to make hypotheses on the functional aspects of intonation, and to test these in appropriate experiments. In the next sub-sections, some functional aspects will be dealt with, most of them illustrated with the aid of the most frequently occurring basic pattern of Dutch.

2. Description of intonation patterns

2.1 Description of a basic non-emphatic pattern

a. Non-emphatic declaratives

Given a sequence of syllables forming an utterance consisting of one clause, a typical pattern for the intonation of a short non-emphatic declarative phrase in Dutch is what we have called the hat pattern. In our corpus of quasi-spontaneous and spontaneous speech, which was reported on in 't Hart and Collier (1975), it has appeared that variants of the hat pattern are used in almost 70% of the clauses. Figure 2 gives an example of the F_0 curve as measured in the sentence *Ik moet EERST mijn FIETS wegzetten.* (I must first my bike away-put) with pitch accents on the capitalised syllables, together with the stylised pitch contour.

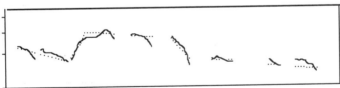

Figure 2. F_0 curve (solid) and stylised contour (dotted) for the sentence *Ik moet EERST mijn FIETS wegzetten.* (I must first put my bike away). It is an example of the hat pattern. Ordinate: divisions (logarithmic) of 50 Hz.

The hat pattern is characterised by an alternation of definitely specified types of rises and falls, in that order. If there is only one accent, there is a rise-fall combination on the single syllable at issue: a "pointed" hat. Two (or more) accents can be made by means of two (or more) pointed hats. Far more often, however, at least part of the rise-fall combinations will be split up into separate rises and falls. Particularly the penultimate and the last pitch accent are given a rise and a fall respectively, with high syllables in between: a "flat" hat. In cases with more than two pitch accents, only the last one has a fall, each of the other ones has a rise.

Between two rises, F_0 falls in one of three different ways: (a) abruptly and immediately after the rise, (b) gradually until the next rise begins, or (c) abruptly but postponed. In the latter case, this so-called non-final fall should not give rise to an extra accent. This is taken care of by its position, which is typically between adjacent syllable nuclei, whereas the accent-lending, final fall takes place during a syllable nucleus. The non-final fall may mark a syntactic boundary between the two rises, in most cases the deepest one (Collier and 't Hart 1975). To circumvent the need of an automatic syntactic analysis in order to locate the non-final fall correctly, a simple text-to-speech system typically uses the gradual fall: the "saw tooth" variant (see figure 3b).

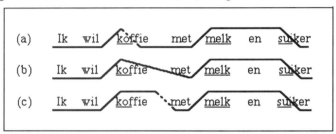

Figure 3. Three ways of lowering F_0 between two accent-lending rises in the sentence *IK wil KOffie met MELK en SUlker* (I want coffee with milk and sugar). (a) abrupt, immediately after the first rise; (b) gradually, saw tooth-like; (c) abrupt and postponed, marking a boundary. Declination omitted.

b. Modification possibilities

Quite a number of variants can be derived from the basic shape of the hat pattern. The resulting contours are often in free variation, *e.g.* with respect to the three ways of falling between two rises as explained in §2.1.a; however, in some cases, for instance within subordinate clauses, marking of a boundary by means of a postponed, non-final fall is unacceptable, since it wrongly suggests a return to the main clause. An example is the third sentence of the Fable of the North Wind and the Sun, in Dutch as follows:

> 1 Ze kwamen overeen, 2 dat degene 3 die het eerst erin zou slagen 4 de reiziger zijn mantel te doen uittrekken, 4 3 de sterkste zou worden geacht 2 1.

A non-final fall between *zou slagen* and *de reiziger...* sounds unacceptable, the best solution is a rise-fall on *eerst*. Interestingly, one is not obliged to mark the boundary between ... *uittrekken* and *de sterkste...*; the tendency to make a flat hat for the last two pitch accents may overrule the need of an intonational boundary marker (a temporal cue will be likely, though).

An example of free variation will be given in §2.4. These observations seem to imply that, since the speaker has a free choice among different variants, the constraints imposed by syntactic, semantic or pragmatic factors are not numerous, nor very strict.

In principle, it is very possible that strings of the same words give rise to different interpretations solely owing to a difference in intonation. But since it is the interplay between word content and prosody that may favour one interpretation over another, such a switch is not always possible (cf. 't Hart 1976). Nevertheless, a shift of a pitch accent from one word to another, and a shift of a syntactic boundary, will generally lead to a change of the implication, or the possible context of an utterance.

2.2 Questions

Figure 4. Two possible contours for the interrogative sentence "Heeft Peter een nieuwe auto gekocht?" (Has Peter a new car bought?). Declination omitted.

There is no specific intonation pattern characteristic of questions. Questions may be marked by means of a final rise, but in our corpus (of about 1400 utterances) only half of the about 100 questions contained such a rise. On the other hand, quite a number of non-questions had a final rise as well (*e.g.* utterances with tags, or vocatives). A hat pattern with a final rise is still judged to be a member of the family of the hat pattern in our "sorting" and "matching" experiments ('t Hart and Collier 1975). If a hat pattern plus final rise is used for a question, the rise does not replace the fall on the last pitch accent, but it is added to it; it comes very late in the last syllable (see figure 4a). An alternative pattern used in questions, but again not exclusively, contains a rise on the last accented syllable (see figure 4b), and in most cases there is also a final rise (otherwise it sounds gruff or impatient). This pattern is also used in non-questions, giving an implication of unfinishedness.

As will become clear in §2.4, exactly the same features that figure in questions may occur at syntactic boundaries, be it that the final rise after the rising last pitch accent is found less frequently.

2.3 Focalisation, contrast

It is certainly possible to use intonation to focalise or contrast an element without any modification of the syntactic structure. To bring about contrast, it is sufficient to reduce the number of pitch accents to one. Of course, the converse need not be true: if, for some reason or other, the number of accents is already restricted to one (in case all the other information is **Given**, in cases of integrative accent where the entire utterance is in focus, or in cases of **default accent**, see *e.g.* Fuchs 1984), one may not conclude that this accent is a contrastive accent. The often observable larger size of the pitch movements is only a concomitant feature, not necessary and in itself not sufficient to bring about contrast. The interpretation of contrast is evoked by considering the entire utterance in its context; it is not visible or audible by the shape of the pitch movement(s) alone.

We might broaden the scope of the notion of contrast by including situations in which the reduction of the number of pitch accents does not lead to a contour with only one pitch accent: if we start with an utterance in which the minimum number of pitch accents adequate for its being judged neutral is three, a reduction to two accents may give rise to an interpretation in terms of contrast as well. For example:

(a) AmsterDAM is de HOOFDstad van NEderland
(b) AmsterDAM is de HOOFDstad van Nederland
(c) AmsterDAM is de hoofdstad van NEderland
(Amsterdam is the capital of the Netherlands)

Version (b) can be used to express that another city in the country has a different important status, as is the case with The Hague, which is the royal residence. Version (c) can be used to express contrast with *Brussels is the capital of Belgium.*

2.4 Breaking up of longer utterances

As was mentioned in the beginning of this chapter, it is convenient to consider the clause as the domain of the intonation patterns. As a consequence, this unit is a suitable one for breaking up longer utterances. But speakers do also introduce boundaries within clauses, *e.g.* by using the postponed, non-final fall. To give an account of the intonational marking of these less deep syntactic boundaries it is useful to apply an analysis in terms of phrases (NP, VP, *etc.*). Sometimes, speakers map an entire contour (the concrete realisation of a pattern) on only a part of a clause, *e.g.* on a prolonged Subject. We must conclude that there is not always a one-to-one relationship between a syntactic and an intonational clause.

Clause contours can be concatenated by means of continuative intonation features. These are dealt with in the rest of this section.

In the traditional literature, separate mention is made of continuative intonation features ("weiterweisend" in German). Delattre *et al.* (1965) thought it useful to make a distinction between major and minor continuations. We may look at this issue from a somewhat different point of view by talking of the ways in which syntactic boundaries are, or can be, marked intonationally, and by asking whether particular types of syntactic boundaries require specific ways of being marked.

The melodic facts for Dutch are that at least three ways of marking syntactic boundaries can be distinguished. They can be characterised as follows:

(1) The last pitch accent before the boundary is a rise, the syllables between the accented one and the boundary remain high, at the boundary F_0 falls to the baseline (see §1.2biii). We have seen this already as the most common way of marking boundaries between phrases within clauses, but it does also occur at clause boundaries, about as frequently as shape (2). In case a clause boundary is at stake, a small, late final rise may be added just before the boundary. Such an extra rise is not usual at phrase boundaries within clauses.

(2) The last pitch accent before the boundary is a fall, the syllables between the accented one and the boundary are low, but the last one contains a very late rise, the continuation rise, immediately followed by a fall to the baseline.

The following shape can be considered to be a variant of (2): the full-size fall is replaced by a half-fall, and the continuation rise is omitted. The frequency of occurrence of this variant is very low. In all likelihood, this variant is only used if the number of syllables between the last accent and the boundary is restricted to one or two.

A common property of both (1) and (2) is that the contour is not low before the boundary, and is low after it.

(3) Regardless of what happens in the last accented syllable, the main feature is a declination reset, *i.e.* the lower declination line, or baseline, takes a new start, considerably higher than its position before the boundary (for declination, see 1.2biii).

One of the ways in which the effect can be obtained is by omitting the resumption of low pitch immediately after the continuation rise as mentioned in (2), but declination resets can also occur in isolation. In such cases, the contour is low before the boundary, and physically high(er) after it; but in view of what follows, it should be considered a raised low: the first pitch accent after the boundary is a rise (or a rise-fall).

One may ask what determines, or perhaps influences, the choice between these types of boundary marking, or their variants, or their possible combinations. With respect to type (3), there is a fair amount of evidence to support the hypothesis that a declination reset is made in order to signal that what follows after the boundary does not link up with the part of the sentence immediately preceding it, but with an earlier constituent. The following example was recorded from a radio broadcast (on 25 June 1984):

> De communistische partij in China, gisteren precies 63 jaar oud, heeft de
> afgelopen vijf jaar 4.8 miljoen nieuwe leden ingeschreven
> (The communist party in China, yesterday exactly 63 years old, has in the past five
> years 4.8 million new members registered.)

In this sentence, a declination reset occurred after the apposition *gisteren precies 63 jaar oud* to link up the finite verb *heeft* with its subject.

The choice between continuation types (1) and (2) appears to be less systematic, although some trend has been observed. As we have seen in §2.1a, a non-final fall can be used to mark a phrase boundary within a clause. Intonationally, such a melodic shape is exactly the same as continuation type (1), used to mark a clause boundary (in the latter case, it is likely that pre-boundary lengthening occurs as well). This might lead us to suppose that continuation type (1) will more often be used for not very deep clause boundaries, and the more "achieved", type (2) for deeper boundaries, such as between main clauses. The facts, until now, are that irrespective of the kind of clause boundary, the frequencies of occurrence of the two types are equal. However, a frequent use of type (2) for phrase boundaries within a clause is considered unacceptable.

Further research is under way to find out whether indeed type (2) is preferable for deeper boundaries; this could give support to a notion of a certain hierarchical principle. From the observations mentioned above we can already predict that this principle should not imply a compulsory choice between the two types of continuation, deterministically dependent on the depth of the syntactic boundary. We might expect, however, that in *e.g.* a succession of a less deep and a deeper boundary, the use of type no. 2 for the former, and of type no. 1 for the latter, can sometimes lead to misunderstandings, and should therefore be avoided.

2.5 Other patterns

a. Stereotyped patterns

In Dutch intonation, one of the melodic possibilities is a pattern which differs from the hat pattern in the size of the final fall. Whereas the final fall in the hat pattern comes down to the baseline, the one in the alternative pattern is typically half sised, to the effect, in the words of Isamu Abe (1962), that it seems to be "suspended in mid-air". The more than 25 years since then have brought to light that in languages possessing this feature, it is not only used in special instances of calling, but in many more situations. Nowadays, *e.g.* in the view of Ladd (1980), the more general idea of "stereotype" or "routine" has been put forward, and very convincingly. A striking impression the half-fall gives is that it sometimes seems to make a musical interval, which is almost never the case with the other pitch movements. Indeed, there is a tendency to keep the pitch steady after the half-fall (*i.e.* no declination), and we may suppose that it is this tendency that gives the main contribution to the impression. Meanwhile, there is no need to believe that the interval is always near a minor third, as was our original impression. As we pointed out a few years ago (Cohen, Collier, and 't Hart 1982), the main cue for a fall of this type is that after its occurrence, F_0 has audibly not reached the baseline.

Another characteristic of this movement is that it is early in the syllable: it is typically completed at the onset of the vowel. For instance, in *Waar is Peter?* (where is Peter), there may be a rise on *waar* (pitch accent), and a half-fall on *Pe-*, in which syllable the pitch is already (half) low before the vowel /e/ begins. The half-fall gives a (light) pitch accent on *Peter*. If the utterance is no longer than *Peter*, the use of the same pattern allows the speaker to use the pitch accent rise on the syllable *Pe-*, but forces him to locate the half-fall early in the syllable *-ter*. Since that syllable has no lexical stress, the half-fall loses its accent-lending capacity. If we now try to use the same pattern on a monosyllabic word, or on a word with its lexical stress on the last syllable, this leads to a conflict: we cannot make a full rise and a half-fall at the same time (*viz.* early in the syllable). The solution consists of a reduplication of the vowel, as in a melisma in singing: *Jahan* instead of *Jan* (John). Note that such a measure is never taken if a pointed hat is used.

As we have seen in §2.4, the half-fall is also used in signalling continuation, but only rarely. A further occurrence of the half-fall, or of a series of them, is found in terrace-shaped contours, between an initial rise and a final fall, as a variant of the hat pattern. In neither of these cases, however, is a "stereotyped" interpretation at stake.

b. Some remarks about other patterns

In Dutch, six basic patterns can be distinguished. Two of them have received rather extensive attention here, the hat pattern since its frequency of occurrence is very high, and the stereotyped pattern since its implications are fairly well understood. To other patterns, such as the one in figure 1b (characterised by its late rise and clause-final fall, which does not lend a pitch accent), and to the hat pattern itself, can (as yet) not be attributed single inherent implications or most likely interpretations. For instance, although the hat pattern is the most adequate pattern to be used in neutral declaratives and interrogatives, it has been observed in many situations of which it was clear that peevishness, irony, preponderance, restrained anger or consolation was at stake. It may well be that this multiple application has something to do with the pattern's high frequency of occurrence; but the other patterns have also been observed in quite a number of differing situations.

Since it is as yet unknown what the most suitable pattern is in a given situation and context, a text-to-speech system can only make use of (variants of) the hat pattern.

3. Comparisons with other systems

3.1 Comparisons within the same language

Dutch, like many other languages, is spoken in a number of different ways. But apart from dialects, it possesses, roughly spoken, two distinct standard forms, *viz.* Netherlands and Flemish. Therefore we can put forward two different questions about comparisons within the same language:

(1) Do dialectal variations also contain intonational variations?
(2) Can we decide whether or not the intonation systems in the two standard forms of the Dutch language have developed differently?

The answer to the former question is: undoubtedly; but we have not studied the intonation in dialects of Dutch in any systematic way. This precludes us from the possibility to give the answer more reliably than on a mere impressionistic basis.

The answer to the latter question can be given with more authority. Our course of Dutch intonation (Collier and 't Hart 1981) has been used for years with Flemish students of Dutch at the University of Antwerp. They were confronted with specimens of all kinds of intonation as based on the analysis of our corpus, in which all the speakers originated from the Netherlands. Practically none of the many hundreds of students had any problems in recognising, or in producing, these specimens. Although it may well be that the frequency of occurrence of the various patterns differs in speakers in the two countries, there seems to be no reason to suspect that the underlying systems are different.

3.2 Comparisons with other languages

In De Pijper (1983) and Willems, Collier and 't Hart (1988) an account is given of investigations, using the same methods as applied for Dutch (see §1.2), on British English intonation. Earlier, Collier inspired Maeda (1976) to apply the same methods in his study of American English intonation. By using these results, Klatt (1980) was able to improve the intonational quality of his synthesis-by-rule system substantially (although critical listeners of eight years later may say that it still sounds far from natural). At IPO, the intonation systems of German and Russian were studied as well.

The use of the same theoretical framework makes cross-language comparisons feasible and meaningful. Although it is not possible to give a full account of the differences between *e.g.* British English and Dutch intonation here, a limited number of the most important differences can be dealt with.

For a description of British English intonation, it was necessary to introduce a grid of three reference lines, Low, Mid, and High (declination lines, see §1.2biii), whereas for the description of Dutch intonation two reference lines are sufficient. Sizes of movements are typically larger in British English than in Dutch, and slopes are steeper. For further details, see Willems (1982). British English uses more falls than rises for pitch accents (as already noticed by Delattre *et al.* 1965, and by Meinhold 1972); Dutch pitch accents are more often rises than falls.

A striking difference is the following: in both intonation systems a pattern can be distinguished which is mainly characterised by a feature that may be called "delay". In British English, a rise starts from the baseline rather late with respect to the vowel onset of the accented syllable, the peak is (in many cases) not reached until the next syllable has started, and is immediately followed by a steep fall back to the baseline. The pattern is called Tone 5 by Halliday (1970), and The Jackknife by O'Connor and Arnold (1973). In Dutch too, the rise starts rather late, and the highest pitch is in the next syllable, but the fall has to be postponed to a clause-final position, is not very steep, and need not reach the baseline (see figure 1b). British listeners, when presented with English utterances provided with the Dutch pattern (by means of the analysis-resynthesis technique), judge this kind of intonation to be "very unacceptable", from which it may be concluded that the requirement of having the fall occur immediately after the rise is a genuine aspect of the English intonation system.

German intonation appears to differ more from Dutch than we had anticipated. Like British English, it is more appropriately described by means of three reference lines, and also the sizes of the movements are usually larger than in Dutch, although not as large as in British English. As in Dutch, pitch accents are more often rises than falls; continuation rises are used very frequently, also for marking less deep syntactic boundaries.

A striking difference with both Dutch and British English is the small slope of the movements, which, since their size is rather large, must have a long duration. As a result, in rapid successions of movements, there is not enough time to make them full-sised. For instance, a fall followed by a continuation rise on one syllable or on two adjacent syllables, is stopped at the middle level, from where the rise starts.

4. Conclusions

One of the main elements of the research method presented here is standardisation. The application of this technique has consequences of two different kinds, one theoretical and one practical. On the one hand, it helps in finding sufficient generalisations in order to establish a moderately extended inventory of pitch movements that make it possible to describe the quasi-continuous course of F_0 in terms of discrete events. On the other hand, since the contours resulting from standardisation should sound acceptable, analysis-by-(re)synthesis is implied which, by virtue of the acceptability experiments, eventually yields reliable precepts for synthesis-by-rule, to be used, *e.g.*, in text-to-speech systems.

The development of a text-to-speech system has never been considered by us as a goal in itself. Rather, it is viewed as a research tool, mainly because it shows the gaps in our knowledge in a merciless way. Starting one day to provide entire texts with artificial intonation, we saw ourselves confronted with a number of unexpected problems, some of which will be dealt with here.

In the acceptability tests done so far, the stimulus materials consisted of isolated sentences, which deliberately had been provided with many different variants of each of the six basic patterns, in view of the aim that the acceptability should be verified of as many of the variants as possible. In a contiguous text, this kind of variation should be assigned by rule. But unfortunately, not enough is known about what determines, in natural speech, the speaker's choice of a particular basic pattern, or of a particular variant of a basic pattern. Therefore, we restrict ourselves to variants of only one basic pattern (the hat pattern, being the most frequently occurring one in natural speech). In this way, we can at least try to examine experimentally whether or not listeners are in want of an alternation of variants, whether or not this alternation may be randomised, and if not, in what circumstance which variant sounds best.

A second difficulty is constituted by the increasing lack of agreement between the judges, or even that of consistency within them. In the tests with isolated sentences, the extents of agreement and consistency are surprisingly high, even if the listeners are chosen among non-experts. The same holds for the question whether alternation of variants is desirable in texts: the repeated application of the same variant all the time, with standardised excursion, leads almost unanimously to a lower appreciation than was found in the earlier experiments with isolated sentences. Finding answers to the other questions mentioned above is hampered by the lack of inter-subject agreement. This can only be remedied by the use of expert listeners; they may agree reasonably well on serious shortcomings, and they may, moreover, locate them. On the other hand, it is doubtful whether such experts can be taken to be representative of the more general public: if they are too critical, they might well cause those involved in the development of text-to-speech systems to invest much effort into subtleties which the average listener is totally unaware of.

Much of what has just been mentioned about the melodic course in general applies more particularly to pitch accents and boundary markers. Here, too, variation is desired, and preliminary experiments have already shown that random variation is not adequate. On the other hand, it has appeared that syntactic considerations offer only limited help in developing rules for such variations.

Part of the desired variation could be brought about by the application of rules that prescribe what measures have to be taken whenever there is not enough time for the execution of the standard movements. Research on what happens in natural speech at high speaking rate is under way. The results should help to develop such rules.

Another kind of variation could originate from widening and narrowing the range within which F_0 changes take place, and from raising and lowering the average F_0. As yet, no research has been done on these phenomena in naturally spoken Dutch. Possible future results could, at the same time, help to explain how, with only six basic patterns and a limited number of variants, nevertheless the so many shades of meaning can be given that we presume to hear in the intonation of a skilled elocutionist.

Although in this chapter fairly much attention has been given to functional aspects, it is apparent from these considerations that we know too little about them. This is only partly caused by the fact that the correspondence between the course of F_0 on the one hand, and the interpretative possibilities on the other, is no doubt a very complex one. As was said in the beginning of §2, in a bottom-up approach the functional aspects take second place. This may seem to be a serious disadvantage of such an approach. Nevertheless, it remains our conviction that experimental research on functional aspects of intonation can only bear fruit once a suitable overview has been made available of the melodic possibilities in the language at issue. In that sense, we may consider the bottom-up approach to constitute the necessary tool for further research.

6

Intonation in
Swedish

EVA GÅRDING

1. Background

Swedish, together with Danish, Norwegian, Icelandic and Faroese, belongs to the Nordic group of Germanic languages. It is spoken by 8 million people in Sweden and about 300,000 people in Finland.

Within this group the Scandinavian languages, Swedish (except Finland Swedish), Danish and Norwegian, are prosodically famous for having two distinctive prosodic patterns connected with stressed syllables, in Swedish called Accent 1 (acute) and Accent 2 (grave), in Norwegian Toneme 1 and Toneme 2 and in Danish stød and non-stød. Historically the two sets of patterns are linked with Old Norse words of different syllabic structure.

The immediate phonological factors determining Swedish intonation are word level accents and accentual and tonal features at the phrase, sentence and text level. These in turn are conditioned by syntax, semantics and pragmatics.

Intonation will be used as a general term for the fundamental frequency pattern of a stretch of speech. Defined in this way intonation covaries with a rhythmic pattern, formed by the sequence of accented and unaccented syllables. The main points of co-ordination between intonation and segments are the accented syllables and the boundaries.

2. Description of intonation patterns

In my description of Swedish intonation the presentation is divided into sections dealing with the word level (2.1), the phrase and sentence level (2.2) and the text level (2.3 and 2.4). Within sections, the communicative functions of intonation serve as an ordering principle. These are the lexical-distinctive function, the grouping function with both demarcative and connective features and the weighting, modal and expressive functions. Section 3 deals with dialectal variation. Behind my analysis is an intonation model which can be applied to analysis as well as synthesis. It will be summed up in the final section.

2.1 Word level: Stress and accent. Rules and basic patterns

a. Stress and accent
Since every syllable with primary stress carries one of the two accents, the term "stress" is not necessary. I will use the term "accent" for primary stress (A1, A2) and "reduced accent" for the secondary stress of compounds and derivatives which does not permit any accent contrast.

As in other Germanic languages, accent is used to express semantic weight and demarcation. Thus, as a general rule, root morphemes, the main carriers of information, are accented, whereas affixes are not. The accented syllable of the first root morpheme is primary, marking the beginning of the construction, *e.g.* `svensk-ar-na` (the Swedes). Reduced accent appears in compounds and derivatives in the accented syllable of the last lexical morpheme (roots and a handful of affixes) *e.g.* `smör-gås-,bordet` (the smorgasbord). The rest of the syllables have lower levels.[1] In contrast to German, a different location of a constituent boundary in such low level syllables has no effect on the accent pattern. A pair of compounds like *[små][landsvägar]* (mini roads) and *[Smålands][vägar]* (Småland roads) is ambiguous in pronunciation (Elert 1981 p. 47).

In lexicalised phrases the accented syllable of the last lexical morpheme is primary and marks the end of the construction. One of the preceding syllables may now be the carrier of reduced accent, whereas other syllables have lower levels, *e.g.* ett,håll-i-`gång` (a going on). Low level accents become for all categories of constructions a connective signal.

An accent pattern may also be influenced by rhythm as is evidenced by polysyllabic loans which do not lend themselves to morphemic subdivision. Here the first heavy syllable is primary and the other syllables appear in rhythmic alternation between lower levels, *e.g.* en,ma-ri'mek-ko (a dress from Marimekko).

The majority of Swedish words are accented on the first syllable. However, there are a considerable number of polysyllables accented on a non-initial syllable. French loans, particularly of recent origin, are oxytones. Only a few pairs of words are distinguished by accent location.

Accented syllables, including those with reduced accent, are heavy. This means that they have either a long vowel or a short vowel followed by consonant(s). Low level accents may be light or heavy (see below under levels of accentuation). In a sequence of such syllables, the principle of open syllabicity is adhered to.

b. The two accents
The two accents Accent 1 (A1, acute) and Accent 2 (A2, grave), are assigned to words according to the rules given below (see Linell 1972).

Phonological rules
> A1 can occur in any accented syllable regardless of position.
> A2 never occurs in the last syllable of a word. From this follows that only polysyllabic words can have an accent contrast.

Morphological rules
> Monosyllabic roots and polysyllabic roots accented on the last syllable have A1. Disyllabic roots have either of the two accents. A2 is the basic pattern for compounds.
> Most inflectional and derivational suffixes are unaccented and require A2 from the preceding root. Hence an A1 root will change to A2 when part of such a form. The definite-article suffix for nouns does not bring about any accent change.

The syllable is a natural domain for the assignment of accents. For the total effect of the accentual manifestation, however, also neighbouring syllables are involved (see below and figure 1).

There are only about 350 pairs with distinctive accent patterns (Elert 1981). From the predictability of the accents, it follows that they are not important in communication. The speakers of Swedish in Finland communicate easily without distinctive accents and a great number of immigrants in Sweden speak Swedish fluently without following the accent rules. The correct location of accent is far more important for word recognition than the correct type of accent (Bannert 1986a).

For a native listener the accent pattern gives information about the phonological and morphological structure of the word, at least when it is pronounced in a familiar dialect. Exposed to a sequence like ´tanken (the tank) or `tanken (the thought), a native listener can refer it to a monosyllabic or disyllabic stem guided by the accent pattern. In fact, in a familiar dialect only a small fraction of the first syllable is needed for correct identification (Johansson 1970, for Norwegian Jensen 1961).

The accent rules are highly productive. Speakers easily integrate new words into the language, compound them and inflect them by means of the old suffixes and their concomitant accent rules.

The present accent rules reflect the situation in Proto-Scandinavian when the accents were not distinctive and when cognates of words with A1 were monosyllabic and cognates of words with A2 were polysyllabic. At a later stage, in the 12th or 13th century, when the influence of Low German was at its peak, changes in lexicon, word structure and reduction of stress in certain suffixes resulted in two pitch patterns for polysyllabic words. This development has been summed up by Haugen as follows (for "tone" read A2):

In the basic native pattern of the language, the incidence of tone is rigidly prescribed by the phonological, morphological and syntactic structure... If it were not for the definite article, the quasisyllabic /ə/[2] and the intrusion of loan words, it would still be (as it was in Proto-Scandinavian) an automatic accompaniment of polysyllabicity. (Haugen 1967, p. 201)

For the origin of the accents see also Oftedal 1952. A summary is given in Gårding 1977b, chapter 7. The origin of the stød is treated by Fischer-Jørgensen (1989, chapter 1).

c. Representation

Almost every Swedish linguist or phonetician has been concerned with the accents and their place in the phonological system of Swedish.[3]

Malmberg suggested the representation "high" and "low" for the two accents since the distinguishing factor in experiments with synthetic speech had turned out to be pitch, and since one accent was physically high when the other one was low at a critical point in the accented syllable (Malmberg 1967).

Elert emphasised the connective function of the accents and compared the following now famous examples (1970, p. 45):

(1)	en `stormans 'dräkt	(the costume of a magnate)
(2)	en ´stor `mansdräkt	(a large costume for men)
(3)	en `stormansdräkt	(a costume of a magnate)
(4)	en ´stor ´mans ´dräkt	(the costume of a big man)

In all these examples, Accent 2 shows that at least one syllable more than the stressed one belongs to the same word.

In his dissertation *Swedish Word Accents in Sentence Perspective*, Bruce analysed the representation of the Stockholm Swedish accents as combinations of "high" and "low", HL, phonetically a fall with a different timing depending on the accent (Bruce 1977, 1983). A similar analysis was later applied to all dialectal categories (Bruce and Gårding 1978).

Comparisons with accentual phenomena in other dialects and languages led us to believe, however, that a phonological representation ought to focus not on the time-shifted fall, common to all dialects, but rather on the accented syllables which have dialectically different, often diametrically opposite accent shapes with a strong effect on the perceptual impression. From a perceptual point of view, then, the accents ought to have different representations in the dialects (Gårding and Bruce 1981, p. 38).

The association of "highs" and "lows" with a particular syllable is similar to the autosegmental approach advocated by Goldsmith (1979). Following his method of analysis, the accented syllable of a southern dialect would be connected with HL for A1 and H for A2 followed by L for the post-accented syllable. In other dialects there would be more complications. For analyses along these lines of Norwegian accents, see Endresen (1983). The feature "delayed peak" for accentual timing differences is discussed by Ladd (1983b). For experiments with a shift of accent peaks for German see Kohler (1987).

d. Manifestation of basic patterns

Differences in fundamental frequency, intensity and duration have been shown to accompany the two accents. Figure 1a is an example in which the accents have been pronounced in declarative intonation by one speaker from the south. To arrive at the full accentual manifestation, let us first discount the features in the record which are caused by the articulation (for a comprehensive treatment of such phenomena see Di Cristo 1985). The gap produced by the voiceless consonants will be filled in since the pitch control proper is not essentially disturbed by the glottis opening for voiceless consonants (Sonesson 1968, Löfqvist *et al.* 1984). The steep fall caused by the glottis beginning to open for the following voiceless consonant /k/ will be ignored. With these modifications, the accented syllables appear as similar humps added to a global slower movement, which we regard as a manifestation of sentence intonation. Physiologically an accentual hump corresponds to a brief period of tension and relaxation in the pitch controlling muscles, in particular the cricothyroid (Gårding *et al.* 1970 and 1975).

For A1 the hump is timed in such a way that there is a fall over the vocalic segment. For A2, on the other hand, the timing has produced a rise. The intensity envelope does not look very different for the two accents, but a close inspection will show that the intensity peak follows the early F_0 peak of A1 but precedes the late one of A2. This seems to be a regular phenomenon. The accents can often be identified in the acoustic record by the intensity curve. Like tones they can be recognised in whisper (Hadding 1961, Segerbäck 1966).

However, pitch is the most important perceptual cue to the accents as was shown by Malmberg in a series of experiments with synthetic speech (Malmberg 1967). His results showed that the location of the fundamental frequency peak is a primary cue to the identification of accents in the dialect exemplified in figure 1.

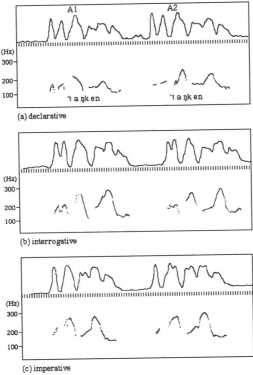

Figure 1. Lexical and modal function. Three sentences: (a) *Att ha tanken* (A1,A2) *redo* (A2) (to have the tank (thought) ready (b) *Har du...* (have you) (c) *Ha* ..(have). intensity (top) and F_0 curves (bottom) according to mingograms. Southern dialect.

2.2 Phrase and sentence level: Weighting, grouping, modality, expressivity

For accentuation at the phrase and sentence level the term focus occurs in the literature together with phrase and sentence accent. I shall make the following distinction. The term **focalisation** will be used for the accentuation giving weight to a special part of the utterance and relating it to the message as a whole. It will therefore be treated in the following §3. The terms **sentence** and **phrase accent** will be used when the accentuation is demarcative and has a grouping function.

a. Weighting
We have seen how accentuation is used at the word level to give special weight to a certain part of the word (root morphemes) and for demarcation. Similar phenomena occur at the phrase and sentence level. Words which are main carriers

of information, *i.e.* content words (nouns, main verbs, adjectives *etc.*) are accented while words which connect and relate them to each other, function words (prepositions, conjunctions *etc.*), are unaccented.

It is usually assumed that four levels of accentuation may be used in a phrase. These levels can be analysed as in the matrix of table 1 below.

Table 1. *Levels of accentuation*

level	syllabic weight	pitch movement	expansion	functional carrier
1	+	+	+	FA,SA,PA
2	+	+	-	FA,SA,PA,WA
3	+	-		A
4	-	-		-A

A syllable is considered to be heavy (+) when it contains either a long vowel or a short vowel followed by consonant(s). Otherwise it is light (−). A pitch movement over an accented syllable is (+) if it is large enough to carry an accent contrast. Otherwise it is (−). The movement is expanded (+) when it dominates a large pitch movement of the same phrase. The abbreviations FA, SA, PA, WA, A, -A stand for focal accent, sentence accent, phrase accent, word accent, reduced accent (deaccentuated) and no accent respectively. All accents of levels 1 and 2 are either A1 or A2.

We notice that there is no unique correspondence between the functional carrier and the level of accentuation. An accent in a monosyllabic utterance normally receives level 2 while a higher level under the same circumstances creates an impression of contrast or emphasis. On the other hand, if the phrase accent occurs in an utterance with more than one accent, it receives level 1 in order to stand out. The same situation reoccurs in a sentence with many phrases. Here the sentence accent (or focal accent) may receive a level higher than 1 or else level 1 while the remaining accents are subdued to a lower level. Behind the assignment of accentuation level in a particular syllable there is, apart from the phonological, syntactic and pragmatic factors, a principle of economy relative to the message.

b. Grouping
In most Swedish dialects, a demarcative accent is assigned to the last accented syllable of a phrase or sentence when no other place is marked for focus. Focal and demarcative accent may coexist in this syllable but in any other place the focal function becomes predominant.

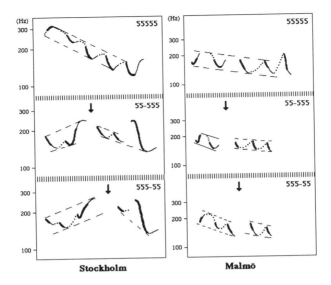

Figure 2. The grouping function. Groupings of *fem* (five) in two dialects. Broken lines denote grids, arrows denote pivots.

The assignment of a demarcative accent to the last accented syllable of the phrase is often combined with a weakening of preceding accents. There is also a rhythmical rule at this level, comparable to the one demonstrated at the lexical level, which works against the encounter of two main accents (Bruce 1984b).

Figure 2 illustrates groups of numbers produced by speakers representing two different dialects. The goal of the corresponding experiment was to force speakers to perform groupings by means of intonation only, without any influence of syntax and semantics. The numbers, here a sequence of the number *fem* (five), were uttered as an ungrouped series or as groups of 2+3 and 3+2, all in declarative intonation. The speakers were asked to think of the series as a telephone number, to give equal weight to the numbers and to avoid pauses.

One conclusion we can draw from this investigation is that speakers use both dialect-dependent and dialect-independent features apart from universal ones. The dialectal difference in accent manifestation is responsible for the most conspicuous part of the variation.

The devices used for grouping will be summed up below. Most of them apply to other languages as well.

i. *Demarcative features.* Pauses, pause-like gaps, large-range pitch movements in terminal syllables (accented or unaccented), changes of direction and/or range of intonation. The term **pivot** is used to cover the demarcative features.

Eva Gårding

ii. Connective features. Reduction of accents with concomitant reduction of pitch movements so as to create special patterns. Similarity of elements of a group.

Perceptual tests with equidistant synthetic stimuli of the same duration have shown that all the intonational features mentioned above are efficient markers of groups (Gårding and House 1986; for continued work along this line see House 1990). The results also indicate that linguistic rules apart from auditory processes influence the grouping decisions. Swedish listeners, for instance, interpreted large-range pitch movements as group-final markers in accordance with the final demarcative accent rule. Another result of our investigation was that we could define a prosodic phrase as a stretch of speech surrounded by pivots.

In analysis of natural speech, one has to distinguish between precise boundaries and boundary regions. Precise boundaries are possible to detect in the acoustic record only when two accented syllables meet with an internal juncture between them (Gårding 1967a, chapter 9; for English, see Lehiste 1960). In other cases we have the same situation as in compounds, namely that precise boundaries are replaced by boundary zones consisting of low-accented syllables some of which may be enclitic and others proclitic. I shall give one example. In the two sentences *[Ander][tankar på gården]* (Anders gets gas in the yard) and *[Anders tankar på gården]* (Anders's thoughts of the yard) with main accents on *Anders* and *gården*, the different syntactic structure is often left unmarked by prosody, which, if there is no support from the context, results in ambiguity. In such cases the intonation forms a bridge over the boundary zone between the two accented syllables which is constructed according to a principle of economy: the shortest way. The implication is that a precise boundary cannot be detected by acoustic criteria. What listeners do, then, if they are asked to segment into phrases, is to let syntactic and semantic criteria be their guide (Gårding 1967b, p. 53 ff.).

The stretch of speech between one accented syllable and the next in connected speech is an important unit in most analyses of intonation and rhythm. It has been given various terms: stress group (Thorsen 1978), foot (Fretheim and Nilsen 1987), speech tact (Strangert 1985), accent domain (Gårding and Lindblad 1988).

Patterns of accentuation and their intonation are important cues in speech recognition as has been shown by Lindblom and Svensson (1973), Svensson (1974) and Risberg (1974). Risberg studied the combined effect of intonation and lip-reading on hard-of-hearing listeners. The result was improved understanding.

Automatic recognition of prosodic features was the object of a joint Lund-Stockholm project (House *et al.* 1988).

c. Modality

The preceding parts of §2 have shown how intonation is used to group words into phrases. In the remaining parts we will consider how intonation turns such phrases into speech acts, conveying the speaker's attitude, emotion and selected centre of the message (focus, see next section). In such acts there are contributions also from lexicon and syntax. However, the modal and expressive signals of intonation are so strong that they may override other cues.

The modal function will be studied in three categories, the declarative, interrogative and imperative modes. Their effect on intonation is shown in figure 1. For the illustrations, short utterances without focus have been used.

i. Declarative mode. Figure 1 illustrates how the accent pattern can be seen as added to a slower movement, in this case a falling baseline expressing declarative mode. Also the topline, defined as a line connecting the main accentual peaks, is falling. The slope of the declination is dependent on the length of the sentence. The declination has a physiological background but it has also a communicative value. If the falling line is levelled out, the intonation seems to reflect an uncertain attitude.

ii. Interrogative mode is most often expressed by word order with the finite verb preceding the subject or by lexical means, and one of these arrangements is enough to make the sentence function as a question. Intonation is also sufficient to convey the interrogative mode in an otherwise declarative sentence. This way of asking questions is not unusual in Swedish. It is found in casual questions for which the answer is expected, *e.g. Du har inte sett Kalle?* (You haven't seen Kalle?). An added speech act adverbial *händelsevis* (by any chance) would bring out the casualness of this speech act even more clearly.

An investigation of syntactically marked and unmarked questions shows that for question intonation the topline is raised and the total range of the curve is widened by focus (Gårding 1979). The widening is timed differently in relation to the intonation curve depending on the rules that govern the manifestation of sentence accent in the particular dialect. As in the analysis of statements, the modal intonation could be separated from the word accent for which the manifestation rules would remain unchanged. Acoustically a question can be signalled by a bundle of features, global as well as local, a shifting up of the whole pattern combined with an optional terminal rise (Bredvad-Jensen 1984).

The presence or absence of focus splits up interrogative intonation into two basic rising types with different semantic connotations. With focus, the rise starts from the focused word and continues to the end. The slope of the rise is determined by the length of the part following after focus. This is the ordinary pattern of a yes-no question and is used when the speaker expects the interlocutor to ponder the answer.

The other pattern occurs in focus-free questions and is characterised by a continuous rise. It is used in questions when the speaker expects a quick answer (*e.g.* echo-questions). Figure 1b is a case in point. The rise is most clearly expressed by the topline of the accent humps in combination with the unaccented syllables.

iii. Imperative mode. Like the other categories the imperative mode can be expressed by lexical, syntactic and intonational means. Figure 1c illustrates the imperative mode expressed by intonation.

It is clear from the figure that the interrogative and imperative modes are distinguished from the declarative one by the overall direction of the curve, noticeable mainly in the topline and in the unaccented syllables. Only with added voice quality and intensity features is a Swedish imperative clearly distinct from a question.

An overall impression of figure 1 is that the modes deform the accentual patterns in characteristic ways and that in this process the turning points of the accents remain fixed to the segments according to certain rules.

d. Expressivity

Intonation gives the speaker the possibility of expressing emotion and attitude. Such effects can be achieved by using an intonation pattern or a voice quality which deviates from a neutral standard. The terms **emphatic** or **contrastive** are often used in connection with such patterns.

Some examples of expressive function are given in figure 3 where a four-digit number, 2510, is the carrier sentence. The intonations have expressed reactions labelled neutral, angry and happy, to different situations. The neutral case has a falling statement intonation with a small range. The angry intonation is almost level and has a much larger range up to the end. In the happy expression a large range is given only to the beginning, actually to the part corresponding to "two thousand". Experiments have shown that the emotional attitudes are not well established and that an angry reaction cannot be distinguished from a happy one by means of intonation alone. Voice quality features are needed (Gårding and House 1986).

To conclude this section let me underline some important observations connected with the examples of figure 3. Just as for modality the neutral case can be regarded as the pitch part of a basic accentuation pattern which is deformed in various ways by the sentence intonation. In spite of these deformations, however, the highs and the lows of the accents, the turning points, are similarly located in the vocalic segments in all cases. These observations, the fixed positions of the turning points and the deformations of the accentual pattern due to sentence intonation, are two of the cornerstones of the intonation model to which I will come back in §4.

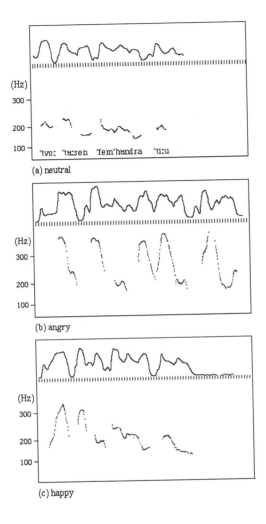

Figure 3. The expressive function. The sentence *Tvåtusen femhundra tio* (2510) in (a) neutral, (b) angry and (c) happy moods. Southern dialect.

2.3 Sentence and text level: Focalisation

Focalisation is used to give weight to the most important parts of a message. It makes these parts stand out above the rest and connects them by a similarity of their accentuation levels. The essence of a text is shown by its focused parts.

Special weight can be given to a part of an utterance by using lexical, syntactic and intonational means. When syntactic and lexical means are used, there is no need for a special accentuation. However, a focal accent can highlight any part of the sentence without assistance from syntax or lexicon. The effect is enhanced when this accent is combined with reduced and compressed patterns of the surrounding accents. It should be remembered that focal accent, as it is used here, is a functional term and need not be phonetically different from sentence accent or phrase accent. Its level of accentuation follows the economy principle mentioned earlier.

As in other languages, the position of phrase and sentence accent in a sentence is mainly determined by syntax and can be predicted with some degree of certainty. In contrast to this, the occurrence and position of focus is determined by the speaker's intentions, for instance of giving weight to new information (informative focus) or to a word acting as an intensifier (expressive focus). In a broad context informative focus expresses semantic relations between discourse referents (Halliday 1967b, Gussenhoven 1983, Rossi 1985, Horne 1987).

a. Manifestation
The phonetic manifestation of focus in different positions in the sentence and its effect on the surrounding accents was the main topic of Bruce's thesis (1977). Test sentences were constructed in such a way that focus could occur in any one of three different positions. The manifestation of focus in the Stockholm dialect was analysed as a rise, differently timed depending on the accent (p. 49). Thus, according to Bruce's theory, the accent distinction is in all cases a question of timing of a pertinent part of the pitch curve, a fall for the word accents and a subsequent rise for the sentence accent.

Bruce's method of analysis made it possible to isolate with great precision the contribution of focal accent from that of the word accents. The focal accent had little effect on the preceding accents but after focus the accent manifestations were reduced in relation to distance from focus. A closer study of declination effects on accents after focus in declarative intonation showed that there are constant frequency ranges in the rises of neighbouring accents but varying ranges in the falls (Bruce 1982a).

The frequent occurrence of focal pitch accents in spontaneous speech makes them strong dialect markers. This motivated continued investigations (Gårding 1993).

b. Manifestation of focal and other accents
Figure 4 illustrates my interpretation (Gårding 1993) of word accent, phrase accent, sentence accent and focal accent in the sentence *Madame Marianne Mallarmé har en mandolin från Madrid* (M.M.M. has a mandolin from Madrid), produced without and with focus on *Mallarmé* by a speaker from the south. In

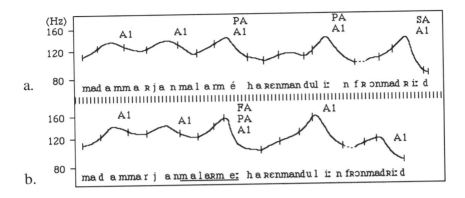

Figure 4. The weighting function. *Madame Marianne Mallarmé har en mandolin från Madrid* (M. M. M. has a mandolin from Madrid) (a) focus-free (b) focus on *Mallarmé*. All accented syllables have A1. The abbreviations PA, SA, FA stand for word, phrase, sentence, focal accent respectively. Southern dialect (from Gårding 1991).

the focus-free production (a), the subject and predicate are delimited from each other by a light turn from fall to rise in connection with the first phrase accent. The predicate phrase has a second phrase accent in *mandolin* and the whole sentence concludes with a sentence accent. Together with the unaccented syllables there are four accentuation levels in this sentence.

In (b), which has three levels, there is a sharper division of the two main constituents effected by a focal accent on *Mallarmé* falling from a high pitch level. The first accent of the second constituent starts from the same high level as the focal accent and the phrase has neither phrase nor sentence accent. Yet, in contrast to what happens in many other languages after focus, the accented syllables retain their pitch manifestations.

2.4 Sentence and text level: Textual organisation

Intonation is used to group and arrange sentences into text units with a variety of semantic implications. When two sentences, separated by a tonal, local juncture, are given a global unidirectional intonation, the second sentence is heard as an added comment. The intonational arrangement has a function corresponding to the text-linguistic category "additive". When the second sentence is uttered with a reset of intonation and a subsequent fall, the impression is extra weight and a new topic (Bruce 1982b). This puts it on a par with the first sentence, an arrangement which may correspond to the text-linguistic category "equivalence". Thus, not only local accentuation but also intonation over a stretch of an utterance contributes to the weighting of different parts of the message.

Eva Gårding

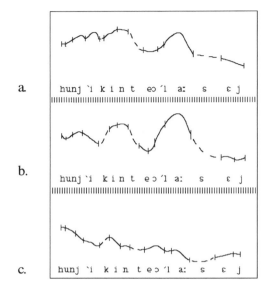

a. hunj 'i k i n t eɔ 'l aː s ɛ j

b. hunj 'i k i n t eɔ 'l aː s   ɛ j

c. hunj 'i k i n t eɔ 'l aː s ɛ j

Figure 5. Text level connections. *Hon gick inte o(ch) la sej.* (She did not go to bed) as a follow-up sentence of different contexts (a) equivalence (b) adversative (c) de-emphasis. Southern dialect.

A study of such phenomena showed that there is a limited number of possibilities for intonation to behave in a major syntactic splice (Gårding 1982a). A third possibility is the encounter of a falling intonation with a rising-falling one. This arrangement expresses contrast to what can be expected in the context given by the first sentence. The corresponding text-linguistic concept is "adversative".

A parenthetical effect is achieved by a compressed range for the part of the utterance which is de-emphasised. Similar effects can be obtained by lexical and syntactic means, such as a subordinating conjunction like *since* in the first additive case above, co-ordination by *and* in the second and by *but* or *on the other hand* in the third case and a subordinate consecutive clause in the fourth.

The semantic implications of such intonational arrangements are recognised by speakers as well as listeners (Gårding 1982a. For French cf. Fónagy 1981a. For the text-linguistic aspects of newscasting see Enkvist and Nordström 1978).

Figure 5 shows the sentence *Hon gick inte o(ch) la sej* (She didn't go to bed), uttered as a follow-up sentence in three contexts, elicited by different preceding sentences. The falling intonation of (a) is an example of equivalence, syntactical co-ordination. Intonation (b), with its rising topline up to the sentence accent, is

126

typical of adversative (superordination) and the compressed range of (c) is an expression of de-emphasis (subordination).

Intonation in text and dialogue has been a special challenge to the development of automatic speech synthesis programs, see *e.g.* Bruce and Touati 1992 and Bruce *et al.* 1994.

3. Comparisons

3.1 Dialectal variation

Intonation is a strong dialect marker in Scandinavian dialects.

Ernst A. Meyer was the first to make instrumental analyses of the accents pronounced by speakers of different Scandinavian dialects (1937 and 1954). Based on his material a prosodic dialect map was set up with four categories apart from the Swedish dialects in Finland and in the north which do not possess any distinctive accents (Gårding 1970). The patterns were divided into two groups, each with two subgroups depending on the number and locations of the pitch peaks in relation to the syllable. The map showed that the geographical distribution of the manifestation types co-occur with well-known dialect areas, established mainly on lexical and morphological criteria. There are single-peaked A2 in the south (formerly Danish provinces), in Bergslagen and Gotland (formerly exposed to contact with Finnish and German) and double-peaked A2 in central dialects.

A new investigation of accents in different dialects and sentence intonations corroborated Meyer's data. The results were presented in a scheme which generated the observed patterns with phonologically motivated rules (Gårding and Lindblad 1973).

A similar analysis of intonation in which rules for word accents and global intonation were separated was carried out on material representing the five dialectal categories established earlier. The dialectal variation could be referred to the different manifestations of sentence accent. A two-peaked A2 is found in dialects in which sentence accent is separated from the word accent manifestation and in the southern dialects with one-peaked A2 there is an overlap of word accent and sentence accent manifestation (Bruce and Gårding 1978).

3.2 Swedish and some related languages

To conclude this section, I shall sum up what I find characteristic of Swedish intonation. (As before I disregard the rhythmic pattern).[4]

1. Typical of Swedish are the word accents. They cause the intonation to go up and down more often than it does in an intonational system like English for instance, which gives the language and its dialects some of their most striking melodic characteristics.

2. From the distinctiveness of the accents it follows that their turning points are fixed to the intonation curve in a regular way. A high stays a high and a low stays a low in relation to the accented syllables and the tonal grid which the model uses to express intonation over a stretch of an utterance (see below). This is not the case in English or German where rising accents are preferred in a rising intonation and falling in a falling one.

3. In many West Swedish dialects, as in East Norwegian ones, the main accent is followed by a rise extending to the next accent or to the end of the sentence. The impression is one of rising intonation for both statements and questions, a feature which is very striking to foreigners. The difference between the two speech acts is that for questions the intonation goes to a still higher level than it does for statements. For a more detailed comparison see Gårding and Lindblad (1988) and Gårding and Stenberg (1990).

Although all these characteristics only have to do with the word level they seem to dominate the total impression of Swedish intonation. Our analysis suggests that if the accents are disregarded, the communicative functions of intonation and their expressions on the other levels are of a very general nature.

4. Conclusion

a. The model

In the background of my analysis of Swedish intonation is a general model which has been described earlier (Bruce and Gårding 1978, Gårding 1979, Gårding and Bruce 1981, Gårding 1983, 1985). The basic principle is that global intonation stretching over a phrase or a sentence is separable from local intonation bearing on accents (and tones). This principle becomes clear in analysis of material in which prosodic features are varied systematically. As was shown in figure 1, the accent humps can be analysed as being added to or superimposed on a global phrase intonation component. The timing of the accent humps is crucial for the separation of accents from sentence intonation, for the accents from each other and for the distinction of different dialects. Another effect of superposition is that the deformation of accent shapes in a given accentual pattern can be explained as due to sentence intonation (Gårding 1984). (For the use of superposition in intonation analysis see Öhman (1967) where it was introduced and Carlsson and Granström (1973). For Danish see Thorsen (1978).)

A very important observation is that some of the turning points have rather fixed positions relative to specified acoustic segments. From this follows that certain falls and rises are also relatively fixed. As a result, an intonation curve can be economically described by giving the time and frequency positions of some specified turning points. This is the main principle for the generative part of the model.

Another principle is to base the global analysis of phrase and sentence intonation on the notions of **tonal grid** and **pivot**. A grid is obtained by fitting two nearly parallel lines to the local main maxima and minima of the curve in such a way that they enclose the main part of the tonal movements derived from normal-sised accents. That part of the grid where the direction or width is changed is a pivot. A pivot marks the boundary between two prosodic phrases.

These concepts, grid and pivot, can be seen as descriptive tools, which can be used to analyse intonation in any language. They are illustrated in figure 2. The pivots are marked by arrows and the grid by broken lines.

The model can also be used to generate intonation for an input sentence equipped with markings expressing lexical accent for the content words, for phrase and text level accents and markings for speech act and dialect area. The input is first treated by a rhythmic component which operates on the same markings as the pitch component and gives the syllables the durations that fit the pitch pattern.[5]

Characteristic of the intonation-generating scheme is that sentence and phrase intonation are generated first from the speech act markings and the boundaries in the form of a grid. The grid lines move within the outer bounds of the normal register, which is about one octave. The direction of the movement is determined by speech act and the position of the phrase in the sentence. The slope of the movement is conditioned by the length of the phrase. Highs and lows are given their proper positions relative to the accented syllables and relative to the grid from specifications for the dialect. Accents with a high level of accentuation reach the outer bounds. Finally, the curve is obtained by interpolation over the voiced segments through the points generated earlier in the program.

Attempts to quantify the accentuation levels relative to the grid have been made by Shi Bo for a Chinese text-to-speech system and by Merle Horne[5] for English (Shi 1989, Horne 1987).

b. Hierarchy
The concept of hierarchy is a salient feature in phonological prosody. In my analysis of Swedish, intonation is given a hierarchical structure in the following way. Phonetic features and their functions observed at the lexical level appear also at the phrase and sentence level. Take the turns of the intonation pattern, for instance. They are first observed at the lexical level and their proper timing in relation to the syllable is decisive for marking different groupings of morphemes and giving them different weights and meanings. At the phrase and sentence level, we encounter turns of the larger phrase-like pattern, the pivots, which again are associated with different groupings and meanings.

Also the range and direction of the intonation movements are used at different levels to bring out relations between parts of the message. The large range of a sentence accent for instance makes it possible for it to dominate over a phrase accent which by the same token dominates over the word accents. Further, the direction of pitch over a syllable may have a certain connotation at the word level (for instance, terminality *versus* non-terminality) which is repeated at the phrase and sentence level.

The hierarchical structure of intonation has been recognised by many linguists and phoneticians (*e.g.* Bolinger 1986b, Thorsen 1978 and this volume). The model presented here can handle such a structure. It has been applied with some success to other prosodic systems such as French and Greek (Gårding, Botinis and Touati 1982, Touati 1987), Chinese (Gårding, Zhang and Svantesson 1983) and Hausa (Lindau 1986).

Notes

1   Acute / ´ / and grave / ` / accent symbols at the beginning of the stressed syllable mark primary stress expressed as A1 and A2 respectively. Secondary stress is marked by a vertical subscript stroke /,/. Note that accents are only marked by orthography if the location deviates from the basic rules as it may do in new family names *Bylén* or in French loans *armé, café*.
2   This /e/ developed in monosyllabic roots ending in an obstruent followed by a sonorant consonant, *e.g. vatn > vatten.*
3   The classical treatment of the accents is Axel Kock's dissertation (1878). For a survey of accent research in Scandinavia, see Gårding (1977b). A comprehensive phonetic study of the stød is given by Fischer-Jørgensen (1989). For surveys and other investigations of intonation see also *Nordic Prosody* 1–7, Gårding 1982b and Jahr and Lorentz 1983.
4   The interaction of tonal and temporal features has been the object of a lot of research. See *e.g. Nordic Prosody* 1–3. Rhythmic patterns are efficiently illustrated by Bannert (1979).
5   Merle Horne showed how accentuation levels can be assigned to words in an English discourse according to a rule system in which grammatical function interacts with coreference relations (1987).

7

Intonation in Danish

NINA GRØNNUM*

1. Introduction

The major part of the investigations which are accounted for summarily below**
deals with intonation in Standard Danish as spoken in the larger Copenhagen
area by young to middle-aged, middle-class speakers. Unless otherwise specified,
it is Copenhagen I refer to when I speak of (Standard) Danish in §1. and §2.

By intonation I mean speech melody, *i.e.* either the fundamental frequency
(F_0) variation as it appears in F_0 curves from frequency analysers, or the closely
correlated perceived pitch course. When I do not wish to make explicit the
acoustic or the perceptual aspect I will talk about "melodic" phenomena. (I have
previously used the term "tonal", which is perhaps better avoided because of its
allusion to lexical tones.)

1.1 Hierarchies in Danish intonation

It is my basic assumption, derived from the results reported below, that Danish
intonational phenomena are structured in a hierarchically organised system,
where components of smaller temporal scope are superposed on components of

---

* Formerly Thorsen.
** Work carried out since the completion of this chapter is reported in Grønnum
    (1990, 1992, 1995).

larger temporal domain. Such an organisation creates global tendencies with more local modifications.

The following components can be discerned:

(a) the **text** contributes an overall textual contour

(b) the **sentence/utterance** yields a sentence intonation contour

(c) the **prosodic phrase** adds a phrasal contour

(d) the **prosodic stress group** (or **foot**) contributes a stress group pattern

(e) the **stød** (see §2.1.2.b below) may involve a melodic modification of the stress group pattern

(f) individual **segments** have intrinsic F_0 characteristics (the microprosodic component).

These components are simultaneous, parametric, non categorial and highly interacting in their actual production.

This view of intonation as a hierarchically organised, layered system of components is not uncontroversial. *E.g.* Pierrehumbert (1980), Liberman and Pierrehumbert (1984), Ladd (1983b, 1986, 1989), and van den Berg, Gussenhoven and Rietveld (1989) take a different approach and describe intonation in terms of a linear sequence of categorially different, non-interacting (high and low) tones (pitch accents). For a discussion of the relative merits of the two approaches, see Ladd (1983a, 1983b) and Thorsen (1983a, 1983b, 1985, 1986, and 1987b).

The reader is referred to Thorsen (1979) and Fischer-Jørgensen (1987) for further treatment of microprosody and stød, respectively.

1.2 Corpora and procedures

The results summarised below derive from systematic, empirical acoustic investigations of the speech of a total of ten Copenhagen speakers. My experiments have had certain intrinsic limitations. They deal with utterances which have been read by the speakers in a sound treated room. The material is to a major extent composed of severely limited and manipulated utterance types, *i.e.* typical "laboratory speech". Such a procedure may seem inappropriate in view of the fact that the final goal is a description of the intonation of spontaneous speech. However, the method may be defended on at least two grounds. Firstly, it is convenient to investigate the course of F_0 in syntactically and pragmatically simple structures which have been produced under controlled circumstances, because this allows you to single out the parameter under scrutiny without interference from other factors which may influence F_0. Secondly, you may reasonably expect that natural, spontaneous speech can be described, at least to a certain extent, with the same categories and prosodic structures which have been discovered in edited, read speech. In other words, the intonation of free speech ought later to be accounted for with the same descriptional devices as the controlled speech material, although you may find that the inventory of parameters will have to be supplemented.

2. Stress group patterns and intonation contours

2.1 The prosodic stress group

Basbøll (1977) has defined a **syntactic** stress group in Danish as a group of words with one main stress, which is on the *last* word in the group (with certain exceptions – personal pronouns are unstressed even in stress group final position). The same definition is implicit in Andersen's (1954) description. The **prosodic** stress group, the foot, on the contrary, consists of a stressed syllable and all succeeding unstressed syllables (if any) – *i.e.* the prosodic stress group boundary lies immediately *before* the stressed syllable – independently of the number and type of syntactic boundaries in the phrase/utterance. The parsing of a short utterance into prosodic stress groups can be illustrated with the following example (/ depicts the boundaries between two main clauses and between verb phrase and complement within each clause; + denotes prosodic stress group boundaries):

(1)   Han lagde sig /på chaiselongen / og tændte / en Caminante.

Han + LAGde sig på chaise + LONGen og + TÆNDte en Cami + NANte.
(He lay down on the sofa and lit a Caminante (a cheroot).)

The definition of the prosodic stress group as a stressed syllable plus any succeeding unstressed syllables within the same intonation contour derives from the analysis of **melodic patterns**. The prosodic stress group is the carrier of recurring and fairly constant F_0 pattern consisting of a (relatively) low stressed syllable followed by a high-falling tail of unstressed syllables. Thus, the three underlined sequences below are all realised with the same F_0 pattern:

(2)   HÅNDboldspil er MEget ANstregende.
         (Handball-playing is very strenuous.)

(3)   BaNAnerne i KASsen er RÅDne.
         (The bananas in the box are rotten.)

(4)   AllerGI er en inFAM SYGdom.
         (Allergy is an infamous disease.)

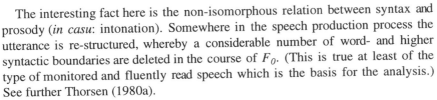

The interesting fact here is the non-isomorphous relation between syntax and prosody (*in casu*: intonation). Somewhere in the speech production process the utterance is re-structured, whereby a considerable number of word- and higher syntactic boundaries are deleted in the course of F_0. (This is true at least of the type of monitored and fluently read speech which is the basis for the analysis.) See further Thorsen (1980a).

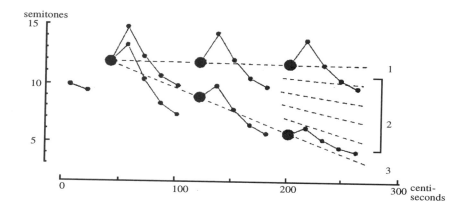

Figure 1. A model for the course of fundamental frequency in short sentences in Standard Copenhagen Danish. (1) Syntactically unmarked questions. (2) Questions with word order inversion and/or interrogative particle; non-final declarative and interrogative clauses. (3) Terminal declarative utterances. Large points denote stressed syllables, small points depict unstressed syllables. Full lines represent the F_0 pattern of prosodic stress groups; broken lines indicate the sentence intonation contours.

If melodic relations are accepted as criteria for locating boundaries, it is clear that the prosodic stress group cannot, *e.g.*, *end* with the stressed syllable: the relation between a stressed syllable and the preceding unstressed one is highly variable, as is apparent from figure 1. The preceding syllable may be higher than, on a level with, or lower than the stressed syllable, depending on how many unstressed syllables precede. I have not investigated rhythmic structure, nor have I looked at segmental cues to syntactic boundaries, and the general relevance in speech production and perception of the prosodic stress group as defined here must be corroborated by investigations of timing.

a. Stress group pattern variation
The prosodic stress group pattern is subject to a certain quantitative variation, depending on:
(i) its *position* in the utterance (the magnitude of the rise from stressed to post-tonic syllable decreases from beginning to end, *ceteris paribus,* cf. figure 1).
(ii) the *intonation contour* upon which the pattern rides (the rise is higher on less falling contours, cf. figure 1).
(iii) within the realm of non-emphatic, non-contrastive stress there is apparently a certain margin for varying the degree of *relative prominence*, which is proportional to the rise in F_0 from stressed to post-tonic syllable, cf. Thorsen (1987a), and see §2.1.c below.

Furthermore, the number of unstressed syllables in a prosodic stress group may vary between zero and rather large numbers, which naturally influences both the F_0 pattern and the time interval between the stressed syllables. If, *e.g.*, there are no unstressed syllables in the stress group, there is no material on which the pattern can rise (and fall), so the F_0 pattern is truncated (rather than being compressed in time to be contained within the single stressed syllable). Finally, there is an interspeaker variation in the magnitude of the low-to-high interval and in the steepness of the slope of the falling unstressed syllables. See further Thorsen (1984a and 1984b).

b. Alignment of segments with F_0 patterns

It is implicit in what has been said above, that Danish resembles the other Germanic languages where stress is concerned. *I.e.* stressed versus unstressed is a meaningful dichotomy in the phonology and phonetics of the language. Danish may even be an extreme case, when compared with its nearest (Swedish, Norwegian and German) neighbours, where the reduction of unstressed syllables is concerned. Firstly, we have a vowel, /ə/, which is exclusive to unstressed syllables. Secondly, on the surface, in fluent speech, this vowel assimilates to a neighbouring sonorant consonant, to the effect that the only trace left of an unstressed syllable may be in (duration and) the course of F_0. See further Brink and Lund (1975) and Thorsen (1984a). This rather drastic phonetic reduction – compared to the full underlying forms (and the orthographic representation) – contributes much to make Danish difficult to understand for Swedes and Norwegians, in spite of the obvious similarities between the Scandinavian languages.

Danish has a phonological distinction in stressed syllables between long and short vowels, *without* the complementary consonantal length characteristic of, *e.g.*, Standard Swedish. Stressed syllables also carry a phonologically relevant stød/non-stød distinction, corresponding to the word tone distinction of Swedish and Norwegian. However, the manifestation of the stød, which exhibits a good deal of dialectal and individual variation, is not generally considered to be primarily melodic. In Copenhagen it may be described as a kind of creaky voice which attacks the final part of a long vowel, or the succeeding consonant if the preceding vowel is short. See further Basbøll (1985), Fischer-Jørgensen (1987), and Gårding (1977b). Stress and stød, both, are to a very large extent predictable from the morphosyntactic structure and from the segmental composition of the underlying lexical forms, cf. Basbøll (1985) and Rischel (1969).

To the extent that stød has an influence upon the course of F_0 it will generally introduce a local falling movement. Stress has a much more invariable and considerable effect upon F_0, as can be inferred from the stylised model in figure 1. In Copenhagen, the stress group is associated with a low + high-falling melodic pattern, whose trough is timed to coincide approximately with the offset

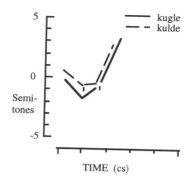

Figure 2. Fundamental frequency tracings (averages over 5 recordings) of two utterance medial words, *kugle* and *kulde* [g̊ʰuːl g̊ʰulˌl]. The vowel-consonant boundary is indicated with a vertical stroke. Zero on the logarithmic frequency scale corresponds to 100 Hz. Male speaker.

of the stressed vowel if it is short, or else about halfway through a long vowel, see the example in figure 2.

The peak of the pattern is generally aligned with the first post-tonic syllable. It is entirely possible to view the F_0 pattern associated with prosodic stress groups as a basically time- and frequency-invariant pattern: segments and syllables are superposed on the wave in straight succession, like pearls of varying length onto an undulating string. Thus, the rise-fall is more or less complete according as the prosodic stress group is longer or shorter, and may be lacking altogether in short, monosyllabic stress groups. See further Thorsen (1984a, 1984b), and see §3.1.a below.

There is a further phenomenon to be noted in the delimitation of prosodic stress groups: Figure 3 depicts the course of F_0 in the underlined sequence of

(5)   DEN ØL ER LUNken   (That beer is tepid)

i.e. [' øl ʔ'æʌ 'lɔ]. The initial [l] in *LUNken* behaves very much as if it were part of the preceding prosodic stress group: together with the stressed diphthong it performs the characteristic low + high-falling pattern. (The high consonant is not due to intrinsic F_0 level differences between the [l] and the vowels, because, if anything, the consonant has an intrinsically lower F_0.) In fact, the initial [l] in *LUNken* behaves qualitatively exactly as the final [l] in *ØL*. Its more ample rising movement is due to the longer total duration of the sequence [æʌl] *versus* [øl], which allows for a more complete gesture before the downward course towards the next stressed vowel. In other words, the melodic syllabification seems to be V́C-V́ rather than V́-CV́, irrespective of phonological and morphosyntactic boundaries. To summarise: an initial voiced consonant in a stressed syllable will be dissociated melodically from the stressed vowel and

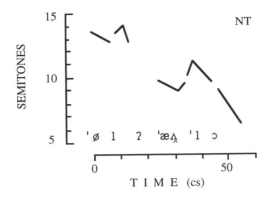

Figure 3. Fundamental frequency tracing of the underlined sequence in the utterance: *DEN ØL ER LUNken*. Zero on the logarithmic frequency scale corresponds to 100 Hz. Female speaker.

continue the F_0 pattern of the preceding context, if any. The perceptual relevance of the melodic association of an intervocalic consonant with the preceding or succeeding vowel has been tested, and it turned out that when vowel duration cues are ambiguous, the frequency location of the [l] alone can shift listeners' identification of synthetic stimuli between /'bilisd/ and /bi'lisd/. See further Thorsen (1984c). It seems, thus, that as far as its melodic manifestation goes, *stress begins with the vowel.* This matches observations from some tone languages, that post-vocalic consonants may carry the final part of the distinctive tonal course, but prevocalic consonants do not seem to be included, cf. Pike (1948, pp. 10–30), Selmer (1928).

Prosodic segregation of initial consonants may not be a purely melodic phenomenon. Fischer-Jørgensen (1982, p. 159) presents evidence that under certain circumstances the pattern of segmental duration indicates a boundary between a prevocalic consonant and a stressed vowel. Recent experiments on Swedish indicate that the most reasonable account of rhythmic phenomena is achieved if the onset of the rhythmical unit is taken to be the onset of the stressed vowel rather than, say, the onset of the first prevocalic consonant. This was one of the conclusions drawn by Lubker *et al.* (1983) from data on articulatory compensation in bite-block experiments, and Strangert (1983) likewise found that the most appropriate segmentation for an account of inter-stress intervals is the onset of the stressed vowel.

c. Stress group patterns in a non-edited, read text

It is worth pointing out, once more, that what has been said above is based on analyses of highly edited, read speech. The preliminary results (Thorsen 1987a) to be summarised in the following are based on a text which was read, but which

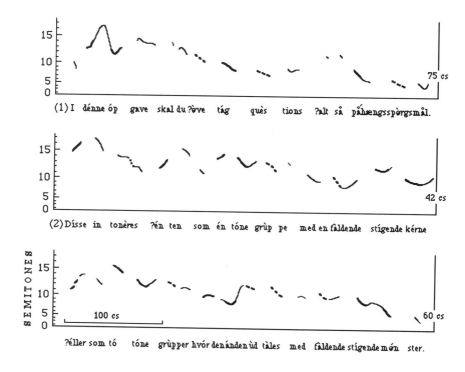

Figure 4. F_0 tracings of the first two sentences in a long text. The stressed vowels have been touched up with thicker lines. Syllables with secondary stress are indicated with broken lines. Vertical bars indicate pauses, with pause duration in centiseconds added. Zero on the logarithmic frequency scale corresponds to 100 Hz. Female speaker.

was not edited for intonation analysis purposes. The investigation represents a first, cautious step on the road to analyse free, spontaneous speech. The text is the tape-recorded instruction to a language laboratory exercise, amounting to a total of five type-written pages. It was recorded once, by one speaker, the author of the programme.

Figure 4 shows F_0 tracings of the first two sentences in the text. I have been particularly interested in the melodic pattern associated with prosodic stress groups: whether they would appear in the same regular and predictable shape as in the pragmatically much more restrained texts analysed previously. The answer is both yes and no. The text contained 341 polysyllabic prosodic stress groups. Only 32 of those, or 9%, do not have an associated F_0 rise. So it appears justified to conclude that a sequence of stressed plus unstressed syllable(s) is normally accompanied by a rise in F_0. The magnitude of the rise, however, varies a good deal, and I cannot assert that it decreases in a monotonous and simple fashion through the phrase or utterance, as it does in short, pragmatically restricted sentences. Nor have I been able to disclose any other systematic trend in the vacillation of the low-to-high interval. I venture to propose that varying the magnitude of the pitch rise from the stressed syllable – as this speaker does – serves pragmatic purposes in that it lends slightly varying degrees of prominence to the stressed syllables, without their falling out of the range of what may be termed neutral, non-emphatic main stress. Thus, greater prominence would be associated with a higher rise after the stressed syllable.

It is important to note that rise in pitch from a stressed syllable to the post-tonic is not the only cue to its stressedness. This is evident in the case of monosyllabic stress groups, where there are no post-tonics to carry such a rise. Instead, I propose, the relation to surrounding stressed syllables may determine a syllable as stressed. That is, if a syllable falls into place in a rhythmic pattern and on an intonation contour, established by preceding and/or succeeding stressed syllables, and if its duration, its vowel quality, and its lack of stød do not contradict it, such a syllable will be perceived as stressed. It may further warrant a characterisation as **accented** if it is succeeded by one or more post-tonics and has an associated pitch rise; if there is no such pitch rise to post-tonics the stressed syllable is **non-accented**. The distinction between accented and non-accented stressed syllables, accordingly, would not apply to monosyllabic stress groups.

The distinction, if it is tenable, between stress and accent as outlined above would bring Danish on a par with German as described by Bannert (1985b), with British English as described by O'Connor and Arnold (1961), and with Dutch as described by 't Hart and Collier (1979), where a similar distinction can be made between stressed syllables which are melodically prominent (accented) and stressed syllables which are not (non-accented).

It appears then that in read speech in Danish, at least the speech I have analysed so far, stressed syllables are *normally* also accented. In the materials I had looked at before this (1987a) one, that had been true without exception, which is why I had not thought to introduce a distinction between stress and accent before. In retrospect, the behaviour of stressed syllables surrounding an emphasis for contrast could have provoked a discussion of accented *versus* non-accented: stressed syllables which are neighbours to an emphasis for contrast suffer a reduction or deletion of their F_0 pattern, cf. §2.3.b and figure 6 below. However, I am not sure whether this reduction is not also a true de-stressing (which is how it has been treated previously). This is clearly a point where empirical research is called for, both in terms of acoustic and perceptual studies.

There is one snag about the dichotomy accented/non-accented, if it is to apply to stressed syllables only. There are 104 syllables with (syntactically determined) secondary stress in the text. 95 of those are succeeded by unstressed syllables. 21 of those 95, i.e. 22%, are associated with a rise in F_0! Does this mean that secondary stresses may also be accented? Or does it mean that the stress reduction is only partial? Previously, secondary stresses have been characterised prosodically as lacking the pitch rise typical of main stress, but retaining all other stress cues (duration, quality, stød). If accented/non-accented is a relevant distinction in stressed syllables, then lack of pitch rise is not a feature confined to secondary stresses. Conversely, if there are secondary stresses with associated pitch rises, then accentuation is not confined to stressed syllables. Note that this would give accentuation a somewhat different connotation from what it usually means when applied to, *e.g.*, English.

There is obviously a vast amount of research to be done on stress and its (melodic) manifestation in Danish, not least perceptual experiments, before the descriptive categories can be definitively established.

2.2 Sentence intonation contours

When the stress group pattern is a recurrent, predictable, qualitatively constant unit, the intonation contour can be defined in terms of the stressed syllables alone (which is entirely in line with the theory of Danish intonation where global tendencies carry more local modifications). That is not to say that the course of the unstressed syllables is irrelevant for listeners' identification of intonation contours, only that they are redundant in the strict sense of the word. See further Thorsen (1980b). In short utterances, the intonation contours approach straight lines whose slopes vary in close correlation with the type and function of the utterance, as shown in figure 1: terminal declarative utterances have the steepest slopes, syntactically and lexically unmarked questions have horizontal contours. In between we find other types of questions as well as non-terminal sentences, with a tendency towards a trade-off between syntax/lexicon and intonation: the more syntactic or lexical information about the interrogative or non-terminal function of the sentence, the more falling, *i.e.* the more terminal declarative-like, is the intonation contour, and *vice versa*, a tendency also noted by Bo (1933, pp. 82–83) and Jespersen (1897–99, p. 592). A similar trade-off has been observed for other languages too, see *e.g.* Bolinger (1962), Cohen and 't Hart (1967), Daneš (1960), von Essen (1956b), Hadding-Koch (1961), and Mikoš (1976). Furthermore, it appears that the melodic course is the same in utterances with identical prosodic structure, independently of syntactic constituents. See above, §2.1., about the prosodic stress group.

It is perhaps expedient to stress once more the fact that the description of Danish sentence intonation above implies that sentence intonation is signalled globally rather than locally, *i.e.* the difference between, *e.g.*, a declarative and interrogative utterance does not reside in a special movement at the end, but is distributed over the whole utterance. In this matter Copenhagen Danish is different from most of the related Germanic languages, and from some of the regional variants of Standard Danish as well, cf. §3.1.b. below.

2.3 Sentence accents and emphasis

a. Default and focal sentence accents

In the course of analysis of materials from Bornholm (a Danish island just off the southern Swedish coast) and Central Swedish (Thorsen 1988a), I came to distinguish two types of sentence accents, which are different as to their function and to a certain extent also in their phonetic form: the prosodically or syntactically determined, final, **default** accent (in isolated, "neutral", utterances) and the contextually or pragmatically determined **focal** accent. A focal accent in final position (which is the only position to allow a comparison) may be characterised by a somewhat larger F_0 excursion, though not invariably so, it entails a certain lowering/diminishing of preceding F_0 patterns, and it shortens the whole utterance more than default accents do. Focused *versus* non-focused items in non-final position have more comprehensive F_0 movements and delete or diminish F_0 patterns on succeeding (but not preceding) stress groups, see §3.1.c. and figure 9 below.

Copenhagen by contrast, (as well as other areas, cf. Thorsen (1988b) and Grønnum (1989)), lacks a compulsory default accent. In pragmatically neutral speech, all stressed syllables have the same prominence. An extra prominence finally in the utterance is not present acoustically, nor perceptually. Such pragmatically and prosodically neutral utterances are neither incomplete nor unnatural. Furthermore, the prosodic means to signal focus is also less generous, *i.e.* the focused item is not F_0 boosted, only the F_0 patterns on succeeding stress groups are shrunk or deleted. Isolated utterances and utterances from context which invites a final focus are not distinguishable in the F_0 course, cf. figure 5. This difference between, *e.g.*, Copenhagen and Bornholm in the means to signal focus led to a distinction between focal sentence accents proper, and focus signalling by stress reduction (of succeeding stressed syllables). Alternatively, we might speak of focus signalling by deaccentuation, cf. §2.1.c. above.

b. Contrast and emphasis

I would like to make explicit that my investigations of sentence accents *etc.* were never conceived as a contribution in the more syntactically or semantically/pragmatically oriented debate about what determines focus placement; when and whether a focus is "broad" or "narrow"; what is focus and what is contrastive stress or emphasis; what determines the default location of sentence accents, *etc.* For an excellent treatment of these questions, see Ladd (1978) and the references therein, and for a more recent overview, see Fretheim

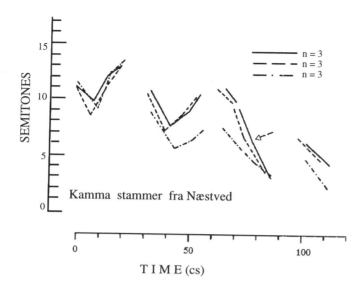

Figure 5. Average fundamental frequency tracings of three utterances, by a female Copenhagen speaker. The full line tracing depicts *KAMma STAMmer fra NÆSTved* uttered in isolation, the broken line tracing is the same utterance uttered in a context which invited a final focus, and the dotted/broken line is the utterance uttered in a context which invited an initial focus. The arrow points to the onset of the last stressed vowel. Zero on the logarithmic frequency scale corresponds to 116 Hz.

(1988). But I would like to note that the distinction between focal accents and emphasis for contrast may not always be clear-cut semantically or pragmatically in spontaneous speech. There will doubtless be many instances where a prominence is open to both interpretations. However, the results presented summarily here are derived from utterances where the contrasted item is explicitly stated (*e.g.: Sorry, what did you say? – Do the buses leave from Tiflis or from Grosny? – There are many buses out of Tiflis. – As far as I can see there is no connection from Grosny at all.*, or: *Does pipípi have shorter syllables or just shorter vowels? – pipípi has shorter syllables.*).

You will see from the stylised tracings in figure 6 (from Thorsen 1980c) that emphasis for contrast is achieved melodically by making the stressed syllable of the emphasised word stand out clearly from the surroundings. This is brought about by raising, *i.e.* boosting, it and by lowering and shrinking the F_0 deflections in the surrounding, *i.e.* both preceding and succeeding, stress groups in a manner so that the immediate surroundings – except occasionally the first post-tonic syllable – fall away sharply from the emphasised one. (There are hints in my data that stress groups further removed from the contrasted element do not

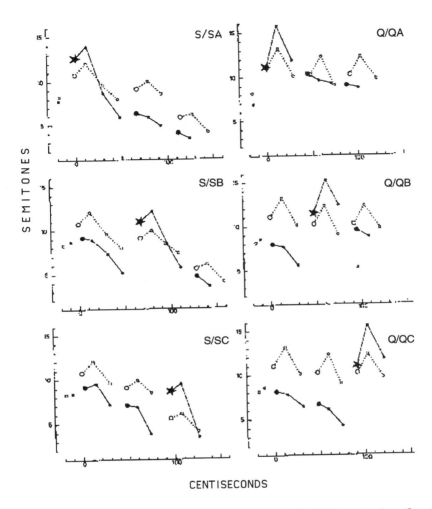

CENTISECONDS

Figure 6. Stylised tracings of the course of F_0 in statements (S – left) and questions (Q – right), which are prosodically neutral (open circles and dotted lines) or have emphasis for contrast (stars, points and full lines) in initial position (top), medial position (mid) and final position (bottom). Stars denote the emphatically stressed syllables, large points denote other stressed syllables, and small points depict unstressed syllables.

suffer a similar shrinking, which is what motivates the restriction of the following generalisation to *short* utterances.)

The changes induced by contrast, when compared with the prosodically neutral editions, can be formulated thus: in short utterances with emphasis for contrast, the utterance reduces melodically to one prosodic stress group. That is, only one low + high-falling F_0 pattern occurs in them. An informal experiment with LPC-analysis and re-synthesis showed that the perceptually salient feature of contrast emphasis resides in the shrinking of the surroundings, rather than in the upward boosting of the emphasised syllable itself. Thus, in an utterance like

(6)   Det er SIDste BUS til TIFlis.   (It is the last bus for Tiflis.)

it is the shrinking of the F_0 movements associated with *SIDste* and *TIFlis*, rather than a higher F_0 location of *BUS*, that will make *BUS* appear as the contrasted element. In other words, the distinction between emphasis for contrast and focus resides possibly in a more comprehensive F_0 boosting of the emphasised as opposed to a merely focalised element, and in the suppression also of *preceding F_0* patterns.

2.4 Phrasing and textual organisation

a. Longer utterances – prosodic phrasing

If a declarative utterance contains more than three or four stress groups, most speakers will decompose the contour into several shorter phrase contours, each with its own declination, which together describe an overall falling slope, cf. figure 7. The discussion of the results which underlie figure 7 was a very involved one, cf. Thorsen (1983a), especially as far as the interplay between prosodic structure, syntactic structure and semantics was concerned. Suffice it here to summarise that there are fairly strong grounds for claiming that some prosodic categories (*in casu*: prosodic stress groups and prosodic phrases) are distinct entities in the phonology that do not have an isomorphous relation to syntactic structure. That is, prosodic boundaries will be affiliated (but not coterminous) with syntactic ones (prosodic boundary location is a combined result of balancing the length of the syntactic constituents in the utterance while taking into account their semantic content), but syntactic boundaries, inversely, need not leave any trace in the intonational structure of syntactically unambiguous, non-compound sentences. Whether syntactic boundaries can be traced in the time structure or in segmental cues is another question, and one that should be addressed.

How and to what extent this description would be applicable to spontaneous speech I cannot say. Spontaneous speech is rarely so fluent and so syntactically well structured as the edited, read speech which was investigated, and prosodic boundaries may be more evident (also when not accompanied by pauses) in free speech and may take more and different shapes than encountered in my (1983a) material.

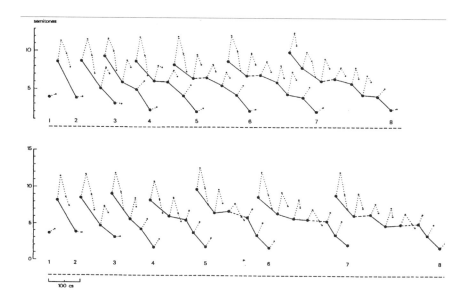

Figure 7. Intonation contours (full/broken lines) and stress group patterns (dotted lines) in two groups of terminal declarative utterances, consisting of one to eight prosodic stress groups. Average over four speakers. Large points denote stressed syllables, small points unstressed syllables. Broken lines denote the boundaries between prosodic phrases.

b. Textual intonation

There are data from several languages that prove paragraphs or texts to have an overall intonational structure to which the constituent sentences are subordinated, cf. Bruce (1982a) (Swedish), Lehiste (1975); Cooper and Sorensen (1981) (American English); Uyeno *et al.* (1980) (Japanese). So is also the case in Danish. (A "text" here is a sequence of semantically but not necessarily syntactically co-ordinated sentences.) Figure 8 summarises the analysis of texts consisting of one, two, or three sentences containing three stress groups each. These sentences were semantically coherent (they described what various members of a family were doing during their summer holidays). In one set of texts they were syntactically uncoordinated, *i.e.* each sentence was a terminal declarative, separated orthographically from its neighbours by periods. In another set the same sentences occurred as coordinate main clauses, separated by commas and *og* (and). For instance:

(7)   Amanda skal afsted på camping. Hendes mor skal på kursus i Tyskland.
        (Amanda is going away camping. Her mother is taking a course in Germany).

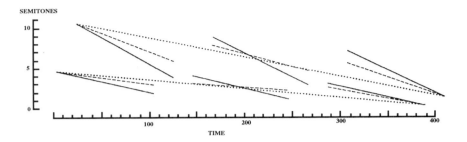

Figure 8. Stylised model of the course of F_0 in texts with three terminal declarative sentences (full lines) and three co-ordinate main clauses (broken lines). The lower lines connect the stressed syllables, i. e. they represent the intonation contours (cf. figure 1), the upper lines connect the first unstressed syllable in each stress group. The dotted lines represent the overall slope through the text. A text with two components is arrived at by leaving out the middle component. An isolated sentence arises when the dotted lines are suitably compressed in time.

(8)   Hendes far skal vandre i Lapland, og Amanda skal afsted på camping, og hendes mor skal på kursus i Tyskland.
        (Her father is going hiking in Lapland, and Amanda is going away camping, and her mother is taking a course in Germany).

Figure 8 reads as follows, see *e.g.* the full lines: the lower line in each of the three pairs of lines corresponds to the broken lines in figure 1, that is, it is the line which supports the stressed syllables of the sentence. The upper line, similarly, is the one which would carry the first post-tonic syllable in each stress group, *i.e.* the local "highs" in the course of F_0. In other words, upper and lower lines delimit the space within which F_0 performs its undulating course through each sentence (disregarding the fact that with a sufficiently large number of post-tonic syllables they may transgress the lower line connecting the stressed syllables). The full lines pertain to sequences of terminal declaratives, the broken lines depict syntactically coordinate main clauses. The dotted upper and lower lines describe the overall textual contour.

Clearly, each sentence is associated with its own declining sentence intonation contour, but together two or three such contours describe an overall downward trend, *i.e.* the onset and offset of upper and lower lines, respectively, decrease gradually through the text. Furthermore, the different syntactic arrangement is reflected in a difference of subordination to the overall contour: the broken lines, pertaining to syntactically coordinate structures, are less steep than the full lines describing syntactically uncoordinated sentences, *i.e.* the coordinate sentences deviate less from, are less slanted with respect to the overall contour than are the terminal declaratives. See further Thorsen (1985).

In a supplementary experiment (Thorsen 1986), where the number of terminal declaratives in a text was varied (between one and four) and where, furthermore, the length of individual sentences was varied (between two and four prosodic stress groups), it was proved that the overall trend described in figure 8 is not the result of a special "initial high" and "final low" effect: a sequence of four declarative sentences also shows a gradual decline. However, it appeared that the textual contour is sensitive, not only to the number of sentences that make up the text, but also to the length of individual sentences. This is due to the fact that, apparently, a declarative sentence must have a certain negative slope associated with it in order to serve appropriately as a declarative. This demand may conflict with a lowering of sentence onsets through the text: the longer the sentence, the higher its onset must be in order to preserve a suitable slope and simultaneously prevent the speaker from falling through the floor of his F_0 range.

3. Comparison with other systems

3.1 Regional variation

a. Stress group patterning

There is a very great deal of variation across different regional variants of Standard Danish, both in the shape of the F_0 pattern associated with prosodic stress groups, in its typical F_0 range, and in the exact alignment of segments and syllables with the tonal pattern. However, this presentation would burst at its seams if a full account were to be given. The reader is referred to Thorsen (1988a, 1988b) and Grønnum (1989) for results from Bornholm, South Zealand, North and South Jutland. However, I do wish to call attention to what appears to be a principled difference between regional variants which compress/expand their stress group patterns with variations in time, and those that truncate them. "Compression/expansion" means that the qualitatively same pattern is performed, the same target frequency values attained through movements of the same magnitude, only those movements are quicker or slower, more or less steep, according to the shorter or longer duration of the stress group. "Truncation" is the term reserved for those that develop greater or lesser parts of a given pattern according to the time available, which truncate F_0 patterns when time is cut short. I would also like to emphasise that differences in F_0 patterns and in the principles which produce them are probably what contributes most to a Danish speaker/listener's immediate recognition and localisation of regional variants. The more so since Bornholm is the only variety so far investigated which differs radically from the prosodic system of Standard Copenhagen. The other varieties, which are auditorily just as different from Copenhagen as Bornholm, share with Copenhagen the lack of default sentence accents, focus signalling by stress reduction, global signalling of sentence intonation, and

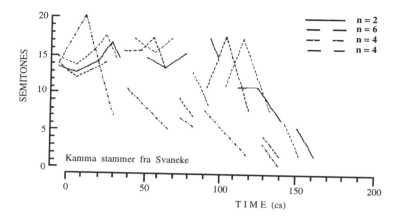

Figure 9. Average fundamental frequency tracings of *KAMma STAMmer fra SVAneke.* by a Bornholm speaker. The full line depicts the isolated utterance with no perceived default accent. The thin broken line is the same utterance in isolation with a perceptible default accent. The heavy broken line is the utterance with a final focal accent, and the dotted/broken line is with an initial focal accent. Zero on the logarithmic scale corresponds to 70 Hz.

rather modest and not ever-present final lengthening, with the exception that in Sønderborg (South-Eastern Jutland) sentence intonation function seems to be signalled locally rather than globally.

b. Sentence intonation

Global signalling of sentence intonation is shared by most, but not all regional varieties investigated: as mentioned just above, Bornholm and Southeast Jutland are exceptions. Compare the full line tracings of figure 5 and figure 9: by far the most extensive F_0 movement in the terminal declarative utterance in figure 9 (a Bornholm speaker) is located within the last stress group *SVAneke*, whereas the preceding F_0 patterns are superposed on a near level global trend. With the Copenhagen speaker (figure 5), on the contrary, local F_0 deflections, associated with the prosodic stress groups, are of approximately equal magnitude (note that the last stress group onsets with the stressed vowel, indicated with an arrow, cf. §2.1.b. above), and they ride on a slant whose slope is evenly distributed over the whole utterance.

c. Sentence accents

As mentioned in §§2.3.a. and 3.1.a. above, Bornholm stands out from other investigated variants of Standard Danish by having sentence accents proper, both default and focal, though neither is compulsory. Figure 9 depicts average tracings from a male Bornholm speaker of 4 different editions of the "same" utterance: one produced without any perceptible default accent (full line), one produced with a perceptible default accent (thin broken line), both uttered in isolation, one produced with a contextually conditioned final focal accent (heavier broken line), and one produced with a contextually conditioned initial focal accent (broken/dotted line). Note the contrast to figure 5, where full and broken lines are hardly discernible, and where the initial focus leaves the focused item itself unaffected but diminishes the F_0 patterns on the two succeeding stress groups. The difference in figure 9 between the final stress group with and without sentence accent is obvious: final default and focal accents both have more comprehensive and more complex movements and a different relation to the preceding unstressed syllable than the non-final-accent case. The difference between default (thin broken) and final focal (heavier broken) accent in this sample lies partly in the relation between the preceding unstressed syllable *fra* and the onset of the sentence accent, which is more distant in the focal accent, thus putting it into greater relief, but mainly in the greater shortening of the prelude to the focal accent (which shortening is *not* only due to the focal accent utterance having been produced in context, cf. Thorsen 1988a, pp. 64ff), *i.e.* in a more accelerated speech tempo.

d. "Final lengthening"

Although final lengthening was not made a separate issue in the description of Copenhagen Danish above, it was mentioned in §3.1.a that it is slight and non-compulsory. Bornholm is interesting again, because it turned up with predominantly *shorter* final syllables, *ceteris paribus*. This is remarkable for the light it throws upon the discussion about the reason for the relative lengthening of phrase- or utterance-final syllables. Several languages, among them Central Swedish, are reported to have longer syllables preceding a phrase or utterance boundary. This lengthening has been taken by some (*e.g.* Lyberg 1979) to be a consequence of the more elaborate F_0 movements finally (due to default accent). The explanation has been refuted by Bannert (1982) and certainly its universal validity is flatly denied by my Bornholm data, where a final element with (default or focal) sentence accent is generally significantly shorter than non-final elements, *ceteris paribus*, though its F_0 movement is considerably more extensive (and therefore considerably quicker and steeper), see further Thorsen (1988a, pp. 130 ff).

3.2 Danish intonation in international perspective

It will be apparent from the preceding sections that Danish shares some important features with its nearest Germanic neighbours: the basic units of prosodic description are, or can be made to be, identical, namely text, utterance/sentence, phrase, stress group/foot, and syllable. It is also a common feature that prominence (stress or accent) is signalled with a melodic change

Table 1. *Summary of the presence and manifestation of prosodic parameters for regional variants of Danish and neighbouring languages.*

	SENTENCE INTONATION SIGNALLING	DEFAULT SENTENCE ACCENTS	FOCAL SENTENCE ACCENTS	FOCUS BY STRESS REDUCTION	FINAL LENGTH-ENING	STRESS GROUP PATTERNS TRUNCATION /COMPRESSION
CENTRAL SWEDISH	local	compulsory	compulsory	-------	extensive	weak compression
BORHOLM	local	optional	optional, frequent	-------	shortening	compression
COPENHAGEN	global	no	-------	optional, never finally	modest	truncation
SOUTH ZEALAND	global	no	-------	rare, never finally	optional, modest	truncation
NORTH JUTLAND	global	no	-------	optional, rare finally	optional, modest	truncation
SOUTH EAST JUTLAND	local	no	-------	optional, never finally	not unex-ceptionally	truncation
STANDARD NORTH GERMAN	global and local	optional	compulsory, except finally	-------	yes	truncation and compression

which centres in or at the lexically stressed syllable. But most varieties of Danish differ from our nearest kin in lacking default sentence accents, in signalling focus merely by stress reduction and in signalling sentence intonation globally rather than locally. Bannert and Thorsen (1988) carried out a specific comparison between Standard Copenhagen Danish and Standard North German, based on our respective previous work with German and Danish. Thorsen (1988a, 1988b) and Grønnum (1989) compare the various prosodic systems, some of which are presented in table 1, in a more direct fashion, *i.e.* based on recordings of identical materials.

This overview states, in rather telegrammatic style, the presence and manifestation of the prosodic parameters treated in the various sections above. Two classificatory remarks may not be self-explanatory: the "weak compression" in Central Swedish refers to the fact that the tonal patterns pertaining to the word accent difference are orchestrated roughly within the stressed and first post-tonic syllables. Succeeding post-tonics continue at a level course where the word tone pattern lands them. This latter bit is simply truncated or continued in accordance with the composition of the stress group, whereas the word tone pattern is compressed/expanded under the rather slight differences that may occur in the total duration of the relevant disyllabic stretch. In standard North German, on the contrary, the falling part of the basically rising-falling stress group pattern may expand over any number of post-tonics, but below one or two post-tonic syllables, any further compression is ruled out, and the fall gets truncated.

Clearly, there is a lot more to be said about the parameters in this schema than what has come through in this and the sections above. For reasons of space, I must, however, refer the reader to the publications in the references.

4. Conclusion

There is not much left to conclude, by way of facts, after table 1, but that does leave room for speculation about the rather considerable prosodic differences in otherwise closely related languages/regional variants. These cannot conceivably be due to corresponding differences in syntax. Danish, Swedish and German are not that different syntactically, and – particularly – the materials recorded for the comparative analyses were near identical, both semantically and syntactically. It is possible, though not very likely, that somewhat greater differences would be found in the syntax of spontaneous speech (*versus* read "laboratory speech"), and that the prosodic systems are basically tuned to the latter speech style. This is an empirical issue, and leads me directly to state that the most obvious lacuna in our present knowledge of Danish prosody is the prosody of free, spontaneous speech. A research project was conducted at our institute, in 1990, whose title was, precisely, *Prosody of spontaneous speech*, cf. Rischel and Basbøll 1995. Its most immediate concern was with various stress phenomena and intonational junctures, and their interplay with syntactic/pragmatic factors. However, there is no evidence that spontaneous Danish syntax is so much richer in structure (compared with Swedish and German) to reasonably compensate for the rather poorer inventory of prosodic parameters and their manifestation. Instead, I propose that some languages/variants simply go down as less expressive prosodically than others. Copenhagen Danish would then lie at the lower end of that continuum, and Bornholm and Central Swedish at the other, something which matches rather accurately the linguistically naïve prejudice that Copenhagen Danish is "flat" and "monotonous", whereas, *e.g.*, the Swedes "sing" a whole lot more.

8

Intonation in Spanish

SANTIAGO ALCOBA and JULIO MURILLO

1. Background

The Spanish language has attracted considerable attention from phoneticians and phonologists; functional as well as articulatory and acoustic descriptions are quite numerous. Studies of the prosodic characteristics of Spanish, however, are far fewer, and differences between authors are such that certain publications and handbooks present the different approaches and points of view – at times contradictory – without explicitly propounding any one in particular. These deficiencies and the diversity of points of view oblige us to approach the question of prosody with great caution.

There are few works of a general nature. In Navarro Tomás (1944) we find the first extensive corpus of Spanish intonation, and virtually the only attempt at a general description of the Spanish intonation system, although its focus is fundamentally on reading and interpreting literary language. Later studies have been carefully described in Kvavik and Olsen (1974), and in the different sections of this chapter we refer to the most important of them. A recent (though summary) attempt at a general presentation of the Spanish intonation system is contained in the chapter which Quilis (1993) dedicates to the subject.

1.1 General prosodic characteristics

There is general agreement that there are four main features which characterise the Spanish intonation system: stress, juncture, rhythm and tonal variation or melody.

The presence or absence of stress in a syllable constitutes an especially relevant characteristic for the description of the Spanish intonation system. Spanish is a free stress language: *va'lido* (court favourite) *vs. 'valido* (valid); *sa'bana* (savannah) *vs. 'sabana* (sheet); *'canto* ((I) sing) *vs. can'to* ((He) sang).

All Spanish words can be classified as stressed or unstressed according to the presence or absence of a stressed syllable. Evidently, this distinction applies only to words that form part of a sentence or other sequence. Any word mentioned or used metalinguistically becomes stressed, if it is not already inherently so. Stressed words contain only one accented syllable, except for derived adverbs in *-mente*: /teɣnika'mente/ [technically], /'faθil'mente/ [easily], /satisfaɣ'toria'mente/ [satisfactorily], which maintain the stress of the original adjective in addition to the stress on the first syllable of the suffix.

In Spanish, stressed words represent 63.44% of the lexical material in spoken language (Quilis 1978). Accented words can be stressed on the final, penultimate or antepenultimate syllable, but the relative frequency of these patterns is very unequal. Even ignoring monosyllabic stressed words and adverbs in *-mente*, final-stress represents 17.68%; penultimate stress 79.50% and antepenultimate stress 2.76% of the total number of stressed words (Quilis 1978). These figures reveal the eminently paroxytonic character of the Spanish language and explain the tendency of speakers to place stress on the penultimate syllable of a new or unknown word (*'Nobel, 'chofer*).

In a stressed word, the location of the accented syllable can be explained by diachronic or morphological reasons (Academia 1973, pp. 64–84), but given a sequence of phonological segments, it is not possible to establish on the basis of the nature of these segments alone which one will be stressed.

Nevertheless the presence of an accented syllable in a Spanish word is not random: it depends, in the first place, on the lexical category (noun, verb, *etc.*) to which the word belongs, on the morphological structure (primitive or simple, derived or compound), on the syntax (possessives placed after a noun are stressed, while those before it are unstressed), on the modality of the sentence (interrogative and exclamatory pronouns are stressed, while relative and declarative pronouns are unstressed) and finally on the difference in function or meaning that an element can have in a sentence: *e.g. luego* (later) adverb [+stress] / (so) conj. [-stress]); *aun/aún* (even / still); *mientras* (while) adverb [+stress] / conj. [-stress]); *medio* (middle) noun [+stress] / adj. [-stress]); *mas/más* (but/more) (Quilis 1978, 1981, 1993).

Given what has been said above, it can be stated that the stressed syllable of Spanish words can only be one of the last three syllables of the word (the Three

Syllable Window Restriction). Generative phonologists have tried to regulate the identification of the tonic syllable of each word in a series of studies, culminating in the extensive studies by Harris (1983, 1987, 1988, 1989, 1992, 1995).

In these studies it has been possible to establish the following generalisations: firstly, in order to identify the stressed syllable of each verb form, the segmental characterisation, representation, and morphological structure is a sufficient and necessary condition for the form in question; secondly, for non-verbal word classes (noun, adjective, adverb), the segmental representation and morphological structure is a necessary but not a sufficient condition to identify the stressed syllable, and further information, therefore, is required in the lexical entry; thirdly, as far as markedness is concerned, words ending in a vowel with a stressed prefinal syllable are considered as unmarked, as are words with final syllable stress which end in a consonant; fourthly, stress is assigned cyclically in each cyclic constituent of a derived word.

Given those observations and in harmony with certain principles and theoretical conditions of metrical phonology (Halle and Vergnaud 1987), Harris (1989) puts forward (1) as a definition of the general algorithm for stress in the non-verbal word classes of Spanish.

(1)   i. Stressable elements are syllable nuclei (rhyme heads).
ii. The rightmost stressable element is extrametrical iff word final or followed by an inflectional consonant.
iii. Form constituent(s) on line 0 and mark head(s) on line 1; Parameter settings: a) unbounded, right-headed (general case); b) binary, left-headed, right-to-left (special case)
iv. Form constituent(s) on line 1 and mark heads on line 2; Parameter settings: unbounded, right-headed
v. Conflate lines 1 and 2 (= remove asterisks in columns that have no line-2 asterisk).

With this algorithm Harris establishes the metrical grids of the examples *republicano* in (2a) (accent of Type A, or general case) and *democrático* in (2b) (accent of Type B, or marked, special case).

(2)   a   [(re.pu.bli.ca.n)o]   b   [(de.mo.cra.ti.c)o]
      line 0   . . . (*) <*>   . . (* .) <*>
      line 1   . . . *   .   . . (*) . .
      line 2   . . . *   .   . . * . .
                    = *republiCAno*   = *demoCRAtico*

Roca (1988) examines in detail the stress algorithm of Harris (1983), without reaching a definite decision as to the possibility of a unified stress algorithm for the non-verb word classes (Harris 1992, 1995). Concerning verb forms, Harris (1987) and (1989) tries to combine the general stress algorithm of (1) with the specific morphological structure and various segmental processes of the verb forms in the different paradigms. However, contrary to the proposal of Núñez-Cedeño (1985) and of Harris (1987), the data seems to indicate a distinction between three different forms of accent (Alcoba 1990):

(3)   a. The forms of the Theme of Preterit (simple past, past imperfect indicative, past imperfect subjunctive, future subjunctive, participle and gerund) belong to the general case.

        b. The forms of the Theme of Present (forms of the present indicative, present subjunctive, imperative and infinitive; with some dialectical variation: in some dialects the stress is moved to the thematic vowel of the first and second person plural) are marked and belong to the special case.

        c. The forms of the Theme of Future (forms of the future indicative and conditional) are marked as general case exceptions.

On the study of stress in Spanish, the seminal work is the article by Bolinger and Hodapp (1961). Its conclusions that the parameter F_0 is the principle defining factor of accent in this language, with intensity and duration playing secondary roles, were corroborated by Quilis (1981, pp. 330–332) who concludes that, from the acoustic point of view,

the most important indication for the perception of stress in Spanish is the fundamental frequency... Length would be a secondary component.

The values related to intensity constitute a very minor factor in the acoustic definition of stress.

The timing of our phonological system has long attracted the attention of phoneticians. Most studies, however, are based on written language or on the oral production of written language. The first study on the subject was that of Navarro Tomás (1939), which is based on the consideration of Spanish as a syllable-timed language and concludes that prosodic groups of five to ten syllables comprise 67.60% of the prosodic groups, and that of these those of seven or eight syllables form 26.32%. It is on these calculations that Navarro Tomás bases some of his hypotheses about the tendency to use octosyllabic verse in Spanish popular lyrics. Matluck, however, considers that prosodic groups of ten to fifteen syllables predominate in familiar registers of educated speech. The conclusions of Canellada and Madsen (1987, pp. 103–104) are contradictory in this respect, as their calculations on syllable counts in prosodic groups differ considerably from those of working-class Madrid speech, represented by a *sainete* or short theatrical comedy, by Arniches, which was also written.

2. Basic intonation patterns

2.1 Description of a basic non-emphatic pattern

The intonation system of the Spanish sentence is mainly characterised by the different patterns and distribution of stressed syllables of the sentence: according to whether the stressed syllable is the first, the last or in an internal position of the utterance, and according to whether the word is stressed on the final syllable or not.

Given a sequence of stressed and unstressed syllables which constitute a non-emphatic declarative utterance, L. Fant (1984) proposes a model which we outline briefly as follows adapting his representations to the INTSINT transcription system (Hirst and Di Cristo this volume) In sentences such as (4), with two stressed syllables the intonation forms two tonic groups (TG):

(4)   (la saCAron)$_{TG}$ (del gaRAje)$_{TG}$ (they took it out of the garage)

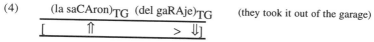

For sentences such as (5) with three stressed syllables, the intonation forms three TGs:

(5)   (saCAron) $_{TG}$ (la MOto) $_{TG}$ (del gaRAje) $_{TG}$

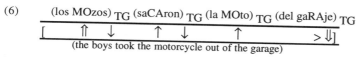
(they took the motorcycle out of the garage)

For sentences such as (6) with four stressed syllables, the intonation forms four TGs.

(6)   (los MOzos) $_{TG}$ (saCAron) $_{TG}$ (la MOto) $_{TG}$ (del gaRAje) $_{TG}$

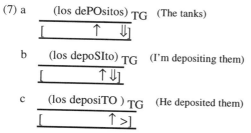
(the boys took the motorcycle out of the garage)

Finally, in expressions such as (7a–c) with only one stressed syllable, the intonation follows the same diagram with a single TG.

(7) a   (los dePOsitos) $_{TG}$ (The tanks)

b   (los depoSIto) $_{TG}$ (I'm depositing them)

c   (los depoSiTO) $_{TG}$ (He deposited them)

Given examples (4–6), and the tonal realisation of word stress which can be characterised as **T** [⇑], **H** [↑], **D** [>] or **B** [⇓], the typical model of short declarative non-emphatic intonation is characterised by, first the presence of an initial stressed syllable at a level near **T**; second, by the presence of a last stressed syllable before the final pause, which maintains the F_0 at level **D**; and, third, by the presence or absence of internal TGs in which the F_0 is situated at level **H**. In the case of utterances such as (7), with a single TG, the interaction between the ascending orientation of the stressed syllable and falling orientation of the unstressed one, produces the effect that the only stress in the sentence does not reach the **T** level because of a "truncating" or "compressing" effect due to the tendency to reach levels **D** and **B** before a final pause.

Finally, the stress pattern of a word also influences the pattern of the melodic curve. If the accent of a final TG (8a), an initial TG (8b) or an internal TG (8c) is on the final syllable of a word, then the intonation pattern of the corresponding TG undergoes some variations (L. Fant 1984, p. 31).

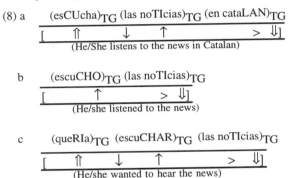

To summarise, non-emphatic short declarative utterances in Spanish present a melodic line whose pattern depends, on the one hand, on the number of stressed syllables or TGs which make up the utterance; and, on the other, on whether the word is stressed on the final syllable.

In addition to the number and differing distribution of the stresses in the sentence and the respective **T** level, of the first, the **D** level of the last and the **H** level of the internal ones, the distinct orientation of the final juncture, falling or rising, interphrastic (with or without pause), and strongly falling or rising end juncture with pause affects the description of Spanish intonation. With respect to the terminal juncture or terminal contour the short declarative intonation is usually (Canellada 1941; Fontanella 1980) closed in Spanish by a falling terminal juncture.

In short declarative utterances, the interphrastic juncture or interior juncture does not usually appear and the utterance closes with an absolute terminal juncture. Nevertheless, this intonation pattern of the declarative sentence can be altered by syntactic, semantic or pragmatic factors.

The presence of a falling internal juncture can change the syntactic incidence of an adjective or adverb, as can be seen in (9) (illustrated in figures 1a and 1b)

(9) a   ¡ NO CIErre la venTAna.! (Don't close the window)

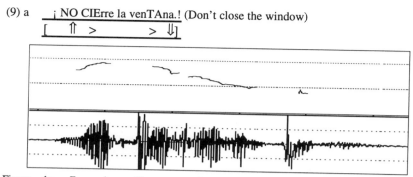

Figure 1a. *F₀* and oscillogramme for example 9a: *¡No cierre la ventana!*. Horizontal lines on the *F₀* curve correspond to 100 and 200 Hz.

(9) b   ¡ NO,   CIErre la venTAna! (No, close the window)

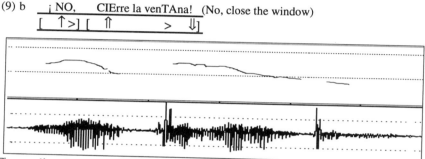

Figure 1b. *F₀* and oscillogramme for example 9b: *¡No, cierre la ventana!* Horizontal lines on the *F₀* curve correspond to 100 and 200 Hz.

Similarly, the different placing of the interphrastic juncture can affect the interpretation of a word, as in (10), or a phrase (11):

(10) a   Cuando HUbo haBLAdo,   JUAN se FUE.

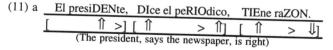

(When he had spoken, Juan left)

   b   Cuando HUbo haBLAdo JUAN, se FUE.

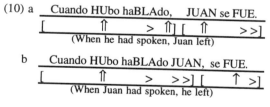

(When Juan had spoken, he left)

(11) a   El presiDENte, DIce el peRIOdico, TIEne raZON.

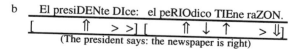

(The president, says the newspaper, is right)

   b   El presiDENte DIce: el peRIOdico TIEne raZON.

(The president says: the newspaper is right)

In this respect, the difference between restrictive and non-restrictive relative clauses is a classic case (Garro and Parker 1983).

As Quilis (1981) indicates, the redistribution of stresses can also produce a change in grammatical category of the constituent words. Nevertheless it should be made clear that these changes are produced, not only by the redistribution of stresses, but also by the resultant modifications of the intonation patterns of (12), as we have proposed:

(12) a   DIle QUÉ HAS leIdo. / DIle que HAS leIdo.
         (Tell him/her what you've read/ Tell him/her that you've read.)

     b   El TÉ GUSta MUcho. / ÉL te GUSta MUcho.
         (Tea is enjoyed a lot. / You like him a lot)

2.2 Modality and expressivity

As in many other languages, the presence or absence of certain interphrastic junctures, generally rising, makes clear (Quilis 1981, 1993) if an utterance is direct (13a), indirect (13b) or vocative (13c) [for the first two cf. figures 2a, 2b]:

(13) a   <u>JUAN preGUNta QUIÉN VA a enTRAR.</u>
         [⇑ ↓ ↑   >   >   > >]
         (Juan is asking who's going to come in)

     b   <u>JUAN preGUNta: ¿QUIÉN VA a enTRAR?</u>
         [⇑   > >] [⇑ >   > >]
         (Juan is asking: "who's going to come in?")

     c   <u>JUAN, preGUNta QUIÉN VA a enTRAR.</u>
         [↑>] [⇑   > >   > >]
         (Juan! Ask who's going to come in!)

Differences of quantity or mere changes of direction of a terminal juncture can also indicate substantial semantic and pragmatic changes, as in (14):

(14) a   <u>SI,   SI</u>   (= Yes, OK)
         [↑ >] [↑>]

     b   <u>SI SI</u>   (= No, only a fool would believe that)
         [↑ > >]

     c   <u>¿SI?</u>   (= Is that so?)
         [↓ ⇑]

Similarly, changes in intonation permit the expression of a single utterance with varying modality: declarative, as in (15a) or imperative as in (15b):

(15) a   <u>En el AUla NO se FUma</u>   (One doesn't smoke in class.) [= declarative]

     [⇑   >   > ⇓]

   b   <u>En el AUla   NO se FUma</u>   (One doesn't smoke in class!) [= imperative]

     [⇑ >⇑] [⇑   > ⇓]

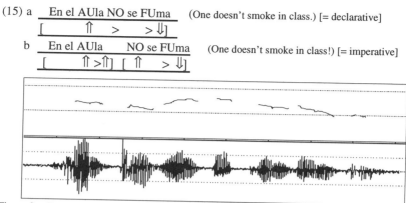

Figure 2a. F_0 and oscillogramme for example 13a: *Juan pregunta quién va a entrar.*

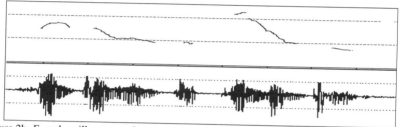

Figure 2b. F_0 and oscillogramme for example 13b: *Juan pregunta "¿Quién va a entrar?"*

Intonation can also play an essential role in the realisation of the interrogative modality. There should also be a clear difference between two types of interrogative utterances. If the question presents a grammatical element, either pronominal or of a different type which manifests the interrogative sense of the utterance, the intonation is manifested in a pattern which is substantially identical to the declarative:

the terminal juncture is falling, and the tonal levels that precede it, are low; that is to say, a similar pattern to declarative utterances. (Quilis 1981, p. 420).

On the other hand, yes/no questions, absolute or not pronominal (cf. 16b) present a model of intonation which substantially coincides with the characteristic pattern of incomplete utterances, with a rising terminal juncture (cf. figure 3).

(16) a   <u>¿QUIÉN VIEne maÑAna?</u>   (Who's coming tomorrow?)

     [⇑   >   > ⇓]

   b   <u>¿MaRIa VIEne maÑAna?</u>   (Is Maria coming tomorrow?)

     [⇑   >   > ⇑]

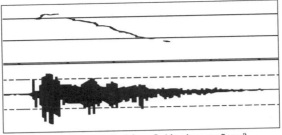

Figure 3. F_0 and oscillogramme for example 16a: *¿Quién viene mañana?*

Now that this difference has been made, it is interesting to note that these general intonation patterns of Spanish questions can undergo alterations to show different secondary meanings such as "courtesy", "repetition", "confirmation" or "order" (Quilis 1981, pp. 435–442, 1993, pp. 448–453). These different interrogative meanings are expressed by different procedures, such as the presence of a maximum level in some of the stresses in the utterance; by the change in corresponding direction in the juncture; or by a combination of the two.

2.3 Focalisation and contextual effects

Variations in the intonation patterns can occur without any syntactic motivation, simply with the purpose of focalising or highlighting an element, without any alterations in syntactic structure. This is the role which sentential stress plays in other very well-known languages.

Contreras (1977, pp. 121–123) supposes the existence of a special accent of melodic peak, which is assigned to the last rhematic element in all sentences in Spanish. The function of this peak consists precisely in focusing on this rhematic element. When there is more than one rhematic element, Contreras proposes a Melodic Peak Assignment Rule, with inter-dialectal validity, to also assign a melodic peak to that rhematic constituent. For this reason Contreras (1980) argues that sentential stress and the word order of the sentence depends at least in part on the information structure, theme/rheme, of the sentence.

Other studies, however, claim that not all sentences present this special maximum level accent, and that it only appears in emphatic declarative utterances and emphatic pronominal questions. This type of utterance, and only this type, is characterised by the presence of a maximum level stress in one of its words, which becomes the rhematic element:

the intonational pattern of emphatic pronominal questions coincides with that of emphatic affirmations. The distinction between these intonations is made only by the grammatical structure: the presence or absence of grammatical words (pronouns or interrogative elements). (Quilis 1981, p. 437, cf. also Quilis 1993, pp. 447–450)

L. Fant (1984, p. 49) considers that the strongest candidate for the function of sentential stress is the **T** stress (which he calls H+ stress), which normally appears in the first TG of the sentence; but after presenting various arguments and studies, he concludes from a test using the expression *botellas en el frigorífico* (bottles in the refrigerator) shown in (17), and its comparison with equivalent data from other languages, that unlike German and Swedish, Spanish, like Danish, does not manifest sentential stress in all utterances, at least in the central peninsular variety spoken by his Spanish informants.

(17) a – Tengo sed. ¿Nos queda cerveza en el sótano?
       – No, pero hay un par de botellas en el frigorífico.
       – Tómalas si quieres.
         (– I'm thirsty. Do we have any beer left in the cellar?
         – No, but there are a couple of bottles in the refrigerator.
         – Would you get them?)

    b – Oye, Juan Carlos. Hay un par de botellas en el frigorífico.
       – ¿Me las quieres traer, por favor?
         (– Hey Juan Carlos. There are a couple of bottles in the refrigerator.
         – Would you bring me them?)

In any case, it is clear that interphrastic junctures serve to emphasise the preceding constituent, especially if that juncture is rising and coincides with the extraposition of a syntactic constituent of the sentence. The **T** stress, which is usually the first accent of the utterance, is interpreted as a signal of emphasis if it appears in a non-initial TG.

2.4 Phrasing and textual organisation

Examples such as (11–14), above, show how the interior breaks of the utterance can be motivated by semantic, pragmatic (presupposition and emphasis) and, in general, syntactic factors. In this respect, L. Fant indicates, correctly, that, the hierarchy of a syntactic limit in a compound sentence, utterance, clause or phrase, in addition to the syntactic and semantic determinants of the different interior junctures in (11–14) and similar ones such as relatives (as he points out with the test of the absent commas) is essential for the presence of an interphrastic boundary (L. Fant 1984, pp. 46–48).

In the breaking up of long utterances into shorter phonic groups, we find the intervention of **tempo** factors. The length of the sequence of syllabic segments, however, or of the TG defined by a stressed syllable, is the principle factor which determines the presence of internal boundaries in long utterances (Alcoba *et al.* 1993). In this respect, L. Fant accepts the arguments of Borzone de Manrique and Signorini (1983) against the traditional hypothesis that considers Spanish a syllable-timed language (probably on the basis of observations of speakers reading from literary texts) and tends more toward the theory (which he considers not yet sufficiently demonstrated), that Spanish is a stress-timed language and that

it is the number of stresses and not that of syllables which counts in terms of the division of an utterance in prosodic phrases. (L. Fant 1984, pp. 46–48).

L. Fant also argues in support of this hypothesis by stating the obvious fact that:

with a longer duration of the prosodic phrases which characterise a rapid *tempo*, there results a reduction in the number of stresses.

Spanish cannot be strictly classified as a stress-timed language (like English, Dutch, *etc.*), nor as a syllable-timed language (like Italian cf. Bertinetto 1983) as Toledo (1988) has shown, so that neither the syllable nor the foot seem adequate operational segments for a phonetic description of Spanish intonation. Unlike English or Dutch, Spanish seems to behave as a trailer-timed language, with sequences of phonetic segments distinct from the syllable and the foot, in which the stressed syllable together with the preceding syllables forms a unity whose behaviour is distinct from the melodic units of leader-timed languages (Wenk and Wioland 1982).

The operative rhythm unit of Spanish is, then, the **tonic group** (TG), providing an explanation for the well-known phenomenon of syllabic reduction via vowel contact between words (Toledo 1988).

The existence of different prosodic groups in long utterances carries in itself the question of hierarchical levels of terminal junctures. To characterise the different boundaries, the presence or absence of a pause must be taken into consideration as well as the rate of slowing down (Quilis 1981, 1993; L. Fant 1984). L. Fant (1984, p. 44) distinguishes three types or levels of interphrastic boundaries: a "strong" boundary [+syllabic turnover; +pause]; a "medium" boundary [+syllabic turnover; -pause], and a "weak" boundary [-syllabic turnover; -pause].

2.5 Other patterns

In Spanish, as in other languages, there exist intonation clichés or stereotyped patterns, which are manifested in child language, as in (18), a children's choosing chant (cf. "eenee meenee minee mo") which resembles chanted more than ordinary speech.

(18) Ṕlto   Ṕlto   C̈Olo   RIto   DOnde VASto   TAN bo NIto

[⇑→   >   ][⇑→   >   ] [⇑   →   >   ] [⇑   →   >]

In these cases, the prosodic structure imposes a certain stress figure on the distribution and structure of the feet, whereas in normal speech it is the distribution of the accents which determines the melodic pattern of the utterance.

3. Comparisons with other systems

3.1 Dialectal variations

It is obvious that the tonal characteristics of Spanish described above vary according to dialect not only throughout the Hispanophone world in general, but even within the Peninsular. However, few studies have addressed this subject.

The first study of dialectal variation of Spanish intonation is that of Canellada (1941), which pointed out the existence of rising intonation contours in declarative utterances in the Spanish of Extremadura (Spain). In Argentina, the difference in tone between the Spanish of Buenos Aires, Tucumán and Córdoba has been studied. The melodic Spanish of Buenos Aires is less complex than that of either Tucumán or Córdoba. In the Spanish of Tucumán, the fourth contrasting position is only discerned in utterances which end with an unstressed syllable. With regard to the number of pitch levels, in Buenos Aires and Tucumán, there are thought to be three, and in Córdoba four.

In Tucumán Spanish (…) there are only two terminal contours: rising and level. The absence of falling contours, together with the existence of glides that are always rising and the frequent occurrence of very high final unstressed syllables in statements, cause certain sequences to appear as interrogative ones to Buenos Aires ears.

While the acoustic analysis of the Argentinean Spanish of Tucumán and that of the Peninsular Spanish of Extremadura confirms the hypothesis of Fontanella (1980) and Canellada (1941), respectively, it is evident that it constitutes an argument against the hypothesis of Lieberman (1967) which considers the "falling terminal frequency contour" of statements as a "linguistic universal". Finally,

Buenos Aires Spanish has a definitely syllabic rhythm, in Tucumán Spanish there are height and quality differences between stressed and unstressed syllables, a compression of the central part of the macrosegment, and glides in the stressed syllables that produce a typical stressed-time rhythm. (Fontanella 1966, 1971 and 1980, pp. 124–125).

The investigations carried out by Kvavik (1974, 1975) dealt with Mexican Spanish. Some of Quilis's studies and investigations collected in L. Fant (1984) have been made with spontaneous speech or recording of informants in the centre of the peninsula. In Quilis (1985) the different forms of the F_0 in the Spanish of Puerto Rico, Mexico and Madrid were studied. Puerto Rican Spanish has a circumflexed F_0 both in declarative statements and pronoun interrogatives.

Castillian and Mexican dialects are the same in that both have a terminal rising contour in absolute interrogatives. But for Quilis, the small difference that can be perceived, is one of the different treatment of F_0 in the syllable which precedes the absolute terminal juncture; in the configuration of the F_0 in the penultimate TG of the utterance; or in the different positioning of the beginning of the terminal rising.

Mexico, Madrid and Puerto Rico are all the same in their presentation of one of the complete forms of declarative utterance, by moving the final circumflex. (Quilis 1985, pp. 166–167).

Finally, Quilis (1989) studies the intonation in the Canary Islands and Sosa (1991) is a general study on American Spanish.

3.2 Comparisons with other languages

With regard to the melodic system of Spanish in relation to other languages of the same geographical area, what stands out is the trochaic character of the rhythm of the Spanish language, and its tendency to converge with the Greek language, while there is a divergent tendency between French and Spanish which manifests itself not only in the phonemic systems, but in the saw-like aspect of Spanish melody, as opposed to the isosceles figure in French melody.

In recent years, and particularly since L. Fant (1984), a greater interest in the phonetic and acoustic characterisation of Spanish intonation can be observed; however no published acoustic studies exist which enable one to quantify, or even simulate, the tonal variations characteristic of Spanish. In this sense, in works synthesising the Spanish voice (Santos 1981; Olabe 1983; Pardo *et al.* 1987) a representative number of oral productions have been analysed. Resulting values permit an acceptable simulation of pitch variations. Nevertheless, Pardo *et al.* (1987: 175) admit that at present they are only

creating an algorithm for text to speech conversion and they hope to use their data to create a theory about intonation in Spanish.

In this sense we must consider studies such as those by Cid and Roach (1990), Prieto *et al.* (1995) and Garrido (1996). As far as sentence rhythm is concerned, L. Fant considers that Spanish is a stress-timed language, following the arguments made in Borzone de Manrique and Signorini (1983), indicated above. But, independently of the evident effects of **tempo** on the greater or lesser number of syllables of a prosodic group or of the number of stressed syllables which form a given prosodic group, the question of the timing of the different intonation models of Spanish, based on the analysis of continuous spoken spontaneous Spanish are still in need of systematic studies, such as Toledo (1988), in order to define the valid parameters statistically and the operative units and sequences for an adequate description of the melodic system.

Unlike stress-timed languages like English or Dutch or syllable-timed languages like Italian, Spanish seems to behave like a trailer-timed language. The tonic syllables group together with the preceding unstressed syllables to constitute a unit which behaves differently from the syllable or the foot.

The operative rhythmic unit should be the "tonic group", a set of syllables grouped around the tonic syllable of a word and circumscribed by the final borders of the stressed words (Alcoba *et al.* 1993, Hirst *et al.* 1993).

4. Conclusions

In the research into the phonetic representations of intonation, two basic types of models can be seen: perception-based models (like the one developed in Eindhoven), and production-based models (like the one developed in Aix-en-Provence).

A perception-based model gives no information, from a theoretical point of view, about the nature of phonological representations, and its representation of intonation is essentially syllabic. But, as has been shown, the intonation contour is not restricted to the confines of the syllable. In any case, while the perception-based model may be perfectly adequate for describing the melodic system of stressed-timed or syllable-timed languages, it does not appear to be so appropriate for a trailer-timed language like Spanish.

For languages like Spanish, where the stress group is the operative rhythmic unit, and where there seems to be no correspondence between the syllables and the contours of phonetic constituents of the intonation, an intonation model based on production seems more appropriate.

The lack of a general consensus as to what constitutes a phonological representation of the sentence also privileges a production-based approach in phonetic research into intonation. The results of a perception-based approach would be difficult to evaluate within a phonological model, because without an explicit phonological model it is difficult to see how to handle the results of a process of stylisation whether we use the empirical (Dutch) or quantitative (French) model. In any case, a representation of intonation, like the one proposed by Hirst (1987, §4.4), when reduced to a sequence of significant points distributed in two or three different levels and calculated from a declining reference line, without being adapted to a specific operative rhythmic sequence, would be perfectly adequate for one language type or another, for English, French or Spanish.

9

Intonation in European Portuguese

MADALENA CRUZ-FERREIRA

1. Introduction

This chapter presents a description of the basic intonation system of (European) Portuguese, as it is spoken in Portugal and specifically in the Lisbon area.

General features of stress, rhythm and prominence are dealt with in the first sections. The bulk of the chapter deals with intonational features of Portuguese.

1.1 General prosodic characteristics

a. Stress

In Portuguese, lexical stress is not restricted to one fixed syllabic position in all words, as for example in French or Polish. In Portuguese, as in Spanish, words may be stressed on one of the last three syllables, although the vast majority of words are stressed on the penultimate syllable. In analyses of lexical stress in Portuguese, penultimate stress is either taken as the "unmarked" general rule from which the assignment of stress to other syllables can be derived (Mateus 1975), or it is viewed as being assigned by a "default" rule, after the application of rules dealing with final and antepenultimate stress (Agard 1967).

Lexical stress is distinctive in Portuguese. Several minimal word-pairs can be found, where stress alone distinguishes the grammatical category:

(1) a dúvida /'duvidɐ/ (a doubt)
    b duvida /du'vidɐ/ (he/she doubts)

In these examples, stress distinguishes between two otherwise identical words, with no difference in vowel quality. With the vowels represented graphically by *a*, *e* and *o*, however, stress and vowel quality are interdependent. When stressed, these vowels have an open quality which is absent in unstressed syllables. Thus the stress marks of ordinary Portuguese orthography indicate both stress and open quality. An example is:

(2) a   cópia /'kɔpiɐ/ (a copy)   b   copia /kʊ'piɐ/ (he/she copies)

b. Vowel quality and devoicing

The relationship of stress and vowel quality in Portuguese is important for intonation. Portuguese, compared with French, for example, is a language with an overall rather lax articulation. Many plosives are spirantised, particularly if voiced and in intervocalic position, and the articulation of most vowels is undershot, and this not only in informal or careless speech.

There is a very strong tendency in standard Portuguese, particularly in the Lisbon dialect, to devoice and/or reduce the quality of all vowels in unstressed syllables to a vowel in the area of [ə] (see Delgado Martins 1988). Additionally, both in syllables containing underlying /ə/ (which is phonemic in Portuguese) and in syllables where schwa occurs as a result of reduction, there is a tendency to omit the vowel altogether:

(3)   catedral (cathedral) *phonemic:* /kɐtə'dɾal/ *pronounced:* [k{ɐ̥}t'dɾal]

c. Rhythm

The fact that phonological syllables are blended together through the collapse of weak syllables in connected speech has obvious effects on the prosody of the language. For one thing, it determines the rhythm of Portuguese. Taking rhythm as the way in which prominent syllables recur in utterances, the syllable obviously cannot be taken as the unit of timing in Portuguese, as is commonly claimed for French (though for criticism of this widely held view see Wenk and Wioland 1982). Portuguese seems in fact to fit more readily into the pattern of stress-timed languages, its rhythm being given by the recurrence of perceptually salient stressed syllables. In the following example, the number of rhythmic beats remains the same, regardless of the number of syllables in between:

(4) a   'Ela dei'xou um re'cado   b Isa'bel esteve na 'praia ontem à 'tarde
         (she left a message)   (Isabel was at the beach yesterday evening)

The rhythmic alternation of weak and salient syllables also has obvious importance for the way in which intonation patterns are accommodated to particular lexical sequences. As Halliday (1967b) pointed out, no choices in intonation are independent of rhythm. Intonation may be regarded as the way in which variations in pitch merge with the syllables of an utterance. In

Portuguese, as in English, the nuclear tone, that is, the most significant pitch turn in the intonation group, always begins (or takes place) on a stressed syllable, typically the last stressed syllable in the intonation group. Being a language with free but predominantly penultimate stress, the nuclear syllable is often not the last one in the intonation group, and is followed by one or two weak syllables. In these cases, the nuclear pitch movement will be continued on these weak syllables. Only for intonational purposes are weak syllables pronounced in Portuguese, and their voiced segments kept.

The nuclear tones take different shapes depending on whether the nucleus is the final syllable in the word or whether weak syllables follow. For example, a rise-fall on a word like *café* (coffee), stressed on the last syllable, will take the shape of a glide on that syllable, whereas on a word like *câmara* (city hall) the rise-fall will take the shape of successive steps in pitch on each syllable.

d. *Accent and nucleus*

The term **stress** describes prominence at word level, a "potential for pitch accent" in Bolinger's (1958) terms. The term **accent** designates prominence at utterance level, which is achieved through the mapping of intonation patterns onto the potentially accentable syllables of an utterance. The interplay of intonational features with potentially accentable syllables is effected in several ways, and results in different degrees of prominence. Accordingly, for the purpose of describing prominence in Portuguese, four degrees of accent are set up, all accented syllables keeping their full vowel quality:

- **primary accent**: nuclear accent with pitch prominence
- **secondary accent**: non-nuclear pitch prominence
- **tertiary accent**: prominence achieved through loudness and/or length
- **weak accent**: unaccented (or "non-prominent").

As regards nuclear prominence, the nucleus typically affects the last stressed syllable in the intonation group, "stress" being defined lexically. This syllable usually marks the beginning of a gliding pitch, that is, a change in pitch direction which takes place *on* or *after* the nucleus. Bolinger (1957/1958, 1958) proposed three types of pitch accent for English, according to how and from where the nuclear syllable is approached. Accent type C seems to account for the majority of salient pitch turns in Portuguese: the nuclear syllable is consistently jumped *to* and frequently *down* to. The nuclear tone commonly begins on a lower pitch than what precedes it. The first type of Bolinger's accent B, where the nucleus is jumped *up* to, accounts for nuclear prominence where the nuclear tones have high-pitched starts, as with high-fall and high-rise, which start on a higher pitch than what precedes. The second type of accent B as well as accent A, where the nucleus is jumped up and down *from*, respectively, do not seem to occur in Portuguese: all nuclei involve a step-up or a step-down.

The nuclear syllable is made prominent through primary accent. Other salient pitch turns within intonation groups occur at the beginning of **head** tunes. Heads begin on the first stressed syllable within the intonation group, preceding the nucleus, made prominent by means of secondary accent which also usually involves a jump in pitch to the accented syllable, but not a following nuclear glide. Other prominent syllables within the intonation group bear tertiary accent.

1.2 Outline of the approach adopted in the chapter

Since earlier descriptions of the intonation patterns and intonational meanings of Portuguese are not available, most of the data presented in the chapter are drawn from my own speech (Lisbon dialect) and from several tests performed with native informants in a study described in Cruz-Ferreira (1983).

The framework for the following analysis of the intonation of Portuguese takes two formal units of intonation as basic: the **intonation group,** corresponding to what may be called a melodic and rhythmic phrase; and the **nucleus,** the syllable melodically predominant within the intonation group. It is assumed that the pitch movement starting on the nuclear syllable is the most significant pitch movement taking place in the intonation group and the one contributing most to the intonational meaning of the intonation group.

Nuclear tones may be preceded by heads, which may in turn be preceded by preheads. The beginning of heads is marked by secondary accent: a head begins on the first non-nuclear accent in the intonation group and stretches up to the nucleus.

Preheads are constituted by the weak syllables preceding the first accent in the intonation group, corresponding to the anacrusis (see §2.4. below).

2. Description of intonation patterns

In the following examples, {...}, where relevant, indicates possible typical contexts for the utterances, intended as merely suggestive.

2.1 Description of a basic non-emphatic pattern

A low-falling tone is by far the commonest falling tone in Portuguese. It is the typical statement tone and typical Q-word question tone. In statements, the low-fall is preceded by a low prehead and a high head:

(5)   <u>está a choVER outra VEZ</u>   (it's raining again)
       [⇓   ⇑   > ⇓]

In Q-word questions, the pre-nuclear pattern has an overall high pitch:

(6)   porque É que não DIzes o que PENsas?   (why don't you speak your mind?)
        [⇑   →   >   ⇓]

2.2 Modality and expressivity

a. Questions

Yes/no questions typically bear a nuclear low-rising tone. The low-rise has a much wider pitch range in Portuguese than, for example, in English, being comparable to Jassem's (1952) "full-rise", starting low and often ending at high level. The low-rise may also be used in Q-word questions, to mark politeness. In both types of questions the low-rise is preceded by high prehead and high head. Example (yes/no question):

(7)   tu SAbes quem É aquele TIpo?   (do you know who that chap is?)
        [⇑   →   >   ⇑]

Another rising tone, the high-rise, also consistently conveys a questioning meaning. It is typically used with echo-questions or with questions requiring repetition of a previous utterance. It is the tone occurring with the wordless "hummed" question [ɛ̃], requiring repetition. The high-rising nucleus is consistently jumped *up* to, although preceded by high level syllables throughout:

(8)   o que É que diSSESte?   (what did you say?)
        [⇑   →   <   ⇑]

In other uses, as for example with tag questions which otherwise bear a low-rising tone, the high-rise gives a very "pressing" overtone to the question, and conveys the strong expectation of the speaker towards agreement with his assumption (see Cruz-Ferreira (1981) for details on the intonation of tags in Portuguese). Example:

(9)   ela NÃO te coNHEce,   pois NÃO?
        [⇑   >   ⇓ [<   ⇑]

        (she doesn't know you, does she?) {it's obvious she doesn't}

b. Imperatives and exclamations

Commands and exclamations are usually conveyed by the extra low-fall, a falling tone beginning at the bottom of the speaker's range and ending below his usual lowest range, usually in creak. This nuclear tone is typically preceded by a low prehead and a falling head. The extra low-fall (which I transcribe here with the symbol ⇓ followed by a double final bracket) is commonly associated with meanings conveying "strong assertiveness":

(10)　　SAI daQUI!　　　(get out of here!)
　　　[⇑　　>⇓]]

(11)　　que DIa LINdo!　(what a beautiful day!)
　　　[　⇑　　>　⇓]]

c. Attitudinally marked patterns

A high-falling tone may be used in declaratives and in Q-word questions, but consistently conveys attitudinally marked overtones, as is typical of tones which are jumped *up* to. The tone is usually preceded by high level syllables:

(12)　　está a choVER outra VEZ　(it's raining again) {and I can't stand it}
　　　[　　　　↑　→ < ⇓]

(13)　　porque É que não DIzes o que PENsas?
　　　[　　↑　　　→　　< ⇓]

　　　　　(why don't you speak your mind?) {you're an idiot if you don't}

The high-fall may also occur with exclamations and commands, replacing the extra low-fall, for added emphasis. By its use, the speaker expresses impatience or even rudeness:

(14)　　SAI daQUI!!　　(get out of here!!) {I won't tell you again}
　　　[↑　< ⇓]

The high-fall may end at any level between mid and the bottom of the speaker's range. When it ends above the bottom level, it is similar to the "stylised fall" described by Ladd (1978) or to Jassem's (1952) "high-fall". When it ends at the bottom of the range, it is similar to Jassem's "full-fall". The high-fall may also end below the bottom level, as a creaky variety which is always emphatic and conveys an "aggressive" overtone, especially if preceded by an emphatic rising-falling head; this head pattern is composed of a series of successive falling glides or steps, each beginning on an accented syllable, and each on a higher level than the preceding one. For example:

(15)　　onde É que puSESte o meu caSAco?!
　　　[⇓ ↑　↓ ↑　↓　< ⇓]

　　　　　(where have you put my coat?) {I'm sick and tired of you misplacing it!}

Other attitudinal overtones are conveyed by a rising-falling tone, the only bidirectional nuclear tone in Portuguese. The rise-fall can occur with different sentence types, declarative, interrogative or exclamative, and is always attitudinally marked. In declaratives, the rise-fall is preceded by a high prehead and a rising head, in a sort of "stretched" mirror-image of the tone itself. The use of a rise-fall in statements implies some reservation on the part of the speaker regarding his utterance:

(16)   eu viVI na CHIna dez Anos.

    [⇑   ⇓   ↑ → >⇑⇓]

    (I lived in China for ten years) {though I never learned the language!}

The rise-fall may also convey surprise, or a patronising or even spiteful overtone, depending on the context. It is also the typical tone for "gossipy" talk. In questions, the rise-fall is preceded by high level syllables throughout the intonation group. Example:

(17)   tu SAbes quem É aquele TIpo?

    [↑   → > ⇑⇓]

    (do you know who that chap is?){he's the one who was jailed for bigamy}

2.3 Focalisation and contextual effects

In Portuguese, the nucleus typically corresponds to the word of highest informational content in the intonation group, that is, the word marking (the end of) the"new" information, or expressing a contrast of some sort.

Portuguese closely follows the principle of **end focus** (Quirk *et al.* 1972, p. 938) for the placement of the nucleus in the intonation group. Accordingly, the organisation of informational content within the intonation group is "given information + new information", in that order. Since the nucleus signals new information, the end focus principle means that the word of highest informational content tends to be placed at the end of the intonation group. In Portuguese, the rule is that the nucleus is always the last lexical item in the intonation group. Example (nucleus underlined):

(18)   eu prefiro que ela venha (I would prefer her to come)

Whereas in English, for example, the nucleus may be moved within the intonation group in instances of contrast or givenness (where the last lexical item corresponds to "given" information), Portuguese does not allow for nucleus movement. However, Portuguese seems to have greater mobility of word order than English, and this will allow the shifting of the "new" word to final position within the intonation group, where it can take the nuclear accent. For example, subject and verb may often change positions, to express meaning contrasts rendered by nucleus shift in English:

(19)   eu preFIro que ela VEnha (I would prefer her to come)

(20)   eu preFIro que venha Ela (I would prefer her to come)

or:

(21)   o foGÃO <u>avarIOU</u>-se   (the cooker broke down)

(22)   avarIOU-se o <u>foGÃO</u>

In (21), *fogão* (cooker) is "given", perhaps because it was recently bought and its breaking down is unexpected. Sentence (22) would be used if a few other things had been breaking down around the house, and the recent addition to the list were the cooker.

These examples show that in some cases it is difficult to speak of a "neutral" word order in purely syntactical terms, in Portuguese. Word order needs to be related to the information structure and organisation of utterances, and to be explained in terms of which word occurs in the nuclear position. It will relate to what precedes a particular sentence, thereby expressing the relevance of each sentence for that context. Out of context, we are of course unaware whether a certain word order is meant as contrastive or not. The same is true of an English sentence with "unmarked" nuclear placement like *John saw Mary*, which may be understood as having contrastive accent on *Mary* if it is a reply to *John saw Jane*, or as being "neutral" if it is a reply to *What happened?*. Contrastiveness is not a property of utterances themselves, but a descriptive label for the effect of sentences in their context, a description of how they are relevant to the context.

Alternative syntactic structures are in fact the commonest way of achieving prominence for emphatic or contrastive purposes in Portuguese. But freedom of word order has its limits, and intonational devices take over in cases where grammatical constraints forbid the shift of the nuclear word to final position in the utterance. In these cases, in Portuguese too, any word within an utterance with a given word order may be given prominence, and hence take the nucleus. However, the division of the utterance into intonation groups will be affected whenever the speaker wishes to accent one item which would not be the last one. The utterance is broken up into two intonation groups, in order to place the accented item in final position within the first one, thus complying with the fixed nucleus rule. Supposing that the speaker wishes to emphasise the word *prefiro* in the sentence *eu prefiro que ela venha*, his utterance may be:

(23)   eu <u>preFIro</u> / que ela <u>VEnha</u>

where an intonation group boundary is provided after the emphasised word, so that an otherwise "non-final nucleus" will not occur.

2.4 Phrasing and textual organisation

Utterances are divided into intonation groups. Formally, and internally, each intonation group is defined by the presence of a nucleus. Externally, the intonation group is defined by the presence of one or both of the following rhythmical elements: (i) **pause**, occurring at the beginning and end of the intonation group; (ii) **anacrusis**, occurring at the beginning of the intonation group. The anacrusis comprehends the sequence of weak syllables preceding the first accented syllable in the intonation group. These syllables are pronounced very rapidly and out of the rhythmical beat of the utterance. Example (where underlining indicates the anacrusis and / indicates pause:

(24)   então ela coMEU a gaLInha / e dePOIS comeu um BOlo

   (then she ate the chicken, and afterwards she ate a pastry)

Semantically, each intonation group corresponds to a unit of information, usually a "clause". The speaker will divide his utterance into as many intonation groups as the number and type of information units he wishes to convey, as in (24). Moreover, it is possible to construct minimal pairs differing in number of intonation groups only, reflecting different syntactic organisations and relations:

(25)   ela coMEU a gaLInha (she ate the chicken)

(26)   ela coMEU / a gaLInha (it ate, the chicken)

where a separate intonation group marks the second noun phrase *a galinha* as an apposed subject and not a direct object; or:

(27)   ela acorDOU e vesTIU o FIlho (she woke her son up and dressed him)

(28)   ela acorDOU / e vesTIU o FIlho (she awoke, and dressed her son)

where the two intonation groups indicate two coordinated sentences and not two coordinated verbs.

Other constituents apart from the clause may be given separate intonation groups, principally for grammatical reasons. These include adverbs which are sentence modifiers, and non-restrictive post-modifiers of the noun phrase.

2.5 Other patterns

a. Continuation
The low-rise is the typical tone to mark continuation or incompleteness, signalling that the utterance is not finished. Example:

(29)

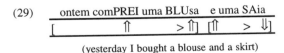

   (yesterday I bought a blouse and a skirt)

b. Stereotyped patterns

In this section, I will not go into detail on the more "local" or specific uses of intonation in Portuguese. To quote but two examples, intonation distinguishes the alternative meanings in the pairs:

(30) <u>eu não fui ao MÉdico por esTAR doENte</u>
[⇑   →   >   ⇓]

(I couldn't go to the doctor, because I was ill)

(31) <u>eu não fui ao MÉdico por esTAR doENte</u>
[⇑   ⇓   ↑   >   ⇑ ⇓]

(I went to the doctor, but not because I was ill)

and the contrast low-fall/high-fall distinguishes the pair

(32) <u>eu SEMpre aCHEI que Ele VInha</u> (I always thought he'd come) {and so he did}
[⇑   >   >   < ⇓]

(33) <u>eu SEMpre aCHEI que Ele VInha</u> (I always thought he'd come) {but he didn't}
[⇑   >   >   < ⇓]

c. Pre-nuclear patterns

Pre-nuclear patterns in Portuguese, about which little is known, will be described only briefly.

Portuguese has four simple heads:

- **high head** – mid/high level throughout;

- **low head** – low level throughout;

- **falling head** – starts high, goes to mid;

- **rising head** – starts low, goes to mid.

Cf. also the complex rising-falling head mentioned in example (15) above.

There are two preheads in Portuguese:

- **high prehead** – high level throughout, or falling pitch from high to mid;

- **low prehead** – low level throughout, or rising pitch from low to mid.

3. Comparisons with other systems

Moraes (this volume) provides a description of the intonation of Brazilian Portuguese. For a more detailed comparison of the intonation systems of European Portuguese and British English see Cruz-Ferreira (1985).

4. Conclusions

a. Pre-nuclear patterns

There are to date no detailed data either on possibilities of co-occurrence of pre-nuclear patterns and nucleus or on the different meanings possibly conveyed by different combinations of the same nuclear tone with alternative pre-nuclear patterns. However, the available data do indicate that, where prehead and head occur in one intonation group, the prehead will show a contrasting shape to that of the head, either as to pitch height or as to pitch direction of the head pattern.

The exceptions to the typically dissimilar sequencing of prehead and head occur in questions, where the pre-nuclear pitch is high throughout, whether in yes/no questions or in Q-word questions (see §§2.1. and 2.2. above).

b. Nuclear tones

For the description of the nuclear tones in European Portuguese it was assumed that there are two basic types of nuclear pitch movement, corresponding to two different sets of meanings:

- **falling tones** – conveying meanings of statement, finality and/or certainty, that is, a "closed" set of meanings;

- **rising tones** – conveying meanings of interrogation, doubt and/or hesitation/continuation, that is, an "open" set of meanings.

For a discussion of closed/open meanings associated with falls *versus* rises, see Cruttenden (1981), and for discussion of falls *versus* rises as linguistic universals, see Bolinger (1978b).

To conclude, the following set of tables summarises the formal characteristics of the nuclear tones of Portuguese.

i. Nuclear falling tones. The three simple falling tones are:

High-fall	**Low-fall**	**Extra low-fall**
[...< ⇓]	[... > ⇓]	[... > ⇓]]
jumped *up* to	usually jumped *down* to	jumped *down* to
starts high	starts (mid) low	starts at bottom of range
ends (mid) low or at bottom of range	ends at bottom of range	ends below lower range
may have creaky end	usually has no creak	usually has creaky end

The only bidirectional tone in Portuguese is the:

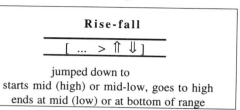

Rise-fall

[... > ⇑ ⇓]

jumped down to
starts mid (high) or mid-low, goes to high
ends at mid (low) or at bottom of range

ii. Nuclear rising tones. Portuguese has two simple rising tones:

Low-rise	High-rise
[... > ⇑]	[... < ⇑]
jumped *down* to	jumped *up* to
starts rather low	starts (mid) high
ends at mid, often at high	ends at top of range

10

Intonation in Brazilian Portuguese

JOÃO ANTÔNIO DE MORAES

1. Background

Portuguese is one of the ten most widely spoken languages in the world, being spoken by some 200 million people, 160 million of whom live in Brazil. The other Portuguese-speaking nations are Portugal, Angola, Mozambique, Guinea-Bissau and Cabo Verde. A comprehensive description of the functioning of its suprasegmental phenomena has yet, however, to be undertaken. Most existing works on Brazilian Portuguese deal with specific aspects of prosody, especially with modal intonation (Aubert and Hochgreb 1981, Hochgreb 1983; Moraes 1984, 1991; Gebara 1976) and word stress (Fernandes 1976; Moraes 1987, 1995a, 1995b; Leite 1974; Costa 1978). Researchers have focused very little attention on the interface between prosody and such areas as syntax, information organisation, or conversation analysis.

This chapter is an attempt to provide a panoramic view of the prosody of Brazilian Portuguese. I will rely chiefly on previously published or unpublished data which I have analysed instrumentally,[1] supplemented with observations made by other authors. In addition to presenting melodic contours of some of the examples, a phonological interpretation is also given, transcribed using INTSINT (Hirst and Di Cristo, this volume).

1.1 General prosodic characteristics

a. Stress

In Brazilian Portuguese, acoustic correlates of lexical stress vary as a function of a word's position in an utterance and, less significantly, as a function of the word's stress pattern. When a word is found in a weak position (*i.e.*, inside a prosodic group), stress prominence is expressed as a combination of intensity and duration (cf. fig. 1). Intensity behaves differently from duration, however, dropping off on the post-tonic rather than increasing on the tonic syllable. It is also worth noting that when an oxytone is found in a weak position, there will be no explicit acoustic stress cue. This means that when a sequence of syllables inside a prosodic group is uttered with one constant prosodic weight, stress is perceived as falling on the final syllable. In a strong position (*i.e.*, at the end of a prosodic group), where phrase or sentence level accent is superimposed on lexical stress, fundamental frequency joins duration and intensity as a stress cue (cf. fig. 2).

Fundamental frequency is indeed the correlate par excellence of phrase or sentence accent but it also indirectly provides a further cue of lexical stress in a strong position, since there is necessarily a movement in pitch on the stressed syllable of the accented word. The shape of the pitch contour on this syllable varies according to the intonation pattern of the utterance. For further details on the acoustic projection of stress/accent in Brazilian Portuguese see Moraes

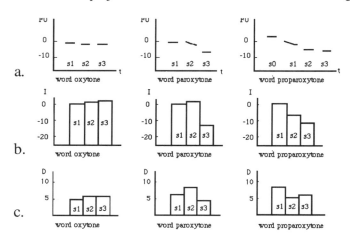

Figure 1. Acoustic correlates of lexical stress inside theme of a statement: (a) F_0 in quarter tones; (b) intensity [I] in decibels; and (c) duration [D] of vowels in centiseconds. Values were obtained using sentences that contained a nonsense word *pipipi* in the location where manifestation of stress was investigated. sl, s2, and s3 represent first, second, and third syllables of word. In the proparoxytone pattern, s0 represents the last syllable of the word that immediately precedes sl.

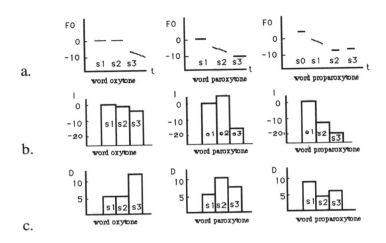

Figure 2. Acoustic correlates of lexical stress at end of a statement: (a) F_0 in quarter tones; (b) intensity [I] in decibels; and (c) duration [D] of vowels in centiseconds (see figure 1).

(1987, 1995b); in European Portuguese see Delgado-Martins (1982).

Results of perceptual tests involving localisation of the stressed syllable in synthesised nonsense words in fact strongly suggest that in the final position of the utterance F_0 is a more effective mark of stress than duration, which in turn is a more effective mark than intensity (Moraes and Espesser 1988).

We have so far been looking at primary word stress. Pretonic syllables, however, do not all receive the same prosodic prominence. In addition to the primary stress (') which falls on one of the final three syllables of a word, a secondary stress (ˋ) is observed over pretonic syllables. In Brazilian Portuguese this secondary stress is governed by a rule of rhythmic alternation of strong (S) and weak (W) syllables, counted from right to left starting from the final tonic:

(1) a   a ˋpro xi 'mar   but   b   ˋa pro ˋxi ma 'ção
        W S W S   S W S W S

Perceived as early as 1895 by Said Ali, this rhythmic alternation often extends beyond the boundaries of a single word, influencing the stress pattern of a prosodic group (PG) consisting of more than one word. As Oliveira (1989) has pointed out, this may prompt a shift in primary stress in the word(s) preceding the final word in the prosodic group, so that two stressed (left shift) or even two unstressed (right shift) syllables will not occur contiguously:

(2) a   **left shift**   Je 'sus, 'Cris to → ˋJe sus 'Cris to
                          W S   S W   S W   S W

João Antônio de Moraes

b   **right shift**   'on tem, ce 'di nho → on `tem ce 'di nho
                        S W W S W   W S W S W

b. Accent

Although one of the syllables of any word with two or more syllables will necessarily be more prominent, only some stressed syllables will effectively be perceived as accented at utterance level. For example, when an utterance like:

(3)   Ele saiu de casa porque teve um compromisso.
       (he left the house because he had an appointment.)

is stated as a reply to the question *Por que Pedro saiu de casa?* (Why did Peter leave the house?), accents will occur on *CAsa*, *TEve*, and *comproMIsso*. In:

(4)   Ele saiu de casa ontem porque teve um compromisso.
       (he left the house yesterday because he had an appointment.)

uttered in response to *Por que Pedro saiu de casa ontem?* (Why did Peter leave the house yesterday?), the first accent is shifted to *ONtem*.

Phrase and sentence accents act at a higher level than word stress, indicating that the elements dominated by one accent present greater syntactic cohesion. Accent is superimposed on lexical stress since the accented syllable coincides with a stressed syllable of a word. Conversely, an unstressed syllable cannot be accented within an utterance, except as a metalinguistic tool, to emphasise an unstressed morpheme for example:

(5)   Ele falou em IMportar, não em EXportar.
       (He was talking about importing, not about exporting.)

Contrast between stressed and unstressed syllables is irrelevant in monosyllabic words, which will receive an accent depending on whether or not they occur at the end of a prosodic group. Some grammatical particles traditionally classified as atonic, or unaccented – such as *de* (of, from); *por* (by, for); *para* (to, for) as opposed to tonic words such as *dê* (give); *pôr* (to put); *pára* (stops) – owe this atonicity not to any intrinsic characteristic but to their role as links between other words in an utterance, marking their grammatical relationship, and this role does not allow them to appear at the end of a syntactic unit. In a metalinguistic context where they can occupy such a position, however, these particles will gain an accent:

(6)   Você disse DE ou PAra? (Did you say FROM or TO/FOR?)

As stated previously, phrase or sentence accent is expressed by a variation in pitch on the accented syllable. The shape of the pitch contour on this syllable varies according to the intonation pattern of the utterance.

182

c. Rhythm

In standard Brazilian Portuguese, switching from a stress rhythm to a syllable rhythm on a certain word (usually accompanied by a ritardando) is used as a device to emphasise that word. It is in the realm of phonostylistic, indexical functions, however, that rhythmic shifts play their most evident role. These rhythmic alterations, which may lean more towards either syllable-timing or a stress-timing, can provide us with information about the speaker's geographical roots (Southern Brazilians, for example, tend more towards a syllable-timed rhythm (Cagliari 1982)) or indicate the use of a certain register (Major 1985) or even of a specific vocal style. A good example of this is the effeminate style, where an exaggerated lengthening of accented syllables as compared to standard Portuguese is offset by an exaggerated shortening of unaccented syllables, creating a very specific stress rhythm characterised by sharp contrasts between the duration of accented and unaccented syllables (Moraes 1998a).

2. Description of intonation patterns

2.1 Basic non-emphatic pattern

In Portuguese, as in most known languages, the neutral declarative pattern is characterised by a drop in fundamental frequency (F_0) at the end of the utterance (more precisely, on the final tonic) while the initial pitch is at a mid level. Therefore, in an utterance such as:

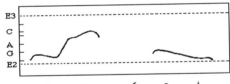

Figure 3. F_0 contour for the declarative sentence *Já foi*. (He has already left)

(7)   Já FOI   ([he] has already left)
       [⇒   ⇓]

in answer to the question *E o José?* (And what about José?), the mid level falls on the first syllable *já* while the drop occurs on the following syllable *foi* (fig. 3). In the case of a monosyllabic utterance such as *Foi*. ([He] has left) in answer to *Ele já foi?* (Has he already left?), the pattern /M L/ is compressed into a single syllable, as can be seen in figure 4.

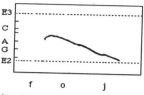

Figure 4. F_0 contour for the declarative sentence *Foi.* (He has left.)

In longer utterances there is a kind of overall behaviour, responsible for the moderate continuous drop in pitch over the entire sentence and especially over the unstressed syllables (that is, the declination line; cf. fig. 5).

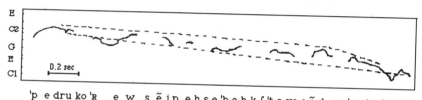

'p e dru ko 'ʀ   e w   s ẽ j p e h s e 'b e h k ʃ 't a v a s ẽ d s e 'g i d u

Figure 5. F_0 contour for the declarative sentence *Pedro correu sem perceber que estava sendo seguido.* (Pedro ran without realising that he was being followed) showing declination. Topline connects accented syllables; baseline, unaccented syllables.

2.2 Modality

a. Interrogative patterns

Although word order or grammatical particles may at times serve this purpose, intonation is the chief question-signalling device in Portuguese (Hochgreb 1983; Moraes 1984). Like the great majority of languages whose intonation patterns have been described (Hermann 1942; Bolinger 1964a, 1978), average pitches are higher for interrogatives than for declaratives in Portuguese. The shape of the interrogative melodic contour depends basically on the question's underlying logical structure. The yes/no question displays a pitch rise on the last accented syllable:

(8)   Ele FOI lá HOje? (Did he go there today?)

In addition to this characteristic final tonic – a melodic pattern which is clearly the opposite of that of a declarative statement both in terms of melodic level (H *vs.* L) and in terms of shape (ascending *vs.* descending) – two other contrasts in the intonational patterns of these two modalities should be mentioned: a) the initial pitch of the yes/no question is slightly higher than in the case of a declarative; b) on the other hand, the final pretonic of a yes/no

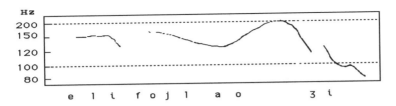

Figure 6. F_0 contour for the yes/no question *Ele foi lá hoje?* (Did he go there today?)

question is lower than the final pretonic of a declarative, thus creating a greater contrast with the final tonic.

While descending in a question, any existing post-tonic syllable(s) will be even lower in a declarative.

Although such melodic markers on the initial and pretonic syllables may at times serve to anticipate the modality of the utterance before it has been completely uttered (Fónagy and Galvagny 1974, Fónagy 1981a), speech synthesis experiments show that it is over the final tonic that the opposition between these two patterns is effectively manifested (Moraes 1984). In tests of sentence-modality perception using synthesised variants, where only the melodic levels of the final tonics (cf. fig. 7) were varied, results indicated that:

a) oppositions in modal intonation are effectively located at precise points along the utterance (key syllables) rather than over the entire utterance,

b) the interpretation of sentence modality changes at a certain, perfectly definable point along the continuum of height levels.

It was also noted that in the interpretation of sentence modality it is not pertinent whether the shape of the intrasyllabic melodic contour is ascending or descending, meaning that this feature should be seen as redundant. When there is a rise in pitch on the final tonic of a sentence but the average melodic level of this syllable remains low, the utterance will be perceived as a declarative; inversely, when the pitch of the final tonic falls but the average melodic level of this syllable remains high, the sentence will be interpreted as a yes/no question.

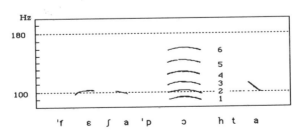

Figure 7. F_0 contours for six synthesised variants of the sentence *Fecha a porta* (Close the door).

Figure 7 shows six synthesised variants of the modality-ambiguous sentence *Fecha a porta* (Close the door), which can be interpreted as a declarative, order, request, yes/no question or request for confirmation, *etc.* The melodic level of the final tonic was modified in one-tone steps and this syllable was given a slightly convex pitch contour, intermediary between the contour of a declarative and that of an interrogative.

Results (fig. 8) show that stimuli 1 and 2 were not perceived by any of the listeners as questions but were interpreted by 75% and 67%, respectively, as declaratives, the remainder having chosen the option "Neither is correct." The threshold for a reversal of the interpretation lies between stimuli 2 and 3: from 3 on, the stimuli are interpreted as questions by 67% of listeners.

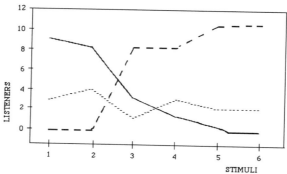

Figure 8. Interpretation of six synthesised stimuli shown in figure 7 by twelve listeners (statement = solid line; yes/no question = dashed line; other = dotted line).

In order to investigate the melodic importance of the pretonic syllable, I synthesised two utterances: a declarative statement using a lowered pretonic (typical of a yes/no question) and, inversely, a yes/no question using a raised pretonic syllable (typical of a declarative). The interrogative displaying a declarative pretonic was interpreted as a yes/no question by 94% of the listeners, and the declarative displaying an interrogative pretonic was interpreted by precisely 50% as a declarative and by the other 50% as a yes/no question. However, the significant number of affective attitudes attributed to the latter utterance, including confirmation, ambiguity, indecision, *etc.*, suggests that the pretonic has a relevant role in the area of expressivity.

In the WH-question which begins with a question word, the rise occurs on the first accented syllable of the utterance:

(9)   QUANdo você SOUbe? (When did you find out?)
     [⇑   >   ⇓   ]

When the interrogative particle is placed at the end of an utterance, however, there is a rise in pitch on the accented syllable immediately preceding it:

(10)   Você SOUbe QUANdo? (You found out when?)
     [⇑ >   ⇓]

This same pattern is used in alternative questions. Here, a higher pitch rise on the accented syllable preceding the alternative particle "ou" tells us the utterance is a question and not a statement:

(11)   Ele quer DOce ou FRUta? (Does he want sweets or fruit?)
     [⇑ >   ⇓]

Figure 9 shows the ambiguous utterance *Como doce ou fruta,* interpretable as either (I eat sweets or fruit) or (Just like sweets or fruit) expressed as yes/no, wh- and alternative questions.

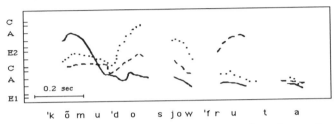

'k õ m u 'd o   s j o w 'f r u   t   a

Figure 9. Superimposition of F_0 contours for ambiguous utterance *Como doce ou fruta* expressed as a yes/no question (dashed line); WH-question (solid line); and alternative question (dotted line).

Although there are a large number of variations of interrogative patterns, one deserves closer attention because of the frequency with which it is observed: the double-rise pattern in a yes/no question, where the first rise occurs on the first accented syllable and the second, slighter one on the final accented syllable. This pattern appears in many different situations, including rhetorical yes/no questions, questions introduced with *Será que* (I wonder / Do you think), and requests:

(12)   SeRÁ que vai choVER? (I wonder if it will rain?)
     [⇑   >   ↑↓]

The double rise is also the yes/no question pattern most often used to begin a dialogue, where the entire question is being presented to the listener as new information.

b. Illocutionary acts and intonation
In addition to distinguishing between statements and different types of questions, intonation is heavily relied on to distinguish directives (Searle 1976). Intonation alone will tell us whether a specific locutionary act such as:

(13)   Fecha a porta (Close the door)

should be interpreted as a command, request, suggestion, piece of advice, threat, *etc.* Command, request, and suggestion contours for this utterance are superimposed in figure 10.

'f ɛ ʃ a 'p ɔ h t a

Figure 10. Superimposition of F_0 contours for the utterance *Fecha a porta* (Close the door) expressed as command (solid line), request (dotted line) and suggestion (dashed line).

2.3 Focalisation and contextual effects

a. Message articulation in theme-rheme

Like many other languages, Portuguese uses intonation to segment the discursive continuum into "information units" and to indicate whether this information is new or given.

This means intonation allows us to distinguish between theme, information already present in the listener's conscious mind, and rheme, new information. This is especially true when theme repeats information already explicitly present in the preceding context.

Rheme is melodically characterised by pitch movement on the final accented syllable – a fall in the case of a declarative sentence and a rise in the case of a yes/no question. The theme's melodic pattern varies according to its position in the utterance. When theme precedes rheme, its melodic pattern will contrast with that of the rheme: there is a rise on the final accented syllable in a statement and a fall-ending in yes/no questions. When theme follows rheme, it reproduces the pitch pattern of the preceding rheme, falling in a statement and rising in a yes/no question. These four possibilities are illustrated below:

(14) a – O que foi mesmo que o Pedro escondeu? (What exactly was it Pedro hid?)
   – O PEdro esconDEU   a pesseGAda. (Pedro hid the peach preserves.)

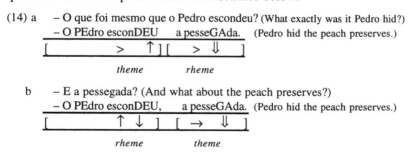

b – E a pessegada? (And what about the peach preserves?)
   – O PEdro esconDEU,   a pesseGAda. (Pedro hid the peach preserves.)

c   – O Pedro escondeu alguma coisa. (Pedro hid something.)
    – O PEdro esconDEU   a pesseGAda? (Did Pedro hide ... ?

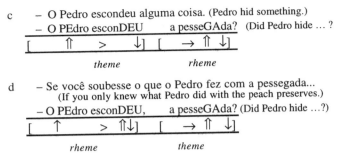

d   – Se você soubesse o que o Pedro fez com a pessegada...
        (If you only knew what Pedro did with the peach preserves.)
    – O PEdro esconDEU,   a pesseGAda? (Did Pedro hide ...?)

Certain classic examples of the use of intonation to distinguish grammatical functions (*e.g.*, subordinate *vs.* coordinate clauses) must in fact constitute examples of different organisations of information in theme and rheme. In a utterance such as *Ele saiu logo porque tinha muito o que fazer* (He left right away because he had a lot to do), for example, the intonation (or pause) pattern of the utterance usually determines whether the clause *porque tinha muito o que fazer* is interpreted as a subordinate adverbial clause or a coordinate explanatory clause. However, these examples would in fact be used in context to reply to two distinct questions, each implying a different organisation of the information:

(15) a   – Por que ele saiu logo?
        – Ele saiu LOgo porque tinha MUIto o que faZER.

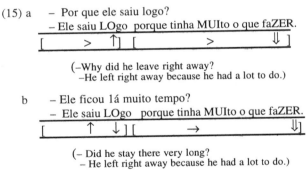

        (–Why did he leave right away?
        –He left right away because he had a lot to do.)

b   – Ele ficou lá muito tempo?
        – Ele saiu LOgo porque tinha MUIto o que faZER.

        (– Did he stay there very long?
        – He left right away because he had a lot to do.)

The order of the information is neutral in 15a: given: *ele saiu logo* / new: *porque tinha muito o que fazer*. In 15b, however, it is the main clause which contains the most important information while the clause beginning *porque* contains supplementary information.

Similarly, and as also occurs in French and in English, an utterance such as *Eu não fui a sua casa porque estava chovendo* (I didn't go to your house because it was raining) – negation in the main clause plus an adverbial clause of reason – is subject to two possible interpretations, depending on the informational structure indicated by the intonation pattern.

(16) a   – Por que você não passou lá em casa?

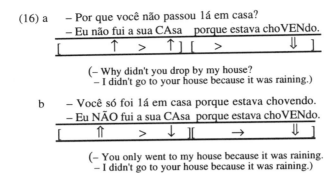

(– Why didn't you drop by my house?
– I didn't go to your house because it was raining.)

b   – Você só foi lá em casa porque estava chovendo.

(– You only went to my house because it was raining.
– I didn't go to your house because it was raining.)

The order of the information is neutral in reply (16a) – theme *eu não fui a sua casa* / rheme *porque estava chovendo* – and we can tell that the second speaker didn't go to the first one's house. In (16b), the speaker is contesting a preceding statement. Since the negative particle *não* stands out from the rest of the utterance, the prosody tells us that it constitutes the new information (rheme) and that the rest is redundant, conveying the meaning I went to your house but not because it was raining.

b. Emphasis for contrast

The intonational characterisation of new information should not be confused with the prosodic prominence that a certain word will receive in an utterance which contests a previous statement with the intent of correcting it. In the latter situation, the new element being introduced will have a particular prosodic pattern, characterising the phenomenon known as emphasis for contrast:

(17)   – Ele cumprimentou a garota de branco. (He greeted the girl in white.)

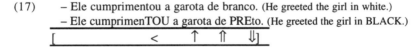

The prosodic profile of utterances which present emphasis for contrast can be summarised as follows:

a) the stressed syllable of the emphasised word is uttered at low pitch.
b) the pitch of the syllable immediately preceding the stressed syllable is high (whether the former is stressed or not), thus producing a contrast between the pitch of the stressed syllable and the preceding one.
c) the pitch pattern of that part of the utterance which precedes the accented word is the same as that of a neutral declarative, while whatever follows the point of emphasis is uttered at a parenthetic low tone.
d) the stressed syllable of the accented word also displays greater intensity and duration.

When an expression longer than one word is contrasted with a single word in the original utterance, pitch will rise on the stressed syllable of the word preceding this expression and will remain high until reaching the stressed syllable of the last word of the expression being emphasised. Compare the melodic patterns of utterances 17 and 18:

(18)   Ele cumprimentou aquela senhora. (He greeted that lady.)
         Ele cumprimenTOU a garota de PREto. (He greeted the girl in black.)

         [> ⇑   →   ⇓]

2.4 Phrasing and textual organisation

The syntactic organisation of a sentence is prosodically expressed through the location of phrase or sentence accents, which allow the utterance to be segmented into prosodic groups. The placement of accents is sufficient to distinguish between:

(19)   A profeSSOra de prosódia brasiLEIra. (The professor of Brazilian prosody)

and:

(20)   A professora de proSÓdia brasiLEIra. (The Brazilian professor of prosody)

In more complex structures, where the length of constituents determines the existence and location of some accents, the relative amplitude of pitch variations provides information on the degree of cohesion between elements of the utterance. Compare the following two examples:

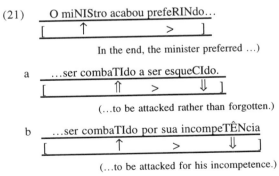

(21)   O miNIStro acabou prefeRINdo...
         [↑   >   ]
             In the end, the minister preferred ...)

a   ...ser combaTIdo a ser esqueCIdo.
      [⇑   >   ⇓]
             (...to be attacked rather than forgotten.)

b   ...ser combaTIdo por sua incompeTÊNcia
      [↑   >   ⇓]
             (...to be attacked for his incompetence.)

Although their accentual patterns are alike, the melodic patterns of these two utterances differ. The amplitude of the pitch variation on *ser combaTIdo* is greater in (21a) than in (21b), indicating that in (21a) the subsequent constituent belongs to a higher level.

3. Dialectal variation

The prosody of Brazilian Portuguese differs greatly from that of European Portuguese both in terms of rhythmic aspects as well as in terms of some of its basic intonational patterns.

a. Rhythmic characteristics

Depending on the application of phonological rules that may vary from dialect to dialect, Brazilian Portuguese sustains, raises (*e.g.* e → i), or lowers (e → ɛ) pretonic middle vowels (Bisol 1981; Silva 1989). However they are never dropped, contrary to what so often occurs in European Portuguese which is interpreted by Brazilians as faster speech. A word such as *prescreveu* /preʃkre'vew/ may be uttered as [prʃkr'vew] in Portugal,[2] something which would never occur in Brazil. This increased "speed" in fact occurs to a greater extent at the phonological level than at a phonetic level. In other words, we can safely refer to the "faster speech" of European Portuguese if we consider the number of phonological syllables underlying the pronounced words instead of considering the number of syllables effectively uttered in a given lapse of time. For what is really observed (as in fast, casual Brazilian Portuguese) is more a reduction in the number of syllables pronounced through processes such as haplology, apocope, *etc.*, than a real reduction in their duration (Moraes and Leite 1989).

b. Intonation patterns

As far as intonation itself is concerned, the most notable difference between the two systems lies in the most prevalent form for production of a yes/no question, in Portugal characterised by a high initial pitch sustained through the pretonic syllable with a fall to a low level on the final tonic and a rise on the post-tonic(s), or on the final part of the tonic if no post-tonics are present (cf. the pattern "high prehead + high head + low-rise nuclear tone" in Cruz-Ferreira, this volume). The variant used in Portugal could be transcribed as:

(22)   A meNIna já SAbe? (Does the girl already know?).
         [⇑   ⇓ ↑]

What we have here is a melodic pattern whose ending is exactly[3] the opposite of the Brazilian pattern, where F_0 rises on the final tonic and drops on the post-tonic:

(23)   A meNIna já SAbe?
         [↑   > ⇑↓]

There is a second quite apparent distinction between Brazilian Portuguese and European Portuguese, this time involving use rather than form. European Portuguese frequently makes use of a pattern characterised by a high pretonic and a mid-level final tonic (cf. the "rise-fall nuclear tone" in Cruz-Ferreira, this volume). Although this is not exclusive of the European variety of Portuguese, its usage there is much more prevalent than in Brazil, where this pattern is interpreted as distinctly attitudinal (probably because it is used to express a smaller range of attitudes than in Portugal) and implies that what is being said is perfectly obvious:

(24)   Quem te ensinou isso? (who taught you this ?)
        O profeSSOR de mateMAtica. (the maths teacher)
        [↑ > ↓]

4. Concluding remarks

I would like to conclude this overview of intonation in Brazilian Portuguese by emphasising that prosodic markers act concomitantly on different levels. While from a more abstract, phonological angle it is possible, and indeed desirable, to isolate the correlates of different prosodic categories, such markers are superimposed during actual speech itself so that the acoustic correlate of an upper-level phenomenon – for example, type of sentence (declarative, interrogative) – indicates both the end of a syntactic-informational unit as well as the location of the word's tonic syllable.

Thus, lexical stress is basically manifested through the conjunction of the parameters duration and intensity. The grouping of words into syntactical informational units is expressed phonetically by the prosodic groups formally defined by phrase or sentence accents. Accent, located on the lexical item farthest to the right in the prosodic group (more precisely, on the tonic syllable), has as its physical correlate pitch, which thus comes to constitute a supplementary indication of the acoustic projection of lexical stress in this context. Lastly, it is the melodic level on certain syllables of the sentence, and especially on the final tonic, which will define whether the utterance is a declarative or an interrogative, for example, or if the information conveyed is presented by the speaker as given, new, contrastive, *etc.*

I would again like to stress that studies on prosody in Portuguese are recent and that not even introductory work has been conducted yet in many areas. In filling in the most apparent gaps of knowledge, I believe that priority should be placed on these areas of study:
a) the prosodic behaviour of segments that express different classes of information units (new, old, given, secondary, contrastive, corrective information, *etc.*) in spontaneous discourse and the resolution of any conflicts between syntactic structure and the organisation of the message.

b) the participation of prosody in conversational interaction and, more specifically, its correlation with phenomena such as turn-taking, change of discursive topic, *etc.*

c) prosodic modifications which result from expressivity (emotions and attitudes).

These are areas where – through prosodic variations at certain points in the speech chain, delimiting chunks of the discourse, or through the assignment of one of various possible prosodic profiles to a given segment – intonation participates actively in the construction of the meaning of the text.

Notes

1 The pitch contours were obtained at the phonetics laboratories of the universities of Paris III (Jean Perrot, Director) and of Lund (Gösta Bruce, Director). The analysed material consisted of read speech. Synthesised speech experiments were conducted at laboratories of the universities of Uppsala (Sven Öhman, Director) and of Aix-en-Provence (Mario Rossi, Director). I am grateful to the directors of these labs.

2 Example suggested by Maria H. Mira Mateus.

3 It should be mentioned that in the Portuguese dialect of Northeastern Brazil the common melodic profile of a yes/no question is closer to the European pattern.

11

Intonation in French

ALBERT DI CRISTO

1. Background

French, which belongs to the Romance family of Indo-European languages, is spoken (according to the "Ministère de la Francophonie") by about 140 million people in the world. Nearly 60 million of these are located in France, where a dozen dialects ("parlers regionaux") are numbered (Carton *et al.* 1983).

This chapter deals with the description of the intonation system of **General French** which can be considered equivalent to Received Pronunciation for British English or to General American for American English. General French is characterised by the absence of dialectal marks and is mainly used by educated people as well as by professional radio and television speakers.

French prosody has up to the present been the object of numerous studies, most of which are mainly concerned with particular aspects such as emphatic stress, the intonation of questions and/or continuations, rhythmic patterns and pauses (for a comprehensive study of pauses in French, see Grosjean and Deschamps 1972; Duez 1987; Guaïtella 1991). Some studies, however, present a more general account of the system as a whole (Coustenoble and Armstrong 1934; Zwanenburg 1964; Delattre 1966a, 1967; Kenning 1979, 1983; Leach 1980, 1989; Rossi *et al.* 1981).

Traditional studies of French intonation are to some extent of a descriptive nature and many of them can be considered examples of the "concrete approach", as defined by Ladd and Cutler (1983). Attempts have, however, been made to develop phonological descriptions of French intonation (Martin 1975, 1981; Crompton 1978; Hirst and Di Cristo 1984, 1986; Nicaise 1987; Mertens 1987).

1.1 General prosodic characteristics: stress and rhythm

a. Final (primary) stress

French is usually described as a language with **fixed stress**. The lexical representation in French thus includes neither tonal segments (as in tone languages), nor metrical structure (as in languages with free word stress). This follows from the fact that on the lexical level, French stress, in contrast with other Romance languages, is not distinctive either for words or for morphemes and that moreover this generalisation is completely exceptionless.

Most traditional prosodic studies agree that French has a single rhythmic stress (also called: logical, objective, tonic, normal, or internal stress) regularly assigned to the final full syllable (*i.e.* not containing a schwa) of the last lexical item of a **stress group**. Following Garde (1968), we can assume that stress placement in French is based on three elementary principles. A principle of *accentogénéité* (stressability) selects lexical items (generally content words) that are stressable; a grouping principle specifies that a stress group is constituted by a stressable word and by adjacent pro/en-clitics governed by it; a right-heading principle assigns stress to the last full syllable of the construction so formed. The last two principles explain why clitics, which are not usually stressable, can occasionally be stressed in French, as in the following where stress is shown by capitals, intonation unit boundaries by ([...]) and stress group boundaries within an intonation unit by (|).

(1) a   [Crois TU | que c'est BIEN?]   b   [Dis LE | a ton jeune FILS]
        (Do you think it's all right?)   (Tell it to your young son)

It has often been claimed that the stress group in French does not always correspond to one single lexical item, but may comprise several, only the last of which carries stress on its final full syllable.

(2) a |La majeure parTIE | b | Le petit gars BRUN |
        (the greater part)   (the little dark-haired lad)

This means that the final rhythmic (or primary) stress tends to give rise to a **phrasal stress** (Grammont 1933; Nyrop 1955; Marouzeau 1956; Sten 1963; Garde 1968), the main function of which is the grouping together of lexical items bearing close syntactical and/or semantic relations into a single stress group. As with many languages, it has been suggested that there is in French a close link between syntactic structure and stress patterning. Thus Martin (1979) proposes stress rules based on dependency relationships, while according to Dell (1984) the stress pattern of a phrase or a sentence is determined by its surface constituent structure. Dell suggests that each word in French contains an accent whose force is proportional to the strength of the following syntactic boundary as in the example.[1]

(3)   Un marCHAND d'éTOFFES naTIF de PaRIS (A cloth merchant native to Paris)
          3   2   3   1

where the numbers 1...3 represent relative degrees of stress from the strongest downwards. Similar principles of analysis are to be found in Martin (1977, 1981) and Rossi (1980).

All these authors, however, admit that syntactic criteria are not by themselves sufficient to account exhaustively for stress patterns in French. Thus Dell (1984), building on the notions of metrical grid and stress clash, invokes a general principle of **eurhythmicity**, independent of syntactic structure, which tends to favour stress alternations in order to avoid the production of rhythmically unbalanced utterances. A similar idea has been developed by Martin (1986) who proposes a formula to calculate an "index of disrhythmicity" making it possible to generate well-formed rhythmic structures even when they are in conflict with the syntactic ones.

To conclude with final (primary) stress, it has been claimed that its syntactic determination leads to a syncretism between stress and intonation, since the final syllable of the stress group is also the point where the pitch contour will be realised when the stress group is final in the intonation unit. This syncretism, together with the non-distinctive character of stress in French, has led some authors (Hjelmslev 1936–1937; Togeby 1965; Pilch 1972) to take the extreme view that French is a **language without stress** (for recent discussion of this issue cf. Rossi 1980). Vaissière (1991) argues that, compared to English, French seems to be more a "boundary language" than a true "stress language".

b. Non-final (secondary) stress

Besides the obligatory final primary stress, French also possesses an optional non-final **secondary** stress. Not all authors agree on the distribution of this secondary stress, however. Fónagy (1979a) attributes to it a **probabilistic** character, suggesting that French stress is at present in a period of transition (cf. also: Fónagy and Fónagy 1976; Fónagy 1989). Verluyten (1984) maintains that the underlying rhythm of French words (not counting word-final schwa) is based on alternating weak (**w**) and strong (**s**) syllables. So, the basic stress pattern of French words is with **antepenultimate** secondary stress (cf. Mazaleyrat 1974). A number of authors, however, agree that secondary stress in French is more generally assigned to the first syllable of a content word (Vaissière 1974; Hirst and Di Cristo 1984; Milner and Regnault 1987; Pasdeloup 1990). Note that this view, like Verluyten's analysis, predicts that simple trisyllabic words will be stressed on the first syllable which is also the antepenultimate and that disyllabic words will possess only one stress on the last full syllable. Monomorphemic words of more than three syllables are relatively infrequent in French.

This secondary initial stress, in my opinion, should not to be confused with emphatic stress, in particular with focal stress for intensification (cf. below §2.3.), a dynamic stress which can occur in the same place. Unemphatic initial stress can be interpreted as a rhythmic stress tending to generalise to different speech styles of contemporary French, although it was signalled as early as the beginning of the century in 1912 by Scherk (quoted by Fónagy 1979a; p.124) and in 1929 by Pernot.

To explain this tendency of stress patterning in French, Fónagy (1979a) hypothesises a "centrifugal force" attracting a secondary stress to the first full syllable of a phrase-initial word and a primary stress to the last full syllable of a phrase-final word, in order to maintain the semantic and syntactic cohesion of the phrase. Example (2a) can thus be pronounced:

(4)   [la MA- | jeure parTIE]

Moreover, the occurrence of secondary stress in utterances seems to be strongly dependant on rhythmic constraints (Pasdeloup 1990), both within stress groups (mainly the regulation of the number of syllables in this unit which tends not to exceed three, according to Wenk and Wioland 1982 and Fletcher 1991), and across boundaries of stress groups (in particular the strong tendency to avoid two adjacent rhythmic stresses in the same intonation unit)

In a preliminary phonological description of French intonation (Hirst and Di Cristo 1984) we proposed the following post-lexical rules:

(I) **Initial Prominence** (optional): form a stress group up to and including the initial syllable of each lexical item.

(II) **Final Prominence** (obligatory): form a stress group up to and including the final syllable of each lexical item.

The following example illustrates the application of these two rules:

(5)   [Un FA- | briQUANT| de MA- | téRIAUX | de CONS- | trucTION]
         (A maker of building materials)

A third optional rule can then apply (depending on such factors as speech rate and pragmatic constraints) to readjust some of the stress patterns produced by the other two rules:

(III) **Readjustment**: When a monosyllabic stress group is both preceded and followed by a stressed syllable in the same intonation unit, combine the last two groups into one.

This has the effect of transforming an utterance like:

(6)   [Un BEAU | CHAT | GRIS] (a beautiful grey cat)

into:

(7)   [Un BEAU I chat GRIS]

Note that all these rules must be applied once the focal (rhematic) part of the utterance has been selected and boundaries of Intonation Units affected.

c. Realisation of rhythmic stresses
Both primary and secondary rhythmic stresses are generally manifested in French by pitch prominence (see §2). Primary stress, however, contrary to secondary stress, is also manifested by temporal cues. This means first that the syllable bearing final stress is lengthened and, secondly, that the following unstressed syllable is noticeably shorter than the preceding ones.

d. Prosodic units in French
Since the main cue for rhythmic stress is pitch prominence, Hirst and Di Cristo (1984) used the term **Tonal Unit** (TU) to refer to what I have so far here called the stress group. The phonological model we proposed thus made use of a hierarchical structure built up from two basic phonological prosodic constituents: on the higher level **Intonation Units** (IU) and on the lower level **Tonal Units** (TU) defined by the rules presented above. From the discussion in the preceding paragraph, however, it appears necessary to take into account temporal factors in order to define rhythmic structure which cannot always be determined solely by tonal characteristics. In order to give a full account of the prosodic structure (*i.e.* including temporal organisation) and thus, of the rhythmic pattern of French, it seems necessary to postulate a category containing exactly one primary stress intermediate between the Tonal Unit and the Intonation Unit. A unit of this type is often called the **Prosodic Word** (PW) (Martin 1977a; Fletcher 1991; Vaissière 1991) and it can be considered equivalent to the Phonological Word as defined by Selkirk (1972) and by Horne (1978). The following examples, where (TU), (PW) and (IU) are indicated respectively by (I), (II) and ([...]), illustrate some possibilities of prosodic grouping in French for utterances articulated at a "normal" rate of speech.

(8)   [Sa SEI créTAIRE] [m'a TÉI léphoNÉ]
          (His secretary phoned me.)

(9)   [Mon FILSII et son voiSIN] [se sont DISI puTÉS].
          (My son and his neighbour had an argument.)

In the remainder of this chapter, we shall be concentrating on melodic rather than temporal patterns and we shall consequently use the more general term stress group without making a distinction between (TU) and (PW). (For more discussion cf. Di Cristo and Hirst 1993, 1997.)

1.2 Outline of the approach

The description of French prosody proposed in this chapter is not based on the analysis of any one specific corpus. It takes into account the results of a number of studies dealing with different kinds of material, including both laboratory and spontaneous speech, which have been carried out by specialists of French prosody from a number of different institutions. In fact, this chapter is an attempt to present as complete a view as possible of the essential characteristics of French intonation, drawing both on the major studies of the subject as well as on original research.

2. Description of intonation patterns

2.1 Description of a basic non-emphatic pattern

The intonation pattern of a simple declarative sentence, *i.e.*, syntactically formed by a noun phrase (NP) followed by a verb phrase (VP) has been described as globally rising-falling or circumflex (Di Cristo 1975b, Rossi and Di Cristo 1982). However, since such a sentence is usually divided into two Intonation Units (see §2.4), a basic intonation pattern is better illustrated by minimal utterances consisting of a single syntactic phrase and hence one single Intonation Unit. This type of utterance is both semantically simple and statistically frequent in spontaneous speech.

In monosyllabic or disyllabic utterances, such as *Non* (No) or *Maman* (mother), consisting of a single stress group, the rising-falling pattern is equally often observed. The peak of the rise is aligned with the end of the nasal consonant in the monosyllabic *Non* (no) (figure 1a) and with the end of the first syllable in the disyllabic *Maman* (mummy) (figure 1b). The final fall occurs on the nasal vowel of *Non* and on the last syllable of *Maman*.

In a longer NP utterance consisting of two stress groups as in (10), the same global rising-falling pattern is found once more (figure 1c), the pitch rise being aligned with the end of the first stress group. The pitch of the syllable *de* is intermediate between the high pitch of the syllable *fils* and the low pitch of *le* and *Jean*.

Using INTSINT (cf. Hirst and Di Cristo this volume), this example can be transcribed:

(10)   Le FILS de JEAN   (John's son)
     [⇑   >   ⇓]

With longer utterances, as in (11), comprising, for example, three stress groups, but still a single Intonation Unit, (figure 1d) a saw-tooth pattern emerges with the pitch peaks corresponding to the first two stress groups. The

initial syllable of the last stress group is realised on an intermediate pitch level
between the maxima and minima of the pattern.

(11)   <u>L'aMI du voiSIN de JEAN</u>   (John's neighbour's friend)
   <u>[⇑   ↓   ↑   >   ⇓]</u>

The last two examples can be accounted for by a general rule: a basic pitch
pattern (*i.e.* an Intonation Unit) ending on a final low pitch (such as a statement)
contains a rising pitch movement (from low to high) at the end of each stress
group except the last, which is pronounced with a falling pitch movement from
mid (or lowered high) to low.

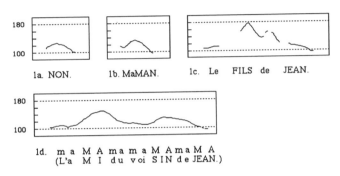

Figure 1. F_0 curves for short declarative utterances in French (see text). Dotted lines correspond
to 100 and 180 Hz.

Phonetically, in such utterances, a global declining effect can be observed
joining the maxima. It is not clear whether this effect is specific to this type of
utterance or, more generally, whether it is simply a characteristic of the type of
speech material analysed (read *vs.* spontaneous speech).

2.2 Modality and expressivity

a. Intonation and questions
In French, as in most languages, there exist different ways of asking a question,
using both morphological, syntactical and intonational devices. In this section,
we shall concentrate on two basic interrogative forms of French: **total** (Yes/No
or polar) **questions** and **partial** (WH-) **questions**.

(i) Total questions. In French, total questions can be syntactically unmarked or
marked either by inversion of a pronoun subject and verb, or else by means of
the expression *Est-ce que....?* (Is it that...?) The unmarked form is the most
interesting both because it is the most frequent one in contemporary French and

also because it raises the question of a specific interrogative intonation pattern. Some authors maintain that so-called "interrogative" intonation is nothing more than a contextual variant of "continuative" intonation, since the former occurs only in text final position and the latter in text non-final position, with the sole exception of alternative questions such as: *Tu veux du vin ou de la bière?* (Do you want wine or beer?), where the first question is non-final.

There is a long tradition of research into the specific characteristics of interrogative intonation (Delattre 1966a; Autesserre and Di Cristo 1972; Fónagy and Bérard 1973; Grundstrom 1973; Boë and Contini 1975; Rossi *et al.* 1981; Wunderli 1984; Léon and Bath 1987). Some of the results presented by these authors seem contradictory. According to Delattre (1966a), the fundamental difference between continuatives and questions is to be attributed to the general shape of the pitch pattern which is described as convex for continuatives and concave for questions. This distinction was not confirmed however in studies by Di Cristo (1976b) and Rossi (1978). More recently, Roméas (1992) has shown that a distinction between convex and concave pitch patterns can be found in certain types of corpus but that this is not necessarily associated with the distinction between continuative and question. Wunderli (1984) claimed that interrogatives are distinguished from continuatives by a considerable lengthening of the final stressed vowel in interrogatives. This effect was not confirmed however in a recent study dealing with spontaneous speech (Léon and Bath 1987).

Other studies have mentioned various characteristics of questions, such as higher final pitch and faster tempo although these are not reported to occur systematically. In fact, all these studies point out the use of a final rise as a characteristic of total questions. What seems to distinguish this rise from that used for continuatives is greater range (Rossi 1981b), steeper slope (Léon and Bath 1987) and higher final pitch (Boë and Contini 1979). It has been shown (Di Cristo 1971) that if this final rise is shortened by regular steps the interrogative meaning changes to a continuative one, not gradually but categorically.

Interpreting an utterance as a question often depends on the communicative context. It follows that an utterance perceived as a question in a given context may no longer be perceived as a question when taken out of that context and presented in isolation. My own observations (Di Cristo 1978) are compatible with the idea that there is a single overall intonation pattern for both continuative and interrogative utterances in French. This resemblance is particularly evident in figure 2 which illustrates both declarative and interrogative versions of two sentences with the same syntactic structure.

It can be seen from figure 2 that the Intonation Units in continuative structures: *Le fils du directeur* (The manager's son): (figures. 2a and 2b) and *Le fils du président* (The president's son): (figures. 2c and 2d) are pronounced with the same global patterns as the Intonation Units used for questions: *a vu le*

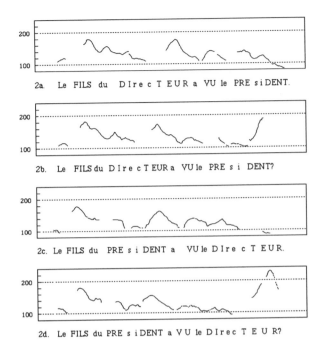

2a. Le FILS du D I r e c T EUR a VU le PRE s i DENT.

2b. Le FILS du D I r e c T EUR a VU le PRE s i DENT?

2c. Le FILS du PRE s i DENT a   VU le D I r e c T EUR.

2d. Le FILS du PRE s i DENT a V U le D I r e c T E U R?

Figure 2. F_0 patterns for declaratives and questions in French. Dotted lines correspond to 100 and 200 Hz.

président (saw the president): (figure 2b) and *a vu le directeur* (saw the manager): (figure 2d). This pattern can be described as an initial pitch peak situated on the last syllable of the first stress group followed by a declining pitch until the final rise. It appears, furthermore, that the final rise is of greater amplitude and reaches a higher final pitch in the case of the question pattern than in the case of the continuative pattern. Nevertheless, it would be interesting to verify whether the distinction observed for isolated utterances is maintained in other speech conditions, in particular in discourse, where it has been demonstrated for other languages (Bannert 1985b; Botinis 1989b) that continuation rises which end larger units (such as turn or sub-turn units) may frequently reach an extra high pitch.

In fact, we can distinguish two basic types of total questions in French: Yes/No questions for **confirmation** (where one specific response is expected) and Yes/No questions for **information**. Yes/No questions for confirmation, which have been carefully analysed by Fónagy and Bérard (1973), are characterised by a final fall, preceded by a pitch peak associated with the penultimate, as in:

Albert Di Cristo

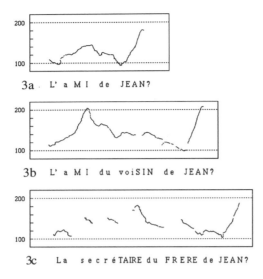

3a L' a M I de JEAN?

3b L' a M I du voiSIN de JEAN?

3c La s e c r é TAIRE du FRERE de JEAN?

Figure 3. F_0 patterns for continuative structures in French (see text). Dotted lines correspond to 100 and 200 Hz.

(12)   Il s'en VA?   (Is he leaving?)

In Yes/No tag questions – or biased questions (Cruttenden 1986) – ending with terminators such as: *oui?*, *si?*, *non?*, *hein?*, *n'est-ce pas?*, which are frequently used in spoken French (Andrews 1989) and which are also used for confirmation, we find the same rising-falling pattern located at the end of the sentence. But a subsequent rise is associated with the terminator. Note that the negative *non* is usually employed with the declarative form and the positive *si* with the negative. The interjection *hein*, which is not marked as positive or negative, can be employed indifferently with either form.

(13)   Elle est maLADE, NON?   (She's ill, isn't she?)

Yes/No questions for information are generally marked, as we saw above, by a rising pitch associated with the last stressed syllable of the utterance. In a simple question of this type, for example a NP utterance consisting of two stress groups, such as *L'aMI de JEAN?* (John's friend) (figure 3a).

The overall pitch pattern is similar (except for the final rise) to that of the corresponding declarative utterance (cf. figure 1c.). If we look at example (14), however, which contains three stress groups, we observe that while the first

204

stress group *L'aMI* contains a pitch rise, the second one *du voiSIN* is characterised by a lowered (downstepped) pitch plateau on its last syllable. This example can be transcribed as follows:

(14)　　L'aMI du voiSIN de JEAN?　　(John's neighbour's friend?)
[　　⇑　　　>　　>　⇑]

A similar pattern can be observed in (15) (figure 3c):

(15)　　La secréTAIRE du FRÈRE de JEAN?　　(John's brother's secretary?)
[　　　⇑　　　　>　　>⇑]

where *La secréTAIRE* constitutes a single stress group. If this lexical item is pronounced with a secondary stress on the first syllable: *La SEcréTAIRE*, only this syllable and the last stressed syllable of the Intonation Unit, *JEAN*, receive a pitch rise. Other stressed syllables are manifested as a sequence of downstepped pitches (each of them lending prominence) along a declining line:

(16)　　La SEcréTAIRE du FRERE de JEAN?
[　　⇑　>　　　>　　　>　⇑]

To summarise: if a question is formed of one or two stress groups, its pitch pattern (except for the final rise) is similar to that of the corresponding declarative utterance. On the other hand, if the question contains more than two stress groups, the recurrent pitch pattern of stress groups between the first and the last tends to be different from that of the corresponding declarative utterance, consisting of a sequence of lowered pitches or downstepped tones.

(ii) Partial questions. Question word interrogatives or Partial (WH-) questions are grammatically marked by the presence of an interrogative morpheme (*qui* (who), *quand* (when), *pourquoi* (why), *comment* (how), *où* (where)...) which is enough to indicate the interrogative form of the utterance. In everyday speech, two main types of partial questions are used: **neutral partial questions** (NPQs), to obtain new information and **echo partial questions** (EPQs), by which a speaker asks for the reformulation of a response which he has not understood or which seems curious to him.

EPQs are usually characterised by an overall high pitch and by a final rise similar to that of Yes/No questions for information. In contrast, NPQs exhibit a final low pitch, as in statements. I shall be dealing only with the pitch patterns of NPQs in this section.

In NPQs containing an initial non-focused question word, we usually observe the presence of a pitch accent on the stressed syllable of the question word. After this initial prominence the pitch drops regularly until the final syllable, which is pronounced in the speaker's low register (figures 4a, 4b).

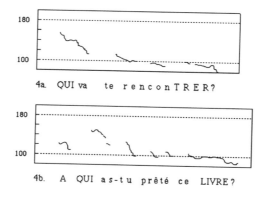

4a.   QUI va   te r e n c o n T R E R?

4b.   A QUI a s-t u   prêté ce   LIVRE ?

Figure 4. F_0 curves for neutral partial questions in French (see text). Dotted lines correspond to 100 and 180 Hz.

When the part of the utterance following the question word contains two or more stress groups, it can be realised either in the same manner as in the preceding example (in this case, intermediate potentially stressed syllables are accentless) or by the use of a recurrent lowered pitch on the last syllable of each stress group, which is then accented. These realisations can be transcribed as (17) and (18), respectively.

(17)   A QUI as-tu prêté ce LIVRE ?   (Who did you lend this book to?)
       [⇑   >   ⇓]

(18)   A QUI as-tu prêTÉ ce LIVRE ?
       [⇑   >   > ⇓]

When the question word is in sentence-final position, as in: *Vous voyaGEZ coMMENT?* (How are you travelling?), the overall pitch pattern is similar (as noted by Wunderli 1983) to that of a statement, comprising an initial rise up to the end of the VP followed by a terminal fall on the question word.

(iii) Other question types. In **alternative questions**, the first term is realised with a rising final contour, similar to that of a yes/no question, and the second term with a globally falling pattern in which accented syllables are signalled by the same recurrent lowered pitch (or downstepped tone) illustrated in the preceding examples (17 and 18). It has been observed (Rossi 1981b) that in alternative questions, the absolute pitch peak can be aligned, either with the conjunction *ou* (or), when the two terms are closely linked, or with the last full syllable of the first term, when they are separated by a pause.

Elliptical questions, introduced by *et* (and) or *mais* (but), such as *Et ta fille?* (what about your daughter?), *Mais, ta voiture?* (But, your car?), which are highly frequent in spontaneous speech, are also characterised by a globally falling pattern including downstepped accented syllables. These questions are often genuinely elliptical in the sense that the addressee needs complementary information which he may formulate as: *Quoi ma fille?* (What about my daughter?), *Quoi ma voiture?* (What about my car?) which, in turn, triggers from the speaker a yes/no question such as *Elle habite ici?* (does she live here?), *Tu l'as vendue?* (have you sold it?).

b. Other modalities: imperative and vocative
Figure 5 illustrates some typical F_0 configurations for interrogative (figure 5a), continuative (figure 5b), imperative (figure 5c) and vocative (figure 5d) realisations of the same segmental sequence: *Anne-Marie*.

Delattre (1966a), in his presentation of ten basic intonation patterns of French, describes an imperative intonation pattern ("commandement") corresponding to a rapid drop in pitch from high to low. According to Delattre, this pattern is distinguished from interrogative and exclamative patterns by its global shape, as illustrated in figure 6.

Other studies have mentioned the following features as characteristic of imperative intonation: high onset with a fall to a final low register (Léon 1974); steeper slope than that observed on declarative utterances (Martin 1973; Léon 1974). Some of these characteristics are to be observed in figure 5c, namely a relative high onset preceded by a slight initial rise and a steep overall slope. (Note that a global rising-falling pattern – the rising part being located at the onset of the utterance – has also been described by Kahn (1968), for Parisian French and by Szmidt (1970), for Canadian French.) Figure 5c also shows a step down from the penultimate to the final syllable which is produced with static

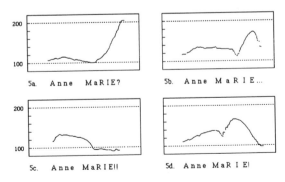

Figure 5. F_0 curves for interrogative, continuative, imperative and vocative realisations of the utterance *Anne-Marie* in French. Dotted lines correspond to 100 and 200 Hz.

pitch. All these observations tend to confirm the idea that while there are pitch features characteristic of the imperative modality, there is no overall specific imperative pattern. Thus Léon (1974) claims that phonologically there is no specific imperative intonation pattern, but rather a modality of imperative enunciation including a number of pitch features which can apply to other types of utterance. Furthermore, as Léon points out, the imperative modality shows similar realisations in a great number of languages which suggests a non-arbitrary, motivated origin.

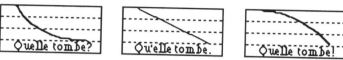

Figure 6. Pitch patterns for interrogative, imperative and exclamative utterances in French (Delattre 1966a).

In a study of the acoustic and perceptual correlates of vocatives in French (Di Cristo 1976a), it has been shown that the overall pitch pattern is once more rising-falling. The rising part, however, begins right from the first syllable and the final syllable is pronounced with a rising-falling pitch movement, the fall, starting from a high plateau, being greater than the rise (figure 5d). Perceptual experiments carried out using synthetic stimuli showed that the final fall does not simply correspond to a final drop in tension but is necessary for the vocative modality to be recognised.

c. Expressivity

It is a well known fact that both intonation and non-verbal gestures are used to convey attitudinal meanings. The expressive and attitudinal functions of French intonation have been studied extensively by Léon (1971) and by Fónagy in a number of studies (see particularly Fónagy and Bérard 1972). Callamand (1973) has proposed a great number of examples of expressive intonation patterns illustrated by stylised curves and by an audio tape.

The attitudinal pitch pattern most frequently used in French seems to be one which has been called "implicative" by Delattre (1966a, 1967). It is mainly characterised by a large rise-fall movement on the last syllable of the utterance and by deaccentuation of preceding stressed syllables (figure 7).

This implicative pitch pattern generally means that the speaker wants to insist on a fact which seems particularly evident to him. However, as pointed out by Delattre, this pattern may convey different meanings, depending on the syntactic structure with which it is associated. For example, with the syntactic structure of a partial question, it means some kind of exasperation; with that of an imperative, a polite invitation, and so on. This suggests that expressive pitch patterns are not always meaningful by themselves. This is not the case, however for "clichés" (cf. §2.5) which carry a strong unambiguous attitudinal meaning.

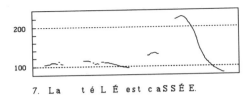

7. La   té L É est c aS S É E.

Figure 7. F_0 curve for an expressive pattern in French for the sentence *La télé est cassée* (the TV set is broken). Dotted lines correspond to 100 and 200 Hz.

On the other hand a comprehensive description of expressive patterns needs a more sophisticated frame of analysis than the simple one adopted for this chapter, and would include parameters such as pitch range, register, complexity of syllabic tones, loudness, speech rate and voice quality.

2.3 Focalisation and contextual effects

a. Focalisation
I shall concentrate here on only two points: focalisation and the given/new (or theme/rheme) distinction in French.

I shall use the term **focus** here as equivalent to what is sometimes called **narrow focus** when the "weighting function" (Bruce 1985, Gårding this volume) applies to a single lexical item or a phrase and I shall assume that the notion of **broad focus** is equivalent to that of new information or rheme (cf. Hirst and Di Cristo this volume).

French speakers can use focal accents either for intensification or for contrast. In the first case, a particular syllable of a word, or a lexical item as a whole, can be highlighted by an extra pitch prominence as in examples (19a) and (19b), respectively. Adverbs and even clitics are often focused in this way in spontaneous speech.

(19) a   C'est FORmiDAble! (it's fantastic)
  [⇑   > ⇓]

  b   Il ne DIT JAmais RIEN. (he never says anything)
  [↑ ⇑ → >⇓]

Focalisation can also be used for a contrastive purpose, implying an exclusive selection (*i.e.* a paradigmatic opposition). As a general rule, an item focused for contrast is characterised by a global rising-falling pitch pattern. While the fall is always associated with the rightmost full syllable of the item in contrast, the timing of the rising movement lending prominence depends on the objective or expressive character of the focus.

In the case of an objective contrastive focus, the rise can be aligned with any syllable of the focused item (except the last), as for example in :

(20) a   Le profeSSEUR a la clé...pas l'étudiant

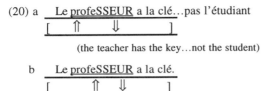

(the teacher has the key...not the student)

   b   Le profeSSEUR a la clé.

In the case of an expressive contrastive focus, the rising-falling pattern occurs on the final stressed syllable of the focused item (20c). This circumflex pitch movement is similar to that of the intonation of implication described above (§2.2.3.).

(20) c   Le profeSSEUR a la clé.

From the point of view of phonological interpretation, following Hirst (1983b), focal contrastive stress could be analysed as an autonomous Intonation Unit embedded within a higher-level intonation unit constituting the utterance as a whole:

(21)   [[Le professeur] a la clé]

The same interpretation can be applied to interrogative forms, as in the case of the focalisation of an interrogative morpheme in partial questions, as in (22).

(22)   QUI va te renconTRER?.   (Who is going to meet you?)

As far as the parts of the utterance outside of the focus are concerned, it should be noted that before focus pitch accents are reduced in amplitude, and after it they are deleted (Touati 1987). In the post-focal part, which is produced with a slightly declining parenthetic pitch pattern without pitch prominence, rhythmic units are mainly signalled by temporal organisation.

b. Theme/rheme organisation
Utterances produced by speakers in different communicative acts can be analysed, from a semantic/pragmatic point of view, as information units or messages (Perrot 1978). It is often possible to distinguish within a message what a speaker (in accordance with the hearer's state of knowledge) has decided to signal as given information (or theme) and what he wants to present as new information (or rheme). These notions have been extensively discussed in different approaches (see Hirst and Di Cristo this volume).

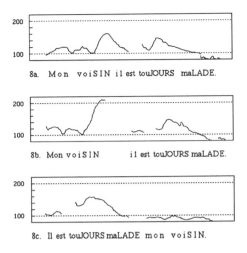

8a. Mon voiSIN il est touJOURS maLADE.

8b. Mon voiSIN   il est touJOURS maLADE.

8c. Il est touJOURS maLADE mon voiSIN.

Figure 8. F_0 patterns for thematic constituents in French (see text). Dotted lines correspond to 100 and 200 Hz.

A number of studies of French intonation (Martins-Baltar 1977, Rossi 1985) have shown that both word order and intonation patterning contribute to the identification of the theme and the rheme as constituents of the message as well as to the hierarchical organisation of these elements.

In **statements**, thematic constituents are mainly signalled in French by three pitch patterns which can be either in complementary distribution (depending on word order) or can enter into a paradigm (depending on the presence or absence of emphasis on the thematic constituent).

Example 23 (see figures 8a, 8b) represents two possible responses to a question about the health of a person's neighbour. In these examples, the thematic constituent *Mon voisin* is syntactically moved from the main clause by left dislocation and replaced by a pronoun.

When the dislocation is signalled by a syntactic mark (the resumptive pronoun *il*), the theme can be pronounced either with a typical continuation pattern:

(23) a   Mon voiSIN, il est touJOURS maLADE (my neighbour, he's always ill)

or with a question pattern:

(23) b   Mon voiSIN? il est touJOURS maLADE (my neighbour? he's always ill)

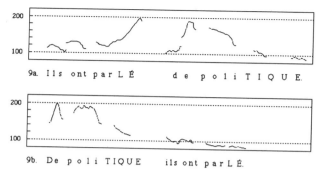

9a. Ils ont parLÉ de poliTIQUE.

9b. De poli TIQUE ils ont parLÉ.

Figure 9. F_0 patterns for the same sentence with theme-rheme and rheme-theme word order (see text). Dotted lines correspond to 100 and 200 Hz.

with an additional character of emphasis. When there is no syntactic mark (no pronoun), only the continuative pattern is possible, not the question pattern:

(24)   Mon voiSIN   est touJOURS maLADE.   (My neighbour is always ill)
       [→↑] [⇑   > ⇓]

Since (23a) and (23b) form a paradigm, the observation of F_0 curves supports the idea (as mentioned in §2.2) that the main cue for distinguishing a continuative pattern from a total question in French is the range of the final pitch rise.

The postposed thematic constituent is characterised by a parenthetic intonation pattern, which has been called a "low parenthesis" (Delattre 1966a; Wunderli 1979), and takes on the form of a low, flat, slightly declining line from which all pitch accents and boundary tones have been deleted (figure 8c).

A rhematic constituent is signalled, whatever its position, by a conclusive pitch pattern (*i.e.*, a final fall for statements and partial questions and a final rise for total questions) and, most often, by a rhematic accent (a pitch rise) marking the onset of the rheme. The value of the rhematic accent is neither emphatic nor contrastive, but demarcative. Figure 9 illustrates the F_0 curves of two utterances which constitute the responses to a question such as *De quoi ont-ils parlé?* (What did they talk about?). Note that the rhematic constituent *de politique* (about politics) shows the same pitch pattern (a rhematic accent on *de* plus a conclusive fall) in figure 9a which is in theme + rheme order and in figure 9b which is in reverse order: rheme + theme. It can also be seen that the thematic constituent *Ils ont parlé* retains a continuative pitch pattern when it is anteposed (figure 9a) and a parenthetic one when it is postposed (figure 9b).

In Yes/No questions, an anteposed theme or topic is generally pronounced with a global pitch pattern similar to that found in basic declarative utterances. This is the case for figure 10a, where the thematic constituent *Ta belle maison*

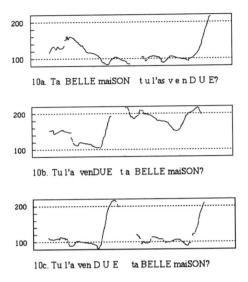

10a. Ta BELLE maiSON   t u l'as v e n D U E?

10b. Tu l'a venDUE t a BELLE maiSON?

10c. Tu l'a ven D U E   ta BELLE maiSON?

Figure 10. F_0 patterns for thematic constituents in Yes-No questions. Dotted lines correspond to 100 and 200 Hz.

(Your beautiful house), which contains two stress groups, shows a similar pattern to *Le fils de Jean* (John's son) illustrated in figure 1c. Thus, if the thematic constituent contains more than two stress groups, as in (25), the pitch pattern organisation of the part preceding the final fall becomes identical to that of a basic Yes/No question. That is to say only the first stress group retains a final rise and all the others (except the final one) are realised with a lowered (downstepped) pitch movement. This recurrent pitch pattern can thus be considered typical of interrogative utterances in general.

(25)   La maiSON de l'aMI du couSIN de PAUL, elle est GRANDE?

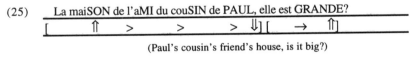

(Paul's cousin's friend's house, is it big?)

If, in a Yes/No question, the theme (or topic) is postposed, it is pronounced either with a flat slightly declining line in a high register (high parenthesis), or with a reduced copy of the question pattern of the rheme, also produced in a high register (figure 10b). The effect is not to be confused with a double interrogative pattern as in figure 10c, which contains two rhematic constituents.

It seems reasonable to treat figure 10c as containing two intonation units, but this analysis is less suitable for figure 10b. A more satisfactory analysis would perhaps be that mentioned above (§2.3), which makes use of recursive prosodic categories, so that figure 10b would be analysed as:

(26)   [[Tu l'as vendue] ta belle maison?] (have you sold your beautiful house?)

A similar interpretation could apply to the declarative example shown in figure 8c, which would be analysed as:

(27)   [[Il est toujours malade] mon voisin.] (he is always ill, my neighbour)

2.4 Phrasing and textual organisation

A description of prosodic **phrasing**, the way in which a stretch of speech is divided up by prosodic means, involves two basic questions; on the one hand the specification of the prosodic constituents derived from the autonomous level of representation of intonation (cf. Hirst and Di Cristo this volume) and on the other hand the alignment of these units with those derived from other levels of linguistic representation such as syntax and semantics.

As stated above (§1.1) this description of French intonation is based on a hierarchical model formed by a basic three level structure including, from the highest to the lowest: Intonation Unit, Prosodic Word and Tonal Unit. This approach thus differs significantly from the traditional one (illustrated by Delattre 1966a, 1967 and followed by a number of specialists of French intonation), which introduces degrees, such as minor and major continuation into a single prosodic category. Our approach is also different from the hierarchical classification of minimal prosodic units (intonation words) proposed by Martin (1975, 1981) in which the number of hierarchical levels is theoretically unlimited.

The organisation of stress groups and prosodic phrases which determines the rhythmic structure of French utterances appears to be neither speaker-dependent nor situation-dependent, but mainly governed by language specific phonological and phonotactic constraints. In contrast, the planning of intonation units seems to be both less language-dependent and more probabilistic (*i.e.*, speaker- and situation-dependent). From this point of view, the list of syntactic candidates which can constitute an intonation unit (clauses, sentence adverbials, NP subjects, topicalised items and parenthetical remarks) as described by Cruttenden (1986) for British English is also fully applicable to French.

Many studies devoted to French prosody have shown that intonation phrasing is strongly correlated with the organisation of information units in utterances (theme/rheme, topic/comment, *etc.*). It also appears, however, that syntactic structure imposes a number of constraints on intonation patterns (Di Cristo 1981; Boulakia 1983; Rossi 1985). As a general rule, major syntactic constituents (NP, VP, P.P., sentence adverbials) can be delimited by intonation unit boundaries. There is a major exception to this rule: when the subject NP belongs to the clitic class, it is always integrated into the following Intonation Unit. For example, a sentence like *Il mange au restaurant* (He eats in a restaurant) is generally pronounced with a single intonation unit. With the exception of this case, it can be said that intonation phrasing contributes to the identification of the syntactic structure and segmentation, as can be illustrated from the following examples where only intonation units are indicated for simplification.

(28)   [PAUL] [a téléphoNÉ au cuRÉ] [du viLLAGE]
       (Paul phoned the priest from the village)

(29) a [PAUL] [a téléphoNÉ au cuRÉ du viLLAGE]

   b   [PAUL] [a téléphoNÉ] [au cuRÉ du viLLAGE]
       (Paul phoned the village priest)

Inserting an Intonation Unit boundary in front of the phrase *du village* as in (28) has the effect of indicating that this phrase is treated as an immediate constituent of the sentence.

Although, as these examples show, there is some interaction between syntax and intonation, it cannot be concluded that the two levels of representation are perfectly congruent (see Di Cristo 1981; Martin 1981 and Rossi 1981c, for discussion of this issue). It is worth stressing that most studies dealing with the relation between intonation and syntax are based on the analysis of isolated utterances. Rossi (1987) claims that the same basic rules also apply to spontaneous speech. Fónagy and Fónagy (1983), however, point out that in the case of spontaneous discourse several syntactic units can be pronounced in a single intonation unit. They suggest that in spontaneous speech the fundamental role of intonation is to mark the paraphrastic relationships of discourse. A complementary point of view is put forward by Mertens (1987) who suggests that the intonational structuring of spontaneous speech is carried out progressively while it is being constructed. According to him, intonation units tend to coincide mainly with syntactico-semantic constituents of the utterance as conceived and planned by the speaker in a particular communicative situation.

In fact, a great deal more research in this field will be necessary in order to firmly establish the criteria (rhythmic, syntactic, semantic and pragmatic) which govern the prosodic phrasing of isolated sentences, paragraphs, continuous texts and spontaneous speech.

2.5 Other patterns: intonation clichés

Intonation clichés, which constitute stereotyped pitch patterns used by speakers belonging to the same linguistic community in particular situations, have been carefully classified and described by Fónagy et al. (1983). Intonation clichés are mainly characterised by a high degree of melodicity and syllable pitch stability. Consequently, they sound more like singing than do other attitudinal

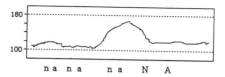

Figure 11. F_0 patterns for a taunting intonation cliché used by children. Dotted lines correspond to 100 and 200 Hz.

pitch patterns. A typical intonation cliché is the *Na-na-na-na* frequently employed by children to make fun of someone (figure 11).

This temporally expanded pitch pattern characterised by a rising movement on the penultimate and a sustained tone in the mid register on the last syllable, is also occasionally applied by adults to different utterances, such as *Tu as perdu!* (You've lost) or *Elle est partie!* (She's gone), to convey a similar meaning. A similar pattern can be found in particular highly connoted expressions of French vocatives, which are illustrated by Figures 12a and 12b.

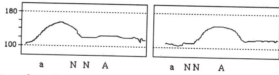

Figure 12. F_0 patterns for an intonation cliché used on vocatives. Dotted lines correspond to 100 and 180 Hz.

These two examples exhibit a similar global pitch pattern, the main difference consisting in the timing of the rising pitch movement which precedes the final sustained mid tone: the rise is aligned with the onset of the first syllable in figure 12a and with the onset of the second syllable in figure 12b. Despite this difference, the two realisations appear to be employed indifferently to capture the attention of a person in a kindly manner. The same patterns (especially that in 12a) can be used for friendly greetings and announcing calls such as *Bonjour!* (hello) or *Coucou!* (literally "cuckoo": a lexicalisation of the sound of this intonation cliché which is reminiscent of the cuckoo's call) As shown by Fónagy *et al.* (1983), there exist several other complex intonation clichés in French. A number of questions remain, however, concerning these patterns. Do intonation clichés really constitute a closed inventory? How many intonation clichés can be counted in contemporary French? Are dialectal intonation clichés different from those of General French? As yet, these questions remain unanswered.

3. Dialectal variations

The main prosodic differences between General French and the different dialects spoken in France, as described in a recent survey (Carton *et al.* 1983), are both quantitative and qualitative. They also seem to be distributed more locally than globally.

Dialects of the North are mainly characterised by a strongly marked stress (by pitch and loudness) on the first syllable of lexical items (Alsace, Lorraine, Jura), or on the last (Normandy and Burgundy). This stress tends to be interpreted by speakers of General French as emphatic.

Stress is not so strongly marked in the South of France, particularly in the dialects of Provence and Languedoc, where the stress falls on the penultimate syllable when the last syllable of a lexical item or a prosodic phrase ends with a schwa as in *mon PÈre* (my father), *la camPAgne* (the country) which, contrary to General French, is usually not elided. Some dialects of the South make use of a rising-falling pitch movement on lexical words, especially when they contain a long final vowel (Gascony). The same circumflex pattern can be found on the last syllables of a non-final intonation unit (Corsica) or of a final intonation unit (Auvergne). In two neighbouring dialects of the South, Provence and Languedoc, the final contour of an intonation unit ending with an unstressed syllable can be spread over the last two syllables. The post-tonic generally tends to be somewhat longer in the Languedoc dialect, giving the impression that most of the final contour is located on this syllable, while in the dialect of Provence, the most prominent part of the final contour is located on the stressed syllable.

4. Conclusions

Our present-day knowledge of French prosody (stress, intonation and temporal organisation) and of French microprosody (Di Cristo 1978; Di Cristo and Hirst 1986), seems sufficient to capture the basic features on which tentative models could legitimately be founded. Furthermore, the data collected from experimental studies (both on production and on perception) as well as their formal interpretation have been successfully applied to technological domains such as speech synthesis by rule (Bailly 1989; Di Cristo *et al.* 1997) and automatic speech recognition (Di Cristo *et al.* 1982; Vaissière 1988). Despite these positive results, there are still a number of quite important gaps in our knowledge.

We know very little about prosodic variability of idiolectal and dialectal origin. As yet, no published data is available on declination in French, although this has been extensively investigated in many other languages. Not enough is known about tonal and temporal interplay. On this subject further research is needed concerning, in particular, the timing of pitch movements and the prosodic basis of rhythmic patterning in French (for a review of studies on rhythm in French, see Caëlen-Haumont 1983 and Pasdeloup 1990, as well as Guaïtella 1991 for a recent study of rhythm in spontaneous speech).

Psycho-acoustic experiments dealing with prosodic parameters (F_0, duration, intensity) have been carried out with the aim of developing methods of stylisation (Rossi *et al.* 1981), but there is a need for a more thorough investigation of the prosody-based strategies used for lexical access and the decoding of larger units in speech understanding.

Prosodic studies of French have up to the present often been concerned with the analysis of isolated (read) utterances in carefully controlled laboratory conditions, and consequently the extent to which the results will be applicable to other speech situations and conditions remains to be seen. It seems in this connection that two main issues are in urgent need of investigation in the future: **Text Prosody** in particular with the aim of improving synthesis-by-rule in text-to-speech systems, and, obviously, **Discourse Prosody**. Projects in these fields are in progress at our Institute using recently developed research tools. These will be reported on in forthcoming publications.

Note

1 The convention of transcribing stress using capitals runs into a problem with words like *étoffes* ending with a so-called "mute-e" which is either pronounced (schwa) or else is elided, depending on a number of stylistic, dialectal and phonotactic criteria. For simplification, these words are systematically transcribed here as in ÉTOFFES /e'tɔf/ although of course the variant pronunciation /e'tɔfə/ is also possible.

12

Intonation in
Italian

MARIO ROSSI

1. Background

The problem of how to define the Italian language has often been raised, both before and after the late unification of the peninsula. Tullio de Mauro, in his *Storia linguistica dell'Italia unita* (1970) provided a complex answer, appropriate to the complexity of the question. If we consider the written language, the answer is relatively easy: the basis of Italian is the dialect of Florence stripped of the characteristics which are specific to Tuscan dialects. For the spoken language, purists claim that Standard Italian should also follow the phonological rules of the Florentine system. It is this variety which for a long time was imposed on the speakers of the Italian radio and television (RAI) in particular and which is still imposed in schools today.

But what about the intonation system? Does Standard Italian include Florentine intonation? The answer is almost certainly not. The Tuscan language was first established as a written system and speakers of different dialectal origins, when they use Standard Italian, cannot easily get rid of a system like that of intonation, which has been firmly established since early childhood. In a context where Standard Italian was being formed on the basis of the Florentine dialect, with considerable regional and foreign contributions, and where the native language of each Italian speaker is a regional language composed of a patchwork of dialects, to describe the intonation of Italian appears an impossible task.

Serious and exhaustive research in this domain would require an Atlas of regional intonations.

Because of this situation, I shall not attempt to describe the intonation system of Standard Italian but rather the intonation of some speakers whose regional origin will be indicated. I thus follow the precious advice given by Tullio de Mauro:

La persistenza della prosodia dialettale nell'uso regionale dell'italiano crea, a livello prescientifico, la possibilità facile ed immediata di riconoscere la provenienza regionale d'un parlante. Per le future ricerche sulla prosodia dell'italiano comune tutto ciò impone che si tenga conto della provenienza regionale dei parlanti sui cui usi si fonda l'analisi: tale accorgimento è stato qualche volta trascurato.

(The persistence of dialectal prosody in regional varieties of Italian creates, on a prescientific level, the possibility of identifying immediately and without difficulty the regional origin of a speaker. For future research on the prosody of common Italian, this implies that the regional origin of the speakers on whose speech the analysis is based will need to be taken into account, a condition which is sometimes overlooked.) (De Mauro 1970, 417)

1.1 General prosodic characteristics

Italian, in both its regional and standard forms, is a free stress language with final, penultimate and antepenultimate word stress (although see §3.1 below). The word, in Italian, can be defined as an accentual domain in which stress rules and the stress characteristics of morphemes apply (Rossi 1981a). Clitics, which are not part of the lexical word, cannot, consequently, affect the word-internal stress rules. As a general rule, stress occurs on the stressable syllable of the rightmost morpheme carrying an underlying accent.

(1) a   il CONT + IN + o $\Rightarrow$ il conTIno   (the little count)
    b   conSIder + a $\Rightarrow$ conSIdera   (consider)
    c   conSIder + a # lo $\Rightarrow$ conSIderalo   (consider it)

a. Lexical level

Lexical morphemes carry stress (') on one of the last two syllables of the word. Formally this means that only the final syllable needs to be marked for presence (') or absence (°) of underlying stress:

(2) a   mi # cro°giol + o $\Rightarrow$ mi CROgiolo   (I snuggle up)
    b   cro'giol + o $\Rightarrow$ croGIOlo   (melting-pot)

b. Morphological level

Grammatical morphemes and formatives may or may not be stress-bearing:

(3) a –°o (verbal suffix, 1st pers. sing. present indicative) *CANto* (I sing)

  b –'o (verbal suffix, 3rd pers. sing aorist.) *canTO* (he sang)

  c –'e (nominal suffix with collective value) *assemblEa* (assembly)

  d –°e (adjectival suffix of matter) *FERReo* (made of iron)

Plurisyllabic suffixes (such as *-evol- -ibil-*) where the final syllable is not identifiable as a stress-bearing monosyllabic suffix, are without underlying stress. A very general stress rule of Italian will however apply to words with these suffixes and attract stress onto them in certain cases (diminutives, nominalisers *etc.*). This rule states that all thematic constructions consisting of a lexeme or a lexeme+formative (marked in the following examples with square brackets [...]), must carry stress on one of the final two syllables of the construction. If there is no underlying stress on one of the last two syllables of this construction then the stress on the root is shifted to the right.

(4) a ['lod + °e°vol]+°e ⇒ [°lo'de°vol] + °e ⇒loDEvole (praiseworthy)

  b [pam°pin + °e] + °o ⇒ [°pam'pin°e] + °o ⇒ pamPIneo (of vine-leaves)

  c [mum°mi + °fic] + °o ⇒ [°mum'mi°fic] + °o ⇒ mumMIfico (I mummify)

Since nominal and adjectival thematic constructions can only be combined with a single monosyllabic grammatical morpheme, this rule has the effect of ensuring that stress occurs on one of the final three syllables of the resulting unit. The same is not true of verbal thematic constructions which can combine with bisyllabic grammatical morphemes or with two stressless morphemes:

(5) a [mum°mi + °fic] + °a + °no ⇒ mumMIficano (they mummify)

  b [consi°der] + °a + °no ⇒ conSIderano (they consider)

Contrary to nouns and adjectives then, verbs can carry pre-antepenultimate stress when they combine with morphemes of the third person plural.

1.2 Outline of the approach

a. Previous research on Italian prosody

Research on the prosodic characteristics of Italian has been devoted to rhythm, accentuation, and intonation. Following Bertinetto's (1981) extensive study of rhythm and accentuation in Italian, Farnetani and Kori (1983) showed that:

the rhythmical structure of a word mirrors the lexical stress pattern; likewise duration is usually the most powerful cue for locating lexical stress.

Vayra, Avesani and Fowler (1984) and Bertinetto and Fowler (1989) have argued that Italian should be considered a syllable-timed language since, on the one hand, "unstressed vowels cause little foot-level shortening" and, on the other hand, reportedly (Bertinetto 1981), unstressed vowels reduce less in Italian than in stress-timed languages.

Studies of Italian intonation have been devoted to such aspects as the relationship between syntax and intonation, the F_0 contours of pragmatic pieces in sentences, the prosodic organisation of discourse as well as applications to Text-to-Speech synthesis. Magno Caldognetto *et al.* (1974, 1978) studied the acoustic characteristics of emphatic and interrogative structures in Italian together with their regional variants. Kori and Yasuda (1991) studied the effect on F_0 movements of such syntactic factors as branching constructions and the head/modifier relation. Cresti *et al.* (1979) proposed stylised F_0 contours for Topic and Comment. Kori and Farnetani (1983a, 1983b, 1984) studied the contextual organisation of utterances as signalled by phonetic devices and demonstrated by means of a perceptual approach the importance of the global shape of the F_0 contour as a cue for focus. Avesani and Vayra (1988) showed that the prosodic organisation of discourse is structured hierarchically in accordance with the hypothesis of Grosz and Sidner (1986), and argued that criteria for intonational phrasing are founded on non-linear principles of cross-sentence organisation. Avesani (1990) proposed a model for the automatic synthesis of Italian intonation. This model, inspired by the theory of Pierrehumbert (1980), represents an F_0 contour as a sequence of tonal elements aligned with the text and operates at different levels of prosodic phrasing (accent units, intonational phrases).Tortorelli (1990) presents a detailed study of the intonational, syntactic and lexical marks of rhematisation in Italian. A recent paper by Bertinetto and Magno Caldognetto (1993) is dedicated to rhythm and intonation in Italian and various dialects.

Besides these studies devoted to Italian, it is worth mentioning some studies concerned with the intonation of regional varieties or dialects: Rossano in Northern Italy (Rossi 1974), Sardinia (Schirru 1982, Profili 1987, Contini and Profili 1989), and Sicily (Grice 1992). Canepari (1983) gives the basic simplified intonation templates for 22 dialects.

b. Theoretical background

In this chapter I present a morphological prosodic analysis of stress and intonation. The stress and intonation morphemes which structure utterances are briefly presented below. For more details cf. Rossi (1981c, 1985, 1987, 1993, 1995).

Lexical stress or internal accent (henceforth **AC**) is a property of morphemes and thus a potential which is realised under certain conditions. It can be combined with an intonation morpheme either in the same syllable (syncretism in *le parole tronche* stressed on the final syllable) or on two successive syllables (in *le parole piane, sdrucciole etc.* stressed on the penultimate, antepenultimate *etc.*); in both cases, the relationship between stress and intonation is one of selection, since the intonation morpheme presupposes **AC**, whereas the latter does not necessarily

Table 1. *Stress and intonation morphemes used for the description of Italian and French intonation.*

AC	internal **AC**cent (lexical stress)
IC	melodic **IC**tus
CC	major **C**on**C**lusive (terminal) intoneme
cc	minor conclusive (terminal) intoneme
CA	non-terminal "**CA**lling" intoneme
PAR	**PAR**enthetical intoneme
CT	major **C**on**T**inuative intoneme
ct	minor continuative intoneme
PA	**P**ragmatic **A**ccent

presuppose the intonation morpheme. It is thus necessary to determine the place of stress before the interpretation of intonation.

The melodic ictus (**IC**) is a rhythmic prominence which modulates phonetic sequences containing neither **AC** nor intonation morphemes, and which are longer than a given number of syllables.

Intonation morphemes, or **intonemes**, can have as their domain:

a.   the syntactic constituent
b.   the utterance
c.   the theme (*i.e.* the presupposed element of the utterance)
d.   the rheme (*i.e.* the new information).

In this description I assume the following intonemes:

i.   a major (**CT**) and a minor (**ct**) continuative intoneme. The main function of these is to create a hierarchical organisation of the constituents of an utterance;
ii.   a non-terminal vocative or "calling" intoneme (**CA**), a marker of the theme;
iii.   a parenthetical intoneme (**PAR**), a marker of a postposed theme.
iv.   a major terminal intoneme (**CC**) which marks the end of an utterance and carries a rhematic value; a minor terminal intoneme (**cc**) which marks a syntactic dislocation inside a parenthesis.
v.   a pragmatic accent (**PA**) which, in competition with **CC,** focalises an element of an utterance.

These stress and intonation morphemes are summarised in table 1 above.

In this study I take into account only the dimensions of pitch and duration, not those of intensity. In order to interpret the pitch values I refer to the model of pitch levels without microprosodic corrections presented in Rossi and Chafcouloff (1972). This study showed from psycho-acoustic and psycho-semantic experiments that French listeners divide a speaker's pitch range into six levels, from **Extra High** (*suraigu*) to **Extra Low** (*infra-grave*) with intermediate levels **High** (*aigu*), **Mid High** (*infra-aigu*) **Mid** (*médium*) and **Low** (*grave*). In French, the speaker's voice is generally pitched on the Mid level. Continuative and Conclusive patterns use the High, Mid High and Low levels respectively, while Extra High and Extra Low are restricted to expressive intonation patterns. The research reported in the present study suggests that these six levels are also adequate for the description of Italian intonation.

The duration of vowels was corrected using the coefficient of intrinsic duration (Di Cristo 1988); contextual or co-intrinsic corrections are not however made, since there is not sufficient data available concerning the effect of consonants on vowel durations in Italian. Vowel durations are subsequently converted into **Perceptual Units** (PUs) of duration.[1]

c. Corpus

The reference corpus is made up of 149 utterances extracted from broadcasts (interviews or round tables on radio and television). For reasons which will be explained below, the corpus was selected on the basis of the position of the subject noun phrase. Speakers consisted of schoolteachers, members of parliament, doctors, and journalists of the RAI, their socio-cultural profile consequently defines a fairly homogeneous linguistic level. The great differences in the regional origins of the speakers, however, means that a systematic and homogeneous study of their intonation system is practically impossible. The following procedure was consequently adopted: a schoolteacher (A.S., 28 years old) from Perugia (Umbria) listened to the recording from which the selected utterance was taken; he was asked to imitate the behaviour of the speaker and to reproduce the utterance in the context of the broadcast; a validation test with students of the University of Perugia demonstrated the reliability of this method: only a small number of sentences were eliminated.[2]

As a control, a second corpus was used consisting of:

a. A conversation between two speakers: B.M. (30 years old) from Florence and R.D.P. (34 years old) from Genova, both associate professors.
b. A corpus of answers to questions on syntactic ambiguities (speaker: A.B., 29 years old, from Bologna, schoolteacher).

It seemed interesting, for reasons given above in the introduction, to compare the intonation system which we assume to be that of Standard Italian with dialectal intonation patterns as produced by speakers from a rural community. This comparison makes it possible in particular to explain certain deviant forms produced by the Bologna and Genova speakers of the control corpus. For this reason the dialect chosen was one from the North of Italy in order to explain variants such as those just mentioned. The dialectal corpus is made up of spontaneous conversations recorded in a predominantly Emilian region of the

Apennines situated on the crossroads of the Tuscan, Ligurian and Emilian influences (Rossano, province of Massa Carrara). For a detailed phonological and phonetic description of this dialect cf. Rossi (1974).

2. Description of intonation patterns

In Italian the basic syntactic order is [NP VP]; this order is obligatorily reversed under certain conditions without any change of pragmatic meaning (Camugli, 1971; Burzio, 1986).

Before I study the prosodic organisation for each syntactic order, it will be necessary to define the criteria for the discrimination of accent and intonation. In French, there are no prosodic criteria to distinguish **A C** from intonemes because of the syncretism holding between these two levels.[3] This syncretism results both from the word-final nature of stress in French and from the relationship of reciprocal presupposition which holds between accent and intonation. In Italian, on the other hand, partly because of the predominantly penultimate position of word stress in the language and partly because of the relationship of selection between accent and intonation, the syncretism between the two levels is only partial. In so far as stress is not word-final, this syncretism is non-existent: **A C** occurs on the penultimate (or antepenultimate) syllable while the intoneme occurs on the final syllable. There are thus objective prosodic criteria, in Italian, for the distinction between accents and intonemes.

The continuative intoneme, for example, will manifest itself on the last syllable of the intonation unit as a contour whose pitch is equal to or higher than that of **AC** (see figure1).

The duration of the vowel under **A C** and the continuative intoneme is longer than of the unstressed vowels by 6 and 3 PUs respectively.[4]

When the pitch on the last unstressed syllable is lower than that on **A C**, we are faced with three possibilities:

i.   The duration of the final vowel is significantly longer than that of the atonic prestressed vowels and the falling pitch contour is pronounced at about one tone below the **AC**. In this case the continuative intoneme is realised.
    Ex.: *quello che ho notato* (cf. figure 13).
                ACI CT
ii.   The duration of the final vowel is significantly longer than that of the atonic prestressed vowels and the falling pitch contour is realised in the Low level. In this case the terminal intoneme **CC** is realised indicating the end of the utterance.
    Ex.: *e consuma molto.* (cf. figure 4).
                ACI CC
iii.   The duration of the final vowel is not significantly different to that of the atonic prestressed vowels. Here, whatever the pitch, no intoneme is realised.

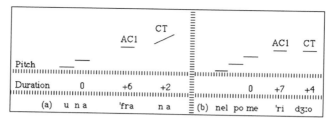

Figure 1. AC1: Primary stress occurring together with an intoneme on the post-stressed syllable. The durational values indicate the number of perceptual units as defined in the text (cf. footnote 1). Utterance a: *Una frana* (a landslide); b: *Nel pomeriggio* (in the afternoon).

Ex.: *ragioni (fondamentali)* (cf. figure 2)
AC2 Ø

On the other hand, as in French, a syncretism is observed between accent and intonation in units with word-final stress. In this case, the only objective criterion which indicates the presence of an intoneme is the difference in duration: in this case the **AC** duration prominence is +6 PUs as when **AC** is syntagmatically tied to the intoneme.
Ex.: *Il mulino sul Po.*
ACI
CC

2.1 Description of a basic non-emphatic pattern

a. Temporal pattern of the intonation unit

The sequence **AC {CT; ct; CC}** concludes the intonation unit; when **AC** is not followed by any intoneme, this constitutes the mark of a stress group (cf. figures 3, 4, 8, 9). The stress group presupposes the intonation unit (relationship of selection) in which it is necessarily included. The duration of the vowel under **AC (AC2)** at the end of the stress group is longer by 3 PUs than that before and after the stressed syllable[5] (cf. figure 2). Thus from the point of view of duration, the end of the stress group and the continuative intoneme behave similarly.

By contrast, **AC** at the end of an intonation unit (**AC1**) is characterised by a prominent duration of 6 PUs which implies the presence of an intoneme following it[6] (cf. figure 2). Since the duration under **AC2** (end of stress group) shows great stability, I take this as a reference (by default, the intoneme duration) rather than that of the unstressed vowels which is highly variable.

b. Melodic organisation of the intonation unit

The loci of temporal prominence are not synchronised with those of pitch prominence. In a pragmatically and expressively neutral continuative intonation unit, the locus of the pitch prominence is on **AC2**, that is to say at the end of

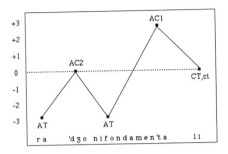

Figure 2. Number of perceptual units of duration relative to AC2 = 0, Unaccented (AT) = -3 ±1; AC1 = +3 ±0.7; {CT; ct} = 0 ±0.5. AC2 corresponds to a stressed syllable occuring without an intoneme. For A1 cf. figure 1. Utterance: *ragioni fondamentali* (fundamental reasons).

the stress group (figure 3). The locus of temporal prominence on **AC1** which implies a following continuative intoneme and the end of the intonation unit, is synchronised with a low pitch contour realised on the same level as that of unstressed syllables. The pitch contour of the continuative intoneme, after **AC1**, may vary freely between the two pitch extremes of **AC1** and **AC2**, that is to say between the **Mid** and the **Mid High** levels. These two extremes define the 3-5 axis (see figure 3), while the AT-AC2 and the AC2-AC1 extremes define respectively the 1-2 and the 2-3 axes (figure 3).

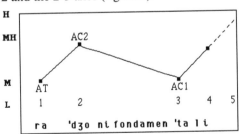

Figure 3. Basic intonation pattern for continuative units. The y-axis corresponds to the pitch levels: High, Mid High, Mid, and Low.

Between AC2 and AC1 no intoneme can be realised; the prosodic values of the unstressed vowels, whatever the morpheme, are consequently adjusted to the temporal and melodic continuums obtained by linear interpolation between these two points. The merging consecutive to this interpolation thus provides the junction between the stress groups and the intonation units. On the other hand, the prosodic features occuring with the continuative intoneme produce a contrast implying a boundary between the intoneme situated on the post-stressed syllable, and the following syllable. Both the temporal and pitch organisation just described (figure 2 and figure 3) represent the basic pattern of the major continuative unit with penultimate and antepenultimate stress.

We saw that intonation units with final stress are characterised by a syncretism between **AC1** and the intoneme realised in an intermediate zone between levels 2 (Mid) and 3 (Mid High) (3-4 axis in figure 3) which are the levels respectively for **AC1** and the intoneme in a continuative unit with penultimate and antepenultimate stress. With the syntactic order NP+VP, the major continuative unit, **CT**, occurs at the end of NP. When the order is VP+NP+X in an unmarked, non-emphatic sequence,[7] **CT** still occurs at the end of NP; in this case VP and NP are not separated by any intoneme and form a single intonation unit. Consequently in pragmatically and expressively neutral sentences, **CT** always occurs at the end of NP, whatever the order of the immediate constituents.

(6)   TUtt'i giornaLIsti   quando TROvano una STOria increDIbile
        AC2   AC1 CT I   AC2   AC2   AC1 ct I...
            (all journalists, when they find an unbelievable story ...)

(7)   arriveRA un moMEnto   che non poTREmo paGAre
        AC2   AC1 CT I   AC2   AC1 ct I .....
            (the time will come when we won't be able to pay)

When the sentence adverb (S-ADV) is in topic position, it attracts **CT**; more generally S-ADV, whatever its place, is separated from the other constituents by a major continuative intoneme.

(8)   in ALtre paROle,   ROma proDUce POco   e conSUma MOLto
        AC2   AC1 CT I AC2   AC2   AC1 ctI   AC2   AC1 CC I
            (in other words, Rome produces little and consumes a lot)

(9)   a FiumiCIno   atTErra un aEreo   ogni miNUto
        AC1 CT I   AC2   AC1 ct I   AC1 CC I
            (at Fiumicino an aeroplane lands every minute)

The immediate constituents in the syntactic order VP+NP are closely linked as shown by the fact that if NP is the last constituent of an utterance, it takes the **CC** intoneme and between VP and NP no intoneme can occur:

(10)   arRIva la doMEnica   (Sunday arrives)
        AC2   AC1 CC I

But if, in this utterance, the constituent *la domenica* is not an NP but a S-ADV, then a **CT** intoneme is realised between VP and the S-ADV.

(11)   arRIva   la doMEnica   (he arrives on Sunday)
        AC1 CT I   AC1 CC I

The highest pitch in the utterance occurs on **AC2** (**CT** by default) in the major continuative unit (see figures 3 and 4). Intonemes and **AC1**s are organised along a declination line as follows. The declination line is determined by a linear lowering of **AC2**s from the Mid-High level on the first **AC2** to **CC** at the end of the utterance (figure 4). Intonemes are produced along this declination line, while **AC1**s are pronounced below it: in the major continuative unit, on average

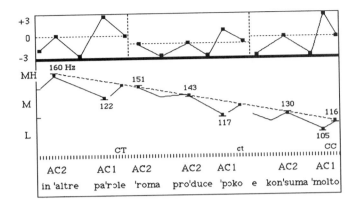

Figure 4. Declination line determined by the sequence of AC2s. The top part of the figure illustrates the temporal pattern expressed in Perceptual Units. The acceleration of tempo in the continuative unit is represented by a shift of the reference line (dotted line) towards negative values in Perceptual Units. The bottom part of the figure illustrates the pitch pattern. The declination line (dotted line) is determined by the AC2s. Note the lowering of the AC1s with respect to this line and the progressive reduction of the ratio AC2/AC1, corresponding to a fourth before CT, to a third before ct and to a semitone before CC. Utterance *In altre parole, Roma produce poco e consuma molto*. (In other words, Rome produces little and consumes a lot).

AC1 is realised at a fourth (4/3) below **AC2** and the following **CT** is raised back up to the declination line. The **AC2/AC1** ratio decreases progressively towards the end of the utterance. The progressive lowering of **AC2s** plus a constraint preventing the realisation of **AC1s** in the Low level before the terminal unit results in a narrowing of the distance between **AC2** and **AC1**. The minimum difference between **AC2** and **AC1** is a semi-tone.

The difference between major and minor continuative units lies, consequently, in a difference of level between **CT** and **ct** as well as in the ratio of **AC2/AC1** (figure 4). The distinction between these two intonation units is also expressed in the time domain by an increase in tempo in minor continuative units.[8]

c. Non-emphatic modifications to the basic pattern
We have to consider first the **AC2** pivot of the stress group. **AC2** is not needed in the intonation unit but occurs only if an underlying internal accent (morphemic stress) is present before **AC1**:

(12)   in ALtre paROle   Coi caPElli GRIgi
              AC2   AC1 CT   AC2   AC1 CT
              (in other words)   (with grey hair)

When no internal accent occurs, there are the following two possibilities:

i.   the number of syllables before AC1 is <= 3: in this case there is no prominence before AC1; AT (atonal or unstressed vowel), AC1 and CT are linearly and successively pronounced on the 3-5 axis, from the Medium to the Mid High levels (figure 5). Here CT represents the top of the declination line.

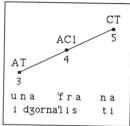

Figure 5. Pitch pattern where AC1 is not preceded by AC2 in the stress group. Utterance: *una frana* (a landslide); *i giornalisti* (the journalists).

ii.   The number of syllables before AC1 is > 3; here in the intonation unit before AC1 a melodic ictus (**IC**) occurs, taking the place of AC2 (figure 6).

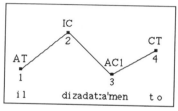

Figure 6. Here AC1 is not preceded by AC2 but the number of syllables preceding AC1 is sufficient to induce a melodic ictus (**IC**). Utterance: *il disadattamento* (dis-adaptation).

The duration of the syllables with the ictus is not significantly different from that of unstressed syllables. From the point of view of their pitch, IC takes the place of AC2 and CT is realised on the 3-5 axis, below the extreme level 5, as when AC1 is preceded by AC2.

In units with final stress, such as:

Il mulino del Po   / è un bel romanzo

ACCENT:	AC1
INTONEME	CT
AXIS-LEVEL	4

the syncretism of AC1 and the intoneme on the last syllable implies the realisation of a pitch contour on the 3-5 axis below the extreme level 5. In terminal units, this syncretised contour is pronounced on the Low level where it represents the lowest point of the utterance. In conclusion, the intonation morpheme resulting from this syncretism is characterised by the temporal prominence of AC1 and the pitch contour of either CT or CC.

The basic pattern I have described so far (figure 7) contains the potential features of the terminal unit as well of the continuative one. These two units

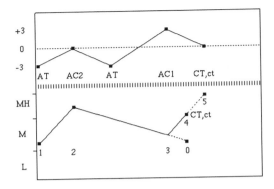

Figure 7. Prosodic organisation of the basic unmarked intonation pattern for Italian. Top: temporal pattern expressed in perceptual units. Bottom: pitch pattern. The continuative intoneme is normally realised on the 3-5 axis. It can also be realised on the 3-0 axis, depending on the intonational content and the context (see §2 case i). Note the contrast between temporal and pitch patterns.

differ in both level and range. As we approach the end of the utterance, the pivots of the pattern follow the declination line. Before CC, AC1 is realised on the Low level. This change of level is paralleled by a narrowing of pitch range: the ratio AC2/AC1 is reduced from a fourth to a tone or a semi-tone (depending on the length of the utterance). The difference between AC1 and CC generally ranges from a quarter of a tone to zero.

In any case, the perceived contour on the post-stressed CC is level; a perceptible rising glissando cannot occur in the basic pattern at the end of the terminal unit since otherwise the basic pattern would be changed into a question.

2.2 Modality: questions

The basic pattern summarised in figures 3 and 7 is also that for questions: with the range of the major continuative unit, and with the final AC1 pronounced on the Low level, followed by a perceptible rising glissando, which is the tonal representation of the question intoneme in a context preceding a silent pause.

The same pattern has a continuative value when immediately followed by another intonation unit but an interrogative one before a silent pause. In order to avoid ambiguity, when the continuative unit occurs before a silent pause followed by a question, the contour on the post-stressed intoneme of the continuative unit is reversed towards the Low level.

(13)   è STAta una FRAna ?   (was there an avalanche?)

ACCENT	CT2	CT1
INTONEME		CT
LEVEL	MH	LOW L-MH
AXIS LEVEL	2	0 3–4
GLISSANDO	–	– +

231

In WH-questions, we have the same declination line as in a declarative utterance but with the pitch peak on the question word in the High level and a realisation of the final post-stressed syllable as a WH-echo above the final CT1 on the 3-4 axis, without any glissando on the final vowel.

(14)   perCHÈ una FRAna ?   (Why an avalanche?)

ACCENT	CT2	CT1	
INTONEME			CC
LEVEL	H	LOW	L-M
AXIS LEVEL	5	0	3-4
GLISSANDO	–	–	–

Before a silent pause, the pitch pattern is maintained from the unstressed syllables up to level 5 (High) as in figure 5 in a question with implications.

2.3 Focalisation and contextual effects

Any significant distortion of the basic pattern is a cue for a pragmatic or an expressive content.

In continuative units with penultimate and antepenultimate stress, AC1 has the possibility of moving up the 3-5 axis. If AC1 is pronounced at the same level as CT, either at the top level of AC2 or higher, the speaker is drawing the listener's attention to the topic which is then marked but not presupposed. We may interpret this focalisation of the topic as an effect of the pragmatic accent (PA):

This use of PA to focalise NP is not possible in French for an accent carrying an intoneme, in French NP focalisation is generally completed by the rheme operator CC followed by the intonation parenthesis PAR. This possibility can also be found in Italian but with the meaning of an exclusive choice only.

We said above that CT (or ct) can move freely up the declination line without any effect of focalisation between the points 3-4 on the 3-5 axis, where it is often pronounced as a perceptible glissando. If the pitch goes beyond the 4 point

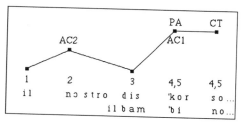

Figure 8. The realisation of AC1 with higher pitch than AC2, between levels Mid High and High, can be considered a focalisation of the topic by PA (Pragmatic Accent), different from marking due to presupposition. The intonation units are extracted from the utterances: *il nostro discorso, si avvia alla conclusione* (our speech is coming to its conclusion); *il bambino ne verrà danneggiato* (the child will not be traumatised).

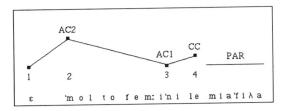

Figure 9. Prosodic pattern with postposed theme in the case of exclusive choice. The CC intoneme marks the rheme on which the exclusive choice focuses, the postposed theme is accompanied by the parenthetic intoneme PAR realised in the Low pitch level. Utterance: *È molto femminile, mia figlia.* (she is very feminine, my daughter).

up to the 5 point or continues on the 3-0 axis below the Medium level (figure 7), the intonation content is modified. In the first case (on the 3-5 axis) the intonation has the meaning of an indirect call by which the speaker asks the listener for his approval; the listener is supposed to know what is being talked about. This version of the pitch pattern of CT above AC2 endows the intonation with a marked thematic value similar to that which is carried by the calling continuative (CA) intoneme in French, as in the following French example.

(15)   Aristote? C'est un grand penseur   (Aristotle? He is a great thinker.)

Generally this pitch contour occurs after a marked theme, introduced or not (figure 10), by a thematic morpheme, but it is not itself a mark of extraction.

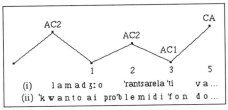

Figure 10. Realisation of the CA (non-terminal calling) intoneme on the 3-5 axis with higher pitch than AC2 between levels M-H and H. CA is a mark of presupposition. Utterances: (i) *La maggioranza relativa ... non ve la vuol togliere nessuno* (The relative majority? No-one will take it away from you) (ii) *Quanto ai problemi di fondo ... sono problemi sempre d'ordine politico* (as for fundamental problems, they are always problems of a political nature).

In Italian, the form of the CA intoneme is that of a question asking for confirmation, whereas in French, in the same situation, the intonation of the neutral question is used. This difference between these two languages may be linked to the fact that in Italian, the continuative intoneme is the same as that of the neutral question, whereas in French a different contour distinguishes continuative and question intonemes (Rossi 1981b).

In the second case where the continuative intoneme is realised below AC1 (3-0 axis), in the Low-Medium level, it carries a marked thematic value, but, unlike the realisation above AC2, has no calling content (figure 11); it is a mark of extraction.

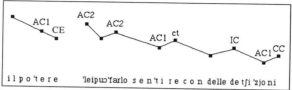

Figure 11. Realisation of the CE (Continuative Extraction) intoneme on the extracted theme: the pattern is inverted on the 3-0 axis. Utterance: *Il potere, Lei può farlo sentire con delle decisioni* (power, you can make it felt with decisions)

This intoneme is also a mark of theme extraction in questions (figure 12); for this reason I shall refer to it as **Continuative Extraction (CE)**. **CE** is generally followed by a silent pause.

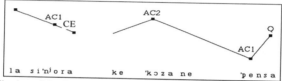

Figure 12. Realisation of the CE (Continuative Extraction) intoneme on the theme in a question. The normal realisation on the 3–5 axis would be ambiguous here since it could be interpreted as a double question. Utterance: *La signora, che cosa ne pensa?* (madam, what do you think?)

In order to understand the mechanism of the modifications in the signifier of intonation with focalisation or emphasis, it is necessary to envisage the prosodic organisation as a superposition of temporal and pitch patterns (figure 7). We can suppose that the temporal pattern may undergo any type of distortion (by contraction or expansion) and that the AC2 and AC1 pivots, together with the intonemes, can move along the temporal pattern while maintaining the duration ratios by which they are defined. As far as its Prosodic Pattern is concerned, AC2 can move along a vertical axis from a minimum (stress deletion) to a maximum in the Mid-High level (realisation of a pragmatic accent PA if AC2 is prominent above the intoneme); AC1 and { CT, ct } can move up and down respectively on the 3-5 and 3-0 axis (figure 7). We observe the patterns summarised in table 2.

Table 2. *Summary of relationships between prosodic forms (signifiers) and prosodic functions (signified) in Italian.*

SIGNIFIER				SIGNIFIED
Rising axis 3 4 5				
Falling axis 3		0		
AC1 CT				**neutral**
AC1	CT			**marked theme** (calling non-terminal CA)
AC1		CT		**Extracted theme** (continuative extraction CE)
	AC1	CT		**Focalisation** (pragmatic accent PA)
	AC1 ∪ CT			**neutral** (with final syncretism)
		AC1 ∪ CT		**Focalisation** (with final syncretism)
			AC1 ∪ CT	**extracted theme** (with final syncretism)

3. Comparisons with other systems

3.1 Regional variants

a. Word stress

In Gallo-Italic dialectal varieties of Northern Italy, stress is limited to the final or penultimate syllable. Antepenultimate stress "sdrucciolo" disappears either through dropping of the post-tonic syllable:

> MANtova ⇒ MANtwa (the town "Mantova")

or through rightward stress shift:

> PALpebra ⇒ parPEla (eyelid)
> LEvanto ⇒ liVANtu (the town "Levanto")

b. Intonation patterns

Both the Tuscan (Florence) and Emilian (Bologna) speakers of our corpus use the basic pattern described above in §2. The Ligurian (Genova) speaker, during the conversation with the Tuscan speaker uses a different pattern, but sometimes resorts to the basic pattern as a variant. This basic pattern seems to be characteristic of Central Italy.

The linguistic behaviour of the Ligurian speaker is easy to understand; that of the Emilian speaker, however, is less obvious. In fact, the Emilian language has predominantly word-final stress which, as explained above, has a profound effect on the basic intonation pattern. The prosodic transfer from one rhythmic structure (word-final stress) to another (penultimate or antepenultimate) is not

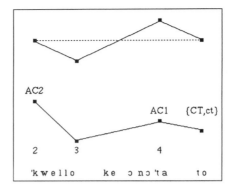

Figure 13. Prosodic contour realised by a Ligurian speaker. Top: temporal pattern. Bottom: pitch pattern. Note the inversion of AC1 and CT compared to the basic intonation pattern of Italian and the parallelism between the temporal and pitch patterns. Utterance: *Quello che ho notato...* (What I have noticed...).

easy; it seems reasonable to assume that the Emilian speaker needs to learn and use the prosodic pattern of the target language.

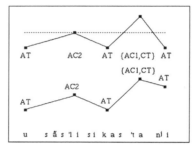

Figure 14. Prosodic organisation in a Liguro-Emilian dialect. The pitch pattern is inverted compared to that of Standard Italian and the post-stressed syllable is here treated as atonic. Top: temporal pattern; bottom: pitch pattern. Utterance: *u s'anslis i castagni* (they graft chestnut-trees).

With the Ligurian language, which has a penultimate stress pattern, the problem is different: this language is characterised by a regional intonation built on a rhythmic structure similar to that of Standard Italian, together with a large pitch movement on AC1. In this case, the transfer of the regional pitch pattern onto the rhythmic structure of Standard Italian is easier than for the Emilian speaker. The result is as follows: the regional pitch modulation on AC1 causes the modification of the AC1/intoneme ratio, the AC1 contour is prominent above the intoneme pronounced at one third below AC1 (figure 13).

The pragmatic value of PA and of the marked theme is expressed by the level reached by AC1 and by the ratio of AC2/AC1. The continuative intoneme is not more prominent than in Standard Italian. AC1 is pronounced between points 4

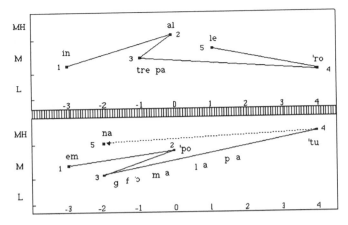

Figure 15. Representation of pitch (y-axis) in function of duration (x-axis). Top: sequence of the basic prosodic pattern in Standard Italian. Utterance: *in altre parole* (in other words). Bottom: sequence of the basic prosodic pattern in a Ligura-Emilian dialect. Utterance /em po g fɔma la patuna/ (and with a little, they make a chestnut pancake). The sequence of the utterance is to be read from 1 to 5. If the (dotted) sequence 4-5 linking AC1 to the post-stressed atonic syllable is excluded in the dialectal utterance, the pattern is identical to that found in French which is reversed with respect to Standard Italian (1: atonic, 2: AC2, 3: atonic, 4: AC1, 5: CT (top) or post-stressed atonic (bottom)).

and 5 and the pitch of CT and ct drops progressively towards that of the unstressed syllables. From now the only difference between AC2 and AC1 is their hierarchy. If AC1 is not focalised, the pitch of AC2 is higher than that of AC1, while the duration of AC1 is greater than that of AC2 as in Standard Italian.

Without a temporal organisation similar to that of Standard Italian, the intoneme, in this regional variety, could not be identified as an independent morpheme. Syncretism between stress and intonation is under way. This syncretism is reached in the dialectal area of Alta Lunigiana, south of Parma, at the cross-roads of Emilian and Ligurian influences. These dialects have eliminated antepenultimate stress and present a stress system where final word stress is predominant over penultimate stress. The syncretism between stress and intonation can be noted in the following facts: pitch and duration patterns on the post-stressed syllable after AC1 are similar to that of unstressed syllables after AC2; AC1 ∪ CT is characterised by duration and a continuative intoneme pronounced on AC1 both as a glissando in the High-Medium or Mid-High levels and a particular ratio between AC1 ∪ CT and the post-stressed syllable. AC1 ∪ CT is greater than AC2 both in its melodic and temporal features.

If the AC2/AC1 ∪ CT ratio is equal to a fourth and if AC1 is pronounced in the Mid-High or High levels, the result is either a question or an expressive intonation, depending on the intensity level on AC1 (Rossi 1974). The pitch contour, compared with that of Standard Italian, is reversed and the post-stressed syllable is now interpreted as an unstressed one.

If we represent the prosodic patterns of the two extremes just described, that is to say of Standard Italian and of the Liguro-Emilian dialect, on the two axes of pitch and duration, we obtain two reversed courses (figure 15). Paradoxically the intonation of this dialect is closer to that of French than of Italian. The cancellation of the post-stressed syllable after AC1 as a domain of the intoneme looks like a transfer from the Emilian and French intonation structure. We thus have an explanation for the behaviour of the speaker from Bologna.

Notes

1 Perceptual Units are calculated as the log of the ratio of the duration of a given vowel to that of the vowel carrying AC in the utterance. This value is then normalised by dividing by $\log(1.22)$, (= threshold of duration cf. Rossi 1972).

2 I should like to express my thanks to two of my former postgraduate students C. Camugli and A. Ben Fadhl. Camugli (1971) made a study of the position of the noun phrase in conversational Italian; Ben Fadhl (1972) used this corpus to study the intonation of the noun phrase in Italian.

3 In the only examples in French where **AC** can be identified as independent of the intonation, **AC** is identified on formal criteria: for example in the noun phrase where we recognise specific constraints (Rossi 1985).

4 Average calculated on 46 occurrences **AC** + { **CT**; **ct** } ; standard deviation under **AC** : 1.5 Perceptual Units and under **CT** : 0.9 Perceptual Units.

5 Average of 81 occurrences, standard deviation : 0.8 Perceptual Units.

6 The formula for calculating Perceptual Units (note 1) is not used with the utterance as domain, but rather with the intonation unit; which allows us to partially eliminate the variability of tempo between intonation units in the utterance.

7 In so-called *pro-drop* languages (= null-subject languages) like Italian, the subject can be moved to the right after V or VP with ergative and passive verbs (Burzio 1986) as in *è arrivato Pietro*. The NP is base-generated after V when it is neither a nuclear nor a contrastive focus. If NP is moved leftwards to the subject position, as in *Pietro è arrivato* it acquires a meaning of nuclear focus. By contrast, with transitive and intransitive verbs, the subject is base-generated in front of VP; if moved rightwards, it will be pragmatically marked as a nuclear focus as in *ha telefonato Pietro, l'ha fatto il gatto.* Concerning the place of NP subject see Camugli 1971, Antinucci & Cinque 1977; Cinque, 1979. If X in VP+NP+X is an adjunction to VP (Beninca 1988), the NP+VP order is mandatory: cf. *è arrivato un emissario* (a messenger has arrived) but *un emissario tedesco è arrivato a Beirut* (a German messenger has arrived in Beirut).

8 This acceleration is not necessarily deduced from the number of Perceptual Units since this is calculated for each intonation unit. The comparison between the intonation units shows a difference of 1 Perceptual Unit between the duration of CT and ct (figure 4).

13

Intonation in Romanian

LAURENŢIA DASCĂLU-JINGA

1. Background

Romanian, the Romance language spoken on the territory of Romania – a country in South-Eastern Europe bordering on Ukraine and Moldova to the North and East, Bulgaria to the South, Yugoslavia to the South-West and Hungary to the North-West – represents a perfect "island of Romanity".

1.1 General prosodic characteristics

As in a great many European languages, stressed/unstressed syllable types are relevant to the description of the Romanian prosodic system. Romanian stress is generally considered a dynamic (intensity) one, and its position in the word is not fixed. Due to its free character, the place of stress may play a distinctive role on lexical and grammatical levels. Minimal pairs such as: *MObilă* (furniture) – *moBIlă* (mobile), or *UMbrele* (shades) – *umBREle* (umbrellas) are relatively few, but the great number of pairs such as: *CÎNtă* (he is singing) – *cînTĂ* (he sang) prove that the place of stress plays a prominent part in verbal inflexion (Guţu-Romalo 1968).

The position of the stressed syllable is to some extent predictable from the phonological and morphological structure of the word; for instance all the morphemes of the nominal inflexion are unstressed, most of the verbal inflexional morphemes and of derivational suffixes are stressed, no prefix is stressed, *etc.* The morphonological rules of Romanian stress have been thoroughly investigated (*e.g.* Vasiliu 1965; Agard 1967; Herslund 1977). Studying the frequency of stress types in Romanian, Cohuţ and Mărd ărescu (1966) report that for plurisyllabic words, penultimate stress is most common (35.13%), followed by final stress (11.95%) and antepenultimate stress (8.04%), whereas other types (on the fourth, fifth syllable from the end of the word) are only "accidental".

The fluctuation of the location of stress, especially in neologisms, has been a permanent object of study (Puşcariu 1959, 1974; Avram 1984; Ulivi 1987) and still remains an open question in Romanian linguistics. A well-known tendency is to avoid two successive stresses, mostly by changing word order (Popescu-Marin 1961; Şerban 1974). In its turn, secondary stress can be used to reduce sequences of unstressed syllables (Tiktin 1905; Puşcariu 1959; Nandriş 1963). In this respect, Lombard (1935) notes that in polysyllabic words there is a tendency to alternate unstressed and secondary stressed syllables both before and after the main stress.

A present-day tendency worthy of mention is a leftward stress shift, especially in the speech of radio/TV announcers (Guţia 1959) or in everyday speech under the influence of affect (Iordan 1934).

The minimal recurrent prosodic unit of Romanian is the syllable; in other words this language exhibits a syllable-timed rhythm. As Chiţoran *et al.* (1984) remark:

Romanian, based on a syllable carried rhythm, is organised into a cursive flow of stressed and unstressed syllables that run after one another at roughly equal intervals of time.

Consequently, Romanian differs strongly from a stress-timed language like English, for instance, so that

to pronounce each syllable clearly but without stressing it too heavily is the main difficulty the English learner of Romanian may encounter when attempting to speak fluent Romanian (*ibid.*).

Very little acoustic information is available on duration. Avram (1971) finds that (i) interrogative sentences have a greater duration than declaratives with the same segmental structure ratio 1.23:1; (ii) the duration of the final syllable is greater in interrogative sentences than in declaratives.

After tentative experiments on pausing in reading broadcast reports, Roceric-Alexandrescu (1963) states that: (i) pause is the paramount means for the segmentation of the speech flow, and adequate phrasing depends on the accurate understanding of the message; (ii) pauses generally separate groups of words bound together into semantic and respiratory units, rather than words alone.

In another preliminary investigation, based once more on reading broadcast reports (Roceric-Alexandrescu 1965), the same author finds that the average speech rate for Romanian is 6 syllables per second.

1.2 Outline of the approach

Most of the following remarks are based on the acoustic analysis of speech material recorded in laboratory conditions.

The text of two dramatic works performed by famous actors was used as the main corpus. Both the actors' linguistic experience as native Romanians and their artistic talent make them unconsciously carry out a linguistic analysis of the text while acting. A second type of material includes different categories of sentences inserted in small dialogues constructed by the investigator in order to analyse the intonation specific to certain types of utterances.

The reported data were exclusively obtained by using the acoustic information contained in narrow-band filter (45 cps) sonagrams. This information has been reduced to the essential rises and falls as transcribed using INTSINT (Hirst and Di Cristo, this volume).

2. Description of intonation patterns

2.1 Description of a basic non-emphatic pattern

The intonation pattern of a short non-emphatic declarative sentence in Romanian seems to be a rising-falling one (Drăganu 1945), regardless of the theme/rheme structure of the sentence:

(1)   <u>MAma VIne</u>   (Mother is coming)
        [⇑ > ⇓]

(2)   <u>VIne MAma</u>   (Mother is coming)
        [⇑ > ⇓]

In fact, the two movements are generally not symmetrical: the fall is lower than the rise; besides, in longer sentences (without emphasis), the second part of the pattern, *i.e.* the fall, is prolonged:

(3)   <u>MAma VIne REpede</u> (Mother is coming quickly)
        [⇑ >   >   ⇓]

so that the basic neutral declarative pattern can be said to be essentially falling.

Declination is easily noticeable on the sonagrams of statements, but this acoustic aspect has not been systematically investigated so far; for the time being we have to be content with merely illustrating it in Romanian. For the sake of comparison, Figure 1 illustrates a sentence with the same meaning as the English, Spanish and French ones quoted by Vaissière (1983):

El a contribuit în mare mă sură la progresul teh nic în ultimii două z eci de ani.

Figure 1. F_0 curve for the sentence *El a contribuIT în MAre măSUră la proGREsul TEHnic în ULtimii DOuăzeci de ANI.* (It has contributed a significant amount to the technical progress of the past twenty years.)

Declination can also be seen in WH-questions, especially in longer ones:

De unde ştii ce să-i s p u i   d a c ă nuţi-am s p u s c e s ă-i s p ui?

Figure 2. F_0 curve for the question *De UNde ŞTII ce să-i SPUI dacă nu ţi-am SPUS ce să-i SPUI?* (How come you know what to tell him when I haven't told you what to tell him?)

2.2 Mode and expressivity

The vocative adds a specific intonation to the basic falling pattern, consisting of a peak on the stressed syllable of the respective word, followed by an abrupt fall (Dascălu 1984a):

(4)   Ana,   VREAU ste rog ceVA.   (Ana, I want to ask you something)
    ⇑ ⇓ [⇑   →   ⇓

Since the intonation of an imperative is similar to that of a vocative, a sentence containing both is characterised by two peaks, each followed by a rapid fall (ibid.):

(5)   VIno,   Ana!   (Come here, Ana!)
    [⇑⇓ ⇑ ⇓

The gradual fall of a long and more intricate statement may be modified by the interpolation of the specific pattern of various kinds of elements. Probably the most typical is the case of parenthetical insertions that interrupt the main contour of the utterance by introducing their own intonation, generally low, ending in a slight rise (Dascălu 1974).

242

(6) ȘtiA, ce e DREPT, că el NU e. (He knew, it's true, that he wasn't)
    [⇑] [⇓ ⇓ ⇑] [⇑ > ⇓]

The intervention of direct speech can also break up the continuously falling pattern; compare (Dascălu 1980a):

(7) MAma SPUne CÎT e de BUN (Mother says how good it is)
    [⇑ > > > ⇓]

(8) MAma SPUne: CÎT e de BUN! (Mother says: how good it is!)
    [⇑ > ⇓] [⇑ > ↑⇓]

Variants of the falling pattern used to express attitudes, shades of meaning or different pragmatic values, are numerous. Thus, for instance, a slightly rising terminal contour sounds indifferent or defensive. On the other hand a rising intonation may add a touch of warmth in greetings. For other examples see Chițoran *et al.* (1984).

A falling pattern is also used in WH-questions. In Romanian the interrogative word, the "lexical focuser by definition" (Bolinger 1986), carries the intonation peak, usually on its stressed syllable. Some authors have claimed that this pattern is identical to the declarative one (GLR 2; Kallioinen 1965). We feel rather that WH-questions are more like statements with emphasis on the word which is in the same position as the interrogative word in the question.

In the following examples it will be apparent that the intonation of question (9) is closest to that of the statement (10) with focus on the subject, not to that of (11) (with no focus), nor to (12) with focus on the verb (Dascălu 1985a). Compare:

(9) CIne VIne? (Who is coming?)
    [⇑ > ⇓]

(10) MAma VIne. (Mother is coming.)
    [⇑ > ⇓]

(11) MAma VIne. (Mother is coming.)
    [⇑ > ⇓]

(12) MAma VIne (Mother is coming.)
    [⇑ > ↑ ⇓]

As far as the terminal contour of statements and WH-questions is concerned, perceptual tests have shown that a sentence obtained by splicing *Cine* from example (9) together with *vine* from example (12) sounds like a kind of "melodic anacolouthon": this strange intonation pattern does not sound acceptable for a single utterance and listeners interpreted it as to two independent segments (ibid.).

Since the question word carries the intonation peak, its position is crucial for the shape of the overall contour (Dascălu 1979b, 1980a):

(13)   CE mai VOR de la MIne? (What else do they want from me?)
        [⇑   >   > ⇓]

(14)   Şi asiguRArile CÎT îi DAU? (And how much does the insurance offer him?)
        [→ ↑   ↑   ⇓]

The negation generally attracts the intonation peak of the sentence (see §2.3); it does not, however, modify the falling pattern of WH-questions. The question word thus takes precedence, intonationally, over the negative word:

(15)   CIne NU VIne? (Who doesn't come?)
        [⇑   > > ⇓]

It seems that the use of a falling pattern with WH-questions is more rigid in Romanian than in other languages, at least as far as genuine questions are concerned (see also §3.2). A WH-question with a terminal rise is rare in this language and its use implies a special connotation, *e.g.*, when a yes-no question is actually presupposed. Questions like:

(16)   Cum o duci?   (How are you?)

(17)   Ce (mai) faci?   (How do you do?)

pronounced with a rising contour, are merely polite formulas, close to greetings, meaning *Is everything all right?*.

In administrative questionnaires (showing a distinct lack of curiosity on the part of the clerk), WH-questions may be pronounced with rising intonation, like items of a list:

(18)   Cum vă numiţi? Unde locuiţi? Ce vîrstă aveţi?
        (What is your name? Where do you live? How old are you?)

A vocative sometimes modifies the falling pattern of a WH-question. When such a question begins with the vocative, an extra peak occurs (Dascălu 1984a)

(19)   MAmă,   CIne VIne deSEAră? (Mother, who's coming tonight?)
        [⇑ ⇓] [⇑ >   > ⇓]

When the vocative is the last word in the utterance, a high plateau may occur between the question word and the stressed syllable of the vocative (ibid.).

(20)   CIne VIne deSEAră, MAmă? (Who's coming tonight, mother?)
        [⇑   ⇑ ⇓]

The vocative may be completely assimilated from an intonational point of view if its addressing value is too slight (Dascălu 1984a, 1979b)

(21)   <u>CIne VIne, MAmă, deSEAră?</u> (Who's coming, mother, tonight?)

    [⇑   >   >   >⇓]

By adding a question word such as *ce* (what) or *cum* (how), before repeating like an echo a part of the other speaker's sentence, a rhetorical question expressing a negative meaning and having a slightly modified pattern may be formed. From the question word peak, the pitch is sustained on a high plateau up to the end, where it falls abruptly or remains suspended (Dascălu 1979b).

(22) –   Adică stră bunul nostru...   (– That is, our ancestor)
      –   <u>CE stră BUN!</u>   <u>CE NOStru!</u>   (– What "ancestor"? What "our"!)

    [⇑   ] [⇑   ⇑ >]

In an informal style, this is, in fact, a common means of rejecting the partner's words: they are repeated as a deliberately ironical imitation, in the lowest register of the speaker's voice (Dascălu-Jinga 1991a):

(23) –   Cred că fratele ei este medic.
      –   <u>CE MEdic!</u>   N-a terminat nici doi ani de facultate!

    [⇑⇓   ]

        (– I think her brother is a doctor.
        – What doctor! He hasn't even finished two years of medical studies!)

The falling pattern may be used with certain questions not introduced by traditional question words. Some complementary questions – with their predicate deleted and adversative meaning – begin with the conjunction *dar* (but):

(24) –   Nu am o zi liberă. (I have no free day)
      –   <u>Dar SEAra?</u>   (What about the evenings?) [literally: But evening?]

    [⇑ > ⇓]

      –   A, seara sînt şi mai ocupată. (Oh, in the evening I'm even busier)

Questions introduced by the conjunction *dacă* (if) derive, probably, from subordinate sentences and retain the falling intonation of their main clause (a WH-question) after its deletion. We have called this phenomenon "melodic transfer". Given a sequence *ab*, we define as melodic transfer the case in which the segment corresponding to *a* is suppressed and its intonation is transferred onto *b*. As a result of this transfer, *b'* (the elliptical sequence) is, from a segmental point of view, an ellipsis with *a* deleted, whereas, from an intonational point of view, it is an ellipsis with *b* deleted.

For instance, the elliptical question

(25)   <u>DAcă PLOuă?</u>   (If it rains?) [= What if it rains?']
[⇑   >   ⇓]

may result from the "complete" question (*ab*)

(26)   <u>Ce-au să FAcă dacă PLOuă?</u>   (What will they do if it rains?)
[⇑   >   > ⇓]

by the deletion of its main clause (*a*) *Ce-au să facă?* which is a proper question; this may be called a "progressive melodic transfer", *i.e.* the elliptical sequence takes the intonation of a sequence which originally preceded it, so that an intonation pattern is "moved" from left to right (Dascălu 1979d, 1984b).

Rising intonation is generally considered (GLR 2) to be typical of Yes/No questions. Such questions can have identical segmental structure to that of statements, the only distictive element being the rising terminal contour of the former. The opposition between rising (interrogative) and falling (declarative) patterns has a high functional load in Romanian, which uses almost no other interrogative devices such as word order, interrogative particles or phrases, *etc.* (Dascălu 1976). There are extremely few cases where rising intonation is redundant: the inversion of the subject and predicate occcurs mainly as a dialectal, archaic or poetical feature. If some modal words such as *oare, cumva* are used with questions, an overcharacterisation of the question results: the intonation remains the distinctive element, these lexical interrogatives being redundant (they may introduce a dubitative shade of meaning but, more frequently, are simply omissible).

An important difference between the two basic patterns is the following: a statement can be uttered completely neutrally, whereas a question is not only more often emotionally marked, but it also contains a certain accented element, which represents the question focus (GLR 2). This phenomenon, which we have called "interrogative emphasis", is a constitutive element of a question, whereas in ordinary statements the accenting of an item is only optional (Dascălu 1975a; 1979a). The special importance of interrogative emphasis is revealed by the intonational aspect of Yes/No questions. The terminal contour of such a question, *i.e.* the intonation of the last stressed syllable in the sequence together with that of any following syllables, is determined by two factors: the position of interrogative emphasis and the position of the lexical stress in the last word. An "absolute rising" terminal contour is observed only when the last word has final stress (Dascălu 1975).

(27)   <u>MAma IA?</u>   (Is mother <u>taking</u>?)
[⇑ ⇓   ⇑]

(28) <u>MAma IA?</u>   (Is <u>mother</u> taking?)

[→ ⇑]

If the last word has non-final stress, the rise is produced only when this word carries interrogative emphasis:

(29) <u>MAma VIne?</u>   (Is mother <u>coming?</u>)

[⇑   ⇓ ⇑]

otherwise the terminal contour is rising-falling:

(30) <u>MAma VIne?</u>   (Is <u>mother</u> coming?)

[↑ ↓ ⇑ ↓]

Since interrogative emphasis is expressed by a negative prominence (falling and/or low pitch), the overall contour of a Yes/No question is generally characterised by low pitch on the stressed syllable of the accented word, and possibly on the following ones (Dascălu 1979a).

(31) <u>Te-ai gînDIT BIne la ce-ai f'aCUT?</u>

[⇑   > ⇓   ⇓ ⇑]

  (Have you <u>thought</u> [literally thought <u>well</u>] about what you have done?)

If interrogative emphasis is placed right at the beginning of a long question, this specific low intonation can be prolonged almost unmodified all over the question up to the final rise:

(32) <u>POT să vorBESC cu FRAtele tău în aCEAStă proBLEmă?</u>

[⇓   ⇓ ⇑ ↓]

  (<u>May</u> I talk to your brother about this problem?)

A negative Yes/No question is generally characterised by the low pitch, specific to interrogative emphasis, which is maintained almost unchanged throughout the whole sentence up to its last stressed syllable, where the final interrogative rise occurs (Dascălu 1981b)

(33) <u>NU VIne la NOI?</u>

[⇓   ⇓⇑]

  (Isn't he coming to our place?)

A conciliatory question can be shaped differently, as D. Bolinger has suggested (personal communication; see also Bolinger (1986) for the "contradiction profile"):

(34) <u>NU VIne la NOI?</u>

[⇑ >   ⇓⇑]

In Yes/No questions with double negation it is not *nu*, but the other negation which is accented: the lowest pitch of the entire contour occurs on its stressed syllable, regardless of the position of the word in the utterance (*ibid.*):

(35)   NU VIne NImeni la NOI? (Is nobody coming to our place?)
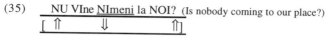
[⇑   ⇓   ⇑]

(36)   NImeni NU VIne la NOI?
[⇓   <   →   ⇑]

If the second negation *nimeni* (nobody) is pronounced on a high or rising intonation, strong surprise or astonishment is implied:

(37)   NU VIne NImeni la NOI?
[⇓ <   < ⇑]

The intonation of rhetorical Yes/No questions is sometimes different from the intonation of genuine ones: it is low, relatively monotonous up to the final rise, which is very slight. This special intonation reflects the false interrogative character of the rhetorical question and the absence of interrogative emphasis in its semantic and intonational structure. Compare the rhetorical question (38) with non-rhetorical questions (39) and (40), identical from a segmental point of view, but containing interrogative emphasis (Dascălu 1982a).

(38)   Se puTEA ALTfel? (Could it be otherwise?)
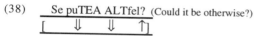
[⇓   ⇓   ↑]

(39)   Se puTEA ALTfel?
[⇓   ⇑   ↓]

(40)   Se puTEA ALTfel?
[⇑   ⇓   ⇑]

If the rhetorical question is negative, it is characterised by a low intonation sustained as such up to the slight final rise.

Compare the rhetorical question (41) and the genuine question (42) with interrogative emphasis on *ea* (she):

(41)   NU-i ea loGODnica lui?   (Isn't she his fiancée?)
[⇓   ⇓   ↑]

(42)   NU-i ea loGODnica lui? (Isn't she his fiancée?)
[⇓ <   → ⇑]

Yes/No questions with an elliptical predicate, which echo a word or a part of the partner's message, have a rising terminal contour preceded by the negative prominence specific to interrogative emphasis; the pattern has a concave shape as compared to an imaginary base line (Dascălu 1979a).

(43) Cu MIne? (With me?)
[⇓ ⇑]

Complementary questions introduced by conjunctions *dar* (but), *şi*, *iar* (and), *nici* (neither) have a similar intonation (Dascălu 1985b).

(44) Nici OAmenii? (Not the people either?)
[⇓ ⇑]

The functional efficiency of the rising intonation pattern in Romanian is even higher if we add certain types of WH-questions which also have a rising intonation. Questions consisting only of the question word can have two different meanings when used with a rising intonation:
(i) asking the partner to repeat some words: *Ce?* (what?), *Cum?* (how?), *Cînd?* (when?);
(ii) expressing surprise, protest, indignation at the partner's words: *Ce?!* (what!), *Cum?!* (how's that!).
The last variant, exclamative, is more marked intonationally: a larger F_0 range, higher peak, longer duration (Dascălu 1980b); compare:

(45) CUM? (How again?)
[⇓ ↑]

(46) CUM?! (How's that!)
[⇓ ⇑]

The intonation of echoed WH-questions is similar to that of Yes/No questions in which the word representing the "key" of the dialogue is pronounced with interrogative emphasis (Dascălu 1985c). Compare the genuine WH-question (47) with the echo question (48) (Dascălu 1980c):

(47) CÎND VIne MAma? (When will mother come?)
[⇑ > > ⇓]

(48) CÎND VIne MAma?
[⇑↓ ↑ ↓ ⇑]

"Reminding" WH-questions are semantically and intonationally distinct from ordinary echos. They are meant to remind the listener of facts or words known and/or discussed previously by the two partners and they imply a presupposition like: question word + did you say + verb. For instance, the question *Cînd (ziceai, era vorba c) vine ea?* (When was she supposed to come?) has a specific intonation: the question word is pronounced with rising pitch, followed by a high plateau up to the last stressed syllable of the sentence, where the pitch rises again (Dascălu 1980c):

(49) CÎND VIne EA? (When was she supposed to come?)
[⇓ < < ⇑]

If the final word has non-final stress, the final peak is followed by a slight fall on the post-tonic syllable(s):

(50) CÎND VIne MAma? (When was mother supposed to come?)
[⇓ < ⇑ ⇓]

The rising-falling pattern is characteristic of alternative questions. The peak is more usually at the end of the first term of the alternative (Dascălu 1983).

(51) BEI VIN ori BEre? (Do you drink wine or beer?)
[↓⇑ > ⇓]

It can also occur on the conjunction *ori, sau* (or), making the question more insistent:

(52) VIne Ana sau MAma? (Is Ana coming or mother?)
[↑ ↓ ↑ > ⇓]

but never at the beginning of the second term of the alternative. It seems that the higher rise at the end of the first term and the smaller fall at the end of the second one are the features that distinguish an alternative question from an alternative statement (*ibid.*); compare:

(53) Ne plimBĂM ori cumpăRĂM caDOuri? (Are we walking or buying gifts?)
[→ ⇑ [⇑ > > ⇓]

(54) Ne plimBĂM ori cumpăRĂM caDOuri. (We are walking or buying gifts.)
[⇑ > > ⇓]

A falling-rising intonation is used with certain "compound interrogative structures"(Dascălu 1981c):

i. Statement + tag:

(55) VII să m-aJUȚI, NU-i aȘA? (You will come to help me, won't you?)
[⇑ ⇓ < ⇑]

(56)   IAR n-am SCRIS BIne, NU?   (I haven't spelt well again, have I?)
   [⇑   > > ⇓ ⇑]

Note that at the end of a number of words in Romanian the letter "i" (sometimes called "pseudo-i") has no syllabic value so that the word *aJUŢI*, in (55) for example, has only two syllables.

ii. By adding a short elliptical Yes/No question to the end of a WH-question, a compound interrogative structure results, which is fairly frequent:

(57)   CUM PLECI, cu TREnul?   (How will you go, by train?)
   [⇑   > ⇓   ⇓ ⇑]

The second part of this structure contains the suggestion of the reply corresponding to the first part (WH-questions), as Bolinger (1957) notes.
   The intonation of exclamation has not been studied separately so far, except for the extent to which certain types of question (rhetorical, echo, imitative, elliptical) have an exclamative shade as well as the distinction between the interrogative value and the exclamative value of certain words such as: *ce* (what), *cît* (how much). In the last case, for instance, intonation plays a decisive role in the opposition, so that the semantic difference between: *Ce surpriză?* (what surprise?) and *Ce surpriză!* (what a surprise!) in Romanian is entirely carried by the intonation.
   The intonation pattern of such exclamations (with elliptic predicate) can have two variants (Dascălu 1981a):

i. a two-peaked pattern: the first peak on *ce*, *cît* and the second one on the stressed syllable of the word "the exclamation (or evaluation) refers to", *e.g.*:

(58)   CE FRIcă!   (What a fright!)
   [↓   ⇑ ↓]

ii. a pattern with a single peak, placed not on *ce* or *cît*, but on the stressed syllable of the other word:

(59)   CÎte eTAje!   (What a lot of storeys!)
   [→ ⇑↓]

2.3 Contextual effects and focalisation

The falling pattern may be modified to emphasise the most important word in the sentence. This kind of contrast is expressed through a positive prominence (high and/or rising pitch on the stressed syllable of the word). Practically any item of an utterance may be emphasised in this way:

(60)   <u>MAma <u>VIne</u> REpede.</u>   (Mother <u>is</u> <u>coming</u> quickly)
      [⇑   >   ⇓]

(61)   <u>MAma VIne <u>REpede.</u></u>   (Mother is coming <u>quickly</u>)
      [↑   >   ⇑   ⇓]

Negative statements are typical cases of emphasising a word, since the negation *nu* (not) is often accented in the sentence (Puşcariu 1959). Usually, negative statements are characterised by an intonational peak on *nu* (Dascălu 1975b):

(62)   <u>De mult NU eRA LAMpă.</u>   (Long ago there weren't any oil lamps.)
      [⇑   > >   ⇓]

If the sentence contains two negations (which is quite normal in Romanian), the intonation peak may be placed either on *nu* or on the other negative word (pronoun, adverb), depending on the speaker's intention:

(63)   <u>N-a veNIT NImeni la NOI.</u>   (Nobody came to our place)
      [⇑   >   > ⇓   ]

(64)   <u>N-a veNIT NImeni la NOI.</u>
      [→ ⇑   > ⇓]

As for WH-questions, when the speaker wants to emphasise some other word for the purpose of contrast, the question word may be fully deaccented:

(65)   <u>Cînd <u>VIne?</u></u>   (When is he <u>coming</u>?)
      [→ ⇑   ⇓]

When the speaker is more insistent, or even irritated for not being understood, the question may have two intonation peaks:

(66)   <u>Cînd <u>VIne?</u></u>
      [⇑ ↓ ↑   ⇓]

where, to use Bolinger's terms (1986a), the first peak corresponds to the "information focus", whereas the second is the "focus of interest".

2.4 Phrasing and textual organisation

The intonation of continuation is, as in many other languages, rising. It differs from the interrogative rise mostly quantitatively, by a narrower F_0 range, a smaller rising interval, as well as a more reduced rate of rise (Dascălu 1971,

1979d). As a rule, a slight rise occurs on the syllable preceding any sentence-internal pause. Since this rise is automatic, the meaning of an example similar to Delattre's one (1966b):

(67)   aCESte Ouă dac-ar fi PROASpete, le-aş cumpăRA.

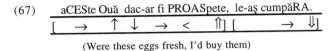

(Were these eggs fresh, I'd buy them)

is not changed by the absence (in rapid speech) of the pauses and/or of the continuation rise. But, in cases of syntactic ambiguity, the relative height of minor and major continuation may become the only distinctive cue. Compare the following examples, borrowed from Bolinger (1986a) and translated into Romanian:

(68)   Dacă te CHEAmă cînd ai să aJUNGI aCOlo, SPUne-mi.

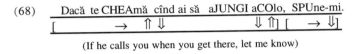

(If he calls you when you get there, let me know)

(69)   Dacă te CHEAmă cînd ai să aJUNGI aCOlo SPUne-mi.

(If he calls you, when you get there let me know)

2.5 Other patterns

"Stylised" intonation frequently occurs in informal, familiar language. The call contour seems the most consistenly used; it differs from the intonation of an ordinary vocative by its "chanted" aspect, *i.e.*, "the stepping-down level pitches as opposed to steadily falling pitch" (Ladd 1980); compare (Dascălu 1985d):

(70)   Ana!   [=vocative]
       [⇑ > →]

(71)   Ana!   [=call]
       [⇑   ⇓]

In the case of monosyllabic words, the two-stepped fall is made possible by splitting up the vowel and pronouncing it as two syllables; compare:

(72)   Vlad! [= vocative]
       [⇑ > →]

(73)   Vla- ad! [= call]
       [⇑   ⇓]

The call contour is the only stylised pattern investigated so far, but we can mention some other uses of this pattern (which typically corresponds to a fall with an interval of a minor third) such as the various shouts of vendors: *MEre!* (Apples!) *GEAmuri!* (Window panes!), as well as some familiar gentle-shaded announcements like *MAsa e GAta!* (Lunch is ready!), *POŞta!* (Postman!), *CIne-i?*(Who's there?), *INtră* (Come in!) *etc.*

Languages may differ considerably in their inventory of intonational clichés and/or specific use. Thus, the French melodic clichés described by Fónagy *et al.* (1983) sound quite strange to Romanian speakers; similarly, not all English examples of "stylised" intonations given by Ladd (1978, 1980) can be translated into Romanian as such.

In turn, Romanian has its own clichés, each of them having a distinct semantic and pragmatic value. For instance, Puşcariu (1976) notes the splitting up of the stressed vowel of a verb in order to express the uninterrupted (durative) course of the action:

(74)   Ai lăsat robinetul deschis şi apa cūrge (= curge mereu).
        (You've left the tap on and water is flowing on and on)

(75)   S-a culcat şi a dormī-it (= a tot dormit) toată ziua.
        (He went to bed and slept and slept all day long).

The author remarks that after the splitting up into two syllables of the lengthened vowel, the first syllable is pronounced with a higher pitch, while the second one "carries the accent" (*ibid.*). Therefore, a simple lengthening accompanied by a special intonation may be used for what corresponds to a periphrastic formula, like that indicated between brackets by Puşcariu: *curge mereu, a tot dormit*, or like the English ones we have used for the translation. Such examples may also be considered stereotyped intonations; these types, among many others, specific to Romanian, deserve a thorough and systematic investigation, which has already been approached (Dascălu-Jinga 1988, 1991b).

We have called "interrogative replies" some fixed structures which originate in rhetorical questions but are actually used – in colloquial and popular language – as categorical, emphatic replies (Dascălu 1982b). Some of them represent affirmative replies, *e.g.cum (s) nu!, de ce nu!* The interrogative reply *de ce nu!* (Why not!) has a different intonation compared to that of genuine WH-questions with the same structure (Dascălu 1988): in the former, there is no fall on *de ce* (why); a slight fall may occur only at the end of the negation *nu*, where, sometimes, even a final rise may be heard;

(76)   – Să facem fiecare cîte o încercare? (– Shall we all try?)
        – DE ce NU!   (– Why not!)
        [↑ → ↓]

or even:

(77) <u>DE ce NU!</u>

    [→ ⇑]

In the genuine WH-question, the high peak on the question word *de ce* is followed by the downskip specific to the WH-questions:

(78) –   N-ai vrea să mergi cu mine la film? (– You won't go to the cinema with me?)
     – <u>DE ce NU?</u>   (– Why "won't"?)

    [→ ⇑   ⇓]

Many fossilised expressions which can function as emphatic negative interrogative replies also originate from rhetorical questions, *e.g.*: *La ce bun?* (What's the use of it?), *Se poate?* (Doubtless! literally: Could it be?) *Ce-are a face?* (It doesn't matter; literally: What matters?), *Ce folos!* (What's the use of it!), *De unde!* (Far from it!, By no means!, Not at all!, literally: From where?), *etc. De unde* is perhaps the most interesting of these expressions, due to the special semantic evolution of the adverb *unde* (where). First, it has lost its primary lexical content (referring to the place of the action); then, after grammaticalisation of the structure and the isolation of *unde*, the interrogative value of it has been lost too, eventually resulting in the fixed formula *de unde!*, with a negative content and an exclamative aspect. The interrogative reply *de unde!* differs from the genuine WH-question *de unde?* from the point of view of its intonation (Dascălu 1988); compare:

(79) –   Ai rezolvat toate problemele? (– Have you solved all your problems?)
     – <u>De UNde! N-am avut timp.</u>   (– Not at all. I had no time for it)

    [⇓   ]

(80) –   A făcut rost de bani. (– She managed to get money)
     – <u>De UNde?</u>   (– Where from?)

    [⇑ ⇓]

     –   De la mama ei.   (– From her mother)

As a matter of fact a great number of idioms which can be found in a phrasal dictionary appear to be used in Romanian at the same time with the free combination of the words they contain. The fossilised expression functions as such only in its own specific linguistic and situational context, where it works as a "bound" utterance, in Fónagy's (1982a) terms.

Besides this essential distinction, noticeable differences between the intonation of "bound" utterances and "free" ones can be observed in Romanian as in other languages (see Fónagy 1982); compare Dascălu 1(988):

(81)   *Bound expression*

    – Pînă la urmă s-au certat îngrozitor. (– Finally, they quarreled awfully)
    – <u>NU MAI SPUne!</u>   (– You don't say!)
    [⇑   > ⇓]

(82)   *Free expression*

    – Va trebui să-ţi faci datoria: să găseşti oamenii, să le explici...
      (– You should do your duty: find the people, explain to them...)
    – <u>NU MAI SPUne.</u> Acum ştiu ce am de făcut.
    [⇑   > ⇓]

        (– Say no more. Now I know what I have to do.)

A special case is that of the idiom *Nici vorbă!* (literally "not a word"), because of the possibility of its use with two semantic values which are completely opposite, *i.e.*, as an emphatic affirmative answer (Of course!, To be sure!, etc), or a negative one (Nothing of the kind!, Certainly not!, etc). Most often the intonation is the only distinctive element: for certain reasons, it seems that the affirmative idiom emphasises the noun *vorb* whereas the negative idiom always stresses the first word *nici*; compare:

(83)   <u>NICI VORb!</u> (Emphatically "yes")
    [→ ⇑ ⇓]

(84)   <u>NICI VORb!</u> (Emphatically "No")
    [⇑   > ⇓]

The analysis of such idioms and their intonation could be extended with many other examples. We are inclined to conclude that for a complete description of a given language, it would also be necessary to include a minimal inventory of these "idiomatic intonations" so that the authors of future phrasal dictionaries could have at their disposal an extra criterion for solving the difficult problem of distinguishing between idioms and "free" combinations of words. (Dascălu 1988).

3. Comparisons with other systems

3.1 Comparisons within the same language

In what follows, some dialectal patterns will be mentioned to the extent they have been investigated so far.

In some regions from the North West of the territory, the last syllable of Yes/No questions is generally falling, regardless of the accentual type of the last word. This fall is sometimes considerable, so that the sentence may end on its lowest level (Dascălu 1986b). On the dialectal terminal fall of Yes/No questions, see also Teiuş (1971, 1980), Dascălu (1975b, 1979c), Ladd (1983b).

Another characteristic of intonation patterns in these regions is the expression of emphasis by means of positive prominence in all types of utterances, including Yes/No questions (Dascălu 1986b). As a direct consequence of this, a peculiar pattern arises: utterances which contain an emphasised word or a negation are characterised by a relatively high plateau beginning with the stressed syllable of the emphasised word and ending with the last stressed syllable of the sentence (something like a reversed U-shape).

This pattern occurs in statements of various kinds: emphatic, negative, imperative, exclamative. The specific declarative fall is not gradual – as in Standard Romanian – but abrupt, in the last stressed syllable of the sentence (Dascălu 1975b, 1986b); compare:

(85) *Maramure*

N-O fost aTÎţia DOCtori (There were not so many doctors)

(86) *Standard Romanian*

N-au fost aTÎţia DOCtori.

A high plateau-shaped pattern also occurs in Yes/No questions. Since in standard Yes/No questions the interrogative emphasis is expressed by negative prominence (see §2.3.), the dialectal Yes/No questions and the standard ones have quite opposite patterns: a high plateau ending with an abrupt fall *vs.* a low plateau ending with an abrupt rise (Dascălu 1986b). Compare:

(87) *Bihor*

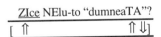

ZIce NElu-to "dumneaTA"?

(Does your Nelu say "dumneata"?) [a more polite form of address in Romanian]

(88) *Standard Romanian*

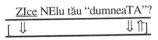

ZIce NElu tău "dumneaTA"?

Although the interrogative high plateau-shaped pattern resembles the declarative one and both of them are used in the same geographic area, they are, of course, different enough to be distinctive: in questions the initial rise is larger and the terminal fall is smaller than in statements; in other words, questions are entirely pronounced on a higher register of the speaker's voice (Dascălu 1975; 1986b).

A special interrogative pattern occuring in Muscel (a South-Carpathian region of Romania) has been thoroughly investigated by Avram (1973). This pattern may be essentially characterised as having a rising terminal contour in all cases, differing thereby from the Standard one, where the final rise is determined by some factors (the place of interrogative emphasis and the accentual type of the last word – see §2.2). The Muscel interrogative pattern is difficult to describe briefly, because of its very odd aspect as compared to the Standard one. It is, probably, most obvious in Yes/No questions ending in bisyllabic words with penultimate stress. Avram sums up his observations on this type – by using arrows to suggest the pitch movement in the last two syllables – as follows:

Question type	Standard Romanian	Muscel
MAma VIne?	↑ ↓	↓ ↑
MAma VIne?	↓ ↑	(↓) ↑ ↓ ↑

In such a case the author assumes that the terminal contour of Standard questions differs from the Muscel one as "simple" *vs.* "complex", *i.e.*: falling-rising *vs.* rising-falling-rising; in other words the Muscel terminal contour of Yes/No questions contains two changes of pitch movement.

Relying on spoken material recorded in Ţara Oltului (a South-Eastern part of Transylvania), we have shown (1986a) the presence of the Muscel-type interrogative pattern in this area of Romania's territory too. Since the interrogative emphasis is expressed by a positive prominence (also as in Muscel – see Avram 1973), a two-peaked overall pattern occurs in this type of question (Dascălu 1986a):

(89)   <u>VEzi BIne?</u>   (Can you see well?)
   [⇑ ⇓ ⇑]

(90)   <u>NU staţi pînă la Unu?</u>   (Won't you stay till one o'clock?)
   [⇑ ⇓   ⇓ ⇑]

3.2 Comparisons with other languages

Chiţoran *et al.* (1984) state that the fact that Romanian negative sentences, unlike their English equivalents, place their most important stress on the negation represents an essential difference between the two languages. Avram

(1972) has shown that a typical characteristic of Romanian speakers of English is a tendency to give excessive prominence to the negative particle *not*.

In WH-questions, the question word is always accented in Romanian, whereas in English it is the last important lexical constituent that carries the sentence stress. This makes Chiţoran *et al.* (1984) predict

a tendency on the part of Romanian learners of English to automatically place the sentence stress on the WH-word in such questions.

Unlike other languages, a rise in the terminal contour of WH-questions appears rather unusual in Romanian. Avram (1972) finds that "it is difficult for Romanian speakers to use a rising tone in this case". This feature opposes Romanian to Italian (Niculescu 1969) and many other languages (Ultan 1969), where a final rise may occur. In fact, it seems that not all languages which record rising WH-questions use them with a primary, neutral interrogative meaning, and that furthermore this pattern is not used by all speakers. In Hungarian, for instance, this phenomenon is somewhat restricted from a sociolinguistic point of view, since such questions are most frequent in the speech of women and young people (Fónagy 1969).

Lehiste and Ivić (1980) think that the low pattern characterising the focus in Yes/No questions (what we have called interrogative emphasis) is "a new Balkanism", which they have also observed in Serbocroatian and Albanian.

The low intonation prolonged as such up to the final rise, specific to Standard Yes/No questions which begin with an emphasised word, seems most typical of Romanian. The very common use of this intonation can explain one of the common mistakes Romanian natives make when speaking English. Pârlog and Popa (1978) have found that the "low prenuclear pattern" is the most frequent error in the pronunciation of English Yes/No questions by Romanian students. Avram (1972) also remarks that "the falling-rising tone is the most difficult one for Romanian speakers".

Unlike English tags, Romanian ones – generally represented by a formula such as *da?* (yes?), *nu?* (no?), *nu-i aşa?* (isn't it?) – are always rising, so that the expected answer is suggested not by their intonation, but by the presence or absence of the negation in the segment that precedes the tag. The use of these interrogative structures is much less systematic and complex than in English, the Romanian type of "tag" seems more like the French *n'est-ce pas* phrase.

4. Conclusions

Instead of conclusions, some desiderata concerning the further study of Romanian intonation are worth mentioning here:

a. theoretical objectives
– the continuation of the study of syntactic functions of intonation, mainly in cases where it helps to remove ambiguity (*cf.* Dascălu-Jinga 1990, 1991c);
– the study of pragmatic functions of intonation (*cf.* Dascălu-Jinga 1991a);
– the development of research aimed at identifying intonation patterns specific to Romanian: (a) by means of a step-by-step constitution of an "inventory of Romanian intonation clichés" and (b) by comparing and/or contrasting Romanian intonation with that of other languages;
– the extension of research into the functions of intonation on a "horizontal" level (geographic variants) and the opening of new paths especially on a "vertical" level (sociolinguistic variants).

Of course there is plenty of room for many other aspects, such as: the relation between the prosody of a spoken message and that of one read aloud (cf. Dascălu-Jinga 1993b, 1994), or the rich field of the affective-attitudinal values of intonation, *etc.*

b. Methods and techniques
The most difficult desideratum still appears to be the finding of some efficient way of recording a real natural, spontaneous corpus; among other desiderata, the improvement of control methods aimed at "validating" the acoustic information (by using more reliable perceptual tests) and the more frequent use of statistical proofs are to be taken in consideration.

14

Intonation in Russian

NATALIA SVETOZAROVA

1. Background

1.1 General prosodic characteristics

In Russian, which belongs to the Slavic branch of Indo-European languages, the phoneme operates as the minimal unit of distinctive opposition. Russian possesses a tendency for open syllable structure, and its word stress does not make use of phonemically contrastive tones. Its prosodic features (length, intensity, pitch) participate in two functionally separate systems: a system of word stress and a system of sentence intonation; within each system, these features perform a primarily organising function as the most important means of grouping sounds and syllables into words, words into phrases, clauses or sentences, and sentences into entire texts. In as much as prosodic grouping can be achieved variously, depending upon which syllable in a word, or which word in a clause, *etc.*, receives prosodic prominence, stress and intonation possess other functions as well: identificatory, delimitative, and distinctive. Certain types of prosodic patterns – elements of expression – can more or less regularly correspond to certain quite highly generalised elements of content. At times, the prosodic patterning of an utterance represents the only expression of certain communicative meanings (question, non-finality, contrast, *etc.*).

The systems of word stress and sentence intonation are both similar and fundamentally different. Their similarity lies in the fact that they both utilise the same means (length, intensity, pitch) in relative (not absolute) quantities, and in the identity of their basic functions. The difference between these systems is explained by the fact that word accent deals with relatively simple signs, whereas sentence intonation deals with signs which are complex both quantitatively and structurally. It is the coordination of intonation with a complex sign, the utterance, which is the reason for the structural complexity of intonation, and also for the use within the framework of intonation of such clause-level prosodic features as pause and phonation type.

Word stress in Russian is free, both in terms of the place of the stressed syllable in the word, and in the relationship of stress to morphemic structure. In principle, stress can fall on any syllable in the word and on any morpheme – root, prefix, suffix, or even desinence. In the IPA transcriptions, the symbol /'/ indicates palatalisation of the preceding consonant and the symbol /'/ indicates primary stress on the following syllable.

(1) a ДОрого   доРОже   дороГОЙ   дорогоВАто
         /'doraga   da'roʒɨ   dara'goj   daraga'vata/
         (dearly   dearer   dear (adj.) rather dear)

     b ХОдит   ходИТЬ   выхоДИТЬ   ВЫходить   выхоЖУ
         /'xod'it   xa'd'it'   vɨxa'd'it'   'vɨxad'it' vɨxa'ʒu /
         (he goes   to go   to go out   to nurse   I go out)

The great majority of Russian words contain only one stressed syllable; secondary stress (transcribed /ˌ/) appears only in some compound words, and even then only optionally:

(2) a водопроВОД   / vadapra'vot/ (water-pipe)
     b сельскохоЗЯЙственный   /s'ilskaxa'z'ajstv'innɨj/ (agricultural)
        СЕЛЬскохоЗЯЙственный   /ˌs'elskaxa'z'ajstv'innɨj/

Despite the apparently random nature of stress placement in modern Russian, there exist certain well-defined paradigmatic regularities based on word class (Fedjanina 1976; Zaliznjak 1985).

One highly characteristic feature of Russian word stress is its mobility, *i.e.*, the tendency of stress to move from one syllable to another under inflection. Although these mobile stress patterns, where for example stress shifts from stem to desinence and from desinence to stem, occur in no more than 5% of all Russian words, these 5% belong to the main core of the lexicon and have a high frequency-rate:

(3)   сеСТРА СЁстры   оСЁЛ оСЛЫ   ЛОшадь лошаДЕЙ
       /s'i'stra - 's'ostrɨ a's'ol - a'slɨ   'loʃit' - laʃɨ'dej
       (a sister – sisters   a donkey – donkeys a horse – horses (Gen. Pl.))

A full accentual description of a Russian word thus consists of its accentual type (mobile, or fixed-stem/-end stress), its morpheme structure *vis-à-vis* stress, and its rhythmic structure.

The phonetic correlates of Russian word stress represent a complex of features, the most important of which are the length and the quality of the stressed vowel. Prominence (greater length, greater intensity, presence of pitch movement) in one of the syllables of a word is always accompanied by a qualitative and quantitative reduction of the unstressed syllables, where the degree of reduction depends on their position in relation to the stressed syllable, as well as to the word boundaries.

The place of word stress and the accentual contour determined by it are obligatory and constant characteristics of word forms. Accentual doublets in Russian are rare, especially for citation forms; when variants exist, they are usually stylistically marked, sub-standard, or emotionally coloured as in the following examples where the second form of each pair is cited in (OSRJ 1983) as a variant:

(4)   твоРОГ – ТВОрог   иНАче – Иначе   далеКО – даЛЁко
/ tva'rok - 'tvorak   i'natʃi - 'inatʃi   dal'i'ko - da'l'oka/
(cottage-cheese   otherwise   far)

The main function of Russian word stress is constitutive and word-identifying: it determines the particular accentual rhythmic structure of a given word, and if that structure is deformed in any way, the word becomes more and more difficult, or even impossible, to recognise. The differentiating and delimitative functions of word stress are secondary for Russian. Although the free placement of stress does result in the existence of accentual minimal pairs:

(5)   МУка – муКА (torment – flour)
/ 'muka - mu'ka/

the possibility of their appearing in the same context is limited. The same feature – free stress – significantly reduces the delimitative function of stress in Russian (as opposed to languages with fixed stress). On the other hand, the accentual unity of Russian words, especially the varying degrees of vowel reduction dictated by the place of stress, to a large extent facilitate the recognition of word boundaries in the flow of speech.

Within the sentence, the accentual-rhythmic structure of a word can vary considerably depending on the degree of its prosodic prominence and its position in the intonational contour. T.M. Nikolaeva has characterised Russian as a language in which word prosody is greatly affected by sentence prosody (Nikolaeva 1977). Nevertheless, full words tend to preserve stress even in the sentence; experimental evidence shows that only in particularly weak intonational positions, such as between two strongly stressed words or following the major sentence stress, does one observe the objective neutralisation of rhythmic differences between words of essentially different accent structure (Svetozarova 1982, pp. 124–126). Syntactic words (prepositions, particles, conjunctions, *etc.*), on the other hand, are for the most part unstressed in the flow of speech, attaching themselves as proclitics or enclitics to fully-stressed words. The fact that Russian does not have functionally opposed types of stress and that its prosodic features are relative rather than absolute, makes it possible to recognise the accentual contour of a word in sentences with various combinations of prosodic features. The melodic component of stress is especially variable: the stressed syllable can have a high or low tone, a rising or falling pitch pattern depending on the general pitch contour of the utterance, and the position of the word within it. Length and intensity have a more direct correlation to stress: in a given intonational position, and with other conditions being equal (for example, the quality of the vowel and its surrounding consonants), stressed vowels as a rule exhibit higher values of these parameters than unstressed ones; the higher the values, the greater the degree of prosodic prominence of the word as a whole. Because this prominence is the result of a complex of prosodic means, the speaker is able to vary their combination depending on the commmunicative situation. Thus, in a request, the vowel receiving main stress owes its prominence more to a greater degree of length than to intensity, while a drawn-out vowel is less compatible with the intonation of a command, and intensity plays a greater role.

Numerous experimental studies have demonstrated the complex interaction of word and sentence prosody, which can be seen to vary: on different parts of a single intonation contour (the intonational centre and the peripheral pre- and post-centric parts); in different types of intonational contours (cf. strongly- *vs.* weakly-centred contours); and in various types of spoken material (read-aloud and spontaneous speech).

1.2 Outline of the approach

The study of standard Russian intonation has a long tradition of linguistic scholarship. The foundations of a theory of sentence intonation are to be found in the works of syntacticians (Peškovskij, Karcevskij, Gvozdev) and specialists of theatrical speech (Vsevolodskij-Gerngross, Volkonskij). Phoneticians turned to the study of Russian intonation relatively late, when the theory of the phoneme was already established. The influence of the latter became in part a stimulus for the development of a theory of intonation, leading to the application of the phonological method to the phenomena of intonation; at the same time it tended to hinder the discovery of fundamental differences betwen segmental and suprasegmental phonetics.

There are two major approaches amongst the numerous descriptions of the Russian intonational system existing in the literature: those that describe the intonational features characteristic of certain sentence types and syntactic categories (declarative and interrogative intonation, intonation of enumeration, contrast, direct address, syntactic isolation, *etc.*); as a rule, such descriptions are not concerned with producing a finite list of intonational units. The other approach is represented by those who describe a limited selection of intonational forms (intonemes, or intonational constructions), determined through the discovery of minimal pairs: segmentally identical utterances which differ only intonationally. Both approaches have advantages as well as disadvantages, and complement one another. The first is found in works of syntax as well as phonetics (see, *e.g.*, Matsusevich 1976), and in intonational studies (Nikolaeva 1977; Svetozarova 1982). The second approach has become well known through the works of Bryzgunova (1977a; Russkaja grammatika 1980) and Ode (1989).

The literature devoted specifically to the study of Russian intonation is extensive. There have been numerous experimental studies using instrumental analysis to discover the acoustic and perceptual correlates of Russian intonation. Such detailed objective descriptions exist for the major commmunicative types of utterances, the intonation of compound sentences, the temporal organisation of connected texts, *etc.* More recently, Russian intonational studies have turned from the investigation of isolated sentences and small prepared texts to work with large extracts from recordings of spontaneous speech, both of conversational and scholarly nature (see references RRR, SRUNR, FSR). There have also been studies investigating the prosody of Russian dialects (Bryzgunova 1977b; Paufo\u0161ima 1983). On the whole, Russian can be counted among those languages whose intonation has been well studied, but there are many important questions of a theoretical and practical nature which remain unanswered.

In this chapter a sample of typical utterances is illustrated by diagrams showing actual fundamental frequency curves (fine line), in combination with the intonational contours arrived at by the calculations used for speech synthesis (bold line). The horizontal lines indicate the range and average height of the informant's voice. The basic model of the pitch contour of a Russian sentence as reflected in the diagrams is that of a declination line with deviations either above or below it corresponding to the stressed syllables of prominent words. For more details, see Svetozarova 1982. The rest of the examples are transcribed using the INTSINT transcription system (Hirst and Di Cristo this volume).

2. Description of intonation patterns

The most common function of sentence intonation, characteristic, it would appear, of all the world's languages, is that of transforming nominative linguistic entities (word and phrases) into communicative entities (utterances). In each language, this is accomplished by a combination of more individual functions. Which of these can be said to be characteristic of a given language depends to a certain degree on the general structural features of that language. The importance of intonation in Russian, its great distinctive possibilities, is connected with the rather free order of words in Russian, and the comparatively rare use of other formal (lexical and syntactic) means for certain communicative categories (theme/rheme structure, and communicative utterance type).

Russian uses a complex of features to combine semantically and syntactically related words into prosodic units of a higher order; the most important of these is the heightened degree of stress on one of the words within such a unit. The kind of sentence stress which performs this organising function can be called *neutral* as opposed to those kinds of stress which apart from organising also perform other functions: that of underscoring, contrasting, emphasising, *etc.* Various terms are used to refer to the stress attached to these functions: contrastive, emphatic, logical; a convenient general term for all of these would be *special prominence*. The phonetic expressions of neutral and special sentence stress in Russian differ from one another, as can easily be seen when they occur in the same position:

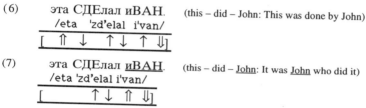

(6)   эта СДЕлал иВАН.   (this – did – John: This was done by John)
        /eta 'zd'elal i'van/

(7)   эта СДЕлал иВАН.   (this – did – John: It was John who did it)
        /eta 'zd'elal i'van/

Neutral sentence stress at the end of a final declarative sentence is characterised by a simple falling tone and increased length of the stressed vowel with relatively low intensity. Special stress in the same position is usually manifested by a high-falling or complex rising-falling tone, a sharp increase in intensity and a possible, though not obligatory lengthening of the vowel. It must be noted, however, that the perception of a special accentual prominence in Russian is often due not so much to heightened prosodic features as to the location of the sentence stress in an unusual position or on a word which would not normally carry it. This is due to the fact that in Russian there exist fairly strict, but as yet inadequately described, rules for the distribution of neutral sentence stress. The research of recent years shows that these rules are based not only on positional criteria (where the last word in an utterance is stressed), or syntactic criteria (where certain grammatical constituents are stressed), but also on semantic criteria (where stress falls on words with a particular semantic structure). Cf., *e.g.*, Nikolaeva 1982, 1987; Paducheva 1987; Skorikova 1987; Svetozarova 1987; Pavlova and Svetozarova 1987.

It is important to emphasise that, whatever means are employed in marking special sentence stress, whether purely phonetic or positional, the effect is in principle the same, namely a kind of "augmented meaning", the actualisation of certain presuppositions, or – to use Nikolaeva's expression – the creation of a communicative halo, a contextual aura (Nikolaeva 1982).

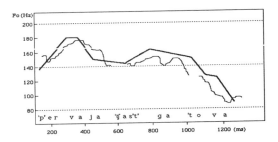

Figure 1. Fundamental frequency curve (fine line), together with the model used for speech synthesis (bold line) for example 8. The dotted horizontal lines indicate the range and average height of the speaker's voice.

Thus, sentence intonation in Russian, in the form of one of its most important subsystems – sentence stress – not only organises words into a single meaningful unit, but, by accomplishing this in a variety of ways, succeeds in transmitting extremely important information of a pragmatic nature as well.

Intonation plays an important role in the distinction of various communicative types of utterances. This aspect of Russian intonation is well described in the literature, both theoretical and pedagogical.

2.1 Description of a basic non-emphatic pattern

The typical intonation pattern of an isolated declarative sentence is constituted by a sequence of pitch rises and falls, coinciding with fully accented words or phrases, and ending with a deeply falling tone on the stressed syllable of the word which carries the neutral sentence stress (see figure 1).

(8) ПЕРвая ЧАСТЬ гоТОва   (the first part is ready)
   /'p'ervaja 'ʧas't' ga'tova/

[⇑   ↓   ↑ > ⇓]

In connected speech, the final falling tone is usually not quite completed, with a possible rising tone on the part of the contour following the sentence stress.

The introduction of special stress into a declarative sentence fundamentally alters its intonational configuration: the bipartite neutrally accented sentence (see above) becomes strongly centralised, and the highly prominent pitch contour of the word receiving special stress is accompanied by reduced melodic prominence on the rest of the words in the sentence (see figure 2).

(9) это Очень СРОчно!   (It is very urgent)
   /eta 'oʧin' 'sroʧna/

[⇑   ↓ ⇓]

267

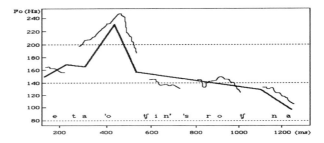

Figure 2. Fundamental frequency for example 9 (*cf.* figure 1).

2.2 Mode and expressivity

Despite the existence of question particles in Russian, a yes/no question is usually formed without them and without special word order. The only indication of the interrogative nature of the utterance is its characteristic intonation: a sharply rising high tone at the beginning of the stressed syllable of the word receiving main stress, and an obligatory deep lowering of tone on the syllables following main stress, while the syllables preceding the main stress are nearly level. (See figure 3.)

(10)   ВЫ меНЯ СЛЫшите ?   (Are you listening to me?)
         /'vɨ m'i'n'a 'slɨʃit'i/
         [↑ → ⇑ ↓ ⇓]

Questions are pronounced with a rapid speech tempo.

There are numerous structural and emotionally coloured variants of the yes/no question whose intonation differs sharply from the type just described. An elliptical question using the conjunction *a* (contrastive "and"), is formed with a low-rising or falling-rising tone:

(11)   (ты приДЁшь?) а МАша ?   (Are you coming? And Mary?)
         /tɨ pr'i'd'oʃ   a 'maʃa /
         [⇓ ↑]

A question used as a self-reminder has a high-rising tone with a continued high tone on the contour following the main stress, *etc.* Emotional connotations such as surprise, doubt, distrust, and irony are usually expressed in Russian by means of various modifications of the question intonation: differences in the length of the sressed syllable, the sharpness and height of the rise, different phonation types (for more details, see Kodzassov 1985).

Opinions are divided concerning the typical intonation of the question-word question. Inasmuch as in these constructions the question element is expresed

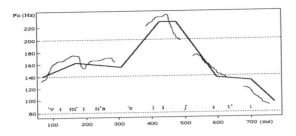

Figure 3. Fundamental frequency for example 10 (cf. figure 1).

lexically, their intonation is often considered to coincide with that of a declarative sentence. However, the part of the contour which precedes the main stress exhibits characteristic differences: a higher rise in tone on the question word, and a high tone without significant lowering on the part between the initial rise and the final fall (see figure 4).

(12)   коМУ переДАТЬ?   (Who shall I give it to?)
        /ka'mu p'ir'i'dat'/
        [⇑   >   ⇓]

A different (and rarer) type of intonation for question-word questions is characterised by special sentence stress on the question word, and a levelling out of the part of the contour that follows.

The same rising tones found in various types of questions can be used in non-final clauses for the expression of continuation. According to several authors, these contours coincide completely. However, the intonation of continuation differs from the typically sharply rising melodic contour of a yes/no question (see figure 3), in having a smaller interval of rising tone. The use of different types of rises and their different realisations allows for diverse kinds of semantic connections between the parts of an utterance with multiple intonational divisions, reflecting their hierarchical structure.

The intonation of imperative and exclamatory sentences, as well as various kinds of responses, reactions, exclamations, and modes of address, is extremely diverse, and cannot be characterised within the scope of this chapter.

2.3 Contextual factors and focalisation

The role of intonation in expressing theme/rheme structure in Russian is extremely large. The unique feature of intonation in this function is its ability to indicate the informational structure of the utterance – its division into theme and rheme, or the lack of such a division – not only independently of special syntactic, lexical or structural means, but even in spite of them by, for example, moving the rhematic predicate from its usual sentence-final position to the

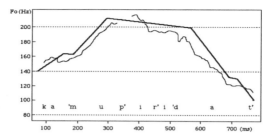

Figure 4. Fundamental frequency for example 12 (cf. figure 1).

beginning. Sentence stress in Russian is the most important means for marking a word or a phrase as belonging either to the theme or the rheme, regardless of their order in the sentence and particular functional-semantic characteristics.

Both theme and rheme, or more commonly, key-words in the composition of polylexemic theme or rheme, are prominent in Russian, and both possess quite specific, although not uniform melodic characteristics.

In a declarative sentence the rheme is characterised by a falling or rising-falling tone, regardless of its position in the sentence.

(13)   иВАН чиТАет (John is reading)
          /i'van t͡ʃi'tait/
          [⇑   ⇑ ⇓   ]

(14)   иВАН чиТАет (It's John who is reading)
          /i'van   t͡ʃi'tait/
          [⇑   ⇓   ]

The melodic composition of the theme, on the other hand, does depend upon its position in the sentence. A theme which precedes the rheme always possesses a rising tone, and the height of the tone increases when the theme becomes isolated in its own tonal group, for example, with the added meaning of *as for X.*, or with a contrastive meaning. Cf.:

(15)   иВАН – ПИшет (а МАша – риСУет)
          / i'van 'p'iʃit   a 'maʃa r'i'suit/
          [⇑ ↓ ↑ ↓] [⇑   > ⇓]
          (John is writing and Mary drawing)

In those relatively rare instances where theme follows rheme, the theme, being highly redundant, does not possess marked prosodic characteristics, and in a final declarative sentence it is pronounced with a low tone.

(16) КТО это там приШЁЛ? – иВАН приШЁЛ.
　　　/'kto eta tam pr'i'ʃol　　i'van　pr'i'ʃol/
　　　[　⇑　　　　⇑　⇓　][⇑　⇓　　　　　　　]

(Who is that who has come? – It's John who has come.)

In non-final clauses and questions, the prosodic expression of theme/rheme structure combines with the characteristic melody of continuation or question: the rheme, as the intonational centre of the utterance, receives a rising tone:

(17)　иВАН приЕхал?　　(has John arrived?)
　　　/i'van pr'i'jexal/
　　　[　↑↓　　⇑⇓　]

(18)　иВАН приЕхал, но ненаДОЛго.　(John has arrived, but not for long)
　　　/i'van pr'i'jexal　no n'ina'dolga/
　　　[　⇑　　↓　↑↓][⇑　　>　⇓　]

In such bipartite sentences, theme and rheme receive a contrastive pitch pattern, and the contrast is heightened as the prosodic opposition becomes more pronounced. In unipartite, all-rheme sentences, intonation expresses a lack of theme-rheme opposition, owing to a unified contour, undivided either by pause or pronounced melodic break. Cf.:

(19)　СВЕтит СОЛНце.　(shines – sun = The sun is shining)
　　　/'sv'et'it 'sontse/
　　　[　　⇑　>　⇓　　]

(20)　поШЁЛ ДОЖДЬ.　(went (began) – rain = It's raining)
　　　/pa'ʃol 'doʃʧ/
　　　[　⇑　>　⇓　]

In Russian, sentence stress, both neutral and special, can be the only means of expressing the informational focus of the utterance – and additionally of expressing such meanings as comparison, contrast, evaluation, degree, *etc.*

2.4 Phrasing and textual organisation

Along with the division into theme and rheme (or the lack of such a division), intonation is responsible for a more subtle structuring of the elements within the theme and the rheme respectively, their internal hierarchy. As noted by Kacnel'son, prosodic devices are analogous to parentheses in an expanded algebraic equation:

grouping various types of segments together and signalling their boundaries, they mark out as it were the complex hierarchical structure of speech on the plane of expression. (Kacnel'son 1971. p. 138)

Equally important information is expressed by the opposite of prosodic grouping: prosodic subdivision. By combining certain words and phrases into conceptual units, intonation by the same token separates them from neighbouring conceptual units and simultaneously determines the hierarchical relationships between them. The universal means of intonational division in Russian as in other languages is the pause. As in other languages the pause as a functional unit is not always expressed by an acoustic zero. It can be achieved by means of abrupt changes in other prosodic features: pitch movement, intensity, length. Experimental data point to the existence of three types of functional pause in Russian: short, medium, and long. The differences between them consist in the length of the pauses themselves, as well as the melodic, dynamic, and temporal composition of the fragments of utterance before and after the pause (cf. Nikolaeva 1969).

The pause, in close combination with the melody, often occurs as a means of isolating, or "setting aside", when parenthetical words or constructions are introduced:

(21)   Я приЕду ЗАвтра, ВЕчером (I'll arrive tomorrow, in the evening)
       / ja pr'i'jedu 'zaftra / 'v'etʃiram /
       [⇑   ↓   ↑ > ⇓] [⇓   ]

(22)   Я приЕду, скоРЕе всеГО, ВЕчером. (I'll arrive, probably, in the evening)
       /ja pr'i'jedu/ / ska'r'ei fs'i'vo / /'v'etʃiram /
       [⇑ ↓ ↑↓][↑   ] [⇓   ]

The place of the pause, together with other intonational devices, disambiguates syntactic structure in homonymous utterances:

(23)   я ВСТРЕтил жеНУ, БРАта и МАТЬ.
       / ja 'fstr'et'il ʒɨ'nu / 'brata / i 'mat'/
       [⇑   ↓ ↑][⇑ ↓][→⇓]

       (I met my wife, my brother and my mother)

(24)   я ВСТРЕтил жеНУ БРАта и МАТЬ.
       / ja 'fstr'et'il ʒɨ'nu 'brata / i 'mat'/
       [⇑   ↓   ↑ ↓][→⇓]

       (I met my brother's wife and (my) mother)

2.5 Other patterns

A distinguishing feature of Russian intonation is its abundance of intonational stereotypes, the prosodic structure of which can be described only in conjunction with their lexico-grammatical structure. There are two basic classes:

a) intonational *clichés*, in which the unique intonation is inseparable from the unique lexico-grammatical configurations:

(25)   НУ и НУ!   (well – and – well) [in the sense of reproach, condemnation]
        /'nu i 'nu/

(26)   ВОТ так ТАК!   (here – so – so) [expressing surprise]
        /'vot tak 'tak/

b) intonational idioms, the intonation of which changes the meaning of the word or the sentence, often to the opposite:

(27)   молоДЕЦ!   (good boy/girl = well done!) [with reproach, irony]
        /mala'd'eʦ/

(28)   ТАК я тебе и скаЗАла!   (So I told you!) [meaning: I won't tell you]
        /'tak ja t'ib'e i ska'zala /

3. Comparison with other systems

3.1 Other dialects of Russian

There is a strong evidence concerning the differences between the intonation system of standard Russian and the intonation of Russian dialects. The peculiarity of nonstandard intonation in different localities in Russia is often reflected in its estimation as "sing-song intonation". However there are surprisingly few experimental studies on this subject. One of the most obvious peculiarities of dialectal prosody is its temporal organisation. Information on Russian dialectal prosody can be found for example in Bryzgubova 1977b and in Paufosima 1983.

3.2 Comparison with other languages

a. Other Slavic languages
In contrast to insufficient knowledge about the intonation of dialects there is much reliable experimental information not only about prosodic characteristics of different Slavic languages but also about the relationship between the prosodic systems in the whole branch of these languages. The most thorough investigation was made by T.M. Nikolaeva in her book describing the sentence intonation of Slavic languages (Nikolaeva 1977). One of the most important conclusions of this work consists in revealing differences in the degree to which sentence intonation affects word prosody.

b. Non-Slavic languages
Such comparisons can be found in the following three directions of experimental investigations which are very popular in the ex-Soviet Union.

The first deals with the comparison between Russian intonation and the intonation of those foreign languages studied at schools and universities (English, German, French). Much valuable information can be taken from the study of foreign accent phenomena in the speech of Russian learners and their estimation by native speakers.

The second direction deals with the influence of native intonation on the intonation of Russian, studied as a foreign language by people from different countries, whose native languages belong to different language families.

The third direction is represented by studies of the interaction of intonation systems (sometimes called prosodic interference) in the Russian speech of bilingual subjects in ex-Soviet republics and autonomous regions also representing many language families (Indo-European, Turkic, Uralic, Caucasian *et al.*).

4. Conclusions

In the pitch contour of Russian sentences there is a base component analogous to the declination observed in other languages (Krivnova 1975; Svetozarova 1975); the dynamic contour also shows a distinct decline from the beginning to the end of speech units. The temporal contour, on the contrary, exhibits increasing relative syllable length, with a strong tendency to prepausal lengthening of both stressed and unstressed syllables. There is a distinct correspondence of dynamic pitch movements (departures from the base contour) to stressed syllables (Ode 1989).

Experimental work has been done on the microprosodic structure of the intonational contour in Russian, including the temporal, intensity and frequency characteristics of vowels, and the influence of the segmental structure and syllabic composition of an utterance on its prosodic features. Microprosodic phenomena in Russian are analogous to those described for other languages. Work in this area continues.

The existing data on the acoustic and perceptual characteristics of Russian intonation are sufficient for the purposes of carrying out research on the automatic analysis and synthesis of speech prosody. In addition, there is an active interest in experimentally based research into the methods of teaching Russian intonation to foreigners, and into specific questions of prosodic interference in learning foreign languages. Development in this area of applied research provides new stimulus for the experimental study of intonation in Russian.

Note

My thanks to Jan Schaffert for his help in translating this text into English.

15

Intonation in

Bulgarian

ANASTASIA MISHEVA and MICHEL NIKOV

1. Background

1.1 General prosodic characteristics

Bulgarian is spoken by approximately 8 million people. The language, which belongs to the Southern branch of the Slavic family of Indo-European, presents free lexical stress: its position in a word cannot be determined from the syllabic structure. There are a number of minimal pairs for stress:

ВЪЛна /ˈvəlna/ (wool)   вълНА /vəlˈna/ (wave)
КУпа /ˈkupa/ (cup, trophy)   куПА /kuˈpa/ (haystack)

Stress is manifested acoustically as a complex interaction of the prosodic parameters of length, loudness and pitch and there are also qualitative spectral changes with reduction of the unstressed vowels.

Phonetic research on Bulgarian intonation has produced a great variety of experimental data concerning the prosodic features of fundamental frequency, intensity and duration (F_0, I, T) of utterances (Tilkov 1981). This makes it difficult to detect clearcut intonation patterns as sets of relevant acoustic features, independently from the accentual and rhythmical structure of the phrase. For example, the pitch contour of a statement consisting of a single word, the simplest case, can be falling, falling + low level, rising-falling or high level + falling. Furthermore the pitch range of the fall which is to be found in most contours associated with a statement, may vary in amplitude, ranging from about two semitones up to a whole octave. The direction of the pitch movement within the stressed syllable itself is not necessarily downwards – it may also be level or rising with the fall occuring on the following unstressed syllables.

1.2 Outline of the approach adopted in the chapter

It is very difficult to provide a description of the intonation system of Bulgarian which will account for the actual variety of F_0 patterns and at the same time unambiguously specify the different intonation patterns without taking into account the prosodic structure of the utterance. For this reason we treat the phonetic aspect of the suprasegmental system as a set of realisation rules for organising the discrete levels of the temporal macrostructure defined with respect to their units: syllables, phonetic words, syntagmas (intonation groups), phrases (sentences), phono-paragraphs *etc.* According to this approach, the suprasegmental system is viewed as a reorganisation of the phonetic segments in order to ensure the phonetic integrity of the macrostructural units conditioned by the goal of speech communication. The suprasegmental system consists of two kinds of rules: distinctive and constitutive, which are differentiated on the basis of their linguistic function or its absence. The intonation system is thus seen as a set of suprasegmental distinctive rules on the level of the phrase. The intonation rules are divided into four types, corresponding to the four linguistic functions described in traditional Bulgarian phonetics: communicatve (speech function or illocutionary force), focusing, delimitative and affective/attitudinal.

In our view, the aim of experimental research on Bulgarian intonation is to unravel the multi-functional phonetic entity of the phrase, considered as the result of an interaction of both types of suprasegmental rules with the sequence of constituent units. We believe that the rules themselves are of a systematic nature, but their application to different structures and the possibility of the simultaneous application of rules results in the observed variety of actual F_0 curves.

2. Description of intonation patterns

2.1 Description of a basic non-emphatic pattern

The position of the stressed syllable in the word, as mentioned above, strongly affects the F_0 pattern of single-word sentences. The pitch fall, typical of statements, regularly occurs on the stressed vowel only if this is late (*i.e.* in the second half) of the word. When the stress is early, (*i.e.* in the first half of the word) the pitch movement on the stressed syllable may be rising or level with the falling part of the pitch movement occuring on the following unstressed syllables. The F_0 peak is usually situated on the stressed syllable itself, but in late stressed polysyllabic words there is a tendancy for it to move onto the preceding unstressed syllables.

The observed differences in the F_0 contours of phrases with the same intonation pattern but different rhythmic structure (as well as the differences between utterances with the same rhythmic structure but different intonation pattern: see §2.2) may be explained by the simultaneous operation of intonation and constitutive rules over the "elastic" unit of the phrase, with the F_0 contour itself behaving like an elastic thread.

Since the constitutive rules are alone responsible for the phonetic cohesion of the constituents of the phrase, we assume that the melodic pattern which directly reflects this phonetic cohesion is a symmetrical rising-falling pattern resulting from a **centripetal** force. For the intonation pattern of statements we hypothesise a **regressive** force acting on the stressed syllable. The effect of this force is to move the F_0 peak back towards the beginning of the unit. For words with late stress, the directions of the constitutive and regressive forces coincide and their values are summed resulting in the regular falling tone on the stressed vowel and in some cases even causing the F_0 peak to shift back to the preceding unstressed syllables (cf. figure 1).

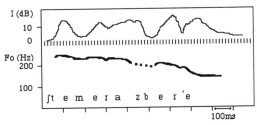

Figure 1. Intensity (top) and fundamental frequency for the utterance /ʃtemerazbeˈre/ (he will understand me).

For utterances with early stress, the two forces are antagonistic and the resulting pitch movement on the stressed vowel results from the difference in degree between the two forces as well as from the position of the stress with respect to the structural centre, so that under certain conditions the pitch movement on the stressed syllable begins on a higher pitch (figure 2a) or may even rise (figure 2b). The degree of the regressive force is probably also related to the attitudinal aspect of intonation. Auditory tests which we have run showed that statements containing early stress with a falling pitch movement are perceived as more confident answers than statements of the same structure with a more neutral rising-falling pattern.

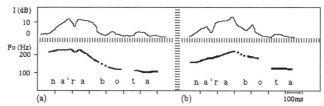

Figure 2. Intensity (top) and fundamental frequency for two intonation patterns for the utterance /na'rabota/ (to work).

2.2 *Modality and expressivity*

The universal tendancy to contrast interrogative and declarative utterances by means of rising and falling contours respectively also applied to Bulgarian intonation. In Bulgarian, however, the rise and the fall do not necessarily occur precisely on the stressed syllable or the terminal part of the sentence. It is thus impossible to represent intonation as a set of patterns defined by determining nuclear tones and specifying boundary tones.

In the case of single-word phrases, the F_0 patterns of statements (S), questions (Q) and commands (C) all show a similar rising + falling pattern, providing the stress does not occur either on the initial or the final syllable. Statistically significant differences between the three pitch contours show up in the pattern of the respective initial, maximum and final values as follows:

Initial F_0:   Command > Statement > Question

$\left.\begin{array}{l} \text{Maximum} \\ \text{Final} \end{array}\right\} F_0:$ Question > Command > Statement.

The pitch movement on the final stressed syllable of a question is always a rise but just as with statements, the peak does not necessarily occur within the limits of the stressed syllable. In polysyllabic words with early stress, a shift of the F_0 peak to the following unstressed syllables is often observed. The terminal interrogative contour thus depends on the position of the final stressed syllable in the utterance – there is a final rise when the stressed syllable is utterance-final, a rise followed by a high level or falling pattern when there are following unstressed syllables.

For single word yes/no questions, we may assume that instead of the **regressive** force observed for statements the intonation rule reflects the action of a **progressive** force acting on the stressed syllable which pushes the F_0 peak towards the end of the unit. The fact that the progressive and constitutive forces act in the same direction for utterances with early stress explains the shift of the F_0 peak onto the following unstressed syllable in polysyllabic words (figure 3). For words with late stress, no shifting of the peak is observed: it regularly occurs within the stressed syllable. This allows us to conclude that the degree of the progressive force, unlike that of the regressive force, is always greater than that of the constitutive force.

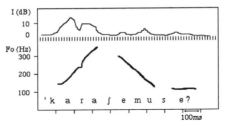

Figure 3. Intensity (top) and fundamental frequency (bottom) for the utterance /ˈkaraʃemuse/ (Did he scold him?).

The effect of the regressive (declarative) and progressive (interrogative) forces on the pitch movement within the stressed vowel can be directly observed in the F_0 contours of phrases where the stress falls on the central syllable, and where the pitch movement is consequently determined by the intonation force alone (see figure 4).

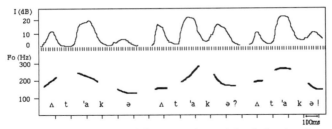

Figure 4. Intensity (top) and fundamental frequency (bottom) for declarative, interrogative and imperative readings of the utterance /ʌˈˌtakə/ (attack).

The regularities of the pitch patterns for single-word statements and questions accounted for by the interaction of a constitutive and an intonational force (progressive and regressive) are also valid for phrases containing several words. In this case, however, the phonetic manifestation of all linguistic functions of intonation has to be accounted for. For example the intonation of questions differentiated either on the basis of their lexico-syntactic structure (lexically unmarked questions, question-word questions, questions with interrogative particles) or according to the expected answer (yes-no questions, WH-questions) may be represented systematically with respect to the degree of the progressive force and the point where it is to be applied.

Figure 5 shows two F_0 contours of yes-no questions with the interrogative particle ЛИ(/li/) which localises the focus of the question onto the preceding word. The progressive force thus applies to the stressed vowel of the first word of the example where a steep rise occurs. The position of the F_0 peak obviously depends on the simultaneous operation of the constitutive and progressive forces: in the first example (5a) the peak occurs at the end of the stressed vowel due to its central position; in the second example it occurs on the particle ли for the same reason.

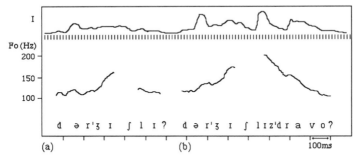

Figure 5. Intensity (top) and fundamental frequency (bottom) for two yes-no questions with the particle ли (a) /dər'ʒɪʃlɪ/ (are you holding?); (b) /dər'ʒɪʃlɪ'zdravo/ (are you holding tight?).

In typical WH-questions (figure 7b) the point where the progressive force is applied is the question word. The F_0 peak occurs at the end of the stressed vowel or on the following unstressed syllable, depending on the position of the stressed syllable within the question word. The F_0 from the peak to the end of the utterance is falling in a neutral sentence. A frequently observed variant both for WH- and for Yes/No questions is a pattern with a low rise on the terminal unstressed syllables, related to the attitudinal aspect of intonation and usually expressing politeness without modification of the communicative function of the utterance (figures 6 a, b).

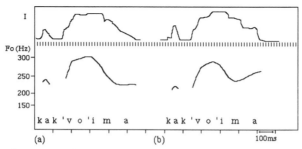

Figure 6. Intensity (top) and fundamental frequency (bottom) for falling (a) and rising (b) patterns for the WH-question /kak'vo'ima/ (What's the matter?).

Echo-questions, which can be of any lexico-syntactic type, are distinguished by a greater degree of the progressive force. In single-word echo-questions, this completely overrides the antagonistic constitutive force in the second half of the utterance and results in a rising or rising + level pattern over the whole utterance. In this case, the steepest slope occurs within the stressed syllable after which the steepness of the slope decreases gradually under the effect of the constitutive force. In echo-questions consisting of two words: a question word followed by a verb (figure 7a), the pitch pattern of both words is formed by progressive forces applying to the stressed syllables. In this way the focus of the question is distributed over the whole utterance transforming the WH-question into a Yes/No question with the meaning "Is that what you said?".

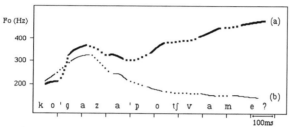

Figure 7. Intensity (top) and fundamental frequency (bottom) for echo (a) and neutral (b) versions of the WH-question /ko'gaza'potʃvame/ (When do we start?).

The intonation of emotionally loaded questions, the function of which is not to ask for information but to deliver information about the speaker's emotions (and which are consequently functionally equivalent to statements), follows the basic regularities determined for statements: the intonation pattern is formed by a regressive force of a greater degree. One peculiarity of emotionally loaded phrases is that the constituent phonetic words retain their own accentual pattern to a higher degree than in neutral statements or questions.

2.3 Focalisation and contextual effects

The manifestation of focus by intonation in Bulgarian follows the universal tendency to phonetic prominence by complex enhancing of the prosodic acoustic features (F_0, I, T) of the stressed vowel in the phonetic word containing the most important information. The linguistic aspects of Functional Sentence Perspective in Bulgarian have been discussed extensively by Penchev (1980) from a syntactic and semantic point of view. In our experience, however, the theory of Functional Sentence Perspective does not always provide a satisfactory linguistic interpretation of the experimental data of phrase intonation.

The regularities of F_0 changes expressing phonetic prominence have been experimentally investigated mainly in simple sentences consisting of three phonetic words and representing the most frequent syntactic structures in Bulgarian with both normal (objective) and inverted (subjective) word order. The interpretation of the acoustic data in terms of **theme** and **rheme** shows that the F_0 pattern depends entirely on the place of the sentence stress determining the rheme of the utterance in accordance with its syntactic, semantic and pragmatic characteristics. In general any of the constituent phonetic words may have the role of rheme.

The melodic prominence of the rheme follows the regularities determined for single-word phrases whereby a regressive force for statements or a progressive force for questions shapes the F_0 movement within and around the stressed vowel creating falling or rising patterns typical for statements or questions.

The part of the F_0 pattern corresponding to the theme is of a monotonic nature without any accentual contrasts. The direction of the pitch movement depends on the position of the theme in the utterance: initial position requires a rising contour and final position requires a falling one due to the action of the centripetal constitutive force. This leads us to conclude that the linguistically relevant phonetic characteristic of the theme is simply the absence of accentual prominence.

A number of different types of accents have been described in the phonetic literature in connection with focalisation, among them: neutral, logical, contrastive, emphatic. The differentiation of these accents is based on the different motives for prominence: syntactic relations, semantics of lexical items, speaker's attitude, opposition, appreciation, insistence and so on. These different accents do not however necessarily correspond to essentially different phonetic realisations. The F_0 patterns are essentially the same, the only difference being in the higher or lower degree of accent contrast between the syllables of the rheme. It seems to us that the different kinds of accents are related to the different degree of the intonation force modulating the F_0 pattern of the utterance. One fairly frequent characteristic of phrases with emphatic accents is the introduction of a pause just before the accented word in contrast to non-emphatic accents where the phrase retains its phonetic cohesion.

2.4 Phrasing and textual organisation

The phonetic segmentation of the speech flow with its usual individual variations may be represented by the general tendencies delimiting the scope of individual deviations in accordance with the specificity of intonation as a structural device in a given language and universal constraints on the speech production process.

The basic regularities in the phonetic manifestation of the deliminative function may be estimated by means of the statistical characteristics of the units which are divided, such as their minimum, maximum and average length, the most frequently used phonetic means for segmentation, the different types of pauses and accents in the units as well as their frequency of occurrence.

Following the Leningrad Phonetic School, we refer to the prosodic units as **syntagma**, understood as referring to a semantic/syntactic unit consisting of one or more phonetic words organised by intonation into a prosodic constituent. The main phonetic condition for a string of words to be grouped into a syntagma is the absence of perceived pauses between the words, these being of two kinds: objective (silent) pauses and subjective pauses, caused by an interruption of the continuity of the prosodic features of the speech signal.

The statistical data given below concerns the segmentation of speech in the particular case of text reading. Figure 8 illustrates the frequency of occurrence of syntagmas of different lengths, the measure of length being the number of constituent phonetic words. The minimal length is of one word containing one single syllable; the maximum length found in our corpus was 6 phonetic words totalling 28 syllables. The average value was 2.35 phonetic words for 8 syllables. The comparison of these values with equivalent data for other languages such as Russian (Zlatoustova 1984; Bratus and Verbitskaja 1983), Spanish (Zmeeva 1968) and English (Antipova 1984) shows great similarity, suggesting that the main factors determining the length of these units are universal constraints on speech production.

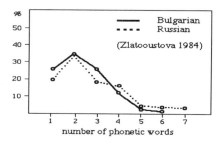

Figure 8. Comparative distribution of number of words in syntagmas in Bulgarian and Russian.

Our data on the length of syntagmas in function of their position in the sentence reveals the following tendencies: short syntagmas (1–2 phonetic words) prefer sentence initial position, the longest ones usually occur in the middle of a sentence while syntagmas of medium length typically occupy final position.

Under our experimental conditions, consisting of reading aloud grammatically well-formed units, silent pauses were found to be used far more frequently (87%) than subjective pauses (13%). Figure 9 shows the frequency of occurrence of silent pauses in function of their duration. The shape of the distribution curve (4 peaks) together with the dependency of the duration of the pauses on the syntactic relations between adjacent syntagmas allows us to distinguish four types of pauses: short, medium, long and extra-long.

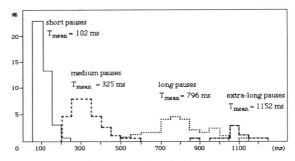

Figure 9. Distribution of duration of silent pauses in Bulgarian.

Short pauses usually separate groups of words in simple sentences: introductory words, nouns and extended attributes, enumerations. It should be mentioned that although closely related, phonetic and syntactic units do not necessarily coincide. For example the syntactic constituent Noun Phrase may be phonetically divided by a short pause between the noun and its attribute simply because of the number of syllables in the two words:

/za ponʌ'tatəʃnoto/usəvər'ʃenstvuvʌne/ (...for further / qualifications)

Medium pauses typically separate clauses in compound and complex sentences, but once again the influence of purely phonetic factors has to be taken into account. Thus when the clauses are of short phonetic structure, they are separated by short pauses:

/zi've jat / ira'botjət / (live / and work)

Medium pauses are also used in simple sentences to separate an extended group of words, the meaning of which is equivalent to a clause:

/.../sledza'vərʃvʌne na obrazo'vanieto/ (after finishing (his) education)

Long pauses occur between separate sentences and a positive correlation between the duration of the pause and the length of the sentence is observed. Extra-long pauses mark the ends of paragraphs.

The auditory and acoustic analysis of our recordings shows that the accent pattern in a syntagma may be realised in two different ways which are perceived as phonetic prominence of equal strength but differing in quality and function, *i.e.* in the nature of the information intended by the speaker. The first type, which we shall call semantic accent, is the result of the phonetic manifestation of the focusing function of intonation; its acoustic correlate is a pitch contrast between the syllables of the prominent word. The second type, which we shall call phrase accent, is connected with the whole intended structure of the utterance and signals either the continuation (continuation accent) or the finality (final accent) of speech and is consequently a result of the delimitative function of intonation. The basic acoustic parameter used in this case is segmental duration; F_0 is generally monotonic, rising for continuation accents with maximum steepness on the last syllable irrespective of word stress and falling without melodic contrast for final accents.

As mentioned above a semantic accent (focus) may reinforce any of the phonetic words in a syntagma, whereas the phrase accent may only occur on the last one. It is possible for the semantic and continuation accents to coincide on the last word of the syntagma. In this case the most typical F_0 contour is a rising convex curve [⌐] with maximum steepness within the stressed vowel, contrasting with the concave curve [⌐] observed on continuation accents alone (*cf.* figures 10a, 10b). The final accent may also coincide with the semantic accent. In this case the increased segmental duration is accompanied by a local F_0 peak (low rise + fall).

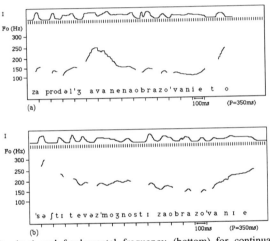

Figure 10. Intensity (top) and fundamental frequency (bottom) for continuation and semantic accent on last word (a) /za prodəl'ʒavanenaobrazo'vanieto/ (for the continuation of studies) and with continuation accent without semantic accent (b) /səʃtɪtevəz'moʒnostɪzaobrazo'vanɪe/ (the same possibilities for studies).

It should be pointed out that both types of accent in Bulgarian depend to a great extent on the speaker's desire to emphasise a given word in the unit as well as to signal whether his speech is continuing or coming to an end. This means that the accents cannot be assigned automatically although it is possible to formulate some non-obligatory rules on the basis of the lexico-syntactic structure of the phrase. In syntagmas consisting of a Noun Phrase where the attribute agrees with the noun, semantic stress usually occurs on the attribute and the noun may or may not be reinforced by a structural accent depending on the speaker's intentions. The negative particle *ne* attracts the semantic accent to the word that follows it. Comparative and superlative forms as well as certain lexical items such as *everybody, all, always, namely, only* and many others are also usually reinforced by a semantic accent.

The general tendencies of phrase accent patterns of Bulgarian syntagmas can be summarised as follows:

(1)   The most frequently used accent patterns consist of a single accent (72% of our experimental corpus), syntagmas with two phrase accents occur less frequently (25%) and those with three are rare (3%). Each of two adjacent words in a syntagma may be accented. In this case there are two centralised accents (following the terminology of Antipova 1984); the two words may also be reinforced as a single accent unit in which case there is a single decentralised accent. Acoustically the difference between the two cases is to be found in the shape of the F_0 peak which is sharp for the stressed syllable of individually accented words (Figure 11a) and takes the shape of a high relatively flat plateau situated between the stressed syllables of the two words (Figure 11b).

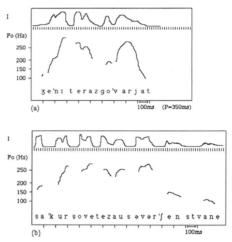

Figure 11. Intensity (top) and fundamental frequency (bottom) for syntagmas produced with two centralised accents (a) /ʒe'nɪterazgo'varjat/ (the women are talking) or as a single decentralised accent (b) /za'kursovetezausəvər'ʃenstvane/ (for refresher courses).

(2)   In Bulgarian, the phrase accents in a syntagma prefer boundary positions. In our experimental corpus the accents are on the first word in 36% of all cases, on the last for 38%, on both first and last words for 12% and on a middle word for 14%. This means that the function of the phrase accent in Bulgarian is essentially delimitative on the level of the syntagma.

(3)   One particularity of Bulgarian which distinguishes it from for example French and Russian is the fact that initial accents are as frequent as final accents.

This means that the classic rule assigning an accent to the last word of a syntagma cannot apply systematically in Bulgarian.

(4)   The main factor responsible for the F_0 pattern of syntagmas is the semantic accent whose presence alone (40%) or in combination with phrase accents (46%) determines the F_0 contours in most of the cases studied.

4. Conclusions

The results described and the illustrations presented make it possible to conclude that in general the F_0 pattern of a question is not identical to the pattern of an unfinished utterance. The two patterns are similar only if the pattern of a syntagma with both a semantic accent and a continuation accent on the last word is compared to the pattern of a question with its focus on the last word. The question will be analysed in more detail in forthcoming work concerning the interaction between intonation and lexical/syntactic information in Bulgarian.

16

Intonation in

Greek

ANTONIS BOTINIS

1. Introduction

This chapter deals with the intonation pattern of (Modern) Greek and its phonetic manifestation as well as its functions at the hierarchical levels of the language associated with stress and prosodic structure. By intonation is meant the way the physical, or prosodic parameter of fundamental frequency is perceived as regular pitch patterns across a sequence of speech units. Temporal and dynamic variations of stress distinctions, as manifested by duration and intensity, respectively, associated with tonal variations as well as their degree of interplay and function are also taken into account.

The investigated language is standard Greek with Athenian Greek as the norm of the current standard. Athens is the capital of Greece as well as the main cultural, political and economic centre of the country with nearly 4 million inhabitants. The Greek language (Ελληνική) is spoken by about 12 million people, 10 million in Greece and approximately 2 million in different parts of the world (διασπορά), mainly in the United States, Canada and Australia. The standard language, apart from Athens, is spoken widely in southern Greece, especially in Peloponnesos. Northern Greek dialects are characterised by differing degrees of vocalic divergence from the standard language, involving raising of unstressed mid vowels and deletion of unstressed high vowels, although major cities are widely adopting the standard language. The islands around the mainland, in addition to segmental dissimilarities, exhibit diverging intonation patterns such as the typical "singing" intonation of Corfu where different types of sentences may sound like questions to speakers of standard Greek, whereas dialects in Crete, Cyprus and those which still exist in Southern Italy are also characterised by a certain preservation of archaic morphological structure.

Greek has a linguistic heritage (κληρονομιά) from the second millennium B.C., being attested in Mycenaean Greek inscriptions and documented continuously from the 8th century B.C. up to the present day. The oldest Greek language stage, Protohellenic (πρωτοελληνική), was spoken by the Hellenes ("Ελληνες, *i.e.* Greeks). Ancient Greek (Αρχαία Ελληνική) is the name given to the language from earlier recorded times up to the 3rd century B.C. with Attic (Αττική διάλεκτος) as the dominant dialect of the Greek world which absorbed dialectal varieties and gave rise to Alexandrian or Hellenistic Koine (Ελληνιστική Κοινή), the international language of the Hellenistic Era, from the 3rd century B.C. to the 4th century A.D. Modern Greek (Νέα Ελληνική), has emerged from Hellenistic Greek through Byzantine Greek and has not undergone major structural changes since the 15th century.

Classical Greek philosophers such as Plato and Aristotle concerned themselves with prosody (προσωδία) and tone (τόνος), reflecting the understanding Greeks had about the prosodic structure of the language as being characterised by (melodic) pitch rather than (dynamic) stress. An acute tone (ὀξύς) and a grave tone (βαρύς), the latter tone denoting in practice the absence of the former tone in a syllable, as well as the combination of an acute-grave within a syllable, referred to as bitone (δύτονος) or circumflex (περισπώμενος), represented the main tonal distinctions in Ancient Greek. These tonal oppositions, largely dependent on morphosyllabic quantity, along with aspiration (πνεῦμα), although not used in classical texts, were later (end of 3rd century B.C.) introduced by Greek grammarians as orthographic symbols, mainly for practical reasons since Greek was the communicative language among peoples with diverging language backgrounds.

By the 4th century A.D. the segmental structure was partly restructured and syllabic quantity neutralised in Greek, resulting in a simplification of the prosodic system. The tonal distinctions had gradually faded away and tonal accents turned into dynamic accents or stress. This change brought about a different approach to the study of prosody which became associated with rhythm and the metrical structure of the language. On the other hand, the prosodic markings, with no distinctive value except for stress, were established and used in standard Greek orthography until the 1980s when the monotonic system was officially adopted, *i.e.* an acute mark usually on the vowel of the stressed syllable.

From the Hellenistic Era on, probably even earlier, the Greek language shows two styles, a formal style resembling to a certain degree the prestigious Attic, and a colloquial style which was the natural development of the Hellenistic

Koine. Up until the 1970s, two forms of the language as a means of communication were distinguished: a written/formal or "puristic" (καθαρεύουσα) style and a spoken/colloquial or "demotic" (δημοτική) style. Finally, the demotic style obtained official recognition and is the norm of the standard language as found in everyday use in Athens. It has absorbed puristic and/or archaic as well as provincial lexical elements and expressions, as a result of the large scale urbanism in Athens in the last few decades, into a unified means of expression. Today, the polarisation of the language has given way to a common form with various styles to fulfil its multi-communicative purpose.

1.1 Prosodic phonology

a. Word stress

Greek shows prosodic variations which have been phonologised at the lexical level as stress distinctions. These stress distinctions are realised within a "stressable zone" comprising the last three syllables (Trisyllabic Constraint) of the grammatical word (Garde 1968), a sequence of morpheme(s) forming the stem and a combination of derivational and/or inflectional suffix(es) forming the terminal. The open form classes (lexical items), regardless of their degree of complexity and/or the number of syllables the word is composed of, appear with only one word stress (Monotonic Principle), *i.e.* the accentual unit (Martinet 1960) in Greek is the word, whereas closed classes (function items), usually unstressed, may appear stressed in a phrase/sentence context.

The traditional view is that word stress in Greek is largely unpredictable (Tsitsopoulos 1973). This is generally admitted by Joseph and Philippaki-Warburton (1987), who nevertheless attempt to associate certain morphological and inflectional processes with the distribution of stress. Recently, it has been proposed (Tseva and Contini 1988) that lexical stress may be predicted in the majority of the cases when the word's ending is taken into account. Nevertheless, even when the prosodic pattern of Ancient Greek (Warburton 1970, Steriade 1988) is considered, from which Modern Greek usually keeps the position of stress, a considerable body of the language's vocabulary has a stress pattern that cannot be predicted. Thus, there are prosodic minimal pairs in words belonging to the same grammatical category, *e.g.* nouns /'nomos - no'mos/ (law - county), verbs /'pino - pi'no/ (to drink – to be hungry), and adverbs /'pote - po'te/ (when – never) as well as in words belonging to different grammatical categories, /'milo - mi'lo/ (apple – to speak), /'poli - po'li/ (town – very), /mi'tera - mite'ra/ (mother – sharp).

Once lexical stress has been provided by the lexicon on semantic and/or morphophonemic grounds, the basic position of stress which is *e.g.* based on the nominative singular for nouns and the first person present singular for verbs, morphoprosodic processes may reassign stress through compounding and inflection/derivation. First, inflectional words may reassign stress to the right when declined (Nom. Sg.) /o 'anemos/ - (Gen. Sg.) /tu a'nemu/ (the wind) as well as when a syllable is added breaking the Trisyllabic Constraint (Nom. Sg.) /to 'maθima/ - (Nom. Pl.) /ta ma'θimata/ (the lesson) (cf. /to 'θima - ta 'θimata/ (the victim)). Second, stress may be retracted to an earlier syllable, as in the formation of the aorist (Pr.) /meɣa'lono/ - (Aor.) /me'ɣalosa/ (to grow up) as well as (Pr.) /'kano/ - (Aor.) /'ekana/ (to make) where the additive /e/ fullfils the antepenultimate stress condition characteristic of certain classes of verbs (Babiniotis 1972). Third, a lexical item's stress in a compound construction is deleted and replaced by a specific compound stress. Sometimes it falls on the syllable of a component word that would have received stress, /kalomaθi'menos/ (spoiled) composed of /ka'los/ (good) and /maθi'menos/ (brought up), and /ka'lopistos/ (honest), from /ka'los/ (good) and /'pisti/ (faith). Compound stress may also fall on another syllable, /xio'noðromos/ (snow trail) from /'xioni/ (snow) and /'ðromos/ (way) in accordance with the requirements of the compound which is stressed as a single accentual unit (cf. /xiono'ðromos/ (snow hiker)).

b. Phrase stress

The Trisyllabic Constraint also operates at the phrase level resulting in a restructuring of the prosodic organisation of the surface constituent structure. But whereas its effect is to move word stress to the right at the word level (cf. /'maθima - ma'θimata/), it may produce an additional stress at the phrase level, the phrase stress. Phrase stress appears in a word + enclitic(s) syntactic structure, two syllables to the right of the word stress, whether this is on the lexical or the enclitic item, whenever word stress is to the left of the antepenultimate syllable with respect to the phrase boundary, *e.g.* in the noun phrases /to 'maθi'ma mu/ (my lesson) and /ta ma'θima'ta mu/ (my lessons) as well as in the verb phrases /pa'raðo'se mu to/ (deliver me that) and /'ðose 'mu to/ (give me that). The verbal constructions may also appear as /pa'raðo'se to mu/ and /pa'raðo'sto mu/ as well as /'ðose 'to mu/ and /'ðosto mu/ which reflects the importance of the number of syllables to the right of the word stress for phrase stress application.

Thus, phrase stress is distributed by rule once the Trisyllabic Constraint is violated in an enclitic construction; it may be used for syntactic parsing as in /to 'onoma tu 'itane ɣno'sto - to 'ono'ma tu 'itane ɣno'sto/ (the name was familiar to him - his name was familiar). On the other hand, in a listening test (Botinis 1989a), proclitic - enclitic syntactic structures with no phrase stress involved (pronounced at a normal to fast tempo) were found indistinguishable; *e.g.* /i 'θia/mu 'pulise to 'spiti/ - /i 'θia mu / 'pulise to 'spiti/ (the aunt sold me the house - my aunt sold the house).

In a series of phonological descriptions of stress in Greek, Philippaki-Warburton (cf. Joseph and Philippaki-Warburton 1987) attributes a primary status to phrase stress whereas word stress is weakened to secondary, in accordance with the principle that in a phonological word (*i.e.* a word + enclitic(s)) there can only be one primary stress (p. 252). On the contrary, Nespor and Vogel (1986, 1989) reserve primary status for word stress, to comply with the requirements of the (prosodic) clitic constituent which has only one primary stress associated with the host (*i.e.* word stress) rather than the enclitic (*i.e.* phrase stress), the stress of which is regarded as a secondary one. Given the relative strength of phrase stress over word stress on the bases of phonetic facts, we have argued elsewhere (Botinis 1989a) that word and phrase stress are different prosodic categories involving different components of the grammar; apart from common properties in prosodic structuring, they have different distributions and functions as well as diverging prosodic manifestations reflected both in production and perception (cf. §2.1.b).

c. Sentence stress
Sentence stress, once the focal domain is provided, is distributed by rule to the last focal item (as in *e.g.* Swedish, Bruce 1977) bearing word/phrase stress. However, the application of sentence stress to a lexical item bearing word stress is neutralised in an enclitic construction with phrase stress, the phrase stress attracting sentence stress. This is a syntactic constraint imposed on Greek prosody, with regard to syntactic/prosodic interaction which may be largely variable in different languages (cf. Rossi 1985 for French). On the other hand, apart from the prosodic distribution of sentence stress, the focal element may be syntactically marked in Greek, *e.g.* through a topicalisation, as long as no syntactic constraint is violated.

1.2 Background

The intonation patterns described below are based on two types of speech material. The first type is the result of our investigations on Greek prosody in the domain of the sentence under well-controlled experimental conditions, with systematically selected speech material from the question - answer paradigm, involving only one speaker at a time (cf. Bruce 1977). An obvious advantage with this method has been the possibility of examining different prosodic categories with minimal influence of other prosodic contributions as well as the interplay of prosodic parameters across an utterance (Botinis 1989a). The second type is the result of spontaneous speech communication, the ultimate goal of any intonation study, where more complicated prosodic structures that may not be encountered in laboratory speech usually appear as a result of discourse factors.

For the laboratory speech, the investigated material consists of meaningful declarative sentences having a relatively simple syntactic structure, an answer to a question, pronounced neutrally as well as with different sentence elements in focus. This was obtained by formulating appropriate questions to make the speaker choose one sentence element as the focus and the carrier of the information required by the question. The segmental composition of the prosodic categories under investigation consists of a nasal+vowel syllabic structure and the principal criteria used in constructing the test data have been semantic naturalness and syntactic simplicity. The results presented here are based on recordings of five speakers of standard Athenian Greek. The parameters of fundamental frequency, duration and intensity were analysed and the data subjected to statistical analysis. One speaker's prosodic categories/structures also underwent six perceptual tests, each of which was submitted to ten high school Athenian students.

For spontaneous speech, a telephone conversation was selected from a local Athenian radio station. It is an extract from an entertainment programme in which programme listeners may phone in and have a short chat with the programme leader, participate in a competition with the possibility of winning a record or a small present, and request their favourite music. The conversation involves the programme leader and a programme participant. This type of dialogue is characterised by non-visual interaction, and time limitation. Furthermore, the programme leader governs the outcome of the conversation to a considerable extent. Our expectation was that in this type of dialogue, prosody plays a major role in structuring the discourse as a consequence of the programme participant's desire to speak and the programme leader's interest in making a lively programme. In this material only fundamental frequency contours were considered.

2. Description of intonation patterns

2.1 Neutral intonation

a. Word stress
Word stress in Greek, apart from duration and intensity, may be associated with a tonal variation, usually a pitch rise, as well as with no variation at all depending on the prosodic organisation of the utterance (cf. §2.3). In the former case, an accurate investigation of the range and timing of this variation seems phonetically justifiable as well as its relation to other tonal variations within an utterance, whereas in the latter case its significance for stress distinctions is questionable. The most regular tonal variations associated with stressed syllables appear in neutral, non-emphatic intonation. By neutral intonation is meant the way a speaker pronounces an utterance with rather equal prominence throughout, as *e.g.* following our experimental procedure to read an isolated sentence written on a piece of paper out of context and with normal tempo and loudness.

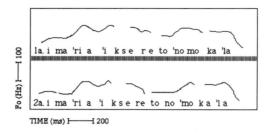

Figure 1: One speaker's F_0 contours of the prosodic minimal pair /'nomo - no'mo/ (1–2) in the carrier sentence /i ma'ria 'iksere to... ka'la/ with neutral intonation.

Figure 1 is an example of one speaker's intonation pattern of the neutral, declarative utterances with the prosodic minimal pair /'nomo - no'mo/ in the same carrier sentence (1–2):

(1)   /i ma'ria 'iksere to 'nomo ka'la/   (Maria knew the law well)
(2)   /i ma'ria 'iksere to no'mo ka'la/   (Maria knew the county well)

Each sentence is composed of four lexical items which each carry a word stress dividing the utterance into four stress groups, according to the traditional definition as a stressed syllable followed by unstressed one(s) (Grønnum [Thorsen] this volume). Every stress group carries a tonal-gesture, constituting a tonal group, which may be partially suppressed as a result *e.g.* of the contribution of the final juncture. The pitch-gesture associated with a stress group is realised as an F_0 rise aligned with the beginning of the stress group whether a consonant or vowel, *i.e.* the stressed syllable. This F_0 rise may form a high F_0 plateau with the following unstressed syllable(s) and decline towards the beginning of the next stress group, to repeat the cycle. The formation of the high plateau is mainly dependent on the interstress interval whereas the post-tonic fall may not be realised, what Bruce (1977) calls an undershooting (*vs.* overshooting) of the realisation of a pitch-gesture.

The declination effect, the tendency of spoken languages to decline in pitch from the beginning towards the end of an utterance (Pierrehumbert 1979) is only evident at the final juncture, which is lower than the initial one, whereas the F_0 tops of both utterances are rather equal in accordance with the semantic salience of the lexical elements composing the utterances which is (following our instructions) equal. Our present conception of the "declination effect" is its global (discourse) realisation and its turn/topic leaving function rather than its local function at the "sentence/utterance" level which may take the appropriate tonal configuration(s) in accordance with the requirements of the spoken discourse. The observed declination and/or final lowering observed in the Greek data as well as often reported in the literature for a number of languages is perhaps an artefact of laboratory speech phenomenon where relatively simple

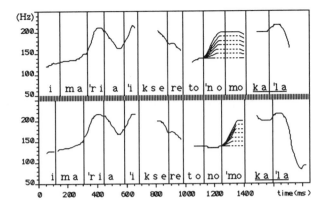

Figure 2. One speaker's F_0 contours in Hz on the vertical axis and syllabic durations in ms on the horizontal axis of the prosodic minimal pair /'nomo - no'mo/ (over - under) in the carrier sentence /i ma'ria 'iksere to... ka'la/; the solid line represents the reference contour and the broken lines six synthetic stimuli for each member of the pair in equal steps of 10 Hz.

utterance(s) are usually involved in only one turn-unit/topic, a subject of ongoing research (cf. §2.4). Microprosodic interference, segmental effects on the prosodic parameters, although well documented in prosodic research (Di Cristo 1982), have not yet been investigated in Greek.

In an extensive study of the effect of intonation contours on stress perception (Botinis 1989a), we carried out perceptual experiments on the pitch range and timing of pitch-gestures associated with word stress. As we found the intonation of neutral sentences, final focus sentences, as well as broad (whole sentence) focus to be similar in structure for a good number of productions, we chose the final focus sentences for perceptual experimentation.

For the pitch range experiment, fourteen synthetic stimuli (St.) of two groups were prepared on a VAX/730 computer system with the api-program of the ILS package for the analysis and the sns-program for the synthesis of the stimuli (figure 2). The first group comprised seven stimuli (St. 1–7) with the test word /'nomo/ as reference in the original sentence /i ma'ria 'iksere to 'nomo ka'la/ (St. 1). The second group comprised seven stimuli as well (St. 8–14) with the test word /no'mo/ as reference in the original sentence /i ma'ria 'iksere to no'mo ka'la/ (St. 8). The pitch range manipulations were strictly restricted to the F_0 plateau of the prosodic minimal pair /'nomo - no'mo/ with six equal steps of 10 Hz, from 200 to 140 Hz, whereas the context as well as the duration and the intensity patterns of the original utterances were unaffected.

The individual judgements of the ten listeners concerning the fourteen stimuli divided the stimuli into two groups; a first group comprising stimuli 1 to 7 and a second group comprising stimuli 8 to 14, in accordance with the production of the test sentences. The F_0 manipulations had no or little effect on listeners; only St. 7 of the first group with a neutralised F_0 contour caused an identification change of 12%, and St. 11–14 of the second group caused less than 10% identification change. It is clear that the F_0 range does not considerably affect the listeners' responses for the two contrastive words which retain their original identity due to duration and intensity.

For the timing of the pitch-gesture, two groups of synthetic stimuli were prepared with the same experimental conditions as in the pitch range experiment; each group comprised eight stimuli of the reference - target type (figure 3). St. 1 had the test word /'nomo/ as reference and with seven succesive stimuli in equal steps (St. 1–8) the timing difference of the pitch-gesture (140–200 Hz) between /'nomo/ and /no'mo/ (the target) was covered. St. 9 had the test word /no'mo/ as reference, and with the next seven stimuli (St. 9–16) the mirror image of stimuli 1–8 was obtained.

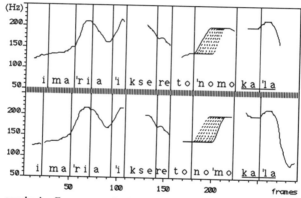

Figure 3. One speaker's F_0 contours in Hz on the vertical axis and duration in frames (1 fr.=6,4ms) on the horizontal axis of the prosodic minimal pair /'nomo - no'mo/ (over - under), in the carrier sentence /i ma'ria 'iksere to... ka'la/; the solid line represents the reference contour and the broken lines seven synthetic stimuli for each member of the pair in equal steps towards the target contour.

The individual responses of ten listeners to the sixteen stimuli divided each group into two categories. St. 1–5 were identified as /'nomo/ with deviations less than 6%, St. 6 was ambiguous, and St. 7–8 were identified as /no'mo/ in the first group; in the second group, St. 9–12 were identified as /no'mo/ with St. 12 deviating by 6%, St. 13 was ambiguous, and St. 14–16 were identified as /'nomo/, St. 14 deviating by 6%. It is interesting to note that the critical point of identification change is not the same for the two groups. Although a pitch-gesture displacement causes an all-or-none identification change in listeners, its timing in one direction or the other has to be clearly away from the mid point to neutralise the effects of the conflicting cues of duration and intensity.

In another perceptual experiment for post-focal word stress distinctions, where the F_0 contours are neutralised (cf. §2.3), listeners identified the prosodic minimal pair /'nomo - no'mo/ by 70% and 90%, respectively. Duration manipulations had a bigger effect than intensity whereas a combination of both duration and intensity at the same time was necessary to bring the change of identification clearly above the guessing level. Apart from stress perception, speech production provides evidence for the dynamic manifestation of stress with a regular distribution of duration and intensity at the syntagmatic and/or paradigmatic level (cf. §2.1.b). Furthermore, an indirect estimation of subglottal pressure, which is directly related to intensity (Isshiki 1964; Stathopoulos and Weisner 1985), showed stress distinctions to be closely associated with subglottal variations in a physiological experiment.

Our accumulated findings on word stress distinctions strongly indicate that intonation and word stress should be kept apart. Duration and intensity, if combined into a single prosodic feature, which has been referred to as "energy integral" (Lieberman 1960) or "total amplitude" (Beckman 1986), are quite constant acoustic correlates, sufficient for making stress distinctions, whereas the variability of fundamental frequency points to a semantic interpretation (cf. §2.3). F_0 is only indirectly related to stress; it involves an F_0 excursion with "turning points" (Gårding 1977a) aligning pitch-gestures with stressed syllables, attributing an appropriate semantic weight to certain stress groups and their corresponding constituent elements within an utterance.

The presence of a suitably F_0 timed event in connection with a stressed syllable is the accent that will mark the stressed syllable as more prominent and distinct from a stressed syllable without an accent. (Bruce 1983, p. 224)

Although prosodic parameters are multi-functional, they may be organised into distinct dynamic features for rhythmic structuring as well as intonative features for semantic weighting. This basic separation of rhythm and intonation as well as their different functions puts into question the traditional view concerning the hierarchical nature of the prosodic parameters (Fry 1958, Berinstein 1979), according to which F_0 prevails over duration and intensity for making stress distinctions.

b. Phrase stress and proclitic vs. enclitic structure

In order to analyse the realisation of phrase stress and the prosodic distinction between a proclitic and an enclitic structure, two test sentences were examined:

(3)   /to 'neo 'maθima tis 'ine 'ðiskolo/ (the new lesson is difficult for her)
(4)   /to 'neo 'maθi'ma tis 'ine 'ðiskolo/ (the new lesson of hers is difficult)

The clitic /tis/ (for her-of hers) is the key syntactic element which forms the proclitic structure with the following verb phrase it is attached to; on the contrary, the attachment of the clitic to the previous noun phrase forms an enclitic structure and modifies its prosodic manifestation creating a new stress, what we have referred to as phrase stress (cf. §1.1.b).

An example of one speaker's intonation pattern of the proclitic - enclitic structure is displayed in figure 4. The proclitic sentence carries four stresses and the enclitic one five stresses, dividing the utterances into four and five stress groups, respectively. Both utterances appear with four pitch-gestures, the final one being a major, focal gesture. The proclitic utterance (3a) has three minor pitch-gestures aligned with the beginning of the corresponding stress groups which are the beginning of the lexical items as well. The proclitic element /tis/ is tonally attached to its prosodic host (stress group), the noun /'maθima/, rather than to its syntactic host (constituent), the verb phrase /'ine 'ðiskolo/. On the other hand, the enclitic utterance (4a) appears with three rather than four minor pitch-gestures aligned with the corresponding stress groups; the enclitic /tis/ is tonally attached both to its prosodic and syntactic host whereas the tonal group it belongs to along with the tonal group of the next stress group /'ine/ are assimilated into a rising pitch contour to the upcoming focal item /'ðiskolo/ which is realised as an anathetic (upstepping), major pitch-gesture.

The proclitic - enclitic phonetic manifestations, apart from their tonal dissimilarity which reflects their rhythmic patterning, exhibit regular dynamic distinctions. At the syntagmatic level, the antepenultimate stressed syllable of /'maθima/ in the proclitic construction has longer duration and higher intensity than its unstressed ultimate, *i.e.* a regular acoustic manifestation of a stressed syllable in Greek. The phrase stressed, ultimate syllable of /'maθi'ma/ in the enclitic construction has a tendency to have greater duration than its word stressed antepenultimate and its word stress - phrase stress intensity ratio is smaller than that of the stressed - unstressed syllables of the proclitic construction. At the paradigmatic level, the dynamic contribution of phrase stress is mainly realised by duration which is greater than that of the unstressed ultimate of the proclitic construction. Furthermore, the enclitic's word stress is remarkably weakened in comparison to the proclitic's antepenultimate stress, both in duration and intensity.

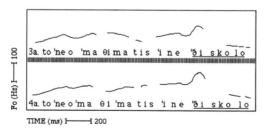

Figure 4. One speaker's F_0 contours of the prosodic/syntactic minimal pair /'maθima tis - 'maθi'ma tis/ (3–4) in the carrier sentence /to 'neo... 'ine 'ðiskolo/.

In a perceptual investigation of the reference – target type (cf. §2.1.a), the F_0 contour has been found to be the strongest perceptual cue for phrase stress in the proclitic – enclitic distinction followed by duration, whereas intensity had hardly any effect. Nevertheless, a combination of all three prosodic parameters was required for an identification change, which indicates the phonetic reality of phrase stress and the listeners' ability to distinguish the proclitic - enclitic realisations and associate them with the corresponding syntactic/semantic structures.

Thus, the all-or-none effect of F_0 on word stress perception appears weakened for phrase stress. The domain of word stress is a stress group coordinated with a local pitch-gesture, the displacement of which is sufficient to cause an identification change, *i.e.* F_0 prevails in a trade-off relation with the energy integral. On the other hand, phrase stress has a larger domain: two stress groups, in which two pitch-gestures are involved in an interdependent adjustment in the trade-off relation with the corresponding energy integrals. Furthermore, phrase stress is morphosyntactically determined to have a fixed position whereas word stress is rather flexible with a lexical function. These phonetic/linguistic facts reflect the different dimensions of word and phrase stress in the relation between rhythmic and tonal structure.

Once the morphosyntactic level has contributed to stress group distribution where prosody and syntax are interrelated, prosody may not leave any traces of boundaries between words and syntactic constituents, at least for simple, one clause utterances. On the contrary, stress group organisation may break up lexical items, *e.g.* in an enclitic construction with phrase stress, or prosodically group together syllables belonging to different lexical/syntactic constituents.

2.2 *Question intonation*

In this sub-section only a sketchy description of intonation observed in questions will be given. This disproportionality in relation to other aspects of Greek intonation we present in this chapter does not mean we attribute less importance to this issue but stems rather from our limited ability/experience to give an overall view, albeit preliminary, to such diverging connotations that the term "question" is associated with. Nevertheless, if we take this term for granted for the moment, we are confronted with the native (Greek) speaker's intuitive preconception that questions *vs.* statements are associated with a (final) rising *vs.* falling intonation contour respectively, especially in a language like Greek where formal lexical/grammatical markers are usually missing. But as earlier investigators for different languages have observed (*e.g.* English, Brown *et al.* 1980), there are vertually no intonation contours for questions, in exclusion of other intonation contours for different types of sentences. In fact, nearly any (final) intonation contour found in questions may also appear in statements and

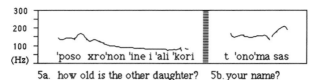

5a. how old is the other daughter?   5b. your name?

Figure 5. One speaker's F_0 contours of an interrogative (5a) as well as a statement (5b) question of a spontaneous speech telephone conversation.

vice versa, and Greek does not seem to be an exception to this phonetic reality. In the present chapter we assume a basic distinction between form (declarative, interrogative, imperative) *vs.* function (statement, question and command) as we have observed no regular correspondence between form and function.

There exists a rich inventory of morpholexical items which may be used as interrogative markers in Greek: /ti/ (what), /ɣia'ti/ (why), /'pote/ (when) /pu/ (where) /pos/ (how) /'poso/ (how much), /pios/ (who), *etc.* These interrogative markers are sufficient to denote a (partial) question without necessarily being combined with syntactic or intonative markers. Syntax is usually neutral in a great number of interrogative sentences as /'pote 'efiɣe i 'ana/ (when did Anna leave?) where the verb phrase /'efiɣe i 'ana/, without the adverb /'pote/, is a well-formed declarative sentence which may function both as a statement and a (total) yes-no question. Even the verb /'efiɣe/ may have the statement - question opposition with hardly any option of a morphosyntactic marker, a typical characteristic of yes-no questions in Greek. This leads to the expectation that Greek may use intonative means to a high degree to denote a question, compared to other languages.

Interrogative questions as defined above usually appear with no final intonative marker (pitch rise) in spontaneous dialogues, the interrogative morpholexical markers being sufficient enough for a question. In laboratory speech however, where questions are rather emphasised in order to elicit a specific focus to an answer, a major pitch rise appears at the final boundaries which, in combination with an initial intonationally marked interrogative item, usually creates an overall falling-rising intonation contour. On the other hand, in spontaneous dialogues, as a rule informative (total) yes-no questions appear with a final pitch rise in the absence of any morphosyntactic marker whereas the same type of declarative questions with a leading/conducive function (when the speaker assumes and/or has high expectations on the directionality of the polar answer to follow) usually appear with a low/pitch fall.

As examples, an interrogative as well as a declarative question from a spontaneous telephone conversation (cf. §1.2) are presented in figure 5. The interrogative question (5a), appears with no final pitch rise whereas the interrogative marker /'poso/ has a minor pitch-gesture at the word boundary rather than the stressed syllable followed by an accentless manifestation of the rest of the utterence. This global prosodic organisation resembles the focal one (cf. §2.3) and the local pitch-gesture is an indication that interrogative morpholexical markers may even be intonationally marked, the perceptual effect of which may be extended to the end of the sentence. On the other hand, the declarative question (5b) appears with two minor pitch-gestures aligned with the corresponding stressed syllables of the phrase /t 'ono'ma sas/, followed by a major pitch rise realised at the (unstressed) enclitic /sas/.

Beyond the above examples, a statement may turn into a question by intonation means in Greek, but this is not a necessary condition even when formal morphosyntactic markers are absent. In the framework of spoken discourse, questions may perhaps best be thought of as part of an open class of propositions, along with greetings, encouragements, suggestions, *etc.*, with a turn-invitation and/or discourse participation function, where a speaker meaningfully leaves his turn but not the topic/conversation which is rather governed by interspeaker mutual agreement. Further research is however obviously needed in this subject.

2.3 Focal intonation

In order to analyse sentence stress realisation, the prosodic category of focus, as well as its effects on the prosodic organisation of the utterance, the test sentences of two previous sub-sections were examined: (1) / i ma'ria 'iksere to 'nomo ka'la/ and (2) /i ma'ria 'iksere to no'mo ka'la/ (Maria knew the law well - Maria knew the county well) as well as (3) /to 'neo 'maθima tis 'ine 'ðiskolo/ and (4) /to 'neo 'maθi'ma tis 'ine 'ðiskolo/ (the new lesson is difficult for her - the new lesson of hers is difficult". In addition, two other sentences were examined:

(5)   /i ma'ria 'estile to 'proto 'γrama stin e'laða/
        (Maria sent the first letter to Greece)

(6)   /i ma'ria 'estile to 'proγra'ma tis stin e'laða/
        (Maria sent her programme to Greece)

The noun phrase /to 'proto 'γrama/ in (5) carries two word stresses and is composed of an article, an adjective and a noun whereas the noun phrase /to 'proγra'ma tis/ in (6) carries a word stress and a phrase stress and is composed of an article, a noun and a pronoun.

Figure 6 displays one speaker's F_0 contours as well as both local and global effects the sentence stress distribution has on the prosodic organisation of utterances (1) and (2). Utterances (1b) and (2b), with four stress groups each, appear with two minor pitch-gestures aligned with the pre-focal stress groups as well as with a major pitch-gesture on the focal items /'nomo - no'mo/, whereas the post-focal stress groups are accentless with a low F_0 plateau. The focal pitch-gestures are the largest ones within the utterances, with the local effect of a major pitch rise aligned with the beginning of the stress group in combination with a pitch fall, the largest within the utterance, which starts already in the stressed syllable and is completed in the first post-stressed syllable and/or at the lexical rather than the stress group boundary. Apart from a constant post-focal accentless organisation of stress groups which is evident also in (1c-2c), the global effect of sentence stress is characterised by a variable intra/inter speaker partial pre-focal accentuation, the effect of which may cause stress groups to appear in an anathetic and/or assimilated rather than alternating F_0 contour.

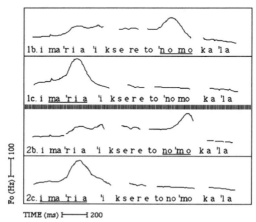

Figure 6. One speaker's F_0 contours of the prosodic minimal pair /'nomo - no'mo/ (1-2) in the carrier sentence /i ma'ria 'iksere to... ka'la/ with different focal organisations (b-c).

The minimal pair /'nomo - no'mo/ which has a rather neutralised F_0 contour in post-focal position (1c-2c; figure 6) maintains its prosodic distinction (cf. §2.1.a) with the dynamic realisation of duration and intensity, *i.e.* the energy integral. The intensity pattern of the word stress distinction is realised with a rather regular higher relative intensity at the syntagmatic and/or paradigmatic level, whereas sentence stress realisation significantly increases this stressed - unstressed ratio in a constant way. The stressed syllables are also longer than the unstressed ones as a rule and this realisation is mainly carried by the vowels whereas the consonants may occasionally vary in the opposite direction. Duration also contributes to focus, increasing the (sentence) stressed - unstressed ratio but with a large intra/inter speaker variability. The non-focal stressed syllables are on the average 24% longer than the unstressed ones, very close to Fourakis' (1986) results, and the focal realisation increases this difference to 39%.

The constancy of F_0 and intensity for sentence stress as well as the combination of duration and intensity for word stress strongly indicate a basic independence of the prosodic parameters although they may be interrelated

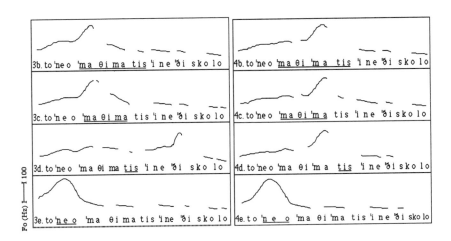

Figure 7. One speaker's F_0 contours of the prosodic/syntactic minimal pair /'maθima tis - 'maθi'ma tis/ (3–4) in the carrier sentence /to 'neo... 'ine 'ðiskolo/ with different focal organisations (b-e).

(Bannert 1986b). Thus, a hierarchical taxonomy of the prosodic parameters for conveying "stress" would appear irrelevant since their contribution is variable across the syntagm depending on the particular function (cf. §2.1.a).

Figure 7 displays one speaker's F_0 contours as well as the effects of focalisation on the prosodic organisation of the minimal syntactic/prosodic pair /'maθima tis - 'maθi'ma tis/. The intonation of the proclitic structure (3b-e) appears with a regular F_0 manifestation, *i.e.* a major pitch-gesture aligned with the corresponding stress groups of the item(s) in focus in combination with a partial accentuation of the pre-focal stress groups (*e.g.* 3d) and an accentless manifestation of the post-focal stress groups (*e.g.* 3e). Different focal domains are neutralised into the same F_0 realisation (3b-3c). On the other hand, when the proclitic /tis/ is in focus (3d), although it is realised as a minor pitch-gesture tonally attached to its rhythmic host (stress group), its focal application is distributed to a stress group of its syntactic host which is in the following verb phrase, *i.e.* a major syntactic constraint is imposed on prosody.

The basic division of an utterance into non-focal - focal parts with a regular distribution of the prosodic parameters is also evident when a phrase stress is involved in an enclitic construction (4b-e). When the enclitic structure /'maθi'ma tis/ is in focus, either as a whole (4b) or a part (4c-4d), sentence stress is constrained to coincide with phrase stress, *i.e.* focal distinctions within an enclitic construction with phrase stress are neutralised, which is another major syntactic constraint on prosody (Rossi 1985). Thus, the prosodic distinction "narrow - broad" focus reported for English (Eady *et al.* 1986) does not affect the F_0 pattern of the investigated material under certain experimental procedures (cf. §1.2)

The focal application may affect the tonal realisation of the preceding stress group(s) into an anathetic or assimilated pitch contour with the focal group as well. Furthermore, post-focal neutralisation of the F_0 contours is rather regular even for phrase stress distinctions (4e) which indicates the global effect of focalisation within an utterance in contrast to the local effects of word and phrase stress within the corresponding domains.

The post-focal word and phrase stress realisations retain their prosodic organisation by a combination of duration and intensity into the corresponding stress groups associated with the distinctive syntactic/semantic structures. Thus, the proclitic - enclitic /'maθima tis - 'maθi'ma tis/, (3e-4e), appears with the regular dynamic distinctions at the syntagmatic and/or the paradigmatic level(s) which are more or less the same in structure as those in the pre-focal position (cf. §2.1.b).

The proclitic - enclitic /tis/ shows a noticeable intra/inter speaker duration variation. Its temporal attachment to the corresponding host is not constant, at least does not conform to the expectations of the cumulative phrase-final lengthening principle (Paccia-Cooper and Cooper 1981) according to which final syllables at word and phrase level should be lengthened in a rather cumulative manner.

Figure 8 is an example of one speaker's raw F_0 data with respect of the focal organisation effect on the paratactic - enclitic structures /to 'proto 'γrama - to 'proγra'ma tis/ (the first letter - the programme of hers'. The paratactic structure

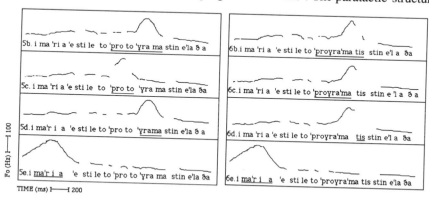

Figure 8. One speaker's F_0 contours of the prosodic/grammatical minimal pair /'proto 'γrama - 'proγra'ma tis/ (5–6) in the carrier sentence /i ma'ria 'estile to... stin e'laδa/ with different focal organisations (b-e).

has two word stresses on two lexical items whereas the enclitic structure carries a word and a phrase stress on one lexical item. The contrastive pair shows predictable similarities as well as striking distinct intonation manifestations. The broad - narrow focus is neutralised in (5b-5d) as well as in (6b-6c-6d). Furthermore, the intonation patterns of the paratactic - enclitic utterances are quite the same except for (5c) and, regardless of dynamic distinctions, there is no intonative cue to indicate the realisation of two word stresses in the paratactic structure or a word and a phrase stress in the enclitic structure. On the other hand, when the adjective /'proto/ of the paratactic structure is in focus (5c), sentence stress with its prosodic manifestation is applied to the adjective leaving outside its scope the rest of the noun phrase, *i.e.* in a noun phrase focus is contextually conditioned and distributed in accordance with its syntactic/prosodic composition.

The above example is an indication that apparently similar stress patterns may take completely different prosodic manifestations when different prosodic categories are involved in focalisation, the enclitic structure with a phrase stress, but not the paratactic structure, imposing a major syntactic constraint on the application of sentence stress. Thus, a syntactic structure may appear with completely different prosodic manifestations as a result of different contextual organisations, and moreover, different contextual organisations may be prosodically neutralised in certain syntactic environments.

The interaction of syntax/context with the prosodic manifestation of an utterance (Rossi 1985) is highly evident as regards the application of sentence stress in Greek. Sentence stress distribution, apart from the semantic scope of focus, is subjected to morphosyntactic constraints, *i.e.* the lower levels of the language are involved in its application, and has global effects on an utterance. On the other hand, phrase stress is context independent, morpholexical and syntactic structure being relevant for its application, and has limited local effects on the phrase domain, *e.g.* a weakening of a word stress in an enclitic construction. Finally, word stress is morpholexically determined with a restricted effect on the stress group it realises. Once sentence stress has been applied there is no further contextual and/or syntactic contribution on the prosodic manifestation of an utterance in Greek, at least for relatively simple, one clause sentences (cf. §2.1.b).

2.4 Phrasing and discourse intonation

In this sub-section, some regular discourse intonation patterns of spontaneous speech are presented, in contrast to the preceding sub-sections (with a partial exception of 2.2) which have dealt with laboratory speech. We have concentrated our attention mainly on patterns which appear interesting to us either because they are familiar from laboratory speech with well documented functions or because they are new to us with, apparently, specific functions. We assume that, regardless of the fact that there is a wide diversity of dialogue types in a language, intonation has a rather limited inventory of patterns to exploit for a great number of communicative purposes and, accordingly, the relation between pattern and function is likely to appear one-to-many.

We have proceeded to the analysis of spoken discourse with some basic conceptions about its organisation (Botinis 1989b). First, discourse participants involved in a conversation are likely to talk rather coherently about one or more **topics** (Brown *et al.* 1980) as well as concentrate on different aspects of it/them, in which case the (main) topic(s) may be sub-divided into several **sub-topics**. Second, discourse participants may proceed to the development of one or several topics by their regular (albeit not necessarily equal) alternation in contributing to the discourse in terms of **turn-units** (Cutler and Pearson 1986). Moreover, a turn-unit may be sub-divided into **sub-turn-units** by external and/or internal prosodic cues as well as grammar and lexis. Third, sub-turn-units may have a relatively autonomous prosodic structure composed of a series of stressed and unstressed syllables in relation to their own lexical/grammatical structure as well as indicating their relation to previous or following turn-units, *i.e.* "look backward - look forward" discourse cues.

For reasons of space, we demonstrate only several typical sub-turn-unit (henceforth STU) extracts of the programme leader from the telephone conversation (cf. §1.2; figure 9). The first three STUs (a-c) have been produced after the customary courtesy expressions and names have been exchanged as well as a compliment on the part of the programme participant to the effect that she has not missed a single programme. The last three STUs (d-f) are part of the next sub-topic in which the programme leader refers to the programme participant's daughter who has just won a record.

STU (a) appears with alternating pitch-gestures aligned with the corresponding stress groups except for the F_0 contour of the last stress group which was not traced; this tonal manifestation across an utterance closely resembles the one of the neutral intonation in laboratory speech (cf. §2.1.a). It is interesting to note that the word /po'te/ in (a) has a pitch-gesture and when part of this STU is repeated in the next STU (b), the very same word /po'te/ reaches the same pitch level (200 Hz) whereas the rest of the STU is manifested by an accentless prosodic pattern. Furthermore, in the following STU (c) the pitch variation of the word /'omos/ reaches the same pitch level (220 Hz) as the word /'kserume/ in STU (a), with the rest of the STU accentless. Thus, the non-focal - focal distinction as well as the sentence stress manifestation and its global effect is quite regular even in spontaneous speech.

STUs (d-f), on the other hand, appear with a mirror-image intonation pattern to that of STUs (b-c), *i.e.* a major pitch-gesture at the final boundary preceded by partial accentuation within the unit which is obviously neutralised in STU (d).

Greek

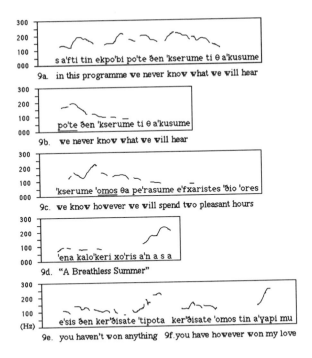

Figure 9. One speaker's F_0 contours of six Sub-Turn-Units (a-f) of a spontaneous speech telephone conversation.

This major pitch-gesture, a turn-keeping rise, is the largest within a STU, as a matter of fact quite regularly the largest (up to 250 Hz) within the entire dialogue, although it is only indirectly associated with a stress group. STUs as well as turn-units may vary from one word to several syntactically complex sub-turn-units separated by various degrees of optional pauses which, in combination with an internal wide pitch-gesture/range and/or an external pitch-change level, provide reliable prosodic cues to the sub-division of a turn-unit. Nevertheless, it is not seldom that there exist neither internal nor external phonetic cues, *e.g.* in intonational sandhi, where it seems reasonable to take syntactic/semantic factors into consideration (Cruttenden 1986).

STUs with an early "narrow" focus may utilise the post-focal accentless stress group organisation as a focal cue, *i.e.* a typical pattern also of laboratory speech, rather than enlarging the focal pitch range in comparison with units with no particular narrow focus. The focal item may be repeated information (Bruce *et al.* 1988) in which case the importance the speaker attaches to this item is emphasised. In our material, the focal item has the largest pitch range within the unit in which it is realised and has a backward reference, *i.e.* it shows the persistance of the speaker in increasing the common ground of the hearer and himself (Brazil 1985), and/or modify the hearer's belief space (Pierrehumbert and Hirschberg 1987).

A STU, apart from a focal gesture may appear with a large pitch rise during the final part of the unit (Bannert 1985b). This pitch rise marks the intention of the speaker to keep his turn, especially in cases where his STU is of complete syntactic structure (Brown *et al.* 1980), in contrast to STU low/pitch fall where the speaker is not so anxious to keep his turn, *i.e.* the hearer may take over. Although the turn-keeping rise clearly denotes more to come, the low/pitch fall does not exclude this possibility, *i.e.* there is an asymmetry in the final STU boundary; in the former case a hearer's turn taking over would be interpreted as an interruption whereas in the second case a take-over would be permitted.

Apart from their different distribution, the two major pitch-changes, focal - turn-keeping, seem mutually exclusive within a S/TU in this material. Both have an exophoric function (for this term in a grammatical treatment cf. Halliday and Hasan 1976; Brown and Yule 1983) but whereas in the focal manifestation the speaker relates the content of the current S/TU to the already developed discourse, in the turn-keeping manifestation the speaker directs the listener's attention towards what is to follow. Moreover, their tonal manifestation is quite distinct; the focal manifestation is realised by a pitch fall onto the post-stressed syllable(s) whereas the turn-keeping manifestation by a pitch rise. Pierrehumbert and Hirschberg (1987) attribute the backward - forward directionality of the sub-turn-unit (intonational phrase) to the (final) boundary tones. Without disputing the significance of the final tones in relation to what follows, we think that earlier (focal) tones are equally important in relation to what precedes. However, further experimental and/or perceptual evidence is required on this issue as well as on the possible coincidence of both focal and turn-keeping realisations at the final boundaries. Furthermore, although we have observed some regular sub-topic intonation cues, we have not discussed the issue further, awaiting a more detailed description of intonation topic/sub-topic contribution in ongoing research.

3. Comparison with other systems

Languages are characterised by prosodic variations in their spoken form which may diverge in distribution as well as in structure and function. Greek shares the focalisation process of highlighting the most important information with the majority of European languages and is semantically motivated like *e.g.* Danish (Grønnum [Thorsen] this volume), in contrast to Swedish which has a default sentence stress rule (Bruce 1977). Encliticisation and its interference in the prosodic organisation of the phrase is rather peculiar to Greek whereas the (tri)syllabic constraint as well as word stress distinctions are shared with Italian and Spanish. On the other hand, the grammatical word as the accentual unit is rather common in non-Germanic languages (*e.g.* Italian, Russian), in contrast to Germanic languages (*e.g.* German, Swedish) where the grammatical word reflects the accentual pattern of the lexical/morphological items composing it.

The prosodic manifestation of a stressed syllable in Greek may be associated with a pitch rise forming a high plateau with several post-stressed syllables whereas in Standard Swedish a stressed syllable may be associated with a pitch fall in which case the relative timing of the fall carries the distinction between the two word accents. Focus in Greek is mainly realised as a pitch rise aligned with the stressed syllable of the element in focus in combination with a major pitch fall into the post-stressed syllable(s) and a regular post-focal flattening at a low plateau. In Swedish (cf. Gårding this volume) on the other hand, focus is mainly realised with a major pitch rise immediately after the fall associated with the stressed syllable forming a high plateau with several post-focal syllable(s) and a successive compression of pitch range for post-focal accent distinctions. In French (cf. Di Cristo this volume), pitch-rises may be associated with minor and/or major syntactic boundaries whereas focus (*accent d'insistance*) is realised on the first syllable of the focal element followed by a pitch fall and a low plateau, *i.e.* post-focal flattening is a regular pitch pattern under comparable experimental procedures in both French and Greek but not in Swedish.

Post-focal pitch neutralisation has also been observed for Danish (Grønnum [Thorsen] this volume), English (Horne 1989), French (Touati 1987) German (Bannert 1985a), among others, whereas the post-focal reorganisation for F_0 contour is minimal in Southern Swedish (Gårding *et al.* 1982). Thus, even though the post-focal F_0 flattening is quite common for a number of languages, it may vary between dialects (Standard - Southern Swedish), between closely related languages (Danish - Swedish), and be the same between more loosely related languages like Danish, French, English, German, and Greek. The above languages associate major pitch-gestures/ranges with focus whereas the contribution of duration, although regular, is not constant. In French (Touati 1987), however, the focal manifestation (*accent d'insistance*) has hardly any effect on duration. On the other hand, the stressed - unstressed duration ratio in Greek is somewhat smaller than the Italian one (Farnetani and Kori 1986), close to the Spanish ratio (Delattre 1966c), whereas in Danish (Fisher-Jørgensen 1984) it is much larger and in Swedish, apart from differences of vowel quality (cf. Engstrand 1986), the stressed syllables are twice as long as the unstressed ones (Bruce 1984b).

4. Conclusions

In spite of the fact that F_0 timing has been found to have an all-or-none effect on listeners, this is interpreted as an experimental artefact which is only indirectly related to word stress. A Greek speaker/listener "knows" that a pitch-gesture is temporally coordinated with a stressed syllable at the lexical level, and the displacement of this has a direct effect on stress identification change, in accordance with the alignment of an F_0 rise with the corresponding stressed syllable. Thus, F_0 is rather thought to be a prosodic parameter the function of which is to attribute to a certain stress group a relative prominence in relation to other stress groups in a speech unit as well as indicate the (bi)directionality and interdependence of speech units in a broader context. In contrast, duration and intensity if combined into a single feature, what has been referred to as the energy integral, may be a constant stress correlate the function of which is to organise the rhythmic structure of successive speech units. In the light of this argument it seems that the idea of a hierarchy of the prosodic parameters for stress perception should be reconsidered. Although a listener may use any prosodic cues available to him/her for the identification of the message, F_0 and duration combined with intensity appear to have basically different functions; moreover, a particular parameter (*e.g.* intensity) may contribute little by itself, but it may turn out to be a decisive cue when combined with the other prosodic parameters.

Our experience with Greek intonation and its interdependence on prosodic structure is mainly based on non-complex, well-controlled laboratory speech; nevertheless, it has been shown to provide a solid framework (cf. Rossi 1987 for French) to approach discourse and the interactive study of prosody. The prosodic contribution to topic organisation and turn interplay units as well as the interactive organisation of spoken discourse are of major interest to our immediate research. This challenging field of prosodic research undertaken by phoneticians has already started at the Phonetics Department in Lund with the acronym KIPROS, based on the original title in Swedish (Bruce *et al.* 1988); it stands for Contrastive Interactive Prosody in which, in addition to Greek, the discourse structure of French and Swedish is investigated in a contrastive perspective.

Note

This contribution was partly supported by a research grant from the Swedish Institute for a year's collaboration with the Institut de Phonétique d'Aix, and is partly within the KIPROS project framework, financed by the Bank of Sweden Tercentenary Foundation. Gösta Bruce and Albert Di Cristo have let me benefit from their comments and Daniel Hirst and Merle Horne have revised my English and made content suggestions.

17

Intonation in
Finnish

ANTTI IIVONEN

1. Background

Introduction

Finnish belongs to the family of Finno-Ugrian languages. The peoples speaking Hungarian or Finnish represent the largest groups in this family. Finnish is spoken by about 4.6 million people as the mother tongue in Finland. In Northern Finland about 4000 people speak Lappish. Swedish is the other official language in Finland and it is spoken by about 300,000 people mainly at the Western and South and Southwestern coasts of Finland and in the Southwestern archipelago. About the same number of people speak Finnish in Sweden, and quite large groups of emigrants use Finnish also in the USA, Canada, and Australia. A great part of the Lappish and Swedish speaking population in Finland is bilingual.

Finnish can be divided into several dialects. The main division concerns the Western and Eastern dialects. They are in regular and vivid use in daily communication, but are partly mixed with elements from Standard Finnish or other dialects. The mixing (switching) of elements is caused especially by the considerable urbanisation and movement of the population within the country, especially to the Helsinki area (Paunonen 1989, Nuolijärvi 1986).

Standard Finnish, which is phonetically mainly based on Häme dialects spoken especially in Central Southern parts of Finland, is a higher social form of language. A considerable amount of competing variants, weak forms, elisions, assimilations, casual speech forms and rhythmical groupings are characteristic of colloquial speech also among speakers from socially higher classes. Variation, elisions and groupings can be illustrated by the following example:

(1)   oletko sinä ollut? (have you been?)

can be shortened maximally in two ways:

(2) a   ots ollu   b   oks ollu

which means that the original sequence

(3)   /ol+e+t+ko # sinä/
          (to be + present tense + second person + question suffix # you)

containing five morphemes, preserves in both of the equivalent variants *ots* and *oks* only three phonemes, each phoneme representing only one original morpheme. Both preserve the indicators for the lexical stems, *i.e.* /o/ and /s/, in addition *oks* also preserves the /k/ of the question morpheme while *ots* keeps the /t/ of the person morpheme.

1.1 General prosodic characteristics of Finnish

a. Phonemes and phoneme combinations
The Finnish phoneme paradigm consists of 13 native consonants and 8 vowels:
    C: /p, t, k, d, s, h, j, v, r, l, m, n, ŋ/
    V: /i, e, y, ø, æ, a, o, u/

Orthographic *ä* and *ö* correspond respectively to /æ/ (an unrounded open front vowel) and /ø/ (a rounded mid front vowel, more open than the French [ø]). Since the orthographic phoneme correspondence is otherwise systematic, in the rest of this chapter, for simplification I use /ä/ and /ö/ instead of the standard IPA symbols /æ/ and /ø/

Vowel harmony restricts the vowel combinations, *i.e.* only /i/ and /e/ can freely be combined with the other vowels in the same word. Otherwise only front vowels can be combined with front vowels or back vowels with back vowels. Hence, such words as *väga* (very) in Estonian (cf. *vähän* (a bit) in Finnish) or *nära* (near) in Swedish (cf. *närä* (resentment) in Finnish) are impossible in Finnish.

b. Quantity
Double (phonetically long) vowels and double (phonetically long or geminate) consonants can phonologically be interpreted as sequences of two phonemes: they are sequences of two identical phonemes (Karlsson 1969, 1983, p. 82). Hence, *sata* (hundred) includes four phonemes (= /sata/), whereas *saattaa* (to escort) includes seven phonemes (= /saattaa/). Double vowels belong to the same

syllable (*väärä* (wrong) = /vää.rä/), whereas a syllable boundary always occurs in double consonants between the identical phonemes (*pakko* (force) = /pak.ko/, *myrkky* /myrk.ky/ (poison)).

The durational mean ratio between single and double vowels V/VV is 1:2.3 which means that the double vowels are about 2.3 times or 135% longer than the single ones (Wiik 1965, p. 113). The ratio depends, however, considerably on syllable position and phonotactic factors. Ratios between 1:2.0 and 1:2.6 are found in the first syllable of bisyllabic words, whereas the ratios are much less prominent in the second syllables of bisyllabic words representing the structure types CVCV/CVCVV or CVCVC/CVCVVC, if the preceding consonant is short (about 1:1.4).

The single/double contrast is also phonetically well preserved in Finnish at fast speech rate (1:2.1), whereas in English the durational contrast becomes smaller (1:1.8) (Marjomaa 1982). In addition, it can be observed that the single/double contrast yields at slow, normal and fast speech rate a double peaked distribution curve for vowel durations in Finnish, but for those in English a single peaked curve.

It has been difficult to find stable microprosodic pitch differences combined with the single/double contrast of vowels. The only difference observed by Aulanko (1985) was a greater F_0 movement in the double (long) vowels. Vihanta (1988) concludes that the systematic F_0 movements observed in connection with the single/double contrasts in vowels and consonants might depend on word structure or sentence intonation, but they might also have some function as an acoustic cue for the quantity opposition.

The ratio between single and double consonants C/CC seems to vary according to the major consonantal classes: the mean ratios for obstruent consonants /p, t, k, s/ 1:1.99 and for sonorant consonants /m, n, l, r/ 1:2.50 were found by Lehtonen (1970, p. 97). This might be connected somehow with the stress/accent signalisation.

c. Double vowels
All vowels occur as single and double in primary stressed and in non-primary stressed position:

i. primary stressed position

V/VV	single (short)	double (long)
i/ii	*sika* (pig)	*siika* (whitefish)
e/ee	*te* (you; pl.)	*tee* (tea)
y/yy	*ryppy* (wrinkle)	*ryyppy* (pull [= drink])
ö/öö	*tötti* (prop) [loan word, techn. slang]	*töötti* (siren) [colloquial]
ä/ää	*värin* (color; gen.)	*väärin* (wrongly)
a/aa	*varat* (funds)	*vaarat* (danger; pl.nom.)

o/oo	*polo* (poor)	*poolo* (polo)
u/uu	*puro* (brook)	*puuro* (porridge)

ii. non-primary stressed position

V/VV	single (short)	double (long)
i/ii	*etsi* ((he) sought)	*etsii* ((he) seeks)
e/ee	*tulen* (fire; gen.)	*tuleen* (into the fire)
y/yy	*hyllyn* (shelf; gen.)	*hyllyyn* (on (to) the shelf)
ö/öö	*särön* (crack; gen.)	*säröön* (into the crack)
ä/ää	*mätä* (rotten)	*mätää* (rotten; partitive)
a/aa	*sata* (hundred)	*sataa* (hundred; partitive) or (to rain)
o/oo	*talon* (house; gen.)	*taloon* (into the house)
u/uu	*surun* (sorrow; gen.)	*suruun* (into the sorrow)

d. Double consonants

Among the consonants /v/, /j/, /d/, and /h/ cannot be doubled in native words. /hh/, however, occurs marginally, *e.g.* huhho (salmon hucho). /ŋ/ has a restricted distribution: it is possible as the only nasal consonant medially before /k/, and as doubled between vowels:

kenkä [keŋkæ] (shoe; nominative)   *kengän* [keŋŋæn] (shoe; genitive)

The single/double contrast C/CC between the other 8 consonants can be exemplified as follows:

C/CC	single (short)	double (long, geminate)
p/pp	nupi (tack)	nuppi (knob)
m/mm	suma (jam)	summa (sum)
t/tt	kato (dearth)	katto (roof)
s/ss	kisa (game)	kissa (cat)
n/nn	peni (whelp, puppy)	penni (penny)
l/ll	palo (burning)	pallo (ball)
r/rr	varas (thief)	varras (spit)
k/kk	pako (escape)	pakko (force)

Syntagmatically again, it is important to note that the double consonants may alternate with single consonants or consonant combinations in the inflectional word forms. This is due to the rich morphophonology, especially the consonant gradation of /p/, /t/, and /k/.

e. Syllable structure and word stress

The number of actually existing syllables is about 3000 (Wiik 1977, Karlsson 1983, p.136). Syllable types /CV/, /CVC/, and /CVV/ are the most frequent ones. They cover 80.6% of all occurrences (40.4, 27.5, and 12.7%, resp.). Other types are /CVVC, VC, V, VV, CVCC, VVC, VCC/.

Word (primary) stress always falls on the first syllable of the word. Word stress therefore assumes a certain role as a word-boundary marker. Because of the great amount of polysyllabic and compound words a secondary stress frequently occurs. The placement of secondary stress depends on quite a number of factors (Sadeniemi 1949, pp. 69–76), but the rules cannot be described here in detail. Some major cases can be mentioned.

Secondary stress occurs in four-syllabic or longer words on the third or fourth syllable, but later in the word on every second syllable, exept the last one (cf. Sadeniemi 1949, p. 72). The word

(4)   'tottele₁matto₁muudes₁tansa /tot.te.le.mat.to.muu.des.tan.sa/
        ((his) disobedience; elative)

includes nine syllables and three secondary stresses. Hence, it can be seen that the long words are divided approximately in bisyllabic foots. Syllable length and derivational structure can influence the placement of the secondary stress. A long syllable contains a long vowel element (double vowel or dipththong) or it is closed with a consonant; a short syllable contains a short closing vowel (*ibid.*, p. 101). If the third syllable is short and the fourth syllable long, the fourth one gets the secondary stress:

(5)   'akvaari₁ossa /ak.vaa.ri.os.sa/ (aquarium; inessive)

If the word structure consists of a stem and a derivational suffix, the secondary stress occurs on the first syllable of the suffix:

(6)   'sirpale₁mainen /sir.pa.le.mai.nen/
        (like shattered) [*sirpale* (splinter) + *mainen* (like)]

The relationships between the elements in compounds resemble the syntactic relationships of words in sentences. Therefore the elements of the compounds play a role in determining the placement of the stress degrees of the compounds (cf. Wiik 1975). Hence, in the compound numeral:

(7)   neljäkymmentäneljä /neljä+kymmentä+neljä/ (44),

the last element /neljä/ gets the strongest stress which causes the highest F_0 peak on the first syllable of the word. The resulting accentual pattern thus resembles *e.g.* the syntactical structure:

(8)   kaljupäiset miehet /kalju+päiset # miehet/ (baldheaded men).

In compounds of two elements the first syllable of the second element gets the secondary stress even if both elements are monosyllabic:

(9)   'puu₁pää (/puu+pää/) (blockhead)

Phonetically, stress is less melodic or tonal in Finnish than in English (Niemi 1984). Against expectation, Niemi (1984, p. 93) also found that duration plays a much greater role in word stress signalling in Finnish than in English. On the whole, Finnish stress is relatively weakly expressed. A frequent pattern is the combination of increased intensity and raised F_0 (cf. Sovijärvi 1958).

Word tone is not distinctive in Finnish, but certain fixed phonetic word tone patterns may occur in Standard Finnish. These might differ in different dialects.

f. Rhythm

Temporal organisation and rhythm of Finnish are strongly influenced by typical syntagmatic rules and structures of the language. These include: the distinction between double vowels and consonants, the existence of diphthongs, vowel combinations, syllable combinations, and long words. The occurrence of long words is due to the relatively long stems, suffixation, derivational and compound words. Typical Finnish word structure includes the stem and the inflectional suffix whereby the morphophonological alternations at the border of stem and suffix are numerous (cf. Hakulinen 1979, Karlsson 1983; Laaksonen and Lieko 1988). The allomorphic alternation in the inflectional suffixes is great.

Typologically, English is often characterised as an intonation language. Finnish could be characterised as an **accent language**.

Within the rhythm typology, Finnish is often included among **syllable-timed** languages (*e.g.* Karlsson 1983, p. 176). This interpretation is, however, controversial. Leino (1986, p. 154) concludes that in the metrical use there exists a tendency towards a **stress-timed** system. Also a characterisation as a **foot counting** language is mentioned (Wiik 1988). In words produced in isolation, the segment duration is shortened systematically in a negative correlation with the phonotactic length of the word (Iivonen 1975). This seems to indicate that some sort of isochrony principle also exists in Finnish.

1.2 Outline of the approach

Prosody has for a long time been described in Finnish, as in numerous other languages, under the vague term "accent" which historically is the Latin equivalent for "prosody" in Greek. Thus the division of the term into **dynamic** and **melodic** types offered a basis for the description of several prosodic phenomena within word and sentence. The term "intonation" was not used in Finnish literature until 1927 in connection with speech (Penttilä 1927; cf. Iivonen *et al.* 1987, p. 24), but its meaning was "accentuation", because Penttilä followed A. Meillet's use of the term. "Intonation", however, began to gain ground among phoneticians at the beginning of the 1930s with a meaning which often covers approximately the same features as "prosody" (cf. Halliday 1970, Cruttenden 1986); it has some specified meaning in the theory (Crystal 1969) or is simply equal to voice pitch (*e.g.* Brosnahan and Malmberg 1970, p. 148).

No specific intonation theory or school is followed in the treatment of Finnish intonation below. Knowledge concerning Finnish prosody available is at the moment more or less fragmentary[1].

2. Description of intonation patterns

2.1 Description of a basic non-emphatic pattern

The basic non-emphatic, non-affective utterance consisting of several words means prosodically a descending F_0 curve which includes rising-falling peaks on the accentuated syllables resembling the American English examples in Lea (1977). In most cases a declination of F_0 can be observed. This pattern is exemplified by means of the following sentence (cf. the corresponding F_0 curve in figure 1).

(10)   LAIna LAInaa LAInalle LAInan. (Laina [= girl's name] lends Laina a loan.)
         [*lainata* (to loan, borrow), verb; *lainaa* (sg. present tense, 3. pers.); *Lainalle* (to Laina (adessive)); *lainan* (loan) (noun; accusative)]

The basic pattern described is common to both statements and questions (cf. their differences in chapter 2.4.). A final rise is rare in Finnish and the rules found in French, English, and German associated with the use of final rise for the expression of interrogativity do not exist in Finnish (cf. §2.4.). In oral reading the declination observed especially in isolated utterances is no longer so evident. In utterance-final positions creaky voice very often occurs.

It has been claimed in several connections that typical Finnish intonation is relatively low, has a narrow variation range and relative small pitch intervals (cf. Hakulinen 1979, p. 33).

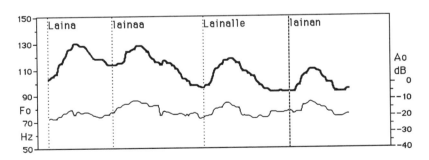

Figure 1. The test sentence (9) produced by a male speaker SL (ca. 55 years). Top (thick curve): the F_0 curve, bottom (thin): the intensity (Ao) curve. Analysis by means of an automatic digital measurement method included in the ISA (Intelligent Speech Analyser) speech processing system developed by Raimo Toivonen. Agaist expectation, no declination can be observed in the Ao-curve. A positive correlation between Ao- tops and F_0 tops can be seen.

Antti Iivonen

2.2 Modality and expressivity

a. Questions

The features of intonation typical of neutral statements were described in §2.1. Concerning questions, it has been problematic, whether a specific interrogative intonation pattern exists in Finnish and how its acoustic cues are located in the utterance. Many reseachers have totally denied the connection between interrogativity and intonation, whereas some others explain that the special prosodic patterns observed in questions are expressive. The problem of interrogative intonation is connected with the fact that there are several grammatical means to express questions in Finnish (Iivonen 1978, p. 45), *e.g.*:

i. particular questions

(11) *m-questions*: Mikä tämä on? (What is this?)

Other m-lexemes are *missä* (where), *miten* (how).

(12) *k-questions:* Kuka te olette? (Who are you?)

Other k-lexemes are *koska* (when), *kuinka* (how)).

ii. general questions

(13)　　Onko hän kotona? (Is he at home?)

with suffix *-ko* or *-kö* (depending on vowel harmony).

Kallionen (1968) concluded, partly on the basis of experimental evidence, that intonation which is associated with a question in a formally unmarked utterance is not distinctive but only expressive, *i.e.* an expressive nucleus (produced by means of rising pitch, increasing intensity, increasing duration) indicates surprise, a final rise indicates a kind appeal.

Hirvonen (1970), applying a more systematic experimental procedure, and relying on a corpus consisting of 70 utterances from a conversation read aloud by two informants, concluded that general and particular questions (and imperatives, too) are consistently characterised by a high initial pitch. Both have otherwise an overall declining pitch like statements. Particular questions (*m/k-*questions) differ from general (*-ko/-kö*-questions) ones on the basis of F_0 contour. In particular questions, the initial high F_0 level is followed by an immediate fall, whereas in general questions the F_0 curve remains on a relatively high level until the first syllable of the most important word of the utterance bearing the main accent. The "most important word" refers to the rheme of the utterance:

(14) *colloquial:*　　TUlek sä TÖIhin huomenna? (Are you coming to work tomorrow?)

(/-k/ = the rest of the question suffix; inverted word order)

318

(15) *standard:*   TUletko sinä TÖIhin huomenna?)

It has been considered an alien feature in Finnish, when the interrogative utterance ends with a final rise. Kallioinen (1968) found, however, several examples with a final rise in colloquial speech. It is also sure that in utterances which end with an interrogative word *vai* (or) the final rise occurs very often. Also in monosyllabic interrogative utterances *niin?* (so?), *no* (well?) the final rise is usual.

The final rise is also possible in **echo-questions** which imply a request for a repetition of the previous statement uttered by the interlocutor, *e.g.*:

(16) – Jussi taittoi jalkansa.   (John broke his leg.)
      – Mitä sitä sanoit?   [with global rising intonation] (What did you say?)

However, the basic problem remains: Are there so called **intonation questions** in Finnish, *i.e.* utterances that totally lack any lexical, morphological or syntactical marker for question? We can look at the following sentences, formally resembling statements:

(17)   Te asutte tässä sisarenne kanssa?   (You live here with your sister?)
(18)   Sinä siis lähdet huomenna?   (So, you are leaving tomorrow?)

According to impressionistic experience, this kind of utterance, which often represent a kind of guessing, may lack any systematic prosodic cue for question, but they may also, in some cases, be uttered using (optional) prosodic features functionally being interrogative. In any case those features are not obligatory, and the final rise is not typically included in them. According to Itkonen (1972, p. 14), direct questions are produced with an overall higher pitch than the statements.

b. Finality and continuation

So called **progredient intonation** or "comma intonation" occurs in Finnish. According to Aaltonen and Wiik (1979) it doesn't only imply a relatively higher level before the boundary (comma) compared with the terminal intonation of statements, but also a higher global F_0 level of the utterance from the beginning as well as stronger intensity before the boundary. Aperiodic voice (laryngealisation, creaky voice) is connected with the ends of the final statements (= terminal intonation), whereas in clauses indicating continuation, periodic voice is observed at the end before the boundary (= non-terminal intonation), cf. the examples:

(19)   Näin eilen purjelaivan.   (I saw yesterday a sailing ship.)

where the underlined syllable is aperiodic, by contrast with

(20)   Näin eilen purjelaivan, joka voitti kilpailun
         (I saw yesterday the sailing ship which won the competition.)

where the underlined syllable is periodic.

c. *Expressivity*

As a special case of expressive intonation a pattern called here delayed F_0 peak (cf. Bruce and Gårding 1978, Ladd 1983b) is dealt with. This pattern, which often expresses some kind of hinting, can be compared with the three accent types described in §2.3. Compared to them, the F_0 peak associated normally with the first stressed syllable is shifted to the right from its normal position (about 100 ms in the example in Iivonen 1987, p. 124). The place of the F_0 peak in the word depends on the segmental structure of the word: if the first syllable is short (*e.g.* /CV.CV/), the F_0 peak is placed on the second syllable; if it is long (*e.g.* /CVV.CV/), the peak occurs at the end of the vowel of the first syllable or on the (resonant) consonant after the vowel. Its production involves laryngeal activity, while an increase of subglottal pressure is suppressed. The typical emphatic accent, on the contrary, involves dominantly an increase of subglottal pressure. Examples (21–22) illustrate the difference between contrastive accent (cf. §2.3.) and delayed F_0 peak:

(21)   *Speaker A:* ⌢Sy＼dänvika se on. (A heart disease it is.)

The word order already indicates a contrastive accent by contrast with:

(22)   *Speaker B:* Sy／dän＼vika se on. (A heart disease it is, sure.)

which is an assertion, but simultaneously a doubt is expressed implying that actually the contrary is true; delayed F_0 peak has often a meaning of hinting.

If an emotion or affect is involved in the speech act, and its scope functionally concerns the whole utterance, the result can be its multi-local appearing in the prosodic composition of the utterance which often happens in cases of an emphatic accent and a delayed F_0 peak (*e.g.* example 28 below).

It is hardly true that the variation range of Finnish intonation is narrow in all circumstances. In expressive function and in intimate discourse, very lively, colourful, and variable use of prosody can be heard. The representatives of the younger generation seem to use more courageous prosody than those of the older generation at the same age. Some observations on the relationships between forms and meanings of the expressive intonation can be found in Lehtonen (1971) and Nieminen (1985).

2.3 Focalisation and contextual effects

a. *Three types of main accent*

Besides the different accentual degrees described above, three accentual classes can be found in utterances in Finnish: **Accent for Rheme** (AR), **Accent for**

Contrast (AC) and **Accent for Emphasis** (AE). All these occur as primary accents in an utterance. The latter two can be characterised as intensified forms of accent. This classification does not mean that they all should be understood as categories which in all circumstances can be functionally and phonetically identified ideally. On the contrary we may merely speak about three different extreme possibilities which mainly differ on the basis of prosodic composition and the specific functional role most often attached to them. In actual speech samples we can easily observe their gradual variants and overlapping between them.

The three main classes can be exemplified as follows. We can imagine an adult teaching a child the letters.

(23)   Tämä on 'A. (This is (the letter) A.)

where /'/ indicates primary accent , i.e. here normal, rhematic accent.

(24)   Tämä on "A. (This is A (not B or some other letter))

where /"/ indicates contrastive accent, phonetically extra high.

(25)   Tämä on "A-"A. (This is A (can't you learn that?!))

Phonetically, the monosyllabic A is divided into two syllables the first A being long, the second one short.)

b. Rheme and theme
In the first category (normal primary accent) often no phonetic indication is used, but very often a higher F_0 peak occurs on the first syllable of the accented word (cf. Hirvonen 1970; Karlsson 1983, p. 170; Niemi 1984). Functionally this type of accent is rhematic in opposite to the thematic part of the utterance which often is produced less accented and at a more rapid speech rate. The unmarked accentuation implies that the last content word is accented. Thus also a verb in this position can be accented, cf. the following sentences:

(26)   Tänään SAtoi.   (It rained today.) [Literally: Today rained.]
(27)   Tänään satoi RAjusti. (It rained today heavily.)

The accentuation of the thematic part of utterances is not very well understood. In some cases, the theme, introduced in fact as a new element in the discourse at the beginning of an utterance, is pronounced with careful and slower articulation and separated from the following part of the utterance by a pause or caesura:

(28)   (")Elefantti / sitä vastoin on (')LAUmaeläin.
        (The elephant, on the contrary, is a gregarious animal.)

where "/" = a brief pause or caesura.

c. Contrast

In the second category (contrast, CA), the most important marking cue is an extra high F_0 peak on the focused syllable. It can be accompanied by stronger intensity, but a more noticeable effect is achieved by means of F_0 peak only. In some cases a lengthening of the syllable is used (Iivonen 1983). The function of the CA is to point to an alternative out of a group of two or more possibilities, whereas the possibilities may be contrastive affirmation or negation (in verbs).

(29)   MATti otti "Omenan. *(contrasted selection)*
        (Matti took an APPLE; not an orange.)

(30)   MATti "EI ottanut Omenaa. *(contrastive negation)*
        (Matti DIDN'T take an apple.)

(31)   MATti "OTti omenan. *(contrastive affirmation).*
        (Matti DID take an apple.)

There exist cases where the segmental structure of two utterances is the same, but the prosodic structure indicates that the group of the alternatives is different, *e.g.*:

(32)   Nämä ovat "PARhaat äidin tekemät KINtaat.
(33)   Nämä ovat "PARhaat, "ÄIdin tekemät KINtaat.
        (*literally:* These are the best mother's made mittens.)

In both cases we may imagine a child speaking about the mittens made by his/her mother, but in (32) the child considers the best mittens made by mother, whereas in (33) he/she considers all the mittens he/she owns. Hence, the literal translations could be:

(34)   (These are the best mittens mother (ever) made.)
(35)   (These are the best mittens (and) mother made them.)

In (32) the underlined passage forms a single intonational phrase beginning with a contrastive accent on the syllable /par/. In (33) the passage is interrupted at the comma and a new phrase begins with a new CA on the syllable /äi/. A short pause or caesura occurs before that syllable.

Intonationally, a downstepped contour (cf. Ladd 1983b, pp. 733–734) occurs after the CA, cf. (37) in the following examples:

(36)   POjalla on UUdet KENgät. (The boy has new shoes.) (rheme underlined)

(37)   POjalla "ON UUdet KENgät.
        (The boy DOES have new shoes.) (CA underlined)

d. Emphasis

In the third accentual case (emphatic accent, EA), increasing subglottal pressure is typically used for its expression and instead of one accented syllable, two syllables are marked (cf. Sadeniemi 1949, Uusivirta 1965). In the cases of monosyllabic words an extra syllable is created for the second marking. As in (25) where the vowel /a/ was doubled, the emphatic form of *on* (is) is /"O."ON/ or /"OO."ON/. In many emphatic utterances every syllable gets the intensified accent:

(38)   No, "OS"TAT"KO!? (Well, do you buy!?).

In several cases the underlying secondary stress of a long word becomes the carrier of the second emphatic prominence, *e.g.* *"Eri"TYIsen kaunis* (especially beautiful). In this example the first syllable can be accented less than the later emphatic syllable. In bisyllabic words the second syllable is fully capable of carrying the emphatic accent, *e.g.* *Tule "HE"TI!* (Come at once!).

Because the emphasis involves the speaker's attitude (often insistence), it cannot be defined as a neutral case of accent. The attitude (connotation) can be expressed by means of paraphrase (cf. Halliday 1970) and can thus be interpreted as an index of an actual speech act. The contrastive accent involves a logical (intellectual) confronting of possibilities (examples 29–37). Therefore it is in principle free from emotions or attitudes.

2.4 Phrasing and textual organisation

a. Accentuation and phrasing
Word structure and the principles of stress placement as well as the importance of maintaining the quantity distinction in all circumstances were described in the preceding sections. These factors are important for the prosodic composition of Finnish utterances.

An utterance consists of minor and major accentual units (feet, stress groups, speech measures, phrases), the status of which is not fully explored. A grammatical word often forms a rhythmical (enclitic) combination with one or two other words in utterances. These enclitic elements often include monosyllabic or bisyllabic verb forms (*on* (is), *oli* (was), *meni* (went)).

For the listener the stress locations form the crucial cues for the interpretation of the utterance. For the utterance /ruiskukannupuissa/ the following two interpretations are possible:
- a syntactic composition consisting of a compound and a single word:

(39)   ruiskukannu puissa   /ruisku/+/kannu/+/puissa/
         (a sprinkling can in the trees; *ruisku* (spray); *kannu* (can); *puu* (tree); *puissa* (pl.inessive))

a compound word consisting of three words:

(40)   ruiskukannupuissa = /ruis/+/kukan/+/nupuissa/
         (in the corn flower buds; *ruis* (rye); *kukka* (flower); *kukan* (sg. gen.); *ruiskukka* (rye flower); *nuppu* (bud); *nupuissa* (pl.inessive))

where the syllabification for both is : /ruis.ku.kan.nu.puis.sa/)

The notation of primary and secondary stresses (accents) disambiguates the structures:

(41)   /'ruiskuˌkannu 'puissa/
(42)   /'ruiskukanˌnupuissa/ or /'ruiskukan 'nupuissa/.

The word level primary and secondary stresses form the underlying basis for the accentuation pattern of the whole utterances. The accentuation pattern consists of a stream of more or less accented and unaccented syllables. The result is phonetically a sequence of different degrees of prominence. The most prominent accents which are produced from semantic or attitudinal reasons (rhematic, contrastive or emphatic accent) are treated in §2.3.

It has been problematic in the literature, how many degrees of prominence can be produced and perceived. A division into maximally six or seven classes is suggested by Bierwisch (1966, p. 124) concerning German; on the other hand some theories suggest a binary system of accented and unaccented syllables only, cf. Bolinger (1958) concerning English. Concerning Finnish, Itkonen (1972, p. 15) suggests a four-degree division (unstressed, secondary-stressed, normal or medium strong primary stress, strong stress) and discusses the possibility of dividing secondary stress into two sub-classes. He concludes, however, that the impression of degree of prominence depends crucially on the length of the surrounding stretch of speech which is considered as the basis of perceptual processing.

How the accentual pattern is planned and executed is a still less investigated area, but it seems plausible to claim that some sequences form quite small rhythm units (feet, measures) beginning with a primary or secondary stressed syllable followed by the unstressed syllable(s). These minor units form larger rhythmical units (speech measures) beginning with a primary stressed syllable and consisting often of a larger grammatical structure (long word, compound word, larger syntactic unit; cf. Sadeniemi 1949).

Still larger prosodic units (phrases) may begin with a more strongly accented syllable and the whole unit may be covered by an F_0 contour beginning on the accented syllable (cf. Trubetzkoy's notion of **culminative function**), whereas the accented syllable of the internal minor unit means a smaller local rise-fall in the larger pattern (Iivonen 1984b). The following example illustrates such a larger unit:

(43)   tohtori Niemisen käyttäytyminen   (Dr. Nieminen's behaviour)

Example (32–33) showed how accentuation can be used for disambiguating the syntax in Finnish (cf. Iivonen 1984b). The following example:

(44)   Tässä on tohtori Niemisen käyttäytymistä koskeva tutkimus.
         (here / is / Dr./ proper noun; genit./ behaviour; partitive /
         concerning / investigation)

can have two (literal) interpretations:

(45)   (Here is an investigation concerning Dr. Nieminen's behaviour.)
(46)   (Here is Dr. Nieminen's investigation concerning behaviour.)

The two meanings and different constituent structures can be disambiguated by means of phrasing and accentuation. The following differences were observed on the basis of five actual repetitions of both examples by a male speaker ML.

In the beginning of both utterances /tässä on/ forms an accentually weak onset. The first syllable of the word /tohtori/ (Dr.) in interpretation (45) shows already quite a high Hz level, whereas with the interpetation (46) the speaker included the same syllable in the weak and low preonset of the utterance. In (45) the main focus word /tutkimus/ has one single complicated attribute consisting of the remaining words /tohtori niemisen käyttäytymistä koskeva/. In (46) the main focus word /tutkimus/ has two independent attributes: /tohtori niemisen/ and /käyttäytymistä koskeva/. The stronger syntactical boundary lying between /niemisen/ and /käyttäytymistä/ could also be indicated by means of a comma:

(47)   Tässä on tohtori Niemisen, käyttäytymistä koskeva tutkimus.

The comma corresponds to the accentual and syntactic division of the two utterances. In (45) this means that the accented word /tutkimus/ practically forms with its attribute one declining F_0 contour, whereas in (46) the same segmental structure shows two F_0 peaks.

Other phonetic consequences of the syntactic structure were as follows: In (45) the word /tutkimus/ with its one complex attribute had a mean duration of 1040 ms, in (46) the same word with its two attributes lasted 1345 ms. In (45) the mean duration of /nieminen/ was only 533 ms, in (46) 754 ms. The increased duration was more obvious on the syllables /nie/ and /käyt/ in (46). At the strong syllable boundary between /niemisen/ and /käyttäytymisen/ in (46) a short caesura (but not a pause) occurred whereas the temporal integration of the same words in (45) can be interpreted as a disjuncture. The relationships between syntax and intonation are discussed also in Aaltonen (1975).

b. Junctures
Prosodic means are used for signalling boundaries. In the following examples the boundary /+/ or /#/ lies between vowel and consonant (48), between vowel and vowel (49), between consonant and vowel (50), or vowel and consonant (51):

(48)   / -V+C- / lintuansa /lintua+nsa/
        (bird; partitive + possessive suffix, 3rd pers.)

(49)   / – V+V- / lintuansa" /lintu+ansa/
        (*compound*: bird + trap)

Antti Iivonen

(50) / – C # V- / "puun eliö" /puun # eliö/
(tree's living being)

(51) / – V+ C- / "puuneliö" /puu+neliö/
(wooden square)

Lehiste (1965, pp. 174–179) found prejunctural, junctural, and postjunctural cues for boundary marking. At the boundary, a brief period of laryngealisation occurred (49). Prejunctural vowel lengthening was not constant, but was observed in one subject (49). Postjunctural secondary stress was accompanied by non-reduced vowel quality (F1/F2 formant structure) and longer duration (49). Example (48) can be interpreted as a non-marked case for the signalling of boundaries.

In (50–51) the coarticulation effects were investigated. In (50), no anticipatory nasalisation of the word-final nasal was observed over the boundary, whereas a strong progressive nasalisation was observed in (51) after the word-initial nasal.

2.5 Other patterns

Stereotyped prosodic patterns and intonation clichés certainly exist in Finnish, but their forms are not known very well.

3. Comparisons with other systems

3.1 Comparisons within the same language

Among the dialects very characteristic quantity differences occur. Especially two of them are important: consonant gemination and so called half-long vowel.

In the general consonant gemination, a single consonant is geminated after a short stressed syllable, if the following syllable contains a long vowel or a diphthong (Nahkola 1987), e.g.

(52) rahaa (money; sg. partitive), in the dialect: rahhaa
(53) kapeita (narrow; pl. partitive) in the dialect: kappeita.

In the special consonant gemination a consonant lengthens before long vowels after a long stressed and unstressed syllable (Palander 1987), e.g.

(54) hiihtämään (to ski; infinitive illative), in the dialect: hiihtämmään

The half-long vowel occurs especially in Southwestern and Eastern dialects (Wiik 1965, 1985). It concerns e.g. the second vowel in muta [muta·] (mud; nominative) (cf. mutaa [muta:] (partitive). A rise-fall intonation pattern additionally occurs on that syllable in Southwestern dialects. The half-long vowel does not occur in the Häme dialects.

Using the rhythm typology of Alfred Schmitt (1924), Penttilä (1927) distinguishes two different rhythm types in dialects: The first (Southwestern)

326

concentrates more attention on the first syllable of the word (= heavily centralising type), whereas the second (Southeastern) is less centralising.

4. Conclusions

Quantity and word stress patterns have been well studied in Finnish. The main features of intonation of the sentence types are known, but not exhaustively. There exist some studies of expressive intonation, of the relation beween syntax and intonation, and that between discourse functions and intonation. How, in fact, accentual concatenation is planned and executed needs to be clarified more extensively. Several other issues need to be investigated more thoroughly: intonation patterns in spontaneous discourses, discourse organisation on the basis of intonational means, intonation clichés, text prosody, as well as prosodic styles and the interplay between these different factors.

Note

1   I should like to thank Terttu Nevalainen and Reijo Aulanko for their collaboration over several years in the field of prosody.

18

Intonation in Hungarian

IVAN FÓNAGY

1.1 Accent and intonation

It is not possible to discuss Hungarian prosody without making a distinction between **intonation** *(hanglejtés)* and **accentuation** *(hangsúly)*. A description of the rules which determine variation in Yes-No question intonation patterns becomes quite simple and clear if this distinction is taken into account. If the two levels are merged using a vague term such as "pitch accent", the description tends to become complicated and counter-intuitive.[1]

I propose to define "accent" *(hangsúly)* as the prominence of a syllable brought about naturally by a greater effort on the level of phonation and articulation which characterises the production of the syllable and which is reflected in the acoustic parameters, both prosodic and segmental. This acoustic image is more or less conventionally coded and is thus to a certain extent independent from its physiological basis; the effort can be mimed or symbolised. Tamás Szende is right when he proposes to distinguishes stress prominence *(hangsúly)* from its natural physiological basis *(nyomaték)*. In this chapter, I shall consequently be using the term **accent** in the sense of *hangsúly* as defined by Szende (1976, pp. 117 ff.).[2]

Intonation, as a functional linguistic entity, is carried by the pitch movements which on the perception level reflect the gradual changes in the fundamental frequency of vocal chord vibration. There is a strict dependency between the perception of intonation contrasts and voice production. Changes in the frequency of vocal chord vibration constitute only one of the possible cues of syllable prominence. This is clear in whispered voice. In Fónagy 1969b, 50 listeners were presented with pairs of utterances which were differentiated on one hand by accent location; *a'pad* (the bench) *vs. 'apad* (water is going down), or *ha'mar* (if he bites) *vs. 'hamar* (early), and on the other hand declarative and interrogative utterances: *Apad vs. Apad?, Hamar. vs. Hamar?*. The declarative *vs.* interrogative modality in whispered utterances was poorly identified: interrogative sentences were taken for declaratives; whereas utterances distinguished by accent location were seldom confused.

Coming back to normal voice, non-differentiation of accent and intonation would oblige us to look for ad-hoc solutions whenever the pitch rise called for by the intonation competes with syllable prominence. Thus, in *'Elhozta a 'széket* (he brought the chair), accent is realised as a F_0 rise on the syllable *szé-*. However, interrogative modality is also marked by a F_0 rise on this same syllable: *Elhozta a széket?* (Did he bring the chair?). In spite of this, listeners were able to distinguish the interrogative *vs.* declarative modality of an utterance in all cases (Magdics and Fónagy 1967, pp. 53–55). The frequency changes due to prominence were never confused with those due to an interrogative tune.

As we were unable to carry out semantic tests using synthesis, we could do no more than analyse and compare the melody of declarative and interrogative utterances.

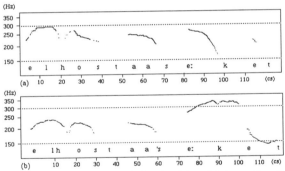

Figure 1. Fundamental frequency curves for declarative (a) and interrogative (b) versions of the utterance *'Elhozta a 'széket* (he brought the chair). Vertical lines correspond to 150 and 300 Hz.

In declarative utterances, the prominence of *szé-* is characterised by greater tension in the articulation of the syllable which is reflected by lengthening of the initial syllable and a higher realisation of the vowel /e:/, by a relatively stronger intensity, and a sharp rise of the fundamental frequency followed by a fall, or by an abrupt fall coming from higher than the preceding syllable (cf. figure 1a). In questions, the melodic movement spreads over the whole utterance. In the first syllables, the tone remains around the same mid-level. This thematic precontour creates an expectancy by behaving like a springboard from which the nuclear tone will leap forward carrying the modal information. The tone gradually rises during the first syllable in *széket* (chair), a rise of 7–8 semitones, followed by a fall of 13–14 semitones on the last syllable (cf. figure 1b).

The rise is gradual, but less important in the case of a short vowel. The distance between the tone level of the syllable preceding the nucleus and the intonation peak is however constant, around 8 semitones. The high degree of melodicity of a question is due to the greater microprosodic regularity (Fónagy and Magdics 1963a, pp. 39–41).

It would be theoretically possible to reduce the contrast to the differences in the F_0 pattern in the syllable but this would be a counter-intuitive analysis. The listener perceives a rise in a question, as part of a global movement, but he only hears a prominence (and no overall tonal movement) in the declarative utterance.

2. Intonation patterns

2.1 The number of intonation units

The number of distinctive intonation patterns identified will vary according to the degree of abstraction of the analysis (Malmberg 1966), or rather according to the nature of the mental contents that intonation is supposed to distinguish. In a grammar of intonation, it is possible to leave out the elementary emotions[3] which are expressed through mobilising the entire vocal apparatus.

According to László Varga (1981, 1983) the inventory of Hungarian prosodemes is made up of 5 tones:

1. falling   /ˎ/   2. rising-falling /ʌ/
3. falling-rising /ˇ/   4. rising   /ˈ/
5. descending   /--/

The distinction between falling and descending cues was introduced by László Deme (1962, p. 508). It makes it possible to distinguish declarative intonation (falling) from exclamative and optative intonation (descending), *De szép ruhád van!* (What a beautiful dress you have!). The latter pattern is characterised by a weak descending contour, almost without any function, which simply reflects the gradual weakness of the air pressure necessary for phonation (Deme *ibid.*).

Applying this clear and simple system to the observed facts allows it to be refined and helps to formulate questions concerning theory and method.

The /ʌ/ pattern is associated with all disjunctive patterns, whether declarative or interrogative utterances. This creates a dilemma: either we have to deny the possibility of intonation making distinction or we have to admit the existence of two distinct circumflex patterns. I will opt for the second solution even if this means we shall need to try to define exactly what it corresponds to on the phonetic level.

There is a series of other distinct syntactic and semantic categories which could be confused on the prosodic level if they were to be represented by the

/∨/ pattern without any further detail. László Varga associates this pattern indifferently with warning *(figyelmeztető)*, imperative order *(nyomatékos felszólítás)*, yes-no questions expressing hope *(reménykedő felszólítás)* or WH-questions (1981, pp. 333, 336) or with a clause which suggests a contradictory opinion *(ellentétes folytatásra utaló közlés)* *(ibid.,* 322)). I would particularly regret in this case that the intonation pattern which has the meaning of *hiszen* (but...) with a clearly defined if complex implication, would be lost and regrouped, for example, with the slight final rise of declarative utterances reflecting various other not very well defined attitudes (such as nonchalance, uncertainty, *etc.*), or indicating that the speaker has something to add. The final rise in WH-questions could be considered as the neutral form in a conversation between women. The identification of these types of utterance cannot be justified either on the level of expression or on the level of content.

This is also true for the /--/ descending pattern, which was rightly distinguished from the /∖/ fall. Varga uses the same /--/ sign for continuity and optative modality (1983, p. 141, utterance 43e). However the latter has a very characteristic pattern: gradual descent in quarter tones from the beginning to the end of the utterance, a legato rhythm, regularity of the F_0 within the syllable (high degree of melodicity). Continuity is signalled by a negative feature: the tone is suspended above the baseline. It is unsatisfactory from both a theoretical and a practical point of view to represent the two distinct categories with the same sign, within the same utterances: *Hogy -- elkésett,* | *-- az mennyire bosszantotta!* (The fact of his arriving late, how it annoyed him!). The first sign represents a variant of continuation intonation whereas the second marks a form of distinctive modal intonation, therefore a "prosodeme", according to Varga.

This example raises an important and interesting theoretical question: is it possible to represent with the same sign both a "prosodeme" and an "allotone"? The /--/ sign corresponds in the example above, first to an "allotone", since the prosodeme of continuity can be expressed through various intonation patterns, such as the /↗/ and the /∨/ patterns, according to Varga's examples and transcription, patterns to which could be added a third one /-/ the level tone (which occurs in Varga, only under the form of an "appended tone", corresponding to the "post-positioned segment" in Michel Martins-Baltar 1977, pp. 137–139). The second sign, on the other hand, represents an exclamative intonation.

László Varga points out the ambiguity of the /∧/ pattern which marks a Yes-no question and which he considers expresses a trifling attitude when it is associated with *Figyelj ide!* (1981, p. 315). I find the ambiguity here less of a problem than in the cases I have just quoted where /∨/ groups melodies which differ on all levels. I believe it would be counter-intuitive to present /∧/ of *Figyelj ide!* as a variant of the imperative prosodeme. It is clearly an interrogative tune grafted on to an imperative utterance which makes it possible to synthesise the two speech acts (see below, page 334).

The two interpretations at the same time illustrate clearly the difference between synchronic static description and dynamic description.

On several occasions we used the tape-splicing method to test the distinctive function of an intonation contour. From our corpus (made up of recordings taken from radio programmes which were added to in the Phonetics Laboratory Studio) we took sentences with the various structures we wanted to test. We copied the utterances only keeping the first part containing the ambiguous structure without the second "disambiguating" part. For example, with the sentence

> Még ott laknak, mert nincs egy fillérjük sem,
> (They are still living there because they have not got a penny),

we only kept the first clause, and we did the same with the other sentences having the same beginning (cf. figure 2):

> Még ott laknak, bár nincs egy fillérjük sem
> (They still live there, in spite of the fact they do not have a penny).

Listeners (9 to 19) had to complete the sentence within the framework of a test with limited choice.

For example the prosodic information on the first three syllables was sufficient to discriminate between a (possessive structure) *vs.* a (subject + verb structure) in 28 out of 30 cases.

It is possible to use the same procedure to demonstrate the anticipatory role of the intonation precontour in the identification of the binary (yes-no) question. We removed the nucleus of 2 declarative utterances and 2 interrogative utterances, only keeping the precontours ,and we played them back to 10 listeners. The falling precontours of declarative utterances were perceived by 10 listeners out of 10 as a potential declarative utterance. The level precontour of a declarative utterance was perceived by 7 listeners out of 10 as a question. The rising precontour of a binary question was perceived as predicting a question.

Our listeners made a mistake in the less frequent cases where the precontour anticipated the rise-falling contour of the nucleus through an inverse echo or pre-echo effect (Fónagy and Magdics 1967, pp. 50–53). Listeners were able to identify 15 to 18 cases out of 19, whether the first clause was to be followed by a copulative clause introduced by *-és,* (and), or by an adversative, introduced by *de,* (but). The number of correct answers fell significantly (12 to 14 out of 19) when we lengthened the first clause from 4 to 11 words (for other tests, see Fónagy 1981).

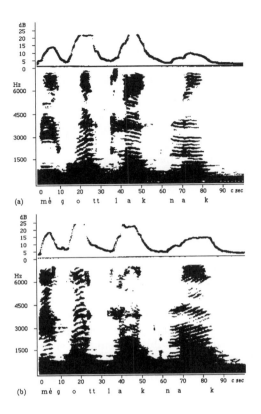

Figure 2. Spectrogram and intensity curve for the two incomplete utterances *Még ott laknak* (They still live /are living there...) used in the test described in the text.

2.2 Modality and mood

a. Modal intonation

Comparing intonation patterns, which on Hungarian utterances differentiate modal values, brings out a problematic case of synonymy and homonymy. The intonation contour which distinguishes Yes-no questions from the corresponding declarative utterances is often rise-falling /∧/ or rising /⁊/. For example *Tett?* (he did), is realised with a rising intonation /⁊/; whereas in *Tette?*, (did he do it?), the melody rises on the initial part of the last syllable, then falls; and in *Tetette?*, (did he pretend to do it?), the rise is on the penultimate syllable and the fall on the last syllable.

The characteristic /∧/ tune which marks a question in *Tetette?* can also be heared on imperative uterances such as *Figyelj ide!* (Listen (to me)), and the rise-fall tune *Jó* regularly occurs in strongly assertive or ironic utterances (Fónagy 1969a).

Such variations and apparently contradictory uses of these patterns seem to completely justify Dwight Bolinger (1986b) and Daniel Hirst (1987, pp. 446ff.) when they cast doubt on the modal function of intonation. This caution on their part, which may be well-founded in the case of English (cf. Uldall 1962), is not valid for Hungarian. From the point of view of the history of linguistics, it would be interesting to find the extent to which the mother tongue of authors determines their approach to general theory.

The straightforwardness of the rules governing interrogative intonation in Hungarian makes it easy to understand the place Hungarian linguists attribute to the modal function of intonation. The diversity of homonymic patterns at the same time favours an analysis which treats patterns in terms of meaning rather than an analysis which would treat meaning in terms of patterns.

Variation in contour which occurs on the Yes-no question *Tett?*, *'Tette?*, and *'Tetette?*, are conditioned by stress position. The tonal movement which characterises the modality always occurs on the last stress group. As Hungarian is a barytonic language (words stressed on the first syllable), oxytonic groups must be monosyllabic and in this case, as in *'Tett?*, the tonic will be rising. In paroxytonic groups, which have to be disyllabic, as in *'Tette?*, the tone rises and then falls on the last syllable. If the group is made of 3 or more syllables, *e.g.* *'Tetette*, the tone rises on the penultimate and falls on the last syllable. We can therefore conclude that these are 3 contextual variants of a modal intonation which could be characterised as a rise-fall ($/\wedge/$) on an abstract prosodic level, following the suggestion put forward by László Varga (1983).[4]

It is necessary to point out however that this form of intonation depends on the actual position of stress in the spoken utterance and not its position in the abstract sentence. If during the actualisation of a sentence, stress is moved from the antepenultimate to the last syllable, the tone will rise on the last syllable instead of falling according to the barytonic pattern 'x x x. Many utterances in fact diverge from this pattern because of stress displacement (Fónagy and Magdics 1963, 1967, pp. 40–47) such as in *Nyolc ora?*, (eight o'clock?), *Gomba?*, (mushroom?), *Elhatarozták?* (they decided?), *Megmentetted?* (you have rescued her?), or because of multiple stressing eg. *Holnap?* (tomorrow?), *Ranktól?* (Rank's?) (cf. figures 3a-f).[5]

It should also be pointed out that interrogative intonation can occur in its pure form, a rise of a fifth followed by a fall of a sixth, on imperative utterances which are 2 or more syllables long.[6]

Some 25 years ago, I was struck by its counter-to-rule occurrence in my children's speech when they were trying to draw my attention or ask for help. *Api, figyelj ⌐ i ⌐de!* Peter said, showing me a strange vehicle that he had just made. As I did not respond immediately he said it again with the sharp fall of the

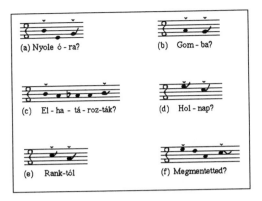

Figure 2. Examples of interrogative utterances with stress displacement or multiple stressing resulting in rising intonation patterns.

imperative modality: *Api ↘ figyelj ide!* (Daddy, listen to me). Later, a semantic test was carried out where the listeners (10 adults and 10 12–14 year old children) were asked to "give a context" for the 2 realisations and the intention of the child-speaker.

According to 8 listeners, (a), the boy was calling his father to ask him a question; according to 10 others, (b), the child had just discovered something extraordinary which called for an explanation, and 2 others (12 year old boys), (c), only picked out the friendly intent of the first utterance in contrast of the second which was unanimously perceived as an imperative call. Recordings of conversations between 9 to 12 year old children have indeed shown that interrogative tune was associated with a problem to solve in most of the cases.

The transfer of the interrogative tune to imperative utterances follows the same dynamic pattern as lexical or grammatical metaphor. The interrogative intonation forces the listener to make a kind of synthesis of the 2 modalities, interrogative and imperative, associated by the transfer of the melodic pattern. Each transfer presupposes clearly defined units both on the level of expression and on the level of content. The homonymy of the neutral interrogative and the intense imperative patterns, far from proving the contingency of modal intonation, implies the existence of 2 distinct intonation patterns.[7]

The presence of certain variants of declarative intonation in Yes-no questions, can be explained in Hungarian (Fónagy and Magdics 1963a, p. 11), as in other languages (French: Marouzeau 1949, Fónagy and Bérard 1973, English: Palmer 1929, Allen 1954, Daneš 1960, Bolinger 1964b, p. 292, German: Zwirner 1952, von Essen 1956, pp. 55 ff.) by the interference of an interrogative tune with a declarative attitude. In our recordings of spontaneous conversations and plays (Fónagy and Magdics 1967, pp. 43–49) we observed 2 predominant types of (quasi-) declarative melodies in Yes-no questions: on the one hand, a fall in 3 steps, and on the other hand an average level about a third higher than that of an assertion. In both cases, the melody is characterised by the absence of downward movement within each accentual group. It is above all this last factor which differentiates the declarative question from a simple assertion.

We have shown that a flat melodic line on a high level followed by a sharp fall (of about a sixth) in the final syllable is a clear indication of a surprise question, in spite of the absence of a rise in the penultimate syllable (Fónagy and Magdics 1963a: 91, Fónagy 1965).

The rise-fall tune /∧/ of the Yes-no question can also be transferred on to other questions. Its presence is clear in WH-questions or in Yes-no questions with a question marker which do not need a melodic cue. In this case, it indicates a putting in question of the question. To the *de re* question is added a second, *de dicto*, that is a "meta-question". The melodic pattern varies little whatever the nature of the meta-question, whether it is an attempt to have an utterance repeated because it was difficult to understand or to believe (repeat questions), or whether it is a question which is quoted for some other reason, to speak plainly or to play for time (with the implication *Is this what you are asking me? I am going to give you a reply*).[8]

The intonation of a Yes-no question which is usually associated with disjunctive utterances, either interrogative or declarative, can be used to suggest a quotation, a (*de dicto*) question, which neutralises the disjunction (the (*de re*) question) by bringing together the alternative terms in a global question: *Fehér vagy fe – ↗ ke – ↘ te?*, ([you said you thought that] it's black or white?). It could also be used to put forward a hypothesis which brings together the alternative terms in order to oppose them to others which are not specified (*de re*).

The quotation of a Yes-no question already marked with an interrogative pattern is not so straightforward. There is no regular linguistic melodic process.

The "quotation" or interrogative repetition of an assertion of an exclamation has the same intonation pattern as the Yes-no question, except when the speaker expresses at the same time an astonished or incredulous attitude which implies a *de dicto* reaction. In Hungarian, there is no preestablished pattern, such as the triangular melodic stereo type, which is used to express an incredulous attitude in French when questioning a previous speaker's words (Fónagy, Fónagy and Sap 1979, p. 9). Here again, in Hungarian the utterance is transformed into an indirect elliptic question (cf. examples in László Varga 1981, pp. 334 ff.).

The contrast in modality of declarative *vs.* interrogative disjunction is not clearly marked by a stable opposition in intonation patterns. Semantic tests involving 5 declarative and 5 interrogative disjunctions read by 10 people of both sexes showed the following tendencies: whereas in the declarative utterances the final contour fell to base level (40 cases out of 50), it generally remained suspended in the disjunctive interrogative at about a third above the base level.

In the interrogative utterances the intonation peak coincided generally with the conjunction *vagy* (or) which was rarely the case for declarative utterances. In several cases the contour rose on the first part of the interrogative disjunction but this was never the case with the assertion. These questions which were clearly marked by contour were correctly identified by all subjects. This pattern however only occurred 5 times out of 50 which indicates that Hungarian has not yet taken full advantage of this potential pitch contour. Despite the absence of systematic distinctive pitch features, the modality of the utterances was recognised in the majority of cases (Fónagy and Magdics 1967, p. 49) not only by the Hungarian subject but also by the 12 non-Hungarian speaking French students to whom we presented the same stimuli. The Hungarian disjunctive question was correctly identified in 51 cases out of 60. At the same time, the modality of 4 French disjunctive utterances was recognised in 72 out of 88 cases by Hungarian students (Fónagy and Bérard 1980, p. 108).

It would appear that the interrogative modality was recognised thanks to prosodic and segmental paralinguistic features which reflect an attitude associated with disjunctive questions. This is certainly the case for the distinction of logical categories, that of inclusive and exclusive disjunction. An exclusive disjunctive utterance is only recognised as such, if it is associated with strongly decisive attitude: polar differentiation of the contours on both parts of the disjunction, strong stresses, glottal stops between the 2 terms, tense articulation (Fónagy and Bérard 1980, pp. 104–108).[9] According to the semantic tests greater melodicity, other things being equal, can also lead to a greater number of utterances being perceived as questions (*ibid.,* 113).

For greater economy, the Hungarian language does not use prosodic cues to signal interrogative modality in Yes-no questions which have the *-e* question marker morpheme nor in WH-questions (marked by interrogative pronouns or adverbs). Intonation therefore cannot play a distinctive role in the rare cases of modal homonymy such as *Mért Ákos?* (why Akos?), *vs. Mért Ákos* (Akos was measuring), or *Ki írta?* (who wrote it?), *vs. Kiírta* (he copied it), *Hánynak?* (for how many people?), *vs. Hánynak* (They vomit). When speakers were asked to read these sentences, they used various strategies to bring out differences which enabled 75 to 81.8 % of the listeners to interpret (them) according to the speaker's intent. (Fónagy and Magdics 1967, p. 94). The possible cues for questions were (a) a wider range (one fourth or one fifth *vs.* one third), (b) a weak final rise, (c) a higher degree of melodicity.

The phonetics laboratory of the Linguistics Institute in Budapest is at present equipped for speech analysis. This was not the case at the beginning of the sixties. We had to rely on makeshift solutions to solve as well as possible the problem we were confronted with.

Thus to abstract away from segmental information we used a "natural filtering technique": After a period of training, 5 male and 5 female speakers produced a total of 67 declarative, imperative, optative and interrogative utterances, at first naturally and then with mouth closed, so as to substitute a nasal bilabial for the sentence. The 670 utterances were then analysed and then played back to 5 male and 5 female hearers who had to suggest a text to correspond to each hummed utterance (Fónagy and Magdics 1967, pp. 90–100). Imperative utterances were understood as orders in 30.8% and as WH-questions in 31.3% (probably due to the prominent accent on the initial syllable in both type of utterance), and understood as neutral assertions in 22.2% and exclamatives in 16.6% cases. The optative utterance *De szeretném már látni!* hummed with a fall on each syllable of a 1/4 tone was identified as expressing a wish for something in nine cases out of ten. However, another optative utterance *Bárcsak 'itt lenne!* with a pattern in 2 parts, fall of a second on *bárcsak*, followed a drop of a third, was understood as a neutral declarative utterance in 9 out of 10 cases.

Experimenting with the possible homonymy of utterances also demonstrated that an "imperative intonation" does not exist. From recordings of a narrative read by 8 men and 7 women, we isolated the utterances *Tanulja a leckét* (he is learning his lesson), *Tanulja a leckét!* (learn your lesson!), *Hozza a könyvet* (he brings the book), *vs. Hozza a könyvet!* (bring the book), and we played them back to 10 listeners(5 female and 5 male). The result showed that declarative utterances produced with a forceful tone of voice were confused with imperative utterances (Fónagy and Magdics 1967, pp. 61–72; *cf.* Deme 1962, p. 507).

The "elliptic" WH-question (Fónagy and Magdics 1963b, p. 98) or interrupted question according to László Varga (*megszakadt kérdés* 1981, p. 335) is clearly marked by a continuously rising contour. These utterances as a rule begin with *és* (and). The WH-morpheme is only present in the underlying form ↗ *És jövö nyáron? (hol nyaraltok)?* (and next year – (where will you spend your holidays?)). In our recorded corpus we found this rising pattern in these contexts. For example, in a WH-question uttered in an encouraging tone by a teacher ↗ *És melyik volt az a király?* (and who was this king?), the interrogative pronoun is not deleted. The utterance is elliptic in so far as it could be completed with *És meg tudnád mondani?* (and could you tell me?).

Questions asked by a policeman or an office clerk are characterised by a weaker rise which does not go higher than a minor second or even stays at the same level: *Neve* (your name?), *Foglalkozása?* (your profession?). This is only a partial homonymy with a different syntax. The utterance is elliptic on the level of discourse and not on the level of the utterance. The missing part must be provided by the addressee. Elliptical utterances of the "form filling" type must be distinguished from elliptical questions beginning with *És.*

This continuous rise also occurs in successive orders: *Állítsd* ↗ *le!* (stop her), *Fordítsd* ↗ *meg!* (turn it!), *Most tedd ↗tiszta sebességre!* (give it full speed!). The pitch rise, the utterance left unfinished, indicates that there are other orders to come and that we are not at the end of the paragraph unit in the discourse.

This explains its continual occurrence in sport reports... (Fónagy and Magdics 1963a, p. 100)

b. Moods and attitudes

In papers about prosody the terms "emotion" and "emotive attitude" are used as synonyms. I believe that we need to distinguish these 2 categories. The 2 are different on the 3 levels of expression, content and function. In the expression of emotions (such as anger, fear, joy) expiratory, laryngeal and articulatory strategies are inextricably linked. Attitudes do not need respiratory features or articulatory and laryngeal expressive distortions; on the contrary they call for constant melodic patterns which have to be clearly delimited. The more highly it becomes organised the more it approaches a linguistic system. Vocal expression of emotions has as its first function the reduction of psychic tensions, whereas attitudes are linked to recurring social situations which intonation is supposed to signal. The expression of emotions is essentially paralinguistic (while not entirely avoiding linguistic regulation); intonations corresponding to attitudes are strictly determined by linguistic rules, even if they are not (completely) arbitrary (Fónagy 1987).

This strong tendency to lexicalisation of attitudes allowed 47 listeners out of 50 to associate the same situation to one of the realisations of the sentence *Hét óra* (it's 7 o'clock), uttered by the famous Hungarian actor Sándor Pécsi: the answer to someone trying to make you hurry, (= but it's only 7 o'clock!). To suggest this situation, Pécsi used an intonation stereotype *(cliché mélodique)*: fall of a fourth, rise of a third with a slight final levelling, low mid level (usually chest register). This intonation has the same value as the adverb *hiszen (csak)* (but as... (it's only)). The equivalence of the intonation pattern with a modal morpheme is characteristic for this set of intonation forms (Schubiger (1965) 1972, Ladd 1978, p. 120). Another attitude, "threat", which is more emotive, closer to emotions, is expressed with a similar pattern: a fall of about a fourth from the first to the second syllable, from a mid low level dropping below the baseline. The rise which follows has a gentle slope and is accompanied by increasing intensity *(crescendo)* .[10]

The status of "discourse moods" could be claimed for those attitudes playing important linguistic roles. They should be called "communicative types of sentences" *(kommunikativ mondat-tipusok)*, according to László Varga who correctly considers them as coming from the expression of attitudes and admits that the boundary line between sentence types and attitudes is unclear, and that the association of an intonation pattern to one or the other category is more or less arbitrary (1981, p. 318 f.).

Admirative utterances of the type *Micsoda hangja van!* (what a voice he or she has!), are a sentence type which he classes with other intellectual intonations labelling them *értékelő – felkiáláltó mondatipus*, (evaluative – exclamative sentence type), whereas other linguists (Kosma 1974, p. 483) consider them as a purely emotive intonation.

The "sound-image" (signifiant) would form a better criterion for classification. Instead of basing classification of intonation patterns on a scale of intellectual meaning, we could base it on the degree to which they are integrated into the linguistic system. A high degree of integration implies that the language system imposes strict limits on variability, as is the case with optative tune.

We could let the language system categorise the contents which are expressed, considering as modal any intonation which is the expression of a grammatical category recognised as such by the language system having segmental morphological markers, such as interrogative, imperative or optative moods. The language system seems to justify László Varga's choice when he gives to *Micsoda hangja van!* the status of a discourse mood. The utterance is introduced by an interrogative adverb which takes on a different modal value, non-interrogative, due to the particular stable tune (fall by semitone): "expression of an admirative attitude". This would allow us to consider that the admirative intonation in such utterances is modal. In the same way, the fall in quarter tones in utterances introduced by an optative morpheme *bár, bárcsak* ought to be considered a modal intonation, used as an optative marker. In a language like Vogul, it would be necessary to distinguish modal intonation for probability, doubt necessity, *etc.*... but it would not be the case for other languages where these moods have no markers.

It would be difficult however not to give the status of a modal intonation to the continuous rise in elliptical questions in spite of the fact that they do not have a segmental marker; a friendly warning marked by a final rise of a third: ⌄*Ki ne ess!*, ([be careful] not to fall out!), would be a similar case.

The initial definition should therefore be modified to give modal status to each intonation pattern which specifies a subset of a grammatical set itself marked by a segmental morpheme.

2.3 Focus

The contrast between accent and intonation is particularly clear in the case of focalisation with implication as opposed to simple focalisation. For the utterances of the unmarked SUBJECT (Nominal) + PREDICATE (Verbal) type, such as *Kati futott* (Kati was running), or *Péter tudta* (Peter knew it), the accent strikes the subject and the predicate with equal force. This makes it impossible to apply the metrical grid analysis proposed by Mark Liberman (1978, pp. 66 ff.) and applied successfully to French by François Dell (1984).

This neutral utterance contrasts with the two marked realisations by either focusing on the subject (it was Kati who was running) or on the predicate (Kati [was not walking, she] was running). Prominence here is above all relating to

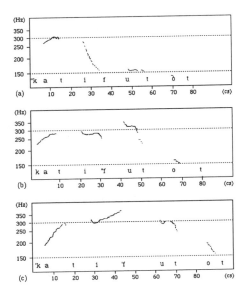

Figure 3. Fundamental frequency for the utterance *Kati futott* (Kati was running) with simple focalisation on the subject (a), the predicate (b) and with focalisation with implication (c).

accent and is easily interpreted in whispered speech. This is not the case with focalisation with implication. *Kati ran* (implying *but not X or Y*); *Peter knew it* (implying *but not V and Z*)). Simple focalisation can be expressed in the written form using some form of graphic highlighting of the syllable in question (italics, bold, *etc.*). This is not the case with focalisation with implication which can only be expressed through melody. In this case the utterance begins on a low level with a strong pitch rise (7–8 semitones) on the first syllable, a weak rise (around a semitone) in the second syllable of *Péter* or *Kati*. This rise contrasts with a fall (of 13 to 14 semitones) from a high tone towards a low level on the predicate *tudta* or *futott* (see figure 3 a, b, c.). This pattern – rise from a low level to high level followed by a fall – reminds us of the melodic arc of the ironic tune (Fónagy 1971).

2.4 Prosodic phrasing and syntax

Melody, together with accent and juncture, is an essential medium for structuring discourse from lower level syntagmatic units and their components up to utterance and paraphrastic units. (Szende 1976, p. 115, Fónagy and Fónagy 1983; Rossi 1985).

Intonation structure may correspond closely to the structure of embedded utterances, as it can indicate that the syntactic groups of an utterance interrupted

341

by the insertion of another utterance, belong to the same level. Double insertions are fairly frequent in lecture style, which gives 3 intonation levels (Fónagy and Magdics 1967, pp. 139–140).

This organisation is an indirect means of differentiating syntactic as well as semantic structures. Thus stress and intonation make it possible to contrast the 2 interrogative sentences *A ⟋ 'kar?* (the arm?), *vs. 'A - ⌃kar?* (does he want to?) (Fónagy 1958, p. 23, Varga 1981, pp. 329–331), by indicating that in the first case we have the structure article + noun, while the second one is a (disyllabic) noun not preceded by an article. In the case *'Szép fiú* (a handsome boy), *vs. 'Szépfiú* (a fop) (Hetzron 1962, p. 199f.), the absence of stress and of a pitch rise indicates that the noun-phrase composed of an adjective and a noun is transformed into a compound.

Intonation can bring out the syntactico-logical structure of the utterance, marking whether a noun belongs to a following or preceding NP (Fónagy and Magdics 1967, p. 120). The iconicity of the two prosodic structures permitted most of the subjects of the semantic tests to interpret the different realisations according to the intonation and intention of the speakers. (*ibid.* 159–160).

Likewise, intonation can indicate whether the adverb is part of the adverbial phrase or not: *Gyorsan fut és úszik* can mean a) (He runs quickly and knows how to swim), or b) (He runs and swims quickly). The rise-fall pattern (melodic arc) bridges together the two verbs in version (b), whereas there is a new rise in the first syllable of the second verb *úszik* in version (a) (*ibid.* p. 120). The listeners correctly interpreted the realisations of both types. (*ibid.* p. 160).

Anacrusis along with deaccentuation makes it possible to distinguish the modal / pragmatic adverb (or sentence adverb) from an adverb proper functioning as a complement to the verb, as with the manner adverb in:

(a)   Biztosan 'futott   *v s.*   'Biztosan futott
         (he probably ran)   (he ran confidently)

(b)   'Tudtommal 'távozott   *v s.*   Tudtommal 'tá vozott
         (he left with my permission)   (He left, as far as I know)
         [complement of manner]   [pragmatic adverb]

(c)   Nekem 'fizethet   *v s.*   'Nekem fizethet
         (As far as I'm concerned he can pay) (He can pay me)
         [pragmatic adverb]   [attributive adverb]

(d)   Felőlem 'jöhetett   *v s.*   'Felőlem jöhetett
         (from my point of view, he could come) (He probably came from where I was)
         [pragmatic adverb]   [adverb of place]

Linking adverbs (Wagner and Pinchon 1962, pp. 416f.) can be distinguished from other types:

    Azért 'dolgozik   *v s.*   'Azért dolgozik
    (Nevertheless, he works.) vs   (That is why he works.)

Egyben 'kérte.   *vs.*   'Egyben kérte.
(At the same time he asked for it.)   (He asked for it in one piece.)

In all these and similar cases (Fónagy 1973), the iconicity of the process is self-evident: An element with a reduced semantic weight is opposed to another having kept its full meaning.

Listing is characterised by a succession of parallel tones (rising or falling) on the terms whether words, phrases or clauses. This parallel patterning is almost perfect in narratives or in recollection, and not so strict in conversation. In narratives, listing is brought out by a greater degree of melodicity. A tune of the / ∨ / type can occur in noun-phrases with a preparatory fall on the qualified noun and a rise on the qualifying term. In clause enumerations, the first accentual group is an anacrusis and the second carries the listing contour (Fónagy and Magdics 1967, pp. 125ff.) which triggers the tune according to László Varga's term *dallamindító* = "tone trigger".

Listing is sufficiently structured to be always recognised even after the suppression of segmental information (Fónagy and Magdics 1967, pp. 181f.). The possibility of metaphoric transfer of the listing tune on to sequences which do not contain a list of elements also confirms its relevance. This transfer expresses an attitude associated with listing and suggests comments such as (it's mechanical), (it's common place), (it's the same old tune) (Fónagy and Magdics 1963a, p. 13, Fónagy 1979, p. 247).

Going on from simple listing, the melody of the term characterised is carried by the expression in apposition, in accordance with the principle of iconicity.

Notes

1   I can see no advantage in the confusion of accent and intonation as is widespread and particularly fashionable at present, such as with Janet Pierrehumbert (1980) or Carlos Gussenhoven (1984).

2   For a critical analysis of definitions of accent and the argument in favour of the definition put forward here, see my previous publications (1958, 1966b and 1980) and also the work of Tamás Szende (1976, pp. 117ff.).

3   In spite of certain earlier differences of opinion concerning the list of primary emotions (Gardiner, Metcalf and Beebe-Center 1937), a consensus seems to have been arrived at on this subject (Izard 1977), particularly within the framework of cognitive theories of emotions (Lazarus, Averill, Opton 1970; Plutchik and Kellerman (eds.) 1980). Plutchik considers primary any emotion which can be linked to an earlier form in the ancestral behaviour of the animal world.

4   Robert Hetzron is the first to have raised the question as to why the interrogative intonation pattern is rise-falling and not rising (1977, pp. 394f.). He thinks he has found the answer within the synchronic history of Yes-No questions by deriving them from disjunctive questions.

5   The study I put forward with Klara Magdics in 1967 is based on recordings of a large number of plays and television panel-games as well as on conversations recorded with hidden microphones, on conferences both read and in natural speaking-style, and recordings made in schools, in the street, on trams and several other types of experiment.

6   According to Lajos Hegedűs the intonation peak is invariably on the penultimate syllable in plurisyllabic utterances. This oversimple rule does not explain all the facts observed. Transylvanian intonation, according to D. Robert Ladd, would seem to differ in several ways from forms found, both in standardised Hungarian (common to all regions) and in dialects; this includes the classic analysis of the Szamoshát dialect intonation by Balint Csüry (1925).

7   László Varga (1981, p. 336) affirms quite rightly that this rise-falling contour is not associated with utterances which encourage people to perform " important" acts and to carry out long term projects. This restriction is probably to be put in relation with the original context in which the transfer took place: problems, call for help, surprising discovery, which has been extended afterwards to polite or friendly invitation.

8   László Varga (1981, p. 336) distinguishes seven types of meta-questions in Hungarian (*idéző kérdés* "interrogative quotations") according to whether the speaker quotes an assertion, an order, an exclamation, a Yes-No question, a WH-question, an elliptical question or a disjunctive question.

9   Varga believes he can distinguish a prosodeme which makes it possible to contrast exclusive and inclusive disjunctions.

10 A sentence from potential Hungarian (consisting of nonsense words, respecting the probability of phonological transitions), pronounced by three Hungarian actors suggesting 18 different attitudes, formed the basis of a first series of tests. The realisations, which had been recorded, were played back to groups of Hungarian, French, American and Japanese listeners (Fónagy 1981). In a second phase, 46 different realisations of the sentence were synthesised on the Formant Synthesizer available at the Research Laboratory of the Compagnie Générale d'Electricité in Marcoussis (see Fónagy *et al.*, 1979). These different realisations were presented within the framework of a test with limited choice, to two groups of Hungarian students (42 school children and 25 students). The realisation type described in the text was the one that had the most answers for "threat" (Fónagy 1981, Fónagy and Fónagy in preparation.)

19

Intonation in
Western Arabic (Morocco)

THAMI BENKIRANE

1. Background

Moroccan Arabic, the Arabic dialect of Morocco, belongs, together with dialects spoken in the other countries of North Africa, to the Semitic family of the Afro-Asiatic phylum, more specifically to the Western (or Maghreb) variety of modern Arabic. Western Arabic should probably be considered a distinct language from Eastern Arabic, as spoken in the Middle East, as well as from Classical Arabic, from which both varieties of modern Arabic originally derive. Historically, Western Arabic is the result of contact between the Arabic tribes who arrived in North Africa between the 7th and 13th centuries, and the original inhabitants of the region whose language belonged to the Berber family (cf. Boukous 1979, p. 12) a different branch of the same Afro-Asiatic phylum. Today with the development of means of communication and the growth of towns (cf. Bounfour 1979, p. 521), Western Arabic has become the common language of communication for practically all Moroccans with the exception of about 10% monolingual Berber speakers (Youssi 1983). The creation of the French Protectorate in Morocco in 1912 had a considerable effect on the sociolinguistic characteristics of the country, with over 10% of the population making regular use of French. After independence in 1956, Classical (Literary) Arabic was proclaimed the official language of Morocco by the constitution of 1961. A striking characteristic of Classical Arabic, as well as of Standard Arabic, a modern version of Literary Arabic, is the fact that it has no native

345

speakers but is learned almost exclusively in school and is used only in formal situations. Moroccan Arabic, on the other hand, due to the fact that it is the native idiom of the population, is used in all normal everyday situations of communication. Estimates of the proportion of the population that use Literary or Standard Arabic systematically vary from about 15% (Bounfour, 1983 p. 521) to about 25% (Youssi 1983 p. 77).

In the Arabic world, a certain degree of bilingualism between Standard Arabic and the various regional varieties of modern Arabic tends to create the impression that there is on the one hand a single invariable and noble Arabic language, and on the other hand a variety of common dialects. This mythical vision is contradicted by the fact that on the level of prosody in particular, the native variety of Arabic has a predominant influence on the pronunciation of Standard Arabic which varies considerably when spoken by a Syrian, an Egyptian or a Moroccan.

The modern pronunciation of classical Arabic reflects the stress patterns of the dialect of the speaker. (Ferguson 1957, p. 474)

It thus seems inescapable that the study of the prosodic and intonative characteristics of Standard Arabic necessarily entails a prior study of these characteristics in the speakers' native language, in our case, Moroccan Arabic.

1.1 General prosodic characteristics

Of all the Arabic dialects, Moroccan Arabic (MA) is that which exhibits the greatest degree of vowel reduction by comparison with the classical language. The classical opposition between three long vowels and three short vowels has completely disappeared from MA due to the loss of the short vowels which had the effect of completely disrupting the internal structure of the syllable (Marçais 1977, p. 24). This loss resulted in the formation of formally impossible consonant clusters. Thus whereas in Classical Arabic the structure of the syllable is always CV, CVC or CVV, that of Moroccan Arabic allows a cluster of consonants to occur as onset. Youssi (1983, p. 81) notes that MA is renowned for its consonant clusters which he compares to those of Berber, and which in his opinion constitute the main obstacle for understanding by speakers of Eastern Arabic. Compare the following illustrative examples:

(1)		**Literary Arabic**	**Moroccan Arabic**	
	a	litaamuhaa	ltæmha	(his/her veil)
	b	nadaa	nda	(dew)
	c	kitaab	ktæb	(book)
	d	katabtu	ktəbt	(I wrote)
	e	musaafir	mṣafəṛ	(travelling)

Phonotactic constraints within the syllable are extremely weak in MA. This can be explained by the fact that originally each consonant of the cluster belonged to a separate syllable. One problem which arises is the way in which these consonant clusters are syllabified in an utterance. A number of different accounts have been proposed (Benhallam 1980; Benkirane 1981, 1982; Benkirane and Cavé 1984, 1987; El-Mejjad 1985; Benkaddour 1986). In MA a syllable with a full vowel is always more prominent and carries more weight than a syllable with a reduced vowel /ə/ which can be treated as epenthetic since its occurrence is entirely predictable. Phonetically /ə/ is an extremely short vocalic segment which is always associated with a following consonant in the same syllable.

While the presence of a consonant in the syllable onset is obligatory in MA, the number of consonants preceding the syllable nucleus does not contribute to the prominence of the syllable which is rather determined by the intrasyllabic relation between the vowel and the subsequent consonants. The examples in (1c) and (1d) constitute exceptionally heavy sequences in MA, with (1c) being the heavier of the two. In MA, sequences with a structure CVC, where V is a full vowel, play, as we shall see, an extremely important role in the prosodic system of the language.

a. CVC sequences

All linguists agree that a CVC sequence makes up a syllable which is heavier than the basic CV structure. These sequences, traditionally described as simple closed syllables, have given rise to a number of original phonological analyses. Benkaddour (1986), for example, notes that this structure is strictly limited to word-final (pre-pausal) contexts, and comments:

The question is how can the final consonant of these syllables be represented in the tree structure. To start with, I shall opt for the solution that makes use of extrasyllabic consonants. An extrasyllabic consonant is one which is not a member of any syllable. (p. 87)

I have suggested elsewhere (Benkirane 1981, 1982) that the sequence CVC should be treated as disyllabic, with the final consonant constituting the onset of a syllable with an empty rime. A number of arguments can be adduced in favour of this solution. First of all, a word such as /dib/ can be realised phonetically either with a final schwa [dibᵊ] or with a final consonant which is devoiced but unquestionably released [dib̥<]. Both the pronunciation of a schwa and the release of the final consonant fulfil the same purpose of detaching the consonant from the preceding syllable. Another argument for this analysis comes from the fact that vowels in absolute final position in MA are produced and perceived as short vowels. This fact was noted by Harrell (1962):

Stable vowels are relatively long except at the end of words, where they are short. (p. 10)

Paradoxically, it is in final CVC sequences that the stable vowels are longest, averaging more than 40% more than the duration of vowels in a CVCV structure. This closed syllable lengthening, which constitutes a counter-example to the closed syllable shortening which Maddieson (1985, p. 206) proposed as a universal tendancy, cannot be explained away as an intrinsic or co-intrinsic effect since the vowel of a sequence such as [blæːt] or [blæːd] is, all other things being equal, always significantly longer than that of a sequence such as [blæ]. It is interesting to note that a similar effect of vowel lengthening in CVC sequences is to be found in several Berber dialects of Northern Morocco (Amazigh dialects of the Rif).

The lengthening of the vowel in a sequence CVC has the effect of reducing the difference between the duration of this sequence and a sequence CVCV. Statistically no significant difference was found in a comparison of the total duration of sequences of this type. This temporal equivalence seems thus a further argument for treating the sequence as disyllabic. It should be noted that there are a number of cases where the pronunciation of the final vowel is optional in MA as in [mʔæja] or [mʔæj] (with me), [ntina] or [ntin] (you), [ṭomobila] or [ṭomobil] (car) and the discontinuous negative morpheme [ma...ʃi] or [ma...ʃ] *etc.* A final argument in favour of this analysis stems from the fact that the lengthening of vowels before final consonants plays an important role in the perception of word boundaries (Benkirane and Cavé 1988):

(2) a [ʃræ#trija]   (he bought a lightshade)
    b [ʃræːt#rija]   (she bought some meat)
    c [ʒæ#bfasu]   (he came with his pick)
    d [ʒæːb#fæsu]   (he brought his pick)

b. Word stress in MA
Regular word stress in MA can be illustrated by the following words:

(3) a ['bæːl] (look out)   b ['bæla] (crafty)
    c [səl'hæːm] (type of coat)   d [bəl'bula] (type of cereal)
    e [bəl'lærəʒ] (stork)   f [ma'gæna] (watch, meter)
    g [miri'kæn] (americans)   h [miri'kæni] (american)

To account for these stress patterns, Lahlou (1982) makes use of two separate stress rules, the first applying stress to "heavy" final syllables (in his analysis CVC syllables) and the second stressing a penultimate syllable in the absence of a final CVC syllable. The analysis of a final consonant as a rimeless final syllable as discussed above makes it possible to simplify the stress rules and to account for all the words in (3) by means of a single rule applying stress to the penultimate syllable in all cases (Benkirane 1982).

The fundamental frequency associated with words like (3a) and (3b) follows in both cases a rising-falling pattern. With the word [bæla] the F_0 peak is reached before the end of the first syllable and the fall begins before the beginning of the lateral consonant and finishes on the final vowel. With [bæl] the maximum and minimum of the curve are both situated on the vowel. The need to produce a complex pitch pattern is perhaps the reason for the extra lengthening observed on the vowel in the CVC context which could be put down to prosodic independence of the parameters of duration and pitch (Lyberg 1979). Gårding (1977b) describes a similar effect for a rising-falling pitch movement which:

> denotes Accent in apocopated monosyllabic forms, *i.e.* forms which can be described as resulting from a reduction of a second syllable. (p. 9)

We can thus conclude that the domain of stress in Moroccan Arabic is the sequence CVC(V). Among the acoustic parameters which contribute to stress, intensity seems to play an important role since a pitch accent is usually a mark both of word accent and of sentence accent: when the word is not in final (pre-pausal) position the presence of a pitch accent on the word is far less evident. Recent investigation has shown that duration is the predominant cue for the distinction between stressed and unstressed syllables of plurisyllabic words pronounced in long utterances, but that this lengthening is not necessarily found systematically in isolated words or short utterances.

c. Sentence accent

From the point of view both of auditory impressions and of acoustic observations, sentence accent in MA tends to be placed on the rightmost word or phrase of an utterance, as in the following examples, where (') indicates sentence accent:

(4) a   [maˈklæːʃ] (he didn't eat)   b   [maˈklæʃi] (he didn't eat)

    c   [ʒæbuˈliːh] (he brought it to him)   d   [ʒæbuˈliha] (he brought it to her)

    e   [ʒæˈbulha]   f   [ʒæbulha lmaˈgæna]

        (he brought it to her)   (they brought her the watch/meter)

As we can see from these examples, sentence accent occurs on the penultimate syllable of the utterance, in other words on the stressed syllable of the final word. As Lehiste (1970) points out:

> It appears probable that word-level stress is in a very real sense an abstract quality: a potential for being stressed. Word-level stress is the capacity of a syllable within a word to receive sentence stress when the word is realised as a part of the sentence. (p. 150)

It should be noted, however, that when a word is not in utterance-final position, the primary cue for the distinction between accented and unaccented syllables is the duration of the stressed syllable rather than its pitch pattern.

Examples (4a) and (4b) on the one hand and (4d) and (4e) on the other hand are syntactically and semantically equivalent. The first pair illustrates the possibility of negative utterances to be pronounced with or without the final vowel. Sentences (4c), (4d) and (4e) are formed from the verb [ʒæb] (bring) followed by one of the clitics [liːh]ə [liha]and [lha]. Only the first two of these clitics have the appropriate structure CVC(V) to receive the sentence accent. As a result, these clitics function as autonomous units which can be preposed in an utterance:

(5) a [liːh ʒæbu lmagæna] (to him, they brought the watch/meter)
     b [liha ʒæbu lmagæna] (to her, they brought the watch/meter)

The unaccented clitic in (4e) however cannot be preposed in the same way:

(5) c *[lha ʒæbu lmagna] to her, they brought the watch/meter)

1.2 Outline of the approach adopted in the chapter

In this study we assume (following among others Di Cristo 1976a, 1985; Lhote 1979 and Thorsen 1987c) that intonation is encoded as a sequence of key points distributed throughout the Intonation Unit and that an intonation contour is perceived as an interpolation between these points as suggested by Thorsen (1987c):

…we anchor our perception of intonational phenomena on certain points in the time varying course of pitch and disregard what lies between such fixed points. (p. 19)

Since intonation is a suprasyllabic phenomenon, it is not necessary to specify a pitch point for each syllable, but we can assume that the key points will vary from language to language depending on the stress pattern of the language. Thus the fact that Di Cristo (1976a) describes the key points of French intonation as occuring on the onset, the pretonic and the tonic is linked to the word-final stress pattern of this language. In the case of Moroccan Arabic, the main pitch movement of the Intonation Unit occurs on the tonic and post-tonic syllables.

This study is based on the analysis of several corpuses of sentences pronounced in an anechoic chamber by eight native Moroccan speakers (all city dwellers). Each sentence was written on a separate card. Speakers were asked to memorise each sentence and then pronounce it without looking at the card. This procedure was found useful to reduce the stereotypic intonation patterns which are often produced by subjects reading utterances directly. The subjects were also asked to produce each utterance in a single breath group to avoid the occurrence of pauses within sentences and to pronounce the sentences without special emphasis and at a normal speed. The recordings thus obtained form the basic material for an ongoing acoustic and perceptual study of intonation in Moroccan Arabic. The description given here is a preliminary account of the major tendancies observed in these corpuses. The transcriptions given, using INTSINT (Hirst and Di Cristo this volume), are based essentially on auditory impression confirmed by examination of the fundamental frequency curve.

2. Description of intonation patterns

2.1 Description of a basic non-emphatic pattern

While there are quite a number of studies concerned with the segmental phonology of Western Arabic, its suprasegmental characteristics have received much less attention. Experimental or acoustic studies are rare: Khomsi (1975); Benkirane (1981, 1982); Benkirane and Cavé (1984, 1987,1988), Lahlou (1981, 1982). There is to date no study specifically concerned with the intonation system of Moroccan Arabic, with the exception of Lahlou (1982). This study is essentially concerned with the microprosodic characteristics of vowels and consonants with a view to obtaining a stylisation of objective data in terms of psycho-acoustic thresholds (as described by Rossi *et al.* 1981). The technique developed is applied to just two utterances taken from a corpus of spontaneous speech. One of these utterances is analysed as follows:

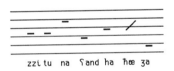

zzɪ tu na ʕand ha ħæ ʒa

Figure 1. Stylised F_0 pattern of the sentence [zziˈtuna ʕandhaˈħæʒa] (the olive tree has a particularity) (from Lahlou 1982).

The first part of the utterance [zzituna] is separated from the second [ʕandhaħæʒa] by a silent pause and the utterance can consequently be analysed as containing two Intonation Units. The first of these finishes on a high pitch signalling non-finality while the second finishes on a low level signalling finality. The sentence accent of the second unit is signalled by a rising pitch coinciding with the penultimate syllable [ħæ]. Using INTSINT this utterance could be transcribed as follows:

(6)   [zziˈtuna ... ʕandhaˈħæʒa] (the olive tree has a particularity)

[→ ⇑] [→   ⇑ ⇓]

In general, neutral unemphatic declarative utterances composed of a single Intonation Unit usually consist of a rising-falling pattern, with the rising portion occuring on the syllable carrying the sentence accent followed by a fall to the bottom of the subject's pitch range. The pitch preceding the stressed syllable generally contains no significant pitch movement. The following example is typical of the pattern characteristic of neutral declarative sentences in Western Arabic and can be considered the basic pattern.

(7)   [ʔamina mreɖa] (Amina is ill)
    [→ ⇑ ⇓]

Phonologically the basic pattern can be described as a sequence of tones [LHL] where the two low tones are associated with the two boundaries of the Intonation Unit and the high tone is associated with the accented syllable. Acoustically, the pitch interval between the onset and the peak is approximately six semitones whereas that between the peak and the end of the utterance is approximately an octave.

When sentence stress occurs on a monosyllabic word of the form CVC, the whole rising-falling pitch movement usually occurs on the vowel:

(8)   ['ʒærna 'mreːɖ] (The neighbour is ill)
    [→ ⇑ ⇓]

It can however sometimes be reduced to a simple falling contour:

(9)   ['ʒærna 'mreːɖ]
    [⇑   ⇓]

This is regularly the case when the nuclear accent occurs on a monosyllabic word of the form CV:

(10)   [ʒæ'bulha 'lma] (They brought him some water)
    [⇑   ⇓]

in which case the peak of the F_0 curve occurs on the unstressed syllable preceding the nucleus. It is in fact impossible to find in Moroccan Arabic a complex rising-falling pitch movement on the final (stressed or unstressed) open syllable of a statement.

In conclusion, a rising-falling pitch movement tends to occur on the last two syllables of a terminal Intonation Unit. Words with the prosodic structure CVC(V) meet the minimal requirement for such a pattern.

The rising-falling pattern at the end of an utterance which is characteristic of all except marked emphatic utterances (see §2.3 below) has the effect of giving the utterance a characteristic rhythm with a crescendo from the onset until the nucleus. The result is that little or no effect of declination is observed in ordinary non-emphatic utterances, since the lowest pitch value before the nucleus is usually on the first syllable. It is possible to find cases of pitch contours which drop slightly from the onset to the nucleus (cf. figure 2):

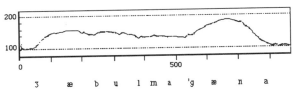

Figure 2. F_0 contour for the utterance [ʒæbulha lmaˈgæna] (they brought her the watch/meter)

This is far less common, however, than a flat or slightly rising pattern as in figures 3, 4.

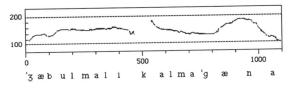

Figure 3. F_0 contour for the utterance [ʒæbul malika lmaˈgæna] (they brought Malika the watch/meter)

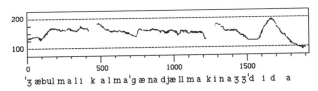

Figure 4. F_0 contour for the utterance [ʒæbul malika lmaˈgæna djællmakinaʒʒˈdida] (they brought Malika the meter from the new machine)

Utterances with a high onset and a falling pre-nuclear pattern are usually either WH-questions or imperatives (see §2.2) or emphatic sentences with a topicalised initial word (see §2.3).

2.2 The intonation of questions

In this section we discuss the intonation patterns associated with WH-questions and Yes/No questions. The emphasis will be on the latter since they illustrate a particularity of the intonation system of Moroccan Arabic.

Rhiati (1984) provides a brief comparative description of the intonation of statements and questions in which he concludes that questions are characterised by a higher onset than statements, that the pitch peak on WH-questions occurs on the question word and that Yes/No questions finish with rising pitch (p. 75).

As we shall see below, this description corresponds in general to our data with the exception of the pattern for Yes/No questions for which none of the subjects we recorded produced a final rising pattern.

a. WH-questions

WH-questions, as in many languages, are characterised by a peak occurring on the question word followed by a rapidly falling pitch on the rest of the utterance as in the following examples:

(11)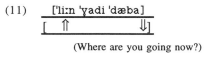

(Where are you going now?)

(12)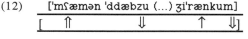

(Who did they argue with...your neighbours?)

Whatever its place in the utterance, the question word is made prominent by the F_0 peak and by a rapid fall on everything following the word in the same Intonation Unit. In example (12) the silent pause between [ddæbzu] and [ʒi'rænkum] has the effect of raising the pitch slightly on the following detached subject which is pronounced with a parenthetical intonation.

The intonation pattern of WH-questions is very similar to that found on imperatives which are also characterised by a high or rising onset followed by a rapid fall to the bottom of the speaker's range.

b. Yes/No questions

Some examples of Yes/No questions are illustrated in Figures 5, 6 and 7. It will be apparent from these figures that the pattern for Yes/No questions is very similar to that observed for statements: in both cases a rising-falling pattern is observed. In particular, the fall at the end of the Yes/No questions was produced by all eight of the speakers we recorded. If we compare the pattern with that of the corresponding statements, however, we notice that there is an overall raising of the whole pitch register including the onset: the average difference between the onset of a statement and the corresponding question being 3.5 semitones (no differences less than 2 semitones were recorded) whereas the difference between the value of the peak on the nucleus was in all cases greater than 6 semitones.

If we examine the pattern of the Yes/No question, we find an interval of 8 semitones between the onset and the nucleus, while that between the nucleus and the following unstressed syllable averages 16.4 semitones. The final falling movement is consequently greater than that observed with statements although for six of the eight subjects the final fall does not reach the lowest level of the speakers' pitch range.

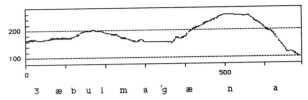

Figure 5. F_0 contour for the utterance [ʒæbu lma'gæna] (Did they bring the watch/meter?)

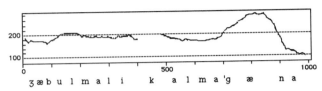

Figure 6. F_0 contour for the utterance [ʒæbulmalika lma'gæna] (Did they bring Malika the watch/meter?)

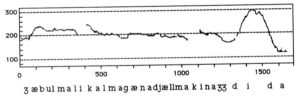

Figure 7. F_0 contour for the utterance [ʒæbu lmalika lma'gæna djællmakinaʒʒdida] (Did they bring Malika the meter from the new machine?)

2.3 Focalisation and contextual effects

The basic unemphatic pattern described in §2.1 is liable to modification when a speaker wishes to focalise a particular item in an utterance. Thus in the following example, it is the non-final word /ma'zæla / ("again"), which is focalised:

(13)   [ʔa'mina ma'zæla 'mreḍa]   (Amina is ill <u>again</u>)
    [⇑ ↓ ↑   >   ⇓]

The final pitch rise occurs on the focalised word. In the same way, to emphasise the negative value of an utterance (Sabia 1982) the speaker may use either of the following equivalent means:

(14) a   [ma kla'ʃæːj]   (He hasn't eaten (at all).)
    [→   ⇑ ⇓]

355

b   [ma ʃiṭbeba] (She's not a doctor (at all).)
[⇑ ↓   ⇓]

As we noted for examples (4a) and (4b), the negative form is usually formed with the discontinuous morpheme [ma...ʃ(i)] surrounding the negated word. In the case of reinforced or categorical negation as in (13a) the negative morpheme takes the form [ma...ʃæːj]. In the case of (13b) there is no longer discontinuity between the two parts of the negative morpheme: [maʃi]. These prosodic modifications follow from the fact that, as we noted above, the minimal structure compatible with prosodic prominence is the form CVC(V).

Focalisation can also be signalled syntactically by the morpheme [lli], which highlights the preceding constituent:

(15)   [lmaˈgæna lli ˈʒdida] (The watch/meter is new.)
[→   ⇑   ⇓]

In sentences of this type the syllable [lli] marks the end of the rising pitch movement and the beginning of the final falling movement which drops continuously without steps to the end of the utterance:

(16)   [aˈmina ˈʒærtna lli ˈmreda] (Amina our neighbour is ill.)
[→   ⇑   ⇓]

The absence of any change of level or slope in the portion following the emphatic morpheme seems to indicate that there are no pitch accents after that occurring on the focalised word.

A comparison of the pitch contours on utterances in which focalisation is expressed both with and without the emphatic morpheme shows that the contour is practically identical in the two cases. The presence of the morpheme [lli] conveys a greater intensity to the focused item.

In all the examples discussed the same basic rising-falling pitch contour as observed on non-emphatic utterances is maintained, the only difference being in the location of the pitch peak which is shifted more or less to the left depending on the position in the utterance of the focused item.

2.4 Longer utterances

Longer utterances are generally split up into two or more Intonation Units the last of which is pronounced with a similar pattern to that described for short unemphatic utterances (§2.1). Intonation Units preceding the final one are usually pronounced with a rising pitch movement on or up to the final syllable of the unit. This rising movement can either cover the whole of the first Intonation Unit as in the following example:

(17)   [bæ'ʕuli] [lma'gæna 'ɣalja] (They sold me the watch/meter at a high price)

[→ ⇑] [→ ⇑ ⇓]

or, particularly when the first Intonation Unit contains more than one stressed syllable, the rising movement can be confined to the final unstressed syllable:

(18)   [ʔa'mina 'wnædja] ['kænutaj 'ddæbzu] (Amina and Nadia were arguing)

[⇑   ↓ ⇑] [→ ⇓]

Syntactically, the first Intonation Unit of (18) contains two noun phrases linked by the conjunction [w]. This syntactic structure is reflected prosodically by a similar hierarchical structure with the form [ʔa'mina] ['wnædja]. It is however possible for the simple rising pattern to occur on a sequence containing more than one stressed syllable as in the first Intonation Unit of:

(19)   [lma'gæna 'ɣalja] [wəl'ma 'ɣali]

[→⇑] [→⇑ ⇓]

(The meter is expensive and the water is expensive)

In general, then, non-terminal Intonation Units are marked by a final rising pitch. There is however a variant pattern with a slight drop in pitch onto the last syllable of the Intonation Unit as in:

(20)   [lma'gæna] [bæ'ʕuha] (The watch/meter, they have sold)

[⇑ >] [→⇑ ⇓]

This pitch drop, which generally does not go below the speaker's medium pitch, is very different from that in the second Intonation Unit which falls to the bottom of the speaker's range. This non-final pitch drop functions very much as equivalent to a filled pause so that (20) is in fact prosodically equivalent to that of example (6) above with, in both cases, a preposed noun phrase functioning as topic followed by a subject pronoun [ha]. The most common word order in MA is VSO (Ennaji 1985).

This variant non-terminal intonation pattern consisting of a pitch peak followed by a slight drop is also fairly common at the end of each item of a list.

3. Comparisons with other systems

3.1 Comparisons within the same language

The vast majority of phonetic or phonological studies of Moroccan Arabic are concerned solely with the segmental level, although there have been a few studies in the framework of non-linear phonology (following in particular McCarthy 1979) dealing with prosodic aspects of various dialects (cf. El-Mejjad (1985) for the dialect of Marrakech and Benkaddour for the dialect of Rabat).

3.2 Comparisons with other varieties of Arabic

A preliminary investigation of the prosody of declarative utterances in Standard Arabic read by Moroccan speakers reveals, as is to be expected, results which are rather similar to the patterns described above for Moroccan Arabic. In particular there is a conspicuous lack of alternating peaks and valleys as observed in many languages. Instead, whatever the length of the utterance, the precontour is practically always flat or slightly rising followed by a single rise + fall situated on the last stressed word of the utterance. There is no apparent effect of declination.

It is interesting to compare these results with those of a recent study of the intonation of Standard Arabic read by speakers from Damascus (Haydar and Mrayati 1985). The acoustic documents accompanying this study show a far greater variety of pitch contours than that observed for Moroccan Arabic. The basic pattern seems to consist of an initial peak followed by a number of rises and falls ending with a final steep fall. The presence of an early peak in utterances results in a distinct declination effect, contrary to what we have observed for Moroccan Arabic. It seems likely that these differences in the prosody of Standard Arabic reflect underlying differences in the phonological and prosodic systems of Moroccan and Syrian Arabic.

There are very few studies of the intonation systems of modern Arabic dialects. Apart from an early instrumental study of Egyptian Arabic by Abdallah (1960), it is worth mentioning a recent pilot study of declarative and interrogative utterances in the dialect of Cairo (Norlin 1989) based on the speech of a single subject. The author concludes:

Cairo Arabic seems to use universally employed means to differentiate between statements and questions. Neutral statements exhibit the expected continuous downdrift in frequency. Statements with any part in focus break the downdrift pattern, marking the focused part by a wider frequency range and a compressed pitch range after focus. Questions also exhibit the expected intonation patterns with a rising intonation at the end of the utterance. (pp. 48–49).

4. Conclusions

This preliminary account of the intonation system of Moroccan Arabic is based on the examination of acoustic documents corroborated as far as possible by the author's intuitions as a native speaker.

It appears that the phonologically relevant portion of an intonation pattern in this language is essentially concentrated on the final stressed syllable and the following unstressed syllable. The different pitch contours appearing on these syllables contribute to the identification of the boundaries of Intonation Units, the position of the sentence accent as well as the form and function of the overall pitch pattern. The pitch of the post-nuclear unstressed syllable appears to play a crucial role in the identification of the type of Intonation Unit: terminal vs non-terminal. The role of the pre-nuclear unstressed syllable requires further investigation: it is worth noting that in examples such as (10) and (11) the final peak occurs not on the final stressed syllable but on the preceding unstressed syllable. This suggests that the function of the rising portion of the contour is simply to prepare for the phonologically crucial falling pitch. This is further corroborated by the fact that, as mentioned above, the difference between declarative and interrogative patterns seems to be based on a distinction between two types of fall: normal and reinforced. The exact nature of the distinction between these two patterns, however, together with a number of other questions which have been raised in this chapter, is the object of research in progress.

20

Intonation in
Japanese

ISAMU ABE

1. Background information

Japanese is the national language of Japan which has a population of approximately 120 million. The language has several varieties or dialects, the major one being the type spoken in Tokyo and its neighbouring areas. This chapter deals with the prosody of standard Tokyo Japanese unless otherwise noted.

The Japanese language, as I have already mentioned elsewhere (Abe 1981), is a tonal language but not strictly a tone language like Chinese or Thai in which all possible phonologically significant distinctions are made within the scope of one syllable. On the other hand, it is not a stress-oriented language, either, in that morphemic distinctions are made primarily by pitch. F_0 used in the domain of morphology is assumed to have a symbolic function, while in sentential and discoursal contexts, it is assumed to have a symbolic/symptomatic function. The term "symptomatic" means that what is said is more or less physico-psychologically constrained, whether it be instinctive or institutionalised.

1.1 General prosodic characteristics

a. The syllable
The syllable is the basic unit of speech that must be considered in connection with the logic of accentuation. The syllable structure of Japanese is either

simplex: (C)V or complex: long V, V plus the moraic nasal "n", V plus geminated obstruent, and some geminated vowels (non-homologous). Complex syllables are counted as monosyllabic or disyllabic. From a **moraic** viewpoint, they are disyllabic in that the term **mora** is a kind of rhythmically defined syllable.

b. Accents and tones

Words or lexical units are either accented or unaccented in Japanese (henceforth referred to as T1 and T2 words respectively if need be). T1 words have, or presuppose, a phonologically significant drop in pitch somewhere either explicitly or implicitly which is also perceptually recognisable as such. T2 words have no such drop in pitch anywhere. In the case of T1 words, all the syllables including and preceding the accented syllable run on a high note except the leftmost one which is low. If none precedes, the accented syllable starts high and the rest runs on a lower note, with a drop in pitch from the initial syllable to the second one. In the case of T2 words, the initial syllable starts low and the succeeding syllable or syllables run on a higher note. This means that Japanese words automatically start low unless the initial syllable is high. The following example illustrates a minimal pair (see figure 1):

(1)　a　*káki* (T1) (oyster)　　　b　*kaki* (T2) (persimmon)

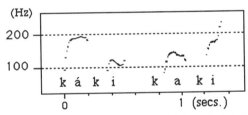

Figure 1. F_0 contours for examples (1a) and (1b). (See §1.2 for technical details.)

There are some exceptions to this rule. Many Japanese pronounce T2 words beginning with V plus "n", or a long V or geminated vowels with the relevant portion on a more or less flat note instead of the expected low to high transition in pitch. Weitzman (1970) shows that the average value of the range of pitch from the first to the second mora (in semitones) as pronounced by 4 native Japanese speakers are +1.2, +1.3, +2.3 and +0.8 for (C) VN words, and +1.5, +1.1, +2.5 and +0.7 for (C) VV words. These values and ranges are to be compared with words with other moraic types. The figures range from +2.6 to +4.6 semitones.

Monosyllabic words pose some problems. For example, the two words hí (fire)(T1) and hi (sun)(T2) do not seem to reveal any clear-cut phonological pitch contrast when they are pronounced in isolation. I have already shown by experimental techniques (Abe 1980) that Japanese words are neutralised as to tone at the monosyllabic level. A method usually resorted to for differentiating the two nouns is to affix the particle *ga* to each word, giving *híga* and *higa* respectively. These then have the same pitch patterns as corresponding bisyllabic words such as *káki* and *kaki* respectively.

The same method also makes it possible to distinguish bisyllabic T1 words with accent on the final syllable, like *kakí* (hedge), from otherwise homophonous T2 words: *kaki* (persimmon), since the resulting trisyllabic compounds *kakíga* and *kakiga* are phonetically distinct.

c. Intonation

Intonation – with its concomitant features – voice quality, articulatory force, *etc.* – serves more than one communicative purpose. The most important functions of intonation are (1) demarcative (indicating whether or where a given message is connected or disconnected, *etc.*), (2) grammatical (determining whether a sentence is declarative or interrogative, *etc.*), (3) attitudinal (revealing the speaker's psychological involvement in what is being said) and (4) focusing (highlighting the portion the speaker particularly wants to stand out).

d. Tones and intonation

Intonation affects tones in a variety of ways (Abe 1972a). Our first concern is how it affects tones. In Japanese, underlying the tone-intonation interplay phenomena is the governing principle that tones are susceptible but usually not subservient to intonation. The same principle basically holds true of tone languages like Chinese or Thai (Luksaneeyanawin 1984a). This means that tones by their nature resist being perturbed by intonation. With this proviso, there are three forms that tones and intonation conjointly generate. I term the three as (1) cumulative, (2) copulative and (3) conflictive. When a given tone – let us assume it is rising – is affected by "declarative" intonation, which is falling in abstract terms, and becomes less rising, this is an example of (1). When the same tone is accompanied by "declarative" intonation in this order, that is rising plus falling, it is an example of (2). And when the same tone is affected by intonation to such a degree that it has completely lost its original shape and becomes falling or whatever, this is an example of (3).

Our next concern is where intonation affects tones. In Japanese we have intonation terminally (*i.e.* as an end-point: falling, rising, *etc.*) at phrase and sentence boundaries, and in this case, it mainly operates as a directional option. The specific location where intonation plays a decisive role as a grammatical device or attitudinal index may be termed as a "pivotal" point. Elsewhere, it mainly operates as a scalar or registral variable. For example, we have intonation with an overall high or low pitch height or with a localised pitch shift either upward or downward. An all-inclusive term "contour" will be used to refer to the shape of pitch movement interpolating each successive turning point, if any (*i.e.* deflection upward or downward) and eventually stretching over the whole sentence.

1.2 Outline of the approach

The description of Japanese intonation given here is based on material drawn from a number of studies that the author has made over the past years (see references). For the purposes of this chapter, I recorded my own pronunciation of all the examples, taking care that the simulated contours fitted as neatly as possible into the context to which they were supposed to apply. There were of course certain limitations on the vocal performance of this kind, particularly when it was attempted in decontextualised experimental conditions.

The intonation pattern of the examples is transcribed using the INTSINT transcription system (Hirst and Di Cristo this volume).

A number of examples are also illustrated by fundamental frequency curves which were obtained from a RION Co. (Tokyo) Pitch Extractor (Model SE-01). Broken/Dotted lines indicate F_0 Unvoiced and devoiced sounds do not appear on the pitchgrams. The approximate positions of the segmentals are shown below the curves. Pitch is shown on the ordinate (in Hz) and time is shown on the abscissa (in seconds).

2. Description of intonation

We have in the preceding section discussed the tonal system of Japanese at the smallest morphemic level. We shall now proceed to the phrasal and then to the sentential level, this time with due consideration of the fact that some pitch modulations are tonal and others are intonational.

2.1 Tonal sequence and intonation

The following example:

(2)   sonokaki   irógaíí   (As for that persimmon, it has a nice colour.)
   [⇑   ↓   ↑ > ⇓]

illustrates how the tone patterns of individual words combine in a sentence (see figure 2). *Sono* (that) is T2, *kaki* is T2, *iró* (colour) is T1, and *íi* (good) is T1. The word *kaki* here emerges as a flat tone because it has undergone a morphological tonal change with another T2 word preceding it. The word *iró* is followed by the particle *ga* and by another T1 word *íi* (with a decreased pitch interval) as shown.

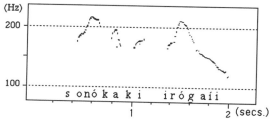

Figure 2. *F₀* contour for example 2.

In the next example:

(3)   sono   kakiirogaíi   (I prefer that bright-red colour.)
     [⇑   ↓ ↑ > ⇓]

(cf. figure 3) the two words *kaki* and *iró* are conjoined to form a larger unit, a compound noun. The accentual rules of Japanese specify that *iró* (T1) used in this environment makes the whole compound unaccented. Hence we have *kakiiro* and not *kakiiró*. There are apparently complicated but in fact quite neat accentual rules in Japanese which dictate the shift of status or position of accents when lexical units are subjected to derivational or inflectional change or to affixation or compounding. We will not however go into more details here.

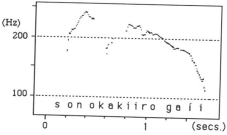

Figure 3. *F₀* contour for example 3.

The next example consists of a sequence of T1 lexical units:

(4)   Kákio tóru ámao míta   (I saw female divers catching oysters.)
     [⇑   ↓   ↑   > ⇓]

kákio (oysters, objective), *tóru* (catch), *ámao* (female divers, objective), *míta* (saw) (see figure 4). There is an upward deflection on *áma*.

364

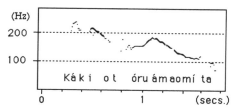

Figure 4. F_0 contour for example 4.

The next example consists of a sequence of T2 lexical units:

(5)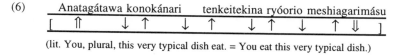

kakio (persimmons, objective), *kau* (buy), *kanega* (money), *iru* (need).

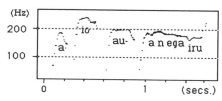

Figure 5. F_0 contour for example 5.

I have just demonstrated two extreme cases of tones in sequence, one consisting solely of T1 words, and one of T2 words. It may be noticed that the overall downward pitch movement is less in evidence in the second example. This is simply because the drop in pitch specific to T1 words is characteristically absent, whereas in the first example there are several downsteps. Both sentences however end with a falling terminal. The end-point appears to be noticeably different as to pitch height in the examples of this nature. This phenomenon is only tonally constrained; the terminal intonation is functionally identical. Pronounced in a more casual manner, the example given in figure 5 may end up nearer to the bottom.

In longer sentences, the usual terminal intonation ("pivotal") occurring at (potential) phrase boundaries is either level or falling.

Figure 6 (taken from Anan 1979) shows the stylised contour of a fairly long declarative sentence. The example is:

(6)

(lit. You, plural, this very typical dish eat. = You eat this very typical dish.)

365

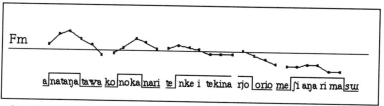

Figure 6. Stylised intonation contour of a fairly long declarative sentence (from Anan 1976). (See example 6.)

The whole contour yields what might be termed as "declination", that is a downtilt of pitch on each succeeding phrase with the first phrase riding on a baseline higher than the second, and the second higher than the third and so on, barring deflection upward. In an unemphatic read-aloud style of speech in the declarative mode, the farther away from the beginning, the lower will be the F_0 employed. For discussion of "declination", see Beckman and Pierrehumbert (1987) and Poser (1984).

In longer sentences of this kind, the intonation occurring at (potential) phrase boundaries is either level or falling. If a rising terminal is used instead in identical position, as in:

(7) Anatagátawa   konokánari...

this may give one the impression that the speaker is calling rather insistently for the listener's attention (equivalent to English "...you see"). This is why this contour is appropriate for the reading of fairy tales to children (Abe 1972b).

2.2 Modality and expressivity

a. Declarative, interrogative and imperative intonation
Examples 8–9 show the contours of the holophrastic sentence *káki* (oyster) pronounced in the declarative mode.

(8) Káki.

(9) Káki...

The first example ends with a falling terminal and the second with a "sustained" level pitch. The fall implies that what has to be said has been said and the level pitch implies that there is still something to follow (*e.g.* oysters, clams...). When the level pitch is not sustained, it is sometimes hard to distinguish between level and falling.

Examples 10–11 show the contours of the holophrastic sentence *káki* pronounced in the interrogative mode: one without and one with the question particle *ka*.

(10)   <u>Káki?</u>
    [⇑ ↓⇑]

(11)   <u>Kákika?</u>
    [⇑↓→⇑]

Both sentences end with a rising terminal as shown. In the first example, the rising terminal is the sole question-signalling device: otherwise there would syntactically be no means to differentiate a question from a non-question.

Thorsen (1978) gives a hypothetical model of Danish questions, and she infers that Danish questions in statement form end higher terminally than questions with the interrogative marker *mon* inserted in sentence-initial position. I have no large-scale systematic instrumental corroboration of the Japanese equivalent of this, but my feeling is that an interrogative sentence with or without *ka* requires no such clear-cut prosodic distinction in the relative height of the terminal pitch. Nor do I subscribe to the view held by some scholars that the presence of the question marker could do away with "interrogative" intonation without doing much harm to the meaning intended. The prosodic picture presented by a number of languages I have surveyed reveals that this is not the case. Yes-no questions with a question marker (the position of which in the sentence is language specific) often end with a rising terminal. To mention a few languages: Arabic: *Hal thahabta ila Boyrūta?* (Did you go to Beirut?); Hindi: *Kyā tum Dillī gae?* (Did you go to Delhi?); Tagalog: *Pumunta ba siya sa Maynila?* (Did he go to Manila?) and Polish: *Czy pojechałeś do Warszawy?* (Did you go to Warsaw?) (Abe 1989).

It cannot be denied, however, that the more rise there is, the more curious or even querulous the question is likely to become. A question with a terminal rise going up to a climatic high would often imply "surprise". Conversely, a Japanese sentence *kákika?* pronounced with the terminal syllable on a very low note would no more be a simple yes-no question. The contour shown in example 12 implies that the speaker has after all been persuaded to believe that they are oysters.

(12)   <u>Kákika!</u>
    [⇑ ↓⇓]

Examples 13–14 show the contours of an interrogative sentence one with and one without the question particle *ka*:

(13)   <u>Kákio tabemáshita?</u>   (Did you eat oysters?)
    [⇑ ↓ ↑↓→ ⇑]

(14) <u>Kákio tabemáshitaka?</u>   (Did you eat oysters?)

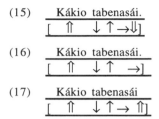

Both sentences end with a rather sharp rising terminal at the end as shown.

Examples 15–17 show the contours of a sentence in the imperative mode. Three basic terminal shapes may be applied here (*i.e.* fall, level and rise). The *sái* is treated as a "diphthongal" vowel.

(15) <u>Kákio tabenasái.</u>

(16) <u>Kákio tabenasái.</u>

(17) <u>Kákio tabenasái</u>

When it comes to describing the attitudinal connotations of the terminals, however, we are on less solid grounds. Subtle emotional overtones are rather elusive and tricky to grasp and Japanese is shackled with syntactical and lexical devices in addition to prosodic ones to express the imperative mode in the best way possible. With this reservation, we may say that the general implications of the falling, level and rising terminals would range roughly from "demanding" to "appealing", either soft or insistent.

b. Addressing and calling

When addressing someone, here again the three basic terminals are likely to occur. Example 18 shows the contour of one such example with a rising terminal.

(18) <u>Hánakosan.</u> [*Hánako* is a female name, *san* is an honorific title of address.]

Examples 19–20 show two of the melodic shapes used in the vocative mode – a calling contour. Proxemic factors demand that the voice be invariably set higher and the syllables lengthened and heavily stressed. (For calling contours in general, see Abe 1962, 1975, 1979a, *etc.* and Ladd 1980).

(19) <u>Hánakosa: n.</u>

(20) <u>Hánakosa: n.</u>

Example 19 shows the normative contour and example 20 a "stylised" contour which is likely to be used by a group of children calling in a loud voice to invite their friend out of his/her house to join them. *Há-* is very high, *-nako* is lower in pitch, and *san* is high again.

c. Attitudinal facets of intonation

Japanese has a variety of devices – prosodic, lexical and syntactical – to express emotional overtones as already stated. To give just a few examples, the word *Anáta* (You) (used by wife to husband) may be pronounced with the final syllable *-ta* kept level or rising or falling, but when the syllable is lengthened and gliding down with heavy stress, the implication would be "irritation" or "anger". The sentence *Hidói kikooda* (Terrible weather) may be pronounced with the portion *hidói* changing from the normative contour (*i.e. -dó-* is merely one step higher in pitch than the adjacent portions) to the intensified contour (*i.e. -dó-* is lengthened and progressively raised in pitch) to highlight the idea of "nastiness". In a certain radio play I heard, a Japanese actor was given the role of a doctor who had to inform the family of a dying patient of his impending death. There was a scene showing the doctor struggling very hard to give the best possible vocal interpretation of the lines he was given to read. The sentence in question was: *Damédesuna.* (lit.: No-good + is + *na,* interjectional particle) (There's no hope). Three versions of the terminal intonation he came up with and had to choose from were as follows, with their possible connotations. (1) The syllable *na* is high rising-falling: authoritative and rather bombastic announcement; (2) the syllable has a normative plain fall: open but more or less sympathetic announcement; and (3) the syllable goes up in pitch and stays level: curt and categorical announcement (Abe 1958a).

2.3 Highlighting and emphasis

The following example is the same as example 4:

(21)   K<u>á</u>kio tóru <u>áma</u>o m<u>í</u>ta.   (I saw <u>female divers</u> catching oysters.)
  [⇑   ↓   ⇑   ↓   ⇓]

but here the word *áma* is emphasised to stand out above the rest (see figure 7).
    Example 22 is the same as Example 5 with the word *kane* emphasised.

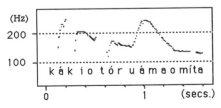

Figure 7. *F₀* contour for example 21.

Isamu Abe

(22)   <u>Kakio kau <u>kanega</u> iru.</u>   (I need the <u>money</u> to buy persimmons.)
[↑   ↓   ⇑   ⇓]

In the above two examples the portion in focus is deflected upwards to form a peak. In the following example:

(23)   <u>Kár<u>uta</u></u> denaku   <u>kár<u>ute</u></u>.   (Not playing cards but medical record.)
[⇑↓↑ ↓→⇑]   [⇑ ↓ ↑]

The word *káruta* (playing cards) is T1, and so is the word *Kárute* (medical record). Here the terminal syllables in contrast (*i.e.* -ta and -te) may be pronounced with heavy stress and pitch raised to a higher register (Abe 1977).

A similar contrast can be made with T2 words:

(24)   <u>Koki denaku   kaki</u>.   (Not "Koki" [a fictitious word] but persimmon.)
[⇑   ⇑] [→ ⇑]

However the portions which stand in contrast cannot be raised in pitch to such a degree as to destroy the otherwise acceptable tonal shapes of the two words (both T2). Here the melodic function is minimised.

2.4 Intonation in connected speech

To sum up what I have been describing so far about tones and intonation in Japanese which are two different phonological entities, I will here attempt to provide some specimens of tones and intonation where they come in contact and where they conjointly serve some specific pragmatic purposes. Numerical figures have been chosen because they are free of any attitudinal associations a "meaningful" sequence of morphemes would otherwise have. The four numerals are *ichí* (one)(T1), *ní* (two)(T1), *san* (three)(T2) and *shí* (four) or *yón* (both T1).

The first example shows the contour of a 4–digit telephone number which the caller is communicating to the other party on the line. A slight pause may be placed between the numerals 2 and 3.

(25)   <u>Ichí   ní   san</u>   yón.   (one two three four)
[⇑   ↓   ↑   → ⇓]

The next example shows the contour of the numerals 1, 2 and 3 pronounced as idependent items:

(26)   <u>Ichí   ní   san</u>.   (one, two, three)
[⇑ > >]

Example 27 shows the contour of the numerals 1, 2, 3... pronounced with the connective particle *to* attached to each item.

370

(27)   Ichíto   níto   santo

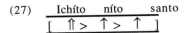

Example 28 shows the contour of the four numerals pronounced in a somewhat deliberate manner. The terminal syllables of the four words are rising. Monosyllabic words are treated like dimoraic ones as shown.

(28)   Ichí   ní: san   shí:

[→⇑] [→⇑] [→ ⇑] [→⇑]

Example 29 shows the contour of the numerals 1 2 3 4... which one would as often as not use while counting things in numerical order in unison and beating time as well. The initial syllable of each item (monosyllabic words being treated as dimoraic again) is lengthened and runs on a higher note than the following syllable and ends with a level pitch at phrase boundaries. The whole sequence would remind one of a "chant" which is something that is halfway between speech and song.

(29)   I:chí   ní:i   sa:n   shí:i

[⇑ ↓] [⇑ ↓]   [⇑ ↓]   [⇑ ↓]

Example 30 shows a contour typically used by a gymnastics instructor. Here the four numerals 1 2 3 and 4 are intoned in descending steps (with staccato effects if s/he prefers). This example shows the figure 3 deflected upward. The instructor often uses this contour with its variants while training his/her students to do exercise that requires some rhythmic action. (Stretch out your arms, bring them back to original position, stretch them out and bring them back again...). A rather mediocre contour I have heard had the four numerals all running on a monotone.

(30)   Ichí ní san shí

[⇑ ↓   ↑ ↓⇓]

Finally, example 31 shows the contour of 1234... pronounced very rapidly and in one breath. This contour is likely to be used when the total count is our first concern rather than the enumeration of the individual items. The four numerals run on a level note as if forming a straight line.

(31)   Ichí ní san shí

[⇑   ]

The examples given above are probably not exhaustive. Different melodic variations are also conceivable. And if the last numerical figure is given as final (*i.e.* no more counting or naming) the whole sequence would end with a falling terminal: otherwise, the intonation occurring at phrase boundaries is either level-sustained, rising or falling as the case may be (Abe 1964).

Finally it is interesting to consider the possible contours that might be superposed on a monosyllabic word (such as *hái* (yes)) used as a holophrastic sentence. A single-word sentence is supposed to carry the least information syntactically next to paralinguistic vocalisations (see §4) and intonation becomes a primary carrier of attitudinal meanings. All examples are in the declarative mode.

A boy would say *hái* (with lengthened -*á*-) on a high level pitch when raising his hand and clamouring for his teacher's attention in the classroom; he would pronounce the same word on a mid-suspended pitch to answer the teacher's roll-call; and the same boy would say *hái* on a low pitch to acquiesce. It is the voice register that does the trick.

A man would say *hái* in a business-like manner with a fall from high to low; he would say *hái* on a terse monopitch when standing to attention in reply to his angered boss.

The word *hái* may be repeated. *Hái hái* with the first *hái* forming a higher peak than the second would imply a "willing" yes, while the same expression with the second *hái* forming a higher peak would imply a "reluctant" yes.

2.5 Intonation clichés

Only very brief mention will be made of intonation clichés in Japanese. The lexical unit *konbanwa* (lit. this evening plus the particle *wa*) used as a formulaic expression of greeting (good evening) is T2, and is used as such in actual discoursal context. Otherwise *kónbanwa* (T1) with its appropriate contour would be used. (*e.g. Kónbanwa...*)(This evening...).

3. Crosslectal comparision of intonation

3.1 Within the language

a. Regional variations

There are several tonal systems in Japanese: Tokyo, Keihan and Ikkei types, among others. The lexical unit *kakiga* is low-high-high in Tokyo, high-high-high in Kyoto and low-low-high in Miya-konojo in Kyushu. Intonation affects all tonal systems more or less alike. Even in the Okinawa vernacular, the sentence *Yaya suinkai suroun.* (You live in Shuri) as pronounced by a group of young native students of Okinawa has a falling and rising terminal when the sentence is read as a statement and as a question respectively. The particle *na* or *mi* may be affixed to the sentence, with either a level-suspended or a rising terminal. So the prosodic picture is just the same as that of the variety of Japanese I speak (Abe 1970a).

Of course, there do exist regional characteristics as well. Yamaguchi (1985) makes a report on the heavily localised features of intonation as used by some speakers of the Echizen dialect (Fukui prefecture). One of the types he refers to has what appears to be repeated pitch downsteps at the end. Thus, *desukedó* (... though) will come out with the portion *-dó* going down twice. The standard type is *désukedo* with the portion *dé-* on a higher pitch and the rest on a lower pitch.

Amanuma (1989) states that the rising terminal of the sentence *Korede íidesune?* (Is this all right?) would elicit, if pronounced softly, a favourable response from another speaker of Tokyo Japanese and the conversation would then go on smoothly. However, speakers of Kyoto and Osaka Japanese cannot be expected to show the same response when they hear the same rising intonation on *ne*. An overwhelming number of them, he says, would take this contour not as a soft pleasing expression but as a curt importunate one. Amanuma concludes from this that intonation would appear to be responsible for the different impressionistic evaluations of the way one dialect is spoken by speakers of another dialect.

b. Socio-linguistic variations

Lectal variations of intonation go not only across the country, they also cross the social network, covering all professions and trades, and up and down the age scale and between the sexes. When a person steps upon someone else's toe by mistake, s/he says *Sumimasén.* (Pardon me.) usually with a completely falling intonation on *sén*. A shop-assistant making his way through the crowd in the supermarket where he works would keep saying *Sumimasén*, with *su-* beginning low, and *-mimasén* running on a higher-pitched monotone with or without a slight fall in pitch on the final *-n*. This is a typical stylised form of apology.

Loveday (1981) points out that Japanese women use a very high register of voice as a politeness formula, which I know often strikes visitors from abroad as very strange.

This prosodic mannerism is not the sole prerogative of females. Even Japanese men in the serving business may be heard using a higher pitch scale as if catering to the taste and wishes of the customer.

People of the younger generation seek and even exploit a new fashion in the way they speak. One of the fads they brought in and somehow has come to stay is the distinctly rising-falling terminal. (*e.g. Sorede* (and) *bókuwa* (I)... with this melody superposed on *de* and *wa*). The contour sounds as if they are doing their utmost to make their point clear. Children also have their own way of intoning (Abe 1980) and adults around them sometimes "talk down" to them and at other times use a kind of "child talk". The Japanese counterpart of the English "Not now" (E.V. Pike 1985) would be *Ím(:)a dam(:)e* – (lit. not now) with the consonant [*m*] and the vowels lengthened as need be.

Isamu Abe

3.2 *Intonational universals*

Bolinger (1964b, 1978b) assumes that intonation is utilised more or less alike in its forms and functions in the many languages of the world. This is the theory of intonation as a universal. Particularly illustrative of this theory is a tendency towards rising pitch in ordinary yes-no questions which he concludes is the dominant strain. Japanese question tunes are no exception to this hypothesis. Recruiting the question particle *ka* does not make the rising pitch on that account redundant (See §2.2.).

Paralinguistic vocalisations are among the most useful devices to examine the workings of intonation – along symptomatic lines in particular. In a survey I made of the various contours that could be imparted to the nasal sound [m], a group of university students from a dozen different countries were asked to give meanings to the contour as the sound was intoned in more than one way. All the subjects agreed that the rising contour on [m] indicated "query" (Abe 1965). (For Japanese contours that might accompany the [m] sound and its variants, see Abe 1958b.) Further experiments of this kind may be attempted, and presumably similar findings will be obtained.

And the way a given message in the declarative mode starts, proceeds and ends also appears to be characterised by a more or less universal trait – rise or level in mid position and fall in terminal position. What I have said about the contours of the numerals arranged in sequence and pronounced in different simulated discoursal contexts is in the main similar to and may even be mistaken for what Pike (1945) says about the enumeration contours in English. Just to clinch the issue, here is one more example. This time it is from Hawaiian (Abe 1970b): *Ekāhi* (one), *elua* (two), *ekolu* (three), *ehā (four)* ... *umi* (ten). All the items have a raised level-sustained contour except the last which falls.

On the other hand, there are scholars (Ladd 1979) who regard the intonational universal theory with a measure of suspicion. They maintain that intonation is idiolectal, dialectal and, on a global scale, language specific. A Russian interrogative intonation, for example, would be the case in point. Lasorsa (1976) gives some examples showing how Italians are likely to be led astray by the Russian contour (*i.e.* a sharp rise in pitch on the portion in focus followed by an abrupt fall in pitch) which evoked a response "slight rebuke or contempt plus confirmation of a fact or decided finality." Any type of contour alien to the native ear is responsible for this kind of misinterpretation of the meaning intended (Abe 1979b, Bolinger 1989, Varga 1975).

4. Conclusion

Japanese exploits pitch to express meanings of various kinds. Tones are mainly symbolic: intonation is symbolic/symptomatic. And these two prosodic entities are layered in neat order – from morphemic to phrasal to sentential to discoursal levels. Tones and intonation interact in a variety of ways – cumulative, copulative and even conflictive. Japanese tones and intonation seem to interact most in the first two ways and in some cases in the third way. In Chinese (Gårding 1987) and Swedish (Gårding 1979) the first way would seem to be the norm.

We have in Japanese a sizable number of affixes that have functions which are syntactic or affective. Coupled with these affixes and accompanied by other prosodic features and even non-verbal cues, intonation has its share of significant communicative weight. More data on intonation at work must be collected and analysed – specifically from a pragmatic point of view: how a message is designed to be given and how it is actually taken. In this era of expanding communication and travel, research on the many "codes of etiquette" intonation involves together with styles and fashions in intonation must be given a more detailed scrutiny – that is, intonation must be viewed in a wider perspective as it is actually observed not only in the classroom or in the experimental laboratory, but also on the streets where people from all professions and trades live and speak. Only by giving a new try on intonation in real action would the phonetician learn (with a nod and probably with a smile as well) that a Japanese shop-assistant's stylised intonation (see §3.2.) has its counterpart in the English *'scuse me* (Ladd 1978) and in the Italian *Mi scúsi tánto* (lit. Excuse me so much.) – an apology formula with the contour ending with mid-suspended pitch which expresses routine politeness as against the contour ending with low-falling pitch which expresses personal regret and sincere sorrow for what has happened (Antonio D'Eugeno, personal communication).

21

Intonation in
Thai

SUDAPORN LUKSANEEYANAWIN

1. Introduction

1.1 General prosodic characteristics of the language

Thai is a tone language. The language has been reported to have stress which has its linguistic function at the phonetic level (Henderson 1949, Thawisomboon 1955, Hiranburana 1971, Noss 1972, Luangthongkum 1977). Later work on the stress behaviour of the language (Luksaneeyanawin 1983, Surinpiboon 1985) suggested that Thai lexemes have a fixed word accent system. Content monosyllabic words are accented and are realised as stressed syllables in neutral or unmarked speech situations. Grammatical monosyllabic words are unaccented and are usually realised as unstressed syllables except in marked situations where contrastiveness or emphasis is given to the word, resulting in stress. Polysyllabic lexemes also have a fixed word accent system, and the primary accent is always on the last syllable of a word. The secondary accent placement is rule governed. In monomorphemic polysyllabic words rules are governed by the structure and the position of the composite syllables of the words. In polysyllabic compound words rules are governed by the morphemic derivative structure of the compounds, and in polysyllabic reduplicatives rules are governed by the morphophonemic structure and the semantic function of the reduplicatives (Luksaneeyanawin 1984b).

Thai has 5 tones; 3 relatively level or static tones: **mid, low,** and **high**; and 2 relatively kinetic or dynamic tones: **falling**, and **rising**. The mid and the low tones of the static set are narrow range continuous fall, but the high tone of this set is a narrow range continuous rise with a slight fall at the end. The fall is a wide range high continuous fall and the rise is a wide range low continuous rise. The following schema illustrates the five tones in Thai:

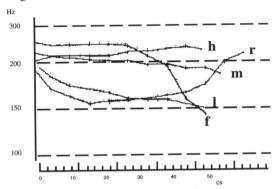

Figure 1. Fundamental frequency (F_0) for citation forms of the five tones: high (h), mid (m), low (l), rising (r) and falling (f) tones.

Thai has no syllable-final consonant clusters; the syllable structure is /(C)CV(:)(C)-T/ where **C** represents a consonant, **V** represents a vowel, ":" represents vowel length, and **T** represents lexical tone. The five lexical tones will be represented with small letters after the hyphen as shown in the following word set:

high tone	/kha:-h/	(to trade)
mid tone	/kha:-m/	(a kind of grass)
low tone	/kha:-l/	(galangale)
falling tone	/kha:-f/	(to kill)
rising tone	/kha:-r/	(a leg)

Phonemic contrastive length is found in Thai vowels and diphthongs. There are 9 vowels and 3 diphthongs. Pairs of vowels and diphthongs which differ quantitatively do not markedly differ qualitatively. Stress has a very strong influence on the realisation of vowel length in Thai. A long accented syllable is always realised as a distinctively long stressed syllable, as opposed to a long unaccented syllable which is always realised as a relatively short unstressed syllable. Duration of syllables is one of the most prominent features used to distinguish stressed and unstressed syllables in Thai (Hiranburana 1971, Luangthongkum 1977).

1.2 Outline of the approach

Two main theoretical questions in the study of Thai intonation are:

(i) How do the two systems of pitch fluctuation, lexical tone and sentence intonation, interplay to form the melody of speech in Thai?

(ii) How are words with lexical tones and accents put together with intonation to form speech sentences?

The answer to the first question can be obtained through the study of the interplay of lexical tone and sentence intonation by the analysis of one-word utterances obtained from the cue card technique which is a combination of the reading and questioning methods of elicitation (Greenberg 1969). The cue cards are used as stimuli to elicit prompt one-word utterances from the subjects without verbal instruction. The meanings which the subjects are expected to convey through their responses to the cue cards are of two types: (1) grammatical, (2) attitudinal.

Two archetypal grammatical meanings, *i.e.* (1) statements or assertions, and (2) yes-no questions, and two other grammatical meanings, *i.e.* (3) the notion of "non-finality" in unfinished utterances and (4) the notion of "continuation" in statements used to signify that the speaker has received the message and "please continue", are the 4 main grammatical meanings used.

Attitudinal meanings used are based on Uldall's (1960, 1964) different dimensions of attitudinal meanings: emphatic/unemphatic, authoritative/ submissive, interested/bored, believing/disbelieving, agreeable/disagreeable, surprised/not surprised (neutral), angry/concealing anger.

The words used to study tonal behaviour under different grammatical and attitudinal meanings represent the five contrastive lexical tones of Thai as described above. They are also chosen on phonetic grounds, *i.e.* all of them are monosyllabic words with initial voiceless stop consonants and long monophthongal vowels.

The tonal behaviour of the five tones in one-word utterances under different meanings are studied and the postulation of the tunes or intonation system of Thai is drawn from the results and conclusion of this study.

The corpus of data used for the analysis of intonation in Thai connected speech is of two groups: the spoken paragraphs are used to investigate the unmarked (non-emotional) intonation system, and the attitudinally marked and unmarked intonation is studied from real conversation dialogues, radio plays, and dialogues read by subjects.

The phonetic analysis is carried both by auditory analysis and instrumental acoustic technique. The 5 auditory pitch levels used are based on phonetic grounds (see detailed discussion in Crystal 1971 and Luksaneeyanawin 1983). A three-term label is used for the auditory pitch: 1) *pitch level* (high, higher mid, mid, lower mid, low); 2) *pitch direction* (level, fall, rise, and combinations of these directions); 3) *pitch range and shape* (wide/narrow range; continuous,

Table 1. *Summary of the tonal behaviour of one-word utterances with different grammatical meanings.*

Phonetic characteristics	Pitch height	Pitch range	Length	Degree of loudness
Semantic contrasts				
1. Statement	normal	normal	normal	normal
2. Question	higher	narrower	± shorter	louder
3. Unfinished statement	higher	narrower	longer	normal
4. "Telephone Yes"	lower	narrower	shorter	softer

delayed, stepping or level-ending shape). The acoustic study of the one-word utterances is the analysis of the fundamental frequency (F_0) done by the PGR progam module (Pitch extraction: Gold and Rabiner 1969) which extracts F_0 using a parallel processing technique for estimating pitch. PGR with 6 pitch period estimators extracts F_0 by estimating the pitch periods of speech at a specified rate (every 10 milliseconds) and gives the inverse of the pitch periods (*i.e.* F_0) in digital form. The program implemented by the Phonetics Laboratory, Edinburgh University works on ILS (Signal Technology Company). The F-J Electronics Aps Pitch Computer and Intensity Meter with the Siemens AB Mingograf 34T are used for the analysis of connected speech. These instruments give a clear visual representation of the relative acoustic value of pitch, length, and intensity and are very useful for the analysis of acoustic silence, the correlate of speech pause. Spectrographic analysis of the utterances is also done when comparison is needed. The spectrographic analysis is done using the DSP Sonagraph.

2. Description of intonation patterns: the interplay between tone and intonation

The tonal behaviour of the five tones in one word utterances elicited from 3 subjects will be given below. The term "normal" is used when the behaviour of the tone is similar to the normal reading pronunciation and the normal unemphatic citation form.

379

Table 2. *Phonetic characteristics of each tone when superimposed with different grammatical meanings.*

Semantic contrasts Phonological tones		Statement	Question	Unfinished statement	"Telephone Yes"
(I)	1. High /phæː-h/	high narrow continuous rise and fall	extra high level	extra high level	mid level
	2. Mid /keː-m/	mid narrow continuous fall	high level	high level	low level
	3. Low /thiː-l/	low narrow continuous fall	mid level	mid level	exta-low level
(II)	4. Rising /kheː-r/	low wide delayed rise	mid narrow delayed rise	low narrow level ending rise	low narrow continuous rise
	5. Falling /caː-f/	high wide continuous or delayed fall	high or extra-high narrow delayed fall	high narrow level ending fall	mid wide continuous fall

2.1 The tonal behaviour of one-word utterances with different grammatical meanings

From table 1 we can conclude that there are 3 types of behaviour:
1. The behaviour found in statements; this is similar to reading and the unmarked citation form.
2. The pitch is raised and the pitch range is narrower. This behaviour, when found in questions, is always accompanied by shortness and loudness, but when found in unfinished statements expressing non-finality, it is always accompanied by longer duration.
3. The pitch is lowered and the pitch range is narrower. This is always accompanied by shortness and a lower degree of loudness. The behaviour is found in the consultative code label of agreement or the "Telephone Yes" intonation.

Table 2 gives phonetic details of the 5 phonological tones grouped into two major classes: the static tones (high, mid, and low), and the dynamic or kinetic tones (rising and falling).

We can see from table 2 that the pitch of the static phonological tone set (set I), which in statements have a narrow range movement, become very static. The pitch is levelled throughout the utterance when superimposed with the question, the unfinished statement and the non-committal answer intonation. Questions are usually marked by other prosodic features, shortness and loudness, and unfinished statements are marked by longer duration (see table 1).

Auditorily, the three static tones are difficult to distinguish from each other when superimposed on question and non-finality intonation. Research on the recognition of the tones in Thai has shown that subjects have difficulties in distinguishing the mid and the low tone from each other, especially when they do not have access to the pitch patterns of the speakers (Abramson 1975, 1978). In terms of pitch pattern, mid and low in reading style are quite similar and both are quite different from high which usually has a narrow rise and a sudden fall at the end. However, in terms of intensity mid and low are quite different. The low tone has a sharp lowering of intensity as compared to the intensity pattern of mid and high. Intensity is another important phonetic cue in recognition of tone, especially in whispering when there is no auditory pitch (Abramson 1972, Gsell 1981). The differences of intensity pattern found in the reading and the statement intonation are not found in the question and the unfinished statement intonation where the intensity is high from the beginning and throughout the utterance. This may increase the problem of recognising the static tones. However perception tests need to be done to answer this question. The argument concerning unmarked and marked "Breath Groups" put forward by Lieberman (1967) is tenable. The acoustic evidence of this study revealed that the question and unfinished statement intonation is marked not only by higher fundamental frequency but also by high intensity towards the end of the utterance.

The two dynamic tones, rising and falling, keep their distinctive pitch patterns under different intonations. With the question and unfinished statement intonation, the pitch of these two tones becomes higher and the pitch range is narrower. Under the "telephone yes" intonation the pitch is lower and the pitch range is narrower. In previous studies of Thai intonation (Abramson 1962, Haas 1964, Rudaravanija 1965) the unfinished statement intonation was postulated as the "sustained contour" as opposed to the "rise contour" of the question intonation. In this study it is shown clearly that the phonological rising and falling tones when superimposed on these two intonations behave differently. "Level ending" is the marked characteristic of the unfinished statement intonation in both tones (see tables 1 and 2).

2.2 The tonal behaviour of one-word utterances with different attitudinal meanings

It is interesting that the attitudinally and emotionally unmarked utterances or the "neutral", which are put on cue cards in a systemic random order in the elicitation process, have similar behaviour.

From the study of the tonal behaviour of one-word utterances when superimposed on different grammatical meanings (tables 1 and 2) and different

Table 3. *Summary of the tonal behaviour of one-word utterances elicited with different attitudes.*

Semantic contrasts	Phonetic characteristics	Pitch height	Pitch range	Length	Degree of loudness
1.	Unmarked or neutral	normal	normal	normal	normal
2.	Emphatic	higher & lower	wider	longer	louder
3.	Anger	higher & lower	wider	± longer	very loud
4.	Agreeable	higher & lower	wider	longer	± louder
5.	Believing	higher & lower	wider	longer	louder
6.	Interested	higher & lower	wider	normal	normal
7.	Disagreeable	higher	narrower	± shorter	± louder
8.	Disbelieving	higher	narrower	± shorter	± louder
9.	Surprised	higher	narrower	± shorter	± louder
10.	Authoritative	lower	normal	± shorter	± louder
11.	Bored	lower	narrower	shorter	softer
12.	Concealed anger	lower	narrower	± shorter	± softer
13.	Submissive	normal	normal	± longer	softer

attitudinal meanings (table 3), we can conclude that in terms of pitch fluctuation, 4 intonation contours or Tunes can be postulated.

Tune 1 The pitch height and the pitch range are similar to that found in the reading citation forms and statements. This applies to utterances which are attitudinally and emotionally unmarked. Utterances marked with a submissive attitude also have this behaviour in terms of pitch but they are also marked by a lower degree of loudness and sometimes by lengthening of the utterances.

Tune 2 The pitch height is higher and the pitch range is narrower. This behaviour is found in questions, unfinished statements, and utterances elicited with disagreeable, disbelieving or surprised attitude. Usually this tune is accompanied by shortness and loudness except in unfinished statements which are accompanied by longer duration, and a level ending pitch configuration is found in the dynamic tones, the rising and the falling.

Table 4. *Phonetic details of each phonological tone.*

Tune contrasts Phonemic tone contrasts		Tune 1	Tune 2	Tune 3	Tune 4
I High	1.	high narrow continuous rise and fall	extra high level	mid level	high wide continuous rise and fall
Mid	2.	mid narrow continuous fall	high level	low level	mid wide continuous rise and fall
Low	3.	low narrow continuous fall	mid level	extra low level	mid narrow delayed rise
II Rising	4.	low wide delayed rise	mid narrow delayed rise	low narrow continuous rise	low wide continuous fall and rise
Falling	5.	high wide continuous or delayed fall	high or extra high narrow delayed fall	mid or high wide continuous fall	high wide continuous rise and fall

Tune 3 The pitch height is lower. In terms of pitch range there are 2 subtypes of behaviour: (1) The pitch range is narrower and accompanied by shortness and a lower degree of loudness. This is found in utterances marked with concealed anger, or bored attitude. It is also found in "telephone yes" statements. (2) The pitch range is normal and accompanied by shortness and a higher degree of loudness. This is found in utterances marked with an authoritative attitude.

Tune 4 The pitch height is higher in the phonological high, mid, and falling tones which have a non-low beginning point. In phonological dynamic tones which have a low beginning point, the rising tones, the pitch height is lower. The pitch range in all tones is wider, the static tones become non-static and the dynamic tones become more dynamic. In other words, there is a marked pitch fluctuation, up and down or down and up, found in both the static and the dynamic tone sets. This behaviour is found in utterances marked with emphatic, agreeable, interested, or believing attitudes. The tune is always accompanied by longer duration and a higher degree of loudness.

Table 4 above gives the details of the behaviour of each phonological tone, grouped into two classes.

It can be concluded here that the "Tune System" of intonation does not contaminate the phonological system of tones in the language. Each phonological tone still keeps its phonetic features distinct from other phonological tones. Under some tunes, the physical acoustic pitches of the tones are similar, but auditorily one can recognise the tones when there is access to the pitch range, pitch height and pitch shape of other phonological tones occurring nearby in the context. It is interesting to find out whether subjects would have more difficulty in recognising these phonological tones when they are decontextualised as compared with previous studies on tone recognition in Thai (Abramson 1975, 1978, Gandour 1978).

Table 5. *Summary of grammatical and attitudinal meanings for the 4 tunes*

Note: the tunes marked * are distinguished from the others in the same group by other prosodic features.

Tune 1	Tune 2	Tune 3	Tune 4
1. Statement	1. Question	1. "Telephone-Yes"	1. Emphatic
2. Citation form	2. Disagreeable	2. Concealed anger	2. Anger
3. Attitudinally unmarked	3. Disbelieving	3. Bored	3. Very agreeable
4. Submissive*	4. Surprised	4. Authoritative*	4. Very interested
	5. Unfinished*		5. Very believing

Results and conclusions as to the tonal behaviour of one-word utterances in Thai give support to the Intonation Universals hypothesis (see §3 for more detailed discussion). If we summarise the tonal behaviour of the traditional grammatical contrasts and attitudinal contrasts in terms of Falls and Rises, we will see a clear connection among the tunes and the meanings they conveyed.

The phonetic falls and semantic finality, found as the core of statements, responses with agreement, neutral or attitudinally unmarked responses to questions, and authoritative answers, is quite explicit and needs no explanation. Responses with concealed anger are realised with a fall, and their semantic finality can be discussed in terms of "hidden" or concealed arguments shown by a lowering pitch. Responses with boredom also show a finality or tiresomeness of arguments by a lowering pitch. Submissive responses show a finality in terms of withdrawal of arguments.

The phonetic rises and semantic non-finality found as the core of questions and responses with disagreement, disbelieving attitude, or in surprised answers is quite explicit and can be viewed as non-finality of arguments. Unfinished statements also show non-finality of arguments.

Falls	**Rises**
1. Statement (Tune 1)	1. Question (Tune 2)
2. Consultative code label of agreement or "telephone-yes" intonation (Tune 3)	2. Unfinished statements (Tune 2*)
3. Attitudinally unmarked response (Tune 1)	3. Marked with disagreement (Tune 2)
4. Marked with concealed anger (Tune 3)	4. Marked with disbelieving attitude (Tune 2)
5. Marked with bored attitude (Tune 3)	5. Marked with surprise (Tune 2)
6. Marked with authoritative attitude (Tune 3*)	
7. Marked with submissive attitude (Tune 1*)	

The question of "questions" considered as a grammatical category is a problematic one (Pope 1977, Searle 1969, 1972, 1979). What is a question? If questions are what we use to ask for new information then polar questions are not really questions. Polar questions are used to express the presupposed belief of the speakers towards the propositions or the matters being asked. In other words, in yes-no questions information about the presupposed belief and attitude towards a proposition is given as well as the request for the hearers to validify the proposition and the speaker's belief of the proposition.

Phonetically speaking, we can divide the Rises into two subclasses: the tense ending rise and the lax ending rise. Questions and responses with disagreement, disbelieving, and surprised attitudes are marked with the tense ending rise *i.e.* they are usually realised with shortness and loudness, and sometimes glottal constriction is perceived. Unfinished statements are marked with the lax ending rise. They are usually realised with longer duration and a normal degree of loudness. The tense ending rise expresses a stronger non-finality and a sign of insistence or more arguments whereas the lax ending rise is used to express a weaker non-finality and a need of tenable arguments both from the speaker himself or from the hearer. Politeness is also observed to be realised with this lax ending rise.

Tune 4 can be considered a complex tune, however: its complicating phonetic features and semantic characteristics need to be explicitly described with a new hypothesis (see discussion in §3).

2.3 and 2.4 Textual organisation: intonation groups and focalisation

In continuous speech, speakers need to divide whatever message they want to convey into smaller units due to the limitation or capacity of human perception and production (Studdert-Kennedy 1979, Lindberg 1979). In the discussion on the mechanism for string simplification of information units or what he calls "speech sentences", Lindberg (1979) proposed the division of units of actual spoken forms as opposed to abstract grammatical sentences. In languages with writing systems, there seem to be graphetic devices used to separate written information into smaller information units. In English and most European languages spaces are found between the smallest divisible units of information, words. Punctuation marks are also used to divide information units as small as words as well as larger information units which correspond to grammatical phrases, clauses, sentences, and combinations of sentences. In the Thai writing system and in many Southeast Asian languages, words are put together to form information units without spaces between them. The only punctuation mark used to divide information groups is spaces.

In the study of spoken prose in Thai (Luksaneeyanawin 1983, 1984a, 1986), it is found that speech sentences or the spoken information groups delimited by pauses and prominent stressed syllables are shorter than the written information groups delimited by spaces. In this style of speech the boundaries of both forms of information groups always correspond to the syntactic boundaries. An average number of syllables per pause-defined unit is 8 with an SD of 4, whereas the average number of words per pause-defined unit is 5 with an SD of 3. In marked conversational speech (Luksaneeyanawin 1983) pauses can be found at any of the syntagmatic boundaries: sentences, clauses, phrases, words, syllables, and even sound segments. Pauses between small units like syllables and sound segments are usually found when the speakers are thinking or hesitating. When there is no pause, "pause fillers" such as /ʔaː/, /ʔɤː/ and /m/ are also found.

The system of intonation grouping in Thai can be discussed in terms of the structure or the distribution of the pause-defined units delimited by phonological pauses and phonological tonics realised as prominent stressed syllables. The same piece of cognitive information can have a different number of points of prominence and this is realised in the way the speakers divide this piece of information. The more points of prominence, the more intonation groups. For example

(1)　/chaːw-m 'naː-m. kam-m 'laŋ-m.　'ŋom-m. 'plaː-m. naj-m.'khuː-m/
　　　[farmer　　　Aux-progr.　　　grope　fish　in　　ditch]
　　　　　(The farmers are groping for fish in the ditch.)

(2)　/'phæŋ-m. 'kɤːn-m.　'paj-m/
　　　[expensive　exceeding　go]　(It is too expensive.)

386

Thai

(3) /chan-r.   'phop-h.   'phan-m   ra?-h 'ja:-m.   khon-m.
     [I   meet   wife   one]
     'su:aj-r. kho:ŋ-r.   khun-m /
     [beautiful of   you]   (I met your beautiful <u>wife.</u>)

In these three examples, each piece of information contains only one point of prominence. The last word of the information group, in (1) a content word /khu:-m/ (ditch), a noun, and in (2) and (3) a grammatical word /paj-m/ (go), a post verb and /khun-m/ (you), a pronoun is prominently stressed which helps to indicate that the information has come to an end. In Thai unmarked intonation groups the last words of the information groups, either grammatical words or content words which are syntactically and semantically unified to the information groups, are prominently stressed. Since Thai has a fixed word accent (the final syllables of the words are the primary accents), the last syllables of the unmarked information groups are always the tonic syllables marking "end focus", or the ending of one information unit.

When the information groups contain more than one point of prominence, the information units can be differently structured, for example, from (3):

(3) a /chan-r. 'phop-h. 'phan-m ra?-h 'ja:-m.   khon-m.
        'su:aj-r. kho:ŋ-r. khun-m / (I met your beautiful <u>wife.</u>)
    b /chan-r. 'phop-h. 'phan-m ra?-h 'ja:-m.   khon-m.
        <u>'su:aj-r.</u> kho:ŋ-r. khun-m / (I met your beautiful wife.)

In (3a) there is one prominent information point, "wife". From the syntactical structure of this information group, the last word /khun-m/ (you), pronoun, which is a grammatical word syntactically and semantically unified to this information unit, is prominently stressed. When the last word of the information group is prominently stressed, it indicates two things: (1) the information is unmarked when there is only one prominent point of information, and (2) the information has come to its terminal position (end-point or end focus).

In (3b) there is one prominent point of information, "beautiful", which is prominently stressed. In this example a pause is used to indicate the termination of information, whereas the prominent point of information is shifted from "wife" to "beautiful" either for sarcasm or to show restrictiveness (the interlocutor has many wives and the speaker wants to refer to this "beautiful" one).

Actually, to mark this restrictiveness one can choose a lexical device as well as the phonological device illustrated above. For example, the word /chv:t-1 'cho:m-r/, which is a literary form of the word "beautiful", can be used to mark the same restrictiveness.

(3) c /chan-r. 'phop-h. 'phan-m ra?-h 'ja:-m.   khon-m.
        'chv:t-1 'cho:m-r. kho:ŋ-r. <u>khun-m</u> /(I met your <u>beautiful</u> wife.)

In (3c) the last word of the information unit, /khun-m/ (you), is prominently stressed. Phonologically speaking, (3c) is similar to (3a). However, the choice of lexical word, the literary word /'chvːt-l 'choːm-r/ as opposed to the ordinary word /'suːaj-r/, is used to mark this point of prominence, showing the same restrictiveness as phonologically marked in 3(b).

(3) d   /chan-r. 'phop-h. 'phan-m raʔ-h 'jaː-m.   khon-m.

    <u>'suːaj-r</u>. /./ khɔːŋ-r. <u>khun-m</u> /(I met <u>your beautiful</u> wife.)

In (3d) there are two prominent information points, "beautiful" and "of you (your)". The information is divided into two pieces by means of a pause. The prominent stress is given to the last word /suːaj-r/ (beautiful) in the first information group, and to the last word /khun-m/ (you) in the second information group. The meaning of (3d) is strongly marked and can be translated as, "I met that beautiful wife of yours."

The following schema concludes how information is grouped:

Actual Meaning
(contextualised)   Utterance
         Real Context of Situation
Potential Meaning   ↑
(decontextualised)   Information Unit
         / | \   (I)
        [....(X) (Y) (Z) ....]
(X, Y, Z, are words which are semantically and
syntactically unified and form an information unit or the
linguistic intonation group)
    / | \   (II)
[(X1...'Xn) (Y1....'Yn) (Z1...'Zn)]
(X1.. n, Y1.. n, Z1.. n are syllables which are
phonologically unified and form a word.)

The diagram illustrates that an information unit is composed of a word or a set of words of which the number is indefinite [X, Y, Z..]. These words are semantically and syntactically unified to form an information unit bigger than a word, *i.e.* a phrase, a clause, or a sentence. If a set of these units are semantically unified, they will form a discourse which in its spoken form can be either spoken prose or a conversation. Each word in the information unit is composed of a syllable or a series of accented and unaccented syllables (X1...'Xn) which are phonologically unified to form a word.

The phonetic rhythmical variation is determined by (1) the phonological structure of the component words of the information unit and the underlying syntactic structure of these words (I and II in the diagram), and (2) the focus of the information unit showing the terminal transition of the unit (end focus) either final (no more to come) or non-final (more to come), and the highlighted point of communicative interest (expressive focus) whether contrastive, new, emotive *etc.*

Information units which are of assertive nature, cognitive, non-contrastive, non-corrective, non-emphatic, non-emotional *etc.*, may have a single focus /man-m. pen-m. 'ma:-r/ (it, is, <u>dog</u>), or multiple foci, /'ma:-r. 'kat-l. '<u>mæ:w</u> / (<u>dog</u>, <u>bite</u>, <u>cat</u>). These units usually have one phonological prominence indicating terminal transition realised as a tonic syllable of the tonic word. The tonic word in these cases is always the rightmost word of the information unit. When expressive information is added to the information unit, there are many linguistic mechanisms that speakers may use, *e.g.*, division of the syntactic structure by phonological pause, choice of lexical items, and placement of the phonological prominence or tonic. The following examples will help to exemplify these points.

(4) a /'dæ:ŋ-m. 'tat-l. kraʔ-l 'pro:ŋ-m. <u>ni:-f</u>/
     [Dang cut dress this] (<u>Dang</u> made this dress.)
    [The speaker noticed that the listener was looking at her new dress]

In the context of (4a) where /kraʔ-l 'pro:ŋ-m/ (dress) is given or known, we can say that /dæ:ŋ-m./ (Dang) is new. The syntactic structure of the information unit is SVO. "Dang" is the grammatical, logical, and psychological subject (Hornby 1972). Judging from the pragmatic structure, the prominent point of information is /dæ:ŋ-m./ (Dang), whereas the phonetic prominence falls on the unaccented monosyllabic grammatical word /ni:-f/ (this), indicating end focus.

In the same situation as in (a), the speaker may say:

(4) b /kraʔ-l ·pro:N-m. ni:-f ·dœ:N-m. <u>·tat-l.</u> /
     [dress this Dang cut] (<u>This dress</u>, Dang made it.)

In (4b) the word /kraʔ-l 'pro:ŋ-m/ (dress), although given or known, has been focalised by shifting this known grammatical subject and logical object to the front. "Dress" has become the psychological subject or expressive focus realised by the marked syntactical structure OSV. The phonetic prominence falls on the last word of the information unit /tat-l/ (cut), indicating end focus.

In the same situation as in (a) and (b), the speaker may say:

(4) c /'dæ:ŋ-m. 'tat-l. ca:w-f. kraʔ-l 'pro:ŋ-m. <u>ni:-f</u>/
     [Dang cut PREFIX dress this] (Dang made <u>this dress</u>.)

In (4c) the lexical prefix /ca:w-f/ is found in a large number of compound nouns in Thai with the morphological structure "PREFIX /ca:w-f/ + noun (-animate) = compound noun (animate)", for example, /ca:w-f/+/thuk-h/ (distress) = "complainant", /ca:w-f/ +/sap-h/ (property) = "proprietor", *etc.* The lexical prefix /ca:w-f/ used here is lexically marked, since /kraʔ-l 'pro:ŋ-m./

(dress) is not animate. The speaker has focalised the word "dress" by marking it with a marked lexical prefix. The phonetic prominence still falls on the last word of the information unit /*ni:-f*/ (this), which is phonologically unaccented, indicating end focus.

So far, we have exemplified how end focus and expressive focus in Thai connected speech are phonologically, morphologically, and syntactically realised. There is another system, the system of "Tune" which has been discussed at length in §2.1. The tune system plays an important role to convey end focus and expressive focus in Thai.

In statements with more than one word, a noticeable lowering of pitch is found. Examples (1) and (2) above are from Noss (1972) and Henderson (1949), respectively, and both are sentences composed of words with the same lexical tone, the mid tone.

The pitch of the first mid tone is much higher than the pitch of the last mid tone. The longer the intonation group, the lower the pitch. This phenomenon has been referred to as "Downdrift". There are 3 classes of tunes in Thai. Tune 1 (a wide range fall) and Tune 3 form "the Fall Class" or "the Downdrift". Tune 2 forms "the Rise Class". And Tune 4 forms "the Convolution Class". The tune system determines the pitch configuration of the whole utterance. Utterances with Tune 1 or Tune 3 have a low pretonic as opposed to the high pretonic of Tune 2 and Tune 4. The lexical tone system operates at the word level. It does not influence the overall pitch configuration of the utterance as a whole. However, each lexical tone behaves differently when superimposed by different tunes. Figure 2 below compares the pitch configuration of the sentences superimposed by Tune 2, 3, and 4. The sentence /'phæŋ-m. 'kɤːn-m. ˌpaj-m/ (It is too <u>expensive</u>.) consists of three stressed mid tones, and the last word, which is the tonic, is prominently stressed.

There is a class of words in Thai, the final particles, which command a flexibility of expressions. They do not have inherent lexical tones as other words do but they have interesting phonetic characteristics when occurring in connected speech. These phonetic characteristics have been described in terms of a prosodic complex of tone, quantity (length), and glottal termination (Henderson 1949, Chuenkongchoo 1956). Variation of these prosodic characteristics changes the grammatical and attitudinal meanings of the utterances. However, the prosodic complex postulated as word prosody in these studies should have been postulated as sentence or phrase prosody, since the complex does not affect only the final particle but the whole utterance. Further research on this aspect of intonation in Thai still needs to be done.

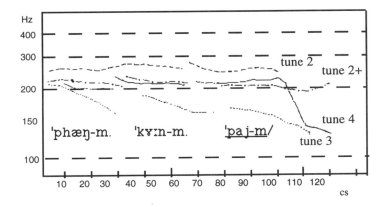

Figure 2. Pitch configuration of the sentence /'phæŋ-m. 'kʋːn-m. 'paj-m/ superimposed with Tunes 2 (tense ending rise), 2+ (lax ending rise), 3 (narrow range fall), and 4 (convolution).

2.5 Stylised intonation

Stylised intonation has been an interest among writers on intonation (Pike 1945, 1948, Chao 1956, Abe 1961, Liberman 1975, Leben 1976, Ladd 1978, Luksaneeyanawin 1983). It has been referred to under different terms, for example, calling or vocative intonation, spoken chant, call contour, and vocative chant.

The term stylised intonation was first introduced by Ladd (1978), whose concept of this system of intonation is not restricted only to stylised or stereotyped forms of speech (calling, chanting, recitation, street cries *etc.*) but is also found in reading pronunciation and conversational speech *etc.* There are two common phonetic characteristics of this intonation system: (1) pitch levelling, and (2) syllable lengthening. When speakers use this phonological process to level and suspend the pitch configuration either in stylised proper or in non-stylised forms of speech, there are some definite semantic elements to be signalled to the listener. Ladd (1978) proposed that the core meaning of stylised intonation is "predictability". In non-stylised forms of speech, this semantic implication is found in situations where speakers want to convey that the message is predictable, routine, known, boring, tiresome, tedious, warning *etc.*

In the study of stylised intonation in Thai (Luksaneeyanawin 1983), it is found that when stylised intonation is superimposed onto speech there are the following common phonetic characteristics: (1) The pitch configuration of the lexical tones is leveled. The three static tones which have a narrow fall or rise in normal speech become level. The dynamic tones which have a wide continuous or delayed fall or rise become a stepping narrow fall or rise. (2) The pitch range of stylised intonation is narrower than normal intonation. The pitch height of the three static tones is very close to each other: higher mid in high tones, mid in mid tones, lower mid in low tones. The dynamic tones have a narrower pitch range. (3) In some extreme cases, such as in chanting, professional callings, and recitation where the meaning of the words is unimportant, the dynamic tones are realised with level pitch. The falling tones are realised with a low level, rising tones with a high level. (4) The extension of the syllable duration is very prominent. (5) The degree of loudness is not prominent, except in street cries and real callings. The following example illustrates stylised intonation in non-stylised forms of speech:

(5)   [The speaker arrives home and finds her child playing with water, making a mess all over the floor.]

/4 '<u>du:-m</u>/   (Look!)

/2 '?aw-m. 'na:m-h. ma:-m. 'len-f. troŋ-m '<u>ni:-h</u>/ (You brought the water here..)

/1 'sok-l ka?-l 'prok-l. paj-m. '<u>mot-l</u>/ (..... it is all a mess.)

/4 'jut-l. 'jut-l. '<u>jut-l</u>/ (Stop, stop, stop!) [The child does not stop...]

/*1 '<u>pho:-m</u> / (Enough.)

/*2 '<u>jaŋ-m</u> / (Not yet?)

/*2 '<u>jaŋ-m</u>. ?i:k-l / (Not listening?)

/*1 'di:aw-r. ca?-l. da:j-f. 'mi:-m. 'khon-m. 'kin-m. kha?-l 'nom-r '<u>pia?-h.</u>
kan-m. maŋ-f. la?-f / (In a minute, someone is going to get a smack... !)

In the acoustic data for this example, the one-word utterances with mid tones superimposed by different Tunes, /4 '<u>du:-m</u>/ (Look!), /*1 '<u>pho:-m</u> / (Enough.), /*2 '<u>jaŋ-m</u> / (Not yet?), are remarkably different. There are 8 intonation groups in this example, all spoken by the same speaker. Stylised intonation (*) is found in the 5th to the 8th group. When the speaker found that the child did not do as she insisted, she started to express herself with a warning tune. "Warning" is stylised in the sense that the speaker expresses that the listener knows what is going to happen (predictable) if he or she does not do as directed. From this last example, we can clearly see that the three systems of pitch fluctuation: tone, tune, and stylised intonation interplay to produce the pitch configuration of the utterances.

3. Comparisons with other systems

The hypothesis on "Intonation Universals" which has interested linguists working on linguistics across languages (Malecot 1974, Bolinger 1978b, Cruttenden 1981) proposes a more abstract level of meanings of intonation. Intonation is looked on as a pitch system of two non-arbitrary signs or ideophones: Falls and Rises. In terms of meanings, Falls convey Finality or

Closedness and Rises convey Non-Finality or Openness. Looking through the past literature on intonation, the classic paper by Beach (1924) mentions three systems of pitch, classified by their functions in speech: (1) the semantic tone or the word tone which is the most arbitrary among the three types and is found only in some languages; the other two types are found in every language, they are (2) the grammatical tone and (3) the emotional tone. The grammatical and the emotional tone discussed by Beach are non-arbitrary and are similar to the system of intonation discussed by contemporary linguists. Beach's discussion on the grammatical function of the pitch system is similar to the discussion on the "discourse function" of intonation (Brazil 1981, Cruttenden 1981). His view of grammatical function is quite different from the notion of Question/Answer grammatical distinction found in earlier British literature and in many recent English textbooks used for pedagogical purposes (Armstrong and Ward 1929, Jones 1918). Beach's view on the function of emotional tone is very similar to our attitudinal function of intonation.

In terms of universality, there is a problem in defining Tune 4 which is found in responses marked with emphasis, anger, strong agreement, belief, and interest. If we postulate only 2 universal tunes as discussed above, we may put this tune under the Falls and discuss its semantic finality. However we should like to propose here the Universal Phonetic Convolution, the combination of Falls and Rises and its Semantic Contrariety, which is a contradiction of finality and non-finality.

Halliday's (1963a,b,c, 1967a) study of British intonation proposed tone 4, a fall-rise, which is discussed in terms of non-finality or containing a "but" about it, and tone 5, a rise-fall, which may be discussed in terms of finality *i.e.* insistence, emphasis, or definiteness. However it is clear that the semantics of tone 4 is different from that of tone 2 and tone 3, found in polar questions, requests, and unfinished statements, and the semantics of tone 5 is different from that of tone 1 with its semantic finality. In both tone 4 and tone 5 there is a contradiction which might be a disagreement between what the speaker believes and what he is informed by or sees from the situation. The contradiction may be within the speaker's mind on the subject being spoken about.

The semantics of emphasis is a problematic one. Why do speakers have to emphasise after all? Emphasis is reported in the literature to show contrastiveness, definiteness, contradiction, anger *etc.* (Coleman 1914, Halliday 1963a,b,c, 1967, Greenberg 1969, Chafe 1976, Enkvist 1980).

Tune 4, postulated here, displays its phonetic convolution, a dynamic pitch movement in the static tone set *i.e.* a rise-fall in the high and the mid tone, and a rise in the low tone. In the dynamic tone set the falling tone is realised with a rise-fall and the rising tone is realised with a fall-rise. It is observed that words with lexical "positive value" such as /di:-m/ (good), /su:aj-r/ (beautiful), /?a?-l 'rɔj-l/ (delicious) are usually taken as sarcastic when uttered with Tune 4, whereas words with lexical "negative value" such as /ra:j-h/ (wicked), /ba:-f/ (mad), /khi:-f re:-l/ (ugly) are usually taken as tenderness and affection of the speaker towards the subject. The study of the complex tunes and their semantic functions across languages needs to be done to verify the hypothesis of The Universality of Phonetic Convolution and the Semantic Contrariety proposed here.

4. Conclusions

The hypothesis of "Intonation Universals" has been discussed at length throughout this chapter. However, it is clearly illustrated that the systems inherent to the words of the language, *i.e.* lexical tones and word accents, which are also realised through the fluctuation of pitch, are not contaminated by the intonation system. The system of tones and accent is primary to the meaning of the word or words in an information unit. The system of intonation adds to these information units the attitudinal and emotional meanings. The stylised system corresponds to the systems of tones and intonations and adds some more meaning to the utterances.

The function of intonation in a language is, undoubtedly, expressive. It adds to the cognitive meaning of the words in the utterance, the attitude and the emotion of the speaker. If speech is not just informative but is also communicative, in order to understand the nature of speech we need to probe into the system of sounds which are used for the expressive and interpersonal functions of speech more deeply. The system of intonation, pause, and tone of voice need to be thoroughly described for a better understanding of this aspect of speech.

The description of the system of Thai intonation in terms of its structure, its phonetic characteristics, and its meanings which is put forward here may provide some answers to the questions in this area of phonetic linguistics. It is hoped that this study will illuminate controversial issues which need exploratory research on this highly sophisticated use of pitch in languages.

22

Intonation in
Vietnamese

ĐỖ THẾ DŨNG, TRẦN THIÊN HƯƠNG
and GEORGES BOULAKIA

1. Background

Vietnamese is the official language spoken by 64 million people living in Vietnam, a country in South-East Asia bordered by China, Laos, Cambodia and the South China Sea.

The linguistic origins of Vietnamese are still controversial; Maspero (1912) considered this language to be related to the Thai family, *i.e.*, Sino-Tibetan tone languages, whereas other linguists, such as Haudricourt (1954a, b), think that it belongs to the Mon-Khmer group of Austroasiatic languages. It is more likely however, as suggested by Vương Lộc (1975), that Vietnamese belongs to a much larger group of languages including the Thai languages and other Austroasiatic languages.

Today Vietnamese is one of the few languages in the region to make use of the latin alphabet, while Khmer, Lao and Thai have kept their traditional writing system. The Vietnamese alphabet was invented by European missionaries in the 17th century. Used for over a century together with Chinese ideograms, which was the writing system of lettered people, it was established as the only way of writing Vietnamese at the beginning of the 20th century and then as the official national system after independence in 1945.

The phonographematic relations are quite simple and there are diacritic signs to indicate the tone of the syllable. The standard orthography corresponds to the Northern variety of Vietnamese which has six lexical tones. Although it is phonemic, the syllabic legacy is maintained as words are transcribed with graphically separate syllables. cf. *Hà Nội*.

1.1 General prosodic characteristics

a. Syllable structure

Vietnamese grammarians and linguists have long considered the syllable in Vietnamese as a fundamental unit with a double structure. On the one hand there is a phonemic skeleton containing a rime with a vocalic nucleus, which can be preceded by a glide and followed by an unreleased stop, a sonorant or a glide; on the other hand there is a "tone", *i.e.* a fundamental frequency variation, spreading over the whole syllable. There are a few constraints: if a syllable ends with an unreleased stop [p, t, k], only the short tones are possible; otherwise in all varieties of Vietnamese, the whole tonal paradigm can occur.

b. The tonal system

From the acoustic point of view a tone is composed of melodic features (register, contour) associated with non-melodic features (intensity, pharyngalisation, laryngealisation...). The number of tones as well as their realisation vary according to dialect. However the written language, which is the same everywhere, follows the traditional representation of the official Northern dialect (in particular that of the capital city Hà Nội) which has become the standard writing system of Vietnamese.

Table 1. *Standard writing system of Vietnamese tones.*

The NGANG tone is also called *Bằng* or *Không dấu.*. The *Sắc* or *Nặng* tones are short.

Tone	Numeric symbol	Keyword
NGANG	1	ma
HUYEN	2	mà
NGA	3	mã
HOI	4	mả
SAC	5	má
NANG	6	mạ

Each tone, which is represented by a diacritic in the written language, is named and described according to the Vietnamese grammatical tradition; the description of the system differs according to contemporary linguists. The Northern variety has received most attention from linguists such as Andreev and Bystrov (1957), Nguyễn Đăng Liêm (1970), Earle (1975), Han and Kim (1974), Đoàn Thiện Thuật (1980), Gordina and Bystrov (1984).

To describe the tonal system on a physical basis most authors have studied tones in isolated syllables where they are likely to be realised as close as possible according to their phonotype. In the Northern system 6 tones can be separated into 2 groups according to register: NGANG, SAC, NGÃ are realised in a higher register while HUYEN, NẠNG, HOI are realised in a lower one. (For example in our data, for female speakers, the mean value of high tones is around 250 Hz whereas that of low tones is around 190 Hz.) For a brief summary of some major differences with other dialects of Vietnamese see §3.1 below.

i. High Tones:

NGANG has an almost flat contour with a slight fall at the end.

SAC, the so-called rising tone, has a slight initial fall followed by a sharp rise in the final two thirds.

NGA also has an overall rising pattern, but interrupted by a glottalisation in the middle; this results in a break in the F_0 curve which then appears to be divided into 3 parts: a short fall, a silence and an abrupt rise.

ii. Low Tones:

HUYEN has a gradual F_0 fall.

NANG has a short fall interrupted by a glottalisation.

HOI is gradually falling then rising in the last third back to the original level.

In terms of distinctive features, Vietnamese tones can be described according to register, contour and glottalisation. Other phonetic features have been mentioned but they are not considered as distinctive:

SAC and NANG are relatively short, and as mentioned above they are the only possible tones occuring on syllables ending with /p,t,k/.

NGA, HOI and SAC are strongly pharyngalised, *etc.*

(c) Tonal range

The tones of a system are generally realised within a well defined F_0 range.

For Gordina and Bystrov, Vietnamese has a range of 2 octaves. In his study of the Saïgon dialect, Gsell (1980) has spoken of a "clearly structured tonal space" consisting of two registers with a fixed bandwidth of approximately 4 semitones each, and separated by an interval of 2 semitones. This is confirmed by the data in Vũ Thanh Phương (1982), Seitz (1986) and Đỗ Thế Dũng (1986) concerning the same dialect, with some individual speaker variation:

The high register is wider than the low register, varying from a 4 semitone range for Seitz's male speaker to 8 semi-tones for one of Đỗ Thế Dũng's female speakers. For all speakers the low register tends to be less wide: for Đỗ Thế Dũng's speakers it varies from 2 to 4 semitones while for Seitz's speaker it is reduced to just one semitone.

Gsell's proposal can be extended to the Northern dialect. But in central dialects the tonal range is reduced: For Vũ Thanh Phương the tones of its so-called "Central Vietnamese" are realised within a 40 Hz range (to be compared with the values he gives for his Northern reference, 128 Hz, and Southern reference, 108 Hz). Seitz's results are comparable; he gives 50 Hz for Huế, 110 Hz for the North and 220 Hz for the South. This reduced tonal range in central varieties of Vietnamese could explain why it is difficult for someone from the North or the South to understand a speaker from the Centre. This gives rise to the common saying "speaking with a level voice" or "speaking with an overall NANG tone" to characterise their way of speaking Vietnamese.

d. Tones in context
In continuous speech, tones seldom reach their target values; they are generally affected by context: stressed *vs.* unstressed syllables; influence of neighbouring tones; tempo... These influences have rarely been studied.

Han and Kim (1974) described tonal variations in bisyllables; there are a few remarks to be found in Hoàng Tuệ and Hoàng Minh (1975), Gordina and Bystrov (1984), Hoàng Cao Cương (1985) and P. Seitz (1986). Đỗ Thế Dũng (1986 and 1989) gave a more detailed account of the relationship between stress and tone.

All authors agree on the absence of tonal neutralisation due to "sandhi" in Vietnamese, a phenomenon which occurs in other tone languages like Chinese and Thai. Tonal variation due to the influence of neighbouring tones can, however, be observed and is described as a type of tonal assimilation or coarticulation. Authors disagree, however, on whether these assimilations are regressive or progressive. Han and Kim find that both exist but they claim that progressive assimilation is predominent; Gordina and Bystrov agree on the existence of both types but insist on the importance of the regressive process. Đỗ Thế Dũng (1986) underlines the importance of progressive assimilation according to the height reached by the tone which precedes it; after a rising tone such as SAC or HOI, any immediately following tone will start one or two quarter tones higher than its normalised target value, and after NANG and HUYEN tones it will start one or two quarter tones lower; this variation is stronger in unstressed positions than in stressed ones; and in spite of this, a relative difference in register and contour is preserved.

e. Stress and Tone
As Vietnamese is a tone language, linguists have rarely been interested in studying "accentuation" or "stress" in Vietnamese. There are a few brief remarks in Jones and Huỳnh SanhThông (1957), Thompson (1965), Nguyễn Đình Hòa (1966), Earle (1975) and Gsell (1980). We know of only 3 somewhat more detailed observations in Hoàng Tuệ and Hoàng Minh (1975), Gordina and Bystrov (1984) and Đỗ Thế Dũng (1986).

According to Hoàng Tuệ and Hoàng Minh and Đỗ Thế Dũng the possible role of "stress" (or "accent") can be pointed to by the study of such minimal pairs as:

(a) Nó lấy xe đạp   đi chơi   (he takes the bicycle to go for a ride)
(b) Nó lấy xe   đạp đi chơi   (he takes a vehicle and goes cycling).

In (a) *đạp* is "stressed" and the first four morphemes make up a phrase ending with the compound word *xe đạp* (bicycle). In (b) the accent is on *xe*, (vehicle) and *đạp* (to cycle) is thus the first, inaccented, part of the following phrase.

Accent marks the end of a phrase or a compound, acquiring thus a distinctive value in indicating different syntactic structures. Accent falls on the last syllable of a phrase unless it is a grammatical morpheme or "clitic". Đỗ Thế Dũng has shown that duration and intensity are the most important parameters for describing stress in Vietnamese. A syllable is longer, by 50 to 100%, in stressed position than in unstressed position whatever the composition of the rime. This usually goes together with a rise in intensity of 10 to 20 %.

Some authors, such as Hoàng Tuệ and Hoàng Minh, or Gsell, consider that the full tonal realisation of accented syllables is one of the "positive marks" of accent. We think that this is a natural consequence of syllable lengthening which allows the tone to reach its target values. We point out that all the descriptions of tones in isolated syllables correspond to those in accented positions. It follows that syllables in unstressed positions are shorter and that there is less time for tonal target values to be reached, particularly in the case of complex movements as in SAC, HOI and NANG. Another consequence is that tones in unstressed syllables are less stable and more subject to contextual variation. In Đỗ Thế Dũng's data, NANG and HOI-NGA tones often lose their initial fall after a low tone and simply become rising in a low register. In the Northern dialect our data show that HOI is just falling, losing its final rise, and that SAC in a high context is just level.

1.2 State of the art and outline of the approach

In a tone language like Vietnamese with 5 or 6 lexical tones which moreover has a system of morphosyntactic markers to express emotions, attitudes, mood and modality (see §2.2 below), it would not be surprising if "intonation" played a lesser role than in languages such as French or English: what is usually conveyed by intonation in many other languages is already marked. This idea was developed by Gordina and Bystrov (1984) following Pechkovskij (1959) (it can also be found in 1968):

The more a language uses morphosyntactic or syntactic means to express mood, modality and emotions, the less it would rely on intonation for the same functions.

This explains why there are very few studies on intonation in Vietnamese. There are a few intuitive remarks in general grammar books, for example: Jones and Huỳnh SanhThông (1957), Hoàng Tuệ and Hoàng Minh (1975).

There are a small number of experimental studies either on interrogative compared to declarative sentences (Trần Thiên Hương (1980), Trần Thiên Hương and Boulakia (1983), Gordina and Bystrov (1984), Hoàng Cao Cương (1985), or on the way attitude and emotion can be conveyed by intonation.

These studies have already given some idea of the role and function of intonation in Vietnamese. The reader should note that the statements about intonation made by grammarians or linguists such as Jones and Huỳnh Sanh Thông, Thompson, Nguyễn Đăng Liêm... are rather intuitive, not based on experimental description, and are in fact directly derived from the analysis of English or French intonation... For example, declarative sentences are said to be "falling" with such descriptive terms as "fading" or "decreasing" (Thompson), "falling" (Nguyễn Đăng Liêm), "normal" or "low pitch" (Jones and Huỳnh SanhThông; whereas interrogative sentences are said to be "rising" (Nguyễn ĐăngLiêm), "sustaining" (Thompson), "higher pitch level 1" (Jones and Huỳnh SanhThông)... Expressive sentences on the other hand are said to have a rising contour with a higher pitch level: "higher pitch level 2 or 3" (Jones and Huỳnh SanhThông), "increasing" (Thompson), "rising-falling" (Nguyễn Đăng Liêm).

Experimental research has in fact shown that the intonation system of Vietnamese is far more complex, bringing in not only prosodic parameters but also taking into account the syllabic structure and the syntactic structure.

According to Gordina and Bystrov, the shorter the sentence, the greater the difference between the intonation patterns.

In their examples:

a   Anh ấy đi sang nước Anh à?   (is he going to England?)
b   Anh ấy đi sang nước Anh.   (he is going to England)
c   Không sách à?   (no books?)
d   Không sách.   (no books)

the difference is greater between the c and d patterns than between a and b, even though in each case a declarative is contrasted with an interrogative.

According to these same authors an interrogative without a morphosyntactic mark has a well differentiated pattern when compared to an interrogative with a marker. In:

e   Không sạch à ?   ([is it] not clean?)
f   Không sạch ?   ([it is] not clean?)
g   Không sạch.   ([it is] not clean.)

the difference between the intonation pattern of g and f is greater than that between g and e.

This fact was also noted in Seitz (1986) and in one of our previous studies. In Trần Thiên Hương and Boulakia (1983) we carried on an experiment to compare the "natural" realisations of declarative *vs.* interrogative short sentences such as *Bao di Vietnam / Bao di Vietnam?* We found that, in fact, while the tonal configuration is maintained, the whole sentence, or part of it, is uttered on a higher pitch. But, there appears to be an important socio-phonetic phenomenon. This work was carried out in France. All the speakers pointed out that these questions were intuitively not very natural, or at least that they could be accepted only as echo-questions, simple or exclamative.

Moreover, it is important to point out that while bilingual speakers, living in France for many years, had no difficulty in producing and differentiating the sentences, speakers who had just arrived in Paris and had not mastered the French language, practically refused to read such interrogative sentences. Either they spontaneously added a final particle, *à*, or they pronounced them in a very emphatic, exclamatory way, or on the contrary like the declarative counterparts. This was confirmed by auditory tests: people just arrived from Hanoi refused sometimes to go through the test because they said that such sentences didn't exist! Those that eventually did the test interpreted the natural "simple" interrogative as declarative (or perhaps exclamatory).

With synthetic speech (LPC),and varying the F_0 parameter, the result was very similar: items going out of the usual "tonal space" (Gsell) were interpreted as exclamative questions, or exclamative sentences. These results led us to say that there is no such thing as (syntactic) interrogative intonation in Vietnamese, except for echo-questions in some situations and with all the reserves we made (in a way a confirmation of what D.B. Fry had said), and the prosodic variations are due to what is usually called expressive intonation and are not related to the morphosyntactic structure for a given tonal sequence.

We may thus consider four types of sentences:

a. Declarative sentences
A description of a "neutral" declarative contour remains controversial. Most authors describe a F_0 declination which is held to be the essential feature of the declarative sentence. However, according to Gordina and Bystrov and Hoàng Cao Cương (1986) this progressive declination is not restricted to the declarative sentence as it also occurs on interrogatives and imperatives. The significant difference between sentence types would relate to average register which, according to most authors, including Jones and Huỳnh SanhThông, is situated in the middle of the range for declaratives and towards the periphery for other sentence types. Gordina and Bystrov pointed out that declaratives are also characterised by the way the low tones HUYEN, HOI and NANG, reach the lowest part of their range.

b. Interrogative sentences

Nearly all authors agree that interrogatives without lexico-syntactic markers have globally a higher register. Conclusions are less clear for interrogatives with "Q-markers". With Trần Thiên Hương (1980) we found that they were similar to declaratives whereas Seitz found that only "open questions" have a declarative F_0 pattern where the interrogative with *Không* would have a rising contour.

For Gordina and Bystrov and Hoàng Cao Cương, interrogative sentences are characterised by:
- higher mid register compared to declaratives (from a second to a fifth, rarely going beyond a fourth);
- greater high tone movement: the rising slope of NGA and HOI is more abrupt and the SAC tone is situated on a higher register. (Trần Thiên Hương has observed that in the Northern dialect HOI only has a rising slope in interrogatives without Q-markers).

c. Attitude conveying sentences

There is little data on this type of sentence. We know of only one phonetic study. LêThị Xuyến (1989) set out to establish whether 6 different attitudinal sentence types (statement, irony, exasperation, anger, sadness and admiration) were differentiated on the prosodic level. Results of her experiments showed that only irony, anger and statement were identified above chance level (75%, 52.5%, 67.5% respectively). According to her the "neutral" declarative is characterised by a low register and a moderate tempo; "irony" has a higher register, a larger tone movement and a slower tempo resulting in increased sentence length; whereas "anger" is conveyed by a speeding up of tempo, greater and more abrupt pitch movement, shortening of the utterance and an increase in the overall intensity.

d. Other types of sentences

Hoàng Cao Cương (1985) has observed that expressive declaratives with the "insistance" marker *Cứ* before the predicate, usually have a higher mid-register than the "neutral" declaratives, whereas imperatives are similar to interrogatives.

Seitz, referring to the work by Trần Phương Mai (1967), claimed that emphatic utterances often have a wider F_0 range than usual with the dynamic tones having sharper movements.

The research described in this chapter is based on a corpus made of three complementary subparts:

i. a set of 6 declarative sentences, with the same simple syntactic structures made of six syllables bearing the same tone, each taken from the 6 tone paradigm. In each of these sentences we then substituted the final tone of one of the other members of the paradigm, giving 36 different sentences. These sentences were then transformed into interrogatives and imperatives with morphosyntactic markers.

ii. a series of 6 long sentences, showing sequences of the same tone.

iii. four expressive dialogues in a narrative context.

The texts were read in recording room conditions by speakers coming from different regions of Vietnam; the results reported in this chapter will, however, be restricted to the Hanoï dialect.

The analysis was carried out in the Laboratoire de Phonétique de l'Université de Paris 7, using the Pitch Analyser designed by Ph.Martin together with E. Keller's program Signalyze running on Macintosh SE and II microcomputers.

Because of the difficulties these pitch analysers have with glottalised speech, we concentrated on the 4 non-glottalised tones, as in:

> NGANG: CôHoa đi thăm ông Tiên
> (Miss Hoa is going to visit Mister Tiên)
>
> HUYEN: Bà Hòa tìm nhà bà Điền .
> (Mrs Hòa is looking for Mrs Điền's house)
>
> SAC: Bé Thúy ngó thấy chú Tiên.
> (Little Thuy saw uncle Tiên)
>
> HOI: Tổ trưởng hỏi tuổi của Điền.
> (The leader of the group is asking Dien his age.)

2. Description of the intonation patterns

A description of intonation patterns in Vietnamese has to take into account the place of accent in the sentence since the pattern of certain tones is considerably modified in unstressed position. For example the fall-rise tone HOI is always realised as a simple fall on unstressed syllables, and only for certain speakers is it fall-rising in accented position (for others it remains falling).

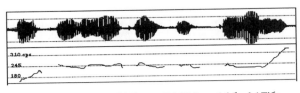

Figure 1. Declarative sentence with the SAC tone. *Bé Thúy ngó thấy chú Tiên.*

In accented position the two fall-rising tones NGA and SAC reach their target values with a sharp final rise, whereas in unaccented position SAC (cf. figure 1) remains high level or high falling (occasionally with a slight final rise), and NGA may be simply high fall-rising with no trace of glottalisation.

If we consider the overall movement of the fundamental frequency on a sentence in which the last syllable bears one of these 3 lexically rising tones, the final contour is of course rising. This would lead us to conclude that there are for example two types of declarative intonation patterns, rising in this case and falling in all others. A unified analysis is possible if we consider other positions as significant for intonation patterns. So as to eliminate the effect of accentuation on tone realisation, we took into account both the mean F_0 value for each tone in a syllable and the mean F_0 value of the first half of the syllable. For this we arbitrarily cut each tone into two equal parts and noted the mean F_0 for each part. This agrees with the hypothesis put forward by Hoàng Cao Cương (1985) and Đỗ Thế Dũng (1986) according to which it is the first part of a tone which contains the cues for the intonation of a sentence.

2.1 Intonation pattern of so-called neutral declarative sentences

In this study we analysed the fundamental frequency pattern of 6 declarative sentences made up of 6 syllables each having the same tone differing from one sentence to the other. (These sentences sound of course unnatural as it is unusual to find such sequences of identical tones in spontaneous speech.)

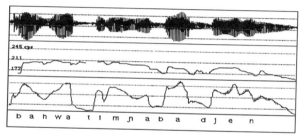

Figure 2. Declarative sentence with the HUYEN tone. *Bà Hòa tìm nhà bà Điền.*

At first sight it seems that only the sentences with the HUYEN or HOI tones have a clearly defined declination line. In other cases, the F_0 of the sentence reaches a first peak then begins to fall gently to the penultimate syllable when it rises slightly at the end of the sentence under the effect of the sentence accent.

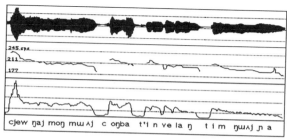

Figure 3. General F_0 declination line in long sentence with the HUYEN tone: *Chiều ngày mồng mười, chồng bà Thìn về làng tìm người nhà.*

Table 2 shows the average fundamental frequency value of tones in neutral (or declarative) sentences.

Table 2. *Mean F_0 (in Hz) of tones in declarative sentences.*

TONE	SYLLABLE					
	1	2	3	4	5	6
NGANG	255	268	250	247	240	249
HUYEN	202	204	207	200	189	184
SAC	204	244	253	249	245	251
HOI	210	184	162	173	153	161

When however we examine the sequence of mean F_0 values measured on the first half of the tones, the relative values are in fact slightly falling to rise at the end, except for the NGANG tone which has a slightly rising F_0 line.

Table 3. *Mean F_0 (in Hz) of the first half of tones in declarative sentences*

TONE	SYLLABLE					
	1	2	3	4	5	6
NGANG	254	268	246	257	242	254
HUYEN	197	207	211	201	191	191
SAC	192	244	251	254	250	238
HOI	214	193	163	180	155	156

As the NGANG tone has to be distinguished from the HUYEN tone (lexically high-level *vs.* high falling) the final rising contour is not surprising. If it followed the mean overall declination line, it would begin at a fairly low level and would therefore be perceived as a HUYEN tone. But even with this final rise, when we take into account the mean F_0 value of syllables 2, 4, 6 (those in "strong" position in the sentence) a gradual declination becomes apparent.

In conclusion we can say that the neutral declarative sentence in Vietnamese is typified by a general F_0 declination line, which becomes more evident the longer the sentence is.

2.2 Modality and attitudes

In Vietnamese there are two possible ways of expressing modality, mood or attitude, the first only using prosodic features, and the second using lexico-syntactic markers, possibly combined with prosodic features. In the first case, as the pragmatic information relies entirely on prosodic structure, it has to be clearly marked; in the second case, as intonation becomes redundant, it is interesting to see if it can still play a role in characterising the pragmatic type.

Intonation being a relative movement between lexical tones in Vietnamese an intonation pattern only develops over a certain utterance-length. It is only in this situation that it would be possible to find phonosyntactic markers indicating the dependency relation between syntactic elements.

Tones cannot be analysed without taking into account the different intonation patterns in which they can occur, their possible relation to accent, and their reaction to their prosodic environment.

a. Modality, attitude and morphosyntactic structures.

The Vietnamese language has a system of syntactic markers which occur mostly at the end (occasionally at the beginning) of a declarative sentence; they are used to express modal and attitudinal meanings.

For example, from a declarative sentence

  Trời mưa.   (it is raining)

we may obtain a Yes-No Question by adding *không*:

  Trời mưa không?   (is it raining?)

With another morpheme: *à* we obtain a question expressing the speaker's surprise:

  Trời mưa à?   (is it raining?!?)

The morphosyntactic elements can be put into three classes according to their semantic value; question, imperative and attitudinal markers.

i. *Question markers.*

Question marking in Vietnamese has been the subject of several studies.(cf. Thompson (1964), Trần Thiên Hương (1980)).

Some controversies remain about the classification of interrogative markers. It seems, however, reasonable to distinguish two types of question.

"True" Yes-No Questions use the following markers:

Không (and its "strong" variant *có không*) expresses a question on the predicative relation itself. (cf. ex.(1) in §1.2. above).

Chưa (and its "strong" variant *đã ... chưa*) has an aspectual value:
  Trời mưa chưa ?   (has it rained (up to now)).

Hay gives an explicit alternative choice:
  Trời mưa hay trời nắng?   (is it raining or sunny?)

Open Questions use indefinite "words" in the same way as "Wh-markers": *A i* (any = who?); *Bao giờ* (anytime = when?); *Bao lâu* (any time period = for how long?); *Bao nhiêu* (any quantity = how many?); *Bao xa* (any distance = how far?); *Đâu* (any place = where?) and its compound *ở đâu* (to be in any place = to be where?); *Gì* (anything = what?); *Mấy* (how many?); *Nào* (anything = which or what?); *Sao* (any reason = why?) and its compounds *Tại sao* and *Vì sao*, meaning "why?" when at the beginning of a sentence, and meaning "how?" when at the end of a sentence or in the compound "*Làm sao*".

All the authors cited have also mentioned a third type of question called "biased questions" (suggesting an expected answer) which are associated with the expression of an attitude. They are syntactically marked with the final morphemes *A*, *U'* (surprise), *Chứ* (logical evidence), *Hả, Hử, Hở* (insisting and astonishment), *Nhé* (supposition, suggestion).

There are arguments for considering that these markers do not have the same syntactic properties as the other markers that are used to obtain alternative and open questions: the first are compatible with negation whereas the latter are not.

From a semantic and pragmatic point of view, the interrogative meaning of these markers is a secondary effect which is derived from their attitudinal value. We therefore prefer to class them with attitudinal markers.

ii. Injunction. Injunction is expressed by the presence of *đi* at the end of a declarative structure:

> Trời mưa đi!   (Let it rain)

A weaker injunction is expressed with *Nhé* and a stronger (insisting) is expressed with the compound marker *Hãy ... đi...*

iii. Attitude and emotional markers. In Vietnamese, a final marker can be used to express speaker attitude. Apart from the words mentioned above, LêThị Xuyến (1989) gave the following list:

A (respect), *Đấy* (admiration), *Rồi* (conclusive), *Mà* (insistance), *Sao* (surprise), *Chăng* (doubt), *Hả* (anger), *Nhỉ* (familiarity), *Vậy* (external obligation).

b. Interrogatives
We consider that only questions with morphosyntactic markers express simple interrogative modality in Vietnamese, and that questions with only prosodic markers (Trần Thiên Hương (1980);Gordina and Bystrov (1984)) are always interrogatives expressing surprise or astonishment and cannot be considered a "neutral" interrogative type (Trần Thiên Hương and Boulakia 1983).

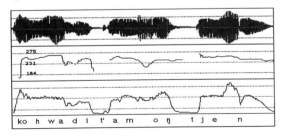

Figure 4. Declarative sentence with the NGANG tone. *CôHoa đi thăm ông Tiên.*

For this reason we will only describe interrogative sentences with morpho-syntactic markers and in particular those ending in *Không*. The one apparent exception is the Yes-No question using "coordinative"_*Hay*.
Examples with *Không*.

As interrogative sentences using a question marker always have the form of a declarative sentence ending with the extra Q-word, there are two possible analyses. The first treats the declarative part of the sentence as independent of the final question marker, the second treats both elements as an inseparable whole.

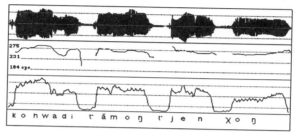

Figure 5. Không question with the NGANG tone. *CôHoa đi thăm ông Tiên không?*

If the first part (with declarative form) of the interrogative sentence ending in *Không* is compared to the corresponding neutral declarative sentence, there is little difference between the two: the F_0 line falls slightly from the peak of the sentence until the penultimate syllable to rise on the last syllable, except for HOI which has a very low average F_0 because it loses its final rise. The interrogative sentence with HUYEN tones, when compared to the corresponding neutral declarative sentence, has a higher F_0 mean value in the end.

The technique of measuring the mean value of the first half of a tone shows that the F_0 pattern is rising at the end of sentences in interrogatives except for the NGANG tone sequence which remains level: we may thus conclude that the intonation pattern of the interrogative sentence in Vietnamese differs from that of the neutral declarative sentence in having a rising contour.

Table 4. *Mean F_0 (in Hz) of declarative and interrogative sentences with Không.*

TONE	DECLARATIVE	INTERROGATIVE
NGANG	248	271
HUYEN	191	211
SAC	241	256
HOI	166	184

The interrogative marker *Không*, with a lexical high-level tone, must in fact be considered part of the interrogative sentence as a whole, and in fact we find that *Không* always has a rising F_0 pattern which is similar to a high rising tone; this is even more obvious in a sentence with SAC tone sequences where

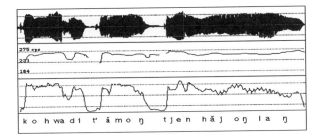

Figure 6. *Hay* question with the NGANG tone. *CôHoa đi thăm ông Tiên hay ông Lang?*

Không has a final rising contour as if it was continuing the general upward movement of the F_0 line.

Most lexico-syntactic question-markers have a high tone such as NGANG or SAC (for example *sao, ai, bao nhiêu, chứ, mấy, nhé....*) and this cannot be entirely arbitrary. This rising F_0 contour in interrogative sentences is confirmed by the analysis of sentences using the coordinative marker *Hay*. All four sentences show an overall similar F_0 movement: a sequence of 2 concave patterns centred on the joining marker *Hay,* as if the two clauses were only marked by an intonation pattern (no Q-marker).

The difference between a neutral declarative sentence and an interrogative is not only to be found in relation to the F_0 slope. A comparison of the mean F_0 value of the sentences shows that interrogatives have a relatively higher register than the corresponding declaratives.

This generally raised level of the mean register of the sentence is due to the higher F_0 value of all the tones in the sentence. In the interrogative sentence, most tones begin on a higher level, and tones which normally have a falling contour such as NGANG and HUYEN often have an almost level pattern, sometimes even rising, particularly when they are unaccented and near to the end. Generally speaking, the tonal movement is less abrupt than in the corresponding "neutral" declarative; this fact was also pointed out in Gordina and Bystrov (1984).

Table 5. *Mean F_0 (in Hz) of tones in interrogatives sentences with Không.*

TONE	\multicolumn{6}{c}{NO. OF SYLLABLES}	Không
	1	*2*	*3*	*4*	*5*	*6*	
NGANG	277	284	274	274	269	271	271
HUYEN	225	214	227	205	197	207	264
SAC	221	261	263	262	259	267	281
HOI	222	219	180	175	162	157	220

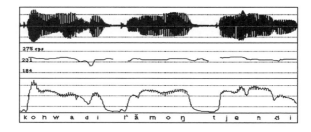

Figure 7. Imperative sentence with the NGANG tone. *Cô Hoa đi thăm ông Tiên. đi!*

Interrogative sentences in Vietnamese have faster tempo than the equivalent declaratives.

To summarise we may say that an interrogative sentence, whether with a question marker or not, is characterised by a rising F_0 pattern, with a higher average register and an insistance on the high components of tones (more abrupt rise and greater intensity) associated with a faster tempo.

c. Imperative sentences

We analysed two types of imperative sentences: on the one hand imperative sentences marked by a final modal morpheme *đi,* and on the other hand "emphatic" imperatives which have an additional emphatic adverb *cứ* just before the verb; we should mention that the imperative sentence generally has the same structure as the interrogative, *i.e.* a basic declarative structure with an additional final modal marker but which in this case is an imperative marker. There are also sentences without imperative markers such as *Đi!* (let's go) or *Đứng lên!* (get up) in which the intonation pattern ought to be particularly distinctive but we have not yet studied these systematically.

On the whole the overall movement of the fundamental frequency of the imperative sentences with the marker *đi* does not differ very much from interrogatives with the marker *không*: the F_0, after having reached the peak of the sentence, gradually falls before rising towards the end of the sentence; this rising movement of course continues with the rising NGANG tone of the marker *đi.*

Table 6. *Mean F_0 (in Hz) of tones in imperative sentences with Đi.*

TONE	NO. OF SYLLABLES						Đi
	1	*2*	*3*	*4*	*5*	*6*	
NGANG	242	244	236	239	239	245	250
HUYEN	203	205	211	206	198	214	238
SAC	231	269	272	275	265	269	290
HOI	191	179	155	161	144	146	182

The F_0 of the imperative part in the long sentence with the NGANG tone sequence has the same pattern. The intonation patterns of these imperative sentences (as in the interrogatives) with a high tone sequence is almost level; the difference between the main peak and the penultimate syllable of the "declarative" part is rarely more than three quarter tones. The emphatic imperatives which occur in our corpus always have a much higher medium register than the *đi*-imperatives, in particular the part which follows the emphatic adverb *Cứ.*

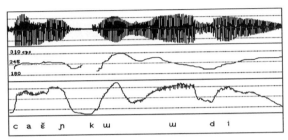

Figure 8. Emphatic imperative sentence with the adverb *cứ.*

It should be noted that in all these sentences low tones such as HUYEN (in *ừ* and *vào*) or NANG (in *mụ*) behave as if assimilated by the intonation context and almost become high tones.

d. Attitudinal and expressive sentences

i. "Logical" evidence. In the third part of our corpus there are a certain number of sentences which seem to express "questioning" ("doubting"). These are mainly sentences with an interrogative marker such as *Thế nào, Sao, Nào, Bao giờ, Đâu.* These "questions" are in fact rhetorical questions either doubting or asserting a logical evidence. Questioning and stating a logical evidence belong to the same semantic category: the first being an implicit negation and the second the assertion of an undeniable truth; it would therefore not be surprising if these sentences had the same F_0 pattern.

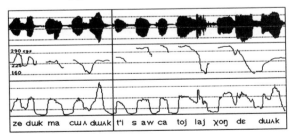

Figure 9. "Logical" evidence sentence *Dê được mà chúa được thì sao cha tôi lại không đề được?* (If a billygoat can do it, why not your father?)

Đỗ Thế Dũng, Trần Thiên Hương and Georges Boulakia

In these sentences, the overall F_0 pattern is higher than in "neutral" interrogative sentences. This higher mean register results from the combination of two phenomena: the rise of F_0 with the high tones NGANG or SAC which are realised within a 250 to 330 Hz range, instead of a 230 to 280 Hz range in the case of interrogatives; and the relatively high initial part of low tones such as HUYEN, NANG or HOI, which start from between 230 to 250 Hz whereas in other sentence types this level is lower than 220 Hz. The stronger upward movement in the high components of tones with interrogatives, mentioned by Gordina and Bystrov, seem to be more pronounced here: levelling out of the NGANG tone in an extra high register; a very abrupt rise of the SAC tones; modification of the contour of certain tones in stressed position, for example the short low tone in *được* which becomes low-rising whereas in other contexts, this tone is low-falling with an abrupt fall down to 160 Hz; or the HUYEN tone in *giờ* which becomes a fall-rise.

The overall movement of the F_0 in these sentences is also characterised by a clause-final raising. If we observe the F_0 in syllables in the final intonation group of each clause, we can notice that it is always rising.

These attitudinally modulated sentences are typified by increased length of their final syllable. Thus the syllable *Được* is 21cs long in one example, and 25cs in another, whereas in other sentence types, this syllable is just 10 to 15cs long.

In conclusion we can say that the intonation pattern of an utterance expressing some logical evidence in Vietnamese is characterised in part by a rising contour but above all by an extra-high register, an exaggeration of the tones and a slower tempo.

ii. Anger. There does not appear to be a morphosyntactic marker for anger. The morpheme *Hả* mentioned by LêThị Xuyến in fact expresses intense surprise which can convey an element of anger. In our corpus all the utterances which express this attitude are either interrogative and imperative with or without morphosyntactic markers, or declarative without markers which indicate intense irritation.

Anger is expressed by a very high register in which high components are particularly well marked. In the following question:

Anh là ai ?   (who are you?)

made up of a sequence NGANG-HUYEN-NGANG, F_0 begins at a fairly high level (269 Hz), rises up to 285 Hz, falls back to 240 Hz on the HUYEN tone, then begins an extremely sharp rise reaching 330 Hz, falling down to 233 Hz.

In other examples the same phenomenon appears. F_0 rises rapidly as we reach the end of the sentence. This F_0 rise always goes together with an increased intensity.

412

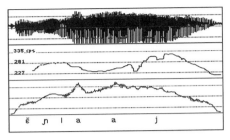

Figure 10. Expression of anger. *Anh là ai ?* (Who are you?).

The F_0 pattern of tones in these sentences is similar to the pattern in sentences expressing logical evidence with a few differences however:
- The level reached by high tones in stressed position is often higher (above 300 Hz);
- Syllables are generally shorter.

Anger can be expressed in Vietnamese on the prosodic level, by an overall raising of the average F_0 value in the sentence. Here, all high tones are well marked with a very high F_0 and the target contour clearly attained: SAC always has here a very abrupt rising contour whereas in other types of sentence it can be level or even falling; the low tones begin at a higher level even though they keep their final fall, reaching their usual level in stressed position. The result of these two phenomena is that tonal range becomes particularly wide. In anger there is also a shortening of syllable length which in our data is in average 170 ms, as against 200 ms for other sentences. At the same time there is a gradual increase of intensity up to the end.

From the study we made we can make a few hypotheses about the way intonation functions in a tone language such as Vietnamese.

The different sentence types are differentiated more by their average register than by their overall intonation pattern. There is a three-level relative scale: declaratives have a mid register, interrogatives and imperatives have a high register whereas the "attitudinal", "expressive" sentences have an extra-high register.

Tones are modified in each type of utterance. In interrogatives and imperatives the high tones are more strongly marked than are the low tones as is the case in "expressive" utterances; in these, however, the low and falling tones do not lose their falling characteristics which gives a wider range to the tone system.

Other parameters such as syllable length and intensity also play a role in the differentiation of these sentence types. Anger for example is marked by a fast tempo whereas "doubting" is much slower.

Intensity is reduced in interrogatives when compared to expressive utterances.

2.3 Focus and its contextual effect

Focalisation in Vietnamese is realised by a strong increase in intensity of the stressed syllable; this goes together with a strong pitch rise as in:

Chỉ ba tiếng trống là ta đã vẽ xong một con vật
(I can draw an animal in the time you need to make three drum rolls)

or as in figure 11:

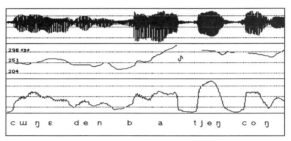

Figure 11. *Chứ nghe đến ba tiếng trống...* (If you need up to three drum rolls...)

In these examples the morpheme *ba* with a NGANG tone has a rising melody which is similar to the one of the SAC tone whereas in other contexts the same syllable has a fairly level contour with a less high register. In another example, the HUYEN tone is falling in the beginning then rises abruptly at the end (250–220–280 Hz).

2.4 Sentence structuring

A sentence in Vietnamese is generally broken up into several intonation groups with patterns differing according to the type of tones which compose the group, or the position of the group in the sentence. In a sequence of high tones the sentence begins on a relatively low level, rising to a high level at the end. With sequences of low tones, the beginning of the group is often higher than the end. When several groups follow each other within the same intonation pattern, however, "downdrift" or "updrift" (which Seitz (1986) calls "resetting") occurs; this consists in lowering the level of a high tone (particularly SAC) or raising a low tone (in particular HUYEN) to avoid going beyond your speaking voice range.

In the case of a declarative sentence, there can be a secondary intonation contour which can be called "major continuation", characterised by raising the F_0 value of the final syllable of a clause as in the following example where the NGANG tone in the middle of the sentence is higher than the NGANG tone at the end of the sentence.

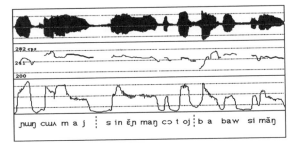

Figure 12. NGANG sentence with 3 intonation sub-contours. *Nhưng trưa mai, xin anh mang cho tôi ba bao xi măng.*

3. Comparisons with other dialects

The dialect described in this chapter is that of the North. There has been less research into the tonal system of the Southern variety; we can mention the work of Thompson (1959), Gordina and Bystrov (1964), Meillon (1967), Gsell (1979) and Đỗ Thế Dũng (1986).

Linguists have paid little attention to the tonal system of the central varieties, possibly because of the range of their variation; there are a few remarks in Maspero (1912) and Gordina and Bystrov (1984), but within a pan-lectal optic, Vũ Thanh Phương (1982) and Seitz (1986) gave more systematic descriptions.

The Southern variety has a 5 tone system where HOI and NGA, the two "fall-rise" are not differentiated. We still can encounter the same tonal register differentiation. NGANG and SAC are high and similar to their Northern counterparts. HUYEN and NANG are low, but NANG is very different from its Northern counterpart being fall-rising with no final glottalisation (Gordina and Bystrov mentioned the presence of a strong laryngealisation whereas for Seitz it is weak and for other authors it is not present). HOI-NGA begins in the low register, falling slightly, then rising rapidly in the last two thirds of its realisation reaching the high register to a level between that of SAC and NGANG; it is unusually associated with a noticeable pharyngalisation. These tones have roughly the same duration probably because of the absence of glottalisation in the system.

A description which takes the traditional basis of one "Central Vietnamese" dialect will encounter difficulties because of the great diversity of dialects covered by this label. The tones of the NghệTĩnh dialect (a Northern province of the central region) are very different from those of Quảng Nam (a province situated in the South of the region). This is why there is little agreement between the conclusions reached by linguists working on so-called "Central Vietnamese". Vũ Thanh Phương's description (1982) for example, could be considered methodologically unsound as it is based on data recorded from different parts of the central region (4 speakers from NghệTĩnh, 12 from Bình Trị Thiên). Paradoxically, Seitz's description (1983) seems more plausible as it is based on only one speaker from Huế.

According to Seitz there are 5 tones in the Huế dialect which are described in terms of 3 registers:

High:	with a level contour:	NGANG
	with laryngealisation:	SAC
Middle:	with a level contour:	HUYEN
	with laryngealisation:	HOI-NGA
Low:	with a level contour:	NANG

This description is very close to that of Maspero (cf. table 2), except that here SAC is not laryngealised and NGA and NGANG are not differentiated. For a detailed description of tones in different dialects according to several authors cf. Gordina and Bystrov (1984).

4. Conclusion

In this chapter we have given an overview of intonation in Vietnamese summing up work on the subject. A critical study of previous authors, including ourselves, has allowed us to define a research paradigm. The necessity of testing different hypotheses makes it necessary to include rather artificial data in the tests, for example reading sequences of identical tones. It is an essential step in our research project before we can go to more "natural" speech which directs us to probable significant phenomena to look for in our future study of spontaneous speech.

Note

We should like to thank A. Hind (Université de Paris 7) for his help with the English version of this text.

23

Intonation in
Beijing Chinese

PAUL KRATOCHVIL

[**Note**: *Like Dwight Bolinger's chapter on American English (chapter two),
Paul Kratochvil's chapter on Beijing Chinese does not follow the outline used in
the other chapters since the author felt that this framework was incompatible
with his strictly empirical approach.* The editors.]

Beijing dialect

Beijing dialect (BD), spoken natively in the capital of the People's Republic of
China and vicinity, is the most prestigious dialect of modern Chinese and the
basis for Modern Standard Chinese (MSC) or *Pŭtōnghuà* (Common Language),
the standard form of Chinese as it has been developed in the PRC since 1949.
This standard is similar to but not in all respects identical with the standards of
Chinese of an earlier period or those which have been developed elsewhere, such
as *Guóyŭ* (National Language), and also the notional world-wide lingua franca of
educated Chinese called Mandarin. For a general description of BD and details on
its relationship to other dialects and standards of Chinese see Kratochvil (1968)
and Norman (1988).

What is said about BD here may apply to MSC and, to some extent, also to
other modern Chinese standards, but it should not be assumed that such
application is possible without risk. Neither should it be assumed that
observations of the normal speech style of BD on which the present comments
are founded must be relevant to isolated citation forms and other forms of edited

speech which are the frame of reference for most existing statements concerning Chinese prosody.

The data

This brief description refers to the normal (that is, spontaneous and unedited) speech style of BD, as reflected in an informal monologue of a native female speaker of this dialect. The speaker, an extrovert and former stage performer who was in her late twenties at the time of recording the monologue, was presented with a large list of BD words and asked to give her views, without any rehearsal, on the meaning and use of the individual words. She was given complete freedom to deviate from her task by telling stories or anecdotes, if she felt that this would demonstrate usage better than a dry explanation. A sample of the monologue consisting of 208 breath groups and containing 1390 syllables altogether was analysed by hand from spectrograms prepared on a 7029–A Kay Sona-graph using analytical procedures presented in Kratochvil (1987a). This sample will be referred to as the GMZ corpus (after the initials of the informant's name). A close copy of the GMZ corpus made by a different female speaker of BD as edited speech in laboratory conditions was prepared later by recording the laryngeal voice output (using the Fourcin laryngograph) simultaneously with the oral-nasal voice output, and this copy was processed by the automatic analytical facility developed in the laboratory of the Institute of Phonetics of the CNRS in Aix-en-Provence.[1] Results obtained from the analysis of the copy served for observing the effect of supralaryngeal resonance on prosodic features, while the original GMZ corpus data reflecting only the oral-nasal voice output were used for reaching quantitatively based generalisations concerning the prosodic features.

Each syllable of the GMZ corpus was treated as a carrier of the segment of the laryngeal voice output coinciding with its tone domain as defined in Howie (1974). The segment was observed in the terms of the three dimensions of the laryngeal voice: duration (T), fundamental frequency (F_0), and amplitude (A). Values were measured in the latter two dimensions at six equally distanced points within each segment, the first and the last points being at the limits of the segment, and the distance between any two points representing 20% of the segment's duration. The tone domain of each syllable, which was understood as carrying the entire part of the prosodic feature complex delimited by the syllable within the given breath group, was thus described by thirteen values: the six F_0 values ($F_0 1 - F_0 6$), the six A values ($A1 - A6$), and the duration value T.

The 1390 thirteen-value strings were then divided into five separate files, one for each group of syllables characterised by one of the four tones of BD, and one for atonic syllables. The division of the syllables in the GMZ corpus into the five files was at first hypothetical, based on the nominal tonal properties of the morphemes represented by the syllables, as given in the semi-normative dictionary of MSC *Xiàndài Hànyǔ cídiǎn* (Dictionary of modern Chinese), Beijing 1977. Reclassification in a small number of cases, due to stylistic, dialectal, and idiolectal deviations from MSC norm, was carried out later when it became possible to test the hypothesis statistically. Two sets of the five files were stored separately, one in the Cambridge University IBM 370/165 mainframe computer, and one on two microcomputers, a Sharp MZ-80B at first, and a Beltron 386 later. Various statistical procedures were then applied in the course of the analysis of the data. Apart from the normal descriptive procedures based on mean value and standard deviation calculations (applied mainly on the microcomputers), three relatively more sophisticated devices were made extensive use of in particular. The first was the discriminant analysis program contained in the SPSS package, as described in the *SPSS(X) user's guide* (1983), which was applied on the mainframe computer and used for classifying or reclassifying data of uncertain affiliation in relation to established classes, on the basis of distinctive configurations of values. The second was a curve fit program used for examining the nature of the relationship between groups of data, which was a modified version of the polynomial analysis program in Lee and Lee (1982). The third was a simple expert system program based on Bayesian inference owing much to various passages in Forsyth (1984), which was applied to the investigation of possible factors involved in observed processes. Both the curve fit program and the expert system program were written for the microcomputers. With the exception of references to other sources, all the statements on the prosodic features of BD made in the following sections of this chapter were based on the results of the analysis of the GMZ corpus carried out with the hardware and software specified above.

Syllable features: tone

Within the complex of features reflected in the prosodic shape of a BD breath group (the prosodic complex), the smallest distinctive configuration coincides with the syllable. This configuration, traditionally referred to as the tone, is primary in the sense that larger configurations up to and including the prosodic complex itself are specific modifications of a string of one or more tones, and that the larger configurations can be predicted given the string and the modifications, whereas they cannot be predicted from the modifications alone. The tone is a configuration because it is polydimensional: as the product of a complex laryngeal gesture, it can be described fully in acoustic terms only by referring to the relationship between all the dimensions of the laryngeal voice, that is, the respective variation of F_0 and A over varying T. It has been demonstrated on experimentally based evidence, such as in Coster and Kratochvil (1984), and in Rose (1984), that A variations in Chinese tones cannot be explained as functions of F_0 variations, and that A variations are used as important cues in tone identification. Because of this and the primariness of tones in the BD prosodic complex, the hypothetical view of F_0 as the sole acoustic dimension of prosodic features, which is still held widely in phonetic research, is no longer tenable for BD.

There are five types of syllables in BD determined by tone. Four of these constitute tonal syllables whose prosodic configurations are traditionally called Tone 1 – 4 or referred to by such labels as **high [level]** (Tone 1), **[mid] rising** (Tone 2), **low [falling-rising]** (Tone 3), and **[high] falling** (Tone 4), which are based on the shape of their pitch curves. The shape of the pitch curves of tones is also reflected in the symbols employed by some phonemic transcriptions (*e.g. mā, má, mǎ,* and *mà* in the Pinyin transcription which has acquired normative status in PRC) and by other devices, such as the so-called tone letters originally designed for modern Chinese by Y.R. Chao, see Chao (1920), but now commonly used in discussions of other tonal languages as well. The fifth type of BD syllables (atonic, also known as "light tone" or "neutral tone" syllables, in the case of which most phonemic transcriptions give no tone symbol, *e.g. ma* in Pinyin) is characterised by the lack of a distinctive prosodic configuration. Since tone or the lack of it is an immediate constituent of a morpheme in BD, segmentally identical (in the phonological sense) syllables belonging to different types determined by tone represent different morphemes (*e.g. mā* (mother), *má* (to be numb), *mǎ* (horse), *mà* (to curse), and *ma* [sentence-final question marker]).

As an illustration of the general acoustic properties of the five types, the mean F_0, A, and T values, together with the corresponding standard deviations in round brackets, of the respective groups of syllables in the GMZ corpus are presented in table 1. It will be noted that Tone 3 is exceptional in that its F_0 contour is characterised by a trough rather than a peak, and that Tones 1–4 differ from each other mainly by the position and concentration of the peak (or trough) in both F_0 and A. In the case of Tone 0 the mean F_0 and A values are of little significance, since the prosodic configuration of these syllables is wholly determined by the overall modification of the syllabic strings containing them. As far as T is concerned, atonic syllables (Tone 0) can be seen to be rather shorter than tonal syllables. The differences in T of tonal syllables are not significant for tone, as they are largely accounted for by the proportion of stressed syllables (usually longer than unstressed syllables, as will be shown further) in the given group. It thus appears that the considerable differences which have been observed in the duration characteristics of isolated citation form BD tones, especially in Howie (1976), cannot be said to exist in normal BD speech.

Chinese

Table 1. Acoustic characteristics of the five syllable types in BD.

	Tone 1	Tone 2	Tone 3	Tone 4	Tone 5
Total	244	228	283	463	172
F_01	240(66.25)	215(59.18)	217(55.21)	263(81.07)	213(63.88)
F_02	236(66.63)	211(62.01)	203(53.35)	257(75.14)	212(62.73)
F_03	233(67.94)	214(66.51)	192(54.19)	247(70.80)	210(64.22)
F_04	231(68.93)	224(71.20)	188(55.41)	235(67.25)	208(65.26)
F_05	229(68.03)	235(76.16)	187(56.16)	223(64.55)	206(65.20)
F_06	225(65.40)	237(76.92)	188(56.64)	214(62.56)	204(62.81)
A1	75(33.47)	74(34.06)	76(38.68)	86(37.08)	92(40.14)
A2	110(42.23)	106(38.97)	106(41.02)	122(41.75)	116(39.61)
A3	115(40.78)	112(37.76)	106(40.66)	130(41.08)	124(38.15)
A4	112(40.49)	114(39.52)	101(40.24)	127(38.79)	121(37.07)
A5	103(38.82)	109(39.86)	95(40.20)	114(36.45)	107(34.14)
A6	81(37.09)	82(29.97)	77(36.77)	84(31.11)	83(30.94)
T	133(59.49)	138(66.04)	129(65.36)	119(64.68)	101(56.14)

F_0 values are given in Hz, A values in dB, and T values in msec. Unbracketed numbers represent mean values, standard deviations are given in brackets next to the respective mean values.

Table 1 obviously does not reflect any possible special relationships between acoustic properties and phonetically, phonologically or otherwise linguistically definable subgroups of syllables within the tonal groups. In the course of analysing the GMZ corpus it was observed that hardly any relationship between T and segmental structure of the kind which had been reported in relation to citation forms, *e.g.* again in Howie (1976), could be established for normal BD speech. Atonic syllables which, unlike tonal syllables, are mostly monophthongal are an exception but it is probable in their case that the monophthongal tendency is the consequence of shortened duration rather than the cause of it. However, segmental structure, or rather the respective variations in supralaryngeal resonance, affect the A characteristics of the tones to such a degree that these characteristics, which can be observed directly from laryngograph recordings of the laryngeal voice, may become masked completely in virtually all syllables except those where the tone domain is a steady-state vowel. This is especially so in syllables the production of which involves changes in the participation of oral and nasal resonance: nasal finals tend to produce uniformly lowered and levelled-off A codas irrespective of tone. As a result, A distinctions of tones in the oral-nasal voice output can only be observed when relatively large groups of segmentally varied BD syllables are taken into account, that is, when the variations in the strong effect of supralaryngeal resonance on A become neutralised. Alternatively, the laryngeal voice output can be used as the source of information on the A characteristics of BD tones, but because it has only been possible to observe the laryngeal voice in laboratory conditions, normal speech could not be analysed that way as yet.

Word and phrase features: stress

The primary prosodic configurations of tones are modified in strings of two or more syllables in BD by the secondary prosodic feature of prominence. This modification precedes the final modification which yields the prosodic complex characterising the breath group. That this is indeed so is demonstrated by the possibility of predicting the prosodic complex from the tone and prominence pattern of the string of syllables contained in a breath group, and the final modification applied to the pattern; the prosodic complex cannot be predicted from the tones and the final modification alone. Prominence is understood here as a feature by which a syllable is made to be perceived auditively by speakers of the given language as relatively more conspicuous than another syllable or other syllables in its immediate vicinity. Phonetically, it is a relative enhancement of the primary tonal properties in BD. Prominent syllables are generally louder, their pitch level is higher (in the case of tones characterised by a F_0 peak, that is, Tones 1, 2, and 4, as well as most atonic syllables) or lower (in the case of Tone 3 characterised by a F_0 trough), and their duration greater, especially in the case of Tone 3, in relation to their non-prominent correlates. The contours of pitch and loudness curves of prominent syllables appear as exaggerations: the peaks are higher, the troughs are lower, and the slopes towards and away from them are more pronounced. The closest acoustic correlate of the relative prominence of a BD syllable is the product of its F_0, A and T values which will be called its syllabic volume (V).[2] In the GMZ corpus, V values are in the range of 0.15 to 19.93. It was noted that relative prominence became difficult to perceive when the V values of all syllables in question were smaller than 1.0 or when the difference between their V values was smaller than 0.1.

Apart from the positive effect reflected in the increased V value of the syllable which is made prominent, prominence in BD produces a negative effect in decreasing the V value of the syllable immediately following a prominent syllable. The decrease varies greatly with style and tempo (it reaches its maximum in very fast emotionally indifferent statements), ranging from nil, in which case non-prominent syllables immediately following prominent syllables do not differ in their prosodic features from non-prominent syllables elsewhere, to a degree at which tonal distinctions become neutralised, syllables affected in this way acquiring a uniform prosodic shape of small duration and unpronounced pitch and loudness contours.

There is a distinct tendency towards regular alternation of prominent and non-prominent syllables, and towards the iambic type of prominence patterning in BD. This tendency prevails especially in unfocused sentences represented by relatively short strings of monosyllabic words. Lexicalisation and formalisation in general, that is, the formation of disyllabic and larger polysyllabic recurrent strings representing words and phrases, is signalled by the formation of relatively stable prominence patterns which may go against the general tendency, at the points where the patterns meet in particular. In such situations of conflict, strings of two or more non-prominent syllables are allowed to resolve the conflict but the immediate sequence of syllables prominent in the underlying patterns is not. Where such a sequence could occur, the prominence of one of the juxtaposed syllables is removed, or a pause is used to separate them from each other, or, if one of the prominence patterns involved is not stable enough, the less stable pattern may be changed in order to remove the conflict.

The choice between the possible solutions depends mainly on syntactical and pragmatic considerations. For example, given the words *tā* (he), *méiyǒu* (there is not/not to have), and *àiqíng* (love), where *méiyǒu* has an iambic pattern of little stability which changes easily to trochaic, and *àiqíng* a relatively stable trochaic pattern, such patterns of prominent (P) and non-prominent (N) syllables would be possible for the string *tā méiyǒu àiqíng* (he has no love), as N PN PN (slow unfocused), N NN PN (fast unfocused), N NP NN (fast focused on *méiyǒu*), P ‖ PN PN (slow focused on *tā*, with a pause after topic), *etc.*, but it would not be possible to use such patterns as P NP NP (because of the stable pattern of *àiqíng*) or P NP ‖ PN (because pause is not allowed in the middle of comment).

The relationship between prominence and its phonemic abstraction of stress in BD is not one of direct correspondence. Stressed syllables are those constituents of recurrent polysyllabic strings (representing words and phrases) which tend to be prominent in most of the occurrences of the strings, although they may become non-prominent as a result of the conflicts spoken of above, or in the kind of conditions of style and tempo which lead to the neutralisation of tonal distinctions. Alternatively, stress patterns can be viewed as abstractions of substrate prominence patterns characterising the respective polysyllabic strings before they are affected by the various conflicts and conditions. Given a sufficiently large amount of data, it is possible to arrive at stress patterns by a statistical process of normalisation in a way similar to that in which norms of tones can be established, as shown in Coster and Kratochvil (1984). The basic stress patterns in BD from which all others can be derived by observing the properties of prominence patterning mentioned so far, are the two patterns of disyllabic words unstressed-stressed (US) and stressed-unstressed (SU). The former is an abstraction of prominence patterns where the first syllable tends not to be affected by prominence positively or negatively, and the second tends to be prominent. Such words as *bùxiǎo* (not to be small), *dǎngwài* (outside the Party), and *fúshū* (to admit defeat), are characterised by the US pattern in the GMZ corpus. In the SU pattern the first syllable tends to be prominent, and the second non-prominent and negatively affected by prominence, such as *àiqíng* (love), *tāde* (his), and *guòle* (to have passed) in the GMZ corpus. These two patterns represent the terminal points of what in historical terms appears as the shift of stress which accompanies word-formative and inflectional processes in Chinese, as suggested in Kratochvil (1974). The US pattern corresponding to the inherent iambic tendency characterises comparatively newly formed words or words which for various reasons remained relatively loosely structured. The SU pattern, on the other hand, represents relatively close morphological constructions. Since the overwhelming majority of word-formative and inflectional devices in Chinese are suffixes and enclitics, many of the morphemes occupying the second position in the SU patterns are largely limited to the position where the syllables representing them are negatively affected by prominence in the total of their distribution in the language. This is the most likely cause of the rise of atonicity in BD: atonic syllables which mostly represent such morphemes are permanently reduced to the extreme shape of syllables negatively affected by prominence, to the point of the complete loss of their tonal features. Atonic syllables retain this shape even when they are not preceded by stressed syllables, and their occurrence in trisyllabic and larger polysyllabic strings generates points of stability around which the strings' stress patterns are built. For example, the SU U pattern of *àiqíng de* (of love), the USU U pattern of *cuòluànle ne* ([it] has certainly become disturbed), and the SUU U pattern of *diàoguolai ba* (turn [it] around towards me), are all made stable against the iambic tendency by the atonic syllables they contain.

In traditional non-experimental descriptions of the prosodic features of BD syllabic strings, the secondary modifications of tones in the respect of pitch (the only perceptual dimension of tones recognised by the tradition) are ascribed to the mutual influence of juxtaposed tones, or tone sandhi in sinological parlance. This is partly due to the tradition not recognising the categories of prominence and stress, and explaining all secondary modifications in the terms of the presence and absence of tones and of their interplay. Largely, however, this is because of the force of rules based on impressions of isolated citation forms of tonal patterns which have become part of the descriptive and pedagogical convention in Chinese linguistics. In normal BD speech, most of these rules do not apply at all, or at least not in the categorical way in which they are formulated. The most notorious case is that of Tone 3 which is posited to change paradigmatically to Tone 2 when it precedes another Tone 3, so that for example, *mǎi mǎ* (to buy a horse) is supposed to become *mái mǎ*, and thus homophonic with *mái mǎ* (to bury a horse), cf. *mǎi* (to buy) and *mái* (to bury). If any tone modification in sequences of Tone 3 syllables takes place at all in normal speech, which is rare and appears to be limited to recurrent strings, the resulting shape is not that of Tone 2 but an idiosyncratic form distinct from both Tone 3 and Tone 2, as noted in Zee (1980) and Kratochvil (1987a). Whatever modifications in the prosodic features of tone contact are actually made in normal speech cannot be explained without reference to prominence patterning, which tone variation cannot be separated from on the level of secondary prosodic modifications, and also to segmental phenomena. The latter concern, in particular, the way in which the continuity of laryngeal voice output is affected by obstructions representing some consonantal syllabic onsets in BD. However, even when these factors are taken into account, it is not yet possible to make a general statement on changes in the terminal parts of tones in polysyllabic strings. It seems likely that the issue has to do with such fundamental matters as the general distribution of peaks and troughs (or turning points, in the terminology developed within the framework of the generative model of intonation by Eva Gårding and others in Lund University), in BD laryngeal voice, as touched upon in Gårding, Kratochvil, Svantesson and Zhang (1986), and the way in which the two strategies of continuous and discontinuous laryngeal voice production are applied in BD. So far, analytical approaches have failed to identify the factors determining the changes in the terminal parts of tones in the GMZ corpus, possibly because the corpus is not large enough for investigating this complex phenomenon, and also because acoustical data may not be sufficient for such an investigation. Perhaps research on the functioning of the speech production mechanism, such as the investigation using Chinese data and carried out on the basis of electromyographic evidence, see Sagart *et al.* (1986), will yield more significant results in this respect.

Sentence features: intonation

The term intonation is used here for the total of the devices which apply globally to the breath group[3] in normal BD speech, giving the final shape to the prosody of strings of syllables of breath group size which are shaped already by primary and secondary prosodic modifications. Since intonation, the same as the other prosodic modifications, has to do with the total output of the laryngeal voice in BD, no prejudice to any particular acoustic or perceptual dimension of the laryngeal voice is applied in the assessment of intonation. In other words, intonation is not assumed here to have to do only with F_0 or pitch.

At least four distinct intonational devices can be identified in BD: channelling, tempo, focusing, and the use of intonation carriers.

Channelling is the overall guidance given to the strings of F_0 and A configurations in a breath group to provide the limits for the execution of the primary and secondary prosodic modifications. It can be compared to the way in which the flow of a liquid is controlled by a canal delimiting depth, width, and direction. Types of channels are the closest phonetic correlate to such phonemically distinct types of intonation as the intonations of declarative sentences and questions in BD. Tempo control is closely related to channelling in that the shape of the channels is determined to some extent by the tempo of speech, that is, the number of syllables produced over a standard period of time. It has been shown, such as in Kratochvil (1971), that there is a minimum amount of time necessary for the correct production and perception of Chinese tones, which in BD appears to be between 50 and 100 msec. for the tone domain of the syllable. In speech segments where the overall tempo allows the syllables an amount of time close to this critical minimum, the channels are, as a consequence, qualified by relatively narrow ranges and small deviations from the overall direction. In the GMZ corpus, the tempo of breath groups varies between 2.92 and 3.39 syllables per second.

Focusing, which is the device for signalling such features as contrastive stress, is a momentary enlargement of a channel. The culmination of a focus coincides with a syllable which is made greatly prominent by it. Depending on the nature of the emphasis signalled by the focus, any syllable may carry the culmination, including atonic syllables, but it is usually the syllable which would be stressed (in the case of recurrent strings) or at least prominent in the given string in an unfocused channel that does. Minor focusing may be limited to a single syllable but it is more common for a focus to spread over several syllables, in which case the culmination is reached by a gradual enlargement of the channel, and, unless it occurs at the end of a breath group, followed by a gradual diminishing of the channel. The underlying prominence patterns in the domain of the focus are modified according to the respective tendency, and occasionally overridden. This is one of the main reasons why the relationship between stress and prominence in BD is not one of direct signalling: stress commonly corresponds to non-prominence in focus domains.

Intonation carriers, mostly but not necessarily monosyllabic items constituting a small closed set in BD, correspond to interjections and what are vaguely referred to as "sentence particles" in some Chinese linguistic terminologies. They are used as replacements of whole sentences or as predominantly terminal sentence constituents. Their most typical position is at the end of a sentence. Since they carry no tone,[4] they are a subtype of atonic syllables, and their prosodic properties are directly determined by intonation. This is of special importance at the end of sentences where channels often change direction rapidly and thus distort very heavily any tones occurring there. Individual intonation carriers may go with a particular channel or they may be chosen to signal the difference between phonemically distinct intonations sharing the same type of channelling and tempo. For example, the sentence *nǐ zěnme bùfúshū a* (how come you don't admit defeat?) (an irritated exclamation) differs in the GMZ corpus from the sentence *nǐ zěnme bùfúshū ne* (why don't you admit defeat?) (an impatient question) substantially only in the choice of the intonation carrier.

From the analytical point of view, the key issue in the description of concrete intonations in BD and in drawing general conclusions from the description is the appropriate way of separating the complex of primary and secondary prosodic modifications from the final prosodic shape of sentences, corresponding to the way in which secondary modifications can be separated from the primary tone modifications in the description of prominence. The statistical device which has proved most useful for approaching this issue is the variable norms of tones. These norms, in opposition to such invariant norms as those presented in table 1, reflect the concept of tones (a concept which may apply to prosody in general) as products of homothetic behaviour. Homothetic behaviour, as referred to, for example, in Viviani and Terzuolo (1980), is any kind of behaviour where an invariant structure is present in learned motor sequences varying in time and space, this structure being the property on which the norm applying to all the variations can be founded, *e.g.* in the case of handwriting. Variable norms of tones are based on the regularities which were found to exist between the varying levels and contours of F_0 and A, an the one hand, and varying T, on the other, for each of the four BD tones. They are valid only for the corpus of data on the basis of which they were calculated; for their description relevant to the GMZ corpus see Kratochvil (1985). The variable norm of a particular tone makes it possible to predict with considerable accuracy the F_0 and A levels and contours of that tone corresponding to a specific T value, that is, the normative shape of the tone modified by a specific degree of prominence and occurring in the conditions of tempo of a specific magnitude. By comparing the given duration variants of the variable norms with the F_0 and A properties of syllables in a real sentence, it is possible to observe and draw conclusions in quantitative terms about the residual prosodic aspects of the sentence which were largely neutralised in the variable norm calculations. These are, on the local level, modifications brought about by such factors as the mutual influence of tones and the influence of the segmental features of syllables, and, on the global level, modifications caused by channelling and focusing.

The example below of two variants of the same short declarative sentence, one non-emphatic and one emphatic, demonstrates the application of variable norms in assessing the residual properties. The two variants occur in different parts of a short discourse in the GMZ corpus where the informant gives an account of an unhappy marriage which finally breaks up, despite the couple's effort to save it. The sentence is *méiyǒu àiqíng* ([but] there was no love), with the emphasis on *méiyǒu* (there was not) in the emphatic variant. On the level of primary and secondary prosodic modifications, the tones in the two variants (Tone 2 in *méi*

Paul Kratochvil

[negative prefix of the verb *yŏu*] and *qíng* [word-formative suffix in nouns which refer to emotional attitudes], Tone 3 in *yŏu* (there is/to have), and Tone 4 in *ài* (to love)) are modified by prominence. Tables 2 and 3 give the acoustic data on the real syllables and the variable norms corresponding to the real durations, and also a graphic representation of the two variants of the sentence.

Table 2. *Acoustic properties of the syllables in the non-emphatic variant of the sentence méiyŏu àiqíng* /meiⁱiouaeitɕʰiŋ/ (there was no love).

	méi	*yŏu*	*ài*	*qíng*
$F_0 1$	165/221	215/218	175/276	165/222
$F_0 2$	185/218	205/208	180/267	160/219
$F_0 3$	200/220	195/199	180/253	155/221
$F_0 4$	210/226	180/194	175/232	145/226
$F_0 5$	220/233	175/191	165/213	145/233
$F_0 6$	225/236	175/190	155/202	150/236
A1	75/74	115/76	170/96	30/74
A2	95/105	160/103	160/144	50/105
A3	105/112	155/106	155/149	55/112
A4	115/113	160/102	135/145	50/112
A5	115/107	180/94	135/129	45/107
A6	115/83	170/78	75/83	30/83
T	110/110	105/105	210/210	105/105
V	2.32/2.5	4.04/2.63	5.04/6.27	0.7/2.4

The values of the real syllables are given first, their variable norms second after a slash. F_0 values are given in Hz, A values in dB, T values in msec., and V values in units reflecting the product of F_0, A and T values. The figure on the right illustrates the F_0 (top) and A values for the real syllables (continuous lines) and the variable norms (dotted lines).

As indicated in an earlier example, *méiyŏu* (there was not) is stressed on the second syllable and has an unstable prominence pattern, and *àiqíng* (love) is stressed on the first syllable and has a stable prominence pattern; in the non-emphatic variant the overall iambic tendency makes the prominence of *yŏu* yield to that of the immediately following *ài*, which results in the NN PN prominence pattern, whereas the tendency is reversed in the emphatic variant with the resulting NP NN prominence pattern. There is also an effect caused by the mutual influence of tones. The raised F_0 peak in the coda of *méi* is induced by the following Tone 3 of *yŏu*, which in its turn has a raised F_0 onset induced by the preceding Tone 2; the bent F_0 onset of *ài* is assimilated to the low F_0 coda of the preceding Tone 3, such bends occurring commonly in Tone 4 syllables with voiced onsets where the laryngeal voice output is uninterrupted.

428

Table 3. *Acoustic properties of the syllables in the emphatic variant of the sentence* méiyǒu àiqíng /mei^{ɟ}iouaeitɕʰiŋ/ (there was no love).

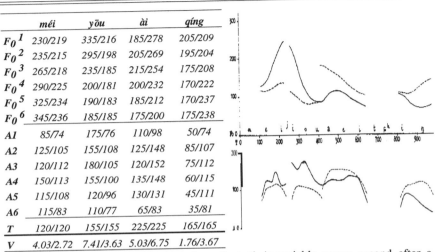

	méi	yōu	ài	qíng
F_0 1	230/219	335/216	185/278	205/209
F_0 2	235/215	295/198	205/269	195/204
F_0 3	265/218	235/185	215/254	175/208
F_0 4	290/225	200/181	200/232	170/222
F_0 5	325/234	190/183	185/212	170/237
F_0 6	345/236	185/185	175/200	175/238
A1	85/74	175/76	110/98	50/74
A2	125/105	155/108	125/148	85/107
A3	120/112	180/105	120/152	75/112
A4	150/113	155/100	135/148	60/115
A5	115/108	120/96	130/131	45/111
A6	115/83	110/77	65/83	35/81
T	120/120	155/155	225/225	165/165
V	4.03/2.72	7.41/3.63	5.03/6.75	1.76/3.67

The values of the real syllables are given first, their variable norms second after a slash. F_0 values are given in Hz, A values in dB, T values in msec., and V values in units reflecting the product of F_0, A and T values. The figure on the right illustrates the F_0 (top) and A values for the real syllables (continuous lines) and the variable norms (dotted lines).

There are also adjustments brought about by changes in supralaryngeal resonance and due to segmental features in general (*e.g.* the lowered F_0 onset of *méi* caused by the switch from nasal to oral resonance, the raised transitions in A from *méi* to *yǒu* and from *yǒu* to *ài* due to the lack of complete obstructions to laryngeal voice output, and the variations in A contours, especially in the case of the coda of *qíng* in the emphatic variant which is the result of relatively heavy nasalisation).

As far as intonation is concerned, both variants show signs of channelling down towards the end of the sentence, with a sharp fall in F_0 imposed on the last syllable. It is interesting to note that this fall actually overrides the inherent rising F_0 tendency of Tone 2.[5] The combination of the downward channelling in both F_0 and A, and the terminal fall in F_0, appears to characterise the intonation of declarative sentences in BD. In the GMZ corpus it also tends to be accompanied by an overall lowering of the F_0 level by about 30–50 Hz, the terminal fall reaching as much as about 100 Hz from the variable norm. The focus on *méiyǒu* in the emphatic variant of the sentence raises the F_0 and A levels of both the syllables, and enhances the secondary prosodic modifications.

In principle, these are the two main properties by which a focus deviates from a basic intonation in BD. It will also be noted that the non-focused part of the emphatic variant is mildly modified as well. The same as the whole emphatic variant, it is a little longer, and the prominence pattern of the word *àiqíng* contained in it is less contrastive than in the case of the non-emphatic variant.

As is perhaps obvious from the preceding discussion, the analysis of the GMZ corpus carried out so far has shown that the general properties of intonation in normal BD speech appear to be very similar to those of intonation in languages which have been exposed to longer and deeper scrutiny of the kind established in Western linguistic tradition. The one aspect which confounds this view is not the properties of BD intonation themselves but the primary tonal modification of the laryngeal voice output. Since this modification, the notion of which is far more deeply rooted in Chinese linguistic tradition, employs the same dimensions as intonation does, it tends to blur the observation of the latter to the point that the very existence of intonation in BD and other Chinese dialects has been seen as dubious at times. The view that Chinese has no intonation to speak of is reflected in most early statements on Chinese prosody, *e.g.* in Karlgren (1918). The more recent general descriptions of Chinese phonetics either do not discuss intonation at all, such as Dow (1972), or make only very brief comments on it, such as Wang (1957) where less than two pages out of 127 are given to intonation.

As far as the specific properties of BD intonation are concerned, this is still an area of much speculation, largely because of the analytical difficulties arising from the nature of the prosodic complex in BD. A sample of data very much larger than that of the GMZ corpus would be required in order to shed some objective light on these features in normal BD speech. This bears upon, on the one hand, the internal properties of BD, and, on the other hand, the way BD relates, in respect of intonation, to other dialects of Chinese and to other languages. As to the former, it is possible to suggest that BD shows signs of possessing such familiar devices as an intonation pattern characteristic of at least some types of questions, and that it probably operates with a relatively small number of basic intonation types. Clichés are known to exist in BD, both in tonal patterns and intonation, but data there are particularly scarce. Similarly, any attempt at discussing the internal structure of intonation patterns, although clear indications of it may be seen in normal BD speech, would be futile at this stage of analytical experience.

It is thus only possible to refer at the moment to statements which have been made on intonation in modern Chinese in sources approaching Chinese data on a basis restricted in objectiveness, whether this is in respect of the nature of the data approached, the quantity of the data, or the way in which the approach was made. Among such sources, linguistic writings on modern Chinese which include comments on intonation based on subjective impression belong to one kind. Of these, Chao (1968) presents the most extensive picture of intonation, including a particularly detailed account of intonation carriers. A similar picture is given in a more concise form in Henne, Rongen and Hansen (1977). Of another kind are experimentally based phonetic descriptions using small samples of isolated citation forms or other forms of edited speech, and limiting the observation largely to the dimension of F_0. The largest and the most comprehensive of such descriptions published so far is Rumjancev (1972). The more recent articles from the University of Lund, such as Gårding, Zhang and Svantesson (1983), and Gårding (1987), also belong to this kind.

Notes

1 The Fourcin laryngograph and its functioning are described in Fourcin and Abberton (1971). For data on the automatic analysis facility at the stage of its development relevant to the analysis referred to here, see Teston and Rossi (1977). The author would like to express his deep gratitude to Professor M. Rossi for the kind permission to use the facility, and for all the help he has received from members of the Institute of Phonetics in Aix-en-Provence.

2 For details on the syllabic volume in BD and the way it was calculated in the analysis of the GMZ corpus see Kratochvil (1969) and Kratochvil (1987b). In the case of Tone 3, the lowered F_0 level accompanying increased prominence is mostly compensated by a greater increase in duration, in relation to the other three tones. It was found that a further global compensation by a factor of 0.3 in the V calculation of Tone 3 syllabic volumes led to an even more realistic result. The example of the two sentence variants in the present discussion makes use of this further compensation.

3 For the purposes of this description, the breath group is taken to coincide with the sentence. The difficulties which arise from this simplistic equation in discussing matters of syntax are obvious but they are of no importance to the description, since no systematic attempt is made here to relate syntactical and intonational structure.

4 The Chinese linguistic tradition sometimes confuses the issue by ascribing to an intonation carrier the tone whose pitch contour resembles the pitch properties of the part of the intonation channel where the carrier typically occurs. This approach has found its way, unfortunately, into many modern dictionaries of Chinese where intonation carriers are commonly given tone values.

5 Distortions of F_0 arising from the overriding effect of intonation do not destroy the phonemic identity of the tone, since the same intonation affects different tones differently. They do, however, make the relationship between the phonetic and phonemic features of tone quite complex, and they are yet another factor confirming the need for not limiting prosodic assessments to the observation of F_0.

References

Abbreviations

ARIPUC   *Annual Report of the Institute of Phonetics (University of Copenhagen)*
BSLP   *Bulletin de la Société Linguistique de Paris*
JL   *Journal of Linguistics*
JP   *Journal of Phonetics*
JASA   *Journal of the Acoustical Society of America*
JIPA   *Journal of the International Phonetics Association*
JSHR   *Journal of Speech and Hearing Research*
L&S   *Language and Speech*
Proc ICL   *Proceedings of the International Congress of Linguists*
Proc ICPhS   *Proceedings of the International Congress of Phonetic Sciences*
PY   *Phonology Yearbook*
RRL   *Revue Roumaine de Linguistique*
SCL   *Studii şi Cercetări Lingvistice*
STL-QPSR   *Quarterly Progress and Status Report, Speech Transmission Laboratory, Royal Institute of Technology (Stockholm)*
TILL   *Travaux de l'Institut de Linguistique de Lund*
TIPA   *Travaux de l'Institut de Phonétique d'Aix-en-Provence*
WIP   *Work in Progress. Department of Linguistics, University of Edinburgh*

Aaltonen, O. 1975. Suomen lausepainon generoimisesta. *Fonetiikan paperit – Helsinki 1975, PPH* 27: 5–17.
Aaltonen, O. and Wiik, K. 1979. Some acoustical observations on the non-terminal intonation in Finnish. In Hurme, P. (ed.) *Fonetiikan päivät – Jyväskylä 1978*, 18: 23–33. Publications from the Institute of Finnish Language and Communication, University of Jyväskylä.
Aaltonen, O. and Hulkko, T. (eds.) 1985. XIII Fonetiikan päivät – Turku 1985. *Turun yliopiston suomalaisen ja yleisen kielitieteen laitoksen julkaisuja* 26: 33–54.
Abdallah, A.G. 1960. *An Instrumental Study of the Intonation of Egyptian Colloquial Arabic.* University Microfilms Inc. Ann Arbor.
Abe, I. 1958a. A Study of English Intonation (in Japanese). 122–123. Tokyo: Kenkyu-sha.
1958b. On Japanese intonation. Lingua 7, 2: 183–194.

1962. Call contours. *Proc ICPhS 4*, 519–523.

1964. Problems of tones and intonation (in Japanese). *Bulletin* 116: 6–8. Phon. Soc. Japan.

1965. Symbolism and symptomatism in speech (in Japanese). *Study of Sounds* 11: 9–16. Phon. Soc. Japan.

1966. General characteristics of Japanese terminal intonation with a presentation of its notational system. *Lingua* 16, 3: 255–262.

1970a. The intonation of Okinawa's vernacular tongue. *Bulletin* 134: 6–7. Phon. Soc. Japan.

1970b. Hawalian accent and intonation. *Bulletin* 100: 107–118. Tokyo Inst. Technology.

1972a. Tone-intonation relationships. *Proc ICPhS 7*, 820–823.

1972b. Intonational patterns of English and Japanese. In Bolinger, D. (ed.) *Intonation*, 337–347. Harmondsworth: Penguin.

1975. Proxemics and phonetics (in Japanese). *Bulletin* 130: 1–5. Tokyo Inst. Technology.

1977. Principles of English and Japanese intonation (in Japanese). *The Gaku-shobo Phonetics Series* 6. Tokyo: Gaku-shobo Publish. Co.

1979a. Melodic patterns of street cries. *Bulletin*, March issue, 19–26. Tokyo Inst. Technology.

1979b. Intonation as a universal in language teaching. *Humanities Review* 5: 245–251. Tokyo Inst. Technology.

1980. How vocal pitch works. In Waugh and Schooneveld (eds.): 1–24.

1981. A Kunimaipa contour model and Japanese intonation. In Léon and Rossi (eds): 89–95.

1989. Language intonation – is there a universal? (in Japanese). *Journal of the Department of Liberal Arts* 40: 1–25. Asia University: Tokyo.

1998. Intonation in Japanese. This volume, 372–387.

Abercrombie, D. 1964. Syllable quantity and enclitics in English. In Abercrombie *et al.* (eds.), 216–222.

Abercrombie, D., Fry, D.B., Mc Carthy, P.A.D., Scott, N.C. and Trim, G.L.M. (eds.) 1964. *In Honour of Daniel Jones*. London: Longmans.

Abramson, A.S. 1962. The vowels and tones of standard Thai: acoustical measurements and experiments. *IJAL* 28.2, Part II.

1972. Tonal experiment with whispered Thai. In Valdman, A. (ed.) *Papers in Linguistics and Phonetics to the Memory of Pierre Delattre*, 31–43. The Hague: Mouton.

1975. Thai tones as a reference system. In Gething, T.W. *et al. In Honour of Fang-Kuei Li*, 1–12. Chulalongkorn University Press.

1978. Static and dynamic acoustic cues in distinctive tones. *L&S* 21.4: 319–325.

1979. Lexical tone and sentence prosody in Thai. *Proc ICPhS 9*, 380–387.

Academia Española Real. 1973. *Esbozo de una nueva gramática de la lengua española*. Madrid: Espasa-Calpe.

Adams, C. 1979. *English Speech Rhythm and the Foreign Learner*. The Hague: Mouton.

References

Adriaens, L.M.H. 1988. A preliminary description of German intonation. *IPO Annual Progress Report* 19, 36–41.

Agard, F.B. 1967. Stress in four Romance languages. *Glossa* 1,2: 150–200.

Alcoba, S. 1988. El morfema temático del verbo español. In Wotjak, G. and Veiga, A. (eds.) 1990. *La descripción del verbo español. Verba*, Anexo 32: 9–22.

1990. Morfología del verbo español: conjugación y derivación de verbal. In Martín Vide, C. (ed.) 1991. *Lenguajes naturales y lenguajes formales*, VI. 1: 87–119. Barcelona: PPU.

Alcoba, S., Le Besnerais, M. and Murillo, J. 1993. Unité tonale et structure prosodique de l'espagnol. *Revue de Phonétique Appliquée* 105: 261–285.

Alcoba, S. and Murillo, J. 1998. Intonation in Spanish. This volume, 159–174.

Ali, M. Said 1895. A Acentuação segundo Publicações Recentes. *Revista Brazileira* (Reprinted in M. Said Ali *Dificuldades da Lingua Portugueza*, Rio de Janeiro, Laemmert, 1908, with the title Phenomenos de Intonação.)

Allen, W.S. 1954. *Living English Speech.* London, New York, Toronto: Longmans.

Allerton, D.J. and Cruttenden, A. 1979. Three reasons for accenting a definite subject. *JL* 15: 49–53.

Altmann, H. 1988. *Intonationsforschungen.* Tübingen: Niemeyer.

Amanuma, Y. *et al.* 1989. *Japanese Phonetics* (in Japanese). Tokyo: Huroshio-shuppan, 157.

Anan, F. 1979. Analysis of the F_0 curves of certain declarative sentences in Japanese (in Japanese). *Bulletin of the Phonetic Society of Japan* 161: 4–7.

1980. *Contribution à l'étude des interferences d'intonation – analyse mélodique et perceptive des réalisations de phrases asservatives françaises par des locuteurs japonais.* Doctoral thesis, Université de Paris.

Andersen, P. 1954. Dansk fonetik. Chapter XV of *Nordisk Lærebog for Talepædagoger.* Copenhagen: Rosenkilde and Bagger, 308–354.

Andreev, N.D. and Bystrov, M.V. 1957. Sistema tonov vjetnamskogo jazyka. *Vestnik Leningradskogo Gosudarstvennogo Universiteta* 8: 132–148.

Andrews, B.J. 1989. Terminating devices in spoken French. *International Review of Applied Linguistics*, 27, 3: 193–216.

Antinucci, F. and Cinque, G. 1977. Sull' ordine delle parole in italiano: l'emerginazione. *Studi di grammatica italiana*, 6, 121-146.

Antipova, A. 1984. *Ritmicheskaja sistema anglijskij rechi.* (The rhythmic system of English speech.) Moscow.

Armstrong, L.E. and Ward, I.C. 1926. *A Handbook of English Intonation.* Cambridge: W. Heffer and Sons.

Aubert, F. and Hochgreb, N. 1981. Preliminares para um Estudo Perceptivo da Intonação da Frase Interrogativa em Português. *Estudos Lingüísticos* I: 9–22. Uberaba.

Aulanko, R. 1985. Microprosodic features in speech: Experiments on Finnish. In Aaltonen, O. and Hulkko, T. 1985: 33–54.

Autesserre, D. and Di Cristo, A. 1972. Recherches psychosémantiques sur l'intonation de la phrase française. *TIPA* 1: 61–98.

Avesani, C. 1990. A contribution to the synthesis of Italian intonation. *Proceedings ICSPL 90* (Kobe) 833–836.

Avesani, C. and Vayra, M. 1988 Discorso, segmenti di discorso i un'ipotesi sull'intonazione. *Quaderni del Laboratorio di Linguistica* (Pisa) 2, 8–58.

Avram, A. 1971. Observaţii asupra duratei sunetelor în limba română (în legătură cu înˇalţimea şi cu intensitatea). *Fonetică şi Dialectologie* 7: 51–58.

1972. Intonation curves in the English of Romanians. In ChiţoranD. (ed.) *The Romanian-English Contrastive Analysis Project. Studies,* 7–41. Bucharest: Bucharest University Press.

1973. Particularităţi ale intonaţiei interogative în graiul din Muscel. *Fonetică şi dialectologie* 8: 43–64.

Avram, M. 1984. Accentuarea substantivelor feminine în -ie. *Limba şi Literatura Română* 13, 2: 3–7.

Babiniotis, G. 1972. Τό Ρῆμα τῆς Ἑλληνικῆς (The Verb in Greek). Philosophical Faculty, University of Athens.

Bailly, G. 1989. Integration of rhythmic and syntactic constraints in a model of generation of French prosody. *Speech Communication* 8, 2: 137–146.

Bailly, G., Benoît, C. and T. Sawallis 1992. *Talking machines:Theories, Models and Applications.* Amsterdam: Elsevier.

Bannert, R. 1979. Ordprosodi i invandrarundervisningen. *Praktisk lingvistik 3.* Ling. Lund University.

1982. An F_0 dependent model for segment duration? *Reports from the Institute of Linguistics* 8: 59–80. Uppsala University.

1983. Modellskizze für die deutsche Intonation. *Zeitschrift für Literaturwissenschaft und Linguistik* 13: 9–34.

1985a. Fokus, Kontrast und Phrasenintonation im Deutschen. *Zeitschrift für Dialektologie und Linguistik* 52: 289–305.

1985b. Towards a model for German Prosody. *Folia Linguistica* XIX: 321–341.

1986a. From prominent syllables to a skeleton of meaning: a model of prosodically guided speech recognition. *WP* 29: 1–31.

1986b. Independence and interdependence of prosodic features. *WP* 29: 31–60.

1987. On the role of accented syllables in speech perception. *Reports from Uppsala University (Department of Linguistics)* 17: 65–71.

Bannert, R. and Thorsen, N.G. 1988. Empirische Studien zur Intonation des Deutschen und Dänischen: Ähnlichkeiten und Unterschiede. *Kopenhagener Beiträge zur germanistischen Linguistik* 24: 26–50.

Basbøll, H. 1977. *Dansk Fonetik og Fonologi – Skitse til en Systematisk Indføring.* Nordisk Institut, Odense University.

1985. Stød in modern Danish. *Folia Linguistica* XIX: 1–50.

Beach, D.M. 1924. The science of tonetics and its application to Bantu language. *Bantu Studies.* vol. II,2: 75–106.

Beckman, M.E. 1986. *Stress and non-stress accent.* Dordrecht: Foris.

Beckman, M.E. and Pierrehumbert, J.B. 1986. Intonational structure in Japanese and English. *PY* 3: 255–309.

1987. Tone structure in Tokyo Japanese (in Japanese). *Studies in Phonetics and Speech Communication* 2: 1–22. Kinki, Soc. for Phonetics.

Ben Fadhl, A. 1972 *L'intonation du groupe nominal sujet en italien.* Mémoire de Maîtrise, Université de Provence.

Benhallam, A. 1980. *Syllable structure and rule types in Arabic*. Ph.D. dissertation. University of Florida.

Benincà, P. 1988. L'ordine degli elementi della frase e le costruzioni marcate. In Renzi, L. 1988. *Grande grammatica italiano di consultazione,* 30–112. Bologna: il Mulino.

Benkaddour, A. 1986. A metrical analysis of some aspects of the phonology of Moroccan Arabic. *Annales de la Faculté des Lettres et des Sciences Humaines:* 83–112. Université Hassan II, Casablanca.

Benkirane, T. 1981. Durée, prosodie et syllabation en arabe marocain. *TIPA* 8: 45–84.

1982. *Etude phonétique et fonctions de la syllabe en arabe marocain*. Thèse de 3° cycle. Université d'Aix-en-Provence.

1998. Intonation in Western Arabic (Morocco). This volume, 357–371.

Benkirane, T. and Cavé, C. 1984. Segmentation syllabique en arabe marocain: étude expérimentale par la méthode du temps de réaction. *TIPA* 9: 85–99.

1987. Hiérarchie de sonorité et segmentation syllabique dans le parler arabe marocain. *Actes des XVI° Journées d'Etudes sur la Parole,* 274–277. Hammamet (Tunisie).

1988. Etude perceptive de la durée vocalique comme indice de joncture en arabe marocain. *Seventh FASE Speech Symposium,* Edinburgh.

Berendsen, E. and Don, J. 1987. Morphology and stress in a rule-based grapheme-to-phoneme conversion system for Dutch. *Proc. European Conf. on Speech Technology,* vol I, 239–242. Edinburgh: J. Laver and M.A. Jack (eds.).

Berendsen, E., Langeweg, S. and Leeuwen, H.C. van. 1968. Computational phonology, merged, not mixed. *Proc. 11th Int. Conf. on Computat. Linguistics,* 612–614. Bonn.

Bergheaud, A. 1986. Dire entre guillemets: voix multiples dans le discours. *Cahiers Charles* V: 139–154. Université Paris 7.

Berinstein, A.E. 1979. A cross linguistic study of perception and production of stress. *UCLA.Working Papers in Phonetics:* 1–59.

Bertinetto, P.-M. 1979 *Aspetti prosodici della lingua italiana*. Padova: CLESP.

1981 *Strutture prosodiche dell'italiano*. Firenze: Academia della Crusca.

1989. Reflections on the dichotomy "stress" *vs.* "syllable-timing". *Revue de Phonétique Appliquée* 91–92–93: 99–130.

Bertinetto, P.-M. and Fowler, C.A. 1989. On sensitivity to durational modifications in Italian and English. *Rivista di Linguistica* 1, 1: 69–94.

Bertinetto, P.-M. and Magno-Caldognetto, E. 1993. Ritmo e intonazione. in A.A.Sobrero (ed.) *Introduzione all'italiano contemporaneo.* Milano, Laterza: 141–192.

Beun, R.J. 1988. Declarative question acts: two experiments on identification. In Taylor, M.M., Néel, F. and Bouwhuis, D.G. (eds.) *The structure of multimodal dialogue*. Amsterdam: North Holland.

Bierwisch, M. 1966. Regeln für die Intonation deutscher Sätze. *Studia grammatica* 7: 99–201. Berlin: Akademie Verlag.

Bisol, L. 1981. *Harmonização Vocálica: Uma Regra Variável*. Tese de Doutorado, Universidade do Rio de Janeiro.

Bleiching, D. 1992. Prosodisches Wissen im Lexikon. In Gürz, G. (ed.) *KONVENS 92*, Nürnberg: 59–68. Berlin: Springer.

1994. Integration von Morphophonologie und Prosodie in ein hierarchisches Lexikon. In Trost, H. (ed.) *KONVENS '94*, Wien: 32–41. Berlin: Springer.

Bloch, B. and Trager, G.L. 1942. *Outline of Linguistic Analysis*. Baltimore: Special Publication of the Linguistic Society of America.

Bloomfield, L. 1933. *Language*. New York: Holt.

Bo, A. 1933 Tonegangen i Dansk Rigsmal. *Studier fra Sprog – og Oldtidsforskning*, 164. Copenhagen: Branner.

Boë, L.-J. and Contini, M. 1975. Etude de la phrase interrogative en français. *Bulletin de l'Institut de Phonétique de Grenoble* 4: 85–102.

Bolinger, D.L. 1955. The melody of language. *Modern Language Forum* 40: 19–30.

1957. *Interrogative Structures of American English*. Publications of the *American Dialect Society* 28.

1957/1958. On intensity as a qualitative improvement of pitch accent. *Lingua* 7: 175–82.

1958. A theory of pitch accent in English. *Word* 14: 109–149.

1964a. Intonation as a universal. *Proc ICL 9* , 833–848.

1964b. Around the edge of language: Intonation. *Harvard Educational Review* 34: 282–293.

1978a. Yes-No questions are not alternative questions. In Hiz, H. (ed.) *Questions*, Dordrecht: Reidel: 87–105.

1978b. Intonation across languages. In Greeberg, J.H., Ferguson, C.A. and Moravcik, E.A. (eds.) *Universals of Human Language, Phonology*, 2: 471–524. Stanford: Stanford University Press.

1986a. Intonation and emotion. *Quaderni di Semiotica* 7: 13–21.

1986b. *Intonation and its Parts: Melody in Spoken English*. London: Edward Arnold.

1989. *Intonation and its Uses: melody in grammar and discourse*. London: Edward Arnold.

1998. Intonation in American English This volume, 49–59.

Bolinger, D.L. and Hodapp, M. 1961. Acento melódico. Acento de intensidad. *Boletín de Filología de la Universidad de Chile* 13: 33–48.

Borzone de Manrique, A.M. and Signorini, A. 1983. Segmental duration and rhythm in Spanish. *JP* 11: 117–128.

Botinis, A. 1989a. Discourse intonation in Greek. *WP* 35: 5–23

1989b. *Stress and Prosodic Structure in Greek*. *TILL* 22.

1998. Intonation in Greek. This volume, 298–321.

Boukous, A. 1979. La situation linguistique au Maroc. *Europe* 602–603: 5–21.

Boulakia, G. 1983. Phonosyntaxe du français. *T.A. Informations* (Paris) 24, 2: 24–63.

Bounfour, A. 1983. l'Etat unitaire et le statut de la langue berbère: les positions de la gauche marocaine. *Annuaire de l'Afrique du Nord* 12: 509–522.

Bratus, B.V. and Verbitskaja, L.A. 1983. Posobie po fonetike dlja inostrannyh studentov-filologov. (Manual of phonetics for foreign students of philology.) Moscow.

Brazil, D. 1975. *Discourse Intonation 1*. Birmingham: University of Birmingham English Language Research.

1985. *The Communicative Value of Intonation in English. (=Discourse Analysis Monograph 8.)* English Language Research, University of Birmingham.

Brazil, D., Coulthard. M. and Johns, C. 1980. *Discourse Intonation and Language Teaching*. London: Longman.

Bredvad-Jensen, A.C. 1984. Tonal geography. Geographical variation in declarative and interrogative intonation along the west coast of Sweden. In Elert, C.C., Johansson, I. and Strangert, E. (eds.) *Nordic Prosody* III,. 31–41. University of Umeå.

Brink, L. and Lund, J. 1975 *Dansk Rigsmål 1–2*. Copenhagen: Gyldendal.

Brosnahan, L. F. and Malmberg, B. 1970. *Introduction to Phonetics*. Cambridge: Heffer and Sons.

Brown, G. 1977. (2nd edition 1990). *Listening to Spoken English*. London: Longman.

1983. Prosodic structure and the given/new distinction. In Cutler and Ladd (eds.) 67–77.

Brown, G., Currie, K.L. and Kenworthy, J. 1980. *Questions of Intonation*. London: Croom Helm.

Brown, G. and Yule, G. 1983. *Discourse analysis*. Cambridge: Cambridge University Press.

Bruce, G. 1977. *Swedish word accents in sentence perspective. TILL* XII.

1982a. Developing the Swedish intonation model. *WP* 22: 51–117

1982b. Textual aspects of prosody in Swedish. *Phonetica* 39: 274–287.

1983. Accentuation and Timing in Swedish. *Folia Linguistica* 17/1–2: 221–238.

1984a. Aspects of declination in Swedish. *Working Papers in Phonetics* 24: 51–64.

1984b. Rhythmic alternation in Swedish. In Elert C.C., Johansson I., Strangert E. (eds.) *Nordic Prosody* III, 31–41. University of Umeå.

1985. Structure and functions of prosody. In Guérin, B. and Carré, R. (eds.) *Proceedings of the French Swedish Seminar on Speech* Grenoble: 549–559.

1987. On the Phonology and Phonetics of Rhythm: Evidence from Swedish. In Dressler, W.U., Luschützky, H.C., Pfeiffer, O.E. and Rennison, J.R. (eds.) *Phonologica 1984*, 21–31. Cambridge: Cambridge University Press.

1988. How floating is focal accent? In Gregersen, K. and Basbøll, H. (eds.) *Nordic Prosody* IV: 41–49.

1989. Report from the IPA working group on suprasegmental categories. *WP* 35: 25–40.

Bruce, G. and Gårding, E. 1978. A prosodic typology for Swedish dialects. In Gårding, E., Bruce, G. and Bannert, R (eds.) *Nordic Prosody, TILL* XIII, 219–228.

Bruce, G., Touati, P., Botinis, A. and Willstedt, U. 1988. Preliminary report from the kipros project. *WP* 33: 23–50.

Bruce, G. and Touati, P. 1992. On the analysis of prosody in spontaneous speech with exemplifications from Swedish and French. *Speech communication* 11: 453–458.

Bruce, G., Granström, B., Gustafson, K., House, D. and Touati, P. 1994. Modelling Swedish prosody in a dialogue framework. *ICSLP*, 1099–1102. Yokohama.

Bryzgunova, E.A. 1977a. *Zvuki i intonacija russkoj rechi*. Moscow.

1977b. Analiz russkoj dialecktnoj intonacii. *Eksperimental'no-foneticheskije issledovanija v oblasti russkoj dialektologii*. Moscow.

Burzio, L. 1981. *Italian Syttax*. Dordrecht: Reidel.

Caëlen-Haumont, G. 1983. Le rythme dans la parole: une revue des études portant sur le français. *4ème Colloque d'Albi: Le Rythme*. (Université de Toulouse-Le-Mirail).

Cagliari, L. 1981. Investigando o Ritmo da Fala. *Anais do V Encontro Nacional de Lingüística*, 290–304. Rio de Janeiro: PUC-RJ.

1982. A Entoação e o Ritmo do Português Brasileiro: Algumas Análises Espectrográficas. *Revista IBM* ano IV, 13: 24–33.

Callamand, M. 1973. *l'Intonation Expressive*. Paris: Hachette.

Campbell, W.N. 1992. *Multi-level Timing in Speech*. Ph.D. thesis, Sussex University.

Camugli, C. 1971. *La place du groupe nominal sujet dans la langue parlée italienne*. Mémoire de Maîtrise, Université de Provence.

Canellada, M.J. 1941. Notas de entonación extremeña. *Revista de Filología Española* 25: 79–91.

Canellada, M.J. and Madsen, J.K. 1987. *Pronunciación del españoľ*. Madrid: Castalia.

Canepari, L. 1983. *Italiano standard e pronuncia regionale*. Padova, CLEUP.

Cao Xuan Hao 1975. Le problème du phonème en vietnamien. *Essais Linguistiques – Etudes Vietnamiennes* 40 Hà Nôi.

1985. *Phonologie and Linéarité*. Paris: Selaf.

Caplan, D. 1987. *Neurolinguistics and Linguistic Aphasiology: an introduction*. Cambridge: Cambridge University Press.

Carlsson, R.and Granström, B. 1973. Word accent, emphatic stress and syntax in a synthesis by rule scheme for Swedish. *Speech Transmission Lab. QPSR*, 2/3–1973, 31–35. Stockholm.

Carton, F., Rossi, M., Autesserre, D. and Léon, P. 1983. *Les Accents des Français*. Paris: Hachette.

Carvalho, J.B. (de) 1989. Phonological conditions on Portuguese clitic placement: syntactic evidence for stress and rhythmical patterns. *Linguistics* 27: 405–436.

Chafe, W.L. 1970. *Meaning and the Structure of Language*. Chicago: University of Chicago Press.

1976. Givenness, contrastiveness, definiteness, subjects, topics and point of view. In Li, C.N. (ed.). *Subject and Topic,* 25–55. New York: Academic Press.

Channon, R. and Shockey, L. (eds.) 1987. *In Honour of Ilse Lehiste*. Dordrecht: Foris.

Chao, Y.R. 1920. A system of tone letters. *Le maître phonétique* 45: 24–27.

1956. Tone, intonation, singsong, chanting, recitative, tonal composition, and atonal composition in Chinese. In Halle, M. (*et al*) *For Roman Jakobson: Essays on the Occasion of his 60th Birthday*, 52–59. The Hague: Mouton.

1968. *A Grammar of Spoken Chinese*. Berkeley.

Chiţoran, D., Augerot, J.E. and Pârlog, H. 1984. *The Sounds of English and Romanian*. Bucharest: Bucharest University Press.

Chomsky, N. 1970. Deep structure, surface structure and semantic interpretation. In Chomsky, N. 1972. *Studies on Semantics in Generative Grammar*: 62–119. The Hague: Mouton.

Chomsky, N. and Halle, M. 1968. *The Sound Pattern of English*. New York: Harper and Row.

Chuenkongchoo, T. 1956. *The Prosodic Characteristics of Certain Particles in Spoken Thai*. M.A. Thesis, The University of London (SOAS).

Cid, M. and Roach, P. 1990. Spanish Intonation Design and Implementation of a Machine-Readable Corpus. *JIPA* 20: 2–8.

Cinque, G. 1979. Left dislocation in Italian: a syntactic and pragmatic analysis. *Cahiers de Lexicologie* 34: 96–127.

Clements, G.N. and Ford, K.C. 1979. Kikuyu tone shift and its synchronic consequences. *Linguistic Inquiry* 10, 2: 179–210.

Cohen, A. and 't Hart, J. 1967. On the anatomy of intonation. *Lingua* 19: 177–192.

Cohen, A., Collier, R., and 't Hart, J. 1982. Declination: construct or intrinsic feature of speech pitch? *Phonetica* 39: 254–73.

Cohen, A. and Nooteboom, S. (eds.) 1975. *Structure and Process in Speech Perception*. Berlin: Springer-Verlag.

Cohuţ, C. and Mărdărescu, M. 1966. Sur la fréquence des types d'accentuation dans le roumain littéraire. *Cahiers de Linguistique Théorique et Appliquée* 3: 43–45.

Coleman, H.O. 1914. Intonation and emphasis. *Miscellanea Phonetica* 1: 6–26.

Collier, R. 1972. *From Pitch to Intonation*. Doctoral Dissertation, Catholic University of Leuwen.

1975. Perceptual and Linguistic tolerance in intonation. *IRAL* XIII/4: 293–308.

Collier, R. and 't Hart, J. 1972. Perceptual experiments on Dutch intonation. *Proc ICPhS* 7: 880–884.

1975. The role of intonation in speech perception. In Cohen and Nooteboom (eds.) 107–23.

1981. *Cursus Nederlandse Intonatie*. Leuven/Amersfoort: Acco.

Connell, B. and Ladd, D.R. 1990. Aspects of pitch realisation in Yoruba. *Phonology* 7, 1: 1–29.

Contini, M. and Profili, O. 1989. L'intonation de l'italien régional – un modèle de description par traits. *Mélanges de phonétique offerts à Péla Simon* (Université de Strasbourg) vol. 2, 855–870.

Contreras, H. 1963. Sobre el acento en español. *Boletín de Filología de la Universidad de Chile* 15: 223–237.

1977a. *El orden de las palabras en español*. Madrid: Cátedra.

1977b. Spanish epenthesis and stress. *Working Papers in Linguistics* 3: 9–33.

1980. Sentential stress, word order, and the notion of subject in Spanish. In Waugh and van Schooneveld, (eds.) 45–53.

Cooper, W.E. and Sorensen, J.M. 1981. *Fundamental Frequency in Sentence Production*. Berlin: Springer-Verlag.

References

Costa, I. 1978. *0 Acento em Português. Estudo de algumas Mudanças no Modelo da Fonologia Gerativa.* Dissertação de Mestrado, Universidade de Campinas, São Paulo.

Coster, D.C. and Kratochvil, P. 1984. Tone and stress discrimination in normal Beijing dialect speech. *New papers on Chinese language use,* 119–132. Canberra.

Couper-Kuhlen, E. 1986. *An Introduction to English Prosody.* London: Arnold.

Coustenoble, H.N. and Armstrong, L.E. 1934. *Studies in French Intonation.* Cambridge: Heffer and Sons.

Cresti, E. 1977. Frase e intonazione. *Studi di grammatica italiana* 6: 45–67.

Cresti, E.; Martorana, F.; Vayra, M. and Avesani, C. 1979. Effets de la prosodie de la phrase sur les variations du *F0* et de la syllabe. *10èmes Journées d'Etude sur la Parole* (Grenoble), 192–201.

Crompton, A. 1978. *A Generative Phonology of French Intonation.* Diss. Univ. of Cambridge.

Cruttenden, A. 1970. On the so-called grammatical function of intonation. *Phonetica* 21: 182–192.

1981. Falls and rises: meanings and universals. *JL* 17, 1: 77–91.

1986. *Intonation.* Cambridge: Cambridge University Press.

1990. The origins of nucleus. *JIPA* 2O, 1: 1–9.

1994. Rises in English. In Windsor-Lewis, J. (ed.) *Studies in General and English Phonetics. Essays in Honour of Professor J.D. O'Connor.* London: Routledge, 155–173.

Cruttenden, A. and Jarman, E. 1976. Belfast intonation and the myth of the fall. *JIPA* 6: 4–12.

Cruz-Ferreira, M. 1981. Tag questions in Portuguese: grammar and intonation. *Phonetica* 38: 341–52.

1983. *Non-native comprehension of intonation patterns in Portuguese and in English.* Ph. D. thesis, University of Manchester.

1984. Perception and interpretation of non-native intonation patterns. *Proc ICPhS 10,* 565–569.

1985. Elementos para um estudo comparativo dos sistemas prosódicos do português e do inglês. In *Miscelânea de estudos dedicados a Fernando de Mello Moser,* 373–388. Universidade de Lisboa.

1998. Intonation in European Portuguese. This volume, 175–186.

Crystal, D. 1969. *Prosodic Systems and Intonation in English.* Cambridge: Cambridge University Press.

1971. Relative and absolute in intonation analysis. *JIPA* 1, 1: 17–28.

1973. Non-segmental phonology in language acquisition: a review of the issues. *Lingua* 32: 1–45.

1988. *The English Language.* Harmondsworth: Penguin Books.

Csüry, B. 1925. A szamosháti nyelvjárás hanglejtésformái. *Magyar Nyelv* 21: 1–21, 159–175, 247–254.

Culicover, P.W. and Rochemont, M. 1983. Stress and focus in English. *Language* 59, 1: 123–165.

Cutler, A. 1984. Stress and accent in language production and understanding. In Gibbon and Richter (eds.) 1984, 77–90.

Cutler, A. and Ladd, D.R. (eds.) 1983. *Prosody: Models and Measurements*. Berlin, Heidelberg, New York, Tokyo: Springer-Verlag.

Cutler, A. and Pearson, M. 1986. On the Analysis of Prosodic Turn-Taking Cues. In Johns-Lewis, C. (ed.), 139–155.

Daneš, F. 1960. Sentence intonation from a functional point of view. *Word* 16: 34–54.

1964. A three-level approach to syntax. In *Travaux Linguistiques de Prague* vol. 1, *L'école de Prague aujourdhui:* 225–240.

1967. Order of elements and sentence intonation. In *To Honor Roman Jakobson (Essays on the Occasion of his Seventieth Birthday)*. The Hague: Mouton, 499–512.

Darwin, C.J. 1975. On the dynamic use of prosody in speech. In Cohen and Nooteboom (eds.) 178–193.

Dascălu (-Jinga), L. 1971. Some remarks on enumerative intonation in Romanian. *RRL* 16, 5: 401–410.

1974. On the "parenthetical" intonation in Romanian. *RRL* 19, 3: 231–248.

1975a. What are you asking about? (On the intonation of emphasis in Yes-No questions). *RRL* 20, 5: 477–480.

1975b. Observaţii asupra intonaţiei graiului din Maramureş. *Fonetică şi Dialectologie* 9: 77–91.

1976. Statistical remarks on question types in Romanian. *RRL* 21, 3: 391–399.

1979a. On the intonation of questions in Romanian. The rising pattern. *RRL* 24, 1: 35–44.

1979b. On the intonation of questions in Romanian. The rising-falling and the falling patterns. *RRL* 24, 2: 111–121.

1979c. Teste de percepţie asupra intonaţiei în limba română. *SCL* 30, 2: 125–139.

1979d. Elipsă şi transfer melodic în limba română. *SCL* 30, 3: 215–228.

1980a. Asupra intonaţiei cuvintelor relativ-interogative în limba română. *SCL* 31, 2: 161–177.

1980b. Despre intonaţia cuvintelor interogative folosite izolat. *SCL* 31, 4: 375–379.

1980c. A "reminding" wh-question and its intonation in Romanian. *RRL* 25, 2: 123–128.

1981a. Despre intonaţia unor enunţuri "cvasi-ecou" în limba română. *SCL* 32, 3: 215–220.

1981b. On the intonation of negative questions in Romanian. *RRL* 26, 4: 329–332.

1981c. Intonaţii interogative "compuse". *SCL* 32, 5: 473–477.

1982a. On the rhetorical interrogative intonation in Romanian. *RRL* 27, 2–3: 207–210.

1982b. Cîteva "răspunsuri interogative" şi intonaţia lor în limba română. *SCL* 33, 1: 39–46.

1983. On the Romanian alternative questions. *RRL* 28, 5: 405–413.

1984a. Asupra intonaţiei vocativului în limba română. *SCL* 35, 5: 440–451.
1984b. On the "melodic transfer" in Romanian. *RRL* 29, 3: 195–202.
1985a. On the interrogative falling pattern in Romanian. *RRL* 30, 3: 209–213.
1985b. An elliptical interrogative rising intonation in Romanian. *RRL* 30, 5: 413–415.
1985c. Intrebările ecou în limba română şi intonaţia lor. *SCL* 36, 4: 299–306.
1985d. Romanian call contours. *RRL* 30, 4: 317–320.
1986a. O intonaţie sud-carpatică în Ţara Oltului. *SCL* 37, 1: 24–49.
1986b. Asupra intonaţiei graiului din Bihor. *SCL* 37, 3: 221–239.
1988. Romanian idiomatic intonations. *RRL* 33, 4: 229–236.
1990. Cîteva cazuri de rezolvare a ambiguităţü sintactice cu ajutorul elementelor prosodice. *SCL* 41, 1: 25–34.
1991a. Romanian rejective intonations. In Stati, S. *et al.* (eds.) *Dialoganalyse III. Referate der 3 Arbeitstagung Bologna 1990*, 2. Tübingen: Niemeyer: 287–293.
1991b. Romanian intonation stereotypes. In *Proc ICPhS* 12, 5: 218–221.
1991c. Despre intonaţia unor exclamative eliptice. *SCL* 42, 1–2: 19–31.
1993a. Prosodic means of dialogue strategies. In Löffler, H. (ed.) *Dialoganalyse IV. Referate der 4 Arbeitstagung Basel 1992*, 1, Tübingen: Niemeyer: 295–300.
1993b. "Repair of prosody" in reading. *Proc ICL* 15, 2: 27–31.
1994. Su alcuni valori della prosodia nel rumeno parlato. *Studi Italiani di Linguistica Teorica e Applicata*, 23, 1: 111–126.
1998. Intonation in Romanian. This volume, 248–269.
De Mauro, T. 1970. *Storia linguistica dell'Italia unita*. Laterza, Bari.
Delattre, P. 1965. *Comparing the Phonetic Features of English, French, German and Spanish*. Heidelberg: Chilton Books, Julius Groos Verlag.
1966a. Les dix intonations de base du français. *French Review* 40, 1: 1–14.
1966b. *Studies in French and Comparative Phonetics*. Janua Linguarum. The Hague: Mouton.
1966c. A comparison of syllable length conditioning among languages. *IRAL* 4: 183–198.
1967. La nuance de sens par l'intonation. *French Review* 41, 3: 326–339.
Delattre, P., Poenack, E. and Olson, C. 1965. Some characteristics of German intonation for the expression of continuation and finality. *Phonetica* 13: 134–61.
Delgado-Martins, M.R. 1982. *Aspects de l'Accent en Portuguais*. Hamburg: Helmut Buske.
1988. *Ouvir falar. Introdução à fonética do português*. Lisboa: Editorial Caminho.
Dell, F. 1984. L'accentuation dans les phrases en français. In Dell, Hirst and Vergnaud, (eds.), 65–122.
Dell, F., Hirst, D.J. and Vergnaud, J.-R. (eds.) 1984. *Forme Sonore du Langage: Structure des Représentations en Phonologie*. Paris: Hermann.
Deme, L. 1962. A hanglejtés *(Intonation)*. In Tompa, J. (ed.) *A mai magyar nyelv rendszere* vol. II: 503–522. Budapest: Akadémiai kiadó.
Di Cristo, A. 1971. Intonation et unités discrètes. *Unpublished Ms*. Institut de phonétique d'Aix-en-Provence.

References

1975a. *Soixante-dix Ans de Recherches en Prosodie*. Aix-en-Provence, Ed. de l'Université de Provence.

1975b. Recherches sur la structuration prosodique de la phrase française. *Actes des 6èmes Journées d'études sur la Parole* (Toulouse), *GALF*: 95–116.

1976a. Des traits acoustiques aux indices perceptuels: application d'un modèle d'analyse prosodique à l'étude du vocatif en français. *TIPA* 3: 213–358.

1976b. Indices prosodiques et structure constituante. *Cahiers de Linguistique, d'Orientalisme et de Slavistique* 7: 27–40.

1978. *De la Microprosodie à l'Intonosyntaxe*. Thèse de Doctorat d'Etat (Univ. de Provence), Publications de l'Université de Provence, 2 vol. 1985.

1981. L'intonation est congruente à la syntaxe: une confirmation. In Rossi *et al.* 272–289.

1982. *Prolégomènes a l'Etude de l'Intonation: Micromélodie*. Paris: CNRS.

1985. *De la microprosodie à l'intonosyntaxe*. Publications Université de Provence.

1998. Intonation in French. This volume, 203–227.

Di Cristo, A. and Autesserre, D. 1972. Recherches psycho-sémantiques sur l'intonation de la phrase française. *TIPA* 1: 61–98.

Di Cristo, A. and Chafcouloff, M. 1981. L'intonème progrédient en français: caractéristiques intrinsèques et extrinsèques. In Léon and Rossi (eds.): 39–51.

Di Cristo, A., Di Cristo, P. and Véronis, J. 1997. A metrical model of rhythm and intonation for French text-to-speech synthesis. In Botinis, A., Kouroupetroglou, G. and Carayiannis, G. (eds.) *Intonation: Theory, Models and Applications*. ESCA, Athens: 83-86.

Di Cristo, A. and Hirst, D.J. 1986. Modelling French micromelody: analysis and synthesis. *Phonetica* 43: 11–30.

1993. Rythme syllabique, rythme mélodique et représentation hiérarchique de la prosodie du français. *TIPA* 15: 9–24.

1997. L'accentuation non-emphatique en français: paramètres et stratégies. In Perrot, J. (ed.) *Polyphonie pour Ivan Fónagy*. Paris: L'Harmattan.

Di Cristo, A., Haton, J.P., Rossi, M. and Vaissière, J. 1982. *Actes du Séminaire: Prosodie et Reconnaissance Automatique de la Parole* (Aix-en-Provence, 7–8 oct. 1982) *GALF*.

Dickinson and Mackin 1969. *Varieties of Spoken English*. Oxford University Press, Oxford.

Đỗ Thế Dũng 1986. *Eléments pour une étude comparative de l'intonation en français et en vietnamien: l'accent de mots en vietnamien*. Mémoire de DEA, Université Paris 3 ILPGA, Paris.

1989. Accent et ton en vietnamien. *Speech Research '89, Proceedings*, 1: 330–334. Budapest, June 1989.

Đỗ Thế Dũng, Trần Thiên Hương and Boulakia, G. 1998. Intonation in Vietnamese. This volume, 408–430.

Đoan Thien Thuat 1980. *Ngữ âm tiếng Việt* Hà Nội: Đại Học and Thcn.

Dow, F.D.M. 1972. *An outline of Mandarin phonetics*. Canberra.

Drăganu, N. 1945. *Elemente de Sintaxă a Limbii Române*. Bucureşti: Institutul de Lingvistică Română.

References

Duez, D. 1987. *Contribution à l'Etude de la Structuration Temporelle de la Parole en Français*. Thèse de Doctorat d'Etat, Université de Provence. (Aix-en-Provence).

Eady, S.J. and Cooper, W.E. 1986. Speech intonation and focus location in matched statements and questions. *JASA* 80: 402–415.

Eady, S.J., Cooper, W.E., Klouda, G.V., Mueller, P.R. and Lotts, D.W. 1986. Acoustical Characteristics of Sentencial Focus: Narrow *vs.* Broad and Single *vs.* Dual Focus Environments. *L&S* 29: 233–251.

Earle, M.A. 1975. *An acoustic phonetic study of Northern Vietnamese tones.* Speech Communication Research Laboratory, Santa Barbara, California.

Ehlich, K. 1986. Formen und Funktionen von Hm. Eine phonologisch-pragmatische Analyse. In Weydt, H. (ed.) *Die Partikeln der deutschen Sprache.* Berlin: de Gruyter: 503–517..

El-Mejjad, K. 1985. *Le parler de Marrakech: quelques aspects prosodiques.* Thèse de III° cycle. Université Paris VII.

Elert, C.C. 1970. *Ljud och ord i svenskan.* Stockholm: Almqvist and Wiksell. 1981. *Ljud och ord i svenskan 2.* Universitetet i Umeå.

Elert, C.C. Johansson, I. and Strangert, E. (eds.) 1984. *Nordic Prosody III,* University of Umeå. Stockholm: Almqvist and Wiksell.

Endresen, R.T. 1983. An alternative theory of stress and tonemes in Eastern Norwegian. In Jahr, E. H. (ed.) *Prosodi/Prosody, Studies in Norwegian Linguistics* 2, 362–387. Oslo: Lorentz O. Novus Forlag.

Engstrand, O. 1986. Durational correlates of quantity and sentence stress: a cross-linguistic study of Swedish, Finnish and Czech. *UCLA Working Papers in Phonetics* 63: 1–25.

Enkvist, N.E. 1980. Marked focus: functions and constraints. In Greenbaum, S. *et al.* (eds.) *Studies in English Linguistics for Randolph Quirk,* 134–152. Longman.

Enkvist, N.E. and Nordström, H. 1978. On textual aspects of intonation in Finland-Swedish newscasts. *Studia Linguistica* 32, 1–2: 63–79.

Ennaji, M. 1980. *The role of Wh-movement in extended standard theory: evidence from Moroccan Arabic.* M.A. Thesis. University of Essex. 1985. *Contrastive syntax: English, Moroccan Arabic and Berber Complex Sentences.* Konigshausen und Neumann.

Faber, D. 1987. The accentuation of intransitive sentences in English. *JL* 23, 2: 341–358.

Fant, L. 1984. *Estructura informativa en español. Estudio sintáctico y entonativo.* Stockholm: Almqvist and Wiksell International.

Farnetani, E. and Kori, S. 1983. Interaction of syntactic structure and rhythmical constraints on the realisation of word prosody. *Quaderni del Centro per le Ricerche di Fonetica* (Padova) 2: 287–318.

Farnetani, E. and Kori, S. 1986. Effects of syllable and word structure on segmental durations in spoken Italian. *Speech Communication* 5: 17–34.

Faure, G. 1962. *Recherches sur les caractères et le rôle des éléments musicaux dans la prononciation anglaise.* Paris: Didier. 1969. Contribution à l'étude des apports du système prosodique à la structuration de l'énoncé en français. *Proc. 10th Intern. Cong. of Linguists* (Bucarest) 2: 1079–1090.

1971. La description phonologique des systèmes prosodiques. *Zeitschrift fur Phonetik* 24: 347–359.

Faure, G., Hirst, D.J. and Chafcouloff, M. 1980. Rhythm in English: isochronism, pitch and perceived stress. In Waugh and Van Schooneveld (eds.), 71–79.

Fedjanina, N.A. 1976. *Udarenije v sovremennom russkom jazyke.* Moscow.

Ferguson, C.A. 1957. Two problems in Arabic phonology. *Word* 13, 3: 461–479.

Fernandes, N. 1976. *Contribuição para uma Análise Instrumental da Acentuação e Intonação do Português.* Dissertação de Mestrado, Universidade de São Paulo.

Féry, C. 1993. *German Intonational Patterns.* Tübingen: Niemeyer.

Firbas, J. 1964. On defining the theme in functional sentence perspective. In *Travaux Linguistiques de Prague* vol. 1, *L'école de Prague aujourdhui,* 267–280.

Firth, J.R. 1948. Sound and prosodies. *Transactions of the Philological Society:* 127–152. reprinted in Palmer, F.R. (1970). (ed.) *Prosodic analysis,* 1–26. Oxford: Oxford University Press.

Fischer-Jørgensen, E. 1982. Segment duration in Danish words and its dependency on higher level phonological units. *ARIPUC* 16: 137–189.

1984. The acoustic manifestation of stress in Danish with particular reference to the reduction of stress in compounds. *ARIPUC* 18: 45–161.

1987. The phonetic manifestation of the stød in Standard Danish. *ARIPUC* 21: 55–282.

1989. *A Phonetic Study of the Stød in Standard Danish.* University of Turku.

Fletcher, J. 1991. Rhythm and final lengthening in French. *JP* 19: 193–212.

Fónagy, I. 1956. Die Eigenart des sprachlichen Zeichens. *Lingua* 6: 67–88.

1958. *A hangsúlyról* (The accent). Budapest: Akadémiai kiadó.

1965. Zur Gliederung der Satzmelodie. *Proc ICPhS* 5, 281–292. Basel, New York: Karger.

1966a. "Api figyelj ide!" Dallammetafora és dallamváltozás ("Daddy, listen! " Metaphor and prosodic change). *Magyar Nyelvör* 64: 121–138.

1966b. Electrophysiological and acoustic correlates of stress and stress perception. *JSHR* 9: 231–244.

1969a. Métaphores d'intonation et changements d'intonation. *BSLP* 64, 1: 22–42.

1969b. Accent et intonation dans la parole chuchotée. *Phonetica* 20: 177–192.

1971. Synthèse de l'ironie. Analyse par la synthèse de l'intonation émotive. *Phonetica* 22: 42–51.

1972. "Il est huit heures" Contribution à la sémantique de la vive voix. *Phonetica* 26: 157–192.

1973. Poids sémantique et "poids phonique". *La Linguistique* 9: 7–35.

1979a. L'accent français: un accent probabilitaire. *Studia Phonetica* 15: 123–233.

1979b. Artistic vocal communication at the artistic level. In Hollien H. and P. (eds.) *Current Issues in the Phonetic Sciences,* 245–260. Amsterdam: Benjamins.

1980. Structure sémantique des signes de ponctuation. *BSLP* 75: 95–129.

1981a. Fonction prédictive de l'intonation. In Léon, P. and Rossi, M. (eds.): 113–120.

1981b. Emotions, voice and music. In Sundberg, J. (ed.) *Research aspects on singing*, 51–79. Stockholm: Royal Swedish Academy of Music.

1982a. *Situation et Signification*. Amsterdam/ Philadelphia.

1982b. Variation et normes prosodiques. *Folia Linguistica* 16: 17–39.

1983. *La Vive Voix. : essais de psycho-phonétique*. Paris: Payot.

1987a. Analysis of complex (integrated) melodic patterns. In Channon, R. and Shockey, L. (eds.) *In honour of Ilse Lehiste*, 75–97. Dordrecht: Foris.

1987b. Emotions, attitudes, modalities. Communication présentée au *XIème Congrès International des Sciences Phonétiques* (Tallin, 1–7 août 1987).

1989. Le français change de visage? *Revue Romane* 24, 2: 225–254.

1998. Intonation in Hungarian. This volume, 339–356.

Fónagy, I. and Bérard, E. 1972. "Il est huit heures": contribution à l'analyse sémantique de la vive voix. *Phonetica* 26: 157–192.

1973. Questions totales simples et implicatives en français parisien. In Grundstrom, A. and Léon, P.R. (eds.) *Interrogation et Intonation*. (= *Studia Phonetica* 8): 53–97.

1980. "BIeu ou vert?" Analyse et synthèse des énoncés disjonctifs. In Waugh and Schooneveld (eds.): 81–114.

Fónagy, I., Bérard, E. and Fónagy, J. 1983. Les clichés mélodiques du français parisien. *Folia Linguistica* 17: 153–185.

Fónagy, I. and Fónagy, J. 1976. Prosodie professionnelle et changements prosodiques. *Le Français Moderne* 44: 193–229.

1983. L'intonation et l'organisation du discours. *BSLP* 78, 1: 161–209.

Fónagy, I., Fónagy, J. and Sap, J. 1979. A la recherche des traits prosodiques dans le français parisien. *Phonetica* 36: 1–20.

Fónagy, I. and Galvagny, M.H. 1974. La Fonction Préindicative de l'Intonation en Français et en Hongrois. *Travaux de l'Institut d'Études Linguistiques et Phonétiques* I: 44–75.

Fónagy, I and Magdics, K. 1963a. Das Paradoxon der Sprechmelodie. Ansätze zur Melodielehre der ungarischen Sprache. *Ural-Altaische Jahrbücher* 35: 1–55.

1963b. A kérdö mondatok dallamáról (On the intonation of interrogative utterances). *Nyelvtudományi Értekezések* 40: 89– 106.

1967. *A magyar beszéd dallama* (The intonation of Hungarian). Budapest: Akadémiai kiadó.

Fontanella, M.B. 1966. Comparación de dos entonaciones regionales argentinas. *Boletín del Instituto Caro y Cuervo* 21: 17–29.

1971. La entonación del español de Córdoba (Argentina). *Boletín del Instituto Caro y Cuervo* 26: 11–21.

1980. Three intonational systems of argentinian Spanish. In Waugh and van Schooneveld (eds.): 115–126.

Forsyth, R. (ed.) 1984. *Expert systems: principles and case studies*. London.

Fourakis, M. 1986. An Acoustic Study of the Effects of Tempo and Stress on Segmental Intervals in Modern Greek. *Phonetica* 43: 172–188.

Fourcin, A.J. and Abberton, E. 1971. First application of a new laryngograph. *Medical and biological illustration* 21: 172–182.

Fox, A. 1973. Tone sequences in English. *Archivum Linguisticum* (New series) 4: 17–26.

1984. Subordinating and co-ordinating intonation structures in the articulation of discourse. In Gibbon and Richter (eds.) 1984, 120–133.

1985. Aspects of prosodic typology. *Working Papers in Linguistics and Phonetics* (Leeds) 3: 60–121.

French, P. and Local, J. 1986. Prosodic features and the management of interruption. In Johns-Lewis (ed.): 157–180.

Fretheim, T. (ed.) 1988. "Broad focus" and "narrow focus" in Norwegian intonation. Unpublished manuscript, Department of Linguistics, Trondheim University.

Fretheim, T. and Nilsen, R.A. 1987. Romsdal intonation: Where East and West Norwegian pitch contours meet. Manuscript.

1989. Terminal rise and rise-fall tunes in East Norwegian intonation. *Nordic Journal of Linguistics* 12: 155–181.

Fromkin, V.A. 1975. The interface between phonetics and phonology. *UCLA Working Papers in Phonetics* 31: 104–107.

(ed.) 1978. *Tone: a Linguistic Survey.* New York: Academic Press.

Fry, D.B. 1958. Experiments in the perception of stress. *L&S* 1: 120–152.

1968. Prosodic phenomena. In Malmberg (ed.) *Manual of Phonetics.* North Holland.

FSR 1988. *Fonetika spontannoj rechi.* Leningrad.

Fuchs, A. 1984. "Deaccenting" and "Default Accent". In Gibbon and Richter (eds.): 134–164.

Fudge, E.C. 1984. *English Word stress.* London: Allen and Unwin.

Fujisaki, H. 1988. A note on the physiological and physical basis for the phrase and accent components in the voice fundamental frequency contour. In Fujimura, O. (ed.) *Vocal physiology: voice production, mechanisms and functions.* New York: Raven Press.

Fujisaki, H., Hirose, K. and Sugito, M. 1979. Comparison of word accent features in English and Japanese. *Proc ICPhS* 1: 376.

Fujisaki, H. and Nagashima, S. 1969. A model for the synthesis of pitch-contours. *Annual report of the Engineering Research Institute,* 28: 53–60. Faculty of Engineering, University of Tokyo.

Gandour, J.T. 1978. The perception of tone. In Fromkin (ed.): 41–76.

Garde, P. 1968. *L'Accent.* Paris: Press Universitaires de France.

Gardiner, H.M., Clark Metcalf, R. and B.D. John, G. 1937. *Feeling and emotion. A history of theories.* New York: American Book Company.

Gårding, E. 1967a. *Internal juncture in Swedish. (=TILL* 6).

1967b. Prosodiska drag i spontant och uppläst tal. In Holm, G. (ed.) *Svenskt talspråk,* 40–85. Uppsala: Almqvist and Wiksell.

1970. Word tones and larynx muscles. *WP* 3: 20–46.

1975. The influence of tempo on rhythmic and tonal patterns in three Swedish dialects. *WP* 12: 71–83.

1977a. The importance of turning points for the pitch patterns of Swedish accents. In L.M. Hyman (ed.). *Studies in stress and accent. (= Southern California Occasional Papers in Linguistics* 4: 27–35.

1977b. *The Scandinavian word accents.* (= *TILL* 11).

1979. Sentence intonation in Swedish. *Phonetica* 36: 207–215.

1981. Contrastive prosody: a model and its applications. *Studia Linguistica* 35, 1–2: 146–165.

1982a. Prosodic expressions and pragmatic categories. In Koch, W. (ed.) *Textstrategier i tal och skrift,* 117–135. Almqvist and Wiksell International.

1982b. Swedish prosody. Summary of a project. *Phonetica* 39, 4–5: 288–301.

1983. A generative model of intonation. In Cutler and Ladd (eds.): 11–21.

1984. Comparing intonation. *WP* 27: 75–99.

1985. In defence of a phrase-based model of intonation. *WP* 28: 1–18.

1986. Superposition as an invariant feature of intonation. In Perkell J.S. and Klatt D.H. (eds.) *Invariance and variability in speech processes,* 292–299. Hillsdale, N.J and London: Lawrence Erlbaum Associates.

1987. Speech act and tonal pattern in standard Chinese, constancy and variation. *Phonetica* 44: 13–29.

1993. Focal domains and their manifestations in some Swedish dialects. In *Nordic Prosody* VI, 65–75. Stockholm: Almqvist and Wiksell International.

1998. Intonation in Swedish. This volume, 117–136.

Gårding, E., Botinis, A. and Touati, P. 1982. A comparative study of Swedish, Greek and French intonation. *W.P.* 22: 137–152.

Gårding, E. and Bruce, G. 1981. A presentation of the Lund Model for Swedish intonation. In Fretheim, T (ed.) *Nordic Prosody* II, 33–40.

Gårding, E., Bruce, G. and Bannert, R. (eds.) 1978. *Nordic Prosody.* (= *TILL* 13).

Gårding, E., Fujimura, O. and Hirose, H. 1970. Laryngeal control of word tones. *Ann. Bull.4 RI Logopedics and Phoniatrics,* 45–53. University of Tokyo.

Gårding, E., Fujimura, O., Hirose, H. and Simada, Z. 1975. Laryngeal control of Swedish word accents. For Kerstin Hadding. *WP* 10.

Gårding, E. and House, D. 1986. Emotion and intonation. Unpublished paper.

1987. Production and perception of phrases in some Nordic dialects. In Lilius, P. and Saari, M. (eds.) *The Nordic languages and modern linguistics* 6: 163–177. Helsinki University Press.

Gårding, E., Kratochvil, P., Svantesson, J.-O. and Zhang, J.-L. 1986. Tone 4 and Tone 3 discrimination in Modern Standard Chinese. *L&S* 29, 3: 281–293.

Gårding, E. and Lindblad, P. 1973. Constancy and variation in Swedish word accent patterns. For Bertil Malmberg. *WP* 7: 36–110.

1988. Eastern Norwegian and Western Swedish intonation in a common descriptive framework. *WP* 34: 50–55.

Gårding, E. and Stenberg, M. 1990. West Swedish and East Norwegian intonation. In *Nordic Prosody* V, 111–130. University of Turku.

Gårding, E., Zhang, J.-L., and Svantesson, J.-O. 1983. A generative model for tone and intonation in Standard Chinese. *WP* 25: 53–65.

Garrido, J.M. 1996 *Modelling Spanish Intonation for Text-to-Speech Applications.* Doctoral thesis, Universidad Autónoma de Barcelona.

Garro, L. and Parker, F. 1983. Relative clauses in Spanish some suprasegmental characteristics. *JP* 11: 85–99.

References

Gebara, E. 1976. *Alguns Aspectos da Intonação no Português*. Dissertação de Mestrado, Universidade de Campinas, São Paulo.

Gelfer, C.E., Harris, K. Collier, R. and Baer, T. 1983. Speculations on the control of fundamental frequency declination. *Status Report on Speech Research* 76: 51–68.

Gibbon, D. 1976a. *Perspectives of Intonation Analysis*. Frankfurt am Main: Peter Lang.

1976b. Performatory categories in contrastive intonation analysis. In Chiṭoran, D. (ed.) *Second International Conference of English Contrastive Projects*. Bucharest: 145–156.

1981. A new look at intonation, syntax and semantics. In James, A. and Westney, P. (eds.) *New Linguistic Impulses in Foreign Language Teaching*. Tübingen: Narr.

1984. Intonation as an adaptive process. In Gibbon and Richter (eds.) 165–192.

1987. The role of discourse in intonation theory. In Dressler, W. (ed.) *Phonologica 1984*. Cambridge: Cambridge University Press and Poznan: Adam-Mickiewicz-University Press: 49–58.

1994. Empirical and semiotic foundations for prosodic analysis. In Quastoff (ed.): 441–479.

1998. Intonation in German. This volume, 83–100.

Gibbon, D. and Richter H. (eds.) 1984. *Intonation Accent and Rhythm: Studies in Discourse Phonology*. Berlin: Walter de Gruyter.

Giegerich, H.J. 1985. *Metrical phonology and phonological structure*. Cambridge: Cambridge University Press.

Gimson, A.C. 1962. *An Introduction to the Pronunciation of English*. London: Arnold. Fifth edition revised by A. Cruttenden 1994.

Gold, B. and Rabiner, L. 1969. Parallel processing techniques for estimation of pitch periods of speech in the time domain. *JASA* 46: 442–448. August.

Goldsmith, J.A. 1974. *English as a tone language*. (ms MIT).

1976. *Autosegmental Phonology*. Ph.D. Dissertation: MIT (distributed by Indiana University Linguistics Club, Bloomington.)

1990. *Autosegmental and Metrical Phonology*. London: Blackwell.

Gordina, M.V. and Bystrov, I.S. 1961. Priznaki sintagmaticheskogo chlenija i frazovaja intonacija vo vjetnamskom jazyke.*Ucenye Zapiski* Leningradskogo Universiteta. Leningrad.

1984. *Foneticheskii stroj vjetnamskogo jazyke,* Moscow: Izdatelstvo Nauka,.

Gramatica Limbii Române. (= GLR) 1963. vol. 1, 2. (2nd ed.) Bucharest: Editura Acadamiei.

Grammont, M. 1933. *Traité de Phonétique*. Paris: Delagrave.

Greenberg, J.P., Ferguson, C.A. and Moravesik, E.A. (eds.) 1978. *Universals of human language,* volume 2: *Phonology*. Stanford: Stanford University Press.

Greenberg, S.R. 1969. *An Experimental Study of Certain Intonation Contrasts in American English*. Ph.D. Dissertation, UCLA.

Gregersen, K. and Basbøll, H. (eds.) 1987. *Nordic Prosody* IV. *Studies in Linguistics* 7. Odense: University Press.

Grice, M. 1992. *The intonation of interrogation in Palermo Italian; implications for intonation theory.* Ph.D. thesis. University College, London.

Grønnum (Thorsen), N. 1989. Stress group patterns, sentence accents and sentence intonation in Southern Jutland (Sønderborg and Tønder) – with a view to German. *ARIPUC* 23: 1–85.

1990. Prosodic Parameters in a Variety of Regional Danish Standard Languages, with a view towards Swedish and German. *Phonetica* 47: 182–214.

1992. *The Groundworks of Danish Intonation.* Copenhagen: Museum Tusculanum Press.

1995. Superposition and subordination in intonation – a non-linear approach. *Proc ICPhS* 13, vol. 2, 124–131.

1998. Intonation in Danish. This volume, 137–158.

Grosjean, F. and Deschamps, A. 1972. Analyse des variables temporelles du français spontané. *Phonetica* 26: 129–156.

Grosz, B.M. and Sidner, C.L. 1986. Attentions, intentions and the structure of discourse. *Computational Linguistics* 12, (3), 175–204.

Grundstrom, A. 1973. l'Intonation des questions en français standard. In Grundstrom, A. and Léon, P.R. (eds.) *Interrogation et Intonation.* (=*Studia Phonetica* 8): 19–49.

Gsell, R. 1979. *Sur la prosodie du thai standard: Tons and accent.* Université Paris 3, ILPGA, Paris.

1980. Remarques sur la structure de l'espace tonal en vietnamien du sud (Parler de Saigon). *Cahiers d'Etudes Vietnamiennes* 4. Université Paris 7.

1981. Sur la realisation chuchotée des tons du Thai standard. *Travaux de l'Institut d'Etudes Linguistiques et Phonetiques, Vol III, Phonetique,* 227–245. Université de la Sorbonne Nouvelle, Paris.

Guaïtella, I. 1991. *Rythme et Parole: Comparaison du rythme de la Lecture Oralisée et de la Parole Spontanée.* Thèse de 3ème Cycle, Université de Provence.

Guierre, L. 1979. *Essai sur l'accentuation en anglais contemporain.* Thèse de Doctorat d'Etat, Université de Paris VII.

Gussenhoven, C. 1983. Focus, mode and nucleus. *JL* 19.2: 377–417.

1984. *On the grammar and semantics of sentence accents.* Dordrecht: Foris.

Guția, I. 1959. Sull'accento nella lingua romena (osservazioni in margine alle trasmissioni di Radio Bucarest). *Acta Philologica* II: 269–277.

Guțu-Romalo, V. 1968. *Morfologie Structurală a Limbii Române (Substantiv, Adjectiv, Verb).* Bucharest: Editura Academiei.

Gvozdev, A.N. 1949. *O fonologicheskih sredvstvah russkogo jazyka.* Moscow-Leningrad.

Haas, M. 1964. *Thai-English Students' Dictionary.* Stanford: Stanford University Press.

Hadding-Koch, K. 1961. *Acoustico-phonetic studies in the intonation of southern Swedish.* (= *TILL* 3).

Hakulinen, L. 1979. Suomen kielen rakenne ja kehitys (4th and enlarged ed.). Helsinki: Otava.

Halle, M. 1959. *The Sound Pattern of Russian.* The Hague: Mouton.

Halle, M. and Vergnaud, J.R. 1987. *An Essay on Stress*. Cambridge, Mass.: MIT Press.

Halliday, M.A.K 1963a. Intonation in English grammar. *Transactions of the Philological Society* (1963): 143–169. Reprinted in Halliday 1967a: 31–49.

1963b. The tones of English. *Archivum Linguisticum* 15: 1–28. Reprinted in Halliday 1967a, 9–30.

1963c. Intonation systems in English. In McIntosh, A. *(et al.)* 1966. *Patterns of Language: Papers in General Description and Applied Linguistics*. London: Longman.

1967a. *Intonation and Grammar in British English*. The Hague: Mouton.

1967b. Notes on transitivity and theme in English. *JL* 3: 199–244.

1970. *A Course in Spoken English: Intonation*. London: Oxford University Press.

Halliday, M.A.K. and Hasan, R. 1976. *Cohesion in English*. London: Longman.

Han, M.S. and Kim, H.O. 1974. Phonetic variation of Vietnamese tones. *JP* 2: 223–232.

Haraguchi, S. 1977. *The tone pattern of Japanese: an autosegmental theory of tonology*. Doctoral dissertation, MIT.

Harrell. R.S. 1962. A short reference grammar of Moroccan Arabic. Washington: Georgetown University Press.

Harris, J.W. 1983. *Syllable Structure and Stress in Spanish. A Non linear Analysis*. Cambridge, Mass.: MIT Press.

1987. The accentual patterns of verb paradigms in Spanish. *Natural Language and Linguistic Theory* 5: 61–90.

1988. *Spanish stress: the extrametricality issue*. ms. MIT, Cambridge, Mass.

1989. How different is verb stress in Spanish? *Probus* 1. 3: 241–258.

1992. *Spanish Stress: the Extrametricality Issue*. Bloomington, IULC.

1995. Spanish Stress. In J. Goldsmith (ed.) *The Handbook of Phonologycal Theory*. Cambridge, Mass. Blackwell: 867–887.

Harris, Z.S. 1944. Simultaneous components in phonology. *Language* 20: 181–205.

't Hart, J. 1976. How distinctive is intonation? In Kern, R. (ed.) *Löwen und Sprachtige*, 367–83. Leuven: Peeters.

1986. Declination has not been defeated: a reply to Lieberman *et al*. *JASA* 80, 6: 1838–1840.

1998. Intonation in Dutch. This volume, 101–116.

't Hart, J. and Collier, R. 1975. Integrating different levels of intonation analysis, *JP* 3: 235–255.

1979. On the interaction of accentuation and intonation in Dutch. *Proc ICPhS* 9, II: 395–402.

't Hart, J., Collier, R. and Cohen, A. 1991. *A Perceptual Study of Intonation*. Cambridge: Cambridge University Press.

Haudricourt, A.G. 1954a. L'origine des tons en vietnamien. *Journal Asiatique* T.242, Fasc. I.

1954b. La place du vietnamien dans les langues austro-asiatiques. *BSLP* .49,, I).

Haugen, E. 1967. On the rules of Norwegian tonality. *Language* 43: 185–202.

Haviland, S.E. and Clark, H.H. 1974. What's new? Acquiring new information as a process in comprehension. *Journal of Verbal Learning and Verbal Behavior* 13: 512–520.

Haydar, Y. and Mrayati, M. 1985. Etude de l'intonation: la courbe mélodique de phrases de l'arabe standard. In *Travaux de l'Institut de Phonétique de Strasbourg* 17: 73–113.

Hayes, B.P. 1980. *A Metrical Theory of Stress Rules.* Doctoral dissertation. Cambridge, Mass.: MIT Press.

1984. The phonology of rhythm in English. *Linguistic Inquiry* 15, 1: 33–74.

Hegedüs, L. 1930. *Magyar hanglejtésformák grafikus ábrázolása – Experimentalphonetische Untersuchungen über den musikalischen Satzakzent im Ungarischen.* (Abstract in German.) Budapest: Egyetemi nyomda.

Henderson, E.J.A. 1949. Prosodies in Siamese. *Asia Major* (new series) 1.2: 189–215. Reprinted in Palmer, F.R. (ed.) 1970. *Prosodic Analysis*, 27–53. Oxford: Oxford University Press.

Henne, H., Rongen, O.B. and Hansen, L.J. 1977. *A handbook on Chinese language structure.* Oslo.

Hermann, E. 1942. Probleme der Frage. *Nachrichten von der Akademie der Wissenschaften in Gottingen, Philologischhistorische Klasse*, 121–448.

Herslund, M. 1977. Remarques sur l'accentuation romane. In Conde, M.V. *et al.* (eds.) *Estudios Ofrecidos a Emilio Alarcos Llorach (Con Motivo de sus XXV Años de Docencia en la Universidad de Oviedo)*, 123–147. Universidad de Oviedo.

Hetzron, R. 1962. L'accent hongrois. *BSLP* 57: 192–205.

1977. Izelitö a magyar tonoszintaksziból (A fragment of a phono-syntax of Hungarian). *Nyelvtudományi Ertekezesek* 104: 389–398.

Hiranburana, S. 1971. *The Role of Accent in Thai Grammar.* Ph.D. Dissertation, University of London, SOAS.

Hirst, D.J. 1983a. Structures and categories in prosodic representations. In Cutler and Ladd (eds.): 93–109.

1983b. Interpreting intonation: a modular approach. *Journal of Semantics* 2, 2: 171–181.

1984. Prosodie et structures de données en phonologie. In Dell, Hirst and Vergnaud (eds.): 43–64.

1987. *La représentation linguistique des systèmes prosodiques: une approche cognitive.* Thèse de Doctorat d'Etat, Université de Provence.

1988. Tonal units as phonological constituents: the evidence from French and English intonation. In van der Hulst and Smith (eds.): 151–165.

1989. Review of Sperber and Wilson (1986) Relevance: Communication and Cognition. *Mind and Language* 4, 1–2: 138–146.

1991. Intonation models: towards a third generation. *Proc ICPhS* 12, 1: 305–310.

1993. Detaching intonational phrases from syntactic structure. *Linguistic Inquiry*. 24, 4: 781–788.

1998. Intonation in British English. This volume, 60–82.

Hirst, D.J. and Di Cristo, A. 1984. French intonation: a parametric approach. *Die Neueren Sprachen* 83, 5: 554–569.

1986. Unités tonales et unités rythmiques dans la représentation de l'intonation du français. *Actes des 15èmes Journées d'Etudes sur la Parole.* (Aix-en-Provence), *G.A.L.F.* 93–95.

1998 A survey of intonation systems. This volume, 1–48.

Hirst, D.J., Di Cristo, A. and Espesser, R. In press. Levels of representation and levels of analysis for the description of intonation systems. In Horne, M. (ed.) *Prosody: Theory and Experiment.* Berlin: Kluwer Academic Press.

Hirst, D.J., Di Cristo, A., Le Besnerais, M., Z. Najim, Nicolas, P. and Roméas, P. 1993. Multi-lingual modelling of intonation patterns, *Proceedings ESCA Workshop on Prosody,* (= *WP 41*): 204–207.

Hirvonen, P. 1970. *Finnish and English communicative intonation.* Publications of the Phonetics Department of the University of Turku 8.

Hjelmslev, L. 1936–1937. Accent, intonation, quantité. *Studi Baltici* 6: 1–57.

Hoang Cao Cuong 1984. Về khái niệm ngôn điệu. *Ngôn Ngữ Ń 2.* Hà Nội : Viện Ngôn Ngữ.

1985. Bước đầu nhận xét về đặc điểm ngữ điệu tiếng Việt (trên cứ liệu thực nghiệm) *Ngôn Ngữ Ń3,* Hà Nội: Viện Ngôn Ngữ,

Hoang Tue and Hoang Minh 1975. Remarques sur la structure phonologique du vietnamien. *Essais Linguistiques, Etudes Vietnamiennes 40,* Hà Nội.

Hochgreb, N. 1983. *Análise Acústico-perceptiva da Entoação do Português: A Frase Interrogativa.* Tese de Doutorado, Universidade de São Paulo.

Hockett, C.F. 1942. A system of descriptive phonology. *Language* 18: 3–21.

1963. The problem of universals in language. In J.H. Greenberg (ed.) *Universals of Language,* 1–29. Cambridge, Mass.: MIT Press.

Holmes, J.N. 1988. *Speech synthesis and recognition.* London: Pitman.

Hornby, P.A. 1972. The psychological subject and predicate. *Cognitive Psychology* 3: 632–642.

Horne, M. 1978. On French stress and intonation (mimeographed). Lund University.

1987. Towards a discourse-based model of English sentence intonation. *WP 32.*

1989. Empirical evidence for a deletion formulation of the rhythm rule in English. Submitted for publication to Linguistics.

House, D. 1990. *Tonal perception in speech.* (= *TILL* 24).

House, D. Bruce, G., Eriksson, L. and Lacerda, F. 1988. Recognition of prosodic categories in Swedish: Rule implementation. *WP 34*: 62–66.

Howie, J.M. 1974. On the domain of tone in Mandarin: some acoustical evidence. *Phonetica* 30, 3: 129–148.

1976. *Acoustical studies of Mandarin vowels and tones.* Cambridge.

Hughes, A. and Trudgill, P. 1979. *English Accents and Dialects: an Introduction to Social and Regional Varieties of British English.* London: Arnold.

Iivonen, A. 1975. Timing of sound duration in negative correlation with phonotactic word length. *Proc ICLS* 11, II: 769–773.

1978. Is there interrogative intonation in Finnish? In Gårding *et al.* (eds.): 43–53.

1983. On explaining the sentence initial pitch height in Finnish. *PPH* 8.

1984a. On explaining the initial fundamental frequency in Finnish utterances. In Elert *et al.* (eds.): 107–119.

References

1984b. Domeeni prosodiikassa: täsmennyksiä ja ongelmia. *PPH* 9.

1987. Paradigm of recurrent accent types of Finnish. In Gregersen, K. and Basbøll, H. (eds.): 115–126.

1998. Intonation in Finnish. This volume, 322–338.

Iivonen, A., Nevalainen, T., Aulanko, R. and Kaskinen, H. 1987. *Puheen intonaatio.* Helsinki: Gaudeamus.

Iordan, I. 1934. Etimologii: Demon. *Dacoromania* 7: 140–148.

Isačenko, A.V. and Schädlich, H.J. 1966. Untersuchungen über die deutsche Satzintonation. *Studia Grammatica* 7: 7–67.

Isshiki, N. 1964. Regulatory mechanism of voice intensity variation. *JSHR* 7: 17–29.

Itkonen, T. 1972. Kuoreveden ja Keuruun murretta. *Tekstejä ja sandhiseikkojen tarkastelua. Suomi* 117:1.

Izard, C.E. 1977. *Human emotions.* New York: Plenum.

Jackendoff, R.S. 1972. *Semantic Interpretation in Generative Grammar.* Cambridge, Mass.: MIT Press.

Jahr, E.H. and Lorentz, O. (eds.) 1983. *Prosodi/Prosody. Studier i norsk språkvitenskap* 2. Oslo: Novus forlag.

Jassem, W. 1952. *Intonation of Conversational English (Educated Southern British).* Wroclaw: Wroclawskie Towarzystwo Naukow.

Jassem, W. and Gibbon, D. 1980. Re-defining English stress. *JIPA* 10: 2–16.

Jassem, W., Hill, D.R. and Witten, I.H. 1984. Isochrony in English speech: its statistical validity and linguistic relevance. In Gibbon and Richter (eds.): 203–225.

Jensen, M.K. 1961. *Tonemicity. Acta Univ. Bergensis.* Hum. Serie No 1.

Jespersen, O. 1887–1899. *Fonetik.* Copenhagen: Det Schubotheske Forlag.

Johansson, K. 1970. Perceptual experiments with Swedish disyllabic accent 1 and accent 2 words. *WP* 3: 47–74.

Johns-Lewis, C. (ed.) 1986. *Intonation in Discourse.* London: Croom Helm.

Jones, D. 1918. *Outline of English Phonetics.* 8th edition: 1956. Cambridge: Heffer.

Jones, R.B. and Huynh Sanh Thong 1957. *Introduction to spoken Vietnamese.* Washington D.C: American Council of Learned Societies.

Joseph, B.D. and Philippaki-Warburton, I. 1987. *Modern Greek.* London: Croom Helm.

Kacnel'son, S.D. 1971. *Fonemy, sindemy i promezhutochnyje obrazovanija. Fonetika. Fonologija. Grammatika.* Moscow.

Kahn, F. 1968. Introduction à l'étude de la mélodie de l'énoncé français chez un jeune parisien cultivé du 16ème arrondissement. *Cahiers F. de Saussure* 24: 15–44.

Kallioinen, V. 1965. Contribution à l'étude de l'intonation roumaine. In Iordan, I. *et al.* (eds.) *Omagiu lui Alexandru Rosetti la 70 Ani,* 433–435. Bucureşti: Editura Academiei.

1968. Suomen kysymyslauseen intonaatiosta. *Virittäjä* 72: 35–54.

Kaplan, E.L. 1970. Intonation and language acquisition. *Papers and Reports on Child Language Development* (Stanford University) I: 1–21.

Karcevskij, S. 1931. Sur la phonologie de la phrase. *Travaux du Cercle Linguistique de Prague* IV.

Karlgren, B. 1918. *A Mandarin phonetic reader in the Pekinese dialect.* Stockholm.

Karlsson, F. 1969. Suomen yleiskielen segmentaalifoneemien paradigma. *Virittäjä* 73: 351–362.

1983. *Suomen kielen äänne- ja muotorakenne.* Porvoo/ Helsinki/Juva: WSOY.

Keating, P.A. 1988. The phonology-phonetics interface. In Newmayer, F.J. (ed.) *Linguistics: the Cambridge Survey. I. Linguistic Theory: foundations.* 281–302. Cambridge: Cambridge University Press.

Kenning, M. 1979. Intonation systems in French. *JIPA* 9, 1: 15–30.

1983. The tones of English and French. *JIPA* 13, 1: 32–48.

Khomsi, A. 1975. *Etude phonétique et phonologique de l'arabe marocain de Casablanca.* Thèse de III° cycle. Université F. Rabelais, Tours.

Kingdon, R. 1958a. *Groundwork of English Stress.* London: Longman.

Klatt, D.H. 1980. Real-time synthesis by rule. *JASA.* 68: 918.

Klinghardt, H. and Klemm, G. 1920. *Übungen im englischen Tonfall.* Cöthen.

Knowles, G. 1979. The nature of phonological variables in Scouse. In Trudgill (ed.) 80–90.

1984. Variable strategies in intonation. In Gibbon and Richter (eds.) 1984.

1987. *Patterns of Spoken English: an Introduction to English Phonetics.* London: Longman.

Kock, A. 1878. *Språkhistoriska undersökningar om svensk akcent I-II.* Lund: Gleerup.

Kodzassov, S.V. 1985. *Intonacija voprositel'nych predlozhenij: forma i funkcija. Dialogovoje vzaimodejstvije i predstavlenije znanij.* Novosibirsk.

Kohler, K. 1987. Categorical pitch perception. *Proc ICPhS* 11, 5: 331–333.

1995. *Einführung in die Phonetik des Deutschen.* Berlin: Erich Schmidt Verlag.

Konopczynski, G. forthcoming. Developmental interactive intonology; theory and applications, in M. Lynch (ed.), *The Cognitive Science of Prosody.* Amsterdam, Elsevier Science Publishers,

Kori, S. and Farnetani, E. 1983a. Acoustic manifestation of focus in Italian. *Quaderni del Centro per le Ricerche di Fonetica (Padova)* 2, 323–338.

1983b. Acoustic manifestation of the contextual organisation of utterance in Italian. *Proc ICPhS* 10, IIA: 583.

1984. Studi percettivo dell'intonazione dell'italiano. *Quaderni del Centro per le Ricerche di Fonetica (Padova)* 3, 217–222.

Kori, S. and Yasuda, H. 1991. Syntax and intonation in Italian noun phrases. *Proc ICPhS.* 12, IV: 194–198.

Kratochvil, P. 1968. *The Chinese language today.* London.

1969. Syllabic volume as acoustic correlate of prominence in Peking dialect. *Chinese linguistics project, Princeton University* 5: 1–28.

1971. An experiment in the perception of Peking dialect tones. *Monograph studies of the Scandinavian Institute of Asian Studies* 6: 7–40.

1974. Stress shift mechanism and its role in Peking dialect. *Modern Asian Studies* 8, 4: 433–458.

1985. Variable norms of tones in Beijing prosody. *Cahiers de linguistique, Asie orientale* 14, 2: 153–174.

1987a. The case of the Third Tone. *Wang Li memorial volumes, English volume*: 253–276. Hong Kong.

1987b. Běijīnghuà zhèngcháng huàyŭli de qīngshēng (Atonicity in normal Beijing dialect speech). *Zhōngguó yǔwén* 5: 330–345.

1998. Intonation in Beijing Chinese. This volume, 431–446.

Krivnova, O.F. 1975. *Sostavl'ajushchaja nesushchego tona v strukture melodicheskoj krivoj frazy. Issledovanija po strukturnoj i prikladnoj lingvistike*. Moscow.

Kvavik, K.H. 1974. An Analysis of sentence initial and final intonational data in two Spanish dialects. *JP* 2: 351–361.

1975. Sense group terminations in mexican Spanish. *Studies in Honor of Lloyd A. Kasten*, 101–115. Madison.

Kvavik, K.H. and Olsen, C.L. 1974. Theories and methods in Spanish intonational studies. Survey. *Phonetica* 30: 65–100.

Laaksonen, K. and Lieko, A. 1988. Suomen kielen äänne- ja muoto-oppi. Loimaa: Finn Lectura.

Ladd, D.R. 1978. Stylised intonation. *Language* 54, 3: 517–540.

1979. On intonational universals. Paper presented at the International Symposium on the Cognitive Representation of Speech, Edinburgh, July 29– Aug. 3.

1980. *The structure of intonational meaning, evidence from English*. Bloomington/London: Indiana University Press.

1981. On intonational universals. In Myers, T., Laver, J, and Anderson, J. (eds.) *The cognitive representation of speech*, 389–397. Amsterdam: North-Holland Publishing Company.

1983a. Peak features and overall slope. In A. Cutler and D.R. Ladd (eds.) 1983, 39–52.

1983b. Phonological features of intonational peaks. *Language* 59, 4: 721–759.

1984. Declination: a review and some hypotheses. *PY* 1: 53–74.

1986. Intonational phrasing: The case for recursive prosodic structure. *PY* 3: 311–340.

1989. The metrical representation of pitch register. In Kingston, J. and Beckman, M. (eds.) *Laboratory Phonology* I. Cambridge: Cambridge University Press.

Ladd, D.R. and Cutler, A. 1983. Models and measurements in the study of prosody. In Cutler and Ladd (eds.) 1–10.

Lahlou, M. 1981. La durée intrinsèque des voyelles en arabe marocain de Fès. *TIPA* 8: 145–162.

1982. *Prolégomènes à l'étude de l'intonation de l'arabe marocain de Fès*. Thèse de III° cycle. Université de Provence.

Lasorsa, C. 1976. Caratteristiche dell'accento italiano nella pronuncia del russo. *Rassegna Italiana de Lingusitica Applicata*, Anno, CIII, n.1: 46–52.

Lazarus, R.S., Averill, J.R. and Opton, E.M. jr. 1970. Towards a cognitive theory of emotions. In Arnold, M.B. (ed.) *Feelings and emotions*, 207–232. New York: Academic Press.

Le Thi Xuyen 1989. *Etudes contrastives de l'intonation expressive en français et en vietnamien*. Thèse de Doctorat, Université Paris 3. (unpublished).

Lea, W.A. 1977. Acoustic correlates of stress and juncture. In Hyman (ed.): 83–117.
1980. Prosodic aids to speech recognition. In Lea, W.A. (ed.) *Trends in speech recognition*, 166–205. New Jersey: Prentice-Hall.
Leach, P. 1980. *Linguistic Aspects of French Intonation*. Ph. D. Thesis, University of Leeds.
1988. French intonation: tone or tune? *JIPA*. 18, 2: 125–139.
Leben, W.R. 1973. *Suprasegmental phonology*. Ph. D. Thesis. MIT.
1976. The tones in English intonation. *Linguistic Inquiry* 21: 69–107.
Lee, J.D. and Lee, T.D. 1982. *Statistics and computer methods in BASIC*. New York.
Lehiste, I. 1960. An acoustic-phonetic study of internal open juncture. *Phonetica 5*, Suppl.
1965. Juncture. In Zwirner, E. and Bethge, W. (eds.) *Proc ICPhS* 5: 172–200.
1970. *Suprasegmentals*. Cambridge, Mass.: MIT Press.
1975. The phonetic structure of paragraphs. In Cohen and Nooteboom (eds.): 195–206.
1979. Perception of sentence and paragraph boundaries. In Lindblom, B. and Öhman, S. (eds.) *Frontiers of speech communication research*, 191–201. New York: Academic Press.
Lehiste, I. and Ivić, P. 1980. The intonation of yes/no questions – a new Balkanism? *Balkanistica* 6: 45–53.
Lehtonen, J. 1970. Aspects of Quantity in Standard Finnish. *Studia philologica Jyväskyläensia* VI. Jyväskylä: Jyväskylän yliopisto.
1971. Puheen sävelkulun muoto ja merkitys. Jyväskylän yliopiston suomen kielen laitoksen julkaisuja 3.
Leino, P. 1987. *Language and metre*. Helsinki: Suomalaisen kirjallisuuden seura.
Leite, Y. 1974. *Portuguese Stress and Related Rules*. Ph.D. Dissert. University of Texas at Austin.
Léon, P.R. 1971. *Essais de Phonostylistique*. (= *Studia Phonetica* 4). Paris, Toronto: Didier.
1974. Modalité impérative et intonation. *World Papers in Phonetics, Festschrift for Dr Onishi's Kiju* 253–280. Tokyo: Phon. Soc. of Japan.
Léon, P.R. and Bath, R. 1987. Structures prosodiques du questionnement radiophonique. *Information Communication* (Toronto) 88–105.
Léon, P.R. and Martin, P. 1980. Des accents. In Waugh and Van Schooneveld (eds.) 177–185.
Léon, P.R. and Rossi, M. (eds.) 1980. *Problèmes de Prosodie, I, Approches théoriques*. (= *Studia Phonetica 17*) Ottawa: Didier.
1981. *Problèmes de Prosodie, II, Expérimentations, modèles et fonctions*. (= *Studia Phonetica 18*) Ottawa: Didier.
Lepschy, G.C. 1978. Appunti sull'intonazione italiana. *Annali della Scuola Normale Superiore di Pisa* 8, 441–456.
Levitt, A. 1993. The acquisition of prosody; evidence from French- and English-learners. *Haskins Laboratories Status Report on Speech Research*, 113, 41–50.
Lhote, E. 1979. Quelques problèmes posés par l'élaboration de règles prédictives de l'intonation. In Hollien, H.and P. (eds.) *Proceedings of the IPS-1977 Congress*, 309–319. Miami Beach, Florida, Amsterdam: John Benjamins, B.V.

Liberman, M. 1975. *The Intonation System of English.* Ph.D. Dissertation, MIT. New York: Garland. Bloomington: Indiana University Linguistic Club.

Liberman, M. and Sag, I. 1974. Prosodic form and discourse function. *Papers from the 10th Regional Meeting, Chicago Linguistic Society,* 416–427.

Liberman, M. and Prince, A. 1977. On stress and linguistic rhythm. *Linguistic Inquiry* 8: 249–336.

Liberman, M. and Pierrehumbert, J. 1984. Intonational invariance under changes in pitch range and length. In Aranoff, M. and Oehrle, R.T. (eds.) *Language sound structure: studies in phonology presented to Morris Halle,* 157–233. Cambridge, Mass.: MIT Press.

Lieberman, P. 1960. Some acoustic correlates of word stress in American English. *JASA* 32: 451–454.

1967. *Intonation, Perception, and Language.* Cambridge Mass.: MIT Press.

1986. The acquisition of intonation by infants, physiology and neural control. In Johns-Lewis (ed.): 239–257.

Lieberman, P and Tseng, C.Y. 1981. On the fall of the declination theory: breath group *versus* declination as the base form for intonation. *JASA ,* Supl. 1 67, S 63.

Lindau, M. 1986. Testing a model of intonation in a tone language. *JASA* 80, 3: 757–764.

Lindberg, C.E. 1979. Is the sentence a unit of speech production and perception? In Mey, J.L. (ed.) *Pragmalinguistics,* 51–60. Mouton.

Lindblom, B. and Svensson, S.G. 1973. Interaction between segmental and non-segmental factors in speech recognition. *IEEE Trans. on Audio and Electroacoustics* vol. AU 21, No 6: 536–545.

Lindsay, D. and Ainsworth, W.A. 1985. Two models of nuclear intonation. *JP* 13: 163–173.

Lindsey, G. 1985. *Intonation and interrogation: Tonal structure and the expression of a pragmatic function in English and other languages.* Ph. D thesis, UCLA. 1991 Bolinger's challenge: melody, meaning and emotion (review of Bolinger 1989), *JL* 29 (1).

Linell, P. 1972. *Remarks on Swedish morphology.* RUUL 1. Department of Linguistics Uppsala University.

Local, J. 1986. Patterns and problems in a study of Tyneside intonation. In Johns-Lewis (ed.): 181–198.

Löfqvist, A., McGarr, N. and Kiyoshi, H. 1984. Laryngeal muscles and articulatory control. *JASA* 76, 3: 951–954.

Lombard, A. 1935. *La prononciation du roumain.* Uppsala Universitets Årsskrift. Lundequistska Bokhandeln. 100–176.

Loveday, L. 1981. Pitch, politeness and sexual role: an exploratory investigation into the pitch correlates of English and Japanese politeness formulae. *L&S* 24, 1: 71–89.

Luangthongkum, T. 1977. *Rhythm in Thai.* Ph.D. Dissertation, University of Edinburgh.

References

Lubker, J., Lindblom, B., Gay, T., Lyberg, B., Branderud, P. and Holmgren, K. 1983. Prosody and compensatory motor behaviour. (abstract), Paper read at *Symposium on Prosody – Normal and Abnormal.* Zürich, April 6–8.

Luksaneeyanawin, S. 1983. *Intonation in Thai.* Ph.D. Dissertation, University of Edinburgh.

    1984a. Tonal behaviour of one-word utterances in Thai: the interplay of tone and intonation. *WIP* 17: 16–30.

    1984b. Some semantic functions of Reduplicatives in Thai. In Tuaycharoen, P. (*et al.*) *Selected Papers from the 1st International Symposium on Language and Linguistics*, 125–144. Chiangmai University.

    1986. *Phonetic correlates and functions of speech pause in Thai.* (Research Monograph, Linguistics Research Unit). Chulalongkorn University.

    1998. Intonation in Thai. This volume, 388–407.

Lyberg, B. 1979. Final lengthening – partly a consequence of restrictions on the speed of fundamental frequency change? *JP* 7: 187–196.

Maddieson, I. 1985. Phonetic cues to syllabification. In Fromkin, V.A (ed.) *Phonetic Linguistics, Essays in Honor of Peter Ladefoged*, 203–221.

Maeda, S. 1976. *A characterisation of American English intonation.* Unpublished Ph. D. thesis, MIT, Cambridge, MA.

Magdics, K. 1964. First findings in the comparative study of intonation of Hungarian dialects. *Phonetica* 11: 19–38.

Magno Caldognetto, E. and Fava, E. 1974. Studio sperimentale delle carateristiche elettro-acustiche delle'enfasi su sintagmi in italiano. *S.L.I.* 2, 441–456.

Magno Caldognetto, E.; Ferrero, F.; Lavagnoli, C. and Vagges, K. 1978. F_0 contours of statements, yes-no questions and WH-questions of two regional varieties of Italian. *Journal of Italian Linguistics* 3, (1), 57–67.

Maidment, J.A. 1983. Language recognition and prosody: further evidence. *Speech Hearing and Language* 1: 131–141.

Major, R. 1981. Stress-timing in Brazilian Portuguese. *JP* 9, 3: 343–351.

    1985. Stress and Rhythm in Brazilian Portuguese. *Language* 61, 2: 259–282.

Makkai, V. 1972. (ed.) *Phonological Theory: Evolution and Current Practice.* New York: Holt, Rinehart and Winston.

Malecot, A. 1974. Cross-language phonetics. In Sebeok, T. (ed.) *Current Trends in Linguistics*, 2511–2523. The Hague: Mouton.

Malmberg, B. 1966. Analyse des faits prosodiques – problèmes et méthodes. *Cahiers de Linguistique Théorique et Appliquée* 3: 99–107.

    1967. *Structural linguistics and human communication.* Berlin, Heidelberg, New York: Springer.

    (ed.) 1968. *Manual of phonetics.* North Holland Publishing Company.

Marçais, Ph. 1977. *Esquisse grammaticale de l'arabe maghrébin.* Paris: Librairie d'Amérique et d'Orient, Adrien Maisonneuve.

Marjomaa, I. 1982. Englannin ja suomen vokaalien kestoista puhenopeuden vaihdellessa. In Iivonen, A. and Kaskinen, H. (eds.) IX *Fonetiikan päivät – Helsinki 1982. PPH* 35: 119–137.

Marouzeau, J. 1949. Quelques effets de l'intonation. *Le Français Moderne* 17: 1–5.

    1956. Accent de mot et accent de phrase. *Le Français Moderne* 24: 241–248.

Martin, P. 1975. Analyse phonologique de la phrase française. *Linguistics* 146: 35–67.

1977. Résumé d'une théorie de l'intonation. *Bulletin de l'Institut de Phonétique de Grenoble* 6: 57–87.

1979. Une théorie syntaxique de l'accentuation en français. In Fónagy, I. and Léon, P.R. (eds.) *L'Accent en Français Contemporain. Studia Phonetica* XV: 1–12.

1981. Pour une théorie de l'intonation. In Rossi, M. *et al.* 1981, 234–271.

1986. Structure prosodique et structure rythmique pour la synthèse. *Actes des 15èmes Journées d'Etudes sur la Parole* (Aix-en-Provence), *G.A.L.F.* 89–91.

Martinet, A. 1960. *Eléments de linguistique générale.* Paris: Armand Colin.

Martins-Baltar, M. 1977. *De l'Enoncé à l'Enonciation: une Approche des Fonctions Intonatives.* Paris: Didier.

Maspero, H. 1912. Etudes sur la phonétique historique de la langue annamite. Les initiales. *Bulletin de l'Ecole Française d'Extrême-Orient* 12, I: 1–127.

Mateus, M.H.M. 1975. *Aspectos da fonologia portuguesa.* Lisboa: Publicações do Centro de Estudos Filológicos.

Matluck, J. 1965. Entonación hispánica. *Anuario de Letras* 5: 5–32.

Matussevich, M.I. 1976. *Sovremennyj russkij jazyk. Fonetika.* Moscow.

Mazaleyrat, J. 1974. *Eléments de Métrique Française.* Paris: A. Collin.

McCarthy, J. 1979. *Formal problems in Semitic phonology and morphology.* Ph.D. MIT.

McCawley, J.D. 1978. What is a tone language. In Fromkin, V. (ed.) *Tone: a Linguistic Survey,* 113–131. New York: Academic Press.

McClure, J.D. 1980. Western Scottish intonation. A preliminary study. In Waugh, L.R. and van Schooneveld 1980, 201–217.

Mehler, J., Jusczyk, P., Lambertz, G., Halsted, N., Bertoncini, J. and Amiel-Tison, C. 1988. A precursor of language acquisition in young infants. *Cognition.* 29: 143–178.

Meillon, M. 1967. *Le système tonal du parler sud-vietnamien.* Mémoire de Diplôme de l'Institut de Phonétique, Université de Paris.

Meinhold, G. 1972. Probleme der Intonationsstatistik. Acta Universitatis Carolinae, Philologica 1, *Phonetica Pragensia* III: 165–73. Universita Karlova Praha.

Mertens, P. 1987. *L'Intonation du Français.* Doctorale Dissertatie, Katholieke Universiteit Leuven.

Meyer, E.A. 1937. *Die Intonation im Schwedischen, I: Die Sveamundarten (= Studies in Scandinavian Philology* 10). University of Stockholm.

1954. Die Intonation im Schwedischen, II: Die norrländischen Mundarten. *(= Studies in Scandinavian Philology* 11), University of Stockholm.

Mikoš, M.J. 1976. Intonation of questions in Polish. *JP* 4: 247–253.

Milner, J.C. and Regnault, F. 1987. *Dire le Vers.* Paris: Le Seuil.

Misheva, A. 1986. Segmentno-strukturej podhod v eksperimentalnoto izuchavanije na intonatsijata. (The segmento-structural approach to the experimental study of intonation.) Publications of Sofia University 79.

Misheva, A. and Nikov, M. 1998. Intonation in Bulgarian. This volume, 285–297.

Möbius, B. 1993. *Ein quantitatives Modell der deutschen Intonation: Analyse und Synthese von Grundfrequenyverläufen*. Tübingen: Niemeyer.

Moraes de, J. 1984. *Recherches sur l'Intonation Modale du Portugais Brésilien Parlé à Rio de Janeiro*. Thèse de Doctorat de 3ème cycle, Université de Paris III.

1987. Corrélats acoustiques de l'accent de mot en portugais brésilien. *Proc ICPhS* 11, 3: 313–316. Tallinn, URSS.

1991. Intonation interrogative et ordre des mots en portugais brésilien. *Proc ICL* I: 487–490.

1995a. Sobre as marcas prosódicos do acento em Portugês. In Pereira, C. and Pereira P. (eds.) *Miscelânea de Estudos Lungüísticos, Filológos et Literáriois in Memoriam Celso Cunha*. Rio de Janeiro: Nova Fronteira: 323–335.

1995b. Acentuação lexical et acetuação frasal em Português. Um estudo acústico-perceptivo. *Estudos Lingüísticos e Literários* 17 (Univ. Fed. de Bahia): 39–57.

1998a. A propos des marques prosodiques du style efféminé en portugais brésilien. in Perrot J. (ed.) *Polyphonie pour Ivan Fónagy*. Paris: L'Harmattan.

1998b. Intonation in Brazilian Portuguese. This volume, 187–202.

Moraes, J. and Espesser, R. 1988. La hiérarchie des indices prosodiques de l'accent en portugais. *Paper presented at the First International Conference on Experimental Phonostylistics, Sociophonology and Speech Acoustic Variability*, Florianópolis.

Moraes, J. and Leite, Y. 1989. Ritmo e Velocidade da Fala na Estratégia do Discurso. *Paper Presented at the III Seminário do Projeto Gramática do Português Falado*, São Paulo: Águas de Lindóia.

Nahkola, K. 1987. *Yleisgeminaatio*. Helsinki: Suomalaisen kirjallisuuden Seura.

Nandriş, O. 1963. *Phonétique Historique du Roumain*. Paris: Klincksieck.

Napoli, Donna Jo (ed.) 1978. *Elements of tone, stress and intonation*. Washington D.C: Georgetown University Press.

Navarro Tomás, T. 1939. El grupo fónico como unidad melódica. *Revista de Filología Hispánica* 1: 3–19.

1944. *Manual de entonación española*, 3ª ed. México, 1966, Colección Málaga.

Nespor, M. and Vogel, I. 1986. *Prosodic Phonology*. Dordrecht: Foris.

1989. On clashes and lapses. *Phonology* 6, 1: 69–116.

Newman, S. 1946. On the stress system of English. *Word* 2: 171–187.

Nguyen Ðang Liem 1970. *Vietnamese pronunciation*. Honolulu: University of Hawaii Press.

Nicaise, A. 1987. *Phénomènes intonatifs en français: de la Perception à l'Interprétation*. Thèse de Doctorat d'Etat, Université de Paris VII.

Niculescu, A. 1969. Per uno studio contrastivo dei sistemi fonematici italiano e rumeno. *Il Veltro* 13, 1–2: 287–302.

Niemi, J. 1984. Word Level Stress and Prominence in Finnish and English. Acoustic Experiments on Production and Perception. *Publications in the Humanities* 1, University of Joensuu.

Nieminen, A.L. 1985. Suomen intonaation identifiointi ja diskriminointi. Helsingin yliopiston fonetiikan laitoksen opinnäyteraportteja 3.

Nikolaeva, T.M. 1969. *Intonacija slozhnogo predlozhenija v slav'anskich jazykah*. Moscow.

References

1977. *Frazovaja intonacija slav'anskih jazykov.* Moscow.
1982. *Semantika akcentnogo vydelenija.* Moscow.
1987. The intonology of the 80's. *Proc ICPhS* 11 vol. 4.
Nooteboom, S.G. and Kruyt, J.G. 1987. Accents, focus distribution, and the perceived distribution of given and new information: an experiment. *JASA* 82, 5: 1512–1524.
Norman, J. 1988 *Chinese.* Cambridge: Cambridge University Press.
Noss, R.B. 1964. *Thai Reference Grammar.* Washington, Foreign Service Institute, Government Printing Office, U.S.A.
1972. Rhythm in Thai. In Harris, J.G. *et al. Thai Phonetics and Phonology*, 33–42. Central Institute of English Language.
Núñez-Cedeño, R.A. 1985. Stress assignment in Spanish verb forms. In Nuessel, F.H. 1985 *Current Issues in Hispanic Phonology and Morphology*, IULC, 55–76.
Nuolijärvi, P. 1986. *Kolmannen sukupolven kieli.* Helsinki: Suomalaisen kirjallisuuden seura.
Nyrop, J. 1955. *Manuel Phonétique du Français Parlé.* 7ème ed. Lund: Gydendal.
O'Connor, J.D. and Arnold, G.F. 1961. *Intonation of Colloquial English.* London: Longman (2nd edition, 1973).
Ode, C. 1989. *Russian Intonation: a Perceptual Description.* Amsterdam-Atlanta GA: Rodopi.
Oftedal, M. 1952. On the origin of the Scandinavian tone distinction. *Norsk Tidsskrift for Sprogvidenskap* 16: 201–225.
Ohala, J.J. 1990. There is no interface between phonology and phonetics: a personal view. *JP* 18: 153–171.
Ohala, J.J. and Gilbert, J.B. 1981. Listeners ability to identify languages by their prosody. In Léon and Rossi (eds.): 123–122.
Öhman, S. 1967. Word and sentence intonation: a quantitative model. *Speech Transmission Laboratory Quarterly Progress and Status Report*, (KTH, Stockholm) 2–3: 20–54.
Olabe, J.C. 1983. *Sistema para la conversión de un texto ortográfico a hablado en tiempo real.* Doctoral Thesis. Madrid: ETSIT.
Oliveira, H. 1989. *Atonização de Vocábulos em Português e Regras Afins.* Tese de Doutorado, Universidade Federal do Rio de Janeiro.
OSRJ: *Orfoepicheskij slovar russkogo jazyka.* 1983. Moscow.
Paccia-Cooper, J. and Cooper, W.E. 1981. The processing of Phrase Structures in Speech Production. In Cole, R.A. (ed.) *Perception and Production of Fluent Speech. Hillsdale*, 399–440. New Jersey: Lawrence Erlbaum.
Paducheva, E.V. 1987. Towards a calculus of intonation contours for sentences of arbitrary complexity. *Proc ICPhS 11* vol. 2.
Palander, M. 1987. *Suomen itämurteiden erikoisgeminaatio.* Helsinki: Suomalaisen kirjallisuuden Seura.
Palmer, H.E. 1922. *English intonation with systematic exercises.* Cambridge: Heffer.

Pardo, J.M. *et al.* 1987. Improving text to speech conversion in Spanish linguistic analysis and prosody. In Laver, J. and Jack, M.A. 1987 *European Conference on Speech Technology*, Edinburgh, 2: 173–176.

Pârlog, H. and Popa, M. 1978. *Intonation errors*. In Chiṭoran, D. (ed.) *The Romanian-English Contrastive Analysis Project. Further Contrastive Studies. Contrastive Grammar. Error Analysis*, 291–297. Bucharest: Bucharest University Press.

Pasdeloup, V. 1990. *Modèle de Règles Rythmiques du Français Appliqué à la Synthèse de la Parole*. Thèse de Doctorat, Université de Provence (Aix-en-Provence).

Paufoʹsima, R.F. 1983. *Fonetika slova i frazy v severnorusskich govorah*. Moscow.

Paunonen, H. 1989. Muuttuvat puhesuomen muodot. In Aalto, S., Hakulinen, A., Laalo, K., Leino, P. and Lieko, A. (eds.) 209–233. Kielestä kiinni.

Pavlova, A.V. and Svetozarova, N.D. 1987. Faktory, opredel'ajushchije stepen'akcentnoj vydelennosti slova v vyskazyvanii. *Sluh i rech v norme i patologii*. Leningrad.

Pellowe, J. and Jones, V. 1978. On intonational variability in Tyneside speech. In Trudgill, 1979.

Peltonen, V. 1901. *Puhetaito*. Porvoo: Werner Söderström.

Penchev 1980. Osnovni intonatsionni konturi v bulgarskoto izrechenje. (Basic intonation patterns of Bulgarian.) Sofia.

Penttilä, A. 1927. Suomen ja sen lähimpien sukukielten painotusoppia. Turun suomalaisen yliopiston julkaisuja B, III, 2.

Pernot, H. 1929–1930. L'intonation. *Revue de Phonétique* 6: 273–289.

Perrot, J. 1978. Fonctions syntaxiques, énonciation, information. *Bulletin de la Sociéte Linguistique de Paris* LXXIII: 85–101.

Peʹskovskij, A.M. 1959. Intonacija i grammatika. *A.M. Peshkovskij. Izbrannyje trudy*. Moscow.

Pheby, J. 1975. *Intonation und Grammatik im Deutschen*. Berlin: Akademie-Verlag.

Pierrehumbert, J. 1979. The perception of fundamental frequency declination. *JASA* 66: 363–369.

1980 *The phonology and phonetics of English intonation*. Ph.D. thesis, MIT.

1981. Synthesising intonation. *JASA* 70: 985–995.

Pierrehumbert, J.B. and Beckman, M.E. 1988. *Japanese Tone Structure*. Cambridge, Mass: MIT Press.

Pierrehumbert, J. and Hirschberg, J. 1990. The Meaning of intonation contours in the interpretation of discourse. In Cohen, P.R., Morgan, J. and Polack, M.E. (eds.) *Intentions in Communication*. Cambridge, Mass.: MIT Press: 371–311.

Pijper, J.R. de 1983. *Modelling British English intonation*. Dordrech: Foris.

Pike, E.V. 1985. The Intonation of American English simplified. *Word* 36, 3: 237–242.

Pike, K.L. 1945. *The Intonation of American English*. Ann Arbor: University of Michigan Press.

1948. *Tone Languages*. Ann Arbor: University of Michigan Press.

Pilch, H. 1972. La mélodie dans les structures linguistiques. *Cours d'Audiophonologie de Besançon*. 43–63.

References

Plutchik, R. and Kellerman, H. (eds.) 1980. *Emotion: Theory, Research and Experience*. vol 1. *Theories of emotion*. New York: Academic Press.

Pope, E.N. 1977. *Questions and Answers in English*. The Hague: Mouton.

Popescu-Marin, M. 1961. Observații asupra topicii atributului adjectival în limba română. *Studii de Gramatică* 3: 161–178.

Poser, W.J. 1984. *The Phonetics and Phonology of Tone and Intonation in Japanese*. 259–289. Ph. D. MIT

Prieto, P., Van Santen, J. and Hirschberg, J. 1995. Tonal Alignment Patterns in Spanish. *Journal of Phonetics* 23, 4: 429–451.

Prince, E. 1981. Toward a taxonomy of given-new distinction. In Cole, P. (ed.) *Radical pragmatics*, 223–256. Cambridge: Academic Press.

Profili, O. 1987. Acoustic investigation of intonation in two regional varieties of Italian: preliminary results. *Progress Reports Oxford University* 2, 47–63.

Pulleyblank, D. 1986. *Tone in lexical phonology*. Dordrecht: Reidel.

Pușcariu, S. 1959. *Limba Română*. vol. 2. *Rostirea*. București: Editura Academiei.

1974. Rostiri și forme șovăitoare. In Pușcariu, S. *Cercetări și Studii*, 404–415. București: Minerva (first published in 1936).

1976. *Limba Română*. vol. 1. *Privire Generală*. București: Minerva.

Quasthoff, U. (ed.) 1994. *Aspects of Oral Communication*. Berlin: Akademie-Verlag.

Quilis, A. 1971. Caracterización fonética del acento español. *Travaux de Linguistique et de Littérature* 9: 53–72.

1978. Frecuencia de los esquemas acentuales en español. *Homenaje a E. Alarcos Llorach*, vol. V: 113–126. 1983.

1981. *Fonética acústica de la lengua española*. Madrid: Gredos.

1985. Entonación dialectal hispánica. *Lingüística Española Actual* 7, 2: 145–190.

1989. La entonación de Gran Canaria en el marco de la entonación española. *Lingüística Española Actual*. XI: 55–87.

1993. *Tratado de fonología y fonética españolas*, Madrid, Gredos.

Quirk, R., Greenbaum, S., Leech, G. and Svartvik, J. 1972. *A Grammar of Contemporary English*. London: Longman.

Reinhart, T. 1981. *Pragmatics and linguistics: an analysis of sentence topics*. Bloomington: IULC.

Reis, C. 1996. *L'interaction entre l'accent, l'intonation et le rythme en portugais brésilien*. Doctoral thesis, Université de Provence.

Reyelt, M. *et al*. 1996. Prosodische Etikettierung des Deutschen mit ToBI. In Gibbon, D. (ed.) *Natural Language and Speech Technology*. Berlin: Mouton de Gruyter.

Rhiati, N.S. 1984. *Etude de l'interrogation en arabe marocain*. Doctoral thesis, Université de Paris III, Sorbonne Nouvelle.

Risberg, A. 1974. The importance of prosodic speech elements for the lip reader. *Scand. Audiol*. Suppl.4: 153–164.

Rischel, J. 1969. Morpheme stress in Danish. *ARIPUC* 4, 111–144.

Rischel, J. and Basbøll, H. (eds.) 1995. *Aspects of Danish Prosody*. RASK Supplement vol. 3. Odense: Odense University Press.

Roca, I. 1988. Theoretical implications of Spanish word stress. *Linguistic Inquiry* 19, 3: 393–423.

Roceric-Alexandrescu, A. 1963. Observaţii asupra pauzei – în citire – în limba română. *SCL* 14, 3: 361–374.

1965. Observaţii asupra debitului vorbirii în limba română. *SCL* 16, 2: 255–262.

Roméas, P. 1992. *L'organisation Prosodique des Enoncés en Situation de Dialogue Homme-Machine Simulé: Théorie et Données*. Doctoral thesis. Université de Provence.

Rose, P. 1984. The role of subglottal pressure and vocal cord tension in the production of tones in a Chinese dialect. *New papers on Chinese language use*. Canberra: 133–168..

Rossi, M. 1972. Le seuil différentiel de durée. In Valdman, A. (ed.) *Papers in Linguistics and Phonetics to the memory of Pierre Delattre*, 435–450. The Hague: Mouton.

1974 *Contribution à la méthodologie de l'analyse linguistique: description phonétique et phonologique du parler de Rossano (Province de Massa, Italie)*. Paris: Champion.

1980a. Le français, langue sans accent?. In Fónagy, I. and Léon, P.R. (eds.) *L'Accent en Français Contemporain*. (=*Studia Phonetica* 15): 13–51.

1980b. Le cadre accentuel et le mot en français et en italien. In Léon and Rossi (eds.) 9–22.

1981a. Continuation et question. In Rossi *et al.* 1981, 149–178.

1981b. Vers une théorie de l'intonation. In Rossi *et al.* 1981, 179–233.

1985. L'intonation et l'organisation de l'énoncé. *Phonetica* 42, 2–3: 135–153.

1987. Peut-on prédire l'organisation prosodique du langage spontané? *Etudes de Linguistique Appliquée* 66: 20–48.

1993. A model for predicting the prosody of spontaneous speech (PPSS model). *Speech Communication* 13, 87–107.

1995. A principle-based model for predicting the prosody of speech. In Sorin, C., Marianai, J., Méloni, H. and Schoentgen, J. (eds.) *Levels in Speech Communication: Relations and Interactions*. Elsevier; Amsterdam.

1998. Intonation in Italian. This volume, 228–247.

Rossi, M. and Chafcouloff, M. 1972. Les niveaux intonatifs. *TIPA* 1: 167–176.

Rossi, M. and Di Cristo, A. 1980. Un modèle de détection automatique des frontières intonatives et syntaxiques. *Actes des XIèmes Journées d'Etudes sur la Parole* (Strasbourg), *G.A.L.F.* 141–164.

1982. En quête des indices de segmentation de l'énoncé. In Di Cristo, A. *et al.* (eds.) *Prosodie et Reconnaissance Automatique de la Parole, G.A.L.F.* 141–164.

Rossi, M., Di Cristo, A., Hirst, D.J., Martin, P. and Nishinuma, Y. 1981. *L'Intonation: de l'Acoustique à la Sémantique*. Paris: Klincksieck.

RRR 1973, 1983, *Russkaya razgovornaja rech*. Moscow.

Rudaravanija, P. 1965. *An Analysis of the Elements in Thai that Correspond to the Basic Intonation Patterns of English*. Doctoral thesis. Columbia University.

Ruhlen, M. 1987. *A Guide to the World's Languages. Volume 1: classification*. Stanford: Stanford University Press.

References

Rumjancev, M.K. 1972. *Ton i intonacija v sovremennom kitajskom jazyke* (*Tone and intonation in modern Chinese*). Moscow.

RG 1980–1982. *Russkaja grammatika*. Vols. I-II. Moscow.

Sabia, A. 1982. *Etude de la négation en arabe dialectal marocain*. Doctoral thesis, Paris III.

Sadeniemi, M. 1949. *Metriikkamme perusteet*. Helsinki: Otava.

Sagart, L., Hallé, P., De Boysson-Bardies, B. and Arabia-Guidet, C. 1986. Tone production in Modern Standard Chinese, an electromyographic investigation. *Cahiers de Linguistique, Asie orientale* 15, 2: 205–221.

Santos, J. 1981. *Contribución a la síntesis por regla de habla*. Doctoral Thesis. Madrid: ETSIT.

Schaffer, D. 1984. The role of intonation as a cue to topic management in conversation. *JP* 12: 327–344.

Scherk, O. 1912. *Uber den Französischen Aksent*. Dissert. Berlin, Schmsow, kirchstrasse, n.l.

Schirru, C. 1982. Analyse intonative de l'énonciation et de la question totale dans l'italien régional de Cagliari. *Bulletin de l'Institut de Phonétique de Grenoble*. 10/11, 169–184.

Schmerling, S. 1976. *Aspects of English Sentence Stress*. Austin, Texas: University of Texas Press.

Schmitt, A. 1924. *Untersuchungen zur allgemeinen Akzentlehre*. Heidelberg: Carl Winter.

Schubiger, M. 1935. *The Role of Intonation in Spoken English*. St. Gall: Fehr'sche Buchhandlung.

1958. *English Intonation: its Form and Function*. Tübingen: Max Niemeyer Verlag.

1972. English intonation and German modal particles. (1965) In Bolinger, D. (ed.) *Intonation*, Harmondsworth: Penguin: 175–193.

1980. English intonation and German modal particles II: a comparative study. in Waugh and van Schooneveld (eds.): 279–298.

Searle, J.R. 1969. *Speech Acts*. Cambridge: Cambridge University Press.

1972. What is a speech act? In Giglioli, P.P. (ed.) *Language and Social Context*, 136–178. Harmondsworth: Penguin.

1976. A Classification of Illocutionary Acts. *Language in Society* 5, 1: 1–23.

1979. *Expression and Meaning*. Cambridge University Press.

Segerbäck, B. 1966. *La réalisation d'une opposition de tonèmes dans des syllabes chuchotées*. *TILL* IV. Lund: Gleerup.

Seitz, P. 1986. *Relationships between tones and segments in Vietnamese*. Ph.D., University of Pennsylvania (UMI).

Selkirk, E.O. 1972. *The phrase phonology of English and French*. Ph. D. Thesis. MIT.

1978. *On prosodic structure and its relation to syntactic structure*. Bloomington: Indiana University Linguistics Club.

1981. The role of prosodic categories in English word stress. *Linguistic Inquiry* 11, 3: 563–605.

References

1984. *Phonology and syntax: the relation between sound and structure.* Cambridge, Mass.: MIT Press.

Selmer, E.W. 1928. Noen bemerkninger om den musikalske aksent i dens forhold til den sterkt og svakt skårne aksent. *Festskrift til Rektor J. Qvigstad, Tromsø Museums Skrifter* 2: 250–262.

Selting, M. 1995. *Prosodie im Gespräch. Aspekte einer Interpretation.* Tübingen: Niemeyer.

Serban, V. 1974. *Teoria şi Topica Propoziţiei în Româna Contemporană.* Bucureşti: Editura Didactică şi Pedagogică.

Sgall, P., Hajiˇcová, E and Panevová, J. 1986. *The Meaning of the Sentence in its Semantic and Pragmatic Aspects.* Dordrecht: Reidel.

Sharp, A.E. 1958. Falling-rising intonation patterns in English. *Phonetica*, 2, 3–4: 127–152.

Shi Bo 1989. A Chinese speech synthesis by rule system. Speech, hearing, language. *UCL* vol. 3: 217–236.

Silva, M. 1989. *As Pretônicas no Falar Baiano.* Tese de Doutorado, Universidade Federal do Rio de Janeiro.

Silverman, K., Beckman, M., Pitrelli, J., Ostendorf, M., Wightman, C., Price, P., Pierrehumbert, J. and Hirschberg, J. 1992. ToBI: A standard for labeling English prosody. In *Proceedings of the 1992 International Conference on Spoken Language Processing*, 867–870.

Skorikova, T. 1987. Functions of accent prominence in speech. *Proc ICPhS* 11. (4).

Sonesson, B. 1968. The functional anatomy of speech organs. In Malmberg, B. (ed.) 1968, 45–75.

Sosa, J.M. 1991. *Fonética y fonología del español hispanoamericano.* Doctoral thesis. Univ. of Massachusetts.

Sovijärvi, A. 1958. Alustavia mittaushavaintoja suomen yleiskielen sanapainosta. *Virittäjä* 62: 351–365.

Sperber, D. and Wilson, D. 1986. *Relevance: Communication and Cognition.* Oxford: Blackwell.

SRUNR. 1985. Sovremennaja russkaja ustnaja nauchnaja rech. Vol. 1. Krasnojarsk.

Stathopoulos, E.T. and Weisner, G. 1985. Effects of monitoring vocal intensity on oral air flow in children and adults. *JSHR* 28: 589–593.

Sten, H. 1963. *Phonétique Française.* Copenhagen: Mundsgaard.

Steriade, D. 1988. Greek Accent: A Case for Preserving Structure. *Linguistic Inquiry* 19: 271–314.

Strangert, E. 1983. Temporal characteristics of rhythmic units in Swedish. In Elert, C.C., Johansson, I. and Strangert, E. (eds.) *Nordic Prosody* III, 201–213. Stockholm: Almqvist and Wiksell.

1985. *Swedish speech rhythm in a cross-language perspective. Acta Universitatis Umensis.* Stockholm: Almqvist and Wiksell International.

1987. Speech rhythm: Data and preliminaries to a model. In Gregersen, K. and Basbøll, H. (eds.) 1987: 91–104.

Studdert-Kennedy, M. 1979. Speech perception. *Proc 9th ICPhS.* (Copenhagen) I: 59–81.

Sugito, M. 1990. Accent and intonation in Japanese and English (in Japanese). *Nihongo to Nihongo Kyoiku.* (Japanese and Japanese Language Teaching) Meiji Shoin, 255–309.

Surinpiboon, S. 1985. *The Accentual System of Polysyllabic Words in Thai.* M.A. Thesis. Department of Linguistics, Chulalongkorn University.

Svensson, S.G. 1974. *Prosody and grammar in speech perception. Monograph from the Institute of Linguistics* 2, University of Stockholm.

Svetozarova, N.D. 1975. The inner structure of intonation contours in Russian. *Auditory Analysis and Perception of Speech.* New York: Academic Press.

1982. *Intonacionnaja sistema russkogo jazyka.* Leningrad.

1987. Linguistic factors in sentence stress. Evidence from Russian. *Proceedings of the XIth Intenational Congress of Phonetic Sciences.* Tallinn. vol. 4.

1998. Intonation in Russian. This volume, 270–284.

Szende, T. 1976. *A beszédfolyamat alaptényezöi* (Les facteurs de base de la parole). Budapest: Akadémai kiadó.

Szmidt, Y. 1970. A la recherche d'un patron intonatif de l'ordre chez huit sujets français de l'Ontario. *Trav. du Lab. de Phon. Exp. de Toronto.*

Teiuş, S. 1971. Delimitarea enunţurilor în graiurile dacoromâne. *Studii şi Cercetări de Lingvistică* 16, 1: 109–120.

1980. *Coordonarea în Vorbirea Populară Românească.* Bucureşti: Editura Stiinţifică şi Enciclopedică.

Terken, J.M.B. 1980. The distribution of pitch accents as function of informational variables. *I.P.O. Annual Progress Report* 15: 48–53.

1981. The distribution of pitch accents as function of informational variables II. *I.P.O. Annual Progress Report* 16: 39–43.

1985. *Use and Function of intonation: Some Experiments.* Ph. D. Thesis, Leyden University.

Teston, B. and Rossi, M. 1977. Un système de détection automatique du fondamental et de l'intensité. *VIIIèmes journées d'études du groupe de la "communication parlée"* 1: 111–117. Aix-en-Provence.

Thawisomboon, S. 1955. *Syllable Junctures within Stress Groups in Spoken Thai.* M.A. Thesis, University of London (SOAS).

Thompson, L.C. 1964. *A Vietnamese grammar.* University of Washington Press.

Thomson, R. 1968. *A History of Philosophy.* Harmondsworth: Penguin.

Thorsen (Grønnum), N. 1978a. An investigation of Danish intonation. *JP* 6: 151–175.

1978b. Aspects of Danish intonation. In Gårding, E., Bannert, R. and Bruce, G. (eds.) *Nordic Prosody.* (= *TILL* 13): 23–32.

1979. Interpreting raw fundamental frequency tracings in Danish. *Phonetica* 36: 57–78.

1980a. Word boundaries and F_0 patterns in Advanced Standard Copenhagen Danish. *Phonetica* 37: 121–133.

1980b. A study of the perception of sentence intonation – Evidence from Danish. *Journal of the Acoustic Society of America* 67: 1014–1030.

1980c. Neutral stress, emphatic stress, and sentence intonation in Advanced Standard Copenhagen Danish. *ARIPUC* 14, 121–205.

1983a. Standard Danish sentence intonation – Phonetic data and their representation. *Folia Linguistica* 17: 187–220.

1983b. Two issues in the prosody of standard Danish. In Cutler and Ladd (eds.), 27–38.

1984a. The tonal manifestation of Danish words containing assimilated or elided schwa. In Elert, C.C., Johansson, I. and Strangert, E. (eds.) *Nordic Prosody* III, 215–230. Stockholm: Almqvist and Wiksell.

1984b. Variability and invariance in Danish stress group patterns. *Phonetica* 41: 88–102.

1984c. F_0 timing in Danish word perception. *Phonetica* 41: 17–30.

1985. Intonation and text in Standard Danish. *JASA* 77: 1205–1216.

1986. Sentence intonation in textual context – supplementary data. *JASA* 80: 1041–1047.

1987a. Text and intonation – a case study. In Gregersen, K. and Basbøll, H. (eds.) *Nordic Prosody* IV, 71–79.

1987b. Intonation and text in Standard Danish – with special reference to the abstract representation of intonation. In Dressler, W.U. *et al.* (eds.) *Phonologica* 1984: 301–309. Cambridge: Cambridge University Press.

1987c. Suprasegmental transcription. *ARIPUC* 21: 1–27.

1988a. Intonation on Bornholm – between Danish and Swedish. *ARIPUC* 22, 25–138.

1988b. Stress group patterns, focus signalling and sentence intonation in two regional Danish standard languages: Aalborg and Næstved. *ARIPUC* 22: 145–196.

Tiktin, H. 1905. *Rumänisches Elementarbuch.* Heidelberg: Carl Winter.

Tilkov 1981. Intonatsijata v bulgarskija jezik. (Intonation of the Bulgarian Language.) Sofia.

Togeby, K. 1965. *Structure Immanente de la Langue Française.* Paris: Larousse.

Toledo, G.A. 1988. *El ritmo en el español.* Madrid: Gredos.

Tortorelli, E. 1990. *Marche intonative sintattiche e lessicali della tematizzazione nella lingua italiana.* Bazigiovani, Bazi.

Touati, P. 1987. *Structures prosodiques du suédois et du francais. Profils temporels et configurations tonales. TILL* XXI. Lund: Lund University Press.

1990. Tonal configurations in Swedish-Accented French. *Nordic Prosody* 5: 306–324

Trager, G.L. and Smith, H.L. 1951. *An Outline of English Structure.* Norman, Oklahoma: Battenburg Press.

Trần Phương Mai 1967. Tone and Intonation in South Vietnamese. *Linguistic Circle of Canberra. Series A.9:* 13–33.

Tran Thien Huong 1980. *Interrogation and intonation en vietnamien.* Mémoire de Maîtrise, Université Paris 7. (unpublished).

Tran Thien Huong and Boulakia, G. 1983. Questions, tones and intonation in Vietnamese (Hanoi dialect). *Proc ICL* 10, 1: 617.

Trim, J.L.M. 1959. Minor and major tone-groups in English. *Le Maître Phonétique* 112: 26–29.

Trubetzkoy, N.S. 1939. *Grundzüge der Phonologie.* French translation by
J. Cantineau: *Principes de phonologie.* (1949). Paris: Klincksieck.

Trudgill, P. 1979. *Sociolinguistic Patterns in British English.* London: Arnold.

Tseva, A. and Contini, M. 1988. Formation de règles d'accentuation du grec moderne:
Prévisibilité automatique. *Journal d'acoustique* 1: 211–213.

Tsitsopoulos, S. 1973. *Stress in Modern Greek.* Ph.D. Dissertation. University of
Michigan.

Uldall, E.T. 1960. Attitudinal meanings conveyed by intonation. *L&S* 3: 223–234.

    1962. Ambiguity: question or statement? or are you asking or telling me? *Proc
    ICPhS* 4: 779–783.

    1964. Dimensions of meaning in intonation. In Abercrombie*et al*: (eds.) 271–
    279.

Ulivi, A. 1987. In legătură cu accentuarea unor neologisme în limba română. *SCL* 38,
4: 310–322.

Ultan, R. 1969. Some general characteristics of interrogative systems. *Working
Papers on Language Universals* 1: 41–63.

Umeda, N. 1982. "F_0 declination" is situation dependent. *JP* 10: 279–290.

Uusivirta, P. 1965. Huomioita emfaattisuudesta. *Virittäjä* 69: 280–288.

Uyeno, T., Hayashibe, H., Imai, K., Imagawa, H. and Kiritani, S. 1980.
Comprehension of relative clause construction and pitch contours in Japanese.
Annual Bulletin of the Research Institute of Logopedics and Phoniatrics 14:
225–236.

Vaissière, J. 1974. On French prosody. *Res. Lab. Electr. Prog. Report, MIT,* 115:
212–223.

    1980. La structure acoustique de la phrase française. *Annali della Scuola Normale
    Superiore di Pisa* X, 2: 529–560.

    1983. Language-independent prosodic features. In Cutler and Ladd (eds.): 53–66.

    1988. The use of prosodic parameters in automatic speech recognition. In Neman,
    Lang and Sagerer (eds.) *Recent Advances in Speech Understanding and Dialog
    System.* Nato Asi Series, Series DF, 46: 71–100.

    1989. The use of prosodic parameters in automatic speech recognition. in Nieman,
    Lang and Sagerer (eds.). *Recent advances in speech understanding and dialog
    systems.* Nato Asi Series, Springer Verlag.

    1991. Rhythm, accentuation and final lengthening in French. In Carlson, R.,
    Nord, C. and Sunberg, J. (Dir.), *Music, Language, Brain and Speech* 188–200.
    Macmillan Press.

van den Berg, R., Gussenhoven, C. and Rietveld, T. 1989. Downstep in Dutch:
implications for a model. In Docherty, G.J. and Ladd, D.R. *Laboratory
Phonology* II, 335–359. Cambridge: Cambridge University Press.

Van der Hulst, H. and Smith, N. (eds.) 1988. *Autosegmental studies in pitch accent.*
Dordrecht: Foris.

    1988. The variety of pitch accent systems: introduction. In Van der Hulst and
    Smith (eds.): ix-xxiv.

Varga, L. 1975. A Contrastive Analysis of English and Hungarian Sentence Prosody.
*Linguistics Institute of Hungarian Academy of Sciences and Center for Applied
Linguistics,* 93–134.

1981. A magyar intonáció – funkcionális szempontból. (Hungarian intonation – from a functional point of view.) *Nyelvtudomanyi Közlemények* 83: 313–339.

1983. Hungarian sentence prosody: An outline. *Folia Linguistica* 17: 117–151.

1986. Vélemények a magyar monda thangsúlyoxzásáról – avag Brassai és a többiek (A point of view on intonation in Hungarian – or Brassai and the others.) *Nyelvtudományi Közlemények* 88: 181–188.

Vasiliu, E. 1965. *Fonologia Limbii Române.* Bucureşti: Editura Ştiinţifică.

Vayra, M; Avesani, C. and Fowler, C.A. 1984. Patterns of temporal compression in spoken Italian. *Proc ICPhS* 10, IIB): 541–546.

Verluyten, P. 1984. Phonetic reality of linguistic structures: the case of (secondary) stress in french. Proc ICPhS 10: 522–526.

Vihanta, V. 1988. Sur le rôle de la F_0 dans l'opposition de quantité en finnois. In Karjalainen, M. and Laine, U. (eds.) *Fonetiikan päivät* – Espoo 1988. Helsinki University of Technology, Acoustics Laboratory, Publ. 31: 13–37

Viviani, P. and Terzuolo, C. 1980. Space-time invariance in learned motor skills. *Tutorials in motor behavior:* 525–533. Amsterdam.

Volkonskij, S. 1913. *Vyrazitel'noje slovo.* Petersburg.

von Essen, O. 1956a. *Grundzüge der deutschen Satzintonation.* Rattingen: Henn. 1956b. Hochdeutsche Satzmelodie. *Zeitschrift für Fonetik, Sprachwissenshaft und Kommunikationsforschung* 9, 75–85.

Vsevolodskij-Gerngross, V.N. 1922. *Teorija intonacii.* Petrograd.

Vũ Thanh Phương 1982. Phonetic properties of Vietnamese tones across dialects. In Bradley, D. (ed.) *Papers in Southeastasian Linguistics* 8: 55–76.*Tonation.* (Pacific Linguistics Series A, N° 62). Canberra: Australian National University.

Vuong Loc 1975. Coup d'oeil sur l'évolution de la langue vietnamienne. In *Essais Linguistiques, Etudes Vietnamiennes N° 40,* Hà Nội.

Wagner, R.L. and Pinchon, J. 1962. *Grammaire du français classique et moderne.* Paris: Hachette.

Waibel, A. 1988. *Prosody and speech recognition.* London: Pitman.

Wang, Q. 1957. *Běijīng yǔyīn chángshí.* (Elementary Beijing phonetics.) Changsha.

Wang, W.S.Y. 1967. Phonological features of tone. *International Journal of American Linguistics* 33, 2: 93–105.

Warburton, I. 1970. Rules of Accentuation in Classical and Modern Greek. *Glotta* 48: 107–120.

Waugh, L.R. and van Schooneveld, C.H. (eds.) 1980. *The Melody of Language: Intonation and Prosody.* Baltimore: University Park Press.

Weitzman, R.S. 1970. Word Accent in Japanese. *Studies in the Phonology of Asian Languages* 9: 43–49, 66–69. Acoustics Phonetics Laboratory, University of Southern California.

Wenk, B.J. and Wioland, F. 1982. Is French really syllable-timed? *JP* 10, 2: 193–216.

Wiese, R. 1988. Silbische und lexikalische Phonologie: Studien zum Chinesischen und Deutschen. Tübingen: Niemeyer.

Wightman, C., Shattuck-Hufnagel, S., Ostendorf, M. and Price, P. 1991. Segmental durations in the vicinity of prosodic phrase boundaries. *JASA* 91, 3: 1707–1717.

Wiik, K. 1965. Finnish and English Vowels. Annales Universitatis Turkuensis. Series B, Tom. 94. Turku: Turun yliopisto.

1975. Lukusanojen painosta. *Fonetiikan paperit* – Helsinki 1975. *PPH* 27: 125–138.

1977. Suomen tavuista. *Virittäjä* 81, 1: 265–78.

1985. Suomen murteiden vokaalien kestoista. In Aaltonen, O. and Hulkko, T. (eds.) 1985, 253–317.

1988. Pohjoiseurooppalaisten kielten entinen yhteinen puherytmi.' XV Kielitieteen päivät Oulussa 13.-14.5.1988. Esitelmät. Acta Universitatis Ouluensis B 14: 277–302. University of Oulu.

Willems, N.J. 1982. *English Intonation from a Dutch Point of View*. Dordrecht: Foris.

Willems, N.J., Collier, R. and 't Hart, J. 1988. A synthesis scheme for British English intonation. *JASA*. 84: 1250–1261.

Withgott, M. and Halvorsen, P.K. 1988. Phonetic and phonological considerations bearing on representation of East Norwegian accent. In Van der Hulst and Smith (eds.): 279–294.

Wunderli, P. 1979. Au sujet de l'intonation du français: la parenthèse en position finale. *Travaux de Linguistique* (Gand) 6: 83–111.

1983. L'Intonation des phrases interrogatives du type: "Il est né en quelle année?" *Romanica Gandensia* XX: 169–181.

1984. L'Intonation des questions sans marque segmentale. *Travaux de Linguistique et de Littérature* (Strasbourg) XXII, 1: 203–250.

Yamaguchi, K. 1985. Intonation of interjectional intonation in Fukui dialect (in Japanese). *Study of Sounds* 21: 213–222. Phon. Soc. Japan.

Youssi, A. 1983. La triglossie dans la typologie linguistique. *La Linguistique* 19/2: 71–83. Paris.

Yule, G. 1980. Speakers topics and major paratones. *Lingua* 52: 33–47.

Zaliznjak, A.A. 1985. *Ot praslav'anskoj akcentuacii k russkoj*. Moscow.

Zee, E. 1980. A spectrographic investigation of Mandarin tone sandhi. *UCLA working papers in phonetics* 49: 98–116. April.

Zlatoustova, L.V. 1984. Sopostavitjelnoje i zuchenije intonatsij russkovo i bolgarsckovo jazykov. (Comparative study of the intonation of Russian and Bulgarian.) Collection of communications by the members of the commission on phonetics and phonology. University of Sofia.

Zmeeva, T.D. 1969. Osnovnyje intonatsionnyje contury ispanskovo jazyka. (The principle intonation patterns of Spanish.) *Bulletin of the speech laboratory of the philology department of the University of Moscow*.

Zwanenburg, W.Z. 1964. *Recherches sur la Prosodie de la Phrase Française*. Universitaire Pers Leiden.

Index of names

Subject index